Design-Tech: Building science for architects

To Mo and Kathy

Design-Tech
Building science for architects

Jason Alread, AIA, LEED
and
Thomas Leslie, AIA

AMSTERDAM • BOSTON • HEIDELBERG • LONDON • NEW YORK • OXFORD
PARIS • SAN DIEGO • SAN FRANCISCO • SINGAPORE • SYDNEY • TOKYO
Architectural Press is an imprint of Elsevier

ELSEVIER

Architectural
Press

Butterworth-Heinemann is an imprint of Elsevier
Linacre House, Jordan Hill, Oxford OX2 8DP, UK
30 Corporate Drive, Suite 400, Burlington, MA 01803, USA

First edition 2007
Reprinted 2007

Notice
No responsibility is assumed by the publisher for any injury and/or damage to persons
or property as a matter of products liability, negligence or otherwise, or from any use
or operation of any methods, products, instructions or ideas contained in the material
herein. Because of rapid advances in the medical sciences, in particular, independent
verification of diagnoses and drug dosages should be made

British Library Cataloguing in Publication Data
A catalogue record for this book is available from the British Library

Library of Congress Cataloging-in-Publication Data
A catalog record for this book is available from the Library of Congress

ISBN: 978-0-7506-6557-5

For information on all Butterworth-Heinemann publications
visit our website at books.elsevier.com

Printed and bound in *Great Britain*

07 08 09 10   10 9 8 7 6 5 4 3 2

Working together to grow
libraries in developing countries

www.elsevier.com | www.bookaid.org | www.sabre.org

ELSEVIER   BOOK AID International   Sabre Foundation

Contents

Contents

Preface

Every architect's office of a reasonable size seems to have one person, usually sitting in the back, still drawing by hand (and often with an advanced nicotine habit) who knows *everything*. This person has been in practice forever, has seen it all, and is often the best kept secret in the firm. When designs get serious, this person gets busy. Designers come to the back of the office with dozens of questions that haven't been much on their minds, but are suddenly critical. How deep does this beam need to be? Can we get by with just one fire exit from these rooms? What material should this component be made from, and who can manufacture it?

We have both worked in offices where a version of this grizzled veteran played a huge role in our educations. When we sat for our respective licensing exams, we passed by pretending to be this person for a few days, to think like they thought, to try for the photographic memory and instant recall that this person seemed to have. It worked.

For whatever reason, the ranks of the technology-fluent seem to have thinned over the past generation. Architects who came up in the tech-heavy 1960s and 1970s are now moving toward retirement, while architects who came up in the theory-rich 1980s (including us) are struggling to take their place. The discipline has undergone immense specialization in the last decade, and we tend to be spoiled by an increasing number of really good engineers with increasingly sophisticated digital techniques that solve a lot of our problems for us.

Solving problems is great, and architects typically pay engineers quite well for it. But we feel that an opportunity is often lost by passing along a conceptually or aesthetically rich design to be 'solved.' In our experience, good design also springs from knowledge and exploration. The more information architects have at the start of a project, the more effective their solutions are likely to be, and – more importantly – the closer in spirit the esthetics and function of a design will come to one another. Integration, in our view, is more than a buzzword, it's a philosophy of design that leads to buildings that appeal on a number of levels – from strict functionality to the intellectual adventure of connecting building form to purpose in both the designer's mind and that of the user or client.

This intellectual adventure is what we've tried to cultivate in developing and teaching a gently radical sequence of technology courses in the Graduate

Architecture Program at Iowa State. From the beginning, we were asked to put together a curriculum that taught what young architects really need to know, in a way that made connections to the design, theory, and history they would get in other coursework. We were both thrilled and inspired by this challenge. Both of us came from very good, rigorous backgrounds in technology education (Florida and Illinois), but we had mixed feelings about replicating traditional 'tech' classes. Our first conversation focused on our thoughts after taking the structures exam, and how over-prepared we had felt. Surely, given the constraints of a 3-year Master's program, the focus and budgeting of time could be adjusted to substitute a bit of breadth for depth. Likewise, we wanted to emphasize the reliance of sub-disciplines on one another. We felt that, rather than separating sustainability into its own course or unit, the entire curriculum should be woven through with issues of environmental and social responsibility. Finally, we wanted to transmit some of the joy and excitement we'd felt in practice when things got figured out – when a subcontractor explained something in a way that gave us an inspiration for design, for example, or when a meeting with a structural and mechanical engineer produced a really clever solution that was neither pure architecture nor pure engineering. We wanted most of the learning to be intuitive, believing that formulae and figures could always be looked up, but common sense or basic understanding could not.

SCI-TECH, the technologies course sequence, has proven remarkably successful. We have enjoyed watching students from diverse, often non-technical backgrounds develop good working understandings of the complex physical issues that arise from building construction and performance. We have seen these issues tackled in parallel studio courses, where integrated designs have arisen based on the student's learning in the technology sequence and studio instructor's recognition that this knowledge is, essentially, another tool in the designer's box. Most importantly, we've seen students with backgrounds ranging from art and music to physics and medicine wrap their heads around some fairly abstruse physical and technical concepts in a hands-on, laboratory-like environment. We believe that this approach is inherently efficient and enjoyable, and we believe it can be easily replicated in a variety of academic – and professional – settings.

In short, we believe the time is right for a reassessment of what 'tech' means in architectural curricula. A new generation of students demands a curriculum that reflects what they're likely to need in their professional lives. This, we think, is important enough that tech might as well lead the way in connecting architecture's 'two cultures' – art and science – in practice and in education. There are dozens of exciting developments in the discipline today, including remarkably effective energy efficiency strategies, new material developments, structural modeling techniques and new ways of assessing and developing building environments. As with previous advances, the hard number crunching for these will inevitably be done by engineers and consultants. But we believe that architects need to know where these developments are heading, what their design implications and possibilities are, and how to work with increasingly sophisticated subcontractors, engineers, and technologists.

Design-Tech offers what we think is a basic framework for integrated knowledge. We've broken down a traditional curriculum into thematic sections – human factors, pre-design, building circulation, structural design, materials, and building systems. For each of these we've put together what we think practitioners need to know, given some history, some technical background, and some case studies that reveal how these aspects have been integrated into well-known or admirable designs. We've included the basic reference information that we think is needed at the desk, and suggested where students or practitioners can go for deeper resources. Our intent has been to focus on the breadth of technical knowledge required, following Vitruvius' admonition that all architects must be educated in a wide variety of fields, or in today's cliché, that architects must be jacks of all trades, if not masters of any.

We are deeply indebted to a generation of technology educators who have gone before us, and whose books have inspired and been constantly used by us. *Design-Tech* is, we think, best seen as an addition to such important, vital books as Ed Allen's *Fundamentals of Building Construction* and (with Joseph Iano) his *Architect's Studio Companion*, Francis D.K. Ching's *Building Construction Illustrated*, Mario Salvadori's *Structures for Architects*, Rowland Mainstone's *Developments in Structural Form*, Harry Parker's *Simplified Engineering for Architects and Builders* (improved and expanded by James Ambrose), Victor Olgyay's *Design With Climate*, Charlie Brown and Mark DeKay's *Sun, Wind, and Light*, Ernst Neufert's *Architect's Data* and the perennial *Architectural Graphic Standards*. We have referenced these books throughout our work, and noted carefully where one might turn to these for further information or elucidation.

Likewise, our careers have been informed by important mentors and teachers. Prof. Leslie owes much of his technical background to teachers at Illinois and Columbia, especially Mir Ali, Tony Webster, and Robert Silman; colleagues at Foster and Partners and Ove Arups, in particular David Nelson, Nigel Dancey, Peter Lassetter, Kevin Dong, Eric Ko, and Jon Markowitz; and a raft of collaborators on the Stanford University Center for Clinical Sciences Research project. Finally, Prof. Leslie would like to particularly acknowledge the teaching and guidance of the late Don Bergeson at Illinois. It is, sadly, too late to propose this book as extra credit for Prof. Bergeson's Environmental Systems class, but Leslie wishes (for many reasons) that this was still possible.

Prof. Alread thanks his good fortune for having started his education under the guidance of Martin Gundersen and Bernard Voichysank at the University of Florida, and later to have the mentorship of Thomas Beeby at Yale. Mentors in practice have continued that education with firm and patient guidance, in particular Rick Rados, John Locke and Mark Schmidt. Prof. Alread must also thank his longtime collaborators, Paul Mankins, Tim Hickman, and Todd Garner, who keep him ever mindful of the need to be humble and relentless in the pursuit of good work.

Finally, our teaching at Iowa State has been influenced and supported by colleagues who have welcomed our attempts at innovation, offered commentary and suggestions for our coursework, and reviewed elements of this book. Clare

Cardinal-Pett, the Director of Graduate Education in our department, deserves the distinct credit for giving us the chance to re-write the tech curriculum within the friendly confines of our Master's program, and for constantly pushing us toward experimentation and innovation. Jamie Horwitz, Marwan Ghandour, Karen Bermann, Kimberly Zarecor, Richard Becherer, and Mikesch Muecke have welcomed the development of our coursework as the Graduate Faculty, and the graduate students who have gone along for this ride deserve special mention for their willingness to serve as guinea pigs, and for their feedback and energy. The Technology Faculty in the Department have also been valuable resources and have supported this project, and we're grateful for the support of David Block, Bruce Bassler, Matthew Fisher, Gregory Palermo, and Jim Bolluyt. Heidi Hohmann very graciously agreed to provide the chapter on Landscape and Paving, and Ann Sobiech-Munson, equally graciously, agreed to save chapters on technical documentation for a future edition. Finally, Cal Lewis, as Chair of the Architecture Department, has given us the academic space and resources to turn our scrappy class notes into this book, and a generous Subvention Grant from Iowa State's Vice Provost for Research's office has provided funding for illustrations and graphics. Speaking of which, we're very grateful for the dedicated work of Anna Aversing and Sade Reed in developing clear (and occasionally quite funny) diagrams from the napkins and post-its we gave them.

Technology, for all the hype, is just how we do stuff. Design is a much higher calling, since it builds *how* we do things into bigger statements that involve the emotions, the spirit, society, and culture. We hope this book helps students, educators, practitioners, and people who are just interested in how – and why – buildings get built connect the two.

Thomas Leslie
Jason Alread

A note on measurement

Throughout this book, we've used both metric and imperial (American) units in parallel. Our hope is that it can be used equally well for both systems.

To do this, we've gone beyond standard conversions and instead tried to translate meaningful units of measure back and forth. In our view, it's not been enough to say – accurately – that a 12-ft span is equivalent to a 3.6576-m span. That may be true, but no metric designer would start with a number like this. Both systems have their 'idioms,' or standard basic dimensions. So in situations like this, we've gone for easy comprehensibility over dead accuracy, and translated 12-ft spans as 3.5 m. Occasionally this gets us into a slightly awkward situation in examples, where translation errors pile up, and we've been forthright about where this happens and about the minor adjustments needed to get things back on track.

That principle applies generally to the formulae, tables, and examples throughout the book. This isn't intended as an authoritative reference, and where we have faced the choice between absolute precision and general understanding we've opted for the latter. One of the great joys of architecture is working with expert consultants, gaining a bit of insight into their field, and assimilating their advice and work. We've intended this book to be an introduction to the various specialties included, and a general reference. In part because of its global scope, the information here is necessarily subject to a wide range of local conditions, and professional consultants should be engaged for any project of reasonable size.

Photo credits

All illustrations by the Authors, Anna Aversing, Sade Reed, or in the public domain, except for the following:

Page	Description	Credit
52	Program Analysis; Cad models	Alissa MacInnes
80	2.1.1	© Josh Lott/Reuters/Corbis
126	2.4.5	© Peter Cook/VIEW Pictures
200	3.5.11	Kimbell Art Museum
220	4.1.2	© Sean Sexton Collection/CORBIS
248	4.2.13	Antoni Gaudi, Sweeney, James Johnson. © 1970. Reproduced with permission of Greenwood Publishing Group, Westport, CT.
266	4.3.19	Benedikt Huber and Jean-Claude Steinegger, *Jean Prouve*. © 1971
278–279	Table 4.4.1	Copyright © American Institute of Steel Construction, Inc. Reprinted with Permission. All rights reserved.
292	Figure 4.5.5	Copyright © American Institute of Steel Construction, Inc. Reprinted with Permission. All rights reserved.
294–295	Table 4.5.1	Copyright © American Institute of Steel Construction, Inc. Reprinted with Permission. All rights reserved.
308	Figure 4.6.2	The Works of Pier Luigi Nervi, Ernesto Rogers. © 1957 Reproduced with permission of Greenwood Publishing Group, Westport, CT.
314–315	Figures 4.6.7, 4.6.8	The Works of Pier Luigi Nervi, Ernesto Rogers. © 1957 Reproduced with permission of Greenwood Publishing Group, Westport, CT.
319	Figure 4.7.1	© Bettmann/CORBIS
325	Figure 4.7.6	Foster and Partners

Photo credits

Introduction: Basic Design Parameters

0.1 Human factors: anthropomorphics

The Body	Range of motion
	Human scale
	The 95th percentile
Ergonomic/Anthropometric Design	How we fit into a built environment
	Human productivity
	Hazards to well being

Design for people

One of the main issues designers face when approaching a project is, 'how big should it be?' This is determined by the intended use, number of users, circulation needs, furniture, and equipment requirements. Once these are accounted for the question becomes, 'How much individual space do the people need?'

There are resources that can assist in determining the typical size and arrangements of people, furniture, and spaces. The human body has been measured and statistically averaged to provide information that can accommodate most of the population. This does not mean you shouldn't measure your own surrounding environment and decide whether or not you think it's adequate, but these resources can help with understanding how others have solved these same problems.

Another primary issue that designers face is when it's appropriate to 'redesign the wheel'. There are arguments for re-examining problems without knowing the standard approach, because that allows for new ideas to emerge. Many times, however, there are problems that have been considered many thousands of times and those solutions are available for your review. Always starting from scratch is impractical, always using the standard approach limits creativity and progress. Be aware of what information is available, and then decide what to use and what to discard.

The body

The laws of physics and the mechanics of the body govern human movements within buildings. We balance in certain ways, walk within a small range of speed, sit comfortably based on our pivot points, and can reach things based on predictable sets of movements. Designing within the tolerances of most people requires an understanding of two issues:

The 95th percentile – is the range of human sizes that are accommodated within typical structures. A 2.1 m (7 ft) tall person falls outside of this range, as does a 180 k (400 lb) person. A 0.9 m (3 ft) tall person may or may not, depending

Introduction: basic design parameters

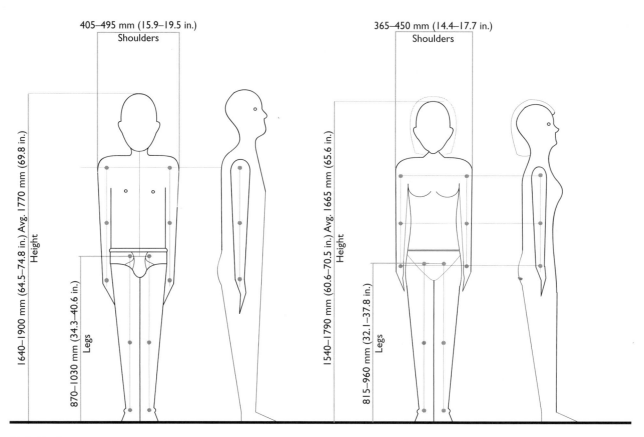

Typical body measurements

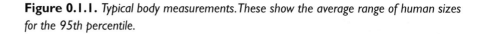

Figure 0.1.1. *Typical body measurements. These show the average range of human sizes for the 95th percentile.*

on whether you are expected to accommodate children. Sometimes it is necessary to duplicate functions at different heights or spacing in order to serve all users. The sizes also evolve as the averages change over time and cultural differences are taken into account (Fig. 0.1.1).

Range of motion – covers how a body can maneuver from a fixed position. Reach, rotation, sight lines, standing and sitting positions all factor into the range of motion.

References/measurement charts

Building guides such as *Timesaver Standards, Architectural Graphic Standards, and Neufert's Architects Data* give you building and furniture configurations with the average sizes of the occupants already factored in. References like Diffrient's (1974) *Human Scale* and Dreyfus' (2002) *The Measure of Man and Woman: Human Factors in Design* allow you to see the detailed dimensions of the body, which provides the opportunity to decide for yourself which layouts work. Typically, the general planning information is adequate unless you're designing furniture or equipment that requires customizing how a person interacts with it. Codes also have requirements for minimum sizes, in the case of fire exit pathways (Section 2.1, Life Safety), or ranges of heights and reach for people with disabilities (Section 2.2, Accessibility).

Body relationship to individual equipment

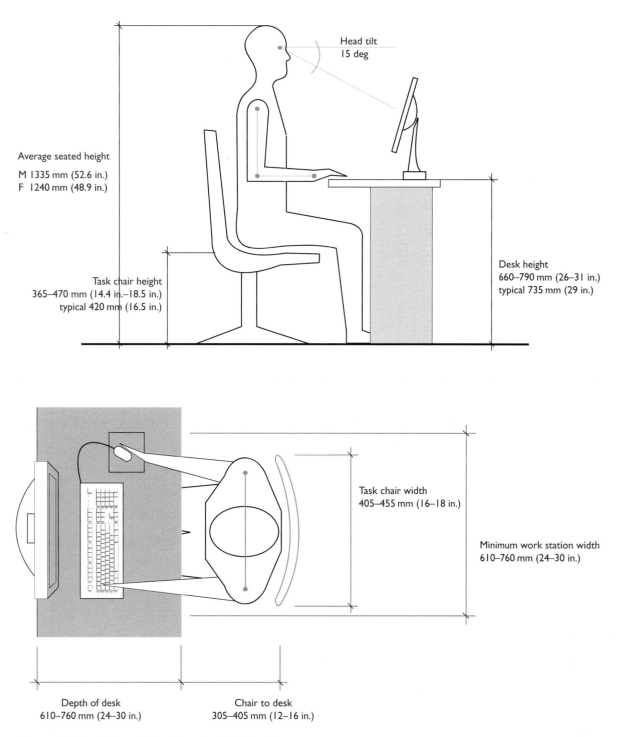

Head tilt
15 deg

Average seated height

M 1335 mm (52.6 in.)
F 1240 mm (48.9 in.)

Task chair height
365–470 mm (14.4 in.–18.5 in.)
typical 420 mm (16.5 in.)

Desk height
660–790 mm (26–31 in.)
typical 735 mm (29 in.)

Task chair width
405–455 mm (16–18 in.)

Minimum work station width
610–760 mm (24–30 in.)

Depth of desk
610–760 mm (24–30 in.)

Chair to desk
305–405 mm (12–16 in.)

Figure 0.1.2. *Bodies relationship to individual equipment.*

There are two methods for figuring out the amount of space people need, but both are based on the same basic idea, that humans take up a certain amount of space and move in similar ways when going about their busy days. The first method is to look at an individual body and the activity they are undertaking, such as working at a computer station (Fig. 0.1.2). Starting from this point you can add up all of the intended users, their activities, required circulation, add in

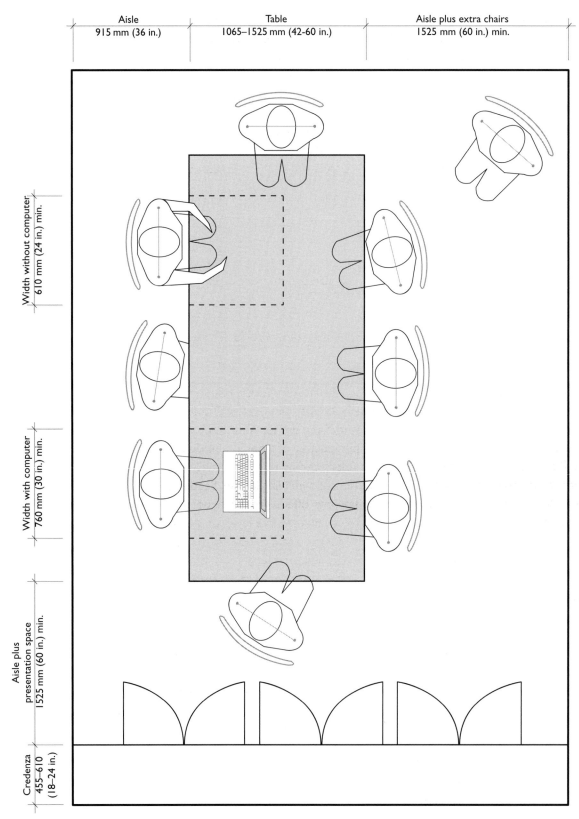

Figure 0.1.3. *Bodies relationship to specific use room.*

service areas, and every other individual area requirement to get the size of a building. This method is impractical for most buildings due to the immense complexity of having to account for every person and their movements. The second method uses guides based on average overall sizes of room types, such as a conference room (Fig. 0.1.3). These room guides have already taken into account the area for individuals, their circulation and other typical needs. The individual method for figuring spaces works for very custom situations, but the guides to typical room size are often more effective because they have used the experience of many previous successful projects to test their validity.

Ergonomic/anthropometric design

Ergonomics are design factors intended to maximize productivity or efficiency by minimizing fatigue and discomfort.

Anthropometrics are the measurements of the human body for use in comparison or design.

Most building projects accommodate people and therefore have a relationship to ergonomics. Taking into account how people interact with a project requires a detailed look at the sizes and heights of everything we see and touch. This is done by considering the design from the perspective of a person inside the space. Plan drawings are only one tool for understanding this, and usually not the most descriptive as no one actually experiences a building in plan. Sections, interior elevations, perspectives, and detail drawings offer a greater opportunity to see the design from a human point of view. Human eye level for standing adults varies between 1.2 and 1.8 m (4 and 6 ft) and seated heights average between 0.9 and 1.4 m (3 and 4.5 ft). These are the points of view that must be considered along with the parameters of how a body moves through and interacts with a space.

The issue of productivity has been carefully studied, thoroughly dissected, extensively tested, and widely published. Still it is an elusive and seemingly moving target. Even the most efficient layout can create overly repetitive actions, become tiresome to the user and begin to hurt efficiency. Adequate light is needed, but efficiency improves when the light levels vary. Consistent environmental comfort can be maintained, but variations in climate seem to improve productivity. In the 1960s and 1970s many elementary and secondary schools were built without windows. This was seen to have many positive impacts, such as higher energy efficiencies and fewer distractions for students. The logic of this was supported by research studies such as C.T. Larson's 1965 compilation *The Effect of Windowless Classrooms on Elementary School Children*, which suggested that there should be no adverse effect in schools without windows. Student performance in these schools briefly increased, and then steadily dropped over time. The children needed mental breaks to improve concentration, and natural light provides desirable variations in the environment. This has been supported in many recent studies such as the Heschong

Mahone Group's report 'Daylighting in Schools,' which shows long term increases of 5–25% in student performance in day lit environments.

The positive effects of some variety in human environments cannot be over-stated. Studies on the ideal consistent work place have consistently shown that people respond well to variations in environment. Rather than find the ideal workplace, researchers realized this basic human tendency; *we like change and we get bored easily*. Add to this that no two people react to changes the same way. So don't get too consumed with determining the perfect consistent solution. Flexibility, variability, individual preference, and the ability to change can be just as important as basic efficiency.

The following are some standard heights and rules of thumb that are helpful to know in order to accomplish many projects dealing with human inhabitation. Be sure to check local building codes for compliance:

Desk/conference/dining table height	710–760 mm (28–30 in.)
Desk depth	610–915 mm (24–36 in.)
Dining table for four depth (square or round)	760–1220 mm (30–48 in.)
Kitchen counter height	865–915 mm (34–36 in.)
Kitchen counter depth	535–610 mm (21–24 in.)
Bar/low bank transaction standing counter height	1065 mm (42 in.)
High bank-ticket transaction counter height	1400 mm (55 in.)
Bath sink height	760–915 mm (30–36 in.)
Guardrail height	1065 mm (42 in.)
Handrail height	840–915 mm (33–36 in.)
Door width	710–915 mm (28–36 in.)
Door handle height	915–1065 mm (36–42 in.)
Light switch height	1065–1220 mm (36–48 in.)
Window mullion height to avoid	1525 mm (60 in.)
Side chair/bench height	405–455 mm (16–18 in.)
Side chair/bench depth	455 mm (18 in.)
Stair riser maximum	175 mm (7 in.)
Stair run minimum	280 mm (11 in.)
Corridor width	760–2440 mm (30–96 in.)
Ceiling height minimums	2130 mm (7 ft) garage, 2440 mm (8 ft) house, 2740 mm (9 ft) office

Frequently asked questions

'Why are rooms in the standard reference books generally square or rectangular?' The reference guides typically demonstrate minimum and common sizes for efficient arrangement of spaces. Because most building components and furniture come in right angles, this tends to be the most efficient way to fabricate and inhabit buildings. Deviations from rectangular volumes generally create less

efficient space, but can offer design advantages when applied skillfully. Don't however assume that spaces that are square in plan must be boring and spaces that are shaped are interesting. The quality of a space has more to do with light, materials, texture, acoustics, articulation, and detailing than it does shape.

'How do you decide how big to make a conference or dining table?'
This is determined by two primary factors, first is the shape of the table and second is the amount of space each person needs. The shape can vary from round to long and rectangular. Round tables tend to democratize participation in discussions and can be placed without concern to orientation; however, when the tables are large, people can be sitting too far away from the person across. Rectangular shapes have ends that favor privileged seating, can fit into narrow rooms, and people sit fairly close to the person across. If presentations need to be made in smaller rooms, rectangular tables are typically used, while in large meeting halls round tables are typically used. Individual space determines the size of table. This ranges from about 610 to 760 mm (24 to 30 in.) per person, with the smaller size for seating only and the larger sizes for full dining or laptop use. Up to 915 mm (36 in.) can be provided, but begins to distance individuals from interaction with one another.

Conclusion

Anthropometrics and ergonomics give designers an idea of how to start a project. No building can be properly conceived without a basic idea of how people will be using it, and we typically use a variety of precedents and references in the initial stages of design. While the reference materials give an idea of the most efficient sizes or layouts, building design involves more factors than pure efficiency or the ability to be flexible. Keep in mind the larger goals of each project. The most efficient church design, laid out by using dimensional diagrams, would look like a low budget classroom, not at all matching the expectations or aspirations of the user group. A designer should be able to deal equally with pragmatics and intangibles when designing a project. Use the references to avoid mistakes and understand common standards but also consider your everyday environment carefully. Catalog the things you see that work well and the things that work poorly. The ability to design great environments is a synthetic process that requires the consideration of many factors at one time. The decision making process must be able to flow naturally from a vast collection of both outside references and personal knowledge.

Glossary and formulas

The 95th Percentile	The range of human sizes that are accommodated within typical structures.
Anthropometrics	The measurements of the human body for use in comparison or design.
Ergonomics	Design factors intended to maximize productivity or efficiency by minimizing fatigue and discomfort.
Range of Motion	How a body can maneuver from a fixed position.

References and further reading

Rumbarger, J. and Vitullo, R.J. (eds) (1994/2000) Human Dimensions (Chapter 1), *Ramse/ Sleeper, Architectural Graphic Standards*, 9th or 10th ed (NY: John Wiley & Sons) p. 2–7.

DeChiara, J. (2001) *Timesaver Standards for Interior Design and Space Planning* (NY: McGraw-Hill).

DeChiara, J. (1990) *Timesaver Standards for Building Types* (NY: McGraw-Hill).

Diffrient, N. (1974) *Humanscale 1, 2, 3–4, 5, 6–7, 8, 9* (Cambridge, MA: MIT Press).

Panero, J. and Zelnik, M. (1979) *Human Dimensions and Interior Space* (NY: Whitney Library of Design).

Dreyfus, H. (2002) *The Measure of Man and Woman: Human Factors in Design* (NY: John Wiley & Sons).

Larson, C.T. (1965) *The Effect of Windowless Classrooms on Elementary School Children* (Architectural Research Laboratory, Department of Architecture, University of Michigan, Ann Arbor).

Neufert, E. and Neufert, P. (2002) *Architects Data* (UK: Blackwell Science). pp. 15–19 and sections on building types.

0.2   Human factors: basic human comfort

Human Body	Reaction to climate changes
	The basic issues of warming and cooling the body
	The 'comfort zone'
Climate Control	History
	Active systems
	Passive systems

The primary issues of human comfort

The human body is capable of life within a fairly wide range of earth's environmental conditions. Outside of the poles, people inhabit virtually every part of the earth. Within the range of overall climatic conditions is a tighter range of coziness that promotes human productivity called the 'comfort zone.' Shelters, constructed or found, are the primary source of attaining human comfort. Shelter modifies the natural environment to create livable environments. In this section we will study the factors of comfort we're trying to control.

The main issue for comfort, or even survival, is temperature. Radiation, air movement, humidity, and precipitation all factor into comfort to a lesser degree and ultimately affect the way the body feels air temperature.

Human body

The human body reacts to hot or cold environments with an attempt to maintain a constant core body temperature. Our natural reactions can accommodate a range of temperatures and still feel comfortable. There are two sets of reactions the body has to extreme conditions at either end of the temperature and humidity scale, from hot-humid environments to extreme cold (Fig. 0.2.1).

Reaction to hot–humid environments

The body gains more heat than it can use and tries to shed the excess. This heat must be moved from the body core to the skin to dissipate to the environment. The heart rate increases to move blood flow to the periphery and blood vessels at the skin dilate to move heat to outer layers of the body. Perspiration occurs to cool the skin, however in humid environments it does not evaporate quickly, limiting its effectiveness. Heat exhaustion, followed by heat stroke, is an extreme case of thermal stress.

Reaction to extreme cold

The body loses heat faster than it can produce it and tries to generate heat by involuntary movement. 'Goose pimples' (small muscle contractions at the

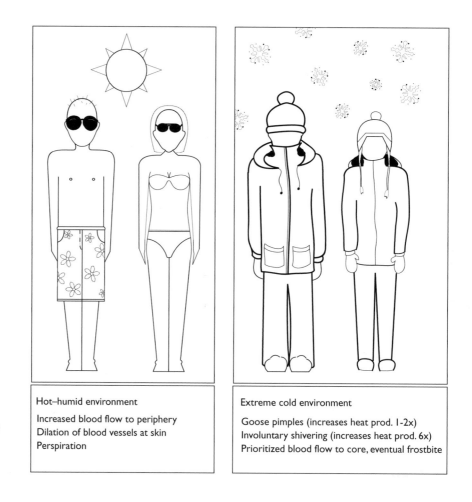

Figure 0.2.1. *The body's reaction to extreme ends of the environment.*

Hot–humid environment

Increased blood flow to periphery
Dilation of blood vessels at skin
Perspiration

Extreme cold environment

Goose pimples (increases heat prod. 1-2x)
Involuntary shivering (increases heat prod. 6x)
Prioritized blood flow to core, eventual frostbite

skin) occur, increasing total body heat production by 1–2 times resting levels. Involuntary shivering can also occur (muscle contractions of whole parts of the body) which increases heat production by 6 times resting levels. In an attempt to keep vital organs functioning, the body prioritizes blood flow. Under extreme stress the body eventually allows limbs to succumb to frostbite while protecting the core and brain functions.

While the body maintains a constant core temperature for efficient functioning, this does not mean that buildings should maintain a constant temperature and humidity all day or all year long.

The human body and its thermal control systems are designed to allow for constant environmental changes. Fluctuations in temperature, air movement and light are beneficial and stimulating. Human senses respond well to some change and our range of daily activities typically changes, making variable environments both necessary and desirable.

The major factors affecting thermal comfort are as follows (Fig. 0.2.2):

1 *Activity* increases your metabolic rate, which raises body temperature.
2 *Clothing* acts as an insulator, allowing your body to retain more heat rather than losing it to the environment.

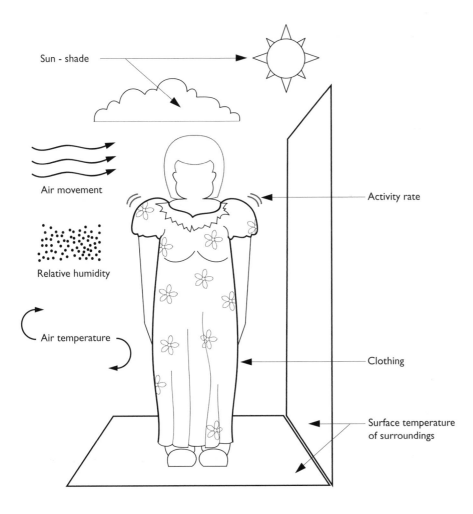

Sun - shade

Air movement

Relative humidity

Air temperature

Activity rate

Clothing

Surface temperature
of surroundings

Figure 0.2.2. *The main factors affecting human comfort.*

3 *Air movement* increases the skin's ability to remove heat by evaporation of perspiration.

4 *Air temperature* is what your exposed skin feels, if it's above your skin temperature it feels warm if it's below it feels cool.

5 *Surface temperatures of surroundings* radiate heat and cold into the fluid medium of air, and conduct heat and cold directly from the body in contact with a surface.

6 *Relative humidity (RH)* is the amount of moisture in the air, which affects how well perspiration can cause evaporative cooling and how very dry air can make the body feel uncomfortable.

7 *Sun and Shade* effect the way your body is warmed by radiant heat from the sun. Air temperature may be the same in sun and shade, but your body surface will heat when directly exposed to the sun's radiation.

The sensation of thermal comfort occurs when the body is in equilibrium with its physical environment. The seven factors listed above all interact to produce relative degrees of thermal comfort in various situations.

For example, if the outside temperature were 72°F (22°C) with a RH of 50% most people would feel quite comfortable at rest. The body, lightly insulated by clothing, is in equilibrium with the surrounding air temperature and air moisture. Going for a run would make you feel hot and sweaty due to the increase in body temperature and the resulting perspiration in an effort to create cooling. If you stop and a breeze is blowing you would feel slightly cold, due to evaporative heat loss without the increased body temperature of running. Now put on a black business suit while the breeze stops and stand on the street in the sun. This will make you feel uncomfortably warm because the suit both over-insulates and absorbs the radiant heat from the sun, raising your skin temperature above 85°F (29.5°C).

The next day if it's a windless 62°F (16.7°C) with the same 50% humidity and you sit outside with a swimsuit on, in direct sunlight, you would likely feel comfortable again. The radiant heat from the sun will increase the skin temperature above the air temperature to a comfortable level; however, any wind will quickly overcome this effect and cause too much cooling effect.

The body also reacts to radiant heat from surfaces like walls. Skin is approximately 85°F, if the walls in a room are over that temperature the body will be warmed, otherwise you will lose heat to the room. Stand next to a cold window in the winter and you will get uncomfortably cold quickly, but even a 65°F (18°C) wall will draw heat from inhabitants. Conduction, or direct contact with the cold or warm materials, quickens the reaction. Stand on a cold marble floor in a 70°F (21°C) house in the winter and your entire body will feel cold quickly.

This illustrates the fact that thermal comfort is affected by all of the seven major factors listed above. No single temperature or humidity is comfortable to everyone in every condition. Typically building environments are designed with a target median comfort level of the air temperature only, and that may or may not be appropriate for the use of the project. Different cultures and regions also tend to react to temperature shifts in various ways, when Americans turn up the heat the British often put on a sensible sweater. People from colder environments tend to react to hot weather with greater discomfort than those from warm environments and the reverse is also true. The popular belief that your blood is 'thinner' and less resistant to cold if you're from a warm environment is not supported by fact, but nonetheless people grow accustomed to their typical discomforts in environmental conditions and are less tolerant of opposite extremes.

The 'COMFORT ZONE' is a defined and charted combination of factors – air movement, air temperature, RH, and radiation where a human body with average clothing at rest in the shade will be comfortable (Fig. 0.2.3).

Looking at the Bioclimatic Chart, the comfort zone is an oval area that exists between 70°F and 82°F (21°C and 28°C) and 20–80% RH. At higher humidity levels the temperature lowers, due to the inability of the body to use evaporative cooling.

The comfort zone can be extended in any direction by using radiant heat, air moisture, wind, and a combination of these factors. For example, 63°F (17°C) dry bulb and 40% RH is below the comfort zone temperature shown on the chart, but within the humidity comfort. A person could be made comfortable by extending the comfort zone down through adding 100 BTU/hr of radiant heat, shown in the horizontal lines below the comfort zone oval.

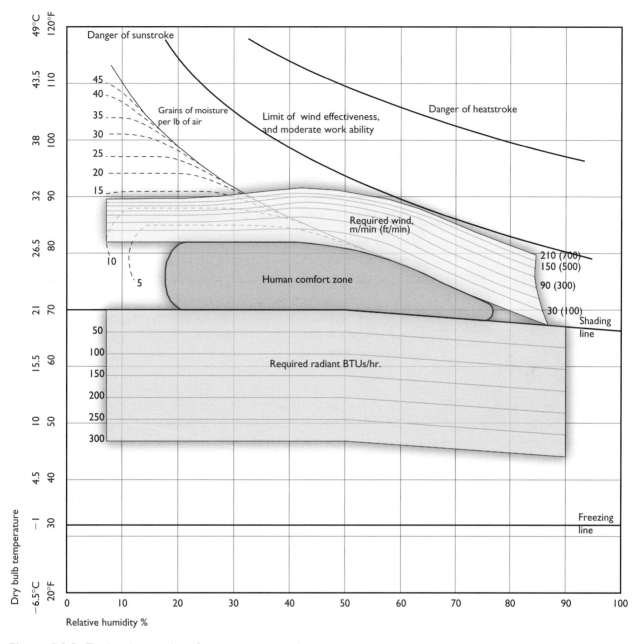

Figure 0.2.3. *The bio-climatic chart for temperate zone climates.*

Eighty-five degrees Fahrenheit and 30% RH are above the comfort zone temperature, but within the lower part of the humidity comfort. A person could be comfortable by three different methods or a combination of them. Adding a wind speed of 60 m/min (200 ft/min) would raise the comfort zone, as shown in the curved wind lines above the comfort zone oval. Adding eight grains of moisture per pound of dry air to the atmosphere would also raise the comfort zone, as shown in the dashed lines in the upper left hand side of the chart. Reducing the mean radiant temperature (MRT) of the surrounding surfaces to 80°F (26.7°C) would again raise the comfort zone, as shown in the vertical bars of temperature on the left hand side of the chart. Depending on the condition it may be preferable to use one method over the others, or a combination of factors. In this example 30% RH is acceptable, but on the lower end of comfort so adding moisture might add most to the comfort of

15

the inhabitants. Adding this much moisture may prove to be difficult, however, so it is possible to add five grains of moisture and a lower wind speed such as 30 m/min (100 ft/min). Once you combine factors it is necessary to interpolate more on the chart, but the primary benefit of using this diagram is to determine appropriate passive strategies for environmental control rather than specific calculations of system design.

The chart also assumes that a person is in normal clothing and at rest in the shade. Active environments like a gymnasium would require lower temperatures, lower humidity, lower MRT, or a combination of all three. Different areas within a building may also require different conditions. The locker room in a gymnasium would not benefit from being colder, but the humidity level may typically be raised due to the use of showers. A grocery store desires colder temperatures and lower humidity to keep food fresher. People in a grocery are normally wearing the coat they had on outside in cold weather and are not at rest while walking up and down the aisles, so it is acceptable to lower temperature and humidity. Keep in mind the specific needs of the inhabitants you are designing for and deviate from the charts as necessary to achieve appropriate comfort.

Climate control

Buildings offer many services to the inhabitants, but one of the automatically assumed functions is modifying climate. While we will cover traditional building types by region later, it should be noted that there are many different ways to achieve the 'comfort zone.' The systems humans use to modify climate are typically broken into two types, 'Active' and 'Passive' systems. Most modern buildings use a combination of the two systems, but the introduction of new technologies has drastically changed the way we approach comfort, frequently for the worse.

Active Systems are mechanically driven heating and cooling systems. These can range from simple fans or hot water radiators to fully air-conditioned and furnace heated systems. The 'Active' part of these systems is the energy required to drive the heating and cooling. None of the active systems could run without a source of power driving them. Even a traditional fireplace has an active component, because the wood it burns is an outside fuel consumed to run the system.

Passive Systems heat and cool with no outside energy or power required to run the system. An operable window is part of a passive system (apart from the fact that you are the power that operates it). Windmills, evaporative water-cooling, fixed sun shading, windbreaks, thermal mass walls, and strategically placed vegetation are all components of a passive system. Not usually considered in the passive definition is the energy used to produce the building components. This is called 'embodied energy' and sometimes can make a passive system more costly or environmentally damaging than an active system; so don't automatically assume all passive is good and all active is bad. These decisions require designers to research which systems are the most appropriate.

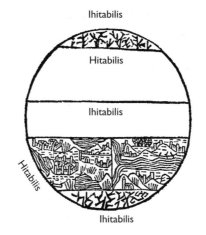

Ihitabilis

Hitabilis

Ihitabilis

Hitabilis

Ihitabilis

Figure 0.2.4. *Socrobosco's diagram of the inhabitable places on the earth, from the 13th century.*

Historically heating has been the easiest modification to handle. Wood or coal burning stoves have been around for ages, whereas cooling has been much more difficult to achieve. This generally drove larger populations to temperate zones, where it never got overly hot and heating to comfort was possible (Fig. 0.2.4). Temperate zones tend to have brief warm summers, longer moderate fall and spring weather, and colder winters. Hybrid building types developed in these areas that allowed for summer breeze cooling, minimal fall and spring environmental needs, and efficient winter wood and coal heating.

More recently systems have been developed that make tropical zone cooling possible, and therefore we've seen large population shifts to regions where previously inhabitation had been limited by heat and humidity. One hundred years ago the notion of moving to a climate like Miami, Florida, or Kuala Lumpur was extreme, while residing in Buffalo, New York, or Helsinki was considered reasonable – now the opposite would be seen as true. Cultural and political reasons aside, people have decided that with adequate cooling it is more pleasant to live in warmer environments. Buildings in general can be built initially more economically where there is no freeze/thaw cycle. Also, when air conditioning is included in homes, vehicles and workplaces, being in the outdoor environment becomes a matter of choice rather than necessity. However, the long-term energy used to enable this transformation has been enormous and increasingly costly. In an effort to lose as little cooling or heat as possible, buildings have been sealed tight – creating unhealthy air quality. Generating power to run mechanical systems is also costly and has a negative environmental impact. Because buildings are one of the primary consumers of energy, intelligent design decisions can have a large effect on long-term costs and environment impacts, while still maintaining reasonable human comfort.

Frequently asked questions

'Why doesn't everyone use passive control systems in the design of new buildings?' While this is the traditional way of creating buildings from the time before modern HVAC systems, concerns about the cost of energy in the 1970s caused most designers to seal buildings tight in an effort to limit heating and cooling losses. Controlled active mechanical systems are very predictable in

terms of managing human comfort, while passive systems can be less certain. These two factors over time caused a loss of the basic knowledge required to create passive structures. With the re-emergence of concerns about the environment and the cost of energy, designers are again engaged in trying to make buildings more passive, but it will take time to educate the profession, consultants and clients.

'If skin temperature is 29.5°C (85°F), why does that air temperature feel hot?' Because we normally wear clothes that allow us to insulate against cooler temperatures. Most shower or bath water is at or above this 29.5°C (85°F) temperature, because this is what feels comfortable to naked skin. Activity rates also generate heat, making this temperature uncomfortable. At rest, in the shade, unclothed, with some air movement 29.5°C (85°F) air temperature would feel neutral.

Conclusion

The reason for understanding the science of human comfort is to create comfortable shelter. During the development of a design project many of the tasks related to attaining comfort will be handled by consulting engineers. Their primary job is to take what the architect has designed and make it comfortable with active environmental control systems, without modifying the building design. Typically they will not make suggestions for changing the design to make it more efficient, not always out of ignorance but because that is how their role has been defined. Most of the decisions about a building's environmental efficiency and ability to use passive systems will have been made by the time schematic design is done, before consulting engineers have even begun work. The goal is to understand what makes people environmentally comfortable and how to most effectively design the building to take advantage of passive systems during early planning. Understanding comfort requires consideration of the specific use and purpose of the proposed building along with the factors that create a comfortable environment.

Glossary and formulas

Air	a mixture of the following gases:
	Nitrogen – 78.00%
	Oxygen – 21.00%
	Carbon Dioxide – 00.03%
	Water Vapor
	Trace elements such as Helium and Krypton in small amounts.
BTU (British Thermal Unit)	The quantity of heat required to raise 1 pound of water 1°F in temperature.
Celsius	Metric temperature scale that measures the freezing point of water at 0° and the boiling point at 100° (at normal atmospheric pressure). $C = (F - 32) \div 1.8$.
Condensation	The process by which a gas or vapor changes to a liquid.

Dew Point	The temperature at which air becomes 100% saturated with moisture and changes state to from gas to liquid.
Dry Bulb Temperature	A measure of the heat intensity at a point in degrees (F, C, or K).
Enthalpy	The total heat (both latent and sensible) of a substance.
Fahrenheit	US temperature scale that measures the freezing point of water at 32° and the boiling point at 212° (at normal atmospheric pressure). F = (C × 1.8) + 32.
Kelvin	Scientific temperature scale where absolute zero is measured as 273° below the freezing point of water. Each Kelvin degree equals one Celsius degree. K = C − 273.
Latent Heat	Heat transfer involved in the change of state of a substance (usually the evaporation or condensation of water, perspiration, or refrigerant).
Metabolism	Burning of fuel (food) to maintain a constant body temperature.
Rate of Metabolism	How much food is burned in a given amount of time is generally proportional to body weight. It is dependent on: Activity – rate increases at higher activity levels. Gender – male rates are typically 15% higher than female rates for the same activity level. Health and Age – older or ill people have lower rates. Amount and weight of clothing. Surrounding atmosphere – temperature, humidity, wind, and radiant heat.
Relative Humidity (RH)	The ratio of the amount of water vapor in the air at a specific temperature to the maximum amount that the air could hold at that temperature, expressed as a percentage.
Sensible Heat	A change in the heat content of a substance that causes the substance to change temperature (measured in BTUs).
Wet Bulb Temperature	A temperature taken with a thermometer whose bulb is surrounded by a layer of wet gauze. The difference between wet and dry bulb temperatures, measured with a sling psychrometer, shows the dew point temperature or the temperature that water condenses (typically on a surface).

Further reading

Olgyay, V. (1963) *Design with Climate: Bioclimatic Approach to Architectural Regionalism* (Princeton, NJ: Princeton University Press).

Neufert, E. and Neufert, P. (2000) *Architect's Data*, 3rd ed (London, UK: Blackwell Science). pp. 19–23.

0.3   Environment: basic climatology

Climate Zones	Cool, temperate, hot–arid, hot–humid Regional climate evaluation methods Thermal, solar, wind, humidity and precipitation factors
Climate Strategies	Traditional regional building types Economical, physical and psychological needs Determining the correct approach
Micro Climates	Site selection factors Working with rather than against your environment

Introduction to climatology

Climatology is the science that deals with prevailing weather conditions. It's important to understand the climactic conditions when designing a structure, in order to create a desirable environment for the inhabitants and to deal most efficiently with the weather's impact on the building.

Systems for mechanically modifying building environments can allow virtually any structure to maintain human comfort, but the efficiency/cost of the system and quality of the interior air are drastically affected by the decisions made during building design.

Regional differences in climate create vastly different requirements for the design of buildings. This may not seem apparent based on the similar 'look' of buildings in varying places, but each region places a different set of forces on a structure. These differences can be clearly seen by studying traditional regional building types that existed without mechanical heating or cooling. Designers are often faced with the issue of borrowing building styles from other regions, regardless of their climactic efficiency. It becomes the responsibility of designers to not only create technically efficient structures, but also to determine what is the regionally appropriate character of a building.

Climate zones

Depending on the source, the earth is usually categorized into four, five or more climate zones. We'll use the four zone descriptions for simplicity, assuming the cool and polar zones on the chart have a similar set of conditions with varying extremes. The descriptions cover the zones in the US and Europe, and the chart shows worldwide areas (Fig. 0.3.1). The UK is mostly in the temperate zone, with northern areas into the cool climates, the US has all four zones represented.

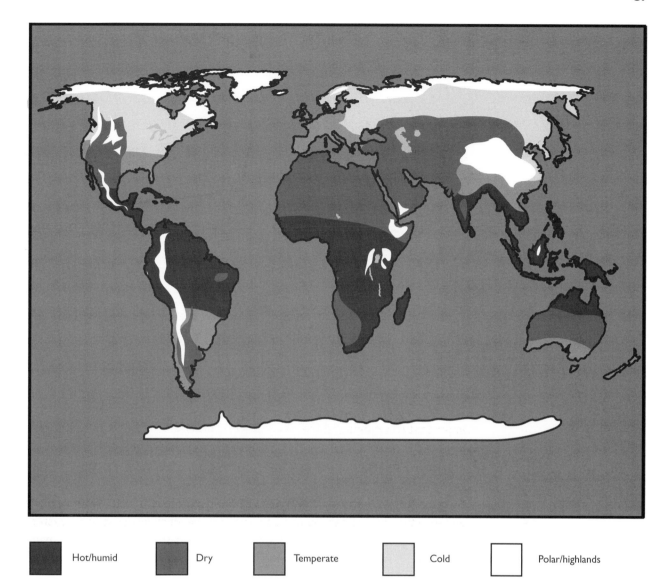

Figure 0.3.1. *World climate zone map, showing hot/humid, dry, temperate, cold and polar areas of climate.*

While most of the variances are a factor of latitude (measurement lines circling the globe *parallel* to the equator and at intervals north and south), there are many variances based on other factors such as altitude, proximity to large bodies of water, prevailing winds, ground surface conditions, and vegetation.

Hot–humid climates

Gulf Coast US, Central Africa, Southern Europe, and Southeast Asia
Summer sun very high in the sky
Winter days relatively long and warm
Long summer
High humidity

Hot–arid climates (Dry)

Southwestern US and inland Central America, North Africa, Middle East, and
Central Australia

Summer sun very high in the sky
Short sunny winter
Minimum precipitation
Large daily temperature swings
Low humidity

Temperate climates

Middle US latitudes, Most of Europe, Southern Russia, and Northern China
Four distinct seasons: cold winter, hot/humid summer, intermediate spring and fall
Moderate length days
Sun changes height in sky more than hot climates
Typically snows and frost layer forms in winter

Cool climates

Forty-five degree north latitude, Northern US and Canada, Northern Europe and Russia, All Areas near the Poles
Very long, cool summer days
Very short winter days – sun very low in the sky
Heavy snow and deep frost layers

Regional climactic analyses can be obtained through local meteorological societies or in resource texts (a good example is in *Sun, Wind & Light* 2nd ed. by Brown and DeKay). The information is extremely helpful in determining how to design for the local climate. The following factors are most important and are shown in many charts:

A. *Thermal analysis* shows the range and distribution of temperatures throughout the year. The dew point (point at which airborne moisture condenses to liquid) and the diurnal cycle (24-h cycle of day to night) of temperatures are also shown and give a good picture of just how comfortable the outside temperatures are.

B. *Solar analysis* shows the hours of sunshine broken up quantitatively for clear and cloudy days. Simply put, knowing how sunny it is provides an essential tool for design. A building in a very sunny place should both utilize and protect from the sun's heat while using the direct light without glare. A building in a cloudy environment will not have as much radiant heat and will need to have more open window area to capture daylight.

C. *Wind analysis* shows wind direction and velocity. Keep in mind that these may be measured in an open field or on top of a building, small site differences like a hill or trees can completely alter this data. Wind can also be blocked or channeled into different directions from the prevailing conditions.

D. *Humidity analysis* shows an average percentage of RH during the day for each month. Humidity affects both comfort and building durability. Condensation, corrosion, mold, and discoloration can be caused by moisture collecting on or inside of building assemblies. Still air, heat, and moisture provide perfect growing conditions for bacteria, mold, and other undesirable problems. Comfort also is largely a factor of dew point, 70% humidity at

70°F (20°C) is comfortable but at 90°F (32°C) is unbearable. This is because at higher temperatures the high RH prevents the body from cooling through evaporation of perspiration.

E. *Precipitation analysis* shows average monthly totals of rain and snow. High and low extreme amounts of precipitation are often shown and help determine if the rain/snow comes steady or in short bursts. Very wet or dry places also require special attention in building assembly. Wet environments need to shed excess water very quickly and the conventional means for accomplishing this, such as gutters and downspouts, are not always adequate. Foundation problems can also occur in wet locations due to the increased hydrostatic pressure of underground water against walls and basement floor slabs. Dry environments can desiccate materials (absorbing moisture out of a material) causing them to shrink and split or crack. Soils in dry environments can also shift unpredictably, causing foundation problems.

Climate strategies

Studying the building types of indigenous people in different climate zones gives a clear picture of what the most important factors are in dealing with the local climate. There is a simple logic that develops, without the use of mechanical means of comfort or the benefit of scientific calculations, which gets right to the heart of the problem. With thousands of years to work on the problem of shelter and the incentive of basic survival, the most efficient solutions developed and were continually refined to high degrees. All of the basic principles of these building types apply to modern designs and most can be adapted easily without needing to copy the style or look of the original building.

Hot–humid climates

In these climactic conditions it's most important to use natural breezes for cooling, while shading from the hot sun. These climates also tend to have heavy rainfall, so large roof overhangs help shed water and keep the sun from penetrating far into the space. Open, operable walls and raised floors promote cooling of the air and the structure. Buildings benefit from being spread out to maximize breezes, and narrow buildings with tall windows promote cross ventilation. The heaviest heat gains are on the west side, from the late afternoon sun in the summer, so narrow orientations east to west are preferred (Fig. 0.3.2).

Traditional buildings of this type are open raised huts with large roof overhangs. Single large rooms with few intervening walls allow for breezes. Tall ceilings allow heat to rise and be carried away with wind.

Hot–arid climates

Desert type climates have high heat gains from the sun in the daytime and frequent cool weather at night. Less ventilation is need than humid climates due to the low humidity, which makes evaporative cooling much more effective.

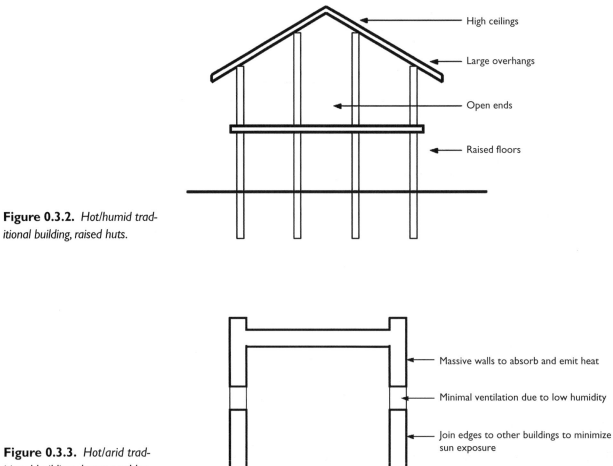

High ceilings

Large overhangs

Open ends

Raised floors

Figure 0.3.2. *Hot/humid trad-itional building, raised huts.*

Massive walls to absorb and emit heat

Minimal ventilation due to low humidity

Join edges to other buildings to minimize sun exposure

Figure 0.3.3. *Hot/arid trad-itional building, desert pueblos.*

Massive walls can be used to absorb heat during the day and emit it back at night. Minimal overall surface exposure to the sun is preferable, joined structures assist in keeping exterior wall surface reduced. Narrow ends are oriented east to west, which minimizes heat gains from low east and west sun while maximizing low winter sun on the south side. Evaporative pools of water near the structure assist in promoting cooling (Fig. 0.3.3).

Desert pueblo and other adobe structures are typical traditional structures in these environments. The massive clay brick walls transfer heat and cooling through thermal shift and are less vulnerable to water disintegration because of the small rain amounts. Small windows allow for some cooling without letting in much heat and the structures tend to be clustered together, minimizing exterior exposure.

Temperate climates

Temperate climates tend to have large shifts between summer and winter temperatures, which favors hybrid building types able to transform themselves. Protection from north winter winds is important with open glazed areas to

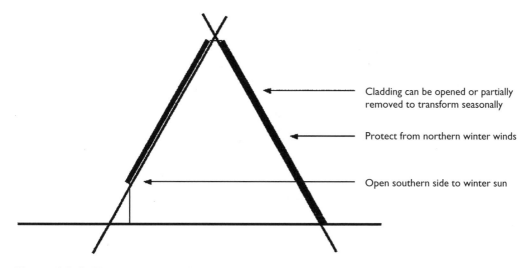

Figure 0.3.4. *Temperate area traditional building type, tipi's and other hybrid building types.*

the low winter sun on the south. Large overhangs on the east and west sides protect from summer sun while shaded outdoor living areas take advantage of temperatures during warm parts of the year. Deciduous trees allow for shading in the summer when leaves are full and warming in the winter when the leaves fall. The windows should be operable to promote summer cooling breezes with good protection from winter cold (Fig. 0.3.4).

Wigwams and Tipis are typical Native American examples of these building types as they were very transformable to more open or closed exterior shells. Bungalow style homes are also hybrid buildings, with projecting sleeping porches that could open on three sides for cooling, and compact central areas that could be heated efficiently.

Cool climates

Colder climates require buildings that will lose as little heat as possible and can protect against large amounts of snow. Protection from northern wind is important in building orientation and entry location. Snow loads can be very heavy, but retaining some snow on roofs is desirable for insulation value. Low winter sun from the south should be used to heat larger southern exposures. Minimum surface areas should be exposed to cold, joined structures are used to retain heat rather than avoid sun. Openings should be well insulated and located for maximum solar heat gain (Fig. 0.3.5).

Igloos and timber huts are common examples of traditional building types. These structures are heavily insulated and often joined together to protect against wind and cold exposure. Roof slopes are designed to shed some snow and retain the rest for insulation.

Apart from the fundamental issues of climate control are both economical and emotional needs. The best solutions to buildings balance these appropriately for the inhabitants. Stone may provide the best material to accomplish

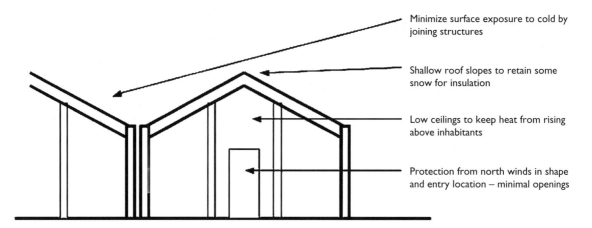

Minimize surface exposure to cold by joining structures

Shallow roof slopes to retain some snow for insulation

Low ceilings to keep heat from rising above inhabitants

Protection from north winds in shape and entry location – minimal openings

Figure 0.3.5. *Cool area traditional building type, igloos and plank huts.*

a task, but may not be affordable or locally available. Minimal windows may improve the thermal efficiency of a structure, but access to view and sunlight are physically and emotionally very desirable.

Determining the correct approach to a project requires a synthesis of information. The limitations of the site or desired arrangement of the program frequently will not allow the building to take maximum advantage of passive climactic strategies. The idea is to keep in mind the environmental factors while dealing with the myriad other requirements of designing a project.

Micro climates

Studying weather data and looking at traditional buildings gives us an idea of regional conditions, however, variations of terrain, vegetation, altitude, and relationships to bodies of water create different localized conditions. These micro climates may be very different from the prevailing regional environment.

Topography affects comfort by a general lowering of temperature at altitude. In tropical conditions it is quite common to build in mountainous regions to find cooler temperatures. In a smaller scale example cool air is heavier than warm and settles in low areas or valleys. Finding the correct location on a slope depends on the region (Fig. 0.3.6).

Hot–Humid regions use the top of the hill. Air movement is most important in these zones as shading can be accomplished through other means.

Hot–Arid regions use the lower slopes to maximize heat loss. Wind cooling is relatively unimportant and south exposure is desirable to trap heat during the day. The southeast side of the hill protects from the hot western afternoon sun.

Temperate regions can move down the slope toward the cooler air, but need more consideration of summer cooling breezes. Careful study of the specific wind vs. cold pool conditions and which is more beneficial needs to be considered.

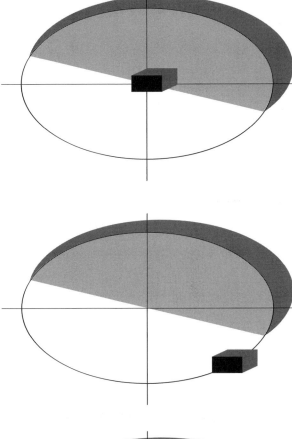

Hot–humid climates

- Open, raised huts are common
- Need large roofs with overhangs to avoid sun and shed rain
- Open walls and raised floors to encourage evaporation of moisture by breezes
- Structures spread out to maximize breezes
- Narrow buildings with tall windows to promote cross ventilation
- Heavy heat gains on east side and higher gains on west side

Hot–arid climates

- Desert pueblos and other adobe structures are common
- Less ventilation needed due to low humidity
- Massive walls used to absorb heat during the day and emit it back during evenings
- Minimal surface exposure to sun – joined homes together to minimize surface area exposed to sun
- Buildings oriented with narrow ends to east and west maximize overhead summer sun on end walls and maximize low winter sun on south
- Near evaporative pools for cooling

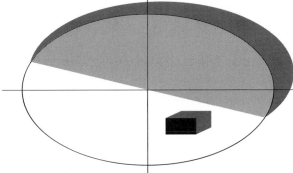

Temperate climates

- Wigwams and tipis are typical Native American examples
- Protection from north winter winds
- Open to winter sun on south
- Shaded open areas with east and west shade overhangs in summer
- Deciduous trees nearby shade in summer and
- Allow winter sun open for summer breezes
- Need to seasonally transform from warm to cold conditions

Cool climates

- Igloos and plank & timber huts are common examples
- Protection from north winds in shape and entry location
- Use low south winter sun to heat walls
- Protect from heavy snow, but retain some for insulating value
- Minimum surface exposure to cold – often joined
- Homes together to minimize exterior area and to retain heat rather than avoid sun
- Minimal un-insulated openings

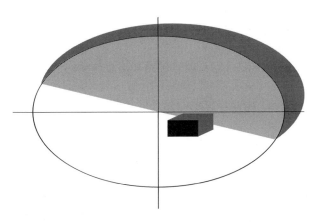

Figure 0.3.6. Climate zone building responses.

Cool regions tend to use the upper slope, out of the cold lower level, facing south to catch winter sun and be protected from north wind.

Vegetation provides a number of micro-climactic effects. Dense coniferous (evergreen) trees or shrubs can provide wind blocks in winter. Deciduous trees provide summer shade and allow sun through in the winter to promote solar heating. Plant and grassy covers reduce temperatures by absorbing the heat and not reflecting it onto other surfaces, conversely urban paved areas are typically warmer than their surroundings.

Water, being dense and having a large surface area touching the ground, is usually cooler in the summer and warmer in the winter than the surrounding terrain. Close proximity to bodies of water tends to moderate temperature extremes. During the day, when the land is warmer than the water, cool air flows from over the water onto the land and the cycle reverses itself at night as air naturally moves from cooler to warmer areas. The moderating effect depends on the size of the body of water, and is more effective on the lee side (the side away from the prevailing direction of the wind).

Frequently asked questions

'How do I determine what the weather conditions are at my site?'
Most cities have information on weather history for a number of previous years. You need to check conditions in the general location for at least 5–10 years previously in order to get an accurate picture of the prevailing conditions. Keep in mind that often these readings are from the local airport or on top of a building, which is normally not the same as the conditions you are designing for. Look at the immediate surroundings to get an idea of how winds, sunlight, water flow, cold air pooling, and snow will be affected. The NOAA (National Oceanographic and Atmospheric Administration) in the US and the Met Office in the UK provide national weather forecasting and meteorological history for most regions.

'What if I'm in between climate zones, or the charts don't match my local conditions?'
The charts are only intended to provide strategies for dealing with climatic conditions. It's more important to be aware of local conditions than to follow an abstract guideline. Generally you use strategies that minimize the mechanical load on a building, so if it's more warm than cold – breezes are most important, if it's more cold than warm – conserving heat and borrowing solar gains are most important. Every different site, even in the same town, should be dealt with first generally then very specifically for it's individual conditions.

Conclusion

The goal of studying micro- and macro-climatic conditions is to work with, rather than against, your local environment. There are always conflicting issues during project development and the designer's responsibility is to conscientiously create a hierarchy of what's most important. These issues must ultimately support one another as a cohesive whole. Basic site orientation, building proportion, consideration of micro-climatic conditions, local vegetation, relationship to the sun and wind are all part of the earliest stages of the design process and have the most dramatic effect on the environmental efficiency and comfort of the project.

Glossary and formulas

Conduction	Heat flow through a homogeneous material (solid, liquid or gas) or between two objects in direct contact.
Convection	Heat transfer by the moving parts of a liquid or gas. This occurs where a river eddy's or the way air diffuses into a room. Natural convection occurs due to heat's natural tendency to move from an area of higher temperature to an area of lower temperature. Forced convection moves the heat by a fan or pump.
Desiccate	Absorbing moisture out of a material, which can cause them to shrink and split or crack.
Micro Climate	Is a climatic condition that varies from the surrounding areas due to variation in terrain, vegetation, altitude and relationships to bodies of water.
Precipitation	Rain and snow. Fog can count as well, but is typically part of humidity. Usually measured in inches using a rain gauge.
Radiation	Transmission of heat energy by electromagnetic waves from a warm substance to a cool one.
Wind	Measured by direction and velocity. Critical to note are the prevailing winds by season.

References and further reading

Olgyay, V. (1963) *Design with Climate: Bioclimatic Approach to Architectural Regionalism* (Princeton, NJ: Princeton University Press). Chapter 1, Part 1, pp. 1–13, 44–52.

Brown, G.Z. and DeKay, M. (2001) *Sun, Wind & Light: Architectural Design Strategies* 2nd ed (New York, NY: John Wiley and Sons, Inc.).

0.4　Environment: solar geometry

The Earth's Rotation	The changing angle and position of the sun
	Solar path diagrams
Sun Control Strategies	Solar gains
	Daylighting

Introduction to solar geometry

Solar geometry follows the study of climatology as a particular area of interest to designers. While the wind, rain, temperature and humidity all affect the design of buildings – the sun typically has the greatest impact on the esthetics of a project. None of the other climactic forces typically offers as much opportunity to harness its power, or creates as many issues to deal with.

The sun provides two distinct issues to confront. The first issue is thermal; the sun is the primary source of all natural heating. This heat can be beneficial or problematic depending on the situation, and in most cases it is both. The second issue is light, and the sun provides the most desirable lighting conditions in most cases. These two factors determine a large part of the shape, site placement and exterior skin of buildings. While artificial lighting and heating systems can replace or offset solar light and heat, the effects of the sun are always too powerful to ignore when designing a project.

There are a number of terms that are important to know in order to understand the way the sun strikes the earth. The first are *Latitude* and *Longitude* which are abstract measurement lines inscribed around the earth. *Latitude* is the angular distance north or south of the earth's equator, measured in degrees along a meridian, shown horizontally on a map or globe. *Longitude* is the angular distance on the earth's surface, measured east or west from the prime meridian at Greenwich, England (Fig. 0.4.1), to the meridian passing through a position, expressed in degrees (or hours), minutes and seconds.

The other important terms to know are sun *Altitude*, *Azimuth,* and *Solstice*. These are the terms used to discuss the measurements of sun position as calculated on a chart later in the chapter. *Sun Azimuth* is the horizontal angular distance of the sun from a reference direction (typically north or south), measured in degrees in a radial pattern (basically, where the sun is east to west). *Sun Altitude* is the vertical angle of the sun, measured in degrees from a horizontal plane. Basically, how high the sun is in the sky. The *Solstice* is either of the two times a year when the sun is at its zenith (directly overhead) over the tropic of Cancer or the tropic of Capricorn. In the Northern Hemisphere the *summer solstice* occurs about June 21st, when the sun is over the tropic of Cancer, the *winter solstice* occurs about December 21st, when the sun is over the tropic of Capricorn. This reverses itself in the southern hemisphere. The summer solstice has the longest daylight of the year and the winter solstice has the shortest (Fig. 0.4.2).

Figure 0.4.1. *The Prime Meridian of the world, located in Greenwich, England.*

Because of the angle of the earth to the sun, the particular latitude of a location will have a different solar orientation. These differences in the angles of the sun throughout the year determine the strategies used to alternatively bring the light and heat in or keep it out. Often times these two desires, light and heat, are in direct conflict with one another and difficult decisions need to be made about which is more important. Understanding the way the sun lights and heats a space is essential to making the right decisions.

The Earth's rotation

The arc of the sun changes throughout the year due to the fact that the earth's rotational axis is at an angle to the orbit of the earth around the sun (Fig. 0.4.3). This change in angle determines the amount of solar radiation any point on the

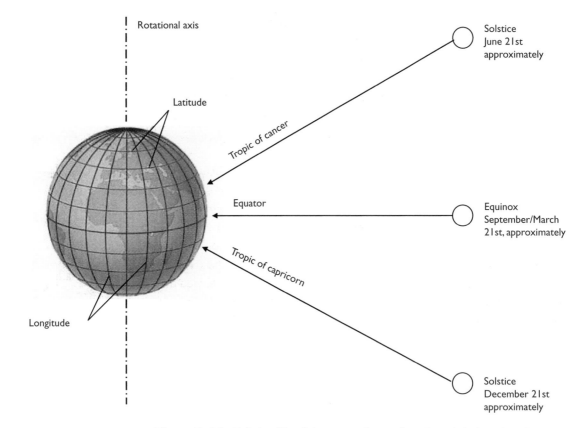

Figure 0.4.2. *Relationship of the sun to the earth at the solstice's and equinox.*

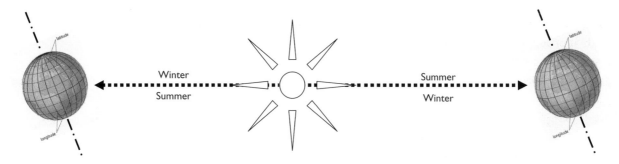

Figure 0.4.3. *Relationship of the sun to the earth during a revolution in orbit.*

earth will receive during a day. The amount of radiation is determined in two ways; the first is the number of hours the sun will strike a point on the surface. The lower the sun angle the less time it will be visible from a point on the earth, the higher the angle the more time it will be visible. The second way the amount of solar radiation is determined is at what angle it strikes the surface of the earth. The more direct the angle, the more heat is absorbed.

As any casual observer notes, the warmest part of the year is typically not the *summer solstice*, and the coldest is not the *winter solstice*. The cold or warm weather typically persists and intensifies past the longest and shortest day of the year by a couple of months. This is primarily due to the ability of mass to retain and transmit heat or cold, commonly called 'Thermal Shift.' We see this phenomenon in many small ways; sunglasses left on the dashboard in summer stay hot after being removed from the sun for a brief period of time while a stone bench remains cold well into a warm day. The larger the heated or cooled mass, the longer it takes to return to ambient air temperature. The mass of the land and water on the earth tends to retain the heat or cold from entire seasons and 'shift' that temperature load past the point of solar heating or lack thereof. This same strategy is used in thermal mass elements on buildings to combat temperature shifts from day to night; the earth simply does this at a much larger scale.

The location of the sun in the sky can be easily calculated for any hour of day throughout the year by using a sun path diagram. Because the height of the sun is dependant on the angle of the earth to the sun, charts are projected by latitude. The higher the degree of latitude, the farther you are from the equator. The equator is 0° and the north and south poles are 90°. All angles between are split between north and south, so a chart labeled 60° latitude can be used for north or south simply by rotating it top to bottom. Some charts are labeled this way and have a set of information both right side up and upside down, to be read for whichever hemisphere (north or south) you are calculating. Typically charts show latitude increments of 4° apart; therefore if you are looking for information at the latitude between two charts it is easy to interpolate the information.

Don't let the initially confusing layout of these charts be intimidating, with some practice they become easy to use. Imagine you are lying on your back looking at the sky so east is to your left. An example follows of how to determine the position of the sun using the chart shown (Fig. 0.4.4).

Naples, Italy, is at 40° north latitude, so the 40° north latitude sun path diagram chart is appropriate. As noted above, the charts can be used for latitudes north and south of the equator simply by flipping them upside down. The dark curved month lines should bow downwards. To determine the position of the sun in the sky at 4:00 pm on Aug. 21st first find the curved August 21/April 21 line on the chart, it should be listed on both sides. Trace this line across the chart until you reach the vertical line that reads 4:00 pm. Afternoon times are right of center, morning times are left, which corresponds to the position of the sun in the east in the morning and west in the afternoon. The intersection of the August 21 line and the 4:00 pm line lands on a radial circle that reads 30°, which is the altitude angle of the sun above the horizon. Lastly find the radial line that runs from the intersection to the outside circle and read the azimuth as 260°, or 10° shy of due west, this is the horizontal angle of the sun from the reference point of 0 directly to the north.

Sun control strategies

Part 1: Solar gains

The angles of the sun are the primary determining factor in solar heat gain for buildings. Depending on the climate or time of year this heat gain may be desirable or not. A basic rule of thumb is that in cold climates you want to maximize winter solar gains, while in hot climates you try to minimize solar gains year round.

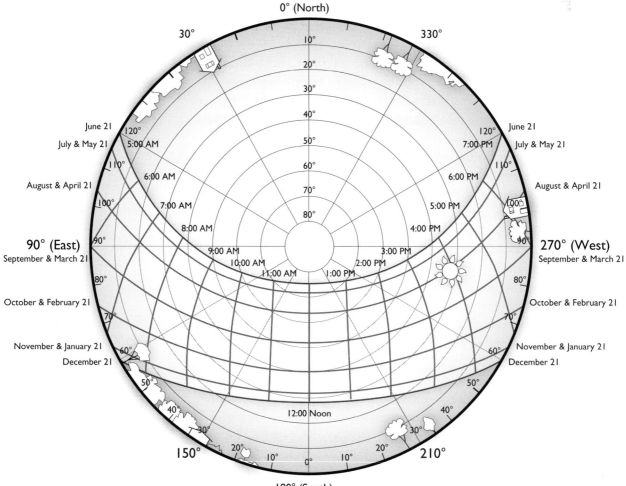

Figure 0.4.4. *40 degree north latitude sun path diagram.*

The variables to be dealt with were covered mainly in the climatology section; however, let's summarize the solar conditions (Fig. 0.4.5):

Hot–humid climates
Need large roofs with overhangs to avoid sun and shed rain
Heavy heat gains on east side and higher gains on west side

Hot–arid climates
Massive walls used to absorb heat during the day and emit it back during evenings
Minimal surface exposure to sun
Buildings oriented with narrow ends to east and west – minimizing overhead summer sun on end walls and maximizing low winter sun on south

Temperate climates
Open to winter sun on south
Shaded open areas with east and west shade overhangs in summer
Deciduous trees nearby shade in summer and allow winter sun

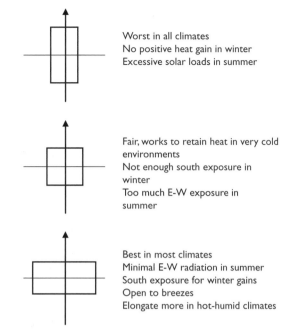

Worst in all climates
No positive heat gain in winter
Excessive solar loads in summer

Fair, works to retain heat in very cold environments
Not enough south exposure in winter
Too much E-W exposure in summer

Best in most climates
Minimal E-W radiation in summer
South exposure for winter gains
Open to breezes
Elongate more in hot-humid climates

Figure 0.4.5. *Relationship of building form to passive environmental responses. North is shown as up.*

Cool climates

Use low south winter sun to heat walls
Minimal un-insulated openings
Where solar gain heat is collected it can be radiated directly into the space by use of passive thermal mass walls, or more actively moved with ventilation systems to distribute the heat. Most of the time a hybrid of passive and active systems can maximize the use of naturally collected radiant solar heat.

Part 2: Daylighting

Almost 50% of the energy use of many modern buildings comes from artificial illumination. While the efficiency of the systems used to maintain building comfort, including lighting, have improved over the last 40 years, the amount of energy used has stayed roughly the same. We're using the energy more efficiently, but we're continually using more of it.

The use of daylighting has often been avoided due to concerns over solar radiation gains, or a desire to keep lighting more consistent. There are, however, strategies that can be used to mitigate both of these concerns.

There are three components of daylighting systems:

1 Exterior Environment – The sky, sun, land and adjacent structures change the intensity of the light. The brightness of the sun changes due to vegetation and clouds, while the direction shifts throughout the year. The ground around the building (i.e., grass or concrete) reflects different amounts of light into the space.
2 Interface Medium – The glazing and building fenestration, or aperture through which the daylight enters the space. Openings act as filters for different

conditions, often times different openings should be used for heat gain vs. daylight.

3 Interior Environment – The shape and reflectance of the space will distribute light in different ways. Deeper, lower spaces get less sunlight, and lighter colored floors tend to reflect light deeper into a space.

The depth of a space affects how well it can be lit. Depths of twice the floor to ceiling height can potentially be day lit. Light shelves and reflectors can allow the light to penetrate deeper into the space without direct radiant solar gain. There are two basic rules to remember – the higher the window the farther the light penetrates, and if you cannot see the sky through the opening, the light level will drop off quickly when it's overcast. A common strategy for minimizing artificial light, but maintaining light levels, is to separate light circuits and put the lights close to the windows on photocell sensors. This allows these lights to be off when the daylight level is high enough and to come on if its overcast or the sun is not in the right position to adequately light the space.

Light travels into openings in a number of ways and slight shifts in exterior openings can have large effects on the amount of light and solar radiation that enters a space (Fig. 0.4.6). Unrestricted openings allow light deep into a space, but can promote heat gain during warm months, when it's undesirable. Small overhangs can limit summer exposure, while allowing winter solar radiation. The amount of overhang can be determined by using the sun path chart to chart the location of the sun for different times of year. Light shelves can solve the problem of limiting summer sun radiation, while reflecting light deeper into a space than a simple overhang can accomplish. Diffusers spread the light evenly throughout a space with patterned glazing. This typically limits vision

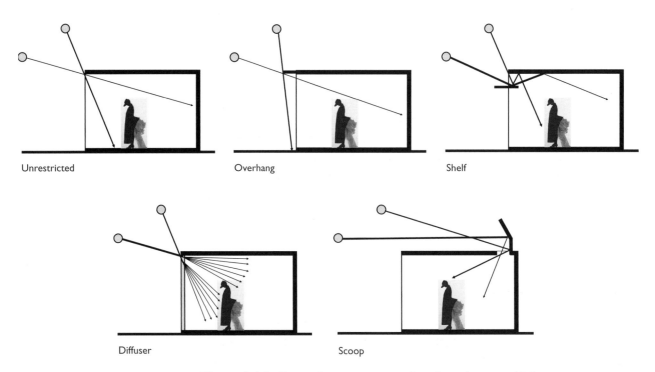

Unrestricted   Overhang   Shelf

Diffuser   Scoop

Figure 0.4.6. *Types of exterior openings for solar radiation and light.*

through the glass, but can produce even and softer daylighting. Light scoops can solve the problem of heat gain vs. light by putting light deeper into a space without large heat gaining window openings at the exterior wall of a building. All methods of building openings offer both design and environmental opportunities. Elegant solutions make these two demands work together.

Frequently asked questions

'How do I find the longitude and latitude of a place?'
Basic information can be found on a typical map or globe that will have longitude and latitude lines indicated at 10-degree intervals. Local maps often show a greater level of detail. Most cities will have an indication of longitude and latitude easily found in the index of an atlas or online.

'How do I determine how the sun will enter a space?'
Find the sun path diagram for the latitude of your site, select the chart closest and interpolate if the exact latitude chart is not available. Calculate the position of the sun for morning, noon and late afternoon hours for the summer, winter and fall/spring. Using the angles and azimuths you've gathered draw a plan and section of the space with window locations and exterior roof overhangs shown. Graphically draw the horizontal and vertical angles of the sun's location for each of the times and seasons as they pass through the window openings, using separate plans and sections for each. The representative sets of drawings will give you a good overview of the amount of sun that enters the space throughout the year, and will allow you to make modifications to achieve the results you desire. Many computer modeling systems also have the ability to calculate sun path projections if the model is built accurately, but keep in mind ground conditions, vegetation and surface colors, which are often not part of a computer model.

Conclusion

The goal of thinking about solar geometry is not only about passive environmental control. The natural environment presents concerns that buildings are forced to respond to, and these environmental factors are the basis on which the first shelters were constructed. The environment offers a means of understanding how to create and express the appearance of a structure. From the factors of the environmental forces placed on a building, a language of form can be created that communicates with the natural world in a very fundamental way.

Glossary and formulas

Latitude	The angular distance north or south of the earth's equator, measured in degrees along a meridian, as on a map or globe.
Longitude	Angular distance on the earth's surface, measured east or west from the prime meridian at Greenwich, England, to the

	meridian passing through a position, expressed in degrees (or hours), minutes and seconds.
Sun Azimuth	The horizontal angular distance of the sun from a reference direction (typically north or south), measured in degrees in a radial pattern.
Sun Altitude	The vertical angle of the sun, measured in degrees from a horizontal plane.
Sky Zenith	The point at which the sun is directly overhead the observer on the earth's sphere.
Solstice	Either of the two times a year when the sun is at its zenith over the tropic of Cancer or the tropic of Capricorn. In the Northern Hemisphere the summer solstice occurs about June 21st, when the sun is over the tropic of Cancer, the winter solstice occurs about December 21st, when the sun is over the tropic of Capricorn. This reverses itself in the southern hemisphere. The summer solstice has the longest daylight of the year and the winter solstice has the shortest.
Thermal Shift	The ability of mass to retain heat or cold and transmit it to a later time.

Further reading

Hawkes, D., McDonald, J. and Steemers, K. (2002) Environmental Design Checklist (Chapter 8), *The Selective Environment* (New York, NY: Spon Press). pp. 122–151.

Brown, G.Z. and DeKay, M. (2001) *Sun, Wind & Light: Architectural Design Strategies* 2nd ed (New York, NY: John Wiley and Sons, Inc.).

Ramsey, C.G. and Sleeper, H.R. (2000) *Architectural Graphic Standards* 10th ed (New York, NY: John Wiley & Sons). pp. 61–62.

Neufert, E. and Neufert, P. (2000) *Architect's Data* 3rd ed (London, UK: Blackwell Science). pp. 151–165.

CHAPTER 1

Pre-Design

1.1 Programming and program/ brief analysis

Programming	Asking the right questions
	Information gathering
	Developing a program/brief
Analysis	Areas schedules
	Bubble diagrams
	Adjacencies and affinities
	Stratification
Solving Towards Design	'Building the diagram' vs. 'finding the fit'
	Building grain

Programming and program/brief analysis

Form Finding from the Inside Out. Programming is the art and/or science of determining the fundamental functional requirements of a designed object. We often assume that this is a simple task, and for well-known building types (single family residences, speculative office buildings, etc.) this may be the case. However discerning the essential requirements for more complex or less deterministic building types (e.g., hospitals or retail shops) may be more difficult. What, for example, is the exact function of an art museum? Certainly we could list a set of rooms with suggested areas, but it is unlikely that this process would set the problem up correctly. The 'function' of an art museum according to Louis Kahn was 'a set of spaces that are good for the viewing of art'. Even this usefully vague description, however, doesn't address the civic, commercial, and educational requirements that today's art museum might face. The building housing such an institution would include functions – branding, public spaces, a civic image – that couldn't be included in a traditional areas schedule.

Programming is, therefore, both an objective and a subjective process. Discerning what our clients need (or want) will invariably involve discussions about square footage/metrage and relationships between spaces. However, it is the architect's task to also figure out the larger issues that underlie our clients' needs, and to see whether those can be addressed architecturally. Typically, developing a program is an additional service for architects in the US and UK, but it does happen frequently. As often as not, we will be confronted on a new job with a program/brief written by a client or a space planner. Even if this is the case, however, good practice suggests that this document be thoroughly questioned.

When architects are asked to prepare a program or brief, we typically rely on several sources of information regarding what elements are necessary in a typical building of the type being designed: how much space each of these may take up (either in absolute or relative terms), what services or qualities these spaces require and what relationships each space should have to one another. This is a process of 'problem seeking', not 'problem solving' in the words of the Texas architectural firm Caudill Rowlett Scott, who pioneered systematic approaches to programming in the 1960s and 1970s. To gain reliable information, architects will often interview clients and users, using existing facilities as a benchmark. Are the spaces being used now large enough? Are there services that should be provided? What does or does not work with the current arrangements, and what suggestions might the day-to-day users have for improving their environment? We may also study other installations of the type, either through a literature search or site visits, to glean information about current space and functional standards. In some cases (for instance, health care) there will be well-published standards that will list much of this information. However, it is almost always beneficial to see these standards in action, and to decide whether good practice will rely solely on these, or whether inherent problems or shortcomings in standard design need to be addressed (Fig. 1.1.1).

Information from this exercise will typically be tabulated in the form of an areas schedule (or program/brief) that lists the space requirements for the proposed design (Table 1.1.1). Usually this will break down required uses into individual rooms, grouped according to how the client sees their functional relationships. The schedule will list room titles or uses, area in square feet or square meters, and may include further information about required proportions, qualities (e.g., daylight), or services. Areas schedules are usually drawn up using spreadsheet software (i.e., Microsoft Excel), which allows users to enter data cells for room names, areas, and qualities, as well as programmed cells that can manipulate, compare, or sort this information. Using spreadsheets we can easily subtotal building areas, compare sizes, or later in the process estimate how close to the original program/brief our developing design may be.

Several rules of thumb for estimating space requirements are shown in Table 1.1.2. These are drawn from daily experience and are thus not universally applicable, but they give a good idea of where a programming exercise might start. All of these assumptions deserve to be tested with any client – for example, a common exercise in an early program/briefing meeting is to tape out on the floor an assumed office size, allowing users or clients to get a sense for what a $10\,m^2$ office actually looks like. Also included are typical 'net-to-gross' ratios. 'Net' space in a building includes all rentable, or assignable areas, such as offices or apartments, clerical spaces or meeting rooms. 'Gross' space includes all 'house' or non-assignable spaces such as hallways, bathrooms, lobbies, and service rooms. Generally the rule of thumb is that any space in a building that could be rented is considered 'net', while any space that cannot be rented is considered 'gross'. Net-to-gross ratios are taken perhaps too seriously by developers, especially considering the qualities that 'gross' spaces such as atriums, cafes, or lounges can add to a building's function. Nonetheless, they are so universally used as benchmarks of efficiency that they are worthy of study. A third type of area, 'construction area' is often assumed or calculated to arrive at a total figure for the 'footprint area' of a building.

Program/Brief Analysis. No matter who creates the program/brief, the first step in our design process is almost always to analyze its implications. Here we are

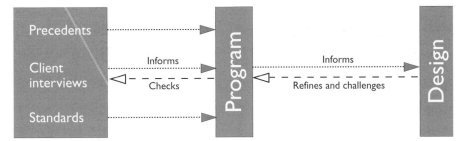

Figure 1.1.1. *The programming and program analysis process is one of asking questions, comparing standards and precedents, and rigorously assessing the results.*

Table 1.1.1. A typical areas schedule, with space names, required areas, and a matrix of requirements.

	Net assignable square feet	Net non-assignable square feet	Gross square feet	Level	Daylight	Public/private	Plumbing
Living room	300			1	1	1	0
Kitchen	150			1	1	2	1
Dining room	150			1	1	1	0
Bedrooms							
Master bedroom	250			2	2	4	0
Child's bedroom	120			2	2	4	0
Child's bedroom	120			2	2	4	0
Office	100			1	1	3	0
Bathrooms							
Downstairs bathroom		60		1	2	3	1
Upstairs bathroom		60		2	2	4	1
Playroom	300			0	3	4	0
Furnace room		120		0	4	5	1
Storage							
First floor closet		20		1	4	5	0
Second floor closet		10		2	4	5	0
Basement storage		110		0	4	5	0
Circulation							
Stairs basement/first		50					
Stairs first/second		50					
Corridors (est.)		100					
Subtotal, NSF	1490	580					
Total, NSF	2070						
Total GSF			2484				

looking for ways to translate a list of requirements into a strategy for form (architectural, landscape, engineering, etc.) As such, architects typically rely on several graphic conventions to help 'spatialize' a program/brief. While these may give the appearance of objective problem solving, they should be approached with great caution. Ideally, these exercises should be seen as ways of questioning and understanding the data in the program/brief. It is very rare that a satisfactory form will

Table 1.1.2. Rules of thumb for estimating space requirements during preliminary design phases.

Use	Allowance, Square meter per person	Allowance, Square feet per person
Standard office	12	125
Clerical office	5	50
Manager's office	14	150
Conference room	1	15
Dining rooms – banquet	1	13
Dining rooms – cafeteria	1	12
Dining rooms – table service	1	16
Retail – ground floor	3	30
Retail – department store	4	40
Library – reading rooms	3	35
Overall	5	50
Museums	1	15
Theatres – fixed seats	1	8
Theatres – movable seats	1	15
Lobby	0.5	3
Backstage is typically as large as seating area		
Elementary classroom	2	20
Secondary classroom	2	25
Large secondary classroom	1	15
Gymnasium	12	125
University classroom	1	15
University seminar room	2	20
University lecture hall	1	12
Apartments	23	250
Hospital	93	1000

emerge solely out of a diagramming process – more often this process will help us understand the problem in spatial terms, and our concepts will emerge from this understanding. It is important to remember, too, that program/brief analysis is an 'inside out' method of strategizing. More often than not, we will *also* be analyzing our site (see Section 2.2) during this phase, and any solutions that emerge will need to be holistic, balancing what we discover from the internal organization and from external forces.

Nonetheless, diagramming is a useful exercise, provided that we understand its limitations. Traditionally, architects begin with 'bubble diagrams', or very loose representations of areas drawn to scale from the program/brief with relationships between these areas noted by lines indicating connectivity. The areas themselves are often color-coded, labeled with names and areas, and typically drawn as ovals or rectangles with curved corners. These shapes remind us that we are not yet designating 'rooms' – we are rather interested in the area that a given activity is likely to take up.

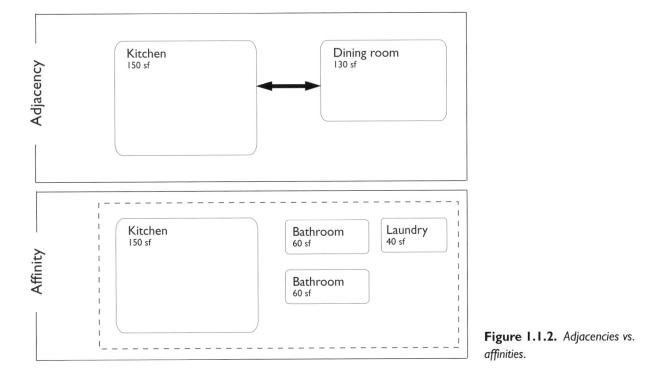

Figure 1.1.2. *Adjacencies vs. affinities.*

Table 1.1.3. A data sort of the areas schedule in Figure 1.1.2 based on daylighting. Note that other important aspects of the spaces (private/public in particular) align with the daylight sort. This may be the start of a possible design strategy.

	Net assignable square feet	Net non-assignable square feet	Gross square feet	Level	Daylight	Public/private	Plumbing
Living room	300			1	1	1	0
Dining room	150			1	1	1	0
Kitchen	150			1	1	2	1
Office	100			1	1	3	0
Bathrooms							
Downstairs bathroom		60		1	2	3	1
Upstairs bathroom		60		2	2	4	1
Bedrooms							
Master bedroom	250			2	2	4	0
Child's bedroom	120			2	2	4	0
Child's bedroom	120			2	2	4	0
Playroom	300			0	3	4	0
Furnace room		120		0	4	5	1
Storage							
First floor closet		20		1	4	5	0
Second floor closet		10		2	4	5	0
Basement storage		110		0	4	5	0

Connectivity is often indicated in one of two categories – *adjacencies* and *affinities* (Fig. 1.1.2). Adjacencies represent relationships between activities that require direct circulatory access. A typical example in residential design is the relationship between a kitchen and a dining room. Here, there are good reasons to locate areas adjacent to one another to enable quick, efficient movement of

Adjacency requirements

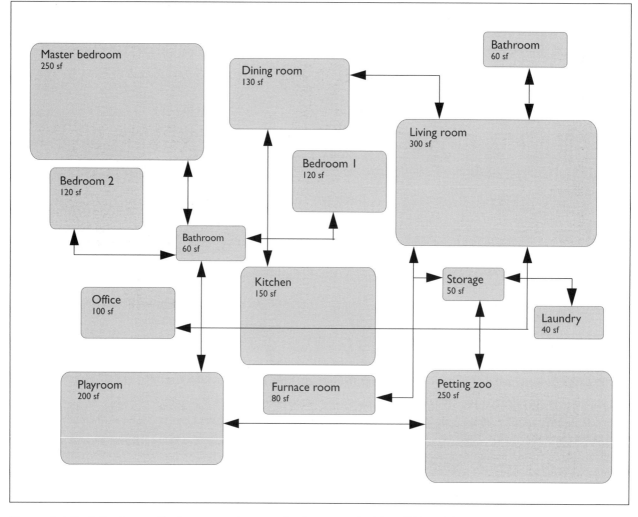

Figure 1.1.3. *A first layout of adjacency requirements for the areas schedule in Table 1.1.2.*

people or goods from one to another. Affinities, on the other hand, indicate activities that share something besides circulatory convenience, and thus may tend toward one another in a building for reasons of performance or constructability. Here, a good residential example is kitchens and bathrooms. While there is no pressing need for circulation between these two spaces, they share a requirement for plumbing. To save the costs involved with excessive piping, 'wet' activities are often grouped near one another, sharing plumbing stacks and drains (see Section 6.4). Other affinities may include the need for daylighting, security, visibility, privacy, fresh air, or sound attenuation.

A useful bubble diagram will often show adjacencies as solid lines connecting one program/brief element to another, while showing affinities as an outline surrounding like elements. In Figures 1.1.3 and 1.1.4, note how spaces relate in terms of circulation (adjacency) and servicing (affinity). In the former, the kitchen and dining room are connected by a solid line, while in the latter the kitchen and bathrooms are circled by a dashed line. These indicate the need for physical proximity due to circulatory and functional reasons, respectively. Through an

Affinities diagram

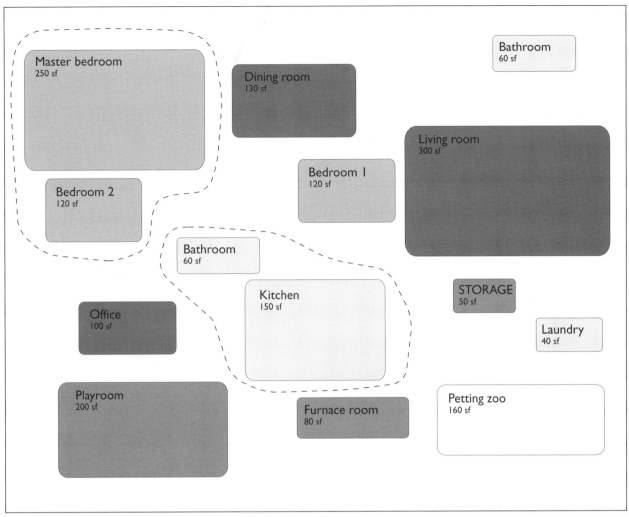

Figure 1.1.4. *A first layout of affinity requirements for the areas schedule in Table 1.1.2.*

iterative process, bubble diagrams will be re-drawn and re-drawn until efficient strategies emerge for deploying spaces and program/brief elements relative to one another. Here, one might think of the connecting and encircling lines as rubber bands, the goal being to tighten these up as much as possible. Figures 1.1.5 and 1.1.6 show several iterations for a small residence. Note that a balance is gradually struck between the ideal circulation scheme and the goal of collecting all wet areas around a single plumbing stack. Note, too, that the 'final' scheme is only an efficient organization – it is hardly 'architectural' and will benefit from a more forceful sculpting of these elements into real spatial proposals.

An additional tool for program/brief analysis is the spreadsheet (e.g., Microsoft Excel). A building program/brief that is entered as a spreadsheet can be manipulated to discover patterns, repetitive elements, or shared requirements in important ways. The areas schedule in Table 1.1.1 contains additional entries representing the spaces' requirements for daylighting, privacy, and plumbing. In each case, the architect has entered a '1' if the requirement

Programmatic layout attempt

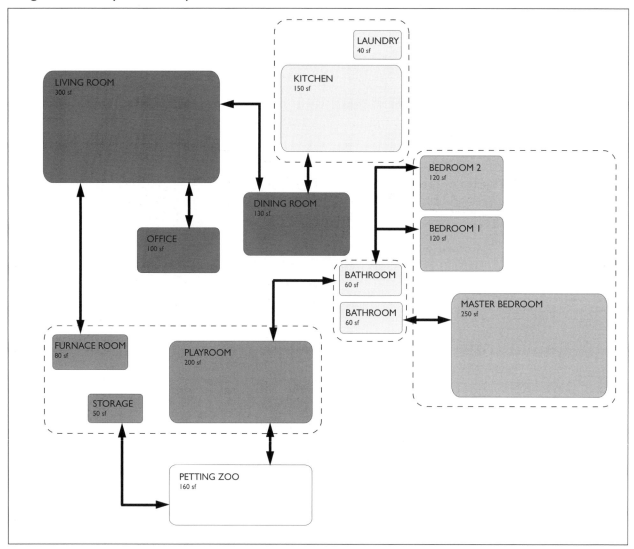

Figure 1.1.5. *Initial layout based on the findings of the first adjacency and affinity diagrams. One way to think of the goals here is that we're trying to 'shrink' the connecting and encircling lines to come up with an efficient arrangement.*

is absolute, '2' if the requirement is desirable, and '3' if the element does not require the attribute in question. The 'Data Sort' tool in a typical spreadsheet program can then be used to show patterns in use, performance, or servicing. By sorting this data by these requirements, patterns emerge that suggest how these spaces might be deployed. The sort shown in Table 1.1.2, for example, indicates what elements require access to plumbing. Note that none of these spaces require daylight. This suggests that these elements might be grouped into a single 'core' in the center of a floor plate, where they will not take up potentially precious perimeter, naturally illuminated space. While the examples shown are simple, this process can be a powerful organizational tool for larger buildings.

Another useful tool during program/brief analysis is a *stratification diagram* (Fig. 1.1.7). This sorts out spaces based on where they 'want' to be in a building's section. In many cases, this will be very simple: an office building, for example,

Programmatic layout attempt

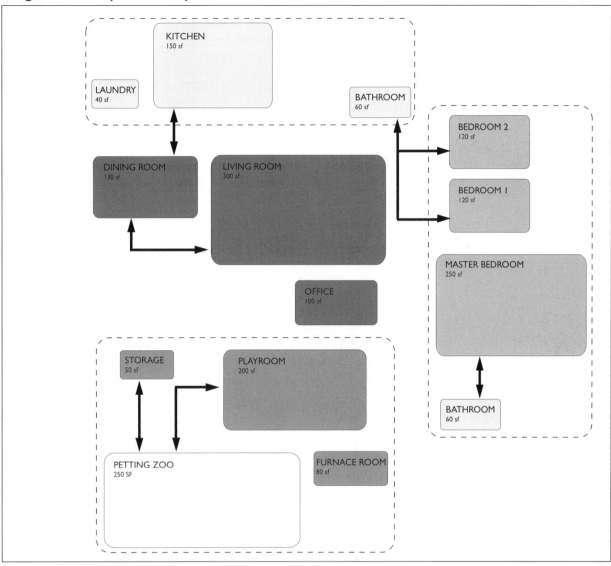

Figure 1.1.6. *Further refinement as the programmatic elements begin to find their place in the overall hierarchy.*

has a set of lobby functions on the ground floor, perhaps parking in the basement, and then a long run of office floors for its remainder. However in many complex program/briefs, such as libraries, museums, sports facilities, etc., it is useful to sort out adjacency requirements relative to ground level; what elements, for example, must be immediately accessible to an entry level lobby, what elements can be one or two floors above and below, what elements can be reached by elevator and have no need to be near an entry level, and what elements can be underground. On a tight urban site where street level space may be at a premium, this exercise can provide valuable opportunities to prioritize space on floor plates, and may give some clues about how the building may be ordered sectionally.

Moving into design. Bubble diagrams and other graphic strategies designed to generate architectural form from objective program data have received a bad

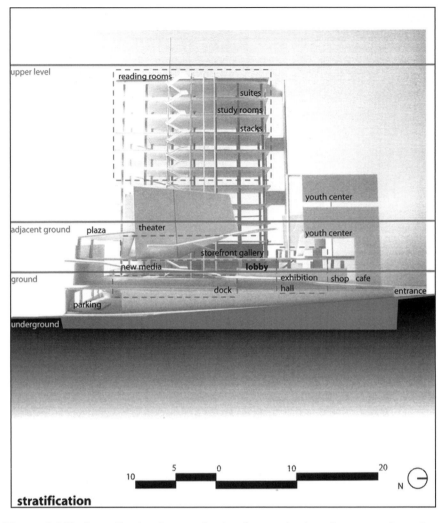

Figure 1.1.7. *A stratification diagram showing the organization of a program in section.*

reputation over the past generation. In our opinion, this is largely due to the late modernist myth that simply figuring out the most efficient solution to a programmed problem, and then 'building the diagram', could produce architecture on its own. This is a very reductivist view. However bubble diagrams and spreadsheets can be powerful methods for discovering the patterns of use and function on which a clever architectural scheme may be based. Very often, initial programmatic assumptions will be altered or questioned as the initial schematic strategies are produced – how close, for example, one is required to meet targets for office sizes or lobby spaces may change dramatically as architectural ideas are explored. Invariably, we'll try experiments from both ends, attempting to find architecturally significant patterns in how the program fits together and looking at how architectural ideas can be fulfilled or matched by the program. Figure 1.1.8 shows two simple organizational strategies applied to the program areas, each having potential as an integrated solution.

An important aspect of turning the corner from data analysis to design synthesis is to recognize just how the spaces required by various activities may be woven together, or how they may 'fit' in three dimensions. Three-dimensional

Linear

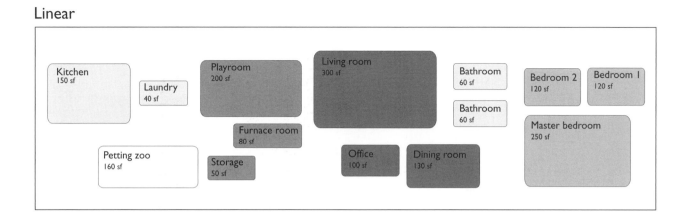

Centralized

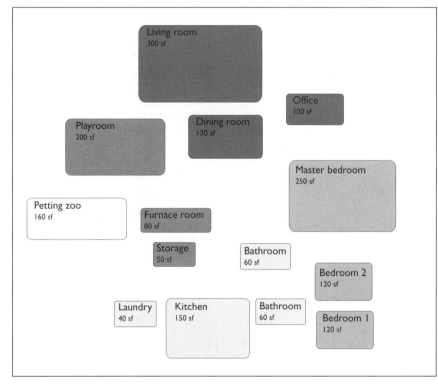

Figure 1.1.8. *Two architectural strategies imposed on the program.*

models – whether physical or virtual – may play a key role in understanding the architectural implications of a diagram produced by analysis. At this stage, volumetric models (boxes) are often less useful than floor-plate models, which can show possible plan arrangements on multiple floors while giving a rudimentary glimpse of what the resulting spaces and building masses might suggest. The computer-aided design (CAD) model in Figure 1.1.9 shows a provocative first step that may well inform the building shape, its major spaces, and its basic organization.

One aspect to look for at this point is clues to the building's *grain*, that is, overlaps of dimensions, bay sizes, floor heights, etc., that may suggest a pattern or

E3.
PROGRAM ANALYSIS
Stratification + Diagramming

10 After organizing the program into clusters and floor plates, these massing diagrams were developed. By extruding the floor plates, spaces formed around the program elements, giving the design a preliminary idea for possibilities of mass and space and vertical organization. These four massings were created for the last four cluster exercises. The tenth massing exercise below became a basic element for the derivation of the schematic design and the first chipboard model.

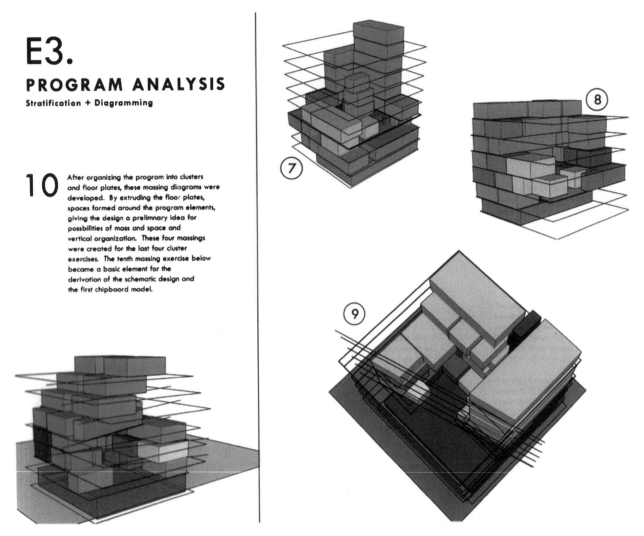

Figure 1.1.9. *A step toward massing, with a complex program laid out in three dimensions, within the confines of a tight site.*

order to the building's spaces and massing. This will become imperative as the design process moves toward structural layout and bay sizes, but may be evident at this early stage. A classic example here is the fortunate coincidence between office dimensions (often 3 × 3 m, 10 × 10 ft) and parking stalls (often 3 × 9 m, 10 × 30 ft). Noticing potential alignments through a building's structure at this point will make subsequent stages of structural design much more efficient and integrated (Fig. 1.1.10).

Frequently asked questions

What's the difference between a program, an areas schedule, and a brief? These are all different names for the same thing. 'Program' is the American term for what British architects call a 'Brief'. To confuse things further, the 'brief' is also often referred to as a 'schedule' in the UK, which in the US refers to the project's calendar.

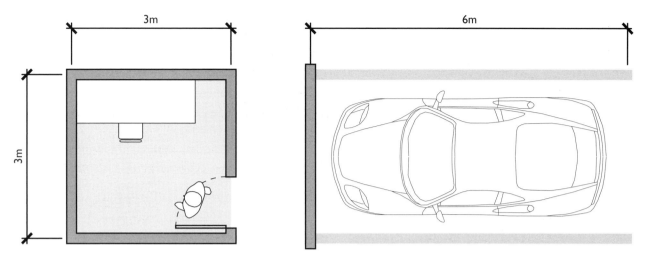

Figure 1.1.10. *Finding the spatial 'grain' of a building can be an important discovery during program analysis. Here, dimensional alignments between two seemingly unrelated program components might suggest a structural module.*

Glossary and formulas

Affinities	Relationships between program elements that suggest physical proximity based on shared qualities or requirements.
Adjacencies	Relationships between program elements that suggest physical proximity based on circulatory requirements.
Bubble Diagrams	Drawings showing the relative areas of programmed spaces and their desired relationship. While often derided, these diagrams can provide a useful first step toward understanding the spatial consequences of programmatic imperatives.
Construction Area	A measure of the floor area taken up by walls, columns, shafts, etc.
Grain	A pattern or order that emerges based on an understanding of typical sizes of elements of the program/brief. Often the primary design goal in analyzing an architectural program.
Gross Area	A measure of building area that includes all spaces – 'assignable' and otherwise (i.e., circulation, toilets, elevators, etc.).
Net Area	A measure of building area that includes only 'assignable' spaces such as offices or apartments.
Net to Gross	A percentage derived by dividing the assignable area of a building (Net) by the total area (Gross). Often seen as a measure of efficiency, but not always accurate in its assessment of how well a building may work.

Program (or Brief)	A written document that lists the required performance aspects of a designed object. In architectural situations, this often takes the form of a list of spaces with areas and qualities ascribed to them, but this is not necessarily a complete description.
Programming	Determining the fundamental functional requirements of a designed object.
Stratification Diagram	A drawing (or model) showing the desired distribution of a given program/brief in a multi-story situation.

Further reading

Peña, W., Parshall, S. and Kelly, K. (1987) *Problem Seeking: An Architectural Programming Primer* (Washington, DC: AIA Press).

1.2 Site analysis

Site analysis

Form finding from the outside in. In program analysis, architects seek patterns and ordering strategies based on the inherent structures of a building's functions and requirements. This is essentially an 'inside out' process. Meanwhile, we are often examining a building's context to see how a project can best fit into its site – an 'outside in' process. In the best cases, the final form, rhythm, massing, and spatial sequences of a project will be a dialog between what we find out from the project's internal and external requirements. Usually, this is a case of balancing, of finding convenient overlaps between competing requirements, and of assessing the relative values and merits of solving both sets of challenges and opportunities.

While getting the functional disposition of a project correct is a major goal in satisfying clients and users, architects have a responsibility to cities, neighborhoods, and surrounding residents, owners and the public to assess how such functional solutions can most appropriately and sensitively nestle in to existing contexts. Site analysis is thus not only concerned with our clients and users, but with the larger community. Much of our work in this area will be concerned with negotiating our clients' needs with the welfare and quality of life of their surroundings. Site analysis is thus a delicate process, and the need for a thorough understanding of a project's physical, social, and cultural contexts in addition to its circulatory patterns, esthetic traditions, and public uses is part of our responsibility beyond simply pleasing a client.

We are also under distinct regulatory pressure in this phase. Many localities have zoning regulations, historic preservation requirements, traffic or pedestrian laws, and review processes to ensure that development takes place within the boundaries of community standards and functions. While the power of development money may occasionally override responsible growth, architects have the power – and the responsibility – to ensure that our work creates buildings that are 'good neighbors,' and that do not simply exploit community resources or environments for corporate or personal gain. While local zoning or esthetic regulations may seem onerous, they represent encoded values that we are duty-bound to recognize. Challenges that adhere to the spirit of such regulations may be welcomed, however this is usually the result of patient, respectful consideration on the part of designers and clients to understand the underlying reasons for what may seem like petty requirements.

Process

Like program analysis, we suggest a diagrammatic approach that emphasizes clear documentation, graphic analysis, and the development of a holistic understanding, rather than an attempt at high-speed form finding. Like program analysis, the successful resolution of site conditions and requirements is more likely to come from a design idea inspired by our integration of this data than directly from the data itself. A typical site analysis package will be documentary in nature, often showing many pages of graphic or tabular information, followed by some very preliminary design diagrams that show strategies likely to best resolve the site's particular issues.

The first steps of site analysis invariably involve gathering data. Often architectural teams will get a detailed aerial photograph or survey map as a base for recording and presenting our findings, as well as for studying the physical context of our site. Direct observation is imperative – architects will almost always need extensive access to the site, often recording activity on and around it for an entire day or more. Topographic surveys that show the shape of the land in plan form are likewise required for sites with significant changes in elevation, and extensive photography is necessary to record the scale of the surroundings, as well as the massing, materials, and styles of surrounding buildings. There are also significant intangible elements to any site analysis that can only be gained by careful observation, by walking not only the site but also its surroundings, and by immersion in the daily activities of its neighbors. What is the pace of life around the site like? Do we sense nearby activities through sound or smell? Are there amenities (restaurants, coffee shops, post offices, cinemas) that might benefit our program, or be reinforced by the sudden infusion of our client's staff? Are there local building traditions that we can respond to, challenge, or simply acknowledge?

Likewise, we need to document the regulatory and legal aspects of the site. Using public records and documents, the site's legal dimensions need to be confirmed, and a full exploration of its allowable uses, building size and type, and required amenities or concessions must be fully documented. Typically, this will come in the form of a zoning designation, which is determined by municipal authorities. A full understanding of this information is vital prior to commencing design work, as obtaining variances may be politically difficult.

Finally, our responsibility to design efficient buildings requires us to study and document the climatological properties of our site. Of particular interest will be the site's relationship to the sun. Ideally, buildings will take advantage of winter sun and summer shade, requiring studies of the sun's position throughout the year. How surrounding buildings, planting, or topography modifies the sun's effects on the site are of particular interest, as are the effects our intervention will have on neighboring properties. To do an accurate solar study, the approximate latitude of the site is needed. From this, solar angles for any day of the year can be calculated using published solar charts that show the position of solar paths on a flattened 'sky chart' (see Section I.4, Environment: Solar Geometry). While this data is particularly useful in designing facades and shading devices, a more holistic overview of the sun's effects on a site can be gleaned by running a solar path study using 3-D CAD modeling. Running typical days for each of the four seasons will give a good idea of the site's exposure during key times of the year, suggesting massing and planting strategies that can take advantage of climate-appropriate techniques to add shade or exposure. This study can also identify likely open areas that will provide direct sunlight, and may indicate areas of the site where glare might be a problem. In addition to solar studies, documentation of daily temperature, precipitation, and cloud cover averages is required to assess insulation,

Location

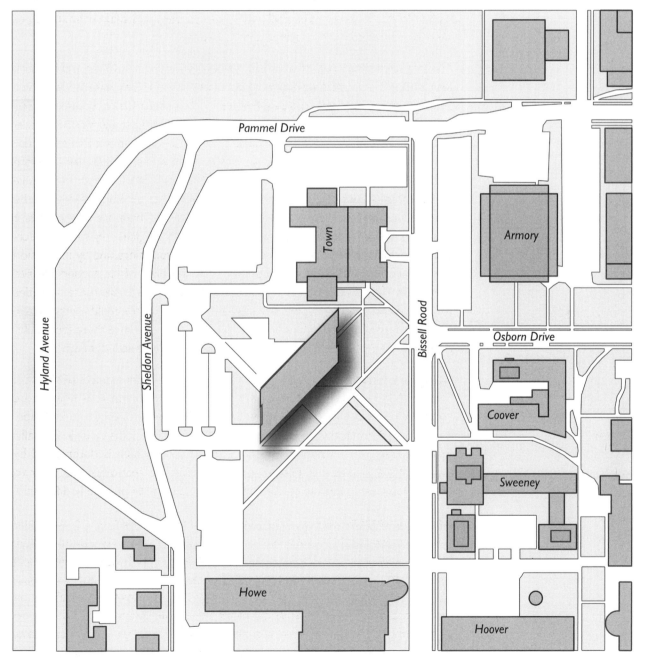

Figure 1.2.1. *A basic map of a project's site, using an aerial photo as an underlay. Key buildings, streets, and paths provide a context for understanding where the project is and what its neighbors are.*

Site boundaries

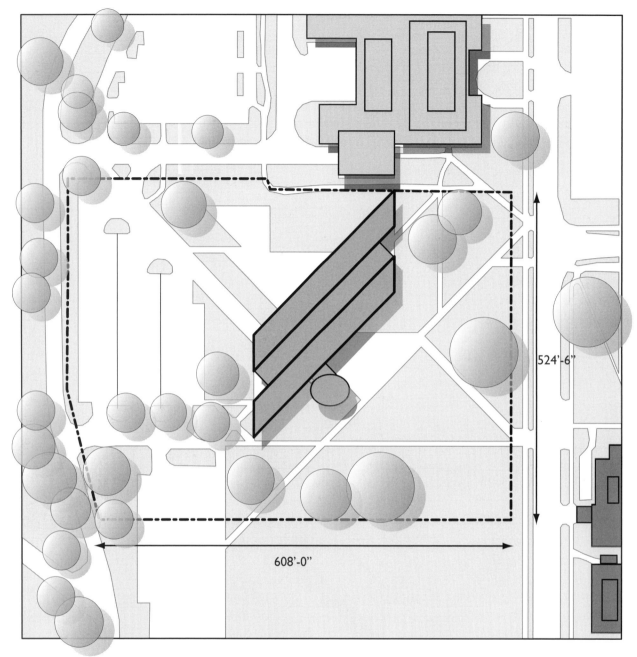

Figure 1.2.2. *Further information on location will include legal boundaries and site dimensions. It may also include setbacks, easements, and other legal restrictions.*

façade porosity and the importance of outdoor exposure. Finally, it is important to study wind patterns on the site, to see if we might be able to take advantage of summer breezes, or to easily block winter winds. Climate data can be found on the web site of the National Oceanic and Atmospheric Administration (www.noaa.gov), or the 'Met Office' (www.met-office.gov.uk).

Documentation

No client will tolerate being confronted with a massive list of traffic, zoning, climate, and historical data. Architects have the responsibility of not only

Topography

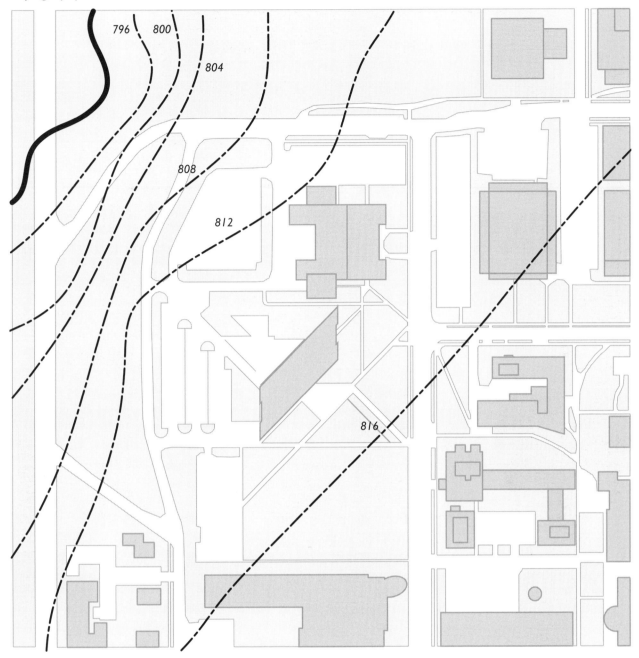

Figure 1.2.3. *Understanding the geography of the site includes a full topographical survey (typically provided) by the client that can be interpreted to show steep slopes, runoff areas, and physical orientation.*

documenting these issues, but also of teasing out patterns and overlaps amongst these areas. Just like Programming, the 'analysis' in site analysis demands that we also make some tentative suggestions about what these findings all suggest.

One way to begin this process is to document our findings in a consistent, graphic method. Architects will often use a set of aerial photographs as underlays for diagrams – or 'vignettes' that summarize the data that we've found in visual ways (Fig. 1.2.1). A traffic diagram, for instance, might layer a set of arrows over an aerial photograph indicating where automobile traffic flows,

Mature foliage

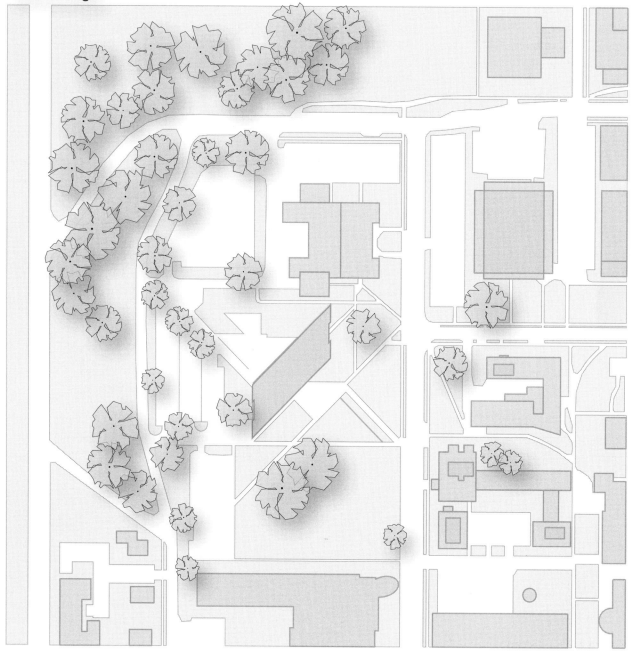

Figure 1.2.4. *Site analysis may include information from landscape architects or arborists on plant types and locations.*

using arrowheads to show direction, line weight to show relative intensities, and color to show types of traffic (truck, vehicular, bike, etc.). The same aerial might underlay diagrams showing pedestrian connections, zoning information, locations of amenities in the neighborhood, etc. (Figs. 1.2.2–1.2.8). A larger scale aerial photograph might show regional traffic connections, population concentrations, or larger amenities such as airports, train stations, or shopping centers. Meanwhile, a larger scale aerial might be used to show more detailed information such as planting locations, data on neighboring structures, or likely entries and exits into the site.

Seasonal Winds

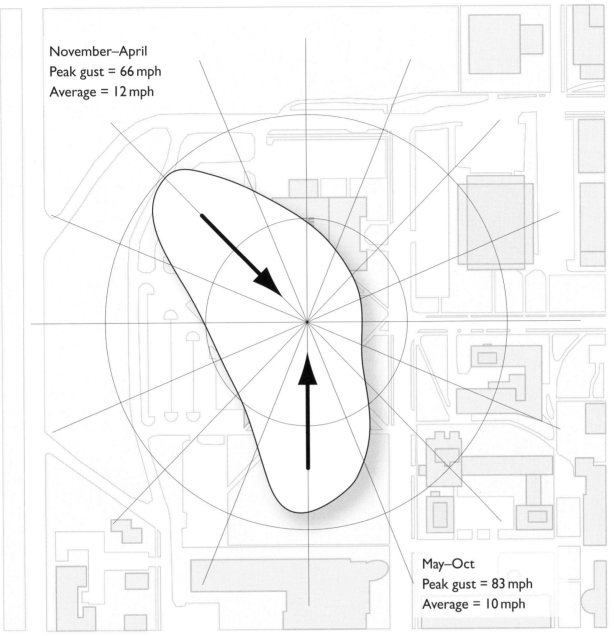

November–April
Peak gust = 66 mph
Average = 12 mph

May–Oct
Peak gust = 83 mph
Average = 10 mph

Figure 1.2.5. *Understanding the local climate and micro-climate is critical to producing an efficient building. Temperature, rainfall, and wind patterns (shown here) can provide clues to the best ventilation, cladding, and orientation strategies.*

In constructing these diagrams, it is important to be both accurate and clear. A good site analysis package will strive to convey the overall themes inherent in the site (Is it automobile-intensive or pedestrian-intensive? Is there a consistent set of materials or styles in its neighbors? Are there portions of the site that offer greater civic presence? Are there opportunities to take advantage of the climatic patterns we've discovered?). It will do this by highlighting the most important information and by presenting an easily graspable graphic package. Consistency in the form of a regularly used set of underlays, a repetition of colors for like types of data, and visual cues that link information with graphic gestures can be helpful in establishing comparative methods – it can

Vehicular and
Pedestrian Access

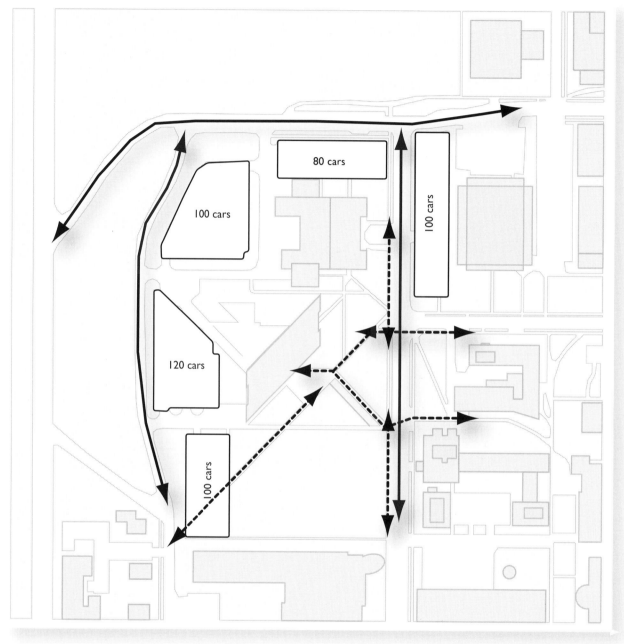

Figure 1.2.6. *Circulatory patterns on a site may provide important clues about where entrances can be best placed, whether new parking or public transit facilities are required, and how the building is likely to be perceived in its context.*

be easy to see parallels between various sets of data this way. By far the best models for good explanatory diagrams can be found in Edward Tufte's (1997) *Visual Explanations*, which offers strategies for presenting data graphically in ways that are rigorously accurate and yet begin to tell the stories that we might otherwise leave for an accompanying narrative.

As this data is assembled, certain patterns may become evident – the site's solar orientation, for example, may suggest a major exterior space that happens to

Service access

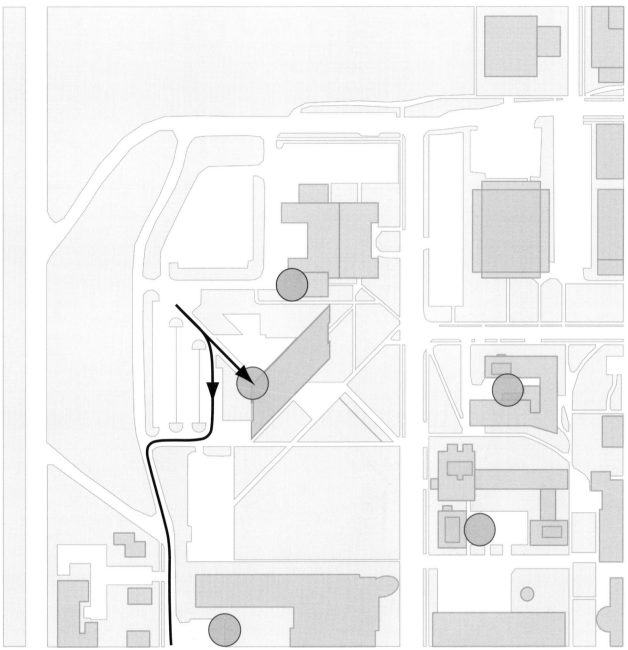

Figure 1.2.7. *In addition to pedestrian and vehicular circulation, service access is an important aspect of siting and program layout. Here, the analysis notes a somewhat difficult truck access, and compares it with other, nearby service areas and truck docks.*

coincide with a good connection to local pedestrian networks. As often as not, of course, we will find sets of information that offer contradictory suggestions – for example, there may be good pedestrian access in the same area that offers the best truck access. In any event, it is now our responsibility to read potential design strategies from the developing large picture of site information. Often the best test of our analysis comes from preliminary schemes – massing, circulatory, or climatic – that will dredge up the inherent contradictions and overlaps in what the site tells us.

Solar path

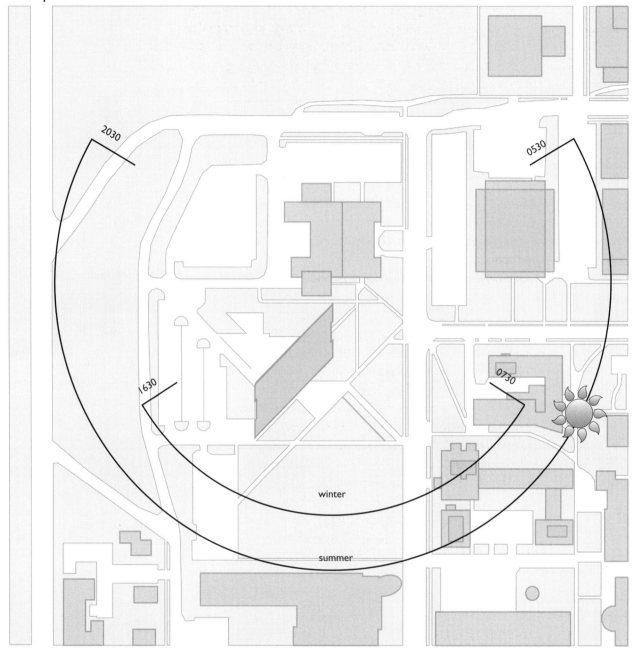

Figure 1.2.8. *A key element in providing efficient daylighting and shading is understanding the sun's path around and over a site. Here, a simple notation shows the sun's arc during the solstices, quickly illustrating the range of solar exposures to which the building will be subjected.*

A typical site analysis package will include both graphic vignettes and an accompanying narrative. It will often parallel a similar package of program analysis. Both studies will present to the client a study of the forces at work on a design – from the inside out (program analysis) and from the outside in (site analysis). Both may suggest initial formal, massing, or circulatory strategies. Often, what we find from one may contradict the other. But these provide the clay from which the final design will be sculpted, and the contradictions we discover will invariably form the challenges of schematic design. Both sets of analysis are concerned with stating the problems of the project clearly; both speak to what the building will be made up from, and what it is designed to achieve. Because these studies are painstaking, they may well seem like they are taking precious time away from the bold gestures and forms that architects may want to jump into early in the process. But, properly executed, they offer the firmest footing for moving ahead. Understanding the external forces at work on a site early in the process is the surest step toward eliminating awkward or insensitive relationships with a project's neighbors.

Typical information contained in a site analysis package

Location   Information from client on site's situation, its legal definition, its size and orientation, and understood jurisdictions.

Context   Photographs, drawings, and studies of surrounding buildings and spaces.

Geography   Documentation of land formations, bodies of water, soil composition (typically done by the client's consultants).

Flora   Information on plants on and around site.

Climate   Information on recorded weather patterns. May include temperature averages, rainfall data, wind speeds and susceptibility to climatic extremes (hurricanes, tornadoes, etc.).

Circulation   Documentation of traffic patterns that affect the site. May include diagrams of automobile traffic, parking inventory, adjacency of arterial streets, rail lines, airports, etc. May also include detailed observations of pedestrian patterns around and across site.

Orientation   Position of site relative to solar path, prevailing winds, and views from and toward itself. Solar orientation is particularly important, as significant energy savings may be realized by a careful development of a design with daylighting and heating patterns in mind.

Further reading

Tufte, E. (1990) *Envisioning Information* (Cheshire, CT: Graphics Press).

White, Edward T. (c1983) *Site Analysis: Diagramming Information for Architectural Design* (Tucson, AZ: Architectural Media).

1.3   Site and building ecology

Site Analysis	Slope (building, planting, paving)
	Soil patterns
	Vegetation
	Wildlife
	Geology
	Surface and sub-surface water
	Climate (Topography)
Soils	Mechanics
	Types and properties
	Geotechnical engineering
	Drainage
	Contour drawings
	Cut and fill
	Wetlands
	Erosion/stabilization
	Topography and building form
Water Movement	Precipitation
	Percolation
	Flow/channels – swales (open system)
	Pipe, Inlet – catchbasin, manhole (closed system)
	Grade slopes for hard and soft surfaces

Introduction to site ecology

All buildings have very specific material relationships to their site. The most basic of these relationships are with the ground and the climate. The physical properties of a site not only affect what can or cannot be built there, but also what is appropriate to construct. As architects, we must know how to thoroughly assess a site – often times very quickly. We also need to be able to judge the probable future of a site – because we operate in this way when designing a structure that does not exist yet, but will operate 20 to 50 to 100 years forward in time.

From a purely functional point of view the site must do two things at a minimum; be capable of supporting the load of a building and keep water flowing away from the structure. Dirt and water have a tremendous impact on every design solution and these factors alone provide great challenges, however, a designer's responsibility goes far beyond these two items.

The notion that we, as humans, exist not just on the ground but also between the space of the earth and sky is made very apparent by the process of building. To place a building on the ground means that you must typically dig into the earth for support. The act of digging moves soil from one place to another – and it must be placed in a stable fashion or it will wash away. You are also replacing open permeable ground with something typically hard and impermeable (a building). This disrupts the flow of water into the ground and creates an imbalance that requires mitigation. Water must find its path between the earth and the sky in ways that allow life cycles to balance. In a sustainable natural system: rain falls onto the earth – nourishes plants, which cleanse the air – percolates into the ground, cleansing and filtering the water – establishes a consistent water table height and ground moisture/humidity level – travels to open water, replenishing streams and lakes – and re-evaporates starting the cycle again. You can see how interrupting this flow with roads, parking, and buildings could be detrimental to the overall environment. To fully understand a site the myriad of other environmental conditions along with social and esthetic concerns must also be taken into account before any design takes place.

Environmental site analysis

The first factor of site assessment is slope. Grade is rarely flat, even when it appears to be, and the amount plus the direction of the site slope often determines both the location and form of a project. In order to judge grade slope a survey is done of the site, resulting in a scaled contour map that can be used to understand the shape of the land. This map becomes the basis for most site assessments, as it allows the 3-D forms to be collapsed into an easy to read plan format. The contour map needs to be augmented with photographs in order to judge the slope perceptually – often a difference of 15 cm (6 in) in height can block a view or run water a different direction, and most contour maps use intervals from 0.3 m (1 ft) to 1.5 m (5 ft) in height. Also, it is very easy to over abstract your perception of a site with plan drawings and be surprised when you see it in person.

Soil Patterns are judged by type and depth. Soil types will be covered later, but typically range from course rock to fine clays. Soils accommodate two different functions between surface and sub-surface material. Soils on the surface determine plant growth possibilities, drainage capability, and erosion potential. Most surface soils can be roughly judged visually, but may also need to be analyzed by a geotechnical engineer or horticulturalist. The soils below grade are judged by their ability to support building load (compressibility), further drainage capacity, plasticity (more plastic soils swell and heave with moisture or frost), underground pollution, and amount of organic vs. inert material. Organic materials cannot support load, due to their tendency to decompose.

Vegetation is considered as the existing plants on the site. Soil patterns determine what is possible in the future. Indigenous plants are judged by size, condition, esthetics, ability to tolerate construction or modifications to the site, and their compatibility with new or planned vegetation. It's also important to understand how the existing plants may stabilize or hold soil in position and promote drainage. Existing plants tell you about the condition of the soil and what types of success future vegetation may have, often it's wise to maintain growth patterns and plant types that have shown to be successful previously.

Existing wildlife is judged in terms of the importance of the site to their movement patterns, and whether the site is critical to their survival. This is not a common issue on most sites but is always important to note, particularly on large site or big planning projects.

Geology in site analysis deals with underground rock layers. These can provide support for building foundations and limit the location of underground construction. Geotechnical engineers, who conduct soil borings and provide an analysis of the soils, rock and load-bearing capacity, do studies of sub-grade conditions. They will also typically make recommendations on the type of suitable foundation systems for the proposed building.

Surface and sub-surface water concerns deal with natural drainage and underground water table levels. Surface drainage can be judged in part through the contour drawings, but viewing the site in person shows the erosion potential of the water movement. Sub-surface water is typically understood through the test borings done by the geotechnical engineer. Boring logs show the depth of the water table at various points on the site.

Climate in relation to siting has been covered previously, but site slope, direction, shading, and ground cover are all parts of the physical properties of climactic site analysis.

Soils

Soil mechanics describe the characteristics and performance of different types of soils under varying circumstances. In extreme circumstances soil conditions can make building impossible on a site. This is largely due to the soil type and its properties.

Soil types and properties dictate the bearing capacity, frost action, and drainage of the site. The range of soil types runs from gravel to clay – the primary differences between the types are the size of particles making up the soil. The coarser and harder the particles, the better it is to build on. Larger particles (like gravel) have higher bearing capacity, little to no frost action, and excellent drainage. Smaller particles (such as clay or shale) shift and move under bearing loads, heave when frozen, and drain poorly. Poor soils often require foundation systems that go to the depth of the rock layer to obtain enough support (Fig. 1.3.1).

Determination of the properties of ground conditions for construction often requires the assistance of a geotechnical engineer. Geotechnical engineers offer both structural and groundwater advice by studying the surface and sub-surface soils along with the rock layers below a site. They use a boring rig to drill, or

Soil types

Type	Classes Letter	Symbol	Description	Value as a foundation material	Frost Action	Drainage
Gravel and gravely soils	GW	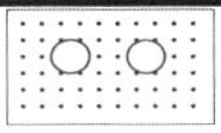	Well-graded gravel, or gravel-sand mixture, little or no lines	Excellent	None	Excellent
	GP	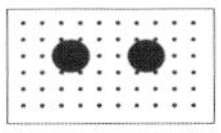	Poorly graded gravel, or gravel-sand mixture, little or no lines	Good	None	Excellent
	GM	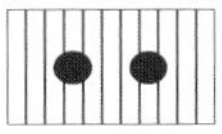	Silty gravels, gravel-sand-silt mixtures	Good	Slight	Poor
	GC		Clay-gravels, gravel-clay-sand mixtures	Good	Slight	Poor
Sand and sandy soils	SW	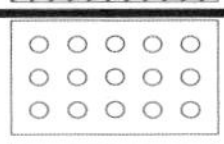	Well-graded sands, or gravelly sands, little or no fines	Good	None	Excellent
	SP	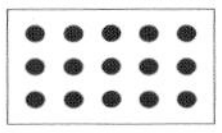	Poorly graded sands, or gravelly sands, little or no fines	Fair	None	Excellent
	SM	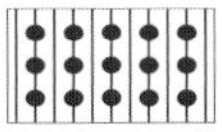	Silty sands, sand-silt mixtures	Fair	Slight	Fair
	SC	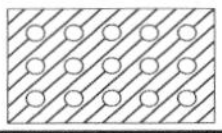	Clay-sands, sand-clay mixtures	Fair	Medium	Poor
Silts and clays	ML		Inorganic silts, rock flour, silty or clay-fine sands, or clay-silts with slight plasticity	Fair	Very High	Poor
	CL	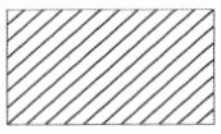	Inorganic clays of low to medium plasticity, gravelly clays, silty clays, or lean clays	Fair	Medium	Impervious
	OL		Organic silt clays of low plasticity	Poor	High	Impervious
	MH		Inorganic silts, micaceous or diatomaceous fine sandy or silty soils, elastic silts	Poor	Very High	Poor
	CH		Inorganic clays of high plasticity, fat clays	Very Poor	Medium	Impervious
	OH		Organic clays of medium to high plasticity, organic silts	Very Poor	Medium	Impervious
Highly organic soils	Pt	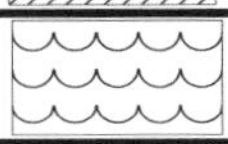	Peat and other highly organic soils	Not Suitable	Slight	Poor

Figure 1.3.1. *Soil types chart, showing the United Soil Classification System (USCS).*

drive a piling tube to pull soil cores out of the ground for study (Fig. 1.3.2). These cores are studied and recorded as a boring log, which shows the type, depth, and condition of the soils below grade. The study of sub-grade soils also determines whether the soils are *undisturbed*, meaning they are well-compacted load bearing material and not recently deposited fill – *recently* in this case can mean anything less than a million years or so. Multiple borings are typically done in various places on the site to get a complete picture of the variance of conditions. These borings go to various total depths depending on the type of building planned, often with big projects the borings are requested to go until they hit rock. Borings to rock depth make multiple attempts to run the bit to refusal. This assures that they are not hitting a thin plate of rock, but a large area of stone capable of bearing load.

Drainage through soils is dependant on the coarseness of the material. Gravels and sands drain well, and clays trap the moisture. This potential for moisture freeze and heave is most critical under the foundations of buildings, and is the

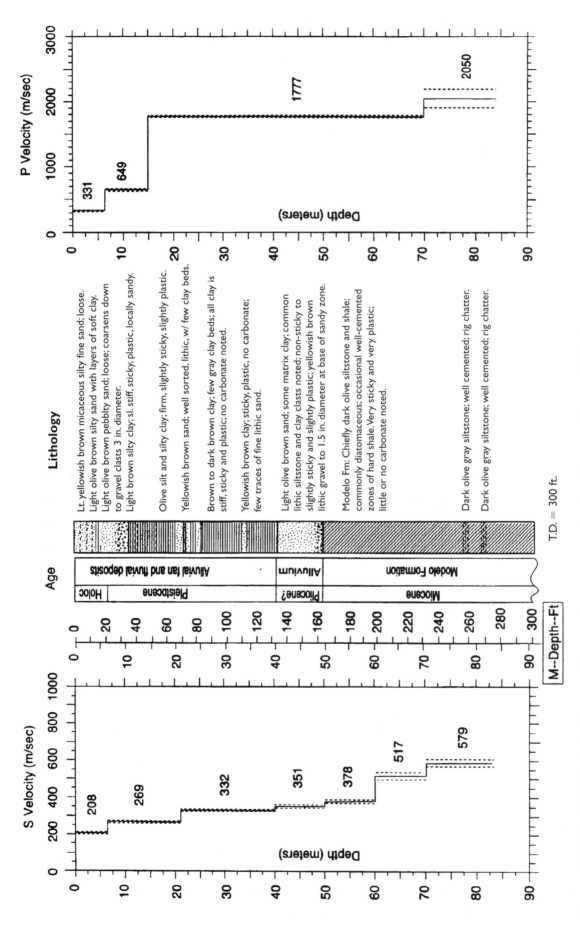

Figure I.3.2. *Typical soil boring log. Showing soil types and pressure required to drive the core to the specified depth.*

reason foundations are always below the frost line. Fine soils that don't drain well also tend to shift and move, which can cause problems in areas close to buildings and under paved areas. In areas where clay is present you would normally specify a deeper layer of gravel and sand under slabs and foundations.

Contour Drawings are the tool used to study the surface shape of the site. Contour maps and plans are done by survey teams using transepts to mark the variations in height across a site. These point heights are recorded relative to a datum height – some cities have standard datum points, other times sea level is used, sometimes the height of a fixed object on the site like a fire hydrant cap is used. The points are then joined into continuous lines that mark a level height across the site. The line curves to follow the specified height, which is normally in 0.3–1.5 m (1–5 ft) increments (Fig. 1.3.3). The more contours desired for precision, the greater the number of points that need to be surveyed.

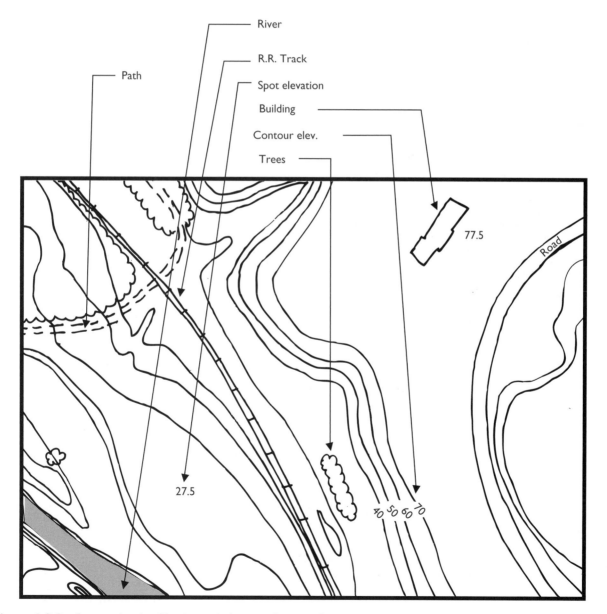

Figure 1.3.3. *Contour drawing. Showing typical range of site conditions.*

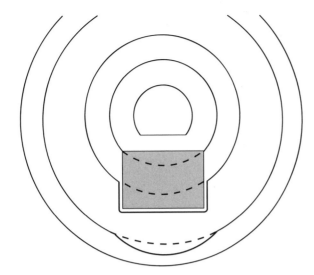

Determining approximate cut and fill volume

– Using contour plan of before and after, calculate area between new and original contours
– Multiply area by contour internal
– If cut or fill stops on a contour level, divide area in half

	CUT	FILL
85		200
90		400
95	300/2 = 150	
100	200	
	350(5') = 1,750 cu.ft.	600(5') = 3,000 cu.ft.

Figure 1.3.4. *Determining approximate cut and fill volume.*

Cut and Fill refers to the amount of soil removed from site areas and added to others during construction. Ideally the amount of soil removed or *cut* equals the amount added or *filled*. It makes little sense and creates unnecessary expense to truck dirt in or out of a site if it can be avoided. This supposes that the fill on the site is *clean*, or without contaminates, and is well-compacted. Determining the amount of cut and fill is done by studying the original and proposed contours on a site plan, and adjusting the location of the contours to equalize dirt movement amounts (Fig. 1.3.4). Keep in mind that building foundations and basements can displace large amounts of earth depending on how deep they go.

Wetlands are designated low-lying areas where water collects and percolates into the ground. These areas need to be protected when developing a site because they often are the primary run-off point for a large area of land, and a problem is created when the water has no place to go. Wetlands are difficult to replace or move, as their ecosystem and soil types have been naturally developed to manage water flow. Code requirements vary, but typically require no modification of wetlands or replacement with an area larger than the size of the original – this is because the new area is likely to be much less efficient at managing water flow. Flow patterns to wetlands also need to be maintained, so the water movement can reach the appropriate low-lying area.

Erosion of grade can occur very easily with even slight modifications to the existing conditions. The natural conditions of a site have usually achieved a balance with the slope, water movement and vegetation holding the soil in place. When forming new slopes the *angle of repose* is the soil angle that will not collapse under its own load to a lower slope. The rule of thumb on this angle is 45°, but that does not take into account erosion by water (Fig. 1.3.5). Moisture in small amounts will percolate into the soil, but in larger amounts will run down the slope taking small particles of dirt along. This eventually creates rivulets and trenches that destabilize ground conditions and become progressively worse. The best way to combat erosion is to keep the slopes low and to prevent the water from channeling into a narrow run. Vegetation

Material	Minimum/slope	Maximum/slope	Recommended/slope
Grass			
Lawn	1–100	1–4	1.5 to 10–100
Athletic	1–200	1–50	1–100
Walkways			
Direction of travel	1–200	1–83	1.5–100
Cross slope	1–100	1–25	1 to 2–100
Accessible Route max		1–12	
Accessible route, not a ramp		1–20	
Street			
Direction of travel	1–200	1–5	1 to 10–100
Parking	1–200	1–20	2 to 3–100

Figure 1.3.5. *Site slope recommendations.*

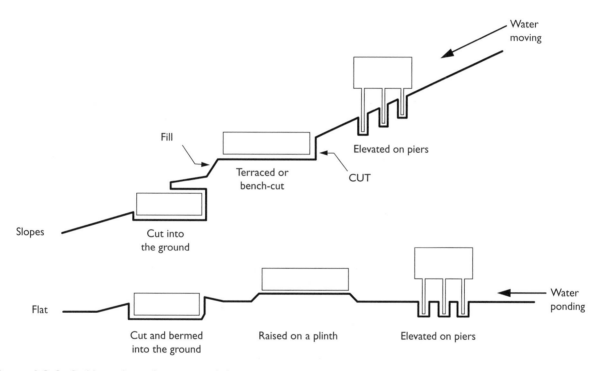

Figure 1.3.6. *Building relationship to ground slope.*

with substantial root systems works most effectively in maintaining stable ground conditions, both holding soil in place and promoting water dispersion and percolation.

Topography and soil conditions can have a tremendous affect on building form. Steep slopes require the building to either float above the ground – dig into the ground or a combination of the two (Fig 1.3.6). Even moderate and low slopes create opportunities for formal responses, as the floors of buildings are almost always completely flat. The flow of water across a site requires modifying the shape of the ground, because all water must flow away from the building and this can be very difficult to accomplish. Sub-grade soil conditions can affect form due to the type of foundation system required to support the building. Avoiding certain areas of the site because of wetland or water flow patterns also affects architectural responses to the site, and is undeniably part of the fundamental design process that begins with site analysis.

Water movement

Precipitation is the primary source of all water movement across a site. The amount can vary, but the situations that cause buildings the most problems are the extreme ends of the spectrum – drought and storms. No rain for prolonged periods lowers the water table and can allow soil to shift and crumble. Storm waters are the bigger problem and move large amounts of water over the ground rapidly. This water can wash away the soil or more significantly run directly into buildings if not considered fully.

Percolation is water moving through the soil surface into the underground aquifer. When a new building is built most site planning ordinances request that the project move water into the ground at the same rate as an undisturbed site. This means a variety of things, but mostly it requires the building keep its water on the site and not run it into the street or adjacent properties. Building roofs and paved areas cause immediate problems, because they no longer allow for water percolation. This water must be sent to an area of the site where it can be collected and allowed to percolate into the site or run into the city storm sewers. The storm sewer system can only handle a certain amount of load at one time, so retention ponds are created on site to hold the water – let some of it percolate – and run the rest into the sewer through a restricted opening that has an allowable flow determined by the city. In urban areas the retention areas can sometimes be bypassed, but storm sewers can only handle so much load. The other concern is that water moved to streams through pipes has lost its ability to naturally filter and clean itself through the ground, plus it has picked up pollutants from the paved areas. This begins a cycle of progressively worsening water quality, reinforcing the desire to keep as much water as possible percolating through the ground.

Channels and Swales are open system methods of shaping the ground to move water in a desired direction. Channels focus the water into a trench that pulls water from multiple directions to send it to a particular destination. Swales are berms that keep the water away from a particular location, such as a building wall. Swales don't normally focus the water; rather they simply discourage a direction of flow.

The Pipe, Inlet – Catch basin, and Manhole is a closed system method of moving water under ground to a storm sewer. The inlet captures the water, sending it into an underground pipe. The pipe slopes to feed the water to the base of a manhole. This water then moves into the storm sewer system that intersects the manhole location. Catch basins typically sit at the curb line of a street and collect water from the open system gutter (Fig. 1.3.7). Pipes can also be used to run water under a structure then bring the water back to an above grade spreader that allows for percolation.

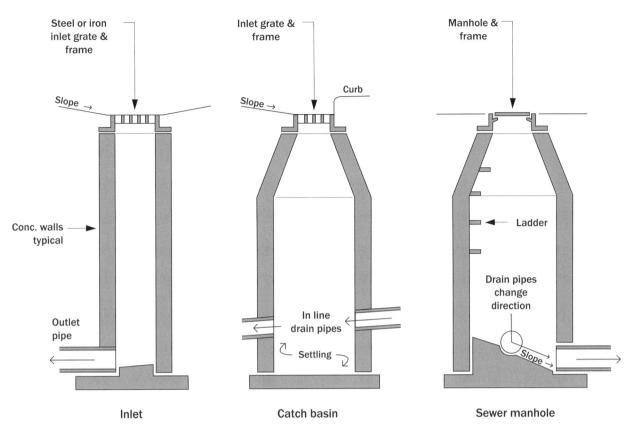

Figure 1.3.7. *Inlet, catch basin, and manhole configurations.*

Grade Slope Minimums are the least allowable angles that surfaces must maintain to keep water moving and to prevent ponding. This slope is a minimum of 2% for planted areas, with 3% minimum recommended. The minimum slope for paved areas is 0.5%, with 1% minimum recommended.

Frequently asked questions

'What makes a site unacceptable to build on?'
Common site problems are poor or unstable soil conditions, contaminated soils, wetland areas that are too large to be avoided, slopes too steep, or difficulty of supplying basic services such as power, water, and electricity. Most of these conditions can be mitigated, but frequently the expense makes it more logical to find another place to build.

'How can you tell how deep a building can go for underground spaces?'
The primary concerns for the depth of underground spaces are the height of the water table and the depth of bedrock. In projects of any significant size (larger than a house) it is common to have a geotechnical engineer drill cores to judge site soil conditions. These borings show the height of the water table and depth of bedrock. The lowest floor normally wants to be above the highest level of the water table otherwise flooding is likely. This can be mitigated with sump pumps, but eventually every pump fails. The depth of bedrock is an indication of how difficult it is to excavate the site. While it is possible to dig out rock, the cost is normally prohibitive if another solution is available.

Conclusion

Site ecology is the component of site analysis that deals with the physical condition of the ground you're building on. Most of these skills need to become part of your integrated ability to see potential opportunities and liabilities quickly when looking at a site. Often architects are asked to look at a number of sites to assist the owners in making a decision of where to locate. The factors covered here are the basics of what you are expected to know, and this does not include cultural and esthetic issues regarding the site. Observe the physical conditions of sites you look at every day and begin to develop a mental reference of how to deal with a large variety of conditions. This skill, like most of the others you've learned about building technologies, must become part of a holistic integrated method of assessing and designing that can weigh many factors at one time. You should be able to look at drawings of a site, visit the actual location, and then have an initial feel for how appropriate the site is for construction and where might be likely locations on the site to explore and avoid developing.

Glossary and formulas

Channels and Swales	Open system methods of shaping the ground to move water in a desired direction.
Cut and Fill	Refers to the amount of soil removed from site areas and added to others during construction.
Geology	In building site, analysis deals with underground rock layers used to support a building loads.
Grade	The level of the ground surface of a site.
Grade Slope Minimums	2% for planted areas, with 3% minimum recommended. The minimum slope for paved areas is 0.5%, with 1% minimum recommended.
Percolation	Water moving through the soil surface into the underground aquifer.
Precipitation	The primary source of all water movement across a site.
Pipe, Inlet – Catch basin, and Manhole	Closed system methods of moving water under ground to a storm sewer.
Soil Types and Properties	Dictate the bearing capacity, frost action, and drainage of the site.
Wetlands	Designated low-lying areas where water collects and percolates into the ground.

Further reading

Neufert, E. and Neufert, P. (2000) *Architect's Data* 3rd ed (London, UK: Blackwell Science). pp. 51–58.

Hawkes, D., McDonald, J. and Steemers, K. (2002) *The Selective Environment* (New York, NY: Spon Press). Chapter 8, Environmental Design Checklist, pp. 122–151.

Ramsey, C.G. and Sleeper, H.R. (2000) *Architectural Graphic Standards* 10th ed (New York, NY: John Wiley & Sons). pp. 61–62.

CHAPTER 2

Circulation

2.1   Life safety

Basic Building Safety	Building codes
	Building integrity
	Fire containment
	Occupant notification
	Escape
Emergency Egress	Occupancy load
	Exiting
	Distance
	Elements

Making buildings safe

A prime responsibility of architects is that of designing out dangerous conditions. Overwhelmingly, we're concerned with what happens in the event of fire, but life safety also covers a variety of daily issues such as falls, collisions, and air quality.

Most of these issues are covered by local *building codes*. These are ordinances adopted into law by municipalities, counties, states, or nations that typically prescribe various parameters of building performance. Public authorities have an interest in making sure that buildings don't present undue hazards, both to their citizens and to their emergency response entities. Europe tends to operate by national codes, while America has long had a tradition of local authorities making their own code (e.g., Chicago and New York), or adopting one of a number of commercially available building codes, often with some modifications to take into account local conditions.

This panoply of code information can be daunting. However, a design that understands the fundamental performance requirements of buildings in emergency situations will often meet the code just by adopting a logical approach. Indeed, there is a movement in some countries away from *prescriptive* codes, which require buildings to be designed to a rigid set of dimensional and material criteria, and toward *performance-based* code compliance, which require designers to assert that their designs will perform correctly. While this adds liability to the design team, it allows for great flexibility in approaching life safety issues, and is likely to lead to better solutions through evolution. Codes typically change in response to disasters, while performance-based solutions often evolve during design.

In addition to government-based building codes, there will often be a number of codes both written and unwritten to which building designs must comply. Worker safety may be mandated by unions or by government labor departments. Buildings for a particular purpose – laboratories for example – may be subject to design guidelines from public or institutional entities. Finally, insurance companies may require policy holders to design to standards beyond those of building codes. In fact, insurance companies have often been at the forefront of code development. While architects will often be responsible for ensuring that their designs meet the letter of these formal and informal regulations, it is again the spirit of the codes that we think is most important, and this chapter will focus on broad principles rather than modeling itself after one particular code or another.

Life safety – the basics

Our overwhelming life safety concern as architects is fire. Over 3000 Americans typically die in house fires each year, and fire can kill or injure by both burning and (more commonly) asphyxiation. Unfortunately, many of the same qualities that make our buildings work – partitioning, enclosure, and security, for example, make them more dangerous in a building fire (Figure 2.1.1).

Figure 2.1.1. *Building fires – especially in multi-story buildings – are usually the gravest danger facing occupants. Building integrity, occupant notification, containment, suppression, and escape are all designed to minimize the potential for death and injury in the event of a large fire.*

We generally have four strategies for ensuring that occupants in our buildings face minimal danger from fire (Fig. 2.1.2). First, we concentrate on *building integrity*, that is, making sure that the building's structure and fabric continue to perform during a fire. Second, we lay out buildings to provide *containment*, preventing the fire from spreading uncontrollably. Third, our buildings must *notify* occupants of the dangerous situation, and fourth, the layout must enable occupants to *escape* the danger quickly and safely.

Building integrity involves the selection of materials and systems that maintain their protective and functional characteristics even in the event of a major fire. Generally, larger-scale buildings will require more robust materials, while smaller buildings permit more flammable construction. Codes require certain types of construction based on the anticipated use of the building – often referred to as the *occupancy type* – as well as the building's size and/or height. The more dangerous the building type, or the larger or taller the building, the more conservative the code is likely to be. This logic accepts that a fire in a small building (e.g., a house) may present a much greater danger to its much smaller number of occupants.

The level of integrity for a given type of construction is measured in hours. This suggests the amount of time that a particular structure or component

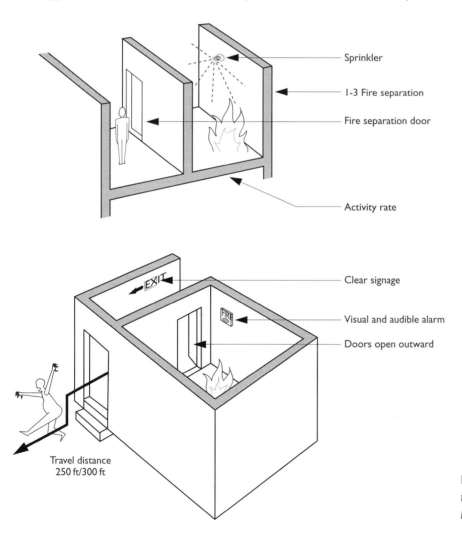

Figure 2.1.2. *Basic strategies to minimize the danger of fire in buildings.*

Table 2.1.1. Typical values for fire ratings of common building materials.

Material/Assembly	Fire rating (hrs)
Timber or metal studs with one layer of gypsum wallboard each side	1
Timber or metal studs with two layers of gypsum wallboard each side	2
Three layers of gypsum wallboard with embedded metal studs	3
Single layer of 225 mm (8″) Concrete Masonry, fully grouted	4
Single layer of 100 mm (4″) hollow clay brick (200 mm total)	1.5
Double layer of 100 mm (4″) hollow clay brick (200 mm total)	2.5
154 mm (6″) poured concrete	4
89 mm (3.5″) concrete slab	1

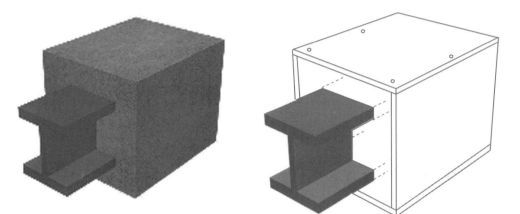

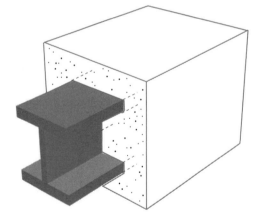

Figure 2.1.3. *Building integrity mandates protective coverings for vulnerable structural materials. Steel is a particularly difficult problem, as it loses its strength in extreme heat conditions. Standard approaches to its protection include spray-on fireproofing, encasement in gypsum wallboard or plaster, and surrounding steel members with concrete.*

will survive a typical building fire, however in practice this may not arise directly from testing. Materials and their typical performance rating are given in Table 2.1.1. In addition to rating components by hours, some codes will further distinguish between 'non-combustible' and 'combustible' construction, essentially dividing types into those that provide fuel for fire (wood) and those that don't (steel and concrete).

Steel presents particular issues of building integrity (Fig. 2.1.3). While it will not ignite in building fires, it is susceptible to softening and eventually melting if the surrounding fire is hot enough. Large building fires can produce temperatures as high as 1000°C (1800°F). Steel loses half of its strength at around 650°C (1200°F) and begins actually *melting* at 1370°C (2500°F). Particularly in tall buildings, therefore, steel must be somehow protected and insulated from the heat of a fire. This can be achieved by wrapping it in another material such as gypsum board, spray-on fireproofing, or concrete.

Containment. Once a fire has begun, our primary concern becomes minimizing the danger area and preventing the fire from spreading. This can be accomplished in two ways. *Passive containment* relies on the integrity of the building's partitioning system to keep the fire compartmentalized, while *active containment* seeks to actually suppress the fire and to put it out.

Compartmentalization relies on robust floor, wall and ceiling assemblies that will prevent a fire from spreading from one space to another. Keeping compartments relatively small ensures that the fire will have a limited fuel supply, thus controlling its temperature. At the same time, a properly assembled fire container will give occupants in adjacent areas time to evacuate the building, and fire fighters time to begin their operations. As with building integrity, fire containment relies on building elements that are fire rated, usually in hours. Depending on the danger inherent in one building program (e.g., storage of flammable liquids), a room or space may trigger a containment requirement. Materials and assemblies range in their performance widely, with concrete providing the best inherent fire separation, followed by masonry, drywall, and timber.

Atria. Multi-story spaces in buildings present particular concerns for fire safety, as they can serve as a conduit for rapid fire spread and can be easily mistaken for safe fire exiting by occupants (Fig. 2.1.4). Nevertheless, they are often architecturally important elements for orientation, daylighting, etc. To ensure their safety, spaces opening into atria must be fully sprinklered, reducing the risk of fire and smoke getting into the space in the first place. Fully fire resistant walls must separate occupied areas from the atrium itself, and exiting must take evacuees *away* from the atrium rather than toward it. Finally, most codes require active smoke evacuation from large atrium spaces (note that this will usually cause extreme air balancing problems and may suck lobby doors shut).

Active suppression usually involves a piped supply of water at high pressure and sprinkler heads located at regular intervals throughout a building area (Fig. 2.1.5). Sprinkler heads rely on heat-sensitive connections to hold a valve closed. If this melts, the valve springs open and water from the piped supply drenches the affected area. Various designs for sprinkler heads can create different patterns of water diffusion, but in most cases sprinklers must be located at approximately 15 ft (5 m) intervals to be truly effective. Additional care must be taken to ensure coverage in corners and where built-in furniture or level changes in ceilings may 'shade' floor areas from a sprinkler's pattern. While sprinklers are effective (the industry claims that there has never been a fatality due to fire in a building with operable sprinklers), they present a constant threat of accidental discharge, which can damage finishes and contents beyond salvage. In programs with valuable or water-sensitive holdings (e.g., computer server rooms, or art

Problems

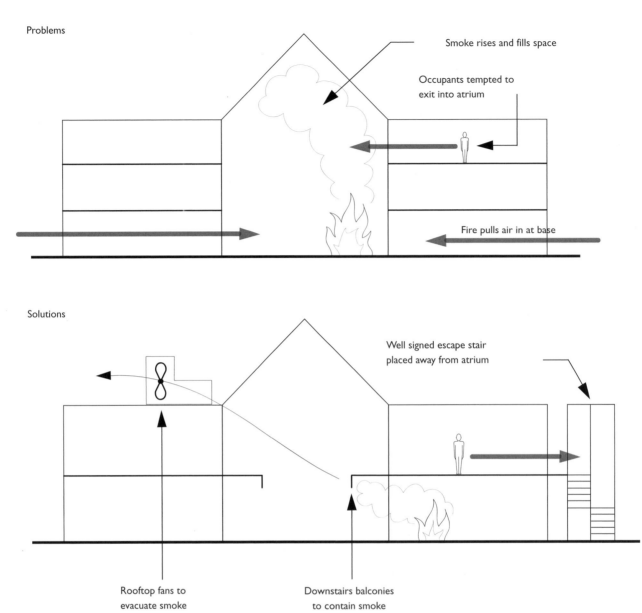

Smoke rises and fills space

Occupants tempted to
exit into atrium

Fire pulls air in at base

Solutions

Well signed escape stair
placed away from atrium

Rooftop fans to
evacuate smoke

Downstairs balconies
to contain smoke

Figure 2.1.4. *Buildings with atriums present particularly serious fire and escape issues.*

galleries), so-called 'dry' sprinkler systems may be installed. These may connect to an empty pipe system that is charged by arriving fire fighting crews, or to a supply of suppressive gas, usually Halon, that replaces the oxygen in the affected area and thus starves the fire. Note that this last option creates a life-threatening condition itself, and thus must be accompanied by an alarm and an adequate time delay to ensure that occupants can safely leave the area before it discharges.

Notification lets building occupants know there is a dangerous situation and, most importantly, can let them know how best to proceed (Fig. 2.1.6). This can be as simple as a battery-powered smoke alarm, which senses abnormal densities of particulates in the air and sets off an attention signal. The most sophisticated notification devices, however, can analyze information from different areas of the building and using public address or signals can inform occupants of the best course of action.

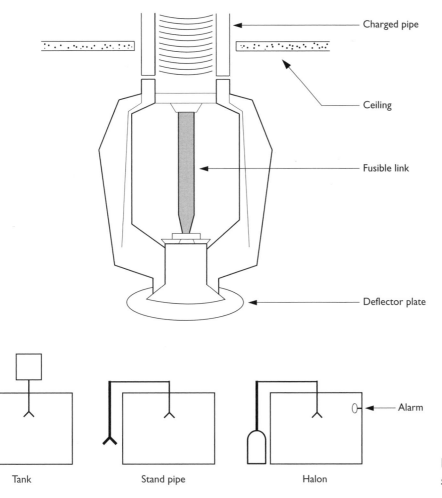

Charged pipe

Ceiling

Fusible link

Deflector plate

Tank

Stand pipe

Halon

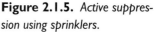

Alarm

Figure 2.1.5. *Active suppression using sprinklers.*

Finally, *escape* is the aspect of life safety that most affects our designs. All buildings must have a circulation system that foresees a threatening situation requiring escape. In some cases this will be coincident with the main functional circulation, but in larger buildings we often have to provide dedicated emergency exiting that allows occupants to efficiently and safely evacuate. Here, we must be concerned with the safety of the route itself and whether it can be protected adequately from an unpredictable fire that may be burning near or around it, in addition to the speed at which people can move through it and the capacity of the area into which it leads. We must also think ahead and ensure that there is never even the possibility that this route could be accidentally blocked, closed off, constricted, or otherwise encumbered. Escape routes from buildings typically involve elements that we recognize instantly – fire stairs and fire exits, for example. However as designers we must always consider the entire occupiable building as a potential exiting path.

Fire safety is one of the great success stories of Western building construction. It is exceptionally rare for a large building fire in Europe or America to cause fatalities, and these usually result from failures to adhere to the local building codes in design, construction or usage. This has not always been the case, and such recent examples as the Torre Windsor building fire in Madrid (2005), the MINFRA tower fire in Caracas, Venezuela, and the Field Building fire in Chicago (both 2004), all of which damaged large areas of building while

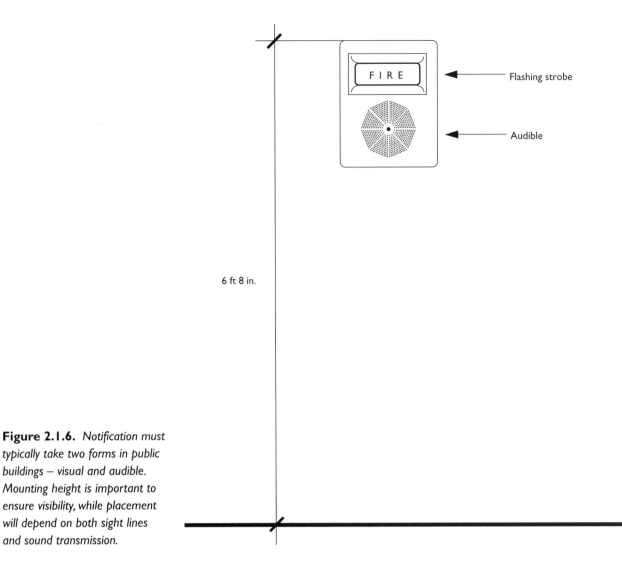

FIRE

Flashing strobe

Audible

6 ft 8 in.

Figure 2.1.6. *Notification must typically take two forms in public buildings – visual and audible. Mounting height is important to ensure visibility, while placement will depend on both sight lines and sound transmission.*

causing no deaths or serious injuries, points to the great success of fire engineering in the 20th century.

Building evacuation

Because of its direct relationship to architectural design, it is worth focusing in some detail on the mechanics and operations of a building's circulation system in a fire. Successful evacuation relies on the above life safety requirements (building integrity, fire containment, and adequate notification) *and* an awareness of the particular circumstances likely to occur in the event of an emergency. Specifically, human nature often results in irrational behavior during a life-threatening event, and buildings that moments before were simply going through their day-to-day operations must suddenly be adequate to safely accommodate large crowds of frightened, often panicking occupants moving at high speeds. When deaths due to fire occur, they are often attributable to exit routes that are either unclear or inadequately sized for the number of evacuees involved.

Most prevalent amongst building codes is a concern for the *number* of exits for a given space or building. For a room with an occupancy of more than 20, it is

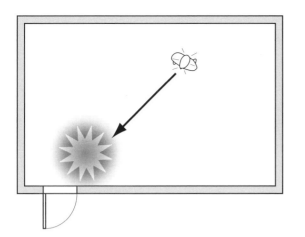

A single exit from a room is a potentially hazardous condition, as the exit may be blocked by fire

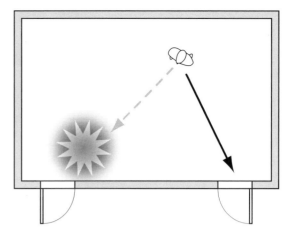

A second exit from a room, if properly placed, offers an alternative exit. This is usually required for occupancies over 50 persons, but is good practice in all circumstances. Larger occupancies may require a third exit

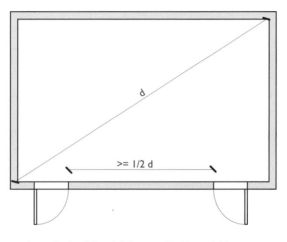

A good rule of thumb (often required by code) is to separate fire exits by at least half the largest diagonal dimension of the space being served. This ensures that no single fire can immediately block all exits.

Figure 2.1.7. *The need for two exits in heavily occupied spaces.*

good practice to provide at least two distinct exits spaced well apart from one another. If a fire blocks one exit, the other should be immediately available, visible, and accessible from all parts of the space. A good rule of thumb is that any two exits should be spaced so that the linear distance between them is more than half of the space's largest diagonal dimension (Fig. 2.1.7). For spaces with higher populations, codes may require more than two exits; generally a third exit is required once the anticipated population reaches 500, while a fourth exit will typically be required once 1000 persons are expected in a space. In addition to number, safe exiting must take into account the exit width. Many early fires (especially the Iroquois Theater Fire in downtown Chicago in 1903) resulted in fatalities despite having numerous exits. When ordered, crowds can move relatively quickly through well-designed spaces. However when panicked, crowds will compress, making movement difficult and often blocking otherwise adequate doorways in particular. A safe width for exiting must take into account the 'tributary' effect of evacuation, as more and more people join a flow toward stairs or doorways.

Generally, life safety codes will again require buildings to be classified by use, and will offer floor-area ratios to determine the likely population, or *occupancy* in a given room or area. Note that these are often quite conservative estimates, as they assume that a fire will occur at a time of maximum occupancy (this is, in fact, often the case). Frequently, codes will also give a cut off point at which two exits must be provided, often 50 persons. However it should be kept in mind that good practice suggests leaving two exits for any significant space; while a single office is small enough to allow rapid exit through one door, even a small meeting room for 10 persons could merit a more robust exiting strategy.

Once the occupancy is determined, minimum widths are generally assigned based on a linear measure per occupant. A typical figure given is 0.5 cm (0.2 in.) per person. An exit for a room holding 300 occupants in this scenario would require a width of:

$$300 \text{ persons} \times 0.5 \text{ cm (0.2 in.)/person} = 150 \text{ cm (60 in.)}$$

or 5 ft–0 in. Note that this requires that a *clear width* serve the calculated population for the entire exiting process. Thus all doors, corridors, ramps, etc., along the exit path would need to be 150 cm clear. There is occasionally an exception made for doorjambs or handrails, which may be allowed to impede the required width by a small amount. For areas of relatively low occupancy, an absolute minimum width is usually required, often 1110 cm (44 in.) in the US. This figure will govern if the occupancy is small, say only 20 persons:

$$20 \text{ persons} \times 0.5 \text{ cm (0.2 in.)/person} = 10 \text{ cm (4 in.)}$$

Here, one can immediately see that the width calculation won't give a realistic figure, and the absolute minimum width must be used. Some circulation elements, particularly stairs, may require a slightly wider width multiplier and/or absolute minimum width. This takes into account the slower pace occupants are likely to take while negotiating stairs, and typically boosts the multiplier to 0.75 cm (0.3 in.) per person.

For reasons of both fatigue and panic behavior, good practice will allow occupants to actually exit the building as quickly as possible. Generally, no exiting path may exceed 75 m (250 ft) of travel distance in an unsprinklered building, or 90 m (300 ft) in one that is sprinklered (Fig. 2.1.8). Note that this typically precludes the use of unprotected ramps or stairs as part of an exiting route, as the distances they add to traverse a vertical story will often push the total over the allowed limit.

There are common circumstances, however, in which stairs in particular can be excluded from the travel route, essentially forming an 'exit' that can serve as the end of a 75 m (250 ft) escape path. If the stair is protected by a robust fireproof enclosure (usually concrete), if it maintains an acceptable width throughout its travel, if it provides adequate landings and if it discharges directly to an exterior space, a stair may be termed as *fire stair*, and most codes assume that the travel distance ends once occupants are protected by this construction (Fig. 2.1.9).

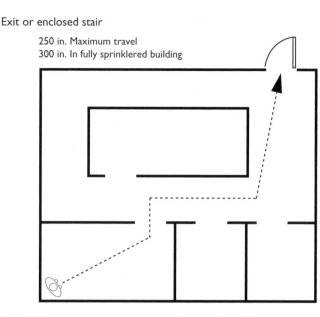

Exit or enclosed stair

250 in. Maximum travel
300 in. In fully sprinklered building

Figure 2.1.8. *Code-mandated travel distances must assume actual routes through rooms and corridors. Furniture is typically not taken into account, but door locations, walls, etc., must be considered in calculating the actual distance from occupied areas to exits or enclosed stairs. Note that a 20% allowance is given for buildings that are fully sprinklered, recognizing the inherent safety of adequately designed active suppression.*

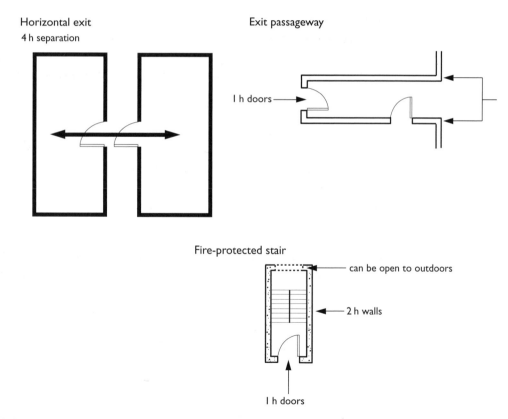

Horizontal exit
4 h separation

Exit passageway

1 h doors

Fire-protected stair

can be open to outdoors

2 h walls

1 h doors

Figure 2.1.9. *Alternative exiting strategies. A Horizontal Exit involves travel from one fire compartment in building to another. Safety is provided by a robust fire separation – usually a 2–3 h wall or a dedicated fire/smoke break between the two compartments. An Exit Passageway is a dedicated 2-h compartment that provides safe travel to an exit or a stair. This is typically used to evacuate occupants from a core stair at the ground floor, but may also be used to 'tunnel' through a hazardous occupancy or to extend an allowable travel distance. Finally, there are strict regulations for containment, accessibility, and exiting for dedicated fire stairs. For high rise buildings, additional requirements may include refuge areas for wheelchair users and/or smoke evacuation.*

Figure 2.1.10. *The fire stair as architectural element. Renzo Piano's Debis Building in Berlin uses fire stairs to articulate its end facades. Because containment requirements only apply to walls between occupied areas and the stair tower, most codes permit glass enclosures for stair walls that are not contiguous with spaces that may burn (there may be restrictions on how close the glass can be to an opening in the building wall, however). Since stairs relate both the horizontal grain of a building (its floor levels) and size of its occupants (the treads, risers, and handrails), they can provide a sense of building and human scale.*

This essentially allows high rise construction, as very tall buildings may require up to half a mile of travel back and forth along flights of stairs to exit from top floors (Fig. 2.10) (see Sections 2.2 and 2.3).

Exits must have adequate *discharge space* once they leave the building. Usually codes require exits to open onto outdoor, public space, although some exceptions permit exiting into yards or courts, provided these again have a clear connection to public walkways, streets, etc. Some high rise codes permit stairs to exit into a fireproof corridor on the ground floor that leads to a street, thus

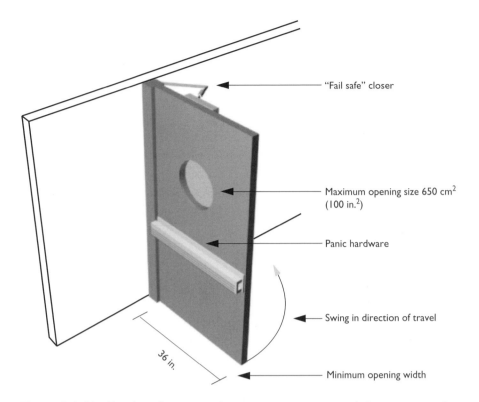

"Fail safe" closer

Maximum opening size 650 cm² (100 in.²)

Panic hardware

Swing in direction of travel

36 in.

Minimum opening width

Figure 2.1.11. *Exit doors have particular requirements to ensure their proper operation during a fire. They must swing in the direction of fleeing occupants, they must be no less than 910 mm (36 in.) wide, and they must have panic hardware to open any latch. This last requirement prevents crowds from piling up against the door and preventing an occupant from operating a handle or button – the panic bar unlatches the door when pressure is applied to it, whether that is from a single user or a growing crowd. Doors that provide fire separation must additionally have 'fail-safe' closers, and have a limited amount of allowable glass area. Note that, despite this limitation, a vision panel is often desirable to allow exiting occupants a view of what's on the other side of the door.*

permitting stairs to be contained within a central core. On rare occasions, some exiting from stairs may be permitted into a building lobby; while convenient, this is not good practice as conditions in the lobby will not be knowable from upper floors, where occupants make their decision about escape routes.

Some considerations when designing for exiting include the following:

Exit travel must be intuitive and unimpeded; therefore any doors (in corridors, to staircases, etc.) must open in the anticipated direction of escape. To prevent crushing, these doors must have *panic hardware* installed that will automatically unlock and open if hit or pressed. Panic hardware must extend across the full width of the door, and is best located at waist level, between 36 in. and 42 in. above the floor so that the body's center of mass will contact it. Arms and hands may well be trapped against other parts of the door (Fig. 2.1.11).

Stairs leading to basements must have clear indications at the ground floor that evacuees should not continue down further, but should exit the stair there. Many codes require a physical gate to prevent panicked occupants from running into the basement, but in practice these are often left open to avoid inconvenience. No matter what the code, signage at the exiting level is a good practice.

Common sense suggests that occupants not be forced to exit through areas of danger (storage, kitchens, machine rooms, factory floors). While codes will often prohibit individual instances of this, good practice again requires architects to consider likely evacuee behavior and to guard against accidental circulation into these areas.

Despite our best efforts, occupants will often evacuate a building through the same route that brought them in – whether or not there is a more convenient or safer path. Codes often require that a building's 'main' entrance thus be sized to allow half of the building's population to escape through it (during the Station Nightclub fire in West Warwick, RI, in 2004 many fatalities occurred within a few yards of illuminated, signed exits as occupants tried to run to the main, rear doors).

Elevators are notoriously prone to failure during building fires. Worse, they are likely to get stuck or even open at a floor that is fully aflame due to its extreme heat. Therefore, elevators never count as code exits, and usually must be disabled when a building alarm goes off, returning immediately to the ground floor and waiting there. Fire fighters may then use a special key to unlock the cabs' mechanisms in order to gain access to the affected areas. Some codes being considered at the time of writing propose to allow elevators as secondary exits if they are encased in fully fire resistant shafts, however this goes against the prevailing wisdom that has consistently discouraged elevator use in a fire.

Conclusions

A building's circulatory design is an important aspect of its architectural impact. Very often we want to use these spaces to celebrate the building's functions or connections. Yet fire codes are often quite rigorous in how these spaces may be used or configured; codes often prohibit furniture or storage in any designated exit route. It is often, therefore, worth considering a second circulatory system in large buildings dedicated to fire escape. This may consist of stairs with dedicated uses, or networks of corridors that are not accessed during typical daily operation. While this may seem wasteful of space and resources, the inherent safety of a properly designed exiting system may allow other, purely architectural circulatory elements to be arranged and developed according to different requirements.

At the same time, the requirements of life-safety systems may align with architectural desires. Fire stairs, for example, may be worthy elements of expression in an overall architectural massing strategy, as they provide both vertical emphasis and (if expressed or clad on the outside in glass) natural human scale. Renzo Piano's headquarters building for Debis in Berlin, Germany, for example, uses a main fire stair as a metaphorical 'prow', offering a distinctive finish to the building mass (Fig. 2.1.11). Life-safety systems, while notoriously onerous in their requirements, are like so many other aspects of building design best considered early in the process, when their particularities may be absorbed into an overall architectural strategy.

Frequently asked questions

Are codes absolute? Or if my design falls just outside of the code's parameters, will it be rejected by code officials? Compliance with codes is interpreted by government and/or institutional officials. Often, municipalities will permit these officials to issue variances that permit single instances of non-compliance. However, this does not come with a waiver of responsibility for the designers, and in the event of a fatality or injury due to fire the design's non-compliance may expose the design team to significant legal risk.

Can fire walls include glass? For low fire ratings (1h in particular) walls and doors may have limited amounts of glass. However this must typically be wire glass, which provides additional structural integrity in a fire situation. Glass products that use chemical interlayers for additional fire resistance are also available and may provide significant protection for larger areas. However this comes at additional expense, and such glass products often have an inevitable color variation that may limit their acceptability.

How do wheelchair users evacuate a multi-story building in a fire? This is a common and slightly chilling problem in reconciling accessibility with fire safety. Most codes assume that wheelchair users can be assisted or carried down short runs of stairs. However, for buildings above three stories, there are generally code requirements for additional space within fire stair enclosures large enough for one or two wheelchair parking spaces. These provisions assume that rescue will come within the rated time for these enclosures, and that these occupants can be carried by fire fighters.

Why do most elevators in newer buildings have fire doors in front of them? Is this to keep people from using them in a fire? Recent codes recognize the potential for elevator shafts to act as very efficient fire chimneys, particularly given their lightweight doors and tall, narrow spaces. Large buildings will often have fail-safe closer doors that will activate and seal off elevator lobbies from occupied or potentially combustible areas to prevent fire infiltration into vulnerable elevator shafts.

Why shouldn't I use fire sprinklers in hotel rooms to hang clothes? Is this a safety issue? Not so much. Most sprinklers contain a small, fragile vial of liquid that, when heated, expands rapidly, breaking the vial and eliminating the only barrier to a fully pressurized pipe system behind. Hangars are notorious for breaking this vial and deluging hotel rooms.

Glossary and formulas

Active Containment	Fire control strategy relying on mechanical systems (usually piped water) to suppress fire.
Building Codes	Regulatory documents that restrict construction to established, safe practices. May be *prescriptive*, giving detailed dimensional and/or material criteria, or *performance-based*, requiring design teams to assert acceptable levels of building performance.

Building Integrity	Element of life safety design that emphasizes the reliability of the building's structure and fabric during a fire or other hazardous situation.
Clear Width	A measure of an escape component's capacity. Often determined by multiplying the worst-case anticipated occupancy by a code-specified width (typically 0.2 in. or 5 mm per person), but generally no less than 44 in. (112 mm) for corridors and stairs.
Containment	Element of life safety design that discourages fire from spreading.
Discharge Space	A public or open area that is sized to accommodate the escaping population of a building.
Escape	Element of life safety design that enables occupants to physically remove themselves from hazardous situations.
Fire Resistance	The ability of a component or material to withstand fire without burning or transmitting dangerous amounts of heat. Usually determined in laboratory settings.
Fire Stair	An staircase that meets all code requirements for access and is separated from any occupied or potentially hazardous area by a significant fire-resistive wall (usually 2 h or more).
Notification	Element of life safety design that alerts occupants of a hazardous situation
Occupancy Type	Classification of a building or building space based on its perceived use. Specified by most building codes as a means of assessing integrity and escape requirements.
Panic Hardware	Bars and latches on doors that enable operation by pressure instead of turning. Usually required by codes on doors in fire exits or corridors to prevent panicking crowds from piling up against them.
Passive Containment	Fire control strategy relying on the fire-resistive nature of construction materials to contain fire.
Travel Distance	The length of a path drawn from a room to the first place of fire refuge – usually an exterior exit or fire-protected staircase. Typically limited by codes to no more than 250 ft or 75 m, occasionally more if the building is fully provided with sprinklers.

Further reading

Allen, E. and Iano, J. (2002) Designing with Building Codes (Chapter 1), *The Architect's Studio Companion: Rules of Thumb for Preliminary Design*, 3rd ed (New York: Wiley), pp. 3–14.

2.2 Accessibility

Accessibility	Definitions Legal history
Anthropomorphic Data	Basic parameters of wheelchair dimensions Fine grained data – grips, etc.
Accessible Design	Principles Requirements
Stairs	Rise and run Code and ADA requirements Detail design – treads, handrails, landings, and guardrails
Ramps	Code and ADA requirements Detail design – surfaces, handrails, and landings

Introduction

In designing for the 'general public,' the profession has had a nasty history of leaving a significant percentage of that public out, either providing routes that are inaccessible to some, or making circulation and function within a building difficult for others.

Nearly one in five Americans or Europeans is unable to fully negotiate or use architectural configurations designed for the average occupant. Disabilities come in a variety of forms, and increasingly our profession has been charged with creating inclusive environments, that restrict fewer individuals from the spaces we design.

There is a long legal history behind the current North American standard of 'universal' or 'accessible' design. Prior to World War II, there was no federal legislation making discrimination against persons with disabilities illegal. As veterans who had been wounded or disabled returned, and as medical care increased both quality and quantity of life for those with disabilities, a movement grew seeking protection against discrimination in hiring. However it was not until 1964 that the federal government took up the problem of environmental discrimination. Employers could still prevent people with disabilities from working, however unintentionally, by providing inaccessible environments and workplaces.

Legislation through the 1960s and 1970s required federally funded buildings to comply with a short list of architectural standards designed to remove barriers to users of wheelchairs. An ANSI standard was developed to provide reliable standards of design. However, the federal government's efforts did not apply to the private sector, and civil rights advocates continued to press for comprehensive accessibility legislation.

The Americans with Disabilities Act (ADA) – the legal climate in America

In 1990, the ADA was signed into law, extending civil rights protection to roughly 43 million Americans with disabilities. It covers broad areas of employment, public services and accommodations and housing.

While the ADA has provided a much needed change in opening up jobs, activities and environments for people with disabilities, it has had numerous critics – not for its intent, but rather for its mechanism. Because the ADA is civil rights legislation, it is enforced by civil courts. Compliance with its prescriptive standards is enforced not by an agency with expertise, but rather by the courts. There is thus no room for 'designed' solutions – rather every place of employment of public accommodation must comply directly with the quantitative information of the ADA, under threat of lawsuit from potentially injured parties.

While numerous building codes have adopted portions of the ADA, it remains the standard for accessibility throughout the US. Compliance is generally mandatory for most employers, government agencies, and 'privately operated establishments in which the public are served.' These entities must make 'reasonable accommodations' for any person with a disability. Case law has generally required *any* new construction for these entities to comply with ADA, and for *existing* construction to be modified on an as-needed basis. Renovation of an existing building is a tricky situation. These projects will generally be required to provide 'reasonable' accommodation.

Note that about the only completely exempt building type is single-family residential housing. Even this, however, has become the subject of code requirements, notably in Naperville, IL, which now has substantial standards for accessibility in all new construction. 'Visitability' is an important idea in residential design, encouraging at least one accessible entry and a suite of rooms (including a toilet room) that can be easily negotiated by wheelchair users.

Other building types pose different challenges. Sports arenas and theaters, for example, present particularly tricky design problems because of their sloped seats. It is not practical to allow accessible routes to every seat in a theater, but it is also discriminatory to cluster all accessible seating at the front, or at the rear. Strategies that offer some variety in locations, views, access to ancillary spaces, and ticket pricing have all been successfully employed in these types of project.

Society has demanded an increased awareness and response to accessibility issues. Thus, like life safety codes, we propose to offer basic strategies that can be incorporated early in the design process, eliminating 'retrofit' solutions and inevitable frustration later on.

Universal design – good practice

'Accessible design' 'disabled design', and 'handicapped-accessible' are all problematic terms, as they imply a special effort being made for users of wheelchairs and other disability-specific equipment or components. Recently the term 'Universal design' has been proposed as a way of pointing out that our buildings should incorporate accessibility principles as a matter of course. 'Clip-on' solutions are not only aesthetically problematic, they stigmatize and often separate occupants with disabilities. The 'stair lift' is a prime example of this. Users of wheelchairs must operate loud machinery to travel a short distance, while their companions who can walk must wait for them to be lifted into place. (Often these require a key, or assistance from a security guard, heightening the problem). A better solution would be to find ways to take up – or eliminate – small changes in level, putting walkers and users of wheelchairs on a 'level playing field.'

With that in mind, recall some basic anthropomorphic dimensions (see Fig. 2.2.1). Allowing for wheelchair passage in corridors, for example, is relatively simple – 910 mm (36 in.) provides enough clearance for operators to comfortable maneuver ahead. Obstructions that limit this distance to 810 mm (32 in.) for brief periods are also acceptable. However, most corridors must accommodate people traveling in both directions. While the code minimum of 110 mm (44 in.) allows someone to move sideways past a wheelchair, this is obviously an awkward situation. Even allowing enough room for someone to comfortably walk past a wheelchair – 1220 mm (44 in.) – does not allow for the obvious case of two wheelchair users passing at the same time. However, 1500 mm (60 in.) allows this to occur comfortably, and therefore from a Universal Design standpoint, this should be an absolute minimum dimension.

Note that the 1500 mm (60 in.) dimension is also the required space for a wheelchair user to turn completely around, based on the width of a typical device. While it is possible to turn a wheelchair in the 'T' shape as shown, allowing room for a full 180° turn allows users to maneuver comfortably. The 1500 mm (60 in.) minimum corridors obviate any tricky or uncomfortable maneuvering. This is also important for elevator cabs; while a 'T' turn will allow a wheelchair user to maneuver in and out, it may require difficult maneuvering to turn around inside the cab. Rather than backing in, frustrated wheelchair users may simply face the back wall and reverse out of a cab in this situation – an awkward and potentially dangerous situation if there is traffic in front of the cab door. If room for a full 1500 mm (60 in.) turn is allowed inside the cab, the user can access the elevator without special effort.

Perhaps the most pressing needs occur in toilet rooms. While some advocates prefer separate toilet rooms that provide full 1500 mm (60 in.) maneuvering clearances, the 'separate but equal' provisions in ADA require some percentage of multi-stall toilet rooms to meet minimum (some would say subminimum) anthropomorphic requirements. Toilet rooms with minimum dimensions required for an ADA-acceptable stall require the user to make a difficult transfer, using grab bars and turning around between the wheelchair and the toilet fixture. (Note, too, that because of planning efficiencies, the dedicated 'accessible' stall is often at the far end of a series of stalls. The user must therefore *back out* down the row of stalls to exit if the stall is in use – hardly a desirable result.) A much better (though more spatially intensive) stall design would allow the user can maneuver a wheelchair parallel to the fixture, and simply transfer laterally, and would include a 1500 mm (60 in.) turning circle as well.

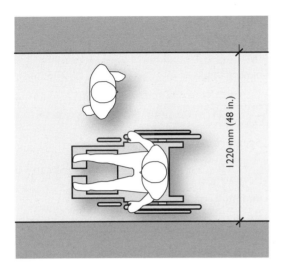

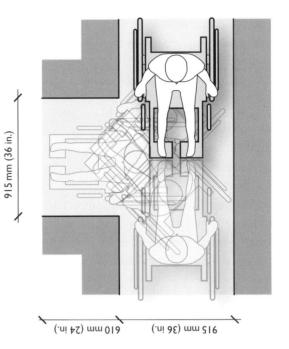

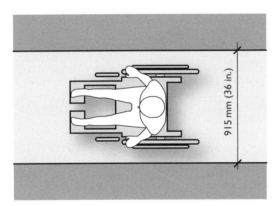

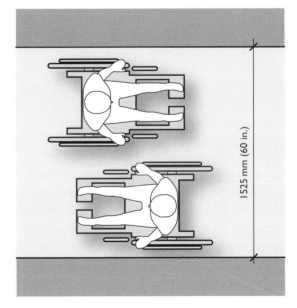

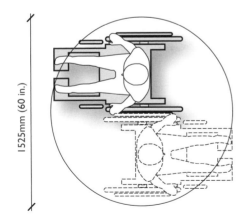

Figure 2.2.1. *Basic planning dimensions for wheelchair accessibility in circulation areas.*

Universal design – fine grain

In addition to these relatively simple planning standards, we need to pay attention to the smaller scale anthropomorphic requirements of a variety of occupants. Most pressing is the need to provide accommodations for persons who need to reach services – shelves, sinks, telephones, door handles, and elevator buttons – from a sitting position (Fig. 2.2.2). While the geometry of the occupant's reach allows greater high and low reach from a 'side approach,' that is, where the occupant can pull alongside the required service. In general, we avoid placing any service – in particular electric outlets – lower than 15 in. from floor height, and try to restrict most amenities – telephones, paper towel holders, etc., to no more than 48 in. above floor height. (Note, too, that there is an overlap between the reach of wheelchair users and persons who are much taller than average, between 910 mm (36 in.) and 1220 mm (48 in.) above floor height.)

Here, again, bathrooms present a unique set of challenges (Fig. 2.2.3). Handwashing requires a front approach, yet this is the least efficient geometry. Countertops must therefore be configured so that a person in a wheelchair can maneuver their legs *under* the countertop, yet comfortably move their hands *above* it. This generally restricts lavatory rims and adjacent counter surfaces to 760–860 mm (30–34 in.) above floor height (also an acceptable range for countertops, desks, and tables) (Fig. 2.2.3). A particular problem here is that persons with limited sensation in their legs can be bruised, cut, or even burned by (sometimes hot) water pipes under the sink. Care must be taken to either insulate these or to configure them in a way that is unlikely to cause injury. Lavatories and counters must also be more than a minimum distance away from the wall – 430 mm (17 in.) – to enable comfortable reach.

Similar principles apply to drinking fountains and telephone booths. In these cases, however, positions that are comfortable for persons using wheelchairs will not be accessible to tall, ambulant users. Therefore, almost inevitably, at least one phone or drinking fountain must be provided at an alternate height.

A final consideration is for occupants who are visually or hearing impaired. Persons who have visual impairments navigate using a cane, which detects changes in floor texture, edges of walls, etc. ADA quite sensibly reminds us not to design corridors with protrusions (such as telephones) that project from the wall without some indication at floor level. Likewise, overhead hazards such as open-stringer staircases are notoriously dangerous to persons using canes, as their first indication that an obstacle is in their way is often by bumping their head.

Universal design – vertical circulation

Perhaps the most pressing requirement of accessibility legislation is the commonsense idea that all major areas of a building (public and the majority of work locations) must be accessible by a common route. This means that persons in

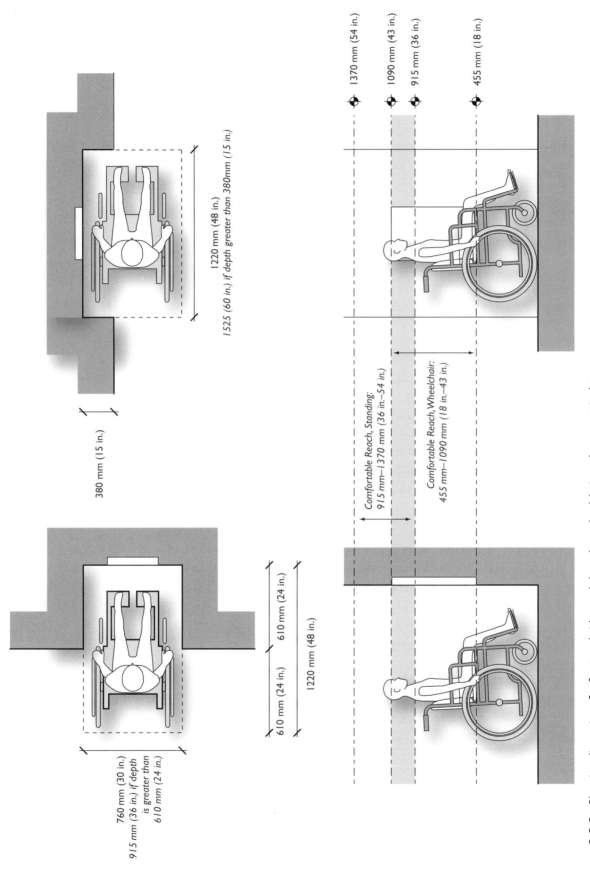

Figure 2.2.2. *Planning dimensions for front and side reach based on wheelchair anthropometric data.*

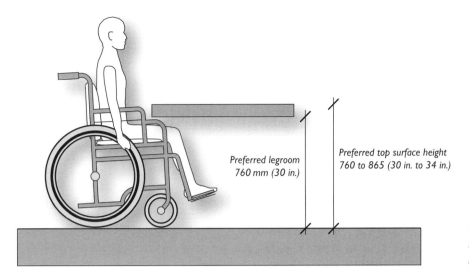

*Preferred legroom
760 mm (30 in.)*

*Preferred top surface height
760 to 865 (30 in. to 34 in.)*

Figure 2.2.3. *Countertop and lavatory requirements for wheelchair use.*

wheelchairs must, for the majority of the design, be able to access rooms and spaces in the same manner as ambulatory occupants.

At a site planning level, this means that certain percentages of parking stalls must be designed to accommodate users who must transfer from their vehicle to a wheelchair. Generally, a space 96 in. wide meets this requirement, although drivers requiring transfer from a custom van generally need a 1500 mm (60 in.)– 2450 mm (96 in.) space parallel to their vehicle to operate a lift. Designated accessible spaces must be signed, must be immediately adjacent to an accessible curb cut, and must be located conveniently to building entries and amenities.

An 'accessible route' may contain no vertical discontinuity of more than 13 mm (1/2 in.). Any change in level greater than this must be traversed by a ramp, or (second best) a mechanical lift. Ramps are divided into two categories – those whose slope is less than 1:20 (1 m of rise for every 20 m of run) and those whose slope is between 1:12 and 1:20 (Fig. 2.2.4). No ramps steeper than 1:12 may be considered accessible. Ramps shallower than 1:20 have no limits on their length or height. Steeper ramps are limited to 740 mm (30 in.) of rise before they must essentially offer a landing to the user of at least 1500 mm (60 in.) in length. This is not only to allow users to rest, but it also breaks the fall of a person who loses control coming *down*, a more serious issue (Fig. 2.2.4).

Ramps with a rise greater than 15 mm (6 in.) must also be provided with handrails that prevent users from falling off the edge, and permit users to grip and pull themselves along. Handrails must be designed for side approach, that is between 860 and 970 mm (34 and 38 in.) from floor level, and must have a gripping surface that is equivalent to a 38 mm (1–1/2 in.) diameter cylinder. Adequate clearance between the handrail and any wall is, of course, required. Handrails must also extend beyond the top and bottom of ramps, parallel with the ground surface, to allow unsteady walkers to grip the rail prior to stepping on to the ramp. To prevent clothing from catching on the end of a handrail, it must typically be returned, either to a post or to a wall, or it must have a connection immediately adjacent to its end. Likewise, guardrails at a slightly higher level must be provided at landings where a fall of more than 460 mm (18 in.) presents itself.

Slopes of 1:20 (5%) or shallower are not limited in length, but may be tiring

20

Slopes of 1:16 (6.25%) to 1:20 (5%) require landings every 40 horizontal feet

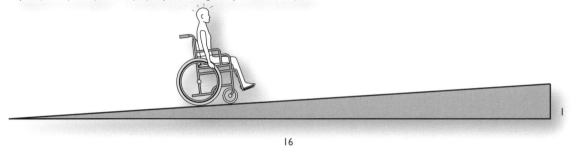

16

Slopes of 1:12 (8.33%) to 1:16 (6.25%) require landings every 30 horizontal feet

12

Slopes steeper than 1:12 (8.33%) are not considered accessible.
Slopes greater than 1:8 (12.5%) are difficult for ambulatory users.

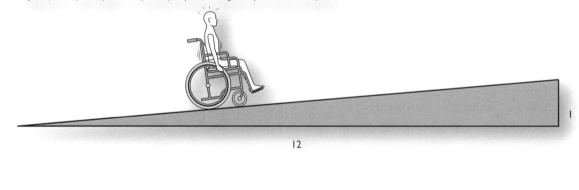

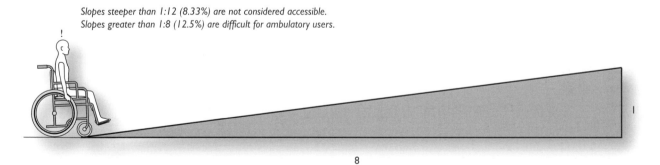

8

Figure 2.2.4. *Ramp slopes rated by accessibility. Slopes greater than 1:20 present varying degrees of difficulty, while slopes greater than 1:12 are not considered accessible.*

Stairs present a more complex set of issues (see Section 2.3 for a full discussion). Even though wheelchair users typically cannot use them, stairs are covered by ADA since a significant percentage of otherwise ambulatory people are nonetheless limited in their range of motion, balance, or visual abilities. In addition, stairs are often the most dangerous public element of a building – the Center for Disease Control estimates that 1300 Americans die every year from falls on residential stairs – and thus the ADA provides standards that account for the difficulty otherwise ambulatory users have on these elements.

The most important attributes of stair design for safety and comfort are the design of the tread and the design of the handrail. Some codes allow risers in interior stairs must be less than 200 mm (8 in.), however this figure is quite tall for people with a limited range of motion and anthropometric data suggests that 180–190 mm (7–7.5 in.) should be the maximum riser height. Adequate space for a human foot must be provided on each horizontal tread, usually no less than 280 mm (11 in.) for interior stairs. Additionally, adequate toe space must be required at each riser, yet the stairs must not present a tripping hazard. Therefore, ADA specifies that nosings should extend no more than 40 mm (1–1/2 in.) from the riser face. Open risers are no longer permitted due to the tripping hazard they pose. To catch falling occupants, it is advisable to have no more than 16 total risers in one run of stairs – most codes will require a landing for every 12 ft of height. Finally, it is critical that the treads and risers in a continuous stair be uniform – changes in riser height in particular can cause serious falls. For exterior stairs, particularly those that might become wet or ice-encrusted, tread, and riser dimensions must be adjusted, usually to 380 mm (15 in.) minimum for treads and 5 in. maximum for risers.

Because doors must be pulled into the occupant's space, they present particular difficulties for wheelchair users. In confined spaces, users may actually become trapped by doors that do not have adequate clearance to allow wheelchairs to travel around the edge of the opening door. Likewise, adequate space should be maintained to the side of any door to allow easy access from either direction (Figs. 2.2.5 and 2.2.6).

Other points to consider

There are typically serious accessibility concerns for a number of other building components, in particular elevator size and layout, configuration and required force for door openers and handles, shower stalls, vending machines, floor grates, and signage. Again, these are often readily achievable if they are considered near the outset of a design, but can cause problems if they are only examined as the design is detailed.

As with codes, a strategic approach is almost always better than a checklist done as the design is in progress. Designs that do the following will stand a better chance of meeting the intent of accessibility legislation in the US or Europe:

- Avoid level changes except where necessary. For multi-story buildings, assume each floor needs to be dead level over its whole area.

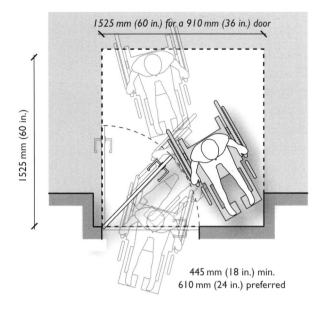
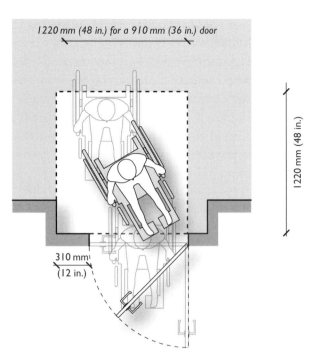

Figure 2.2.5. *Space requirements for wheelchairs at doors.*

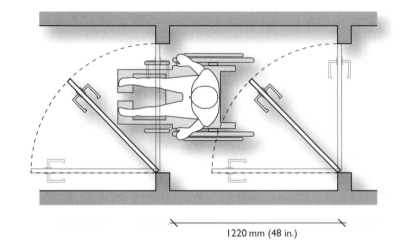

Figure 2.2.6. *Space requirements for wheelchairs in sequential doors.*

- Where level changes are required, understand that space will be required for ramps or lifts. Assume that any level change will have 20 times its height in ramp run (though, in a pinch, this can be reduced to 12 times height, plus landings).
- Allow adequate space in the planning stages for generous toilet rooms, incorporating 1500 mm (60 in.) turning circles for people using wheelchairs. An 3350 mm (11 ft 0 in.) wide bay will (barely) allow a plumbing chase, stall depth and adequate clearance.
- Allow adequate space in the planning stages for generous stairs, incorporating runs as shallow as reasonably possible. As a rule of thumb, allow at least an 3350 mm by 6100 mm (11 ft 0 in. by 20 ft 0 in.) plan area for a scissor stair serving a 4600 mm (15 ft 0 in.) floor to floor height.
- No pubic corridor should be less than 1500 mm (60 in.) wide.

- Doors present particularly difficult issues, as room must be allowed for wheelchair users to approach, open, and pass through without becoming wedged against the door during its travel. On the pull side of doors, a minimum clear maneuvering space of $1525\,mm^2$ (for a 910 mm (36 in.) door allows this comfortably, while on the push side this can be reduced to a 1220 mm (48 in.) square (see Fig. 2.2.5). Doors in sequence must also be designed to allow adequate maneuvering room for opening (see Fig. 2.2.6). Doors arranged in sequence should open in the same direction to prevent wheelchair users from becoming trapped between them.

Unfortunately, common sense is not always insurance against a technical accessibility issue. Case law at the moment suggests that the letter of the law, in addition to its intent, must be followed. However, also keep in mind that lawsuits are only likely to arise in cases where people are inconvenienced, frustrated, or insulted by a building's design. Sensitivity to different levels of motion, vision, etc., is something society demands of us. Like life safety (see Section 2.3), it is not technically difficult to produce an environment that allows access to all, but this does take patience and attention to detail to ensure an integrated solution.

Frequently asked questions

My design has multiple entrances/levels that will require extensive ramps and elevators to make them work. Do all of these have to be accessible to meet American codes? The ADA requires only that half of all building entries be accessible, but that these be the entries most commonly used by building occupants or users. Level changes are a different story. Any part of a building that serves an occupational, commercial, or public purpose should be fully accessible by wheelchair users. While some case law has suggested that offices, in particular, can provide a certain percentage of accessible work areas (a so-called 'program-based solution'), designers should keep in mind that meetings, conversations, or work groups could meet anywhere in a building, and that this could be exclusionary if all areas aren't accessible.

Do I need an elevator? My design has multiple levels but is very small. Perhaps not. Most buildings under three stories, or less than $300\,m^2$ ($3000\,ft^2$) are exempted under ADA (exceptions are shopping centers and health-care providers). Accessibility regulations generally exempt residential uses, although multi-unit facilities will typically be required to provide a percentage of accessible units. This, however, excludes wheelchair users from amenities or occupied spaces on floors above ground, which is not a desirable situation. Adequate accommodation on the ground level must be provided.

Does every seat in a stadium or theater need to be accessible? No. The ADA in particular makes very clear that only a small percentage of seats – about 1% for large facilities – must be accessible, in addition to a certain number of aisle seats with removable arms. However, recent case law has pointed out the need to distribute these seats throughout an arena or theater. Placing all accessible seating at the back of a theater, for instance, has been seen as discriminatory, as wheelchair users have no opportunity to occupy any but the least desirable seats.

My project involves an historic structure. Does the existing fabric need to be totally altered to provide full accessibility? Most accessibility legislation recognizes the impossibility of retrofitting full access into existing, pre-legislation structures. The ADA makes specific exceptions for existing structures, in which any alteration must itself be accessible, and historic structures, in which accessibility requirements are limited to site, entry, and major spaces. Even these, however, are to be balanced with the perceived impact on the building's historic fabric and may be negotiated with local or state historic preservation authorities.

Glossary and formulas

Accessible	Generally, building spaces or elements that allow full use by those with impaired mobility.
Clear	Unobstructed. Usually refers to floor space in which a user can maneuver a wheelchair.
Guardrail	A railing intended to prevent a user from falling at a level change. Must be located at or above the average human center of gravity (about 1060 mm (42 in.) above a walking surface) where there is a significant drop beyond.
Handrail	A grippable surface intended to offer additional stability to a stair or ramp user. Must be located at a comfortable gripping height, usually 860 mm (34 in.) above either stair nosings or ramp surfaces.
Ramp	A slanted surface that enables ambulatory and wheelchair-using occupants access between levels. Slopes less than 1:20 aren't considered ramps, while slopes greater than 1:12 restrict access by wheelchair users.
Universal Design	A design philosophy that eschews 'accommodation' in favor of circulation and accessibility principles that integrate, rather than segregate, users of varying mobility.

Further reading

Osterberg, A.E. and Kain, D.J. (2002) *Access for everyone : a guide to accessibility with references to ADAAG* (Ames, IA: Iowa State University Facilities Planning and Management). Note: This title is available for purchase through Iowa State University: www.fpm.iastate.edu/accessforeverone

Evan Terry Associates, P.C. (2002) *Pocket Guide to the ADA*, Revised edition (New York: Wiley).

Henry Dreyfuss Associates (2002) *The Measure of Man and Woman: Human Factors in Design*, (New York: Wiley). Esp. Differently Abled People, pp. 35–43 and A Universal Work Chair, p. 44.

2.3 Stairs

Principles	Human movement
Stairs – Treads and Risers	Proportions
	Details
Configuration	Flights
	Landings
	Width
	Special stairs
Fall Protection	Handrails
	Guardrails

Vertical movement

Invariably buildings require people to move through them vertically, and even those of one story will often have minute level changes that require careful design. Thousands are injured every year on stairs in particular. While codes and accessibility legislation have prescribed basic dimensional data for both stairs and ramps, it is important to think about these elements from anthropometric principles, which will often suggest more generous provision than typical codes allow.

The average European or American person can lift their foot about 400 mm (16 in.) while standing but will quickly tire if forced to do this repeatedly (Fig. 2.3.1). For about 90% of the population, raising the foot 150 to 200 mm (6 to 8 in.) is relatively easy. However for the remaining 10% (children under 5 years, the elderly, or those with a mobility impairment) this motion is difficult or excessively tiring. Likewise, the average human foot is about 265 mm (10.4 in.) long with the majority of the body's weight concentrated at its rear.

Foot dimensions

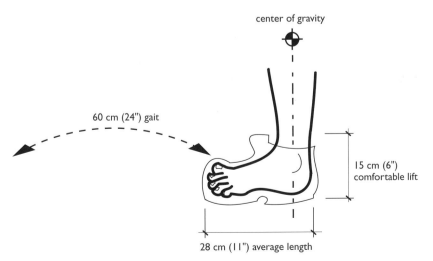

center of gravity

60 cm (24") gait

15 cm (6") comfortable lift

28 cm (11") average length

Figure 2.3.1. *The basics of stair design start with the human foot and gait.*

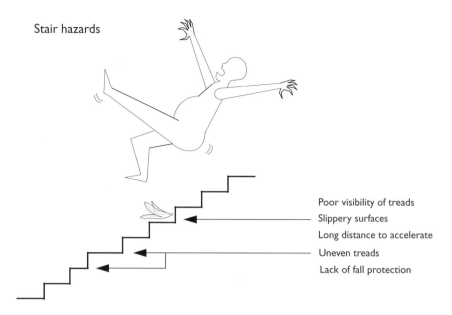

Stair hazards

Poor visibility of treads
Slippery surfaces
Long distance to accelerate
Uneven treads
Lack of fall protection

Figure 2.3.2. *Stairs present some of the most prevalent dangers in buildings. More than 1000 Americans die every year from stair-related falls.*

Stairs in particular can thus easily be too steep or too short. Steep stairs are dangerous both because they can cause fatigue (a contributor to slips and falls), and because they present a difficult descent (Fig. 2.3.2). Short stair treads are dangerous because a climber can easily misplace their step, centering their weight beyond the edge of the stair tread, potentially causing a fall as well.

Ramps present somewhat less dangerous conditions, however their design must likewise be considered in terms of human mobility. In particular, we are typically concerned with wheelchair operation on ramps, as these are often the primary alternatives to stairs that aren't negotiable by wheelchair. Like stairs, ramps can be steep enough that climbing them either on foot or in a wheelchair can be tiring, while descending steep ramps in a chair can present a runaway danger. The change in level that comes with either a stair or ramp often presents a falling danger off the side, as well.

Stairs – treads and risers

The key to designing a safe stair is the careful proportioning of *treads*, the flat pieces of the stair, and *risers*, the vertical pieces. In addition to leg lift and foot size, these two dimensions should be coordinated to match a typical human gait for comfort and ease of use (Fig. 2.3.3).

Treads should be made of a non-slip surface to ensure good traction between foot and stair. While wood is often acceptable, commercial installations should be made of something with greater traction – carpet, vinyl, or concrete, for instance. Smooth surfaces such as glass should be roughened by sandblasting or a similar process. Exterior stairs should additionally provide for drainage, to keep the treads as dry and ice-free as possible.

Minimum tread dimensions vary according to use, however they should generally be no less than 280 mm (11 in.) to ensure full contact between foot and stair. Exterior stairs should be slightly longer, reflecting both the quicker pace

Stair dimensions

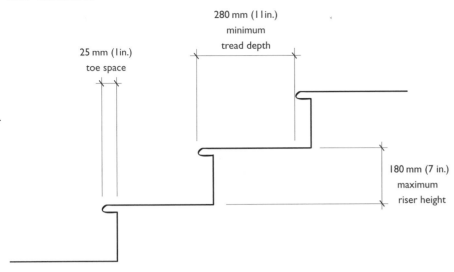

Figure 2.3.3. *Stair dimensions must be based on comfortable walking gaits and foot lengths.*

during outside walking and the possibility of water or snow during inclement weather. Generally, exterior stairs have treads 360 mm (14 in.) or longer, though care should be taken that treads occur at a natural rhythm to the human gait – about 610 mm (24 in.). Some codes make exceptions for stairs connected directly to a building entrance and allow exterior stairs in these cases to have treads 300 mm (12 in.) or larger. Residential construction is generally held to less stringent standards and may have treads as short as 230 mm (9 in.), however this can be a contributing factor to dangerous falls.

Riser heights are usually limited to 180 mm (7 in.), though again some codes will make exceptions up to 210 mm (8.25 in.) for residential applications, although this is still a potentially dangerous condition and not generally good practice. Exterior stairs should have risers no higher than 130 mm (5 in.).

The geometry of the human foot means that a slight overlap between the back of the heel of the climbing foot and the toe of the resting foot must be provided. This is usually done by setting the face of the riser back 25 mm (1 in.) from the *nosing*, or front edge, of the tread above. To prevent catching the toe, nosings are rounded, or include a sloped underside. Nosings greater than 25 mm (1 in.) present a tripping hazard and must be avoided.

Because of the natural walking stride's length, the relation between tread and riser is crucial. Thus, in addition to meeting the criteria for minimum tread and maximum riser size, stair proportion must be calculated. The typical rule of thumb for sizing treads and risers in relation to one another is that the sum of the tread length (measured from nosing to nosing) plus twice the riser height should be as close to 635 mm (25 in.) as possible:

$$2R + T = 635 \text{ mm (25 in.)}$$

Other rules of thumb include adding the tread length to the riser height to get as close to 460 mm (18 in.) as possible:

$$R + T = 460 \text{ mm (18 in.)}$$

And multiplying tread length by riser height to get as near to 1850 mm (73 in.) as possible:

$$R \times T = 1850\,\text{mm (73 in.)}$$

All of these are shortcuts for a brief bit of trigonometry describing the fact that stairs, to be safe, must occur within a relatively narrow range of pitch angles – between about 18° and 35° (Fig. 2.3.3).

Stairs – configuration

While proper tread and riser sizing can create a generally safe, comfortable stair, additional considerations involving the stair's length, landings, and fall protection must also be taken.

First, stairs are generally limited in height, both to prevent acute fatigue while climbing and to arrest any falls that occur while descending. Building codes will often limit the total height of a stair flight to 3600 mm (12 ft), though this height can cause a potentially fatal fall. Better practice is to limit stairs to 16 risers in a straight run, which will translate to just over a 2740 mm (9 ft) height if the above formulae are employed.

To reach floor heights greater than 9 ft 0 in., therefore, an intermediate landing will be necessary (Fig. 2.3.4). Landings must be of sufficient length in the direction

Landings

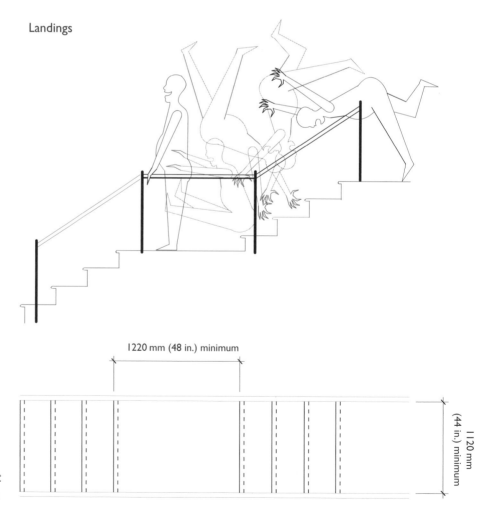

1220 mm (48 in.) minimum

1120 mm (44 in.) minimum

Figure 2.3.4. *Landings provide important fall protection and must be sized to arrest a tumbling user.*

of travel to fully arrest a falling person – usually 1220 mm (48 in.). In multi-story construction, stairs will typically double back at intermediate landings to arrive back at the stair entrance in plan – this is called a *scissor stair*.

Occupants using stairs quickly establish a walking rhythm that must not be disrupted by variations in tread or riser size. Any variation greater than 3 mm (1/8 in.) in either dimension will be noticeable, and may cause stumbling, 'flat-footing' or tripping.

Stair width is often determined by life safety codes based on emergency evacuation conditions. However at minimum stairs should allow the comfortable passage of two users going in opposite directions – 1120 mm (44 in.) – in commercial or public installations. For residences, stairs may be as narrow as 920 mm (36 in.), which allows passage for only one person at a time safely. Stairs that serve as fire exits must additionally be sized for the occupancy they serve, usually 8 mm (0.3 in.) per assumed evacuee. Where 'scissor stairs' are used, landings must be sized to maintain this width throughout the stair (Fig. 2.3.5). This is often shown on plans by drawing an arc from the outside edge of one flight to the other. Any doors entering in to the fire stair must be configured so that they do not open against the path of travel, and typically cannot reduce the required travel width by more than 50% at any point in their swing. Where stairs are likely to be used for evacuating people with motion impairments, their width must be at least 1220 mm (48 in.) to permit carrying room.

Curved or winding stairs present special hazards (Fig. 2.3.6). Where stairs are curved, they present varying tread widths, which can disrupt climbing rhythm if users move from one side to the other. At the tighter radius, care must be taken to ensure adequate tread depth, while the outer radius must be checked to ensure the treads are not too wide. Usually curved stairs are designed by

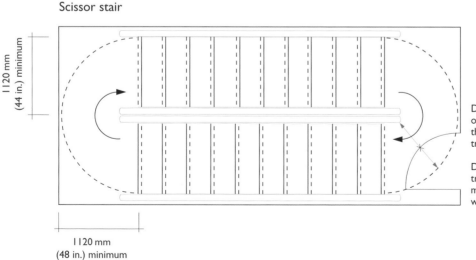

Scissor stair

1120 mm (44 in.) minimum

1120 mm (48 in.) minimum

Door must not obstruct more than half required travelling distance

Door opens with traffic down – no more than 7 in. from wall when open

Figure 2.3.5. *Most high rise buildings will use a scissor stair to provide landings at each floor level in a compact package. These must be designed to allow high volume traffic in an emergency, with adequate space for crowds to turn at each landing, and entries from floors arranged to impede the flow as little as possible.*

Curved and winding stairs

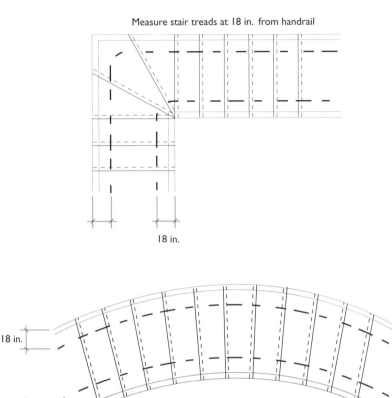

Measure stair treads at 18 in. from handrail

18 in.

18 in.

18 in.

Figure 2.3.6. *Curved and winding stairs present particular hazards and must be designed to allow a comfortable gait at the correct distance from handrails.*

taking the likely centerline of travel, about 355 mm (14 in.) from the handrail, and using that line to determine tread/riser sizes. Winding stairs, which 'turn' through a square 90°, present similar issues with tread depth at their short ends. Spiral stairs are usually not permitted in commercial or public buildings, as their extremely tight radii rarely offer adequate footroom. In general they should be a last resort even in residential or industrial applications because of their serious fall potential.

Handrails and guardrails

Stairways and ramps require two types of fall protection: *handrails* that provide grips for users, and *guardrails* that prevent users from falling off of the inevitable level changes that occur with these elements (Fig. 2.3.7). Handrails must present an easily graspable bar for the hands of those climbing or descending. On stairs, these are required whenever there are more than two risers present, while on ramps handrails are only required for ramps steeper than 1:20 slope. For stairs greater than 1220 mm (48 in.) wide, handrails must be provided on both sides of a stair. For stairs greater than 2240 mm (88 in.) wide, an additional handrail must be provided in the center of the stair.

Handrails are generally placed from 760 to 860 mm (30 to 34 in.) above the tip of the nosing. The ADA does not acknowledge the geometrical difference between a stair and ramp, and requires the handrails to be placed between

Hand and guardrails

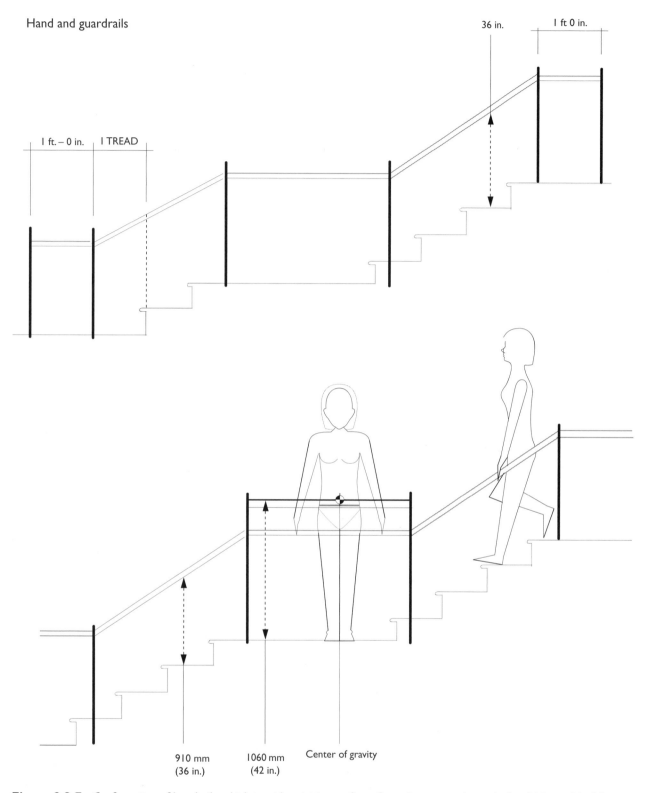

Figure 2.3.7. *Configuration of handrails, which provide gripping surfaces for stair users, and guardrails, which provide fall protection. Note the difference in height between the user's hand and her center of gravity.*

860 mm and 960 mm (34 in. and 38 in.) – thus 860 mm (34 in.) is a good default height for both. Like ramps, handrails must have an equivalent gripping surface to a 38 mm (1.5 in.) diameter cylinder, they must be uninterrupted by posts or brackets, and they must be located a good distance away from side

Handrails and guardrails

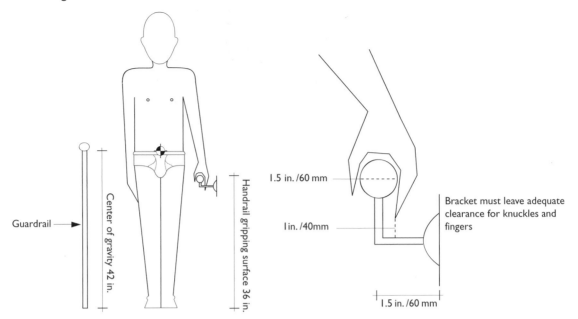

Figure 2.3.8. *Configuration of handrails in particular must allow for a comfortable, obstacle-free grip.*

walls – usually 38 mm (1.5 in.) (Fig. 2.3.8). Handrails that are not continuous must extend beyond the top and bottom stair tread to signal the change in direction and to provide for falls from the last stair. At the topmost stair, handrails must extend an additional 300 mm (12 in.) beyond the last nosing, while at the bottom they must extend 300 mm (12 in.) plus one tread width. As with ramps, handrails must be returned to a post or wall, or must have some way of shedding clothing that might otherwise become caught. Handrails must either be solid between the nosings and rails, or must provide a mesh that will not permit a 100 mm (4 in.) ball to pass through, to prevent small children's limbs from becoming entangled in the handrail.

Most codes require open landings to have a different configuration if they present a falling hazard over 450 mm (18 in.) high. Guardrails in these instances must be 1060 mm (42 in.) high, with the same requirements for solidity as handrails. While this initially seems like a contradiction, guardrails perform a very different function from handrails. The latter must provide a gripping surface for a hand that naturally rests 860–960 mm (34–38 in.) above foot height. Guardrails, however, prevent falls, and must therefore be placed above the average center of gravity of a typical human body. This is about 960 mm (38 in.) above floor height in an average male, 1060 mm (41.8 in.) above floor height in the 99th percentile male. Detailing the connection between hand and guardrails thus presents particular problems.

Two fine points of handrail and guardrail design are worth noting. When laying handrails out on a stair, it is often advisable to stagger adjacent flights of scissor stairs to ensure that their respective handrails hit a common point at the landings. This prevents a vertical discontinuity between flights that is usually unsightly and can create an uncomfortable transition between flights. Usually the upper

Figure 2.3.9. *A carefully thought out arrangement of handrail and guardrail that offers gripping surface well past the final tread and fall protection without sacrificing aesthetics. (Clark Center, Stanford University. Foster and Partners.)*

flight is set back by one tread, so that its handrail 'lands' at the same point in section as the end of the handrail on the lower flight. These two points are then connected by a horizontal segment of handrail, providing a clean detail. Careful thought about the three-dimensional nature of the handrail and guardrail at landings is required to achieve a detail that looks clean while functioning well (Fig. 2.3.9).

A second design consideration involves the difference in height between handrails and guardrails. When designing stairs with landings requiring guardrails, there will be an offset between the required height of the handrail and that of the guardrail. To integrate both elements, systems are often designed that cantilever a steel handrail off of a glass or metal plate designed to guardrail height. This combined element satisfies both requirements in a single assembly. Note, too, that if properly designed the handrail extension at the bottom of a stair may be faired in to a descending guardrail plate, again providing a neat aesthetic fix to a difficult arrangement.

Frequently asked questions

Why are stairs covered by accessibility codes? Surely they can't be traversed by wheelchair users? Mobility is a continuum, not an either/or state. While much accessibility legislation covers wheelchair usage, much of the American–European population is mobile but requires some accommodation for difficult actions such as climbing or descending stairs. Stairs are particularly difficult for many elderly, or those with chronic joint pain, and thus the design of these elements should account for a range of potential usage.

Why aren't open stair treads allowed? And why do stair treads require nosings? I know I've seen open treads somewhere before. Open treads present a serious tripping hazard. Without a riser for the user to sense where treads start and stop, it is much more likely that someone will move their foot too far forward while climbing, and catch the edge of the next riser up with their toe. Unfortunately, a stair presents a series of relatively acute edges to the falling occupant on the ascent, often resulting in facial injuries. This is a relatively recent addition to American codes, so many buildings may still have this dangerous condition. Nosings prevent the opposite occurrence. A natural human stride up a normal staircase does not completely offset one foot from another. A nosing allows a bit of an overlap between toe and heel, the most comfortable (and most balanced) stance.

I'm designing a scissor stair and can't get a satisfactory detail because of all the handrails and guardrails coming together at the landing. What do I do? Offset the upper flight by one tread depth. The handrails will then 'hit' the same point at the ends of both flights, allowing you to design one flat rail between them.

Glossary and formulas

Rise	The vertical distance between stair tread surfaces. Generally no more than 200 mm (8 in.).
Rise-to-Run	A measure of a staircase's ease of use. Not all slopes are easy for human legs to negotiate. While minimum runs and maximum rises help, additional formula are often used to ensure a comfortable stride or gait. In particular, the formula:

$$2R + T = 635 \, \text{mm} \, (25 \, \text{in.})$$

is useful for designing traversable stairs.
Other rules of thumb include:

$$R + T = 460 \, \text{mm} \, (18 \, \text{in.})$$

$$R \times T = 1850 \, \text{mm} \, (73 \, \text{in.})$$

Run	The horizontal distance between stair nosings or risers. Generally no less than 280 mm (125 mm (1 in.))
Nosing	The lip of a stair tread, designed to allow toes enough room underneath while the other foot negotiates the tread. Usually 25 mm (1 in.) deep.

Scissor Stair   A stair that doubles back on itself, usually with landings at
                    floor levels on only one side. Most common in high rise
                    buildings for their efficiency.

Landing   A flat, level portion of a staircase that provides one or more
                    steps of rest ascending, and can arrest falls while descending.
                    Usually a minimum of 1120 mm long (44 in.).

Further reading

Templer, J. (1992) *The Staircase: Studies of Hazards, Falls, and Safer Design* (Cambridge, MA: MIT Press).

2.4 Elevators and escalators

Elevators	History
	Types – hydraulic, traction, and self-contained
	Safety features
	Convenience – number, speed, and capacity
	High rise systems
Escalators	Configuration
	Arrangements

Introduction

Until the 1870s, building owners and users were limited to human power to move freight and people up and down in buildings. This was often cleverly achieved, for instance by using pulleys and ropes to haul merchandise into attic storehouses in Amsterdam, or yoking animal power to winches that moved materials to the top of gravity feed systems in typical agricultural buildings. But the need for human power to move up and down buildings limited most structures to five stories, the limit of typical human comfort. Until the completion of the Washington Monument in 1884 (169 m/554 ft), the tallest manmade structures were all uninhabitable spires.

Platforms for moving freight and people vertically were nothing new in the 19th century, rather the innovations that made the elevator popular were electric and hydraulic motive power, and devices to keep elevator platforms from falling. Safety, rather than actual lifting power, was the key innovation in the development of workable elevators for populated high rise buildings. Teagle elevators were employed in multi-story mills in Britain in the 1840s, using overhead cables, pulleys and side rails to move workers and material. These were relatively sophisticated, using counterweights to offset the weight of the cab itself. However, the rope was the only vertical support for the cab, and if it broke, there was nothing to prevent the cab from falling to the lowest level, crushing whatever was inside.

The first working safety device on a passenger elevator was demonstrated in 1853 by Elisha Graves Otis, involving toothed metal grips attached to the elevator car's main cable or rope by long pawls. If the rope were cut, the pawls would release the grips, which would then grab on to the side rails, stopping the cab. Still driven by steam power, the first Otis Safety Elevator was installed in the five-story Haughwout Store at Broadway and Broome Streets in New York in 1857. Innovations after Otis' death in 1861 included the use of hydraulic pressure, rather than steam, to raise elevator platforms. Comfort remained a serious issue, as stops were sudden and the ride could be disarmingly noisy.

Elevators – principles

Contemporary elevators come in three types (Fig. 2.4.1). Hydraulic (piston) elevators rely on a piston located beneath the cab and require a basement

Elevator types

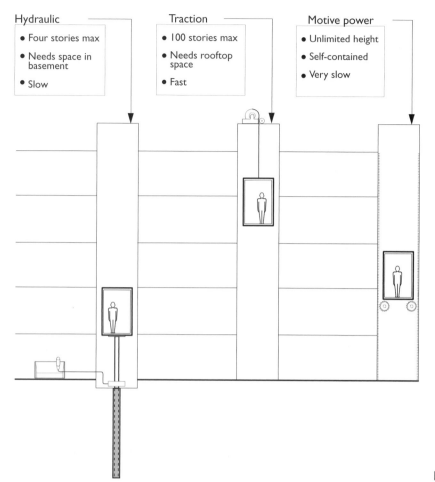

Figure 2.4.1. *Elevator types.*

machine room to provide hydraulic power (now with oil, rather than water, for a smoother ride). Traction elevators use a rooftop machine room to house a system of cables, pulleys (or sheaves), and counterweights. Motive power elevators use traveling systems (such as rack and pinion) to drive the cab itself. In each case, the cab must be supported by guide rails to ensure a smooth, reliable motion. The cab will typically be housed within a steel box that is connected to the driving element, and that contains biaxial rollers that keep the cab true relative to the guide rails.

Some equipment is common to all three types. A hoistway that provides space for travel will run the full height of the building, plus overruns at the top and bottom (Fig. 2.4.2). This shaft poses inherent dangers, in that the tall vertical space makes an ideal fire chimney, and its height will present a grave fall hazard. The fire danger is typically addressed by providing a 2–4 hour fire separation between the shaft and any occupied area, often by means of self-closing fire doors. The fall danger is more complex. Most codes require that elevators have two sets of doors, one mounted on the cab, and the other at each floor level, attached to the hoistway wall. Interlocking mechanisms ensure that the two doors only open when the elevator cab is level with a floor. Power to open the doors is typically attached to the cab itself, by means of a motor and rail attached either above or below the cab doors. The hoistway will usually require solid walls on

Elevator anatomy

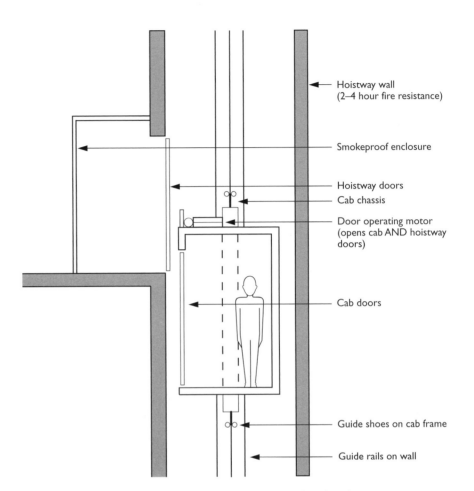

Hoistway wall
(2–4 hour fire resistance)

Smokeproof enclosure

Hoistway doors

Cab chassis

Door operating motor
(opens cab AND hoistway
doors)

Cab doors

Guide shoes on cab frame

Guide rails on wall

Figure 2.4.2. *Elevators are complex mechanical systems, but their basic parts are straightforward. The cab is supported by a structural chassis (usually steel) that is connected to the driving mechanism – a cable, a piston, or a self-contained motor. Guide shoes on the chassis connect to vertical guide rails that ensure the elevator's path stays true. Typically, the cab will contain the operating mechanism for both the cab and hoistway doors, ensuring that the hoistway doors won't open if there's no cab present. Finally, hoistway walls must be constructed of fire-resistive material if the shaft connects more than two floors, and most codes require a smokeproof enclosure to protect the door area from migrating smoke or flame.*

at least three sides, to prevent crushing as the cab runs past floors and to provide adequate support (Fig. 2.4.3). While intuitively obvious, this has implications for atrium and outdoor installations. Within the cabs themselves, control and signal mechanisms must be accessible to both able bodied and wheelchair users.

Hydraulic Elevators. The simplest type of passenger or freight elevator is hydraulic. These use an oil-filled piston to push the cab up through a shaft. When ascending, a pump fills the piston with oil, which can then be slowly released to bring the cab back down. Hydraulic systems require a large machine room at the lowest level of the hoistway to accommodate the pump and oil reservoir necessary. They also typically require a drilled hole to hold the piston when the cab is at its lowest point. Their main advantage spatially is that they do not require

Electric passenger elevators

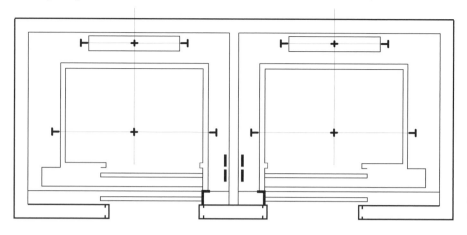

Figure 2.4.3. *Elevators in plan showing location of guide rails, cab and hoistway doors, and counterweight (for traction elevators only).*

any significant space at the top of the hoistway for mechanical equipment. Hydraulic elevators are relatively slow, with a maximum speed of about 60 m/min (200 ft/min), and their travel is generally limited to four stories due to the pressure required in the plunger.

Traction Elevators. Most large-scale installations use an overhead machine room and a system of cables and pulleys to move elevator cabs. Known as traction systems, these provide motors at the top of an elevator shaft to turn metal wheels with grooves known as traction sheaves. Cables sit in these grooves and are attached to the top of the cab's frame below at one end, and a counterweight at the other. The counterweight is sized to balance the weight of the cab, plus a percentage of the anticipated passenger or freight load, and a set of slack cables are usually attached to the base of the elevator cab to balance the changing weight of the cables above as the elevator travels up and down. While a single steel cable would ordinarily be sufficient to hold the load of a typical elevator cab, they are usually ganged into groups of five or six to allow sufficient traction on the sheaves – this also provides a very high safety factor should one of the cables fray. Various roping arrangements can be implemented to both increase traction and to gain mechanical advantage through pulleys. Additionally, a three-sheave system can allow the mechanical room to occupy a basement position. However, all of these come at the expense of extra cable, which must be constantly maintained.

Traction machines are inherently expensive due to their complex roping requirements. Likewise, the placement of heavy motors at the top of a tall shaft necessitates major structure to both hold their dead load and to absorb the constant reactions of cabs starting and stopping. Access is often more difficult, and machine rooms generally require a story and a half above the top of the shaft to hold the motors and allow proper access. Despite the high maintenance required on cables, traction elevators tend to be inexpensive in terms of life cycle cost, in part because they can re-generate electricity when descending – often up to 40% of the power required to hoist them. Likewise, they are much faster than hydraulic elevators, as typical speeds range from 75 to 150 m per minute (250 to 500 fpm). In extreme circumstances, high rise elevators may travel as fast as 600 m/min (2000 fpm), and their rise is limited only to the deflection of steel cables. Technically, there is no reason that elevators could not be fitted into a high rise a mile high or more.

Self-contained motive power: In unusual circumstances, elevators may be required in situations that do not permit a machine room at the top or bottom of the shaft. Several products exist that place the motive power within the cab or counterweight itself, relying on a rack and pinion to raise and lower the cab. This is a particularly good system for observation cabs, as it eliminates the bulky counterweight. Likewise, new products include hydraulic elevators with integral pistons, placed within the hoistway to avoid the excavation required for a large plunger hole. These latter systems are limited in height, usually to three stories.

Elevators – safety

Most systems rely on at least two systems to stop the cab in an emergency. The cab's speed is generally monitored by a *governor*, a wheel connected to a dedicated set of cables that contains a centrifugal switch. If the cab exceeds allowable speeds, the governor trips, first setting into motion a set of friction brakes that rub against the guide rails, slowing the cab's travel. At a catastrophic speed, the governor will trip a second set of switches, releasing spring-loaded steel jaws that will clamp on to the guide rails more tenaciously, stopping the cab quickly. Because of the redundancy of cables and the ability of the motor to brake the cab's travel, this latter event is extremely rare.

More common are accidents involving tripping hazards and crushing. Elevators are required to have floor leveling devices that will nudge an arriving cab to within 6 mm (1/4 in.) of the landing's level, and interlocks that will prevent doors from opening in any misaligned position. Likewise, at the base of the shaft, a significant overrun is required, with buffering springs to absorb any substantial overrun (note that these springs are *not* there to stop a falling cab). All cabs must fully enclose passengers so that limbs are not endangered by passing structure, and all hoistways must be fully enclosed for the same reason. Finally, doors must be equipped with mechanical sensors that will trigger an instant reversal when an object prevents their closure, and they must be limited in the amount of force they can produce. Higher end installations will include an infrared sensor that will detect anything in the doors' paths, causing them to open before hitting a late passenger.

Because they are electronically controlled, elevator cabs have the unfortunate tendency in a fire of stopping at a burning floor because of the intense heat involved. Therefore, elevators are quite dangerous means of 'escape' and must be sent automatically to the ground floor with no intermediate stops if the building fire alarm is triggered. This safely discharges passengers who might have been aboard during the emergency, prevents new passengers from using the cabs, and provides convenient transport to arriving fire fighters, who can override the emergency instructions by means of a special key. Typically, fire crews will take the elevator to a floor just below the suspected fire.

In the event of a power outage, some occupancies (hospitals in particular) must provide emergency power to elevators, allowing them to move to the nearest floor to discharge passengers. However in commercial and most residential occupancies there is often no such requirement. Occupants of any cab must be able to access an emergency phone, usually wired directly to building security or a police operator. Cabs will typically be fitted with an emergency hatch on their roof to allow rescue crews to remove stranded passengers, who can then exit through the closest hoistway door, above. Passenger discomfort can be lessened in these situations by providing a confirmation light indicating that assistance is on the way. Observation cabs that include views out can also make this rare occurrence less stressful. To prevent panicked passengers from attempting to escape into the hoistway, which would become dangerous if the system was suddenly re-energized, hatches must be locked from the outside, and hoistway doors must have a mechanical interlock that prevents their being opened by normal human efforts. In the unlikely event that these doors are opened, hoistway shafts must be designed to prevent limbs from being crushed if the cab does begin to move suddenly. In all cases – even a fire – the cab is a much safer environment than the hoistway.

Elevators – convenience

While a variety of codes will require various safety features as described above, elevators must be designed to comfortably and conveniently move passengers, and this is a more difficult task than might at first be assumed. Building occupants in general have very unrealistic expectations about waiting and travel times – studies have shown that frustration is apparent after only 25 s of wait. Particularly in high rises, which may discharge more than half of their population within 15 min at the end of a work day, the capacities required of elevators are formidable.

Three factors determine the total waiting and travel time for elevators – speed, capacity, and number. While speed in feet per minute seems an obvious component, this is tempered quite a bit by the elevators performance while *on station*, that is, while passengers are loading and unloading. Here, the size of the door and the speed at which it opens and closes has a significant effect, particularly in buildings of considerable height. Doors that open in the center will halve the time that the elevator cab is stopped with no passenger movement, while *two-speed* doors will further decrease this inherent inefficiency by opening more quickly. Likewise, while capacity has a positive effect on efficiency, it is limited by the fact that more passengers will typically require more stops, leading to longer round trip times. Generally, the single greatest variable in determining system convenience is number – that is, a larger number of smaller elevators will always be preferable in a multi-story system. This, of course, is more expensive, as more hoistways, motors, etc., must be purchased, and all elevator companies will provide extensive design services to assist in the realization of an economical balance between cost and performance. The ultimate measure of a system is its *handling capacity* (HC), which is the percentage of a building's population that can be accommodated within a <5-min period and is equal to:

$$HC = 300\, p/l$$

where p is the number of passengers per car and l is the required interval, or waiting time (note that 300 s give us the 5 min capacity). A good rule of thumb in planning, however, is to provide one elevator for every 3000 m^2 (30,000 ft^2) of occupied space, with a minimum of two for any multi-story commercial or institutional building.

In large high rises, control of an elevator system can greatly increase efficiency. The earliest controls involved a single 'call' button that could only be operated while the elevator was idle – each trip was made independently of any other. Control systems have become more sophisticated, first with electro-mechanical systems able to 'log' all requests and collect them as the cab traveled up and down the hoistway, and later with electronic systems that could assign calls to the nearest (or least full) cab. Contemporary control systems are universally microprocessor based, with sophisticated programs that can quickly determine strategies for minimizing overall waiting time, assign cabs for passengers who have been waiting the longest, and gradually learn from traffic patterns.

Another major convenience factor is layout, particularly the arrangement of cab entrances in a lobby. Where there are more than one or two cabs, visibility is a necessity, and passengers should be able to see clearly which elevators are arriving. Long runs of single openings present problems in that passengers must hurry to catch arriving cabs, while double-loaded lobbies require passengers to look in two directions at once. While space-intensive, radial layouts provide the best grasp of the elevator bank's status. Another strategy is to provide screens showing the location, direction of travel, and even likely arrival time for each cab in the system, allowing users to move to the arriving cab's position well before its doors open.

Floor space in front of elevator entrances must be adequately sized to permit entering and exiting traffic to flow freely in the worst (most loaded) situation. Efficiency is dramatically impaired when doors are held open to await passengers who are held up by congestion. In general, 0.5 m^2 (5 ft^2) of immediately adjacent lobby space should be allowed for each anticipated passenger in an elevator lobby, although 0.7 m^2 (7 ft^2) per person is the general threshold of comfort. In no case should opposing banks of elevators be closer than 2500 mm (8 ft), and good practice suggests that a minimum of 3000–3660 mm (10–12 ft) is required to allow for constant flow.

High rise elevator systems

The development of the skyscraper has continued to spur development in elevator systems. As structural techniques improved in the 1950s, several major advances in elevator design followed, permitting the jumbo high rises of the 1960s and 1970s.

The two primary problems with high rise elevator design relate to travel time and floor plate footprint. As buildings pass about 20 stories, travel times become so long that even high speed elevators will not be able to handle the populations such buildings house. To overcome this, more elevators can be provided, however at some point the number of shafts required will take up too much floor

Elevator banks

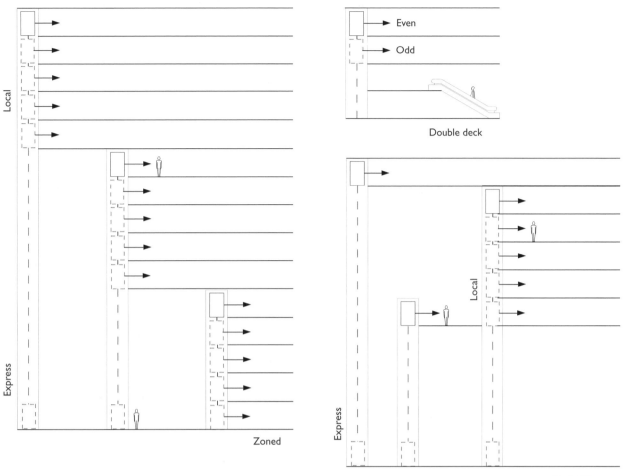

Figure 2.4.4. *Banking strategies for high rise elevator systems. To maximize efficiency, most buildings over 20 stories will employ express/local elevators that skip certain floors and serve others. These cabs are banked at the lobby level so that users can quickly segregate themselves into the appropriate staging areas. Double deck elevators were used frequently in the 1960s but proved unpopular due to the 'downtime' when one cab empties or loads and the other sits idle. Super tall buildings may employ sky lobbies and express elevators that feed regional hoistways.*

area to be economical. Several strategies were therefore developed to essentially increase the passenger capacity of each shaft (Fig. 2.4.4). *Zoned systems* provide banks of low, mid, and high rise elevators that travel directly between the lobby and the appropriate zone. This system uses more floor space, but it provides very efficient service to high rise floors. *Double deck* cabs feature two passenger compartments stacked atop one another, with a two-story entry lobby that segregates passengers according to even and odd floors. While this doubles the capacity of each shaft, it also doubles the number of stops, and leads to disconcerting moments in each cab as the other stopped for passengers. For buildings over about 250 m, the most efficient system is a *sky lobby* arrangement, where express elevators run to a set of transfer floors at roughly even intervals throughout the building. From these transfer floors, local elevators then run to individual floors. Because the local shafts can 'stack' (with appropriate structural

Figure 2.4.5. *Elevator cabs are often showpieces for detailing and mechanical expression. Here, elevator cabs in Lloyds of London (Richard Rogers Partnership, 1985) offer riders a panoramic view of the exterior. (Richard Rogers Partnership.)*

separation), this multiplies the capacity of each shaft by the number of transfer floors.

Freight Elevators. In addition to passenger elevators, any building requiring the movement of goods or equipment will be outfitted with a dedicated freight elevator, typically one for every 30,000 m^2 (300,000 ft^2) of commercial or industrial space. Such elevators should connect as directly as possible to a loading dock, if provided, and to a 'back of house' circulatory system. Freight elevators will generally be sized according to the largest anticipated piece of equipment in the building, and will be outfitted with interior finishes designed to absorb constant cart or dolly traffic. In some situations, a passenger elevator will include hanging elements to hang blankets that can protect higher end finishes, allowing it to be used for freight. In all cases, buildings with elevators must have at least one that will allow a full-sized ambulance stretcher to comfortably move in and out.

Escalators and conveyors

For applications involving only a few stories and high pedestrian capacities, escalators may present a better solution to vertical transport than elevators. Because their start and finish points are usually visible, they provide a more intuitive way

Escalators

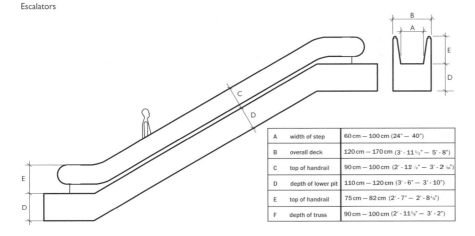

A	width of step	60 cm — 100 cm (24" — 40")
B	overall deck	120 cm — 170 cm (3' - 11½" — 5' - 8")
C	top of handrail	90 cm — 100 cm (2' - 11½" — 3' - 2¾")
D	depth of lower pit	110 cm — 120 cm (3' - 6" — 3' - 10")
E	top of handrail	75 cm — 82 cm (2' - 7" — 2' - 8⅛")
F	depth of truss	90 cm — 100 cm (2' - 11⅜" — 3' - 2")

Figure 2.4.6. *Typical escalator dimensions. Escalator slope has been standardized throughout the US and Europe at 30°. Note that narrower escalators do not permit faster users to bypass standees.*

finding strategy, and their capacities are much higher than comparably priced elevators. Their expense, however (often US$100,000–300,000 per installation) may be prohibitive in many situations.

Escalators operate by a running a continuous chain attached to self-leveling treads around a drive motor, usually at the top of the run. In the US, escalators' slopes have been standardized at 30°. Flat runs at the top and bottom allow the treads to level out, and provide a kinesthetic cue to passengers that the landing is approaching. To prevent catching feet or clothing, the treads must be ridged, and must enter a 'combplate' at both ends. Moving handrails are geared to the drive chain as well, and must return at floor level, again to prevent ingesting hands (Fig. 2.4.6).

The arrangement of escalators in a multi-story building may be based on efficiency, in which case a scissor arrangement may be most appropriate, or on exposure to key elements on a floor (i.e., retail), in which case parallel stacks may work best. The former is essentially a double helix, with up and down traffic separated into distinct paths, while the latter pairs up and down escalators, enforcing a walkaround to go from one floor to the next. In cases where massive efficiency is required (train stations, stadiums), multiple parallel escalators may be set to run predominantly in one direction, depending on the flow of traffic.

The layout of escalators involves figuring both the horizontal run required to achieve a given height, and allowing for the often quite substantial truss that enables them to be self supporting for rises up to 7.3 m (24 ft) (Fig. 2.4.5). The truss is typically hollow, allowing space for the return path of treads. For larger installations, intermediate support may be required. While generally limited to 12.2 m (40 ft) of rise, installations involving continuous support and intermediate drive motors have enabled rises of up to 48 m (160 ft) in unusual situations such as the Washington Metro. An exterior escalator in Hong Kong uses several sequential escalators to move commuters up and down a 400 m height.

Moving Passenger Conveyors are continuous tread surfaces that operate horizontally, moving occupants over large distances with minimal vertical change (no more than 12°). These are most typically used in airports, where distances to gates are often extreme for passengers with luggage. To allow efficient exiting, conveyors are usually limited to 90 m (300 ft). Conveyors must operate at a slow enough speed to allow safe embarking and disembarking. As a result, they generally move at a pace slower than typical walking speeds. While most users will walk on them, doubling their speed, others often see conveyors as a chance to rest. This can block traffic, and therefore good practice is to ensure that faster users can easily pass standing passengers; a minimum clear width of 1000 mm (40 in.) is recommended. Dimensions for handrail heights and thicknesses are typically similar to those of escalators.

Frequently asked questions

Why aren't elevators allowed as exits in a fire situation? Elevators present an extreme fire danger in that they are located in vertical shafts, which can act as chimneys, and offer no alternative exit if the hoistway shaft is broached by flame or smoke. Worse, fire and heat can damage elevator doors, guide rails, or fascia panels, causing cabs to stop at floors that are aflame. Occupants then have no escape. Typically, detailed signage is required at all elevator landings that locates nearby emergency exits or fire stairs.

What is required to have glass elevators? Exterior elevators? Glass (or 'observation' elevators may be exempt from hoistway requirements as they typically occur in atria, or outside. Often a solid wall (or a carefully designed glass wall) will still be required at each landing, and this wall must be continuous to avoid crushing hazards for maintenance personnel or a foot or hand trapped in a door. At the base, a wall or a physical separation is required to avoid occupants reaching in to the path of a traveling car. Guide rails must still be provided, usually on fin walls or columns even with the cab's center of gravity, however in extreme circumstances cabs may be significantly cantilevered from the hoistway wall for dramatic effect – this requires careful location of cable or plunger connections, and often extensive weighting and balancing of cabs to prevent racking. Exterior cabs must be outfitted with extensive (and expensive) waterproofing, as door-operating motors must still be mounted atop the cab itself.

Glossary and formulas

Car or Cab	The enclosure, structure, and mechanics associated-with the traveling, occupied portion of an elevator system. Typically includes guides, structure (usually steel), walls, roof, and floor, control panel, and doors with motor and chain drive. Must meet accessibility standards for wheelchair users (especially turnaround and control panel access), and safety standards to prevent walls, roof, or floor from being breached by panicked occupants in an emergency.
Counterweight	In a traction system, a large weight attached to a cab's cables that balances the anticipated typical traveling weight of the cab.
Dumbwaiter	A small elevator system designed for freight only. Often not subject to many of the safety regulations as a passenger elevator, but limited in size and height.

Governor	A safety device that senses excess cab speed and triggers brakes.
Guide Rails	Precision elements (usually steel) that are typically attached to hoistway walls, on which the cab's guide wheels roll to ensure straight travel.
Hoistway	The 'tube' through which an elevator cab moves. Typically includes a fire-resistive group of surrounding walls and doors assemblies at each landing. Often subject to very stringent fire and safety codes, as they provide ideal chimneys for the spread of smoke and flame, and numerous crushing hazards for anyone within.
Hydraulic Elevator	A vertical transportation system composed of an enclosed cab, a hoistway, and a hydraulically activated plunger system that is usually bored into the ground and filled from a reservoir and pump at basement level.
Landing	An area of floor that is designed to accommodate access in and out of elevator cabs. Subject to building code legislation for fire separation, and accessibility codes for call buttons, alerts, and door configuration.
Motive Power	A system in which an elevator's motors are part of the cab assembly. While rare, this arrangement offers savings in space.
Overrun	A designed space at the top of an elevator hoistway that provides additional travel distance for cabs and for anyone (typically maintenance personnel) who may be on the cab's roof.
Platform Lift	An unenclosed elevator cab, usually traversing a short distance and often used only for wheelchair access. Must typically have a full set of guard and handrails, and must meet additional safety standards to prevent crushing of fingers, etc., that may be extended through rails.
Traction Elevator	A vertical transportation system composed of an enclosed cab and a hoistway. Its motors, sheaves, and cables are usually located at the top of the hoistway.
Two-Speed Doors	On an elevator cab and hoistway, an opening system that moves door leaves at two different speeds, saving space and reducing opening time.

Further reading

Strakosch, G.R. (ed.) (1998) *The Vertical Transportation Handbook* (New York: Wiley).

CHAPTER **3**

Materials

3.1 Materials: wood

Trees	Types: deciduous and coniferous
	Hard vs. soft woods
	Dimensional lumber
	Sustainability
Species	Examples
	Framing/structural
	Finish/cabinetry
History	Laugier's primitive hut
	Framing types
	Traditions
Wood Construction	The carpentry trade
	Framing carpentry
	Light framing
	Heavy timber
	Finish carpentry
	Cabinetry
	Doors–windows–trim
	Paneling
	Floors

Introduction to wood

Wood is one of the most prevalent building materials in the world. Approximately 90% of buildings constructed in the US each year are framed with wood, while that percentage is only 15–20% in the UK. Timber is one of the only 100% renewable building materials and it doesn't naturally produce any toxic by-products in its conversion from tree to product. Trees have one of the longest life spans of all living things – the oldest living trees are 5000 years old. Timber has obvious advantages over other materials: it can regenerate (if properly harvested) and provide an infinite supply for our use; wood is recyclable, waste efficient, biodegradable, and non-toxic. It has proven to be very energy efficient and trees play a major role in soaking up carbon dioxide, reducing the risk of global warming.

There are an immense number of species and types of wood products. Each type has its own character and appropriate use. Many woods are most commonly used for structural purposes, while others are best suited for finish work. The properties, availability, and cost of the many types of wood vary considerably. Some types of timber are also inappropriate to use under any circumstances due to their rarity or the forestry practices used to harvest them. Making the correct decision is a difficult and moving target, which requires some research and careful specifying.

While many technological advances have been made in the development of new materials, few can rival the strength, durability, beauty, workability, and versatility of wood. New technologies in wood production have also modified the ways we can use this material, and it continues to be one of the primary structural and finish materials architects use on projects. Chances are good that you will never work on a project that does not involve wood in one way or another, and in each case you will need to know what species to select and how it will work in the environment you've created.

Trees

Commercial lumber is classified into 'hardwoods' and 'softwoods'. Hardwoods come from broad leaf or deciduous trees and softwoods come from evergreen or coniferous trees. While most commercial hardwoods are physically harder or denser than most commercial softwoods, the classification refers to the type of tree and does not always describe the hardness of the wood.

Wood is cellular material and due to the microstructure of longitudinal cells wood has different structural properties parallel to the grain vs. perpendicular to the grain. Parallel to the grain wood is strong and stiff; perpendicular it is weak and deformable (Fig. 3.1.1). On the basis of performance by unit weight, construction timber is as least as stiff and as strong as structural steel.

Commercially marketed lumber includes dozens of tree species. When trees are commercially cut or 'harvested' the cellular hollows are filled with moisture, commonly called 'sap'. Trees are sawn into rough lumber while in a saturated or 'green' condition. Timber which will be shipped long distances from the sawmill, or be made into finish lumber is 'seasoned', which dries most of the sap. This seasoning is accomplished through stacking the wood in the open air for a period of months or more commonly by heating it in a kiln for a period

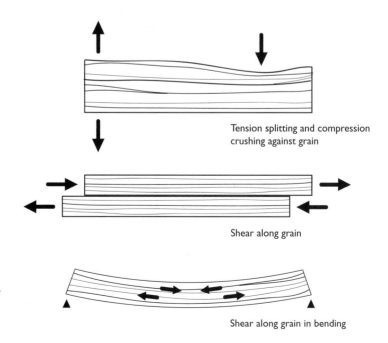

Tension splitting and compression crushing against grain

Shear along grain

Shear along grain in bending

Figure 3.1.1. *Timber resistance to vertical and horizontal pressure.*

of days. The process of seasoning causes the lumber to shrink considerably, and it continues to shrink until it is in equilibrium with the moisture content of the surrounding air. Wood expansion is due much more to moisture than thermal factors, and the changing moisture content needs to be taken into account to allow expansion/contraction in any final assembly.

Most lumber is surfaced after seasoning, which reduces it to its final dimensions and gives the wood smooth faces. The edges are rounded or 'eased' to reduce splinters and make the wood easier to handle.

All of this rough cutting, seasoning, shrinking, and surfacing explains why there is such a difference between 'nominal' and 'actual' sizes of timber in the US. However, in the UK metric sizes are close to the actual size of timber you purchase (Fig. 3.1.2). If lumber is 'sawn' in the UK it is not planed so it is actual size, while planed lumber is 3–5 mm smaller than listed (so a planed 100 × 50 in the UK is about 95 × 47 mm). The most common of construction timbers is nominally called a 2 × 4 (100 × 50) – which implies a piece of wood 2 in. deep by 4 in. wide (100 mm wide by 50 mm deep), by the length, which is normally called out in board feet or meters. Note that when calling out the size of lumber, the thickness is called out first in the US (feet and inches) but the opposite is true in the metric system. For example, a metric 100 × 50 mm equals an imperial 2 × 4 in. A brief size verification of US lumber will show that the depth is actually 1.5 in., the width is 3.5 in., and the length is very close to what is listed. The boards are rough-cut at the actual size, except for the length that is cut at the end of the process. The shrinking and surfacing reduces the nominal size dramatically. The final surfacing process creates boards that follow a standard amount of size decrease: 1 in. nominal = ¾ in. actual, 2–6 in. nominal reduce size by ½ in. – so a 6 in. width is actually 5.5 in., 8 in. nominal sizes and up reduce size by ¾ in. – so a 14 in. width is actually 13¼ in. 16 in. (400 mm) is the typical maximum nominal board width, and board lengths run from 6 ft (1.8 m) to 24 ft (7.3 m) in 2 ft (0.2 m) increments.

How the boards are cut from a log affects the strength and appearance (Fig. 3.1.3). Plain sawn lumber has a variety of noticeable grain patterns and tends to twist, cup, and wear unevenly. It can also have grain patterns on the

Nominal dimensions	Actual seasoned and surfaced dimensions
25 mm (1 in.)	22 mm (3/4 in.)
50 mm (2 in.)	47 mm (1½ in.)
75 mm (3 in.)	70 mm (2½ in.)
100 mm (4 in.)	95 mm (3½ in.)
125 mm (5 in.)	120 mm (4½ in.)
150 mm (6 in.)	145 mm (5½ in.)
200 mm (8 in.)	195 mm (7¼ in.)
250 mm (10 in.)	245 mm (9¼ in.)
300 mm (12 in.)	295 mm (11¼ in.)
350 mm (14 in.)	345 mm (13¼ in.)
400 mm (16 in.)	395 mm (15¼ in.)

Figure 3.1.2. *Lumber nominal and actual surfaced dimensions.*

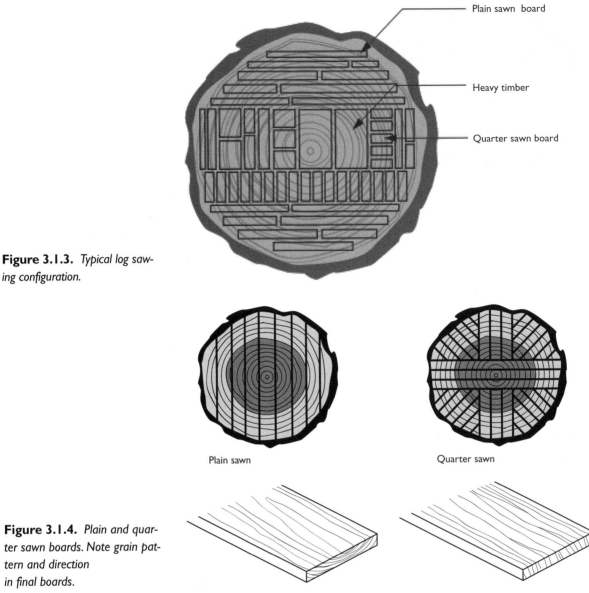

Figure 3.1.3. *Typical log sawing configuration.*

Plain sawn board

Heavy timber

Quarter sawn board

Plain sawn

Quarter sawn

Figure 3.1.4. *Plain and quarter sawn boards. Note grain pattern and direction in final boards.*

surface that peel apart and separate. It is typically less expensive to produce and purchase (Fig. 3.1.4).

Quarter sawn lumber has more even grain patterns than plain sawn, wears better, warps less, and is less affected by surface splitting. It is typically more expensive due to the additional waste materials from the cutting pattern.

Lumber is also milled in ways that resist warping. Tongue and groove floors, door thresholds, and wood sills frequently have *relieved* backs, meaning the side facing down has a notch cut to promote curling down rather than up (Fig. 3.1.5). These notches assist in keeping wood from curling, but the most reliable way to prevent problems like this is to use a better cut of wood (like quarter sawn) and also relieve the back of the piece.

Lumber is graded on both structural and visual scales; each scale is based on the species of wood. Typically hardwoods are rated visually (because they are

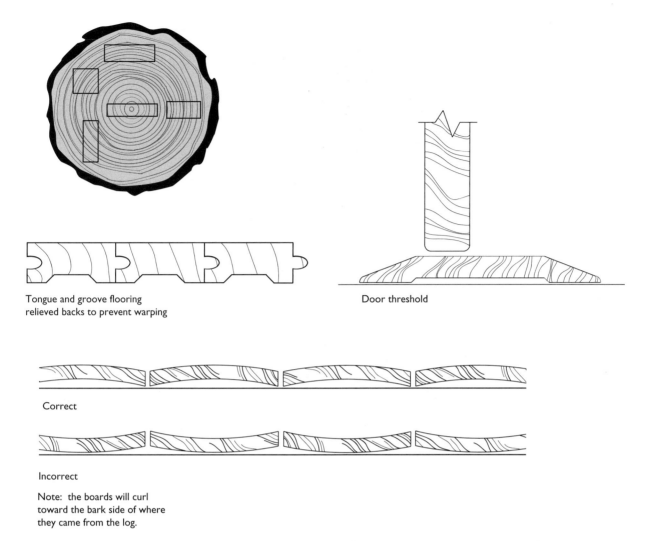

Tongue and groove flooring
relieved backs to prevent warping

Door threshold

Correct

Incorrect

Note: the boards will curl
toward the bark side of where
they came from the log.

Figure 3.1.5. *Board warp. Boards are placed to curl downward and often have relieved backs to prevent curling.*

used for finish purposes) and softwoods are graded structurally (because they are used for framing and construction).

A major issue facing all timber harvesting is sustainability. Entire species of trees have been eliminated due to over cutting, and the environmental impact of clear cutting forests has proven devastating. The general quality of timber has also steadily decreased over the last century and we are just recently beginning to understand how to manage this issue on a global scale. The complexity of these issues makes a simple unchanging list of what trees to use and not use worthless. Wood is the main cooking fuel for nearly half the world's population – so banning species has at times reduced the worth of that tree to the point that it is no longer valued, and therefore used as firewood or cleared for agriculture more quickly than if it was exported for construction. The goal is to stay aware of what timber is being responsibly harvested. What 'responsible' means can be debated, but the goal is to reach zero loss forestry –the cutting and growing need to take place equally. Also, forests need to retain a diverse population of vegetation, rather than becoming single species farms. Some states have banned the use of certain woods in publicly funded projects, but the ultimate responsibility for using appropriate species lies with the designer – only the person designing a structure can determine what goes in and what stays out. The decision requires research, and sources like the US Forest Service, the CITES (Convention on International Trade in Endangered Species – www.cites.org), CFPC (the Certified Forest Products Council – www.certifiedwood.org), and The Nature Conservancy (www.nature.org) and the Forest Stewardship Council (www.FSC.org) can assist.

Species

Most people are familiar with the common species of wood – Douglas Fir and Southern Pine for construction, and Oak, Maple, Cherry, Teak, etc. for finishes. To list all of the types is too cumbersome, but some species descriptions will be helpful.

Certain types of woods are naturally resistant to problems without preservatives or special treatment. Wood in general is decay resistant when its moisture content is below 20%. This can be hard to control in many situations, and all applied treatments eventually fail – so decay-resistant woods are often used for exterior applications. Redwood, Cedar, Bald Cypress, Black Locust, Teak, and Black Walnut are the most common decay-resistant species. Termite resistant species include Redwood, Eastern Red Cedar, and Bald Cypress.

The following are a list of common species, their properties, and typical uses:

Name	Uses	Notes
Western red cedar	Cladding	Weathers to gray, closet linings, resists rot
Douglas fir	Construction to furniture	Grows fast and straight
Southern pine	Construction to furniture	Grows fast and straight
Spruce	const. and scrap	Lower quality and not durable
Yew	Furniture and finishes	Limited availability
Yellow Poplar	const. and moldings	Little grain – paints well
Ash	Finishes and veneer	Decorative, simple to oak
Bubinga	Veneer	African exotic, dark red
Cherry	Finishes, veneer, furniture	Medium color to light red
Elm	Finishes and furniture	Wiped out in US by disease
Mahogany	Finishes and furniture	Dark color, medium grain, resists rot, over forested
Maple	Veneer, flooring, furniture	Light grain, can take stain poorly
Red oak	Veneer, finishes, furniture	Red to brown, course, strong grain
White oak	Veneer, finishes, floors	Lighter brown, hard, stains well, can resist rot
Padauk	Finishes and furniture	Strong red, limited availability
Teak	Finishes and furniture	Warm brown, resists rot, over forested
Redwood	Cladding, furniture	Warm red, resists rot, avoid old growth trees

History

Wood is traditionally known as the first building material. Abbe' Laugier proposed in 1753 that the first human impulse to construct shelter resulted in the 'Primitive Hut' – the first act of architecture (Fig. 3.1.6). This is a wooden four-post structure with a simple roof, fulfilling the most basic need of shelter – but one created by humans rather than found in nature. There are many other traditions of wood design, and its ease of use and prevalence throughout the world gives it a special quality in the realm of design. Stone and masonry were certainly used early on to create monumental works – some of which are our oldest remaining artifacts of early culture, but wood was certainly used for most construction in places that had timber available.

Figure 3.1.6. *Abbé Laugier's primitive hut, from 1753. The traditional first act of architecture.*

The nature of construction before engineering was trial and error. Each generation learned from the previous and transmitted that knowledge forward – refining it to the particular circumstances and cultural heritage of the builders' society. This pattern has been repeated thousands of times – until we are faced with similar problems that have been addressed by our earliest ancestors. This is a knowledge base too powerful to ignore, yet we frequently do, and often times neglect to study our own traditions when we're deciding how to create assemblies. Don't make this mistake – as Bruce Mao says, '*Stand on someone's shoulders. You can travel farther carried on the accomplishments of those who came before you. And the view is so much better.*' Learn the difference between looking back in nostalgia and using tradition to move forward.

Barn construction is a good example to look at to see how this refinement and tradition can work. Entire communities would come together to raise a barn and the lessons were shared throughout the community. These structures have an almost inevitable quality of appearance, each detail has been thought out to maximize the use of local materials, available technology, and need for durability (Fig. 3.1.7).

The method of assembling building frames has responded to the need for fast construction as well. After the Chicago fire of 1871 there was a need to re-construct buildings quickly. Out of this need was developed the *balloon type wood framing system*. This framing system raises an exterior wood frame the entire height of the building, the floors are then inserted inside this exterior

Figure 3.1.7. *Barn heavy timber joint, from the late 1800s.*

frame and it can be sheathed and enclosed quickly. The system only works for two storey structures (due to the available lengths of wooden studs), but it allows for full height wall assembly on the ground, which can then be simply propped up and joined together easily (Fig. 3.1.8).

The more common method currently used is *platform wood frame construction*, where each storey of wall framing is constructed and propped into place. Then the upper floor joists and floor sheathing are constructed, and the next level can commence, building wall frames on the new floor. This allows for more than two floors to be constructed and uses smaller wooden wall studs. There are, however, still limits to the overall height based on building fire safety codes.

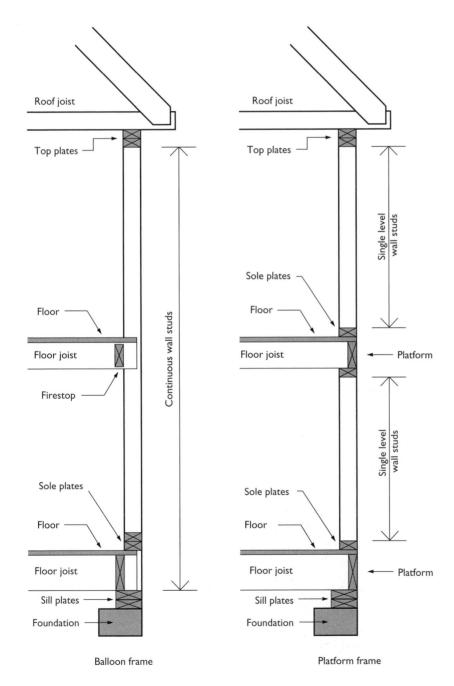

Figure 3.1.8. *Balloon and platform frame types.*

Wood construction

A *Carpenter* is the classification of the tradesperson who will be dealing with the woodwork at a building site or millwork shop. This person has been trained to deal with wood as an apprentice, and knows more than most architects about wood construction. Many project field superintendents were carpenters by trade before they took on more senior roles. Trust these people – ask them how they would do something – watch how they put things together. Many younger architects are immediately discredited on job sites because they draw things that are shown incorrectly or inefficiently, yet they insist on having them built the way they are drawn. Be flexible on assembly and firm on durability and esthetics. Think about how someone would really assemble something – mentally go through the steps, if you can't put it together in your head it will be difficult or impossible in the field.

One of the main roles of a carpenter is assembling the framing. Wood framing is of two primary types: Heavy Timber and Light Frame (Fig. 3.1.9). Heavy timber construction consists of exposed columns, girders, beams, and decking large enough to be slow to catch fire. This type of construction is used in a large range of building sizes and types. The large size of timbers used in this type of

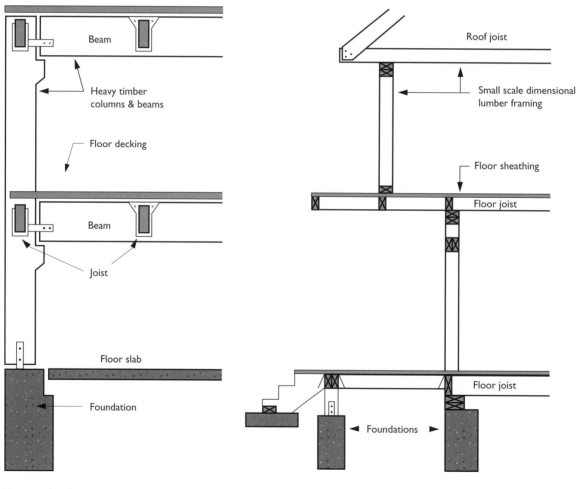

Heavy timber frame

Wood light framing

Figure 3.1.9. *Heavy and light wood framing.*

construction makes it appropriate for regular, repetitive bays, and simple building shapes. Light frame construction, such as the balloon and platform types, is usually made up of nominal 50 mm (2 in.) framing members spaced closely together and concealed. Light frame construction, with its small member sizes adapts easily to more intricate building forms than heavy frame construction. Often metal studs are used in place of wood in light frame construction, which can be less expensive, easier to assemble, and more fire resistant, but they are typically much less rigid. Wood is better suited to making stiffer assemblies, but is not the typical choice for large scale or commercial building types.

Another role of carpenters is in cladding and sheathing the building. This is often done in wood as paneling, siding, shingles, or shakes. Base sheathing is often plywood or other fiber based sheet products, and it can be applied to the exterior walls and roof, along with the interior floors. Waterproofing is placed over this sheathing and then the finish material is applied. Careful attention needs to be shown to the ways sheathing can shift and expand, so appropriate gaps should be built into the assembly. Fasteners also should be selected and placed so not to stain the wood or cause leaks into the area behind the sheathing (see Section 5.1, Building Envelope).

Finish carpentry involves all of the finished or exposed woodworking on the interior and sometimes exterior of the building. Examples of finish work are cabinets, wall paneling, wood floors, stair railings, floor and crown trim, interior doors and frames, and finish window framing (windows are typically premanufactured and installed as part of the exterior sheathing). Much of the finish wood is prepared in a millwork shop and fitted in place at the job site. The more work that can be done at the shop the better the result will typically be. Quality control is much higher in the shop and therefore the level of precision and quality of finish is superior. Certain things need to be done in the field in order to custom fit the space, and a good field carpenter will consistently determine whether a project turns out acceptable or great. Again, don't underestimate these people; learn as much as possible from them. Combative relationships with construction teams always negatively impact your project.

The assembly of wood is much more involved than simply deciding whether to use screws or nails to put pieces together. Wood joinery has a long history of developing different types of joints for different purposes (Fig. 3.1.10). Within the decision of how to join any two pieces of a building assembly together is an attitude about the overall structure. Some joints try to hide the fact that they are two separate pieces, while others accentuate and celebrate the juncture with elaborate details. Considering the juncture of any two pieces or materials should be a design decision, and treated as such. Consistency and intention in detailing tends to hold the overall feel of a building together.

Frequently asked questions

'How do you decide between using plain or quarter sawn lumber?'
Plain sawn lumber is usually less expensive than quarter sawn, but of a lower finish quality. The decision tends to rest on whether the lumber will be exposed

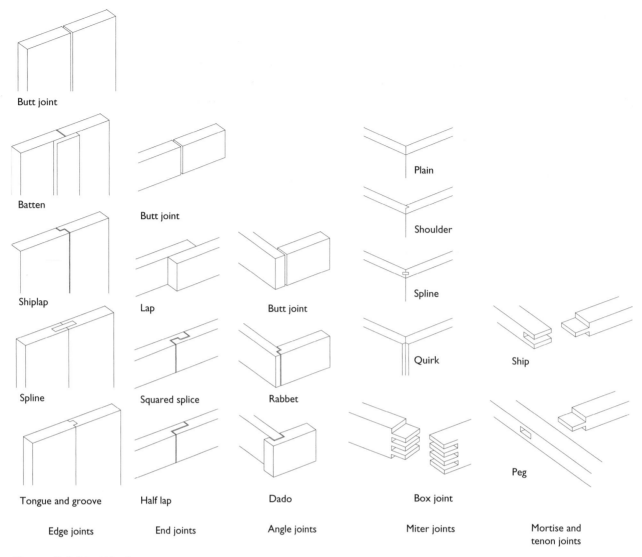

Butt joint

Batten

Butt joint

Shiplap

Lap

Butt joint

Plain

Shoulder

Spline

Spline

Squared splice

Rabbet

Quirk

Ship

Tongue and groove

Half lap

Dado

Box joint

Peg

Edge joints

End joints

Angle joints

Miter joints

Mortise and tenon joints

Figure 3.1.10. *Wood joint types.*

or in a condition where some abrasion or warping will negatively affect performance or esthetics. Concealed structural wood is typically plain sawn, as it is not exposed to view and is normally part of an assembly that will not be affected by small amounts of warping or cupping. Exposed wood, such as decking or finish cabinetry, is preferably quarter sawn because there are less potential impacts of warping and a desire for a higher finish quality.

'Is there a list available for what types of lumber are sustainable?'
The short answer is No. A major issue facing all timber harvesting is sustainability. While there are lists available that recommend what woods to use or avoid, the issue is too complex to be stable over a long period of time, meaning the lists go out of date quickly. This is an area where designers must stay abreast of the latest research and information on lumber acceptability, and one of the reasons why practicing sustainably requires constant re-education.

Conclusion

Wood is one of the easiest materials to work with and one of the most difficult to master. If it had been just invented, rather than naturally occurring, it would be hailed as the most technologically advanced and usable building product ever created. It can do almost every building function well and is remarkably versatile and beautiful. As designers it is our responsibility to use it responsibly – and there is resistance to doing this. Information is not always easy to gather on the best sustainable practices, and architects have been doing things the same way for so long that it's hard to change. This is an area that is a watershed decision for designers; there are so many things to deal with that it is easy to neglect the ones that aren't absolutely necessary. Each designer decides their own ethical responsibilities and how to approach the difficult task of doing things the most responsible way.

Glossary and formulas

Balloon Framing	System that raises exterior studs the full wall height with floors inserted into the frame.
Carpenter	The classification of the tradesperson who will be dealing with the woodwork at a building site or millwork shop.
Easing	Rounding the edges of lumber to limit splintering at the corners.
Hardwoods	Lumber from broad leaf or deciduous trees.
Plain sawn	Lumber cut straight across the log in the most efficient pattern.
Platform Framing	System that constructs single floor height studs with platform floors at each level before proceeding.
Quarter Sawn	Lumber cut toward the centerline of the log in fourths, resulting in more even grain patterns.
Sap	The moisture that fills the cellular hollows of wood.
Seasoning	Drying the sap from recently cut trees until it is at a specified moisture content.
Softwoods	Lumber from evergreen or coniferous trees.
Veneer	Thin wood sheet glued to the face of a core material or to other veneers to form plywood.

Further reading

Levin, E. (1972) *The International Guide to Wood Selection* (New York, NY: Drake Publishers). pp. 12–27.

Lefteri, C. (2003) How to Buy Wood, *Wood: Materials for Inspirational Design* (Mies, Switzerland: RotoVision SA). pp. 12–13.

3.2 Materials: masonry

Masonry Basics	Masonry types
	Production and quarrying
	Properties
	Common uses
History	Early uses of masonry
	Technology developments
	Modern use
Masonry Construction	Assembly methods
	Patterns
	The arch and lintel
	Colors, Finishes, Textures
	Problem issues
	The masonry trade

Introduction to masonry

Masonry is based on the need to build semi-permanent structures from durable individual units that can be stacked and adhered together. We consider masonry to be: clay brick, clay tile, concrete masonry units (CMUs), glass block, terra cotta, adobe, and stonework. Masonry construction has been found that is over 16,000 years old, and has been continually improved for durability, esthetics, and versatility.

Masonry is long lasting, weather resistant, and can provide building structure, cladding or both. Masonry is also fire resistant, provides thermal comfort, resists sound penetration, and can reduce overall sound levels. Systems may be designed as walls, columns, piers, pilasters, lintels, and arches, but always work most efficiently in compression. Masonry is used in virtually every type of building application, and the colors and finishes of masonry are almost limitless.

Typical masonry construction is made up of small building units, which create maximum versatility of building form. Manufactured masonry units are made of clay, concrete, or glass and may be solid or hollow. Solid units have less than 25% open voids and are usually cored or have indentations that reduce weight and provide a better surface for mechanical bonding of the mortar. Hollow masonry units are more than 25% open and the voids, or cells, are large enough to contain reinforcing bars and grout.

Manufactured clay masonry units are molded or extruded and then heated at over 870°C (1600°F). Adobe units are cured at low temperatures, sometimes by sun drying, and gain strength from emulsifiers or other binders. CMUs are molded from low water mixture concrete and gain strength through the chemical hydration of the cement.

Mortar and grout are the bonding materials used to adhere masonry units together. Mortar is spread, or 'buttered', between units by the mason during stacking. Grout is poured or spread into cells and cavities in walls or between tiling units to fill gaps. Mortar and grout are made of a cement, aggregate, and water mixture similar to concrete – but with less aggregate and sometimes more water content to remain workable, spreadable, and pourable. Once the mortar or grout is placed between masonry units it sets quickly, due to the drying absorption of the porous masonry.

Masonry construction is often initially more expensive than other types of construction, but has an excellent life cycle cost. The construction is very durable, long lasting, is low maintenance, and is energy efficient. It also has a low environmental impact and is inert when downcycled as fill material.

Please note that while you may frequently see and hear the term 'masonary,' there is only one 'a' in the word.

Masonry basics

The most common type of masonry is the clay brick. *Bricks* are made in modular and non-modular sizes with specific nominal and actual dimensions (Fig. 3.2.1). The nominal dimensions in brick sizing are based on a completed assembly – meaning the final size in the wall with mortar joints included. The most common brick size is the 'modular' brick that is nominally 8 in. deep, 4 in. wide, and 2⅔ in. high in the US, and $225 \times 112.5 \times 75$ mm for the British Standard co-coordinating brick size. The height/width/depth dimensions are for common reference only, as units may be placed into the wall system in any orientation. The actual size of this unit is 7⅝ in. deep, 3⅝ in. wide, and 2¼ in. high, with a 3/8 in. mortar bed in the US and $215 \times 102.5 \times 65$ mm (or 73 mm), with 10 mm mortar joints in the UK. This makes vertical coursing 8 in. high for every three rows of standard running bond in the US and 225 mm high for three rows in the UK, with 4–8 in. increments of wall length in the US and 112.5–225 mm increments in the UK. Working with these dimensions when designing is called 'using brick module' – understanding that height/openings/corners can only occur at increments of these dimensions. Other brick sizes and mortar bed thicknesses are possible and can be found in Figure 3.2.1. Keep in mind when using any material like brick, that labor costs far outweigh material costs – therefore using larger, more expensive individual units is cheaper overall due to the fact that fewer of them need to be placed to make a wall (this only works up to a reasonable size of unit, i.e., small enough for one person to easily carry). The rough dimensions of the basic modular brick have been in use for over 2500 years because of its size, it is easy to handle, and place with one hand for an entire work day.

Clay Tiles are far less commonly used since the large-scale production of CMUs became widespread. Clay tiles were largely used for structural applications, as they were often larger open cell units that could be easily placed and grouted full if needed. They are also used as interior wall backup with brick veneers placed over top. CMU construction has taken the place of clay tiles in the US because the expense is less and the durability/strength of the

Standard brick sizes and vertical coursing

Unit designation	Nominal dimensions (in.)			Joint thickness	Actual dimensions (in.)			Vertical coursing
	W	**H**	**D**		**W**	**H**	**D**	
Modular	4	2⅔	8	⅜	3⅝	2¼	7⅝	3C = in.
				½	3½	2¼	7½	
Engineer modular	4	3⅕	8	⅜	3⅝	2¾	7⅝	5C = 16 in.
				½	3½	2¹³⁄₁₄	7½	
Closure modular	4	4	8	⅜	3⅝	3⅝	7⅝	1C = 4 in.
				½	3½	3½	7½	
Roman	4	2	12	⅜	3⅝	1⅝	11⅝	2C = 4 in.
				½	3½	1½	11½	
Norman	4	2⅔	12	⅜	3⅝	2¼	11⅝	3C = 8 in.
				½	3½	2¼	11½	
Engineer Norman	4	3⅕	12	⅜	3⅝	2¾	11⅝	5C = 16 in.
				½	3½	2¹³⁄₁₄	11½	
Utility	4	4	12	⅜	3⅝	3⅝	11⅝	1C = 4 in.
				½	3½	3½	11½	

Unit designation	Joint thickness	Actual dimensions (mm)			Vertical coursing
		W	**H**	**D**	
Standard coordinated	10	215	65	102.5	3C = 210 mm
Imperial	10	215	73	102.5	3C = 234 mm
Thin format	10	240	52	115	4C = 238 mm
Standard format	10	240	71	115	3C = 238 mm
1½ Standard format	10	240	113	115	2C = 238 mm
3½ Standard format	10	240	113	175	2C = 238 mm

Note: UK Nominal and actual dimensions are equivalent. Check with masonry manufacturer to verify specifications.

Figure 3.2.1. *Standard brick sizes and vertical coursing.*

concrete units are higher. Tiles are, however, still used in applications such as fireplace flues (where they are more heat resistant than concrete) and underground drainage systems (where they resist leakage better than concrete). They are also used when the glazed tile look is desired or in situations where vandalism is a concern, because they can be cleaned of paint and stains easier than unglazed CMUs.

CMUs are molded from zero-slump concrete and cured with hot water ranging from 38°C (100°F) mist to 175°C (350°F) steam. This makes the units very strong and resistant to cracking and chipping. Most CMUs have hollow cores to reduce weight and allow for grout and reinforcing bars. The most common nominal size for a CMU in the US is 8 in. wide, 8 in. high and 16 in. long, the actual size being 7⅝ × 15⅝ in., in the UK this is 24 cm wide, 23.8 cm high and 49.5 cm long. This makes each block row height the same as three 'modular' bricks and allows the two systems to be tied together easily in composite wall construction. Again, using the standard nominal block dimensions is referred to as designing in 'block module', and many times this module controls the overall

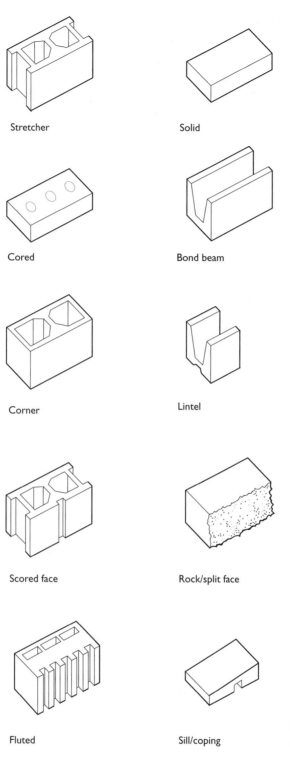

Stretcher

Solid

Cored

Bond beam

Corner

Lintel

Scored face

Rock/split face

Fluted

Sill/coping

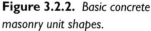

Figure 3.2.2. *Basic concrete masonry unit shapes.*

dimensions of the building you're designing (It's much easier to know this from the start rather than making the mistake of having to go back and change *all* the dimensions on a set of drawings). CMUs come in so many shapes and sizes that it's hard to call the most common 24 × 49.5 cm (8 × 16 in.) size standard (Fig. 3.2.2). The versatility and compressive strength of these units, paired with the fact that they are easily combined with steel reinforcing bars for tension capacity, make them nearly ubiquitous in most construction. They are resistant to corrosion, termites, winds, weather, and can be colored or textured easily.

Terra cotta is used as a part of, or over masonry wall systems. Terra-cotta moldings were used extensively in the 1930s to produce colors and shapes not possible in other materials and much less expensive than stone carvings. This type of construction is no longer common, but may be encountered as part of building restoration, and more modern ceramic glazing systems can reproduce the look of original hand cast terra-cotta moldings. Modern large-scale glazed ceramic tile cladding systems are becoming more common, and provide a durable, attractive exterior finish that is hung in curtain wall fashion rather than grouted onto the surface of a wall.

Glass Blocks act as a hybrid type of masonry, using what was traditionally a thin glazing and making it into a compact translucent/transparent modular wall unit. While not used for load-bearing walls, the versatility of the material creates many types of applications from entire facades, window openings, interior partitions, floors, skylights, and stairways. The glass blocks allow for light to pass, can self support without framing, manage thermal transmission, control sound transmission, and can be made vandal – even bullet resistant. Typical blocks are made from two halves bonded together, although solid block are also available. Common square sizes are from (115–300 mm) 4½–12 in. Rectangular, 45-degree corner, bullnose, and radius blocks shapes are also available by various manufacturers. The surface finishes of blocks range from clear to translucent to various wave and gridded patterns. Cement mortar is normally used to assemble wall systems, however, silicone-based mortars can be used to reduce sound transmission or increase earthquake resistance (Fig. 3.2.3).

Adobe walls are made from mud for both the masonry unit and the mortar. This type of construction uses sun-dried mud bricks layered in a roughly 1:10 ratio of width to height. Actual thicknesses vary from location to location based on the traditional methods of local construction and intentional 'tuning'

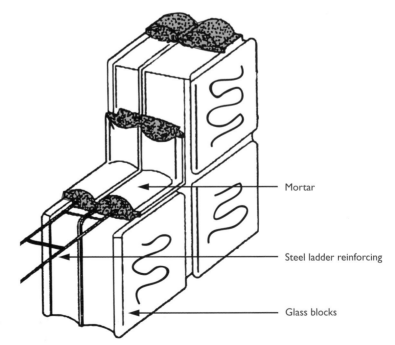

Mortar

Steel ladder reinforcing

Glass blocks

Figure 3.2.3. *Typical glass block assembly.*

of the thickness of the wall for thermal load shifting. The most important consideration with adobe is the control of water, as the sun-dried bricks will dissolve under moisture. Well-built structures dissolve at a rate of 25 mm (1 in.) in 20 years in areas of 254–635 mm (10–25 in.) of rainfall per annum. This type of building system makes sense in dry areas that can effectively use thermal mass walls. Earth walled buildings are very ecologically friendly – taking a minimum of energy to construct, using limitless supplies of natural building material, and recycling themselves back into the earth with no adverse biological impact (Fig. 3.2.4).

Stone Masonry was historically used as a structural material; however, in modern buildings its use is primarily restricted to veneers, facing, flooring, cabinetry, and decorative detailing. This is due to the extreme cost and difficulty of working with large-scale stone pieces – under almost any circumstances construction can take place vastly cheaper and with more consistent results by using the stone as surface rather than structure. Stone is quarried from particular locations worldwide that can produce consistent color, pattern, and texture for production. These qualities are both dependent on the stone type and the methods of fabrication and finishing. Harder stones, like granite, keep their finish and color longer than softer stones, like limestone, that change over time due to exposure. The three rock classes are igneous, sedimentary, and metamorphic, although classifications are made by stone type and name rather than by class (Fig. 3.2.5). The class of stone determines not only how it was formed, but its durability and properties as well – and you should be able to note the type and class of most stones on sight. Unlike brick, common sizes

Adobe wall

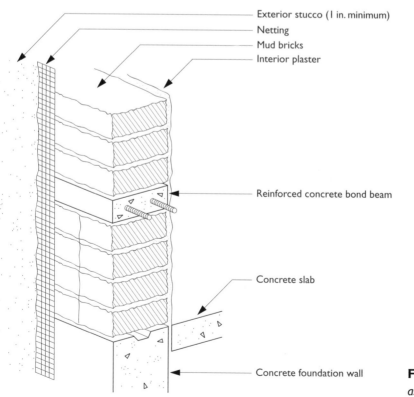

Exterior stucco (1 in. minimum)
Netting
Mud bricks
Interior plaster

Reinforced concrete bond beam

Concrete slab

Concrete foundation wall

Figure 3.2.4. *Adobe wall assembly.*

3 Materials

Stone properties

Physical properties	Igneous rock Granite	Sedimentary rock		Metamorphic rock	
		Limestone	Sandstone	Marble	Slate
Compressive strength (psi)	15,000–30,000	4000–20,000	3000–20,000	10,000–23,000	10,000–15,000
Shear stress (psi)	1800–2700	1000–2000	1200–2500	900–1700	
Weight (psi)	156–170	147–170	135–155	165–178	170–180
Absorption of water (percent by weight)	0.13%	2.63%	4.16%	0.33%	0.23%
Texture	Typical course to fine crystals, often with various colon	Fine crystalline to granular	Granular with sand grain visible	Smooth granular to course crystalline, typically showing veining	Fine crystalline flat layers can show cleft surface

Note: Properties vary considerably, check with quarry for actual appearance.

Figure 3.2.5. *Stone properties.*

of stones vary greatly depending on the type and fabrication. Most stone installations of any scale will be custom fabricated, and the details will be worked out with the fabricator or manufacturer.

History

The first uses of masonry date to prehistoric times and the first molded bricks have been found in Egypt dating to 16,000 years ago. The first fired bricks date from 5000 BC, which is the same time frame as the first quarried and cut stones were used in construction. By 3000 BC brick glazing and coloring was taking place, and with the discovery of bronze around 2500 BC adequate tools were available to cut stone with precision. The use of clay and stone in the production of buildings has taken place throughout the world and these are still some of the most prevalent building materials worldwide.

Sumerian and Babylonian cultures began the more sophisticated uses of masonry around 3500 BC, developing not only baked and glazed bricks, but also early forms of vaulting – setting the stage for the ability to span distances with small modular units, a triumph of intellect and form making. This skill was built upon for thousands of years, being further advanced by the Greeks who manipulated structures with subtle variances in the dimensions of structures to create an 'animation' most evident in the 'entasis' (slight curvature from top to bottom) of the Greek column. The Romans furthered the skill of masonry construction not only in engineering feats, but also in the large-scale production of masonry building materials. Fired brick was an industrially produced product in Roman times and the widespread use of masonry pushed forward ever more impressive projects. One of the most impressive of Roman technical feats is the Pantheon, a concrete cupola spanning 40 m with a masonry

Figure 3.2.6. *Romanesque church tower, from the late 1300s. Rome, Italy.*

drum support resisting horizontal load. Later in the Eastern Roman Empire the Hagia Sophia cupola was constructed, spanning 35 m in a lighter expression than the Pantheon and forming the height of ancient masonry and concrete expression. This knowledge was subsequently lost for 1000 years.

In the middle ages, roughly 1000 AD, Romanesque churches begin to re-discover the use of spanning arches and vaults to create large-scale structures. These structures, however, were still largely dependent on very thick load-bearing wall structures for support (Fig. 3.2.6). The discoveries made at this time also centered on the ability to speed-up the construction process. Stone and brick fabrications were streamlined and made more precise, and it was this precision that made possible the increased sophistication of the Gothic churches.

By the 14th Century the skill of the builders was such and the material properties of masonry were understood well enough to begin to lighten the wall and roof structures significantly. This makes very evident the nature of minimizing the amount of material by maximizing the understanding and effort put into assembling it. The Gothic cathedrals explode the exterior walls into gigantic openings and use lightweight traceries to form the roof vaults as lightweight spider webs of structure that seem to float in the air (Fig. 3.2.7). Further

Figure 3.2.7. *Duomo di Siena, 12th–15th centuries. The lower section of the church was begun in the Romanesque style, with the vaulting done later in the Gothic style.*

sophistication leads architecture into the Renaissance era, where the material properties of construction become less the generator of form, and the ideas of the designer begin to generate formal properties of buildings. This is where we depart from the historical discussion of masonry as a technical development, until the modern era.

With the invention of the iron and later steel frame as the primary structural support for larger buildings, the role of masonry changed. The Monadnock Building in Chicago, from 1891, represents one of the last load-bearing masonry skyscrapers in the US (Fig. 3.2.8). Standing 16 stories tall, its walls at the base are over 8 ft thick, narrowing progressively as the height increases. Most structures after this time would either use masonry as a structural material for low height buildings or as a surface cladding only. We are currently in the ideologically uncertain position of deciding how to use this material; that has fundamentally changed its purpose in the last 100 years from how it was used 16,000 years prior to that.

Masonry construction

Basic assembly methods of masonry are based on the vast history of the material. The standard steps in the industrial production of clay bricks are

Figure 3.2.8. *Monadnock building, 1889–1891, Chicago, Illinois by Burnham and Root. The classic brick load-bearing skyscraper. Sixteen floors tall.*

shown in the chart (Fig. 3.2.9), while quarries typically drill and blast large chunks of stone to be then sawn into sizes suitable for transport to manufacturing facilities or local stone fabricators.

Brick wall types begin with the structural, or solid masonry wall, which is made up of multiple rows of bricks locked together to achieve greater strength. All joints are filled with mortar to create a unified load-bearing wall that can withstand heavy vertical and horizontal forces. The brick can be bonded or mixed with CMU units to create a stronger wall, particularly if the block is reinforced with grout and re-bar (Fig. 3.2.10).

Brick or brick/block cavity walls use two 'wythes' (a wythe is a single row of bricks) of brick with an air space between 50 and 100 mm (2–4 in.) wide. The air space creates additional insulation value for the wall, and acts as a barrier against moisture penetration. Moisture that gets through or around the first layer of brick runs down the air gap – and metal flashing combined with weep holes at the base of the wall release the moisture back to the outside. The

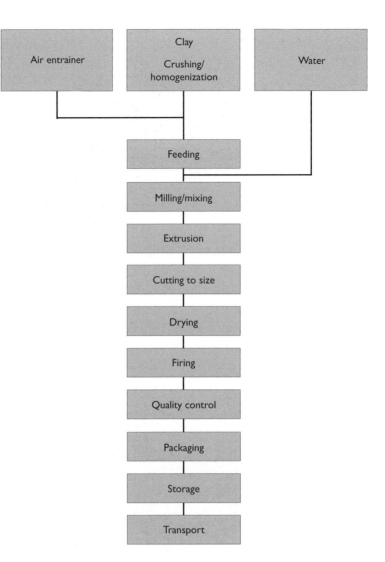

Figure 3.2.9. *Clay brick production.*

two wythes are linked together with metal wall ties embedded in the mortar joints (Fig. 3.2.11).

Reinforced brick walls are constructed with the gap from a cavity wall, but the gap is filled with grout and reinforcing steel. This creates a structurally stronger wall, and is typically used for vertical piers, columns and in horizontal lintels, and bond beams (Fig. 3.2.12).

Brick veneer walls use a back-up system of wood or metal structure and act as the vertical cladding system. The back-up structure assumes the entire vertical load and the brick, or other masonry, provides the weather barrier (Fig. 3.2.13).

The look of any wall surface is determined by both the selection of masonry material and the mortar joints applied by the mason. Different joints provide different looks and weathering capabilities – the primary purpose of the mortar joint at the exterior face of the wall is to prevent moisture from entering the assembly. Figure 3.2.14 shows the types of joints and their relative quality of moisture shedding capacity. Architects tend to like mortar joints that are

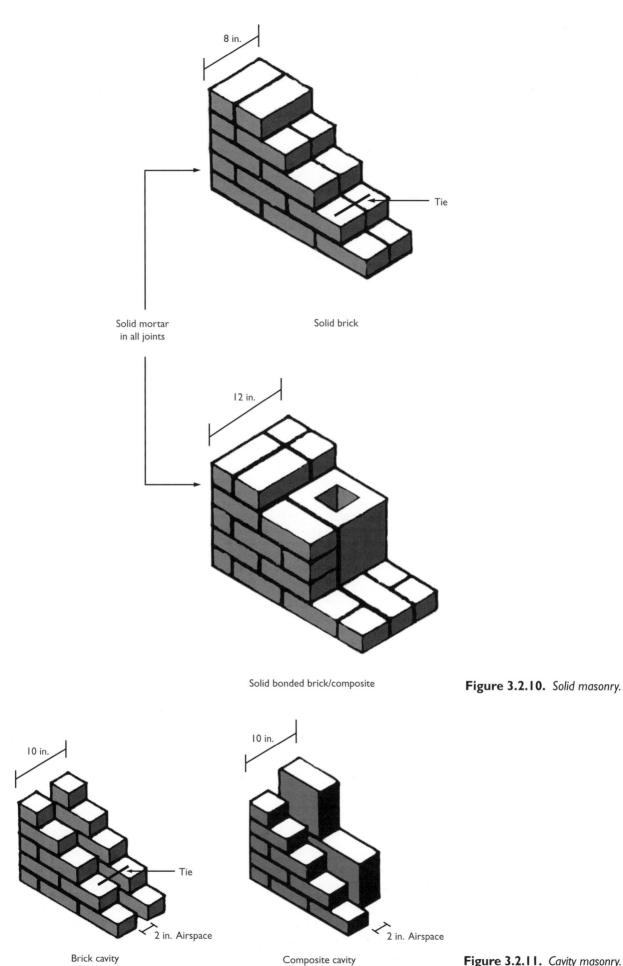

8 in.

Tie

Solid mortar
in all joints

Solid brick

12 in.

Solid bonded brick/composite

Figure 3.2.10. *Solid masonry.*

10 in.

Tie

2 in. Airspace

Brick cavity

10 in.

2 in. Airspace

Composite cavity

Figure 3.2.11. *Cavity masonry.*

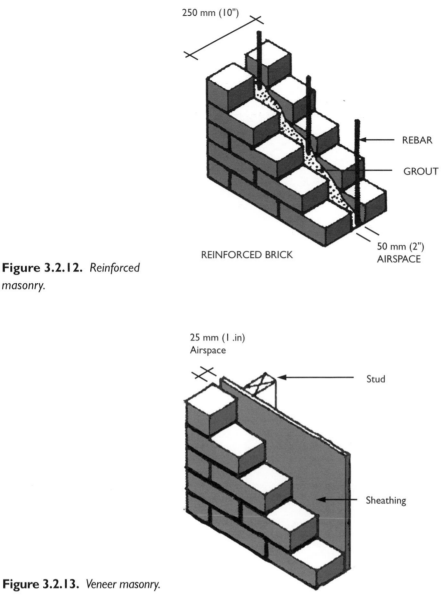

250 mm (10")

REBAR

GROUT

REINFORCED BRICK

50 mm (2")
AIRSPACE

Figure 3.2.12. *Reinforced masonry.*

25 mm (1 .in)
Airspace

Stud

Sheathing

Figure 3.2.13. *Veneer masonry.*

Veneer brick

deeper and cast shadows, Frank Lloyd Wright would rake the horizontal joints on his homes and leave the vertical joints flush to accentuate this effect. These types of joints are usually not as durable, but a weathered joint can often have the same effect with better long-term performance.

The pattern in which masonry is laid out has both structural and historical significance. While the running bond is typically thought of as standard in brick layout, it simply provides the most efficient way to slather brick onto a horizontal surface, while still making it look somewhat structural. The traditional structural bonds always had some bricks turned with their short face or 'header' to the outside, which locked the multiple rows of bricks together (see Fig. 3.2.15 for brick terminology). The various patterns emerged out of historical traditions and the artful skill of the mason in designing various wall patterns that were both attractive and served the technical purpose required. There are many patterns and variations, a few of the most common in stone and brick are shown in Fig. 3.2.16.

| Good | Good | Fair | Poor |
| Concave or rodded | 'V' shaped | Weathered | Extruded |

| Poor | Fair | Poor | Poor |
| Beaded | Flush or plain cut | Struck | Raked |

Figure 3.2.14. *Mortar joint types and weathering quality.*

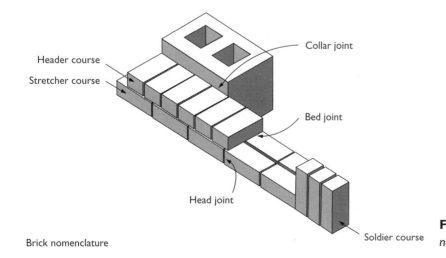

Brick nomenclature

Figure 3.2.15. *Brick nomenclature.*

159

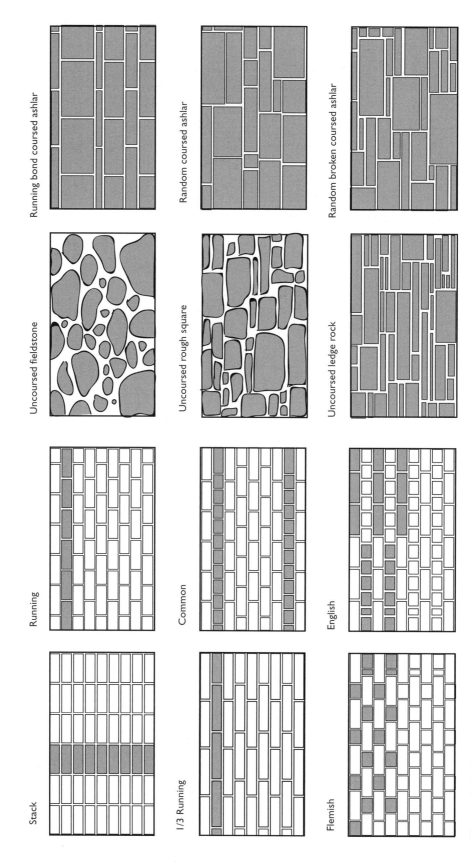

Figure 3.2.16. *Brick and stone bond patterns.*

Running bond coursed ashlar

Random coursed ashlar

Random broken coursed ashlar

Uncoursed fieldstone

Uncoursed rough square

Uncoursed ledge rock

Running

Common

English

Stack

1/3 Running

Flemish

Along with the running wall patterns are the types of openings made in masonry walls. The most basic opening is made with a 'lintel' or beam that spans the top of the opening, allowing the load from above to be transferred to either side and down the load-bearing structure. This strategy is limited by the strength of the material used to span, and the potential deflection that can occur over time. In older brick structures the lintel was often stone or wood, these being the only longer structural materials available. Wood had an obvious problem – in a fire the entire wall fell, which is why even current code requirements do not allow any masonry to be carried on wood support structure. Modern lintels can be made from concrete, steel, or even grouted into the brick with re-bar, giving the appearance of no structure at all carrying the brick.

The development of the arch was instrumental in creating large openings that did not rely on the limited length of solid stone lintels. Arches can be made from brick or stone masonry units (Fig. 3.2.17), and range from completely flat 'jack' arches to tall gothic arches. The arch creates longer spans by the compressive nature of the masonry material and must follow certain rules and formal relationships to function properly. Not only is the opening spanned, but also horizontal force is being placed into the wall below, requiring some mass or other strategy to counteract this force. The frequency with which arches are misused, malformed, and distorted is not only a fundamental structural misunderstanding, but also the loss of a formal language of architecture based on 3500 years of accumulated knowledge.

Colors, finishes and textures are virtually limitless in both brick, concrete and stone masonry. Bricks can be glazed in matte or gloss finishes to create

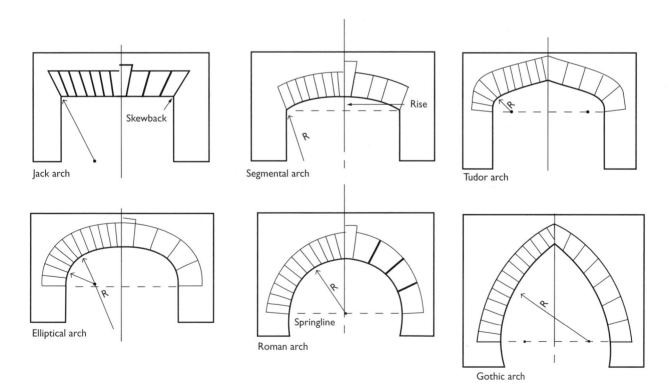

Figure 3.2.17. *Arch types.*

extremely uniform or varied finishes. The surfaces of bricks are often patterned with tools, such as brushes or wires, to create different textures and adhesion of the glazing materials. Concrete can be integrally colored and different surfaces are available, from natural to glazed. Concrete surfaces can also be textured or split, to form very rough finishes. Stone types come in almost every color, and the finishes can intensify and modify the natural color. Standard stone finishes are polished (glossy), honed (smooth but matte), flame finished (rough but close to flat), sawn (showing the circular fabrication marks), or split faced (roughly split and unfinished). Each texture has different qualities depending on the type of stone, and some materials are better suited to some finishing methods than others.

Lastly, all materials pose particular problems that can be effectively dealt with if the designer knows what to expect. Masonry offers a few common problems, some of which are controlled by careful assembly, some are controlled by good design detailing. All involve water penetration.

The first problem is efflorescence, commonly seen as a white staining on the exterior surface of a masonry wall. Efflorescence is a leaching of salt minerals out of the mortar, caused when water gets into the brick assembly and has no path to get out. Eventually the water infiltrates the mortar from the inside, causing the mortar to slowly dissolve. This also commonly happens in basement foundation walls that are painted, the moisture cannot evaporate through the wall, and eventually destroys the mortar – ironically this is typically accelerated by homeowners who don't like the slightly stained mortar in basement walls and decide to 'fix' them with latex paint. Efflorescence is controlled by properly flashing the base of cavity walls and keeping the weep holes unclogged. Often, the weep holes are 'wicked' by placing a piece of rope into the hole to prevent it from getting clogged with mortar during construction and exterior soil or debris after construction. Careless masons can sometimes clog the air gap with excess mortar, keeping the water from reaching the weeps and causing water build-up. The effluent salt deposits can sometimes be difficult or impossible to clean if they bond to the masonry surface – or the water can go through to the interior surface of the wall, creating lingering mold and internal water damage. Be sure to make your intentions clear on the drawings and watch for this condition during field visits.

The other issue for masonry in temperate climates is the freeze/thaw cycle. Water penetrates everywhere it can and expands when it freezes, blowing things apart. Typical reasons for water to enter masonry structures are: bad decisions on mortar profiles which pull standing water into joints by capillary action, insufficient expansion joints that cause cracking of the mortar, foundation movement that causes cracking of mortar and masonry, bad window or door flashing that allows water into the system, and roof leaks that pour water into the system. Minor problems have a tendency to amplify themselves over time, a small crack gets progressively bigger as more water is allowed in – eventually causing failure. Another related problem with water penetration is the internal rusting of steel lintels – which occasionally fail with spectacular results, potentially removing entire walls or segments of buildings.

Frequently asked questions

'What does designing in brick/block module mean?'
Because bricks and blocks are typically modular materials they form wall lengths based on the dimensions of the units selected for construction. Therefore a standard brick wall will normally fall on 8 in. or 225 mm increments of length. It is more expensive and less esthetically pleasing to cut the units to make other sizes work, so most buildings constructed of brick or block have wall lengths and openings placed on these increments of size.

'Why do we now normally only use brick masonry as a veneer rather than a structural material?'
The obvious answer is expense, but that doesn't mean that bricks themselves are costly. The material itself is not prohibitively expensive, brick is rather economical as a raw material. The expense primarily comes from the labor involved to assemble a wall, and as in most building assemblies the labor cost far outweighs the material cost. The other issue with cost is that work on other parts of a building cannot begin until the shell is completed. If the shell has an open frame or block wall exterior it can be assembled and closed in quickly, which allows inside work to occur while the outside brick cladding is applied. Finally, load-bearing masonry needs to be thicker to accommodate structural concerns. This thickness can become problematic for light entering a space in taller buildings, where window openings can get quite deep at the base.

Conclusion

Brick is one of the simplest building products, yet one of the most difficult materials to deal with. Its history spans to the earliest structures built by humans and it has remained essentially the same for millennia. The variations of application and form are nearly endless, yet it has definite rules for how it can be effectively used. The best way to learn to deal with masonry is from the masons on job sites. Along with carpenters, masons are some of the most skilled craftspeople at a construction site. The time it takes to develop skill as a mason is lengthy and they go through an apprenticeship process as part of their training. The craft of building with masonry requires not only knowledge of the material's capabilities but also the ways it can fail. This requires the experience of people like masons, who have seen it perform over time. The other issue with masonry is its fundamental change in the past century from a structural material to cladding. This makes the appropriate use of brick challenging at times. It is certainly a durable building skin, but how should it be represented as a skin rather than structure? These are the types of decisions designers must struggle with while determining what the appropriate expression of a material is.

'The brick is a different master. How ingenious: a small, handy, usable format for every purpose. What logic there is in the bonding. What spiritedness in the joints. What wealth there is in even the simplest wall surface. But what discipline this material demands' *Ludwig Mies van der Rohe.*

Glossary and formulas

Adobe	Unfired mud brick masonry units.
Brick	Clay fired modular masonry unit.
Clay Tile	Open cell clay fired modular masonry units.
CMU	Concrete Masonry Unit. A low water to cement ratio modular masonry unit.
Efflorescence	A leaching of salt minerals out of mortar, causing staining.
Glass Block	Glass masonry units, typically with open cell interior spaces for insulation.
Grout	High water small aggregate concrete mixture poured into block assemblies or used to finish gaps in tile.
Lintel	Beam that spans the top of a wall opening.
Mortar	Low water and no aggregate concrete mixture used to bind masonry units together.
Re-bar	Reinforcing steel bars used in hybrid concrete and masonry assemblies for tensile strength.
Stone Masonry	Stone units quarried to be used primarily as veneer or sitework masonry.
Wythe	A single row of bricks in a wall assembly.

Further reading

Pfiefer, G., Ramcke, R., Achtziger, J. and Zilch, K. (2001) *Masonry Construction Manual* (Basel, Switzerland/Boston, UK/Berlin, Germany: Birkhauser). pp. 9–29.

Ramsey, C.G. and Sleeper, H.R. (2000) Masonry (Chapter 4), *Architectural Graphic Standards*, 10th ed (New York, NY: John Wiley & Sons).

Neufert, E. and Neufert, P. (2000) *Architect's Data*, 3rd ed (London, UK: Blackwell Science). pp. 62–67, 171.

3.3 Materials: steel

Raw Material	Iron ore/carbon
	Alloys
	Strength/stiffness
	Fire/corrosion
History/Production	Discovery to artisan production
	Bessemer – technology
	Carnegie – mass production
	Modern steel mills
Steel Fabrication	Structural elements/shapes
	Structural framing types
	Joining methods
	Finishing

Introduction to steel

The discussion of steel in architecture is fundamentally linked to iron. This, simply put, is because steel *is* iron. Iron becomes steel when carbon is removed, making the material stronger. Humans have used iron for 5000 years, but its substantial use in architecture spans only about 200 years. The first architectural uses were as fasteners and reinforcement, with larger pieces becoming available as production skill increased.

The most significant leap in the use of iron occurs when it begins to become a structural material, replacing wood and masonry as a building's means of support. Like most other new materials, the expression of iron originally takes the form of the materials it replaced, with early detailing looking like masonry or wood elements – but eventually designers created forms that were unique to the material properties of iron and steel. Steel is the material we still use to create most of our large-scale structures, whether it is in the form of rolled structural members or reinforcement in concrete frames. Understanding the material properties of steel is essential to not only the structural design of buildings, but to a formal and ethical approach to making architecture.

Steel is extremely valuable as a building material because it is so strong in both tension and compression. It is much more difficult to fabricate than wood and architects must understand what shapes it comes in and how shops typically work with it in order to design with steel. The decisions of when to use steel, what type, shape, size, thickness, finish, and fabrication method are difficult and can greatly affect performance, cost, durability and esthetics. As with most materials there are complex issues with the appropriate or best use of the material and the rather severe environmental impact of a material that requires vast energy to produce.

Raw material

Common carbon steel is over 98% iron (Fe) with the remainder being primarily carbon (C) and trace elements of silica (Si), manganese (Mn), chromium (Cr), and nickel (Ni). The character of steel differs from iron in its increased strength yet still malleable quality.

The raw material used to form iron comes from mined rock referred to as iron ore. This high iron content rock is placed in a blast furnace for the process of *smelting*, which refines or purifies the iron ore into *pig iron*. As the iron ore reaches melting point and becomes fluid, lime is added to the mixture and combines with the rock portion of the ore forming *slag*. This slag is lighter than the iron, so the furnace is tapped from the bottom releasing the smelted or refined pig iron (Fig. 3.3.1).

Pig iron contains up to 10% impurities, much of it carbon. The pig iron is relatively easy to produce with sufficient heat and is the material we commonly

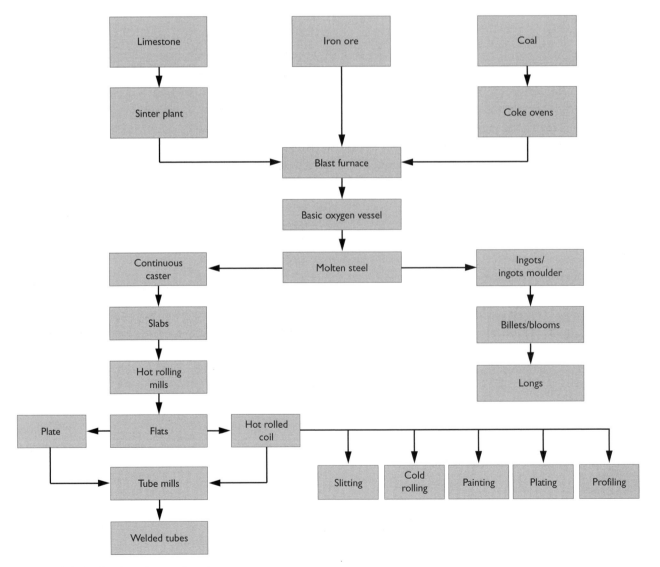

Figure 3.3.1. *Steel production flow chart.*

see as cast iron. Producing steel requires another refining process to remove carbon and other undesired elements, and until the mid-19th century was extremely difficult, time consuming and expensive to make.

Steel is classified into non-alloy, low-alloy, and alloy steel. Non-alloy steel is common carbon steel. This is the material used for most construction, as it is strong, malleable, structurally predictable, and relatively inexpensive (Fig. 3.3.2).

Alloy steel has other metals added into it in sufficient quantity to create unique properties of the resultant metal. The most common steel alloy used in construction is stainless steel, which has up to 20% chromium and nickel added to resist corrosion and improve appearance. All stainless steel is not alike, as there are variations of alloys that change depending on the intended use of the product. Keep in mind that under certain circumstances stainless steel does rust, particularly in seacoast or chemical environments. It is also much harder and more brittle than carbon steel, making it significantly more difficult to cut, drill, weld, and bend. Lastly, stainless steel is much more expensive than carbon steel.

Low-alloy steels are very similar to carbon steel, with small amounts of metals added to increase strength, hardness, and corrosion resistance. One of the most common in architecture is weathering or Cor-Ten steel, which is a corrosion resistant weathering steel. Cor-Ten is carbon steel alloyed with copper, which oxidizes and forms a patina on the surface of the metal – preventing further corrosion. The effect is self-renewing, as any new penetrations or abrasions of the surface will form a new patina and re-seal the material. The visual result is a rusted surface, so care needs to be taken on the

Metal	Yield strength (MPa)	Tensile strength (MPa)	Melting temperature (K)
Iron	50	200	1809
Mild steel	220	430	1765
High-carbon steel	350–1600	650–2000	1570
Low-alloy steel	290–1600	420–2000	1750
High-alloy steel	170–1600	460–2000	1680
Cast iron	50–400	10–800	1403

Metal	Typical uses
Low-carbon ('mild') steel	Low-stress uses, General constructional steel, suitable for welding.
Medium-carbon steel	Medium-stress uses: machinery parts – nuts and bolts, shafts, gears.
High-carbon steel	High-stress uses: springs, cutting tools, dies.
Low-alloy steel	High-stress uses: pressure vessels, aircraft parts.
High-alloy ('stainless') steel	High-temperature or anti-corrosion uses: chemical or steam plants.
Cast iron	Low-stress uses: cylinder blocks, drain pipes.

Figure 3.3.2. *Steel/iron types and properties.*

appropriate situations for use. It also tends to continually shed some of the rusting, causing staining of areas below the rain drip line of the metal.

Carbon steel is sometimes referred to as 'a soft steel' because it is a highly ductile material. It has a high *elastic limit*, meaning it will return to its original shape after deformation under a high load. After the elastic limit is reached it will not return to its original shape, but also does not immediately fail. These properties of reliable stiffness, high elastic limit and ductility allow for reliable calculations of required structural needs. This means that steel can be used economically in buildings, because you can precisely size structural members.

Corrosion occurs because steel is exposed to a thin layer of water and oxygen. Humidity levels below 60% do not promote rust, unless the steel is frequently exposed to water. Salt water and chemicals also create corrosion difficulties; therefore rural desert steel buildings are far less prone to rust than industrial seacoast steel buildings.

Fire affects steel in an entirely different way than it does wood. While steel is essentially fire resistant in terms of burning, it loses strength at temperatures that can easily be reached by building fires. At 480°C (900°F) steel loses 50% of its strength, therefore most structural steel needs to be protected by fire resistant insulation. Ultimately the goal of any building fire code is not to prevent damage, but to provide a reasonable amount of time for escape before failure occurs.

History/production

Iron has been found in human settlements 5000 years old. It is believed the first iron pieces came from meteorite fragments, which had smelted the material through high heat. The remains of Egyptian King Tutankhamen from 3000 BC had large amounts of gold fabricated into objects, but small amounts of iron sewn into the burial garments of the king. In the 13th century the first primitive steels were produced through very crude and imprecise methods. The first method is to heat the iron to over 1350°C (2500°F), which was very difficult to achieve. The other method is through pounding the carbon out of the iron while constantly heating the metal. This was the method used to make high quality armaments, with the blades of swords being heated and pounded to achieve higher strength from the iron.

In the 1700s England had perfected the basic smelting method for making iron and crude steel, but the raw material costs were astoundingly high. To run the kilns for production of 1 ton of iron required ten acres of forest. England was running out of trees and looked to the Colonies for production capacity.

During the first part of the industrial revolution iron was in huge demand, but not strong enough for many applications. The railroads in particular found iron rails too flexible for long-term heavy train loads, with many derailments caused by tracks twisting or bending loose. Steel at the time was seen as strong enough, but still an artisan produced material – extremely time consuming and in small-scale production. Henry Bessemer solved this problem by inventing the Bessemer Converter, which increased the temperature of kilns and removed carbon by introducing cold air into the furnace. The cold air combined with the carbon in iron, ignited and drove up the temperature, then blew free of the furnace removing almost all of the carbon content. Carbon could then be re-introduced in exacting amounts, which made quality control very high.

Andrew Carnegie perfected the mass production of steel at Bethlehem Steel by buying all of the components of steel manufacture – from mining ore to furnace fuel. He then proceeded to increase profits and become wealthy by controlling labor costs. This created some of the most contentious and disastrous early union labor disputes in the US.

The beginnings of steel buildings completely changed the form of modern cities. Between the ability to build much higher than was previously possible with masonry construction, and the invention of the elevator by the Otis Company, building heights soared. This was a building type that had no historical precedent, and the skyscraper became something uniquely identified with architecture in the US.

By the early 1950s 85% of all manufactured products contained some steel, 50 million steel food cans were used every single day. The raw energy and limited life cycle of these products in a time before any recycling is terrifying to imagine. Unfortunately we are no better off now, which is why the life cycle of all products – from pop cans to buildings is a cause for not just concern, but active resource management.

Modern steel mills are virtually completely automated compared to the mills of the first part of the century. This creates not only healthier work environments, but also greater efficiency. Nonetheless, steel production requires a vast amount of energy. This can be offset in life cycle costs due to the extreme strength benefit and durability of steel compared to other materials, but both need to be considered to make responsible buildings. Strength means less material can be used to achieve the same goal as a less impactful material, and durability means the material will not require recycling, or downcycling, for a long period of time.

Fabrication

Raw steel in the mill is poured into forms to create ingots. These ingots are then milled into rough shapes in preparation for rolling into specific shapes. Large-scale rolling operations often times take multiple passes to reach final dimensions. The rolling process also increases the strength of the material through compression and alignment of the metal's grain structure (Fig. 3.3.3). Rolled products are divided into two types – sections and plates. Sections or shapes are heat rolled while in a red-hot state. Plates can be hot rolled or cold rolled. Cold rolling allows for thinner and more even surfaces than hot rolling. The typical shapes available are: bars, plates, W shapes, M shapes, S

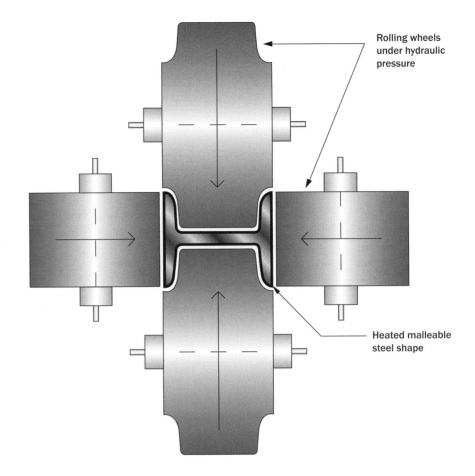

Rolling wheels
under hydraulic
pressure

Heated malleable
steel shape

Figure 3.3.3. *Modern rolling mill diagram.*

shapes, and HP shapes (which are all 'I' shaped sections), channels, angles, tees (which are normally cut from 'I' shapes), pipes, square tubes, and rectangular tubes (Fig. 3.3.4). Steel can also be cast into customized forms, but the expense is very high, casting is more frequently done from easier materials to work with such as iron or aluminum. When non-standard shapes are needed, built-up shapes are created, which are welded from plates or portions of standard sections.

The shapes of steel sections are standardized for both size and strength. Dimensions and properties of commercially available steel sections are available in the *Manual of Steel Construction*, published by the American Institute of Steel Construction and *The Steel Designer's* and *Steel Detailer's Manuals*, published by Blackwell Science in the UK. These books are indispensable for detailing projects as they cover not only the sizes of steel shapes, but also the methods for joining steel elements together.

Structural framing types in steel are more varied than in wood, but fall into several categories. The simplest framing type is post and beam, which is virtually the same as a wood system. Multi-bay truss systems function similarly, with the simple beams being replaced by open trusses. Multi-storey or high-rise construction works on a post and beam system, but lateral loads due to wind forces creates the need for horizontal bracing which can be higher than the gravity loads. Long span construction creates large areas of free space

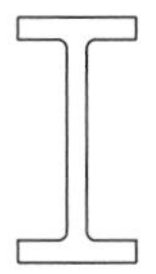

	W shape			WT shape
	The most common shape with greatest variety of size options. It has parallel flange surfaces, with typically unequal web and flange thicknesses.			Structural tee cut from W shapes.

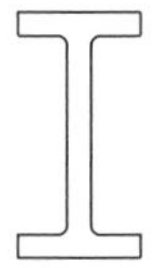

	HP shape			MT shape
	It has parallel flange surfaces with equal web and flange thicknesses.			Structural tee cut from M shapes.

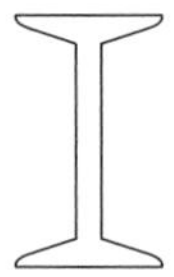

	S shape			ST shape
	American Standard beams have sloped flange surfaces of approximately 17% with both equal and unequal average web and flange thicknesses.			Structural tee cut from S shapes.

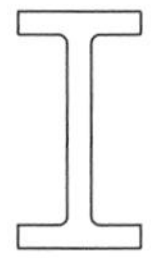

	M shape			Pipe
	Shapes that cannot be classified as W, HP, or S types. Limited shape sizes and production. Flange slopes vary.			Open tubing of various diameters and thicknesses. Sizes typically refer to inside diameter.

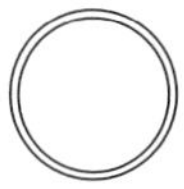

	C shape			Square and rectangular tubing
	American Standard channels have sloped flange surfaces equal to S shapes with both equal and unequal average web and flange thicknesses.			Various dimensions and thicknesses. Sizes typically refer to outside dimension of flat surfaces. Outside corner radius may be up to 3 times the wall thickness.

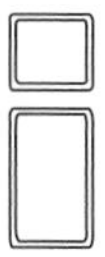

	MC shape			MC shape
	Shapes that cannot be classified as C type. Limited shape sizes and production. Flange slopes vary.			Shapes that cannot be classified as C type. Limited shape sizes and production. Flange slopes vary.

	L shape			Square and round bars
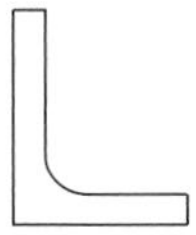	Angles with both equal and unequal leg lengths.			Solid sections of various weights and thicknesses.

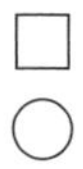

Figure 3.3.4. *Standard rolled structural steel shapes.*

uninterrupted by intervening walls or columns. Steel is particularly well suited to long span construction due to its high strength to weight ratio. Hybrids of all of these systems allow for virtually any building form to be created with steel. No other material offers steel's strength – combined with high performance in tension, bending and compression.

Steel can be joined in two ways – welding and bolting. This decision is based on a number of factors. The basic rule of thumb is, 'weld in the shop – bolt in the field'. Welding can be done much more effectively in a controlled environment, whereas bolting is easily accomplished on site. Esthetic and structural considerations can also dictate the method of assembly; however, most often it can be done either way. Welding has a number of choices in finished appearance. Often the structural requirements of a weld will not match the desire for a clean or consistent finish. Understanding basic weld marks on a

Weld symbols

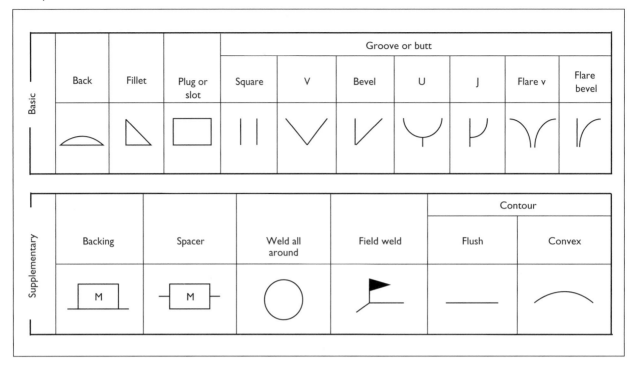

Standard location of elements of a welding symbol

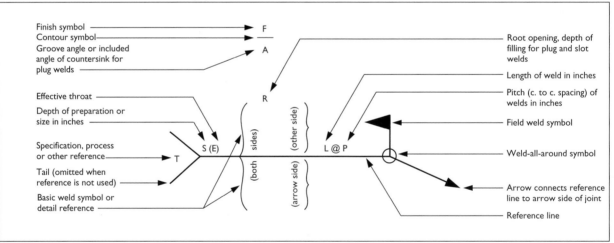

Figure 3.3.5. *Weld symbols.*

shop drawing can save the trouble of having pieces arrive on site in an unsatisfactory manner (Fig. 3.3.5). Basic weld marks to note are field assembly flags, flush or convex weld finishes, and continuous or stitch welds.

One of the factors to consider when designing large steel elements is the size of individual pieces; remember if it can't fit on a truck, it shouldn't be finished in the shop. Many times large portions of an assembly can be made in the shop, with the final form finished by a few simple bolts on site. Keep in mind when detailing bolting that room must be left for the fabrication to take place, meaning there needs to be space for a wrench to fit and for hands or equipment

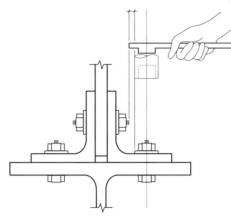

Typically leave at least 1/4 in. clearance for assembly tools, more if rotation or other operation is required

Figure 3.3.6. *Fabrication clearance.*

to operate tools (Fig. 3.3.6). Another factor to consider is the steel finish. Painted or galvanized pieces will have the finish destroyed by welding on site, and then the original finish will be 'matched' with a can of spray paint. This tends to be completely unsatisfactory in appearance. Think through the assembly and finishes carefully to decide how to join steel elements together.

All exterior carbon steel must be finished to avoid corrosion. This goes for most interior carbon steel as well, but not to the same degree. We have previously discussed stainless and Cor-Ten, which have corrosion resistance capabilities, but exterior carbon steel has particular problems with finishes. The primary problem is the durability of the finish; steel is very dimensionally active so it tends to move throughout the year. Most paint cannot stretch to accommodate this movement and eventually cracks – and then the degradation cycle begins. Water penetrating the cracks separates the paint quickly and in freeze-thaw environments it gets progressively worse. Hidden conditions also cause problems, such as the joint between two steel sections thermally moving, removing the protective coating, trapping the moisture, and rusting from within. Galvanizing can help protect steel, as the zinc forms a corrosion resistant coating. However there are two types of galvanizing: electroplating and hot-dip galvanizing. Electroplating is an electrically applied micro-thin coating that flakes off quickly. Hot-dip galvanizing requires the entire piece to be dipped in a zinc bath, making a much thicker, more reliable, and more expensive coating. There is no choice to be made here, long-term durability requires hot dipping. Electroplating is typically ineffective for exterior building components; you are better off using higher quality paint rather than spending resources on the electroplating. Keep in mind that galvanizing tanks are limited in size and will require thoughtful consideration of the size of individual steel pieces you use. Hot-dipped galvanizing can also warp thin steel plates due to the temperatures of the molten zinc. Breaking plates with a minimal cross or 'v' shaped seam can prevent warpage (Fig. 3.3.7). Like many situations in buildings, you must judge the maintenance capabilities of the owner and the life cycle of the project. For high abuse projects, like parking garages or coastal buildings, it is common to use hot-dip galvanized *and then* epoxy coated exterior steel pieces, because stainless steel is cost prohibitive.

Section and axonometric of flate plate
warpage after hot-dip galvanizing

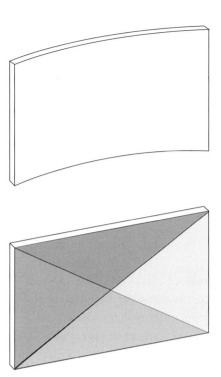

Section and axonometric of flat plate
with 'X' breaks or folds to prevent
warpage

Figure 3.3.7. *Break pattern to prevent warp.*

Frequently asked questions

'What is an Alloy metal?'
Metal alloys are basic materials, like steel, that have other elements added to modify the properties of the original material. This is normally done to either improve the strength or corrosion durability of the metal. Cor-Ten and stainless steel are examples of alloys designed to resist the natural oxidation of standard steel. Cor-Ten has copper added to allow for limited surface oxidation and stainless has chromium and nickel added to resist any oxidation. Chromium Molybdenum steel is an alloy designed to improve the strength of standard steel for particular high strength applications.

'If steel doesn't burn, why does it need to be covered with a fireproof coating?'
While steel is essentially fire resistant in terms of burning, it loses strength at temperatures that can easily be reached by building fires. At 480°C (900°F) steel loses 50% of its strength, therefore most structural steel is protected by fire resistant insulation that will keep the steel from heating up for long enough to evacuate building inhabitants.

Conclusion

The basic benefits of steel are super strength in tension and compression, precise shapes, shop, or field assembly, a limitless variety of formal possibilities, infinite finish options, and a straightforward honesty of structural expression. This is countered by high-embodied energy, difficulty of fabrication, corrosion problems, thermal movement, high thermal conductivity (condensation issues), and fire resistance difficulties. You must understand these factors to use steel effectively, but it is unavoidable in most construction as a structural, cladding, fastening, and finish material. Pay particular attention to steel assemblies that are exposed or vulnerable to corrosion. Rust is a constant issue with steel and must be handled carefully while detailing the material. Exposed fabrications also are an area where detailing skill is important, as there are many options for how to bolt or weld the material together. Steel is very strong and very heavy, so use it in areas where the need for strength is more critical than low weight and keep in mind that energy intensive materials should be used sparingly and appropriately.

Glossary and formulas

Alloy	Metal with added elements to modify its properties.
Cor-Ten Steel	A corrosion resistant weathering steel. Carbon steel is alloyed with copper, which oxidizes and forms a patina on the surface of the metal – preventing further corrosion.
Galvanizing	Zinc coating to prevent corrosion.
Elastic Limit	The point at which a material will no longer return to its original shape after being bent or deformed. Steel has a high elastic limit.
Electroplating	Is an electrically applied micro-thin coating. For steel this is usually a zinc coating. Electroplating is typically not durable enough for most exterior building applications.
Epoxy Coating	Is a process of durably bonding a colored powder to metal. The metal is heated and an electrically charged powder coats the steel, melting and bonding to the surface of the material.
Hot-Dip Galvanizing	Is a corrosion resistance that requires the entire piece to be dipped in a zinc bath, making a much thicker, more reliable, and more expensive coating.
Iron	Basic metal material created from iron ore.
Iron Ore	High iron content mined rock.
Pig Iron	Metal material that comes from the blast furnace after smelting, it contains up to 10% impurities, much of it carbon. This is the material we normally see manufactured into cast iron.
Slag	Lime that has combined with rock in iron processing to purify the metal mixture.
Smelting	Blast furnace process for purifying iron ore into pig iron.
Stainless Steel	An alloy of steel which has up to 20% chromium and nickel added to resist corrosion and improve appearance.
Steel	Iron modified to have a low carbon content, to increase strength.

Further reading

Eggen, A.P. and Sandaker, B.N. (1995) *Steel, Structure, and Architecture* (New York, NY: Watson Guptil Publications). pp. 10–28.

Davison, B. and Owens, G. (2003) *Steel Designer's Manual* (Oxford, UK: Blackwell Science).

Hayward, A., Weare, F. and Oakhill, A. (2002) *Steel Detailers' Manual* (Oxford, UK: Blackwell Science).

Manual of Steel Construction: Allowable Stress Design (Chicago, IL: American Institute of Steel Construction, 1994).

3.4 Materials: glass

Glass Basics	Glass composition
	Glass fabrication
	Transparency
History	The discovery of glass
	Technological developments
Properties/Technology	Strength – heat/laminations
	Color
	Thermal transmission
	Light transmission/coatings
Applications	Windows
	Storefronts
	Curtain walls
	Skylights
	Roofs/canopies
	Other structures

Introduction to glass

Glass is a remarkable material; it is transparent, rock hard, and chemically inert enough to resist the most corrosive acids. Humans first discovered how to make glass about 4000 years ago from the earth's most abundant raw material, sand. Through a lengthy process of trial, error, and perseverance it became possible to make objects of what is essentially transparent rock. Its use was restricted to jewelry and pots until some 2000 years later, when the technology emerged to create flat glass for windows. This solved the basic conundrum of the need for shelter as protection and the need for light as illumination. Glass provided the perfect solution as a strong, durable, and cheap building material.

To be able to successfully use any material you need to understand its properties. Glass has two characteristics, beyond its transparency, that make it particularly useful in architecture. The first is that it resists weathering extremely well; it doesn't scratch haze or degrade under ultraviolet (UV) radiation. The second is its radiation transmission; air temperature moves slowly through glass while solar radiation moves quickly. This offers the designer many possibilities for working with the material. As the technology of glass production improves, we have been able to manipulate both its light transmission quality and its thermally resistive properties. By combining glass with other materials the possibilities for its use have continually increased. The glass we typically use now in buildings is one component of a composite material designed to solve multiple issues, while still retaining the fundamental material properties of simple glass.

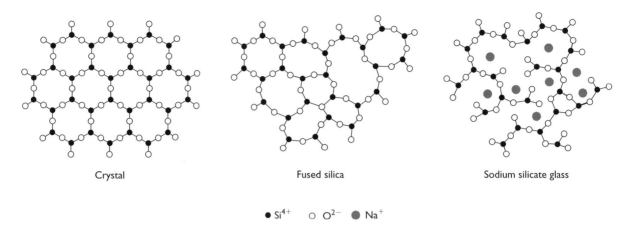

Crystal   Fused silica   Sodium silicate glass

● Si^{4+} ○ O^{2-} ● Na^{+}

Figure 3.4.1. *Glass molecular crystalline structure.*

Glass basics

Glass is most commonly referred to as a 'super-cooled liquid', meaning it is molecularly amorphous, like a liquid, but is in a solid state. The secret to glass transparency is in this molecularly amorphous composition. Most materials form crystalline microstructures between heating and cooling. These crystals are what make materials opaque. Silicon is a material that does not automatically form dense microcrystalline structures (Fig. 3.4.1). Fortunately, silicon in oxide form is silica, which is most commonly referred to as ordinary sand. Sand is not pure in its composition, but some of the other oxides commonly found mixed with the silica make the production of glass easier.

The basic means of producing glass involves melting the silica, then cooling it in very controlled ways. Certain temperature ranges favor the formation of crystals, so the glass is brought through those temperatures quickly and slowed through the rest of the process. Other oxides besides silica are added to the mixture to lower the melting temperature; pure silica melts at over 1700°C. Iron oxide, normally found in sand, reduces this temperature because it absorbs heat more easily. The addition of other materials also assists in melting temperatures, workability, reduced crystal formation, durability, and color. The reason most glass is green is due to the iron oxide in the sand, removing it would be far too expensive so it has become a natural part of the material. The most common mixture of materials is referred to as soda-lime glass, and has been produced with minor variations since the mixture was developed in ancient Rome. The soda reduces the melting temperature to below 800°C and the lime vastly increases durability.

The process of glass making involves more than just chemical properties. The skill of the glassmaker must be precise and originally required both technical prowess and bravery. Both the temperatures and effects of breaking the material proved extremely dangerous at times. Lessons such as never inhaling air from the blowing tube have rarely been forgotten by the few survivors. The three parts of the glass making process are melting, forming, and controlled

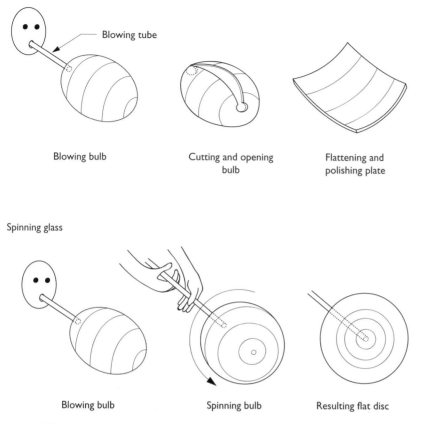

Cylinder forming glass

Blowing tube

Blowing bulb

Cutting and opening
bulb

Flattening and
polishing plate

Spinning glass

Blowing bulb

Spinning bulb

Resulting flat disc

Figure 3.4.2. *Forming and spinning glass.*

cooling. Melting occurs at super high temperatures, where the various components are mixed. Forming takes place as temperatures fall into the zone where glass is hot enough to work and still viscous. The final cooling process is typically referred to as 'annealing', or controlled heating and cooling to achieve a solid state without crystal formation.

For 1000 years, up until about 100 years ago, glass was formed for windows in two primary ways. The first is by 'crowning' or blowing a cylinder of glass, cutting it down the side and flattening it. The second way is called 'spinning', which is done by blowing a bulb and spinning the glass until it forms a disk (Fig. 3.4.2). In the 1700s early plate casting took place, but the surface quality was very uneven. In the late 1800s the first presses were developed to make glass bricks and shortly after – drawing and rolling were developed. All of these methods create difficulties with the quality of the surface of the glass. Anything the molten glass touches creates unevenness and imperfections – which required additional grinding and polishing to remove. In the 1950s 'float glass' was developed by Pilkington, which forms the plate by pouring the glass onto molten tin. The tin melts at a lower temperature than the glass and has a higher density; this makes both sides of the glass pane perfectly flat (Fig. 3.4.3). Most of the glass now produced for building components is created this way. During the 1970s tinting was added to glass in an attempt to improve performance, but the dark glass reduced visible

The float process

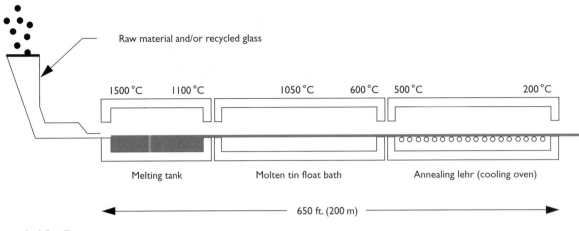

Raw material and/or recycled glass

1500 °C   1100 °C   1050 °C   600 °C   500 °C   200 °C

Melting tank   Molten tin float bath   Annealing lehr (cooling oven)

650 ft. (200 m)

Figure 3.4.3. *Float process.*

light too much and didn't reduce solar gains enough. The newest technologies are now involved with laminating and suspending thin films into the glass assemblies to improve performance.

History

The discovery of glass took place roughly 4000 years ago, the first examples being found in the eastern Mediterranean. It was most likely an accident; silica from pottery kilns melting and mixing with ash from the hearth and forming a crystallized glass. By 3500 years ago, pressed and molded glass vessels were being made in Egypt. Two thousand years ago glass blowing was discovered, which made possible thin transparent sheets durable enough for windows. The Mediterranean climate, however, didn't need glazing to control the interior environment. Vitruvius speaks at length about building materials in his *Ten Books on Architecture*, but glass is absent from the discussion. Its use was more novelty than function; cold weather was not severe and was mitigated by fireplaces, which benefited from openings to clear the smoke. The northward push of the Roman Empire into temperate climate zones sees the first substantial use of glass in architecture, and the development of glass production as an industry in Venice, the Middle East, and Germany.

The most impressive early versions of architectural glass were created during the Gothic age by the primary agency for construction in northern Europe – the Church. Romanesque churches, which preceded the Gothic, had small openings made necessary by the heavy construction and frequent need for defense. Gothic churches shifted to a search for lighter structures and more illumination. The lighter structural frames increased the need for larger panes of glass, and the technology was pushed to meet the demands. Most of the cathedral glass is 'stained glass' – or smaller colored pieces of glass set into larger frames with lead strips connecting them. The glass was tinted with

Figure 3.4.4. *Medieval stained glass window.*

metal oxides during melting and painted with a black pigment to produce the detailed imagery (Fig. 3.4.4).

A shift in patronage during the 16th century made large glass panes more typical in residences of the wealthy ruling class, and during the 17th century the 'conservatory' or greenhouse became an important building type (Fig. 3.4.5). This movement from religious structure to secular and then to public/farm building moved the technology of glass continually forward, eventually making it reasonable and affordable for most structures. The conservatory also created much of the inspiration for the new age of modern architecture, with lightweight iron structures and entirely glass skins. The early modernists envisioned the future world of buildings as transparent, light filled boxes. As Paul Scheerbart writes in 1914 in his influential work, *Glasarchitektur*:

' … we live for the most part in closed rooms. These form the environment from which our culture grows. Our culture is to a certain extent the product

Figure 3.4.5. *Glass Conservatory. Palm House, Kew Gardens, London, 1848.*

of our architecture. If we want our culture to rise to a higher level, we are obliged, for better or worse, to change our architecture. And this only becomes possible if we take away the closed character from the rooms in which we live. We can only do that by introducing glass architecture, which lets in the light of the sun, the moon, and the stars, not merely through a few windows, but through every possible wall, which will be made entirely of glass – of colored glass. The new environment, which we thus create, must bring us a new culture.'

The force that has driven much of modern architecture comes from technology and its relationship to culture. Two of the most influential technological advancements have been lightweight metal frame structure and large-scale glass fabrication.

Glass tempering process

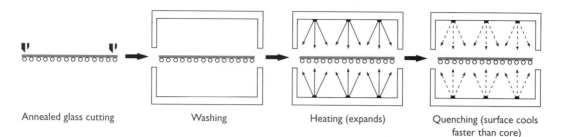

Annealed glass cutting   Washing   Heating (expands)   Quenching (surface cools
                                                                                faster than core)

Figure 3.4.6. *Glass tempering process.*

Properties/technology

The glass we use today in buildings has been highly refined to achieve a few main goals; strength, safety, clarity, size, high light transmission, and low thermal transmission. We are also developing technologies that can embed electronic technologies into glass, making them act intelligently.

Strength and safety are related properties, because the reason for strength is in part due to basic durability and also to concerns about injury if glass breaks. While glass is hard, it is also brittle and tends to fail suddenly. The results of a break, with standard annealed float glass, are sharp, heavy shards of broken material – not what you want to put your hand through or worse, have fall from stories above onto the street below. The property of strength is dealt with in a number of ways: heat-treating, wire embedding, and laminating.

Heat-treating is accomplished through heating and quenching annealed glass (Fig. 3.4.6). This rapid cooling of the surface of the glass hardens it, while the interior is still fluid. During the cooling of the interior it shrinks, putting the surface into compression. The surface compression and interior tension makes the glass stronger and alters its breaking characteristics. Full heat-treating is referred to as 'tempering' and causes the glass to break into small pieces with no sharp edges. While this glass is much stronger than standard annealed. it is vulnerable to small cracks or chips that can explode the entire pane. The side and rear windows in cars are made of this type of material, along with the glass in most building's doors and some windows.

Wire embedded or 'wire glass' is made by pressing wire mesh into the glass during forming. It holds the glass together when broken, creating greater fire resistance, security, and safety. It allowed for glass to be used in some situations where transparency was previously not possible. Wire glass use is frequently discouraged as more advanced laminations replace it and due to safety problems with jagged metal edges protruding from broken panes.

Laminated glass is made by sandwiching a plastic sheet between glass layers (Fig. 3.4.7). This plastic material is typically polyvinyl butyral (PVB), pressed and

Laminated glass

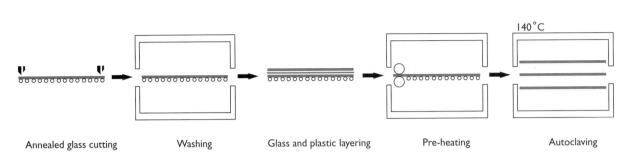

| Annealed glass cutting | Washing | Glass and plastic layering | Pre-heating | Autoclaving |

Figure 3.4.7. *Glass laminating process.*

autoclaved for about 4 h at 140°C at 827 kPa (120 psi). Laminated glass combines the hard, durable, but brittle glass with the elastic PVB. Laminated glass that breaks will adhere to the PVB, making it safer. Automobile front windows are made this way, where breaking tempered glass at high speed would still be dangerous. It also dampens sound transmission and can resist attack and explosion, bullet proof glass is laminated with high strength plastics. Another appealing aspect of laminated glass is that it can be cut after manufacture; tempered glass cannot be cut after fabrication. In more extreme situations tempered glass can be laminated to increase safety.

Clarity has to do with both the finish and color of the glass. The development of float glass has created perfectly flat and consistent surfaces. This, combined with precision annealing and oxide admixtures, inhibits any visible crystalline formations, making common annealed float glass virtually invisible when clean. Color is more difficult to control, as naturally occurring iron oxides in sand give the glass a green tint. While some other oxides reduce the green tint, the complete removal requires separation of the iron from the silica sand. This is a difficult process and raises the temperature at which the silica melts, making the 'water white' glasses very expensive. Another strategy used to make glass less green is by making it stronger, and therefore thinner, so the tint is less dense. This system of thinner stronger glass is seen in cavity glazing, commonly referred to as double-glazing or 'thermopane'; however, the primary purpose of this type of glass is for thermal resistance. At times clarity is not the desired goal, and glass surfaces are intentionally rolled with patterns to create different effects.

Size is dependent on the manufacturing process. Float glass production is very expensive and requires equipment to maintain pools of molten tin. The size of the pool determines the maximum size of the glass. The typical sizes are based on width, as production runs are continuous and can create virtually any length. The problem becomes how big an individual piece can get and still be safely moved. Glass is heavy, difficult to lift, and if the aspect ratio becomes more than about 4 to 1 it becomes much more fragile. Most common float beds are about 3.5 m (11.5 ft) wide, because glass panes much wider are difficult to move and not in high demand. Where double-glazing is used there is also the size limitations of the machinery that vacuum seals and binds the edges

Insulated glass process

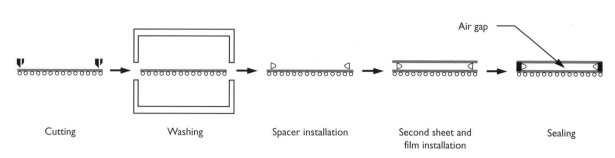

| Cutting | Washing | Spacer installation | Second sheet and film installation | Sealing |

Figure 3.4.8. *Insulated glass process.*

of the glass. Maximum sizes of double-glazing units are typically about 3 m by 3.6 m (10 ft by 12 ft).

High light transmission and low thermal transmission are also related properties. Any clear glass provides high light transmission; the problem is how to limit solar radiation gain and UV color degradation while bringing in daylight. This was originally done with curtains and shades, but these limited view and provided a fire hazard in commercial applications. Dark tinted and reflective glass was the next solution, but proved to limit light too much and produced the undesirable 'fishbowl effect' of not being able to see out at night while those outside could see in. The most effective solution has been through the use of multiple glazing (Fig. 3.4.8). By trapping dry air between panes of glass, the thermal transmission of heat and cold can be significantly reduced. To function properly the air must be dry, clean, and still – to act as an insulator and not cloud the interior surface of the glass. This is achieved by introducing a molecular sieve or desiccant material into the glass cavity to promote dryness. The glass is vacuum-sealed and often higher performance gases, such as argon, replace the air left in the cavity. Into this cavity can also be introduced coated films that reduce and reflect heat transmission and UV rays. This film can be placed onto the inside surfaces of the glass or suspended in the middle of the panes – further reducing air movement. The films are completely invisible, and the total performance of sophisticated multiple glazed systems are similar to the thermal transmittance (*U*-value) of a cavity brick wall.

Smart walls use the basic technology of lamination and expand upon the films used inside the glass to create walls that can transform based on environmental changes and even generate energy. In the most basic form the interior film can be tinted, colored, or patterned to create different qualities of light transmission. The film can also be charged electrically, creating an electrochromic material that changes from transparent to opaque when a charge is applied. The field of laminated materials is where most of the newest technology is being applied. Thin film photovoltaics can generate energy by sandwiching photoelectric generator cells into glass panels, turning unwanted heat gain into power. Other electrical thin films can make skins that have 'intelligent' behavior, sensing the exterior and interior environment and making changes to the window opacity and building's environmental systems to maintain comfort. Glass is also

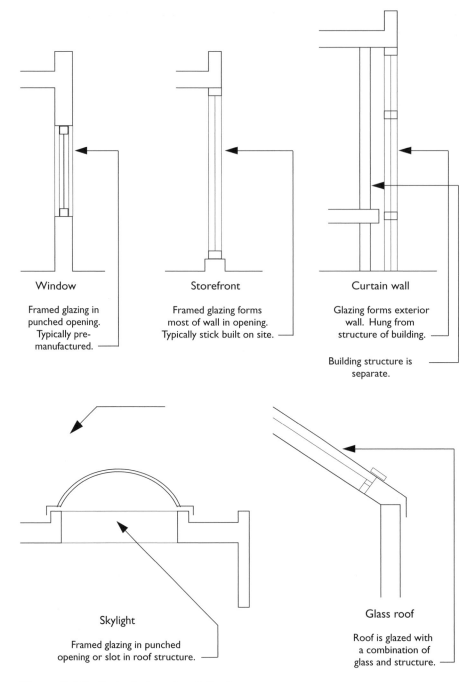

Figure 3.4.9. *Basic glazing type applications.*

becoming part of information transfer, as liquid crystal and heads-up displays can be integrated directly into the skin of a building. The need for this technology has not yet been demonstrated to the degree that makes it cost effective, but we will continually see developments in this area of glass production.

Applications

Windows are the most commonly thought of glass application (Fig. 3.4.9). This is simply a glass pane held into a frame that is supported by the wall structure. All horizontal building glass can be considered windows, but architects usually refer to windows as punched openings in a solid wall plane. This separates them from storefront and curtain wall applications.

Storefronts are multiple window units forming a large or total portion of the wall. They are pieced together in a pre-manufactured frame that supports its own load, but is still framed into a wall structure. Storefront frames are lightweight and usually span no more than two stories, so wind load requirements are low.

Curtain walls are entire walls made of glass panes, or a combination of glass and other materials in a frame or frameless system of support. The curtain wall acts independently from the structure of the building essentially acting as a cladding clipped onto the surface of the building. Most modern high-rise buildings are of this type, as the structural system has been separated from the exterior wall.

Skylights are basically windows that face the sky. They are punched or linear strips of glazing in an otherwise solid roof structure. The demands of weather on skylights can be significantly higher than on windows, and the effects of water and minerals standing on glass can etch or stain it permanently.

Glass roofs make the entire top surface glazed with a combination of structure and glass. This is commonly seen in greenhouses and atriums, but elsewhere it is difficult to mitigate the direct solar radiation enough for everyday use. This type of system is also prone to leaking as it thermally moves in response to variations in temperature from above and below. Lastly, horizontal glass has a tendency to always be dirty and very difficult to clean.

Other structures can be made from glass for architectural applications. We have focused on glass as an exterior cladding material, but its use in other ways is nearly limitless. Glass is commonly used in furniture, as guardrails, partitions, doors, floors, stairs, in tiles, sinks, mirrors, and other places too numerous to mention. It can be made into almost any shape, color, opacity, and has structural capabilities when used properly. It is one of the most versatile materials we use, and the technology of its fabrication is continually expanding.

Frequently asked questions

'Why is glass clear and green?'
The secret to glass transparency is in its molecularly amorphous composition. While most materials form crystalline structures, the basic building material of glass, silica, does not form crystalline structures when heated and cooled in a precise fashion. The green color comes from iron oxides that occur naturally in the silica sand that is melted to form glass.

'What is safety glass?'
Safety glass refers to glass that has been modified by one of two ways to protect from injuring people if it breaks. One type of safety glass is tempered, a

process of heat strengthening that causes the surface of the glass to be in tension. When broken tempered glass shatters into small rounded pieces, rather than the larger sharp plates that standard annealed glass can become. The other method for making safety glass is laminating, which adheres a layer of plastic in-between sheets of glass. When broken, the plastic clings to the glass preventing it from flying free.

Conclusion

Glass is as unavoidable as wood in architecture, and possibly more so as no reasonable alternatives to architectural glass are available. It is a very straightforward material that is being constantly modified and improved with new technology. The majority of glass production causes relatively minimal environmental impact compared to many other building materials, and it has no rivals in performance. Effectively using both active and passive glass technology is essential to sustainable design, and a thorough knowledge of applications and assembly is a necessity for every building designer.

Glossary and formulas

Crowning Glass	Traditional method for making windows by blowing a cylinder and cutting it open to form a flat plate.
Curtain Wall	Entire walls made of glass panes, or a combination of glass and other materials in a frame or frameless system of support.
Double-Glazing or 'Thermopane'	Glass outer layers with a vacuum-sealed inner air gap for thermal resistance.
Float Glass	Modern method for forming flat glass sheets by cooling them on a bed of molten tin.
Glass	A molecularly amorphous material made from melting and cooling silica sand.
Heat-Treating	A method for strengthening accomplished through heating and quenching annealed glass.
Laminated Glass	A type of pane made by sandwiching a plastic sheet between glass layers.
Photovoltaic Glass	A method for generating solar energy by laminating thin film photoelectric generator cells into glass panels.
PVB	Polyvinyl Butyral, a plastic material typically used as the inner layer in laminated glass.
Smart Walls	Use the basic technology of lamination and expand upon the films used inside the glass to create walls that can transform based on environmental changes and even generate energy.
Spinning Glass	Traditional method for making windows by blowing a cylinder and spinning it until it flattens into a thin plate.
Storefront	Multiple stick-built window units forming a large or total portion of the wall.

Further reading

Wiggington, M. (1996) *Glass in Architecture* (London: Phaidon).

Ramsey, C.G. and Sleeper, H.R. (2000) *Architectural Graphic Standards*, 10th ed (New York, NY: John Wiley & Sons). pp. 512–514.

Neufert, E. and Neufert, P. (2000) *Architect's Data*, 3rd ed (London, UK: Blackwell Science). pp. 62–67, 171.

3.5   Materials: concrete

Raw Material	Cement and portland cement
	Aggregate
	Water
	Hydration
	Cement production
	Concrete production
History	Discovery
	Modern rediscovery
Concrete Construction	Reinforced concrete
	Pre-Cast vs. Cast-in-Place
	Pre-Stressed
	Post-Tensioned
	Control joints
	Cold joints
	Formwork
	Placement
	Slump/strength
	Colors

Introduction to concrete

Concrete is a very hard, durable, monolithic building material defined as a mixture of cement, aggregate, and water. It is common to hear the terms cement and concrete used interchangeably; however, cement is just the powder that binds the aggregate together when mixed with water to form concrete. Concrete is a 'plastic' material, as it can be molded into almost any shape – because it starts as a liquid and hardens into solid form. It is remarkably strong in compression and when combined with the tensile properties of steel provides the most versatile of structural building materials. This is a material that we consider commonplace, yet the fact that it is possible to pour a liquid material that dries in hours to the consistency of stone is amazing to consider.

Concrete is relatively inexpensive as a base material, but the difficulty of working with it can make the labor costs high. It is also a very energy intensive material to create, requiring over 80 separate and continuous operations for production. In 1990 cement production was the sixth most energy intensive industry in the US, necessitating 18,700,000 ton of coal burning and 1,398,400,000 kW (worth US$700,000,000/400,000,000 GBP) of power usage.

Raw material

While cement is the key component of concrete it makes up only about 11% of the total mix. The remainder of the mixture is (approximately) 16% water,

6% air, 26% sand (fine aggregate), and 41% gravel or crushed stone (course aggregate). This is the mixture that arrives on a construction site inside the cement mixing truck.

The type of cement that is used in modern construction is called Portland Cement. Portland Cement binds the other materials in concrete together through the process of hydration. Concrete hydration is a chemical reaction that occurs when the cement powder is mixed with water, resulting in heat and a crystallized bond forming between the wet cement and the aggregate. This bond becomes stronger as the water evaporates from the mixture, and concrete never loses this strength, in fact it continues to become stronger over time.

Portland Cement is made by combining ground limestone and shale/clay in a furnace heated to over 1480°C (2700°F). The resulting material is called clinker, which is pulverized and mixed with powdered gypsum to form Portland cement (Fig. 3.5.1). The basic chemical components of Portland Cement are Calcium (Ca), Silicon (Si), Aluminum (Al), and Iron (Fe). The first rotary kilns allowed for economical cement production starting in 1895, with the first large US kilns constructed in 1895. Thomas Edison is credited with developing the first long kilns, which doubled production by lengthening the kiln from 24 m (80 ft.) to 46 m (150 ft.). The kilns are long tubes that continuously rotate to mix and process the raw materials into clinker. This is a massive machine, a 46–185 m (150–600 ft.) long, 3.6 m (12 ft.) diameter, 3500°C (6300°F) furnace that is constantly spinning – an impressive engineering feat (Fig. 3.5.2).

Cement powder is extremely fine; one pound contains approximately 150 billion grains. This is mixed with the aggregate, which can be fine sand or larger pieces of stone. The majority of concrete is this rock, which provides the strength of the material. The size of the aggregate is dependent on the application – small jobs can use sand only, but any substantial structure will use larger pieces of stone. The water is added to the mixture shortly before placement, because the

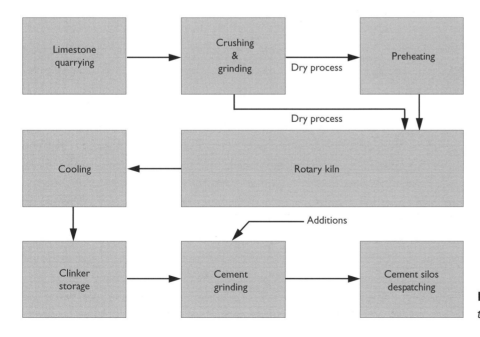

Figure 3.5.1. *Cement production process.*

Figure 3.5.2. *Rotary cement kiln.*

hydration begins immediately. The water needs to be clean for the hydration to take place properly; contaminated water can inhibit or prevent the chemical reaction from taking place. The rule with water is that it needs to be of potable (or drinking) quality. The quality of the stone aggregate also matters, as the aggregate color affects the concrete color – after hydration occurs and the water evaporates nearly 80% of concrete is the aggregate. Aggregate should not contain high contents of iron or other corrosive metals, because they will oxidize and eventually stain the surface. This mixture comes to the site from the concrete plant in trucks that rotate the mixture to keep it consistent and delay hydration, but if the truck is not emptied within a certain amount of time (typically about 90 min or 300 revolutions of the truck cylinder) the driver is forced to dump the mix before it hardens in the cylinder. Most plants have a dump area that collect unused concrete that is brought back, and while this averages about 2–3%; it begins to build up over long periods of time and is wasted material.

Figure 3.5.3. *Pantheon dome, 118–126, Rome, Italy. The coffered concrete dome spans 40 m.*

Timing and quantity orders from the plant to large job sites are an exacting science that requires skill by the job supervisor.

History

The basic form of cement has been around since the creation of the planet as a naturally occurring compound of limestone and shale; however its development as a building material has been by chance at first and later by developing ways to manufacture cement as a reliable and predictable building material. The Egyptians used gypsum mortars from 3000 BC and the Greeks used lime mortars before the Romans developed concrete as an independent construction material. Romans used naturally occurring cement powder from Pozzuoli, Italy near Mt. Vesuvius to build parts of many ancient buildings from concrete, the most remarkable example being the 40 m dome of the Pantheon (Fig. 3.5.3). Pliny

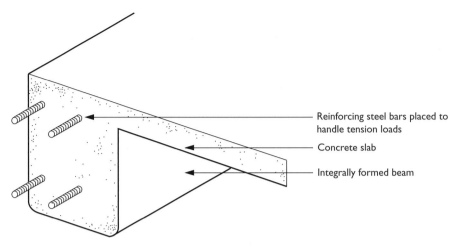

Reinforcing steel bars placed to handle tension loads

Concrete slab

Integrally formed beam

Typical assembly with reinforcing steel concrete

Figure 3.5.4. *Typical assembly with reinforced steel in concrete beam.*

reported a common mortar mixture of one part lime to four parts sand, while Vitruvius reported two parts pozzolana to one part lime.

During the Middle Ages concrete technology had deteriorated, but in the 1700s the first hydraulic cements were developed for the use of stucco finishes. In 1824 a bricklayer named Joseph Aspdin invented Portland Cement by burning ground chalk with clay in a kiln until CO_2 was removed. The resulting material was finely ground and named after the stones it resembled quarried on the isle of Portland, England.

Construction

Concrete has advantages over many other construction materials because it can single handedly solve the primary problems of structure; it works well in compression, bonds with steel to handle tension, can be formed into almost any shape with many surface textures and finishes, and provides fireproof construction.

The development of reinforced concrete is tied to the production of steel. Concrete is inherently strong in compression, but lacks strength in tension. Combining reinforcing steel (re-bar) with concrete works effectively because the cement bonds with the steel to form a monolithic material; the concrete also acts as a fireproofing insulator for the steel (Fig. 3.5.4). Reinforced concrete can be made into post and beam systems as well as shell structures; the durability of concrete allows it to act as both structure and enclosure for a building. The most common limitation on this type of structure (beyond the expense) is the inadequate insulation qualities of solid reinforced concrete – it transmits thermal loads enough to form condensation on the interior surface in extreme conditions. Particular care needs to be taken in situations where this can occur, often the steel re-bar is epoxy coated and the surface of the concrete is sealed to prevent corrosion from happening due to water penetration or condensation.

Concrete for construction can be handled in two common ways, Pre-Cast and Cast in Place. Pre-Cast concrete is made in a factory under carefully controlled conditions. Because both the strength and finish of concrete is partly

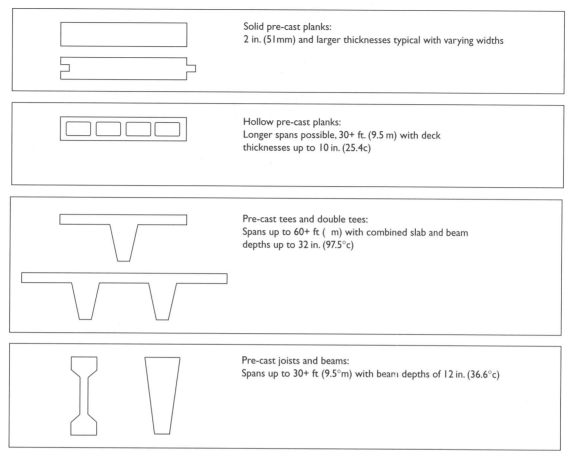

Solid pre-cast planks:
2 in. (51mm) and larger thicknesses typical with varying widths

Hollow pre-cast planks:
Longer spans possible, 30+ ft. (9.5 m) with deck
thicknesses up to 10 in. (25.4c)

Pre-cast tees and double tees:
Spans up to 60+ ft (m) with combined slab and beam
depths up to 32 in. (97.5°c)

Pre-cast joists and beams:
Spans up to 30+ ft (9.5°m) with beam depths of 12 in. (36.6°c)

Figure 3.5.5. *Standard pre-cast deck and beam shapes.*

dependent on the temperature of hydration, field cast concrete can be unpredictable and uneven. Pre-Cast concrete solves many of these problems, because the water to cement ratio is exacting and the temperature of hydration is constant. Factory casting also allows for precise corners, accurate opening locations, and predictable cast-in plates or other desired elements cast into the concrete (Fig. 3.5.5) – as there is no problem of shifting field formwork. Pre-Cast structures can also be constructed at any time of the year and in any weather, whereas rain and extreme cold can delay field cast construction. Lastly, if there is a problem you can see it before construction occurs – often it is impossible to correct a problem once concrete has been Cast in Place. The liability of Pre-Cast is the need to assemble the components on site, which can lose the elegant quality of monolithic construction. The joints are often joined by welding together steel plates cast into the concrete at the joint location, making for cumbersome connection points. This is only an issue in conditions where the structure can be seen, if it is hidden behind cladding there is no problem – however the finish improvement no longer matters if the concrete is hidden. Pier Luigi Nervi was able to consider pre-cast concrete frames in elegant and impressive structures that integrated cast-in-place elements and the necessary joints in the structure (Fig. 3.5.6).

Cast-in-Place construction occurs on site with the concrete poured into forms. This type of construction requires a larger safety factor than Pre-Cast due to the

Figure 3.5.6. *Pre-cast airplane hanger structure, 1940s, Pier Luigi Nervi. Italy.*

aforementioned unpredictability of site conditions. The skill of the contractor along with good detailing and specifying are critical if the concrete is intended to be exposed. While it is possible to reject a concrete pour – it almost never happens unless there is a serious structural problem. Removing concrete pours is very difficult and delays the entire job schedule – both contractors and owners will expect the designer to figure out a way to 'deal' with finish or opening placement problems that occur during casting. In many cases the formwork for one floor has not come off before the next is being cast – meaning two floors would need to be taken down in order to fix a problem. Cast-in-Place concrete has a rougher quality then Pre-Cast which is part of the esthetic, this is generally presented to a client in the same fashion as a blue jeans disclaimer, 'some imperfections and variations in the material are to be expected and give it a unique and desirable quality'. Much of the unique quality of Cast-in-Place structures also comes from the completely monolithic characteristics of the material; it can flow together without interruption at assembly joints. This creates entirely new formal possibilities not available in any other material, as seen in the work of designers like Eero Saarinen and Felix Candela (Fig. 3.5.7).

The method of reinforcement in the concrete has a big effect on its structural performance. While most reinforcement is simply placed into the concrete form before casting, the steel can be manipulated in two common ways to improve performance. Pre-Stressed concrete works by stretching the steel reinforcement and holding it in tension while the concrete is poured. Once the concrete begins to dry the steel is released, which pulls the concrete into tension. This both strengthens the concrete element and limits cracking. This method is most commonly used in Pre-Casting plants, where proper quality control can be maintained (Fig. 3.5.8). Post-Tensioned concrete works in a similar fashion, however, the tension is added by stretching reinforcing cable

Figure 3.5.7. *Thin shell concrete structure, restaurant, Xochimilco, 1958.*

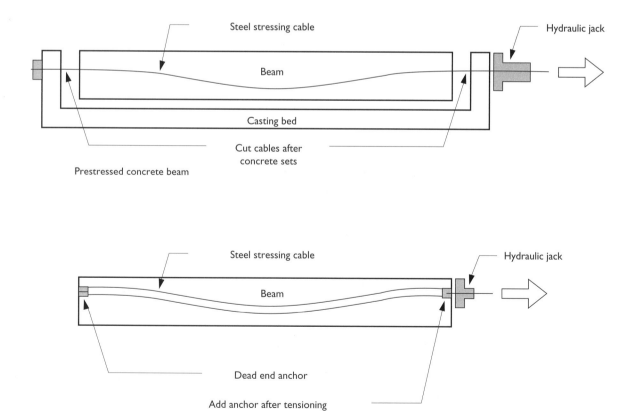

Figure 3.5.8. *Pre- and post-tensioned beam diagrams.*

Control joints

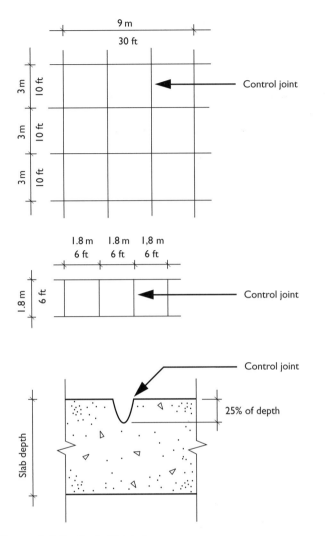

Control joint

Typical concrete slab with control joints at approximately 3 m (10 ft) on center. Keep aspect ratios close to equal in order to minimize cracking outside of joints.

Control joint

Typical 1.8 m (6 ft) wide sidewalk uses 1.8 m (6 ft) control joints to maintain 1:1 aspect ratio.

Control joint

25% of depth

Control joints must be 25% of slab depth to control cracking. Joints can be grooved with a tool before hydration or saw cut after.

Figure 3.5.9. *Control joint diagrams.*

through the concrete after it has begun to set. This is the method used in most Cast-in-Place situations, large hydraulic jacks pull the cable to 9000 kg (20,000 lb) plus tension before wedges are placed to hold the cable taught and the ends of the cable are torched off. Both methods place the reinforcing in pre-determined curves that pull the bottom of the slab in the center and the tops on the ends, following the lines of force placed on the structural element. Tensioning methods are used almost exclusively for beams and slabs, shapes that work mainly in tension rather than compression. Tensioning would have less effect on columns or other compressive structural elements.

Remember that all concrete cracks. Concrete normally hydrates and dries unequally; creating uneven surface tensions, which along with natural thermal and foundation movements in buildings, works against concrete's lack of strength in tension. Steel reinforcement assists in limiting the cracking, but cannot fully prevent it. The idea is to keep the cracks from pulling the concrete apart (which is handled by reinforcement) and to maintain an acceptable esthetic finish. The

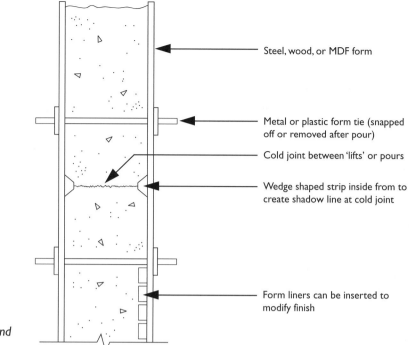

Figure 3.5.10. *Formwork and cold joints.*

Steel, wood, or MDF form

Metal or plastic form tie (snapped off or removed after pour)

Cold joint between 'lifts' or pours

Wedge shaped strip inside from to create shadow line at cold joint

Form liners can be inserted to modify finish

finish cracking of small concrete pieces or structural elements is minimal, but large wall planes and particularly large floor slabs can be problematic. The method of dealing with this is through control joints. Control joints are grooves cut or cast into the concrete that gather the cracks into a 'controlled' location (Fig. 3.5.9). We're all familiar with these joints in sidewalks and driveways, but they follow three particular rules for effective use. First, they need to be cut or cast 25% of the depth of the slab – more lessens strength too much, less doesn't force all cracks to occur there. Second, 3 m (10 ft.) is the maximum distance of slab distance without a control joint. This can be longer in some circumstances, but the 10-foot rule works in almost every circumstance. Last, an even aspect ratio of one to one should be maintained. This means that the control areas need to be almost square, which is why 2 m (6 ft.) wide sidewalks have joints about every 2 m (6 ft.), 3 m (10 ft.) joints would make rectangles that would tend to crack in the middle rather than in the control joint.

Another type of concrete joint is the cold joint. Cold joints are the juncture between two concrete pours. Because concrete can only be transported and placed in limited quantities, there are inevitably breaks between pours. These joints often exhibit different colors of concrete touching one another and overlap of concrete from one pour seeping onto the next. Cold joints are often concealed in vertical formwork by casting a reveal or groove in the surface to hide the joint (Fig. 3.5.10). In thin ground slabs, these joints are often separated from one another with a felt or neoprene material that prevents one pour from bonding with the next. This separation is called an expansion joint. Expansion joints are intended to allow for movement between two areas that are expected to shift or settle unevenly, like an on grade slab meeting a building entrance. The slab will float with the ground expansion, while the building should remain still. The joint prevents the movement of one system from damaging the other. Expansion joints are also built into separate segments of a building that has an irregular or elongated form. The movement of a building's shape should be considered in a similar fashion to a ground slab – aspect ratios of one to one are best. Large-scale expansion joints can sometimes allow for over 300 mm (12 in.) of movement, and more extreme cases can be seen in very long, thin structures like bridges that may need to allow for meters of total movement.

Concrete formwork is the means of shaping all concrete structures. Formwork determines not only the shape, but also the finish of the concrete. Concrete buildings are essentially built twice – first the formwork is constructed in the shape of the building, then the concrete is poured, then the formwork is removed. Custom formwork is often constructed by carpenters and must be precisely built because it needs to be almost waterproof and incredibly strong. Concrete is very fluid when first poured and will leak out of any openings in the form; it is also very heavy (over 135 lb per cubic foot/659 kg per cubic meter) and can destroy a weak form. There are no second chances with most pours, so a thorough knowledge of how forms are made is essential for designers. Forms can be made of wood or metal, lined with various types of materials, and are both pre-manufactured and custom built (Fig. 3.5.11). The material and texture of the form transmits itself onto the surface of the concrete, so even the wood grain from plywood is visible after the form is removed. All forms come in limited sizes, with the standard 1.2 × 2.4 m (4 × 8′) sheet of plywood creating the most common module. Form ties are metal or plastic rods that pass through the formwork, holding the two sides together, and make a

Figure 3.5.11. *Kimbell Museum of Art, concrete construction, 1967–1972, Fort Worth, Texas.*

pattern of indentations in the surface of the concrete. Wooden or metal strips, textured form liners and chemical sprays can be added into the form before pours to change the surface appearance. All of these formwork issues need taken into account, along with the color of the aggregate and cement, to get the desired finish.

Concrete comes from the cement plant in trucks that can pour the material directly into place or into another means of moving the concrete across the site. Given the limited time between water mixture and hydration, the placement must occur relatively quickly. In order to move concrete up onto taller building structures vessels that can lift and pour with cranes are filled, or pumping systems are used. Pumping trucks can take multiple loads from cement trucks and pump the material through hoses and pipes into tall structures. A pumping truck will normally run almost continually throughout the day in a large pour, because it needs to be thoroughly cleaned if not in use. The placed concrete is then sometimes vibrated into place in formwork, or surface finished by screeding (flattening with a long bar or plank), and troweling smooth. Final finishes can be added by brooming, raking, rotary troweling, or sandblasting. All finishing needs to occur at a time when the concrete is soft enough to take the finish, yet hard enough to retain it. Only a limited area can be done at one time, as too large an area cannot be completed before the concrete hydrates beyond workability.

The workability and strength of concrete are at direct odds with one another. The lower the water to cement ratio – the stronger the concrete, however, the more water – the easier it is to work. Concrete develops its strength quickly, up to 75% of total strength in 7 days and full strength in 28 days. Testing of strength is done in two ways. First is a slump test, which consists of filling a plastic cone with the concrete mixture, placing it on the ground and pulling the cone. The amount of collapse, or slump, is used as an indication of water to cement ratio before the concrete is acceptable to be placed. The other test is a cylinder break. Small diameter cylinders are poured from each cement truck that arrives on site; these are numbered and sent to a testing lab where they are crushed after 7 days. If the acceptable strength is reached there is no problem, if not the contractor has the option of deferring to a 28-day break, which typically is much stronger. If the concrete does not meet strength specifications it may need to be removed and replaced, difficult to do 7–28 days after the building has been built on top of it. The typical range of concrete strength is 1150–1800 kg (2500– 4000 lb) of compressive force per square inch, with higher strength concrete available.

To deal with the desire for higher strength concrete, which is much harder to work with, admixtures have been developed that allow for more workability without adding water. Superplasticizers and mid range water reducers are the most common admixtures, they allow the concrete to be manipulated longer without affecting water-cement ratios. Admixtures are expensive and can make structural engineers nervous, due to frequent abuses on job sites of adding water above the specified ratios to keep concrete fluid. They are often necessary, but keep in mind that they can also affect the finish and color of the concrete.

Concrete can be colored through the use of various pigments, stains, and etchings. Integrally colored concrete has the pigment mixed into the cement powder, which has a limited effect due to the high percentage of aggregate in concrete. When concrete cures it tends to send the water and finer cement particles to the edges of the form, making the surface smooth and composed of mostly the cement powder and fine aggregate, so mostly you see the color of these materials, but it is rather inexact and unpredictable. The surfaces of concrete can be sandblasted or acid etched, which removes this layer of cement and fine aggregate, exposing the larger aggregate and dramatically changing the appearance of the surface. Surface pigments can be painted or blown on after curing, which stain the top layer a color, but the inconsistency of the concrete tends to make this a mottled effect. Lastly paints and sealers can color the surface, but wear off and fade after time.

Frequently asked questions

'How do you determine if a concrete pour is strong enough to handle the design load?'
Concrete is specified in various strengths, which determine the mix ratios at the cement plant. Once it arrives on site the contractor must approve that the mix is correct as specified by the structural engineer. There are frequently slump tests, which show an indication of the amount of water in the mix before pouring, and cylinder breaks, which are small pours of concrete from the mix that are brought to a lab and tested for strength by compressing them to failure. Concrete reaches 75% of its strength after 7 days, so after a week they run the test and you typically know if a problem exists.

'How do you know when to use control or expansion joints?'
Control joints are intended to prevent cracking in a random pattern in concrete slabs. The joints focus the normal slab movement onto the weaker joints, causing a 'controlled' crack pattern. Expansion joints are intended to allow for movement between two areas that are expected to shift or settle unevenly, like an on grade slab meeting a building entrance. The slab will float with the ground expansion, while the building should remain still. The joint prevents the movement of one system from damaging the other.

Conclusion

Concrete is a material that fundamentally changes the rules of construction and form making. It can do things no other material can, and has little formal historical precedent. Newer technologies are making the material stronger, which again modifies what was previously thought possible. Like all materials there is an ethical component to the use of concrete, it can do many things but its energy use and environmental impact are large. Cement manufacturing plants have begun the use of burning waste materials for fuel, much of this is harmless, however the use of fuel materials like used automobile tires can have negative environmental impacts. Unsound environmental practices can only be confronted with sound research by designers and subsequent education of the user groups. That may mean specifying only certain cement producers and convincing the client of this – or avoiding the use of a material altogether. The threshold has been raised on what it means to responsibly assemble a project – and this is an integral part of an architect's task.

Glossary and formulas

Aggregate	Stones and gravel added to the concrete mixture to improve strength and durability.
Cast in Place Concrete	Construction that occurs on site with the concrete poured into forms assembled in their final location. This type of construction requires a larger safety factor than Pre-Cast due to the unpredictability of site conditions, and results in a more varied finish.
Cement	A powder that binds the other materials in concrete together through the process of hydration. Concrete hydration is a chemical reaction that occurs when the cement powder is mixed with water, resulting in heat and a crystallized bond forming between the wet cement and the aggregate.
Cold Joint	The juncture between two concrete pours.
Concrete	A mixture of cement, water, and aggregate that hydrates to form a solid building material.
Control Joint	Grooves cut or cast into the concrete that gather the cracks into a 'controlled' location.
Expansion Joint	Joint intended to allow for movement between two areas that are expected to shift or settle unevenly.
Pre-Cast Concrete	Concrete building components made in a factory under carefully controlled conditions. The water to cement ratio is exacting and the temperature of hydration is constant making it more predictable and precise than cast-in-place concrete.
Portland Cement	A commercially manufactured cement made by combining ground limestone and shale/clay in a furnace heated to over 1480°C (2700°F).
Re-Bar	Reinforcing bars of steel used to provide tension strength in hybrid concrete/steel pours.

Further reading

Nervi, P.L. (1965) *Aesthetics and Technology in Building* (Cambridge, MA: Harvard University Press), pp. 1–21.
Ramsey, C.G. and Sleeper, H.R. (2000) Concrete (Chapter 3), *Architectural Graphic Standards*, 10th ed (New York, NY: John Wiley & Sons).

3.6   Materials: aluminum

Raw Material/Production	Bauxite – alumina
	Smelting
	Alloys
	Recycling
	Strength/stiffness
	Fire/corrosion
History	Discovery to small-scale production
	Electrolysis – technology
Aluminum Fabrication	Methods of producing shapes
	Joining methods
	Galvanic action
	Finishing

Introduction to aluminum

Aluminum, in relative terms, is a very recently discovered metal. Copper has been used for over 7500 years, bronze for 4000, iron and steel for over 3000 years. Aluminum was only discovered about 200 years ago, in 1808. Its properties compared to other metals are what have made it so ubiquitous in such a short time. It's a third the weight of steel for the same quantity, highly resistant to corrosion, conducts electricity twice as efficiently as the same weight of copper, forms more easily than other metals and is easier to cut, can be alloyed to rigid or ductile states, finishes very smoothly, can be electrically dyed (anodized), and is easily recyclable. All of this, however, comes at a cost.

Aluminum contains the most embodied energy of any commonly used building material. In fact it has over five times the embodied energy of the same weight of steel, and is over three times as energy intensive as its closest metal, copper (Fig. 3.6.1). The process used to extract the material from the mined ore uses vast amounts of electricity and produces significant amounts of waste and toxicity. This is balanced by the performance of the resulting product. Simply put, no other material can do everything that aluminum does. The use of the material becomes an exercise in appropriateness – deciding when and where the performance outweighs the impact.

Aluminum is typically not used as a primary structural material. This is because it lacks the strength of materials like steel. It requires large sizes to approach the strength of steel, which is impractical, and is not resilient when alloyed to increase strength – making it unable to absorb impact and deflection before failing (low modulus of elasticity). For smaller less demanding support tasks it works very well, and adds less load into the overall structure because of its light weight (Fig. 3.6.2).

	Energy content	
	Joules/gram	BTU/Lb
Sand	42	18
Wood	430	185
Lightweight concrete	2186	940
Gypsum board	4255	1830
Brickwork	5115	2200
Cement	9533	4100
Glass	25,808	11,100
Porcelain	26,273	11,300
Plastic	43,013	18,500
Steel	44,640	19,200
Lead	60,218	25,900
Zinc	64,635	27,800
Copper	68,820	29,600
Aluminum	240,638	103,500

Figure 3.6.1. *Approximate embodied energy of common building materials.*

Figure 3.6.2. *Miss Britain III, one time fastest boat in the world, clad in aluminum.*

Raw material

Aluminum is the most plentiful metal in the earth's crust (8%), but must be mined from bauxite ore. The process begins much like steel with large-scale mining operations, but the process used to extract and refine the metal is much different and more energy intensive. The following is the process as described courtesy of Alcoa, the largest producer of aluminum in the world (Fig. 3.6.3).

1. Mining

   Bauxite is an ore rich in aluminum oxide, formed over millions of years by chemical weathering of rocks containing aluminum silicates. It was first mined in France and has since been found in many locations around the world. Today, most bauxite mining is in the Caribbean, Australia, and Africa.

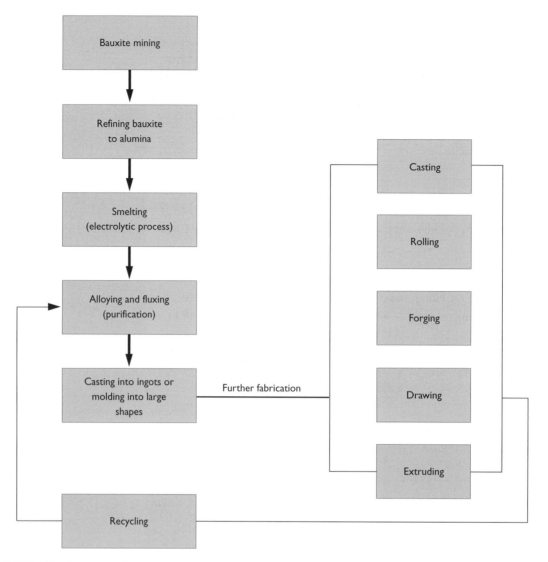

Figure 3.6.3. *Aluminum manufacturing process.*

2. Refining

   To turn bauxite into alumina, the ore is ground and mixed with lime and caustic soda, pumped into high-pressure containers, and heated. The aluminum oxide is dissolved by the caustic soda, then precipitated out of this solution, washed, and heated to drive off water. What's left is the sugar-like white powder called alumina, or aluminum oxide (Al_2O_3).

3. Alumina

   Alumina chemicals are used to purify water and to make refractory bricks, ceramics, adhesives, catalysts, and fire retardant fillers for fabrics and plastics.

4. Smelting

   Alumina becomes aluminum in an electrolytic reduction process known as smelting. Alumina is dissolved in a cryolite bath inside large, carbon-lined cells called pots. When a powerful electric current is passed through the bath, aluminum metal separates from the chemical solution and is siphoned off.

5. Fabricating

Aluminum from the smelting pots goes into furnaces for precise mixing with other metals to form various alloys with specific properties designed for particular uses. The metal is purified in a process called fluxing, then poured into molds or cast directly into ingots. Further fabrication may include casting, rolling, forging, drawing, or extruding – some of the ways manufacturers make thousands of different finished products, from beverage cans to cars to jet aircraft.

6. Recycling

Of the 100 billion or so beverage cans produced annually in the US, roughly two-thirds are returned for recycling (a bit over one-third are returned in Britain). So is 85–90% of the aluminum in cars. Recycling saves 95% of the energy it would take to make new metal from ore, and it lessens the need for solid waste disposal.

Aluminum secondary smelting, *scrap recycling*, accounts for approximately 33% of all primary aluminum produced in the US. There are approximately 68 major secondary processing plants in the US and 22 in the UK. These processing plants are typically located near large urban areas where large supplies of scrap aluminum are available. Aluminum recycling and secondary smelting requires preprocessing of the scrap aluminum to remove impurities, followed by re-melting of the aluminum. To maintain sufficient purity, the re-melted aluminum is mixed with pure aluminum produced in a primary smelting plant (typically a 50–50 mix). Prior to melting various mechanical, thermal, chemical, and magnetic techniques are used to separate contaminants and non-aluminum materials from the scrap. In contrast to the electricity intensive process of primary aluminum smelting, melting of scrap to yield secondary aluminum involves primarily natural gas usage. The argument that it is more expensive to process recycling than it saves is not true of aluminum; to save 95% of the energy intensive raw material process is significant in dollars and environmental impact.

Aluminum corrodes very slowly; it quickly forms a protective oxide skin on exposed surfaces. This can eventually break down, but is typically stable for long periods of time even in marine conditions. Painting or anodizing can extend the corrosion resistance.

Fire affects aluminum earlier than materials like steel. It melts completely at 660°C (1220°F) and loses strength far before that. This makes it impractical as a primary structural material, beyond problems of its low modulus of elasticity.

History

The earliest known uses for alumina date to 7000 years ago, when Persian potters made vessels from a clay containing the oxide to increase strength. Ancient Egyptians used aluminum oxides in dyes, make-up and medicine. There was no use of aluminum as a metal, however, until much later. It is the most abundant metal in the earth's crust, but it doesn't occur naturally as a metal and is hard to transform from raw material to metallic form.

In 1808 Sir Humphry Davy discovered the existence of aluminum. Danish physicist Hans Christian Oersted managed to produce a few droplets of the metal shortly thereafter. Through the course of improving production about 1.8 metric tons (2 ton) were produced by 1869. This brought the cost down dramatically, from £425/kg ($550/lb) to £13/kg ($17/lb). In the early 1880s aluminum was considered a semi-precious material, more rare than silver.

Charles Martin Hall was a student at Oberlin College when he saw aluminum for the first time as a rare metal. After graduation, he experimented with ways to make the material commercially viable. He learned how to make aluminum oxide – alumina – and he fashioned his own carbon crucible. In February 1886, he filled the crucible with a cryolite bath containing alumina and passed an electric current through it. The result was a congealed mass that he allowed to cool then shattered with a hammer. Inside were several small pellets of pure aluminum. This process, electrolysis, is how aluminum is processed today at a much larger scale.

Fabrication

Foundries produce complex metal shapes by melting aluminum or aluminum alloys and pouring the molten metal into a mold to solidify into the desired shape. Aluminum casting accounts for 32% of all metal castings in the US and 8% in the UK, with the majority of these castings being done for the automotive industry. There are four main methods used for casting metals: sand casting, investment casting, permanent mold casting, and die-casting.

Die-casting and permanent mold casting together account for over 80% of all aluminum casting. Due to aluminum's low melting temperature, inexpensive steel and iron can be used for forming the dies and molds. The molten aluminum feeding the casting line is derived from three different sources: ingots from a primary aluminum producer, molten aluminum directing from a smelting plant, or partially processed recycled aluminum scrap.

Casting consists of pouring molten aluminum into molds. Once in the mold, the aluminum solidifies into the shape defined by the mold. Three different casting methods are used: sand casting, permanent mold casting, and die-casting. Molten aluminum is derived from three different sources: ingots from a primary aluminum producer, molten aluminum directly from a smelting plant, or partially processed recycled aluminum scrap.

Sand casting is the most versatile method and the most economical for producing small quantities. Almost any shape mold can be produced from fine sand and binder mixture. After casting, the sand molds must either be hauled to landfills or reconditioned. Thermal sand reclamation processes are available that remove the binder material from the sand and allow the sand to be reused. These processes are typically natural gas fired.

Investment casting uses a ceramic mold that was created around a plastic or wax replica of the desired metal shape. Prior to casting, the ceramic mold is fired which increases the mold strength and burns the plastic or wax replica, removing it from the mold. Investment casting is capable of creating higher precision casts than sand casting.

Permanent mold casting uses steel or other metal molds to shape the molten aluminum. Molten aluminum is forced into the mold under gravity or with the aid of a vacuum. Permanent mold castings are stronger than sand castings and less expensive for large production quantities.

Die-Casting is used for producing accurate components that require little subsequent matching. The molten aluminum is forced under high pressure into steel molds or dies that shape and cool the molten aluminum.

Extrusion is the process of forcing heated aluminum through a die under extreme force to produce the desired shape. Extrusions can be made in literally thousands of complex shapes, but the most commonly used shapes are readily available (Figs. 3.6.4 and 3.6.5). Billets are preheated and forced by a ram through one or more dies to achieve the desired cross-section. The product is long in relation to its cross-sectional dimensions and has a section other than that of rod, bar, pipe, and tube.

Rolling is the process of forming aluminum sheets from slab ingots that are up to 660 mm (26 in.) thick, 6 m (20 ft.) long, and weigh up to 18 metric tons (20 ton). The slab is heated in a furnace and rolled between powered rollers until the plate is approximately 25 mm (1 in.) thick. The plates are further

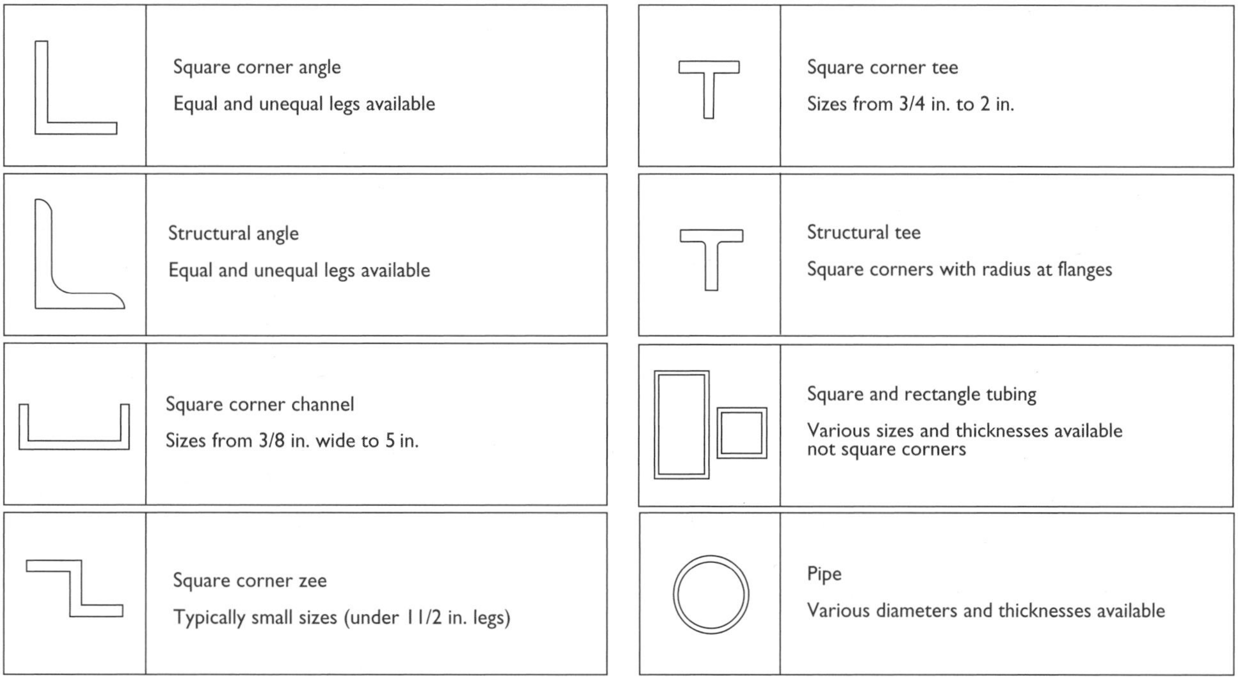

Square corner angle Equal and unequal legs available	Square corner tee Sizes from 3/4 in. to 2 in.
Structural angle Equal and unequal legs available	Structural tee Square corners with radius at flanges
Square corner channel Sizes from 3/8 in. wide to 5 in.	Square and rectangle tubing Various sizes and thicknesses available not square corners
Square corner zee Typically small sizes (under 1 1/2 in. legs)	Pipe Various diameters and thicknesses available

Figure 3.6.4. *Standard aluminum shapes.*

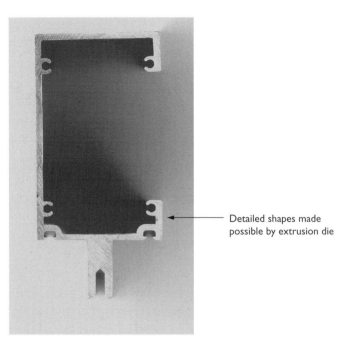

Detailed shapes made
possible by extrusion die

Figure 3.6.5. *Aluminum extrusion.*

reduced in finishing mills where they are hot rolled to a thickness of 6–10 mm (0.25–0.4 in.).

Forging is the process of forming aluminum by impacting and/or squeezing a preheated aluminum blank between two halves of a die. A succession of dies may be needed to achieve the final shape. Forging provides advantages over casting in that internal microstructure can be oriented to improve strength, and internal defects or porosity are minimized. The aluminum blank is typically heated to 315–480°C (600–900°F), but some cold forging is also performed in the industry. Cold forging is performed on billets at room temperature. This process involves high die costs and is typically limited to high production volumes, but results in very strong materials.

Aluminum comes in different classifications from 1000 to 7000 series to be used for varying purposes (Fig. 3.6.6). Each series of aluminum is alloyed with other agents to modify the properties of the material. 1000 series is almost pure aluminum and 7000 series is the strongest, but the numbers do not indicate a progressive strengthening of the material (2000 and 7000 series are the highest strength series). Common types of each series have individual numbers within the series, such as 7075 aluminum, which is the strongest but is not weldable. Many of the highest strength aluminum alloys are not weldable, and even the ones that can be welded do not have the strength of steel welds. Steel welds can be made as strong as the parent material being joined, preventing potential weaknesses at the weld joint. Aluminum welds are never as strong as the parent material, therefore additional material thickness and weld quantities are needed to maintain strength.

Aluminum can be joined in two ways – welding and bolting. This decision is based on a number of factors. The basic rule of thumb is the same as steel, 'weld in the shop – bolt in the field'. Welding can be done much more effectively

Aluminum classification	Primary alloying agent	Characteristics	Uses	Common types
1000	None	Soft, weldable, corrosion resistant	Food/Chemical resistance	1050, 1200
2000	Copper	Heat treatable, non-weldable, strength, poor corrosive resistance	Aircraft construction	2014
3000	Manganese	Non-heat treatable, medium strength, weldable, corrosive resistant	Marine environments	3103, 3003
4000	Silicon		Used as welding rod	
5000	Magnesium	Non-heat treatable, weldable, and very corrosive resistant	Pressurized applications marine environments, including shipbuilding	5454, 5083
6000	Magnesium and Silicon	Heat treatable, medium strength, weldable, corrosive resistant	Architectural extrusions, intricate shapes, structural members	6063, 6061, 6082
7000	Zinc	Heat treatable, age hardens, some weldable, some unweldable, very high strength, poor corrosion resistance	Aircraft construction, motorcycle and bicycle frames, armored vehicles	7020 weldable 7075 non-weldable

Figure 3.6.6. *Aluminum classification series.*

in a controlled environment, whereas bolting is easily accomplished on site. Aluminum welding is significantly more difficult than steel and cannot be easily done on site. As noted above, not all aluminum series are even weldable, so often bolting is the only choice. Esthetic and structural considerations can also dictate the method of assembly because often it can be done either way, but one method can have significant strength or esthetic impact. One of the factors to consider is the size of a metal assembly, remember if it can't fit on a truck, it shouldn't be finished in the shop. Many times large portions of an assembly can be made in the shop, with the final form finished by a few simple bolts on site. Another factor to consider is the metal finish. Painted or anodized pieces will have the finish destroyed by welding on site, and then the original finish will be 'matched' with a can of spray paint. This normally results in a finish less durable and esthetically compromised. Think through the assembly and finishes carefully to decide how to join metal elements together.

A common problem with all metals in the field is galvanic action. This is corrosion caused by dissimilar materials touching one another in a wet environment. An electrical current flows between different metals as one 'sacrifices' itself to the other (Fig. 3.6.7). The galvanic series runs from the more stable or 'most noble' metals to the most corrosive or 'least noble' metals. The least noble metal corrodes when in direct contact with the more noble metal – the farther apart

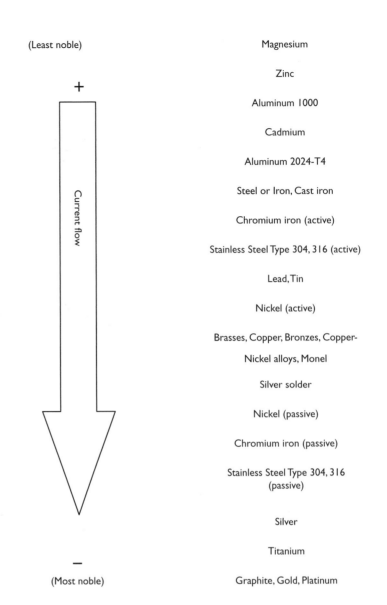

Figure 3.6.7. *Galvanic series.*

they are in the scale the more corrosion occurs (Fig. 3.6.8). This can cause catastrophic failures, such as stainless steel panels eating carbon steel fasteners, resulting in wall panels dropping off of buildings. Chemically active materials can also create galvanic action – the most common being concrete eating aluminum when in direct contact in moisture. The method of limiting this is intelligent selection of systems and isolation of materials. Isolation generally takes place with inert washers or spacers, such as nylon and plastic. Keeping direct contact in check is very important to avoid major problems with corrosion. Aluminum is one of the least noble metals and always needs to be carefully handled.

Aluminum does not always need to be finished when used in building applications, but it normally is. The finish types most commonly used are painting and anodizing. Painting aluminum is similar to most other materials, however, because aluminum has a very high thermal expansion rate the paint can crack over time. Aluminum can also be anodized, which is an oxide coating applied as a dye with an electric current (Fig. 3.6.9). The finish is then chemically bonded to the surface and cannot be flaked off or cracked. It can however be

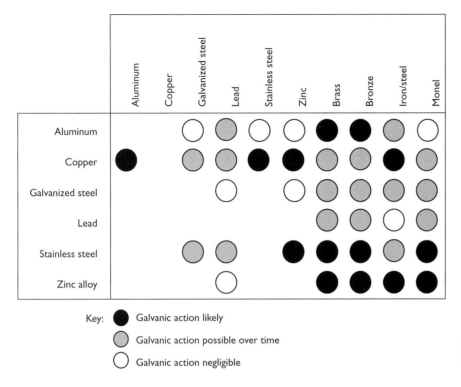

Key: ● Galvanic action likely
○ Galvanic action possible over time (grey)
○ Galvanic action negligible

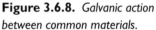

Figure 3.6.8. *Galvanic action between common materials.*

scratched, because it is a thin coating, and this cannot be repaired in the field. Anodizing leaves the finish of the aluminum exactly the texture of the surface of the pre-prepared metal, but tends to be matte. Any color can be obtained and the color stability has improved over the classic fading of red to pink or black to brown that was common 20 years ago. Most aluminum windows and other pre-manufactured building components are anodized.

Frequently asked questions

'How do you decide when it's appropriate to use aluminum?'
Aluminum has a high cost of embodied energy, but it can do many things no other material can. It has a very high strength to weight ratio and can lighten assemblies that require weight reduction. It also has corrosion resistance, and can be used more economically than stainless steel in many corrosion resistant applications. It is recyclable, but often difficult to separate from hybrid assemblies in building systems in order to recycle.

'How do you know whether to use rolled, forged, or cast aluminum?'
Casting allows for very specific shapes due to the molding process, but it typically is not as strong as rolled or forged aluminum. Rolling makes a limited number of shapes (such as angles and bars) because it is a linear fabrication process. Forging presses shapes using dies and can be very expensive, but produces very strong pieces. Typically you're looking for the most economical way to achieve your desired result.

Conclusion

The basic benefits of aluminum are strength to weight ratio, more precise shapes than steel, shop, or field assembly, a limitless variety of formal possibilities,

Aluminum anodizing process

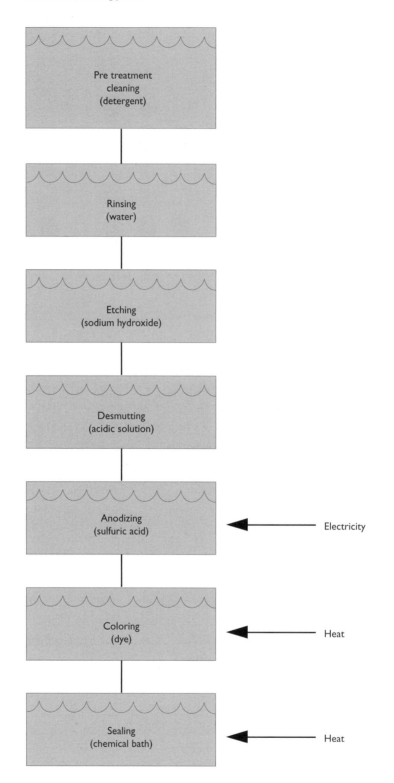

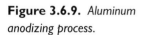

Figure 3.6.9. *Aluminum anodizing process.*

infinite finish options, and a lightweight corrosion resistant material. This is countered by the highest embodied energy of any common building material, difficulty of fabrication, potential for surface abrasion, thermal instability, high thermal conductivity (condensation issues), and fire resistance difficulties. Some people would argue that we should simply stop using aluminum, and it is likely overused, but its economy combined with its unique properties make it difficult to avoid. This is another example of a material that has its appropriate applications, but should be considered carefully before automatically selecting it.

Glossary and formulas

Alloy	Metal with added elements to modify its properties.
Alumina	Aluminum oxide produced from bauxite by an intricate chemical process. It is a white, powdery material that looks like granulated sugar. Alumina is an intermediate step in the production of aluminum from bauxite and is also a valuable chemical on its own.
Anodizing	An electrochemical process for applying a protective or decorative coating to metal surfaces.
Bauxite	An ore from which alumina is extracted and from which aluminum is eventually smelted. It takes four parts bauxite to make one part aluminum.
Brazing	Joining metals by flowing a thin layer of molten, non-ferrous filler metal into the space between them.
Casting	The process of forming molten metal into a particular shape by pouring it into a mold and letting it harden.
Cold Mill	The equipment on which aluminum is rolled into sheet or foil by passing it through pairs of rollers under pressure. In cold rolling, the incoming metal is normally at room temperature.
Extrusion	The process of shaping material by forcing it to flow through a shaped opening in a die.
Fabricate	To work a material into a finished state by machining, forming, or joining.
Flat-Rolled Products	Aluminum plate, sheet or foil products made by passing ingot through pairs of rolls, successively reducing its thickness and increasing its length.
Forging	A metal part worked to pre-determined shape by one or more processes such as hammering, pressing, or rolling.
Ingot	A cast form suitable for re-melting or fabricating. An ingot may take many forms: some may be 9 m (30 ft) long and weigh 13.6 metric tons (15 ton); others are notched or specially shaped for stacking and handling.
London Metal Exchange (LME)	The international trading body that facilitates the worldwide open market buying and selling of metals.
Magnesium	A light, silvery, moderately hard, metallic element used in processing metals and chemicals, and in alloying aluminum to give it desired metallurgical properties.

Mill Products	Metal that has been fabricated into an intermediate form before being made into a finished product. The most common fabricating processes for aluminum are rolling, extruding, forging, and casting Example: aluminum sheet, a mill product, is used to make beverage cans, a finished product.
Pot	In aluminum production: the electrolytic reduction cell in which alumina dissolved in molten cryolite is reduced to metallic aluminum. A series of cells connected electrically is called a potline.
Smelt	To fuse or melt ore in order to extract or refine the metal it contains.

Further reading

Ching, F.D.K. (2001) *Building Construction Illustrated* (New York, NY: John Wiley & Sons).

Ramsey, C.G. and Sleeper, H.R. (2000) *Architectural Graphic Standards*, 10th ed (New York, NY: John Wiley & Sons). pp. 260–263.

CHAPTER **4**

Structural Design

4.1 Forces and loads

Introduction to Structural Design	History
Forces	Definitions Vector representations
Loads	Definitions Types – live vs. dead, gravity vs. lateral
Equilibrium	Definitions (why this is good for architecture) Rotational vs. translational equilibrium How to achieve this – reactions
The Free Body Diagram	Vector geometry Elementary calculations using graphic and algebraic methods

Introduction to structural design

Structural Engineering involves planning for the static forces that will act on a building. Until 1750, Structural Engineering was considered part of the Architect's task, Rules of thumb, intuitive solutions, and 'collected wisdom' created an unofficial – and not always successful – approach. While humans instinctively recognize some forms as structurally sound (Fig. 4.1.1), the complexity of static behavior in building structures demands a professional's knowledge and care.

Since the founding of the *Ecole Polytechnique* in Paris in the mid-18th century, engineering has become its own discipline. Structural engineers are licensed to build a variety of structures, and must be consulted for medium- to large-size buildings.

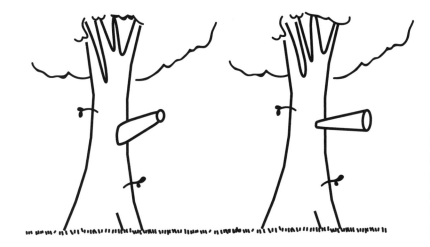

Figure 4.1.1. *At its highest levels, structural design is a complex, highly technical field. At its simplest, it is intuitive and even instinctual. Which branch will support a person's weight?*

Figure 4.1.2. *Structural Engineering and Architectural design fully integrated – the Gothic Cathedral*

The history of Structural Engineering and its relationship to architecture is a complex one, with occasionally successful integration (Figs. 4.1.2 and 4.1.3).

Forces

A *force* is that which produces, or tends to produce, a change in the motion of a physical body. Newton defined a force as mass times acceleration, or:

$$f = ma$$

where m is the mass of the object and a is the resulting acceleration. Heavier masses accelerate more slowly, while larger forces make things accelerate more quickly.

A force consists of three separate, quantifiable variables (Fig. 4.1.4):

Magnitude, or the amount of force. This is measured in units of mass that is kilograms, pounds, 'kips' (a 'kilo-pound,' or 1000 lb), or tons, and represents the 'push' imparted to an object.

Direction, or the orientation of the force. This is usually measured by an angle from a reference axis.

Sense, or whether the force is acting positively along its orientation, or negatively – essentially, whether the force is 'pushing' or 'pulling' the object.

Figure 4.1.3. *While the split of engineering and architecture in the 18th century had serious consequences for the discipline of building, the two fields have a history of subsequent collabor-ation, often producing conceptually seamless buildings. Here, a skyscraper rises in Chicago in the 1890s, a pure statement of structure that would be clad in a minimal architectural skin.*

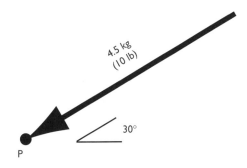

Figure 4.1.4. *A vector representation of a force, showing magnitude, direction, and sense.*

These variables may all be graphically represented by a *vector*, that is, an arrow whose length is keyed to the magnitude, and whose direction and orientation are keyed to the direction and sense of the force in question. Figure 4.1.4 shows a vector representing a force of 4.5 kg (10 lb) 'pushing' point *P* at an angle of 30° from the horizontal. Note that, from Newton's equation, this

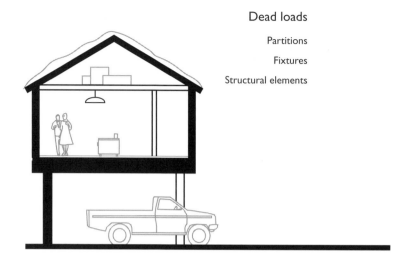

Dead loads

Partitions

Fixtures

Structural elements

Figure 4.1.5. *Dead loads arise from the structure itself and permanently fixed building elements.*

will cause *P* to accelerate in the direction of the arrow. As long as the force is continually applied, and as long as we don't do anything to stop it, *P* will continue to not only move, but accelerate in this direction. Note, too, that the arrow doesn't represent anything spatially, except for a direction and sense. Its length is strictly indicative of the force's magnitude. This ability to quantify forces as mathematical entities allows us to simulate structural behavior, and we can use vector geometry to figure out how forces will affect structural elements.

Loads

Loads are external forces acting on a structure. They can be abstracted into simple forces acting on a structure using vectors, as described above. Loads *deform* or change the shape of the structure – in the worst case, they will cause the structure to fail, or break. The structure resists and channels two basic types of loads:

> *Dead Loads* (Fig. 4.1.5) include the weight of the structure itself, and any elements carried by the structure that are intended to remain in place permanently. Also referred to as *Static Loads*.
> *Live Loads* (Fig. 4.1.6) include all elements supported by a structure that move, or will move during the life of the structure. Live loads that change over time are referred to as *Dynamic Loads*.

Two additional important types of loading are *Repeated Loads*, which occur again and again, often with a regular rhythm, and *Impact Loads,* which occur on a structure during a very brief period of time.

Dead and Live loads may be *concentrated*, or applied essentially at a point, or *distributed* over a continuous area of the structure (Fig. 4.1.7). *Concentrated* loads take the form of a single vector – one 'push' acting at a more or less discrete point in space. *Distributed* loads are represented by a two-dimensional vector – a 'push' that is spread along a line, or across a plane. However,

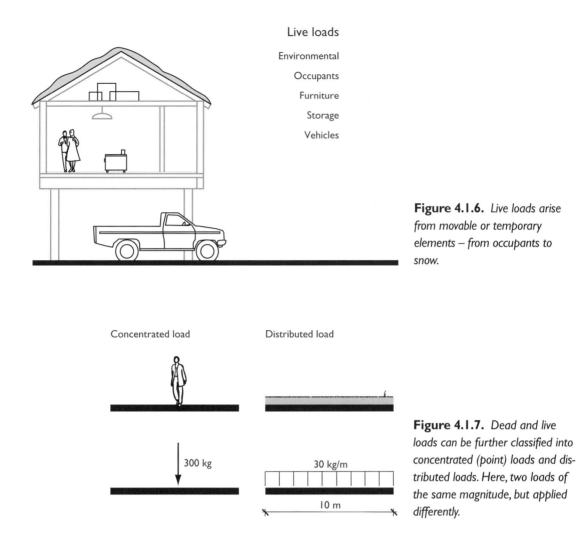

Live loads

Environmental

Occupants

Furniture

Storage

Vehicles

Figure 4.1.6. *Live loads arise from movable or temporary elements – from occupants to snow.*

Concentrated load

Distributed load

300 kg

30 kg/m

10 m

Figure 4.1.7. *Dead and live loads can be further classified into concentrated (point) loads and distributed loads. Here, two loads of the same magnitude, but applied differently.*

a *distributed* load can be 'summarized' as a single concentrated load that will have similar macro-effects on a system. Figure 4.1.7 shows two loads – one concentrated, one distributed – that have similar effects on the structural *system* being considered. In both cases, the structure will have to carry a load of 300 kg – concentrated in the first case, distributed in the second – to its supports on either end. The structure's *supports* won't 'know' whether the load is concentrated or distributed; but, as we'll see, these two loads will be handled differently within the structural *element* itself.

All types of load may be calculated by adding all of the anticipated weights on or in a structure. However there are specified loadings in most building codes. Most commonly, building codes provide live load figures for various types of occupancy, since these loads can only be guessed at or assumed. Live loads are also usually specified for wind, snow, and rain. Dead loads are typically specified for various structural materials. While most structural calculations involve *gravity loads*, there are also typically a number of *lateral loads* acting on a given structure that push or deform the structure more or less sideways. Lateral loads include wind, seismic forces, and soil pressure. Tables 4.1.1–4.1.3 show some common assumptions for typical building loads.

Table 4.1.1. Typical assumptions for live loads.

Usage	Live load	
	kg/m^2	lbs/ft^2
Assembly areas, fixed seats	300	60
Assembly areas, lobbies	500	100
Assembly areas, movable seats	500	100
Stages and platforms	750	150
Balconies	500	100
Balconies, single family residence, smaller than 10 m^2	300	60
Offices	250	50
Lobbies, meeting rooms	500	100
Offices where filing is intensive	600	125
Habitable attics	150	30
Bedrooms	150	30
Residential other than sleeping	200	40
Apartments and hotel rooms	200	40
Apartment and hotel buildings, public areas	500	100
Catwalks	125	25
Corridors, main floor	500	100
Storage, light	600	125
Storage, heavy	1200	250
Dance halls, dining rooms, bars	500	100
Library stacks	750	150
Library reading rooms	300	60
Garages, cars only	250	50
Garages, trucks	750	150
Light manufacturing	600	125
Heavy manufacturing	1200	250
Rest rooms	300	60
Classrooms	200	40
Stadium seating	500	100
Retail, main floor	500	100
Retail, upper floors	400	75

Equilibrium

Fundamentally, Structural Engineering in architecture is concerned with *equilibrium*, or the state of being at rest. While all buildings move to some degree, the desired state for most structures and structural elements is one of limited or no movement – thus the distinction between *statics* and *dynamics*.

We are generally interested in finding ways to counteract external *forces* on a structure to produce equilibrium. This means developing systems and techniques that will *react* against forces, or cancel them out with internal forces within the elements themselves. An example is shown in Figure 4.1.8. In the scenario on the left, a person pulling with 67.5 kg (150 lb) of force on a rope with no resistance will not be in equilibrium. The person and the rope will *translate*,

Table 4.1.2. Typical weights of architectural materials.

Material	Weight kg/m³	lb/ft³
Snow	128	8
Cedar	361	22.5
Soft maple	529	33
Douglas fir	545	34
Southern pine (shortleaf)	561	35
Southern pine (longleaf)	657	41
Teak	689	43
Hard maple	705	44
Particleboard	721	45
White oak	753	47
Ice	913	57
Water	1000	62.4
Earth, loose	1218	76
Earth, packed	1538	96
Sand, dry	1603	100
Damp clay	1763	110
Limestone	2308	144
Concrete	2404	150
Glass	2564	160
Aluminum	2644	165
Marble	2692	168
Slate	2756	172
Granite	2804	175
Wrought iron	7692	480
Steel	7853	490

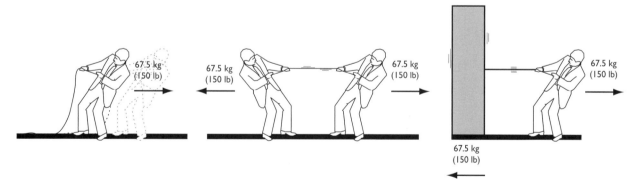

Figure 4.1.8. *Applying a force can result in translation or the development of a reaction in a structural system.*

or move, in a predictable way. On the other hand, a person pulling with 67.5 kg (150 lb) of force on a rope, against another person pulling with 67.5 kg (150 lb) of force will produce *equilibrium*. That is, the two forces will resist one another equally, and no translation, or motion, will occur. While the rope (and the people pulling) will experience internal *stresses* (see Section 4.2), the outside observer will not notice any movement; the system will be in equilibrium.

Table 4.1.3. Typical weights of architectural assemblies.

Material	Weight kg/m²	lb/ft²
100 mm brick	195	40
200 mm brick	390	80
100 mm concrete masonry wall	97.5	20
150 mm concrete masonry wall	136.5	28
200 mm concrete masonry wall	170.625	35
300 mm concrete masonry wall	268.125	55
2 × 4 stud wall with one layer gypsum board each side, insulation	263.25	54
2 × 6 stud wall with one layer gypsum board each side, insulation	287.625	59
Glass curtain wall	316.875	65
25 mm layer of reinforced concrete	282.75	58
25 mm layer of unreinforced concrete	268.125	55
Steel deck	58.5	12
2 × 6 joist floor with plywood deck	121.875	25
2 × 8 joist floor with plywood deck	131.625	27
2 × 10 joist floor with plywood deck	141.375	29
2 × 12 joist floor with plywood deck	165.75	34
Tile in 1/2 in. mortar bed	380.25	78
Granite flooring (3/8 in.)	146.25	30
Hardwood floor	58.5	12
Shingle roof	48.75	10
Built up roof	141.375	29
Clay tile roof	365.625	75
Acoustic ceiling	29.25	6
Gypsum board ceiling	73.125	15

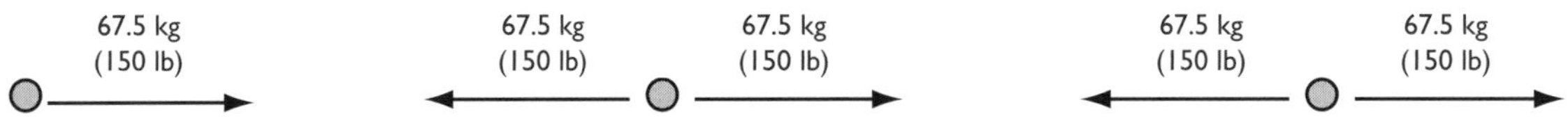

Figure 4.1.9. *A graphic representation of the two conditions in Figure 4.1.8.*

Likewise, a person pulling with 67.5 kg of force on a rope that is anchored, or *fixed*, to a structure may also experience equilibrium. In this case, *reactions* develop within the structure, and between the structure and the ground. In the case shown, the person's pull is resisted by the solid mass of the wall, and the friction developed between the wall and the ground. Again, both the wall and the person pulling will 'feel' internal stresses and pressures, but there will be no visible movement to an outside observer.

These two cases can be represented by the vector diagrams shown in Figure 4.1.9. In the first instance, the pull is not resisted, and motion occurs due to

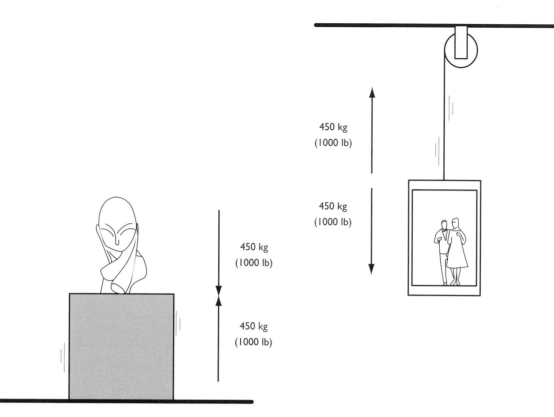

450 kg
(1000 lb)

450 kg
(1000 lb)

450 kg
(1000 lb)

450 kg
(1000 lb)

Figure 4.1.10. *Two systems in translational equilibrium.*

$F = ma$; an external force is introduced into the system without a reaction, and thus acceleration will occur. In the second instance, the pull is *resisted* by a simultaneous, equal and opposite pull. No motion occurs, and we say that the *system is in equilibrium*. In the third instance, the pull is *passively resisted* by the mass and friction of the wall, and again the system is in equilibrium.

A more architectural example is shown in Figure 4.1.10. Here, a sculpture weighing 450 kg (1000 lb) is placed on a pedestal. A gravitational force equal to the weight of the sculpture pulls it down (or more properly, toward the earth's center). This pull is resisted by an internal force – a reaction – that develops within the pedestal's material, equal to the weight of the sculpture but opposite in direction. Note that forces must also develop in the floor to support the pedestal plus the weight of the sculpture, and eventually forces must develop in the earth itself to support the floor, the pedestal, and the sculpture. Likewise, the elevator in Figure 4.1.10, weighing 450 kg (1000 lb), is prevented from falling by a force that develops in its cable, of equal magnitude.

Each of these situations describes *translational equilibrium*, that is, a balanced system of sculpture and pedestal or elevator and cable that are not moving from one position in space to another. (What happens to the sculpture if the pedestal can only develop 400 kg of resisting force? There will be an unbalanced load, and the sculpture will accelerate toward the ground, though somewhat slower than if it were completely unsupported. What happens to the elevator if the cable is made to develop an upward force of 600 kg? Again, there will be an unbalanced force, this time of 150 kg (330 lb) working upward. The elevator cab will accelerate upward. Unlike the sculpture, this is often a desirable attribute in an elevator.)

Translational equilibrium is important; buildings need to stay in the same place, and need to resist accelerating due to gravity (collapsing). Equally important in structural design, however, is *rotational equilibrium*, the stability of a system *around* any given point. *Rotational equilibrium* can be described by a seesaw, as shown in Figure 4.1.11. Here, the combined weights of the riders are resisted by a reaction in the central pylon to keep the system in translational equilibrium. But note that the rider's weights are also *balanced* around the pivot. This requires that the sum of each weight *multiplied by its distance from the pivot* is equivalent to the other weight multiplied by *its* distance from the pivot. The distance from each weight to the pivot is called a *lever arm*. The force acting on the pivot – the product of the weight times the lever arm – is called a *moment* and is measured in kilogram-meters (or foot-pounds).

The example in Figure 4.1.11 thus shows a system that is in both translational *and* rotational equilibrium. The force implied by the two riders is resisted by a *reaction* in the pylon equal to the sum of their weights (45 kg + 90 kg = 135 kg, or 100 lb + 200 lb = 300 lb) to provide translational equilibrium. The force implied by each rider *around* the pylon is equal to their weight *multiplied by their respective lever arms*:

$$45\,kg \times 3\,m = 135\,kg\text{-}m \qquad 100\,lb \times 10\,ft = 1000\,ft\text{-}lb$$
$$90\,kg \times 1.5\,m = 135\,kg\text{-}m \qquad 200\,lb \times 5\,ft = 1000\,ft\text{-}lb$$

Since the two moments are equal and opposite, the net *moment* on the pylon is 0 kg-m or ft-lb, and the system is in rotational equilibrium. If the moment forces are unequal, the system will not be in *rotational equilibrium*, and it will turn about the central pivot.

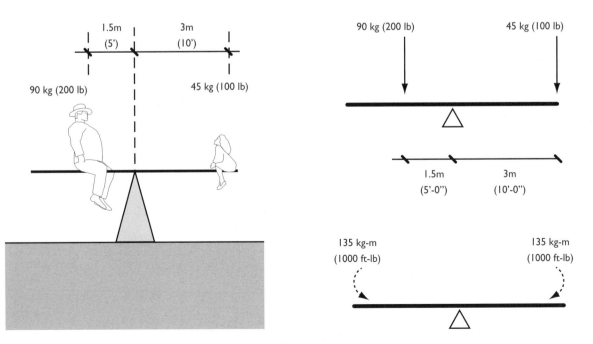

Figure 4.1.11. *A system in rotational and translational equilibrium.*

What would happen if the riders moved position relative to the pylon? If the lighter rider moved toward the pylon by 1 m (3 ft), the seesaw would remain in *translational* equilibrium – that is, it would not move from one position to the other. However, there would be an unbalanced moment around the pivot point:

$$45\,\text{kg} \times 2\,\text{m} = 90\,\text{kg-m} \qquad 100\,\text{lb} \times 7\,\text{ft} = 700\,\text{ft-lb}$$
$$90\,\text{kg} \times 1.5\,\text{m} = 135\,\text{kg-m} \qquad 200\,\text{lb} \times 5\,\text{ft} = 1000\,\text{ft-lb}$$
$$35\,\text{kg-m} > 90\,\text{kg-m} \qquad 1000\,\text{ft-lb} > 700\,\text{ft-lb}$$

This imbalance would cause the seesaw to accelerate around the pivot point in a clockwise direction. Likewise, if the riders maintained their position, but we added a 22 kg (50 lb) weight to the lighter rider's side, we would again have an unbalanced moment.

$$67\,\text{kg} \times 3\,\text{m} = 200\,\text{kg-m} \qquad 150\,\text{lb} \times 10\,\text{ft} = 1500\,\text{ft-lb}$$
$$90\,\text{kg} \times 1.5\,\text{m} = 135\,\text{kg-m} \qquad 200\,\text{lb} \times 5\,\text{ft} = 1000\,\text{ft-lb}$$
$$200\,\text{kg-m} > 135\,\text{kg-m} \qquad 1500\,\text{ft-lb} > 1000\,\text{ft-lb}$$

This time, the seesaw would rotate counter-clockwise.

The free body diagram

The above principles can be used graphically and algebraically to calculate reactions for a given set of forces. To do this, rigid structural systems can be abstracted to a point, a line, or a plane, and forces can be represented by vectors whose length and direction indicate magnitude and direction, respectively.

Using trigonometry and algebra, along with the definitions of equilibrium, we can easily resolve simple situations by breaking down individual forces into horizontal and vertical components, and solving in both directions for the resultant reaction.

In order to abstract forces into a geometrically solvable diagram, we can use the Principle of Transmissibility, which states that forces in a free body diagram can be rearranged spatially, provided that their directions and quantities of all vectors remain the same. Essentially, we can pick up and move the arrows, so long as their sense, direction, and magnitude don't change. Thus, the two diagrams shown in Figure 4.1.12 represent the same static situation, with the element in question reduced to a point and the forces involved arrayed in a geometrically convenient fashion. Furthermore, the forces can be rearranged for solution without regard to the element in question by aligning 'heads' and 'tails' of the vectors and solving for the resultant. (We'll use simple math to solve one of these, but note that these can be easily solved or checked using any vector-based drawing software that allows accurate line lengths and orientations.)

In particular, the Principle of Transmissibility lets us rearrange forces into quadrilaterals and triangles that can then be solved using trigonometry.

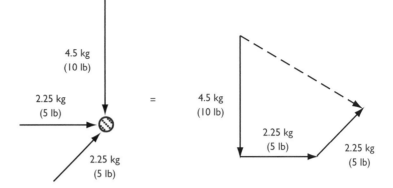

Figure 4.1.12. *Example of the Principle of Transmissibility. These two free body diagrams represent the same static condition, and we can rearrange the positions of the vectors (but not their orientation or direction) to arrive at a geometrically solvable problem.*

Example: A sailboat is anchored as shown in Figure 4.1.13. A wind from due north exerts a force of 270 kg (600 lb) on it, and a simultaneous tide from due west exerts a force of 135 kg (300 lb). Which direction will the anchor chain extend, and what force will be required on it to keep the boat in position?

Solution: First, find the resultant of the two forces. Using the principle of transmissibility, we can rearrange the two forces into a triangle as shown. The resultant force is represented by a vector connecting the 'start' of one vector with the 'finish' of the other, as shown. Since the two forces are operating at right angles, the magnitude of the resultant can be solved using the Pythagorean Theorem:

$$a^2 + b^2 = c^2$$

Or, in this case:

$$(135\,\text{kg})^2 + (270\,\text{kg})^2 = c^2 \qquad (300\,\text{lb})^2 + (600\,\text{lb})^2 = c^2$$

Solving for c,

$$c = \sqrt{(18{,}225\,\text{kg} + 72{,}900\,\text{kg})} \qquad c = \sqrt{(90{,}000\,\text{lb} + 360{,}000\,\text{lb})}$$
$$= 302\,\text{kg} \qquad\qquad\qquad = 670.82\,\text{lb}$$

The direction can be established using trigonometry:

$$\tan \Theta = 135\,\text{kg}/270\,\text{kg} \qquad \tan \Theta = 300\,\text{lb}/600\,\text{lb}$$
$$\tan \Theta = 0.5 \qquad\qquad \tan \Theta = 0.5$$
$$= \text{inv} \tan(0.5) \qquad\qquad = \text{inv} \tan(0.5)$$
$$= 26.57° \qquad\qquad\qquad = 26.57°$$

The *resultant* force, or the sum of the wind and tide forces, is therefore 302 kg (670.82 lb), with a direction of 26.57° from due south – or a compass direction of 116.57°, if true north is 0°.

The *reaction*, or the force needed to keep the boat in place, will be equal in magnitude, but opposite in direction to this resultant, or:

$$116.57° + 180° = 296.57°$$

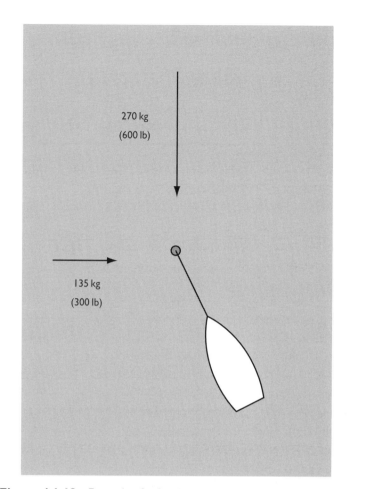
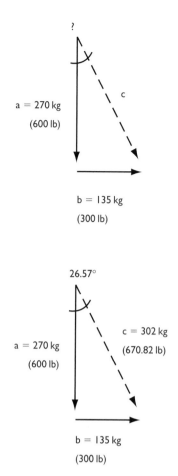

Figure 4.1.13. *Example of a free body and the results of external forces on it (see text).*

A similar algebraic process can be used to solve reactions for rotational equilibrium. Moments can be summed around a given pivot point, with clockwise moments having positive values and counter-clockwise moments having negative ones.

The ability to solve for translational and rotational equilibrium allows us to quickly calculate reactions on structural systems composed of rigid bodies:

Example: A locomotive weighing 9000 kg (20,000 lb) stops two-thirds of the way across a 180 m (600 ft) span bridge (see Figure 4.1.14). What reactions are required at each of the supports to maintain the bridge's equilibrium?

Solution: In order for the bridge to remain at rest, that is to not rotate about either of its supports, the moment induced by the locomotive must be met by an equal and opposite moment induced by the reactions of the two supports. Note that this is related to the seesaw problem, although in this case we have two pivot points and one load. However, we can start by assuming what we hope to achieve – rotational equilibrium, and working backward to figure out what forces we'd need at the two supports to do this.

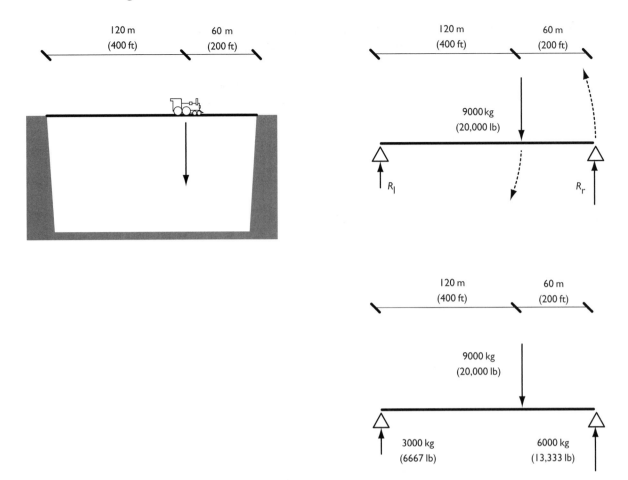

Figure 4.1.14. *Use of rotational equilibrium to deduce reactions (see text).*

Let's first take the moment about the support on the left. Again, we want to figure out a way to make this moment equal zero. We can very quickly figure out the moment that the locomotive imparts, and then figure out what moment we'd need the opposite (right-hand) reaction to impart to counteract that.

The locomotive imparts a moment equal to its weight times its lever arm, or:

$$M_L = (9000\,\text{kg}) \times (120\,\text{m}) \qquad M_L = (20,000\,\text{lb}) \times (400\,\text{ft})$$
$$= 1,080,000\,\text{kg-m} \qquad\qquad = 8,000,000\,\text{ft-lb}$$

This must be resisted by an equal and opposite moment imparted by the support on the right (M_S). Since we know the length of the lever arm (l), and the total moment it must resist, we can solve for the reaction (R_r) by working backward:

$$M_S = M_L$$

$$
\begin{array}{ll}
M_S = L \times R_r & M_S = L \times R_r \\
(1,080,000\,\text{kg-m}) = 180\,\text{m} \times R_r & (8,000,000\,\text{ft-lb}) = 600\,\text{ft} \times R_r \\
R_r = (1,080,000\,\text{kg-m})/180\,\text{m ft} & R_r = (8,000,000\,\text{ft-lb})/600\,\text{ft} \\
R_r = 6000\,\text{kg} & R_r = 13,333.33\,\text{lb}
\end{array}
$$

Notice that the length of the lever arm cancels out the length component of the moment and we're left with a result in pure pounds.

Having solved for the reaction on the right, we have two options for solving for the reaction on the left. We could perform a similar calculation that would give us a moment about the support on the right, and dividing by the length of the span (the lever arm) we could find the reaction on the left support. However, knowing that the bridge must also be in *translational* equilibrium (i.e., not falling straight down), we can also use the weight of the locomotive (W), and the known reaction (R_r), to figure out what the remaining reaction (R_l) must be:

$$
\begin{aligned}
(R_r + R_l) &= W \\
((6000\,\text{kg}) + R_l) &= 9000\,\text{kg} \\
R_l &= 9000\,\text{kg} - 6000\,\text{kg} \\
R_l &= 3000\,\text{kg}
\end{aligned}
\qquad\qquad
\begin{aligned}
(R_r + R_l) &= W \\
((13{,}333.33\,\text{lb}) + R_l) &= 20{,}000\,\text{lb} \\
R_l &= (20{,}000\,\text{lb}) - (13{,}333.33\,\text{lb}) \\
R_l &= 6666.67\,\text{lb}
\end{aligned}
$$

For simple structural situations, it is often enough to remember that the desired outcome is equilibrium – that we don't want the system to either move or rotate. With a limited number of external forces, we can calculate what combination it would take to hold the system in both translational and rotational equilibrium. This is a powerful tool – one we'll use regularly to establish the reactions on beams.

The limitation to this process involves the connections at either end. We have assumed – and will continue to assume – that the connections at the bridge's ends cannot *themselves* help resist the bending moment of the train. In other words, if the opposite reaction weren't there, we've assumed that the connections would allow the bridge to rotate freely (and disastrously). This type of connection is known as a *pin connection*, one that consists of an axle and bearing to hold a structural element in place, but that lets it turn or rotate. Other connection types do exist – *fixed* or *moment* connections can keep the bridge from rotating, and *roller* connections can allow the bridge to rotate and slide freely (see Section 4.8). Moment connections can obviously help our cause, but they create mathematical difficulties, since we can't assume that the sum of loads and reactions around them will equal zero. The moment at either end could actually be fairly large and still be resolved by the strength of the connection. If the nature of the connections doesn't permit us to calculate the reactions algebraically, as shown above, we say the structure is *indeterminate*. Indeterminate structures can still be solved, but the mathematics required are more intensive. Throughout the next three chapters, we'll always assume that the structural members under consideration are pinned rather than fixed, and this will help us get through some basic structural theory.

Frequently asked questions

I don't understand how a reaction can form in a structure – how does the structure know how much to 'push back'? It doesn't, of course. What happens is that the material within the structure becomes *stressed* – this will be discussed in the next chapter. The reaction is mostly a way to visualize how much work the structure has to do. What it really consists of is a state of stress, or pressure, that prevents the load we're imparting from moving the structure. When we draw an arrow as a reaction, we're describing that state of internal pressure in a convenient form, and labeling it in a way that makes sense graphically.

The examples you've given are all in two dimensions – isn't that cheating? How do you analyze three-dimensional structures? It is cheating, to a point. Many of the structures we work with will be two, or even one dimensional. Beams, for example, can be analyzed by thinking of them as single lines. Every structure takes up three dimensions, of course, and every loading situation is, technically, three dimensional. To analyze these situations, we look to provide translational and rotational equilibrium in all three directions and around all three axes: x, y, and z. We can do this by resolving three-dimensional lines of force into their x, y, and z components, and figuring out what it would take in each dimension to provide equilibrium. What's important here, though, are the basic principles. Work in three dimensions uses the same basic theory of translational and rotational equilibrium, but in and around all three axes instead of one or two.

How do we know if the seesaw in Figure 4.1.11 will break? With what we know so far, we don't. The next step (in Section 4.2) is to use logic to figure out what's going on inside the structure itself. Everything we've dealt with so far has to do with external loading – the real essence of structural design is to now think about how best to deploy material in a structural element to resist that loading, to transmit those loads to the earth, and to do both in a way that gives us equilibrium and doesn't break the structure.

If fixed connections are stronger, why wouldn't they always be used? Where would you use a pin or a roller connection? Fixed connections are stronger, but there are plenty of circumstances where we'd actually like to allow structural members to rotate or even translate. In large bridges, for instance, the bending moment at the supports can be extraordinary. If the supports were fixed to their foundations, the resulting torque would try to pry the foundation out of the ground. Over time, as the bridge flexed repeatedly, this could cause major settlement. A pin connection here ensures that the foundation only experiences the reaction force, and is never pried out of its position. Likewise, structures can expand and contract considerably as the outside temperature changes. A roller connection can allow parts of a structure to do this without stressing adjacent elements. Finally, fixed connections tend to be much heavier than pin connections. There are plenty of applications where we just want a slimmer, esthetically more compelling joint, and solve connections using pins rather than bulky moment connections.

Glossary

Concentrated Load	A load that is applied at a discrete point.
Dead Load	Loads that will not change over the course of a structure's life.
Distributed Load	A load that is spread out over a line or surface.
Dynamics	The physics of things in motion. Usually irrelevant to architecture.

Equilibrium	The condition of being at rest. Any forces acting on the object must be balanced by forces adding up to equal and opposite reactions.
Fixed (or Moment) Connection	A connection that does not permit a structural member to rotate or translate.
Force	That which tends to produce a change in the motion of a physical body. Defined by the formula:

$$f = ma$$

	where *m* is the mass of the object and *a* is its acceleration due to the force. Measured in units of weight, that is 100 lb.
Free Body Diagram	A mathematical abstraction of the forces at work on a single, monolithic structure in which the object in question is reduced to a single point.
Gravity Load	Loads acting on a structure along a line between the structure and the earth's center.
Lateral Load	Loads acting on a structure along lines other than those between the object and the earth's center, for example wind, earthquakes, etc.
Lever Arm	The distance between the action of a force and its pivot point.
Live Load	Loads that may change over the course of a structure's life.
Load	Any external force acting on a structure.
Moment	The resultant force about a point, measured by multiplying the quantity of the force by its lever arm. Expressed in kilogram-meters, pound-feet, or similar units.
Pin Connection	A connection that allows a structural member to rotate, but not to translate.
Reaction	A force that develops in resistance to an applied force. Can be active (e.g., pulling on a cable), or passive (a pedestal bearing the weight of something).
Roller Connection	A connection that allows a structural member to translate (slide) and rotate.
Statics	The physics of things at rest.

Further reading

Mainstone, R.J. (2001) Structural Actions (Chapter 2), *Developments in Structural Form*, 2nd ed (Oxford: Architectural Press).

Margolius, I. (2002) *Architects + Engineers = Structures* (Chichester: Wiley-Academy).

Nervi, P.L. (1956) *Aesthetics and Technology in Building: The Charles Eliot Norton Lectures 1961–1962.* (Cambridge: Harvard University Press, 1965).

Salvadori, M. (1963) Structure in Architecture (Chapter 1) and Loads on Structures (Chapter 2), *Structure in Architecture: The Building of Buildings* (Englewood Cliffs, NJ: Prentice-Hall).

4.2   Stresses

Basic States of Stress (1)	Simple tension
	Simple compression + buckling
Simple Tension and Compression Structures (Funicular Shapes)	Cables
	Arches
Properties of Structural Materials	Deformation
	Elasticity vs. plasticity
	'Brittleness' vs. 'flow'
	Isotropic vs. anisotropic
Practical Applications	Elastic Modulus and Hooke's Law
	Ultimate strength and yield point
	Factors of safety and allowable unit stresses
	Design of basic tension and compression members

Structural materials

In Section 4.1 we looked at conditions of forces and loading, and found ways to resist these externally – with forces *outside* of the structural member – to achieve *equilibrium*. In doing so, we *assumed* certain structural members could actually carry the loads we were imposing without breaking.

In fact, the design of structural elements themselves to carry or transfer these loads and forces *internally* is the very essence of structural design. Once we have established the basic performance of the system, we must *design* the elements of that system to safely carry these loads to their resolution. In a typical architectural situation, this may involve designing floors, beams, columns, and foundations, as well as doing calculations to ensure that the soil we are building on can transmit and disperse the weight of our building throughout the ground.

All structural elements are made of materials whose resistance to loading we can confidently predict. In over 250 years of empirical testing, we know enough about the strengths of building materials to have developed useful, reliable data that enable us to predict how structural elements of various shapes and compositions will perform.

There are four basic things (states) that can happen to materials under loading. We will deal with the simplest two – tension and compression – in this chapter, and will look at how these two types of stress affect a range of typical building materials.

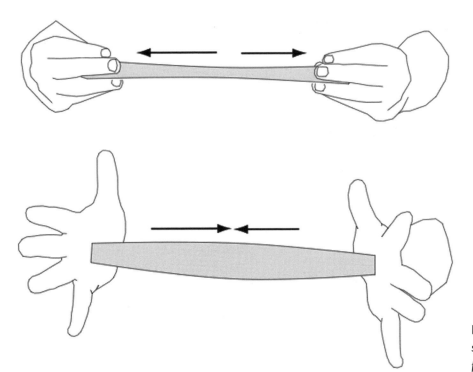

Figure 4.2.1. *Axial loading at its simplest – tension (top) and compression (bottom).*

Basic states of stress

Stress is defined as the effects of force on an object. Whereas Section 4.1 looked at the *external* effects of loading on a structural member – what is being carried and what the reactions are – stress deals with the *internal* effects of loading on a structural member.

Using fairly simple math, we can predict the effects of a well-defined loading on a structural member, and we can map out the effects of this loading, meaning that we can either select or design a structural member based on the forces it is subject to.

The two simplest states of stress are both *axial*, that is, they occur parallel to the axis of a structural member (Fig. 4.2.1). *Tension* is defined as an internal force that tends to pull the particles of a material apart, and *compression* is defined as an internal force that tends to push the particles of a material together (Fig. 4.2.2).

Tensile forces, for instance the forces in a metal cable holding a load from a crane, are relatively straightforward, though *tensile structures* are relatively recent developments. Until the 18th century, there were virtually no materials employed in building construction that could reliably perform under tension. Cast iron, in the form of chains, was used during the Renaissance to resist the thrust of church domes. However, in general tensile structures have the inherent problem that they fail catastrophically; if a tensile element fails the load it supports has nothing to break its fall (Fig. 4.2.3). Consequently, to

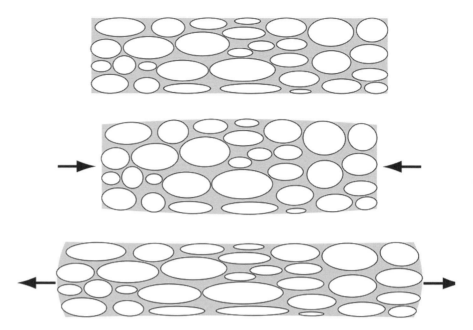

Figure 4.2.2. *A simplified view of the internal results of axial loading. In compression, the material's grains or fibers are pushed closer to one another. In tension, the material's grains or fibers are pulled apart from one another. Note that, in addition to the linear deformation (elongation or shortening) the material will have a secondary deformation – a bulging out in compression and a necking down in tension.*

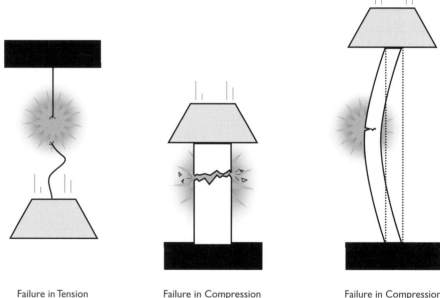

Failure in Tension   Failure in Compression   Failure in Compression
                                   (Crushing)   (Buckling)

Figure 4.2.3. *Failure modes due to axial loading. Failure in tension is sudden, while failure in pure compression tends to be less dramatic. However, a second mode of compression failure, buckling, presents additional complications (see Section 4.5).*

employ materials in tension we need to know with great confidence how they will perform under loading.

Compressive forces, for instance the forces in a table leg, are less straightforward. Historically compressive structures are literally as old as the hills. Materials that

Figure 4.2.4. *Compressive failure in buckling (Charlie Chaplin, after Mario Salvadori, Structure in Architecture).*

reliably perform under compression are easy to find, and compressive structures tend to fail gradually rather than catastrophically; if one member fails the load will be prevented from falling by other elements. While this failure may be complete, it may not be catastrophic. Thus, it is comparatively safe to experiment with compressive forces, and a large body of knowledge based on empirical experimentation was available to builders from an early era.

There is, however, a complication with compressive structures. Whereas tensile structures have essentially one *mode of failure*, that is, the member simply snaps, compressive structures have two modes of failure. They can fail simply, by crushing. This is analogous to a cable snapping. However, they can also fail by *buckling*. This occurs when a relatively thin structural member deforms or bends under loading (see Section 4.4 for a complete discussion of bending). The classic example of this is the cane in Charlie Chaplin's famous 'Little Man' sketch (Fig. 4.2.4). As Chaplin puts his weight on the cane, the load is initially purely compressive. As the load increases, however, the cane *bends*, and Chaplin's weight is no longer resisted by purely compressive forces. It is, instead, resisted by the capacity of the cane in *bending* and the cane will eventually fail by snapping in two instead of crushing.

For the moment, we will leave the problem of buckling aside and deal strictly with tension and with compression. Columns in which compression is the dominant concern are referred to as 'short' columns (or, in extreme cases, 'pucks') to distinguish them from columns in which bending is the major issue.

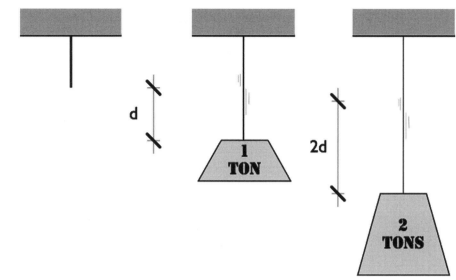

Figure 4.2.5. *Hooke's Law.*
Doubling the load on a structural
member (in this case a
tension rod or cable) will double its
deflection.

Stresses and strains

To understand structural behavior, it is important to know that all materials *deform* under stress. This deformation is often too small to see, but it nevertheless changes the material dimensionally and often physically.

In 1678, Robert Hooke, an associate of London architect Christopher Wren, discovered two key laws of structural behavior. First, the deformation of a material is always proportional to the stress it undergoes, or in Hooke's words, 'Ut tensio, sic vis' ('As the elongation, so is the force'). This means that doubling the force on a given structural member will double its deformation (Fig. 4.2.5). This is a key piece of knowledge, as it allows us to model large-scale structural behavior with small experiments.

Hooke's second discovery was that this relationship between force and deformation (or between 'stress and strain') only applies within limits. Every material will react to stress in two distinct modes. Up to a certain threshold (the material's *elastic limit*) it will deform under stress, but then will spring back to its original shape (Fig. 4.2.6). Beyond the *elastic limit*, the material will deform permanently (Fig. 4.2.7). The first condition is known as *elastic behavior*, the second is known as *plastic behavior*.

We will concentrate on elastic behavior, as it describes materials under what we hope is ordinary loading. Materials that have exceeded their elastic limit and are permanently deformed will often behave differently than materials that haven't had that kind of stress applied. Often, we will want to know how much a structural member will deflect under normal loading; for instance how much a cable will stretch, or how much a beam might bend. These changes are governed by a material's stiffness, or more technically, its *modulus of elasticity*.

The modulus of elasticity of a material is determined by testing, and available in common reference books. It is represented by *E*, which is defined as the ratio of stress to strain or, more commonly, stiffness – resistance to deformation.

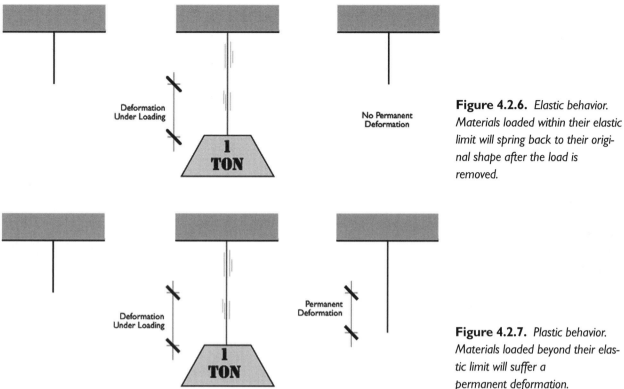

Figure 4.2.6. *Elastic behavior. Materials loaded within their elastic limit will spring back to their original shape after the load is removed.*

Figure 4.2.7. *Plastic behavior. Materials loaded beyond their elastic limit will suffer a permanent deformation.*

Strain is a percentage measure of the change in dimension of a material under stress, or:

$$s = e/L$$

where e is the change in dimension and L is the original length.

It follows that:

$$E = f/s$$

That is, the modulus of elasticity, or stiffness, is the ratio of stress to strain – how many pounds, for example, it takes to stretch a material one inch. By definition, we can expand both f and s, knowing that $f = P/A$ (the total force divided by the area of the member in question) and that $s = e/L$, from above. We therefore get:

$$E = (PL)/(Ae)$$

as a definition of the modulus of elasticity, E. By adjusting the formula, we also get the quite useful relationship:

$$e = (PL)/(AE)$$

which says that the total deformation of a member is proportional to its length and the force it is undergoing, and inversely proportional to its area and its modulus of elasticity. (In common terms, a material will stretch more if we put more force on it, or if it is longer to begin with; and it will stretch less if

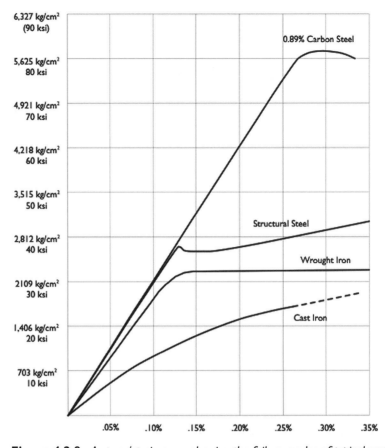

Figure 4.2.8. *A stress/strain curve showing the failure modes of typical metals.*
Up to a certain point (36 ksi for ordinary structural steel), these materials have a reliable
relationship between added load and deformation, as Hooke's Law states. Past their elastic
limit, they will deform out of proportion to their loading. Wrought iron, for instance, will con-
tinue to deform without additional load at around 32 ksi. Safety factors built into calcula-
tions ensure that no structural component will be loaded to its elastic limit, avoiding
permanent deformation and, eventually, failure.

we increase its cross section or make it out of some stiffer material.) In other
words, the greater the cross-sectional area of a member, or the greater its *E*,
the more it will resist deflection. Likewise, the greater the force on a member,
or the longer that member is, the greater the measured deflection will be. Given
that *E* is readily available from references, this makes solving deflection equations quite simple. Relationships between stress and strain are shown for
common building metals in Figure 4.2.8, and a general picture of common building materials' related stiffness and strength is given in Figure 4.2.9.

In addition to a material's *elastic limit*, it is important to know the ultimate *yield
stress*, or the level of stress at which a material will fail entirely. These two modes
of failure – plasticity and yield – must be taken into account when designing
structural elements as failure in either one will ruin the structure. A failure in
plasticity will leave a permanent deformation, while a failure in yield will, perhaps obviously, collapse. Various methods of calculating structural members
rely on knowing either the elastic limit or the ultimate yield stress of a material, and using a *factor of safety* to determine an allowable load as a percentage

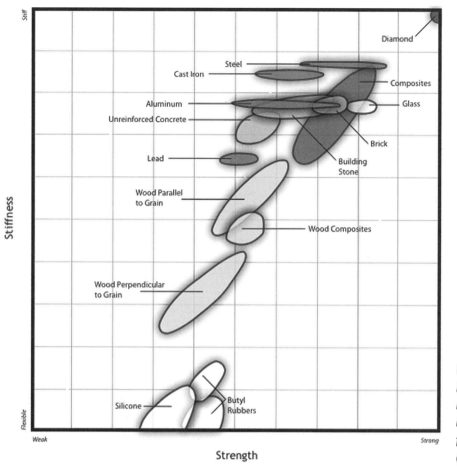

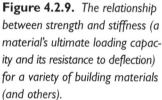

Figure 4.2.9. *The relationship between strength and stiffness (a material's ultimate loading capacity and its resistance to deflection) for a variety of building materials (and others).*

of these numbers. Factors of safety are, understandably, quite conservative, but proven reliable. Factors of safety range from 1.6 for steel and other metals whose composition can be carefully controlled, and whose behavior is well understood, to 5.0 for experimental concrete mixes where quality may be an issue, and where the material does not have a long record of performance. These factors are incorporated into well-publicized Allowable Working Units Stresses, shown in Table 4.2.1.

Strength of a material, then, is not a single number, but a description of the magnitudes and relationships between its elastic limit and its yield stress. Obviously, materials that are too elastic – that deform a lot in comparison to the stress they undergo – are not used structurally, but are often useful as jointing materials or finishes. Materials that have a great deal of elastic resistance – steel in particular – make very good structural materials. However, if the elastic limit and yield stress are very close together, we refer to the material as *brittle*, and tend not to employ it structurally as it will fail suddenly, rather than gradually.

In designing axial members, we look at two criteria: whether the loading will stress the material above its allowable working stress, and whether the resulting deflection will be within specified limits. Designing for allowable stress in

Table 4.2.1 Basic strength properties for typical building materials.

| Material | Weight | | Elastic limit | | Ultimate strength | | | |
| | | | | | Tension | | Compression | |
	kg/cm^3	lbs/in.^{3}	kg/cm^2	psi	kg/cm^2	psi	kg/cm^2	psi
Concrete	0.0023	0.0830	–	–	–	–	176	2500
Brick masonary	0.0021	0.0750	–	–	–	–	141	2000
Cast iron	0.0072	0.2600	–	–	1757.75	25,000	5273	75,000
Wrought iron	0.0078	0.2810	1757.75	25,000	3374.88	48,000	3375	48,000
A36 structural steel	0.0078	0.2830	2531.16	36,000	4921.70	70,000	4922	70,000
Aluminum (6061-T6)	0.0027	0.0980	2460.85	35,000.00	2671.78	38,000	–	–
Douglas fir, structural	0.0006	0.0230	–	–	1054.65	15,000	274	3900
Southern pine, dense structural	0.0006	0.0230	–	–	–	–	281	4000
Oak, 1450 grade	0.0006	0.0230	–	–	984.34	14,000	246	3500
Structural glass Rubber	0.0026	0.0930	–	–	–	–	–	–
Carbon fiber	0.0018	0.0640	–	–	38740.81	551,000	–	–

* Measured parallel to grain for woods. Note: These figures are averages, intended for illustration only. Depending on manufacture and processing, materials may vary significantly from these figures.

axial members is straightforward, since stresses are published in units of load per units of cross-sectional area. For a given load and material, we simply divide the total loading by the material's allowable unit stress to arrive at a required cross-sectional area:

$$P_{allowable} = f_{allowable} \times A$$

P in this formula is the total allowable load, f is the allowable unit stress (see Table 4.2.1), and A is the member's cross-sectional area. For deflection, we use:

$$e = PL/AE$$

to find the anticipated deflection.

To complicate things, a material's elasticity and yield stress are always related to temperature. Colder weather tends to increase resistance to elastic deformation, but it also tends to decrease the yield stress. Hot weather – or fire – can radically alter a material's elastic behavior. This is why steel must normally be fireproofed, as a hot fire can not only weaken steel columns and beams, but actually melt them.

Example: Determine the expected deflection in the structural members shown in Figure 4.2.10. The cable is made of aluminum, the post is made of Douglas Fir. Are either of these loads likely to induce failure? What steps could be taken to reduce the deflection in both cases?

Allowable Working Stress

Tension		Compression*		Shear		Modulus of Elasticity	
kg/cm²	psi	kg/cm²	psi	kg/cm²	psi	kg/cm²	psi
–	–	43.94	625	–	–	210,930	3,000,000
–	–	12.30	175	–	–	914,030	13,000,000
–	–	632.79	9000	316.40	4500	1,054,650	15,000,000
843.72	12000	843.72	12000	703.10	10,000	1,898,370	27,000,000
1546.82	22000	1546.82	22000	843.72	12,000	2,038,990	29,000,000
1054.65	15000	1054.65	15000			632,790	9,000,000
–	–	84.37	1200	7.03	100	112,496	1,600,000
–	–	84.37	1200	9.00	128	112,496	1,600,000
–	–	77.34	1100	8.44	120	105,465	1,500,000
						674,976	9,600,000
						2,327,261	33,100,000

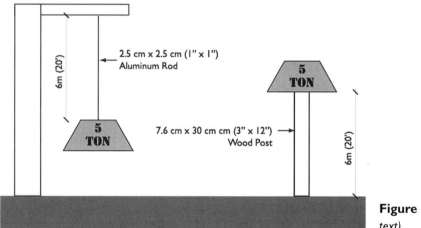

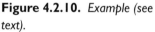

Figure 4.2.10. *Example (see text).*

Solution: For aluminum, we take E from Table 4.2.1 as 632,790 kg/cm² (9,000,000 psi), and get:

$e = PL/AE$
$e = (4500\,\text{kg} \times 600\,\text{cm})/(6.45\,\text{cm}^2 \times 632,790\,\text{kg/cm}^2)$
$\quad = 0.66\,\text{cm}$

$e = PL/AE$
$e = (10,000\,\text{lb} \times 240\,\text{in.})/(1\,\text{in.}^2 \times 9,000,000\,\text{psi})$
$\quad = 0.27\,\text{in.}$

In this case, the allowable working unit stress for aluminum, 1055 kg/cm² (15,000 psi), is far greater than the load induced, 350 kg/cm² (5000 psi). Likewise, it is far below the elastic limit of 35,000 psi. However, the deflection is significant.

For Douglas Fir, we take E from Table 4.2.1 as 112,500 kg/cm^2 (1,600,000 psi), and get:

$e = PL/AE$ $e = PL/AE$

$e = (4500\,kg \times 600\,cm)/(230\,cm^2 \times$ $e = (10,000\,lb \times 240\,in.)/(36\,in.^2 \times$
     112,500 kg/cm^2)   1,600,000 psi)

$e = 0.104\,cm$ $e = 0.042\,in.$

Here, the allowable working stress for Douglas Fir, 84 kg/cm^2 (1,200 psi), is not exceeded by the design load, which works out to 19.5 kg/cm^2 (278 psi). Again, however, the deflection is significant.

In either case, the deflection could be minimized by making the members larger (increasing A), changing material (E), or by lessening either the length of the member or the load.

It is important to note that while ideal structural materials will perform nearly equally under tension and compression, many materials that we build with do not (human bone, incidentally, has identical yield stresses in both, making it particularly suited to the varied loadings that we subject it to). Brick and stone, for example, fail under relatively small tension loads, while being extraordinarily strong in compression. Likewise, steel cables are incapable of taking any compressive force, yet they perform very well in tension. Concrete is a particularly interesting case. It is excellent in compression, yet the nature of its composition – aggregate particles held together by an adhesive matrix – means it is terrible in tension. When using concrete in anything other than pure compression, therefore, it is combined, or *reinforced* with steel to form a composite system (see Section 3.5).

Other materials have more complicated performance factors. Wood, for example, is good in compression, but it is only good in tension if it is loaded parallel to the grain. If it is pulled perpendicular to the grain, it will split well below its expected elastic limit. In this case, the elastic limit is slightly lower across the grain, but the yield stress is much lower.

Wood is considered an *isotropic* material, meaning that it has a structural directionality. Steel and concrete, neither of which have a recognizable direction, are called *anisotropic*. Much like reinforced concrete, materials with directionality can be combined or organized to create particularly efficient structural elements.

Simple tension and compression structures: funicular shapes

For every loading condition, there will be a corresponding shape that can resist the load through only tension or compression. These shapes can thus be designed using the principles just discussed. Such shapes are termed *funicular shapes*.

The simplest funicular shapes are those that resist a single point load. The shapes for these are straight lines, and are referred to as *columns*. Since common parlance uses this term for compressively loaded members, it is customary to refer to axial members under pure tension as *tensile columns*.

Multiplying either the number of loads or reactions will lead to progressively more complicated – though still statically simple – shapes. Each of the examples shown in Figures 4.2.11 and 4.2.12 demonstrate funicular geometry for the loads implied on them.

For constant loading (i.e., a floor slab), the funicular geometry is mathematically complex, but conceptually quite simple. A series of weights hung along a cable supported at two points will, by definition, form a funicular curve – since cables cannot perform in compression. As the distribution of weights becomes more and more consistent, the cable will tend toward a *catenary* shape (from Latin, *catena*, meaning chain). Using principles of translational and

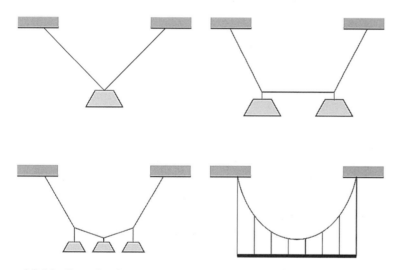

Figure 4.2.11. *Funicular shapes in tension. Each of these shapes experiences only tension, given the loading shown.*

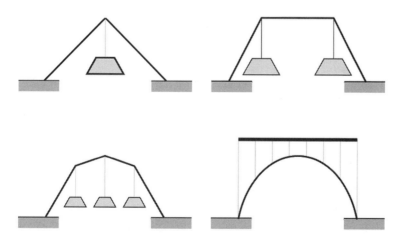

Figure 4.2.12. *Funicular shapes in compression. Note that these are the same for given loading conditions as those in tension. Compressive members must often be more substantial than tension members to avoid the danger of buckling, while tension members can ordinarily be sized for axial loading only.*

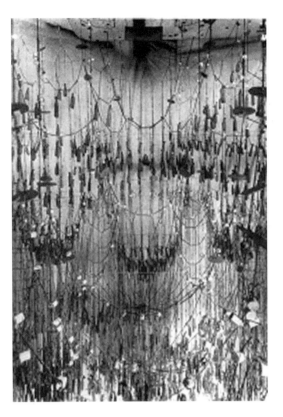

Figure 4.2.13. *Funicular shapes in practice. Catalan architect Antonio Gaudi (1852–1926) used tension nets and weights to determine the funicular arch shapes for the Sagrada Familia in Barcelona.*

rotational equilibrium, one can quite easily calculate the reactions at the supports, and thus the force at any point along the cable.

Flipping the cable upside down will, predictably, show a catenary shape in compression. This principle was used by Antonio Gaudi, a Catalan architect and engineer, to determine the structural shapes for vaults in the Sagrada Familia Church in Barcelona, Spain (Fig. 4.2.13).

Arches are among the oldest high-performance structural shapes, having been used consistently in large-scale Roman buildings. The geometry of Roman arches is not perfect – they are circular instead of catenary, and therefore not purely funicular – but these shapes allowed relatively easy construction. Their relative bulk compared to structurally efficient shapes of the 20th century allowed a wide margin of error in the calculation of load paths, to say the least. Contemporary bridges tend to adopt more purely structural, efficient geometry (Fig. 4.2.14).

Element design

For simple funicular shapes, the design of structural elements can be quite simple. Since allowable loading is given in amount of force over area (pounds per square inch or kilograms per square centimeter), our concern is providing enough cross-sectional area to adequately distribute the force we intend to apply. Generally, we take the given force and divide it by the allowable stress. The result will be an area, the minimum required to spread the force out over an acceptable cross section.

Figure 4.2.14. *Perhaps the most famous funicular of all, the cables of the Golden Gate Bridge (and all other suspension bridges) are pure catenary shapes, reflecting the additive loading of the bridge deck (a distributed load) being transferred through pure tension elements to the towers.*

Example: Design a steel cable to support a tensile load of 30,000 lb (66,000 lb).

From Table 4.2.1, we see that the allowable stress for steel is $1540\,kg/cm^2$ (22,000 psi). This means that for every square centimeter of cross section (perpendicular to the load) we can safely apply 1540 kg. To support a load of 30,000 kg (66,000 lb), therefore, the cable will need to have:

$$P = f_{all}A \qquad\qquad P = f_{all}A$$
$$30{,}000\,kg = (1540\,kg/cm^2)\,(A\ in.^2) \qquad 66{,}000\,lb = (22{,}000\,lb/in.^2)\,(A\ in.^2)$$
$$(30{,}000\,kg)/(1540\,kg/cm^2) = A\ in.^2 \qquad (66{,}000\,lb)/(22{,}000\,lb/in.^2) = A\ in.^2$$

Note here that pounds cancel, leaving us with a figure in square centimeters or inches:

$$19.5\,cm^2 = A \qquad 3\ in.^2 = A$$

So we need a cable with a cross-sectional area of 3 in.^{2} to safely carry the load as shown. Using geometry, we can find the required diameter of a round cable to satisfy this:

$$A\ in.^2 = \Pi r^2 \qquad\qquad A\ in.^2 = \Pi r^2$$
$$19.5\,cm^2 = \Pi r^2 \qquad\qquad 3\ in.^2 = \Pi r^2$$
$$19.5\,cm^2/3.14 = r^2 \qquad\qquad 3\ in.^2/3.14 = r^2$$
$$6.2\,cm^2 = r^2 \qquad\qquad 0.955\ in.^2 = r^2$$
$$r = \sqrt{6.2\,cm^2} \qquad\qquad r = \sqrt{0.955\ in.^2}$$
$$r = 2.5\,cm \qquad\qquad r = 0.977\ in.$$

Here note that square centimeters and inches are reduced to linear measures by taking the square root of the area. Thus, the required radius is about 1 in.

CAVEAT: As mentioned previously, axially loaded compression members (columns) must meet additional geometric requirements to prevent buckling. A general rule of thumb is to make columns relatively compact, that is round or square, to prevent having a weak axis. Likewise, axially loaded members can develop additional internal stresses if their connection to a support is much narrower than either cross-axis. Again, it is generally advisable to make either compressive or tensile members under axial load roughly square, or round, to ensure proper stress distribution at connections. We will discuss slender column design in detail later – for the moment our compression examples will be in a realm that does not induce buckling.

Frequently asked questions

I notice in the tables that some materials have no allowable limit in tension. Are they that weak that they can't take any load at all? These materials (wood parallel to the grain in particular) can take some tension load – often quite a bit. But their performance in tension is often very sensitive to material imperfections; a knot in a piece of wood, for example, might reduce the effective cross-sectional area of a member considerably as it might not be adhered to the fibers around it. Because tension members fail catastrophically, the factor of safety in tension for materials with potential flaws is, essentially, very high. It's not generally safe to rely on a potentially flawed material like wood in these situations (note that in compression, a knot would end up taking part of the load as the member deformed in length).

Why aren't funicular shapes used more often? If they're the most efficient, why do we use flat beams and slabs? Funicular shapes are the most efficient in terms of total material, but they require very large heights to achieve their geometry under distributed loads. To get the proper curve, a catenary arch must typically be about 1/4 as high as its span is long. The Golden Gate Bridge, for example, has 735 ft towers to achieve its 4090 ft span. While its cables are very light, considering the load they carry over so great a distance, this would be waste a lot of space in a multi-story building. As we'll see, designing structures in bending isn't as pure as designing funiculars, but the material penalties aren't high enough to demand such extreme geometry for typical situations.

Glossary and formulas

Allowable Stress	A generally accepted safe load per unit of area for a given material. Often dictated by codes or industry standards.
Anisotropic	Material with a consistent structural behavior in all directions. Steel and concrete are examples of anisotropic materials.
Compression	An internal state of stress in which a material's fibers tend to be pushed into one another.
Deflection Formula	A member will change its length by a calculable amount, e: e = PL/AE. Where P is the applied load, L is the original length, A is the member's cross-sectional area, and E is the material's modulus of elasticity.

Deformation	Change in shape due to loading.
Elastic Behavior	The tendency of a material to 'snap back' to its original dimensions after it is loaded within its *elastic limit*.
Elastic Limit	The stress level within which a material will not permanently deform. Beyond the elastic limit, a material will change shape under loading and not return to its original form.
Factor of Safety	A numerical allowance added into all structural calculations that ensures no structural material will be stressed to an unsafe limit – either to its elastic limit or to its yield stress.
Funicular	Every opera fan's favorite structural term. A shape that functions in pure compression or tension for a given load.
Isotropic	Material with a directional structural makeup, typically with very different abilities to resist tension and/or compression depending on whether a load is applied parallel to or perpendicular to its grain. Wood is the best-known isotropic material.
Modulus of Elasticity	A measure of a material's stiffness, or more technically, resistance to deformation. Measured in pounds per square inch, but not a measure of pressure or stress.
Plastic Behavior	The tendency of a material to deform permanently once it is loaded past its *elastic limit*.
Strain	Deformation, measured in percentage based on the original, pre-loaded dimensions of a structural member.
Stress	A measure of internal loading on a material, defined as the total load divided by the cross-sectional area across which the load is spread.
Tension	An internal state of stress in which a material's fibers tend to pull away from one another.
Yield Stress	The level of internal load per unit of area beyond which the material may fail (break, crush, or shear).

Further reading

Salvadori, M. (1975) Structural Materials (Chapter 3); Basic States of Stress and Tension (Chapter 5) and Compression Structures (Chapter 6), *Structure in Architecture: The Building of Buildings* (Englewood Cliffs: Prentice-Hall), pp. 37–56, 79–134.

4.3   Shear and bending

Shear	Definition
	Examples
	Relationship to tension and compression
	Torsion
Simple Bending	Definition
	Examples
	Relationship to tension and compression
Shear and Bending in Elements	Shear diagrams
	Moment diagrams
	Relationships between shear and moment

Introduction

In addition to tension and compression, structural elements can undergo more complex forms of stress. Understanding these are critical to understanding most everyday structural types, including beams, slabs, etc. The two most common types of structural stress are *shear* and *bending*.

Shear occurs when a force tends to slide particles in a structural material relative to one another. Shear occurs in a bolt or nail when two connected members are pulled along one another, for example. Other instances of shear include a paper punch, or a desktop at its support.

Bending occurs when a member is loaded at a point other than its supports. As a member bends, it will deform slightly, with the top edge elongating and the bottom edge contracting. This creates a characteristic curve in members that are undergoing bending. One edge thus goes into *tension*, while the other goes into *compression*.

Because of the principles of rotational equilibrium, shear and bending are closely related to tension and compression. A shear force in an object will result in internal tension and compression as the object's material tries to maintain equilibrium in both senses. Bending is a more complicated case, as it can be described as the distribution of tension and compression throughout a cross section.

Shear

Like all forces, shear tends to deform, or change the shape of a given object (Fig. 4.3.1). Typically, shear will *skew* a shape, turning a rectangular section into a parallelogram, for example. Because there is no change in length in a

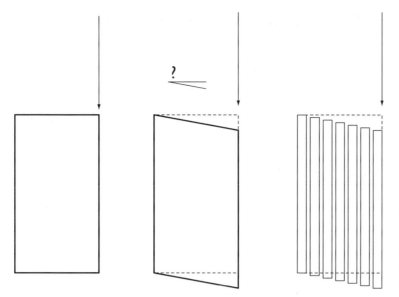

Figure 4.3.1. *Basic shear. Shear tends to force planes of a material to slide past one another. Materials resist shear by developing resistance between 'slices'.*

body undergoing shear, the measure of shear deformation is the *skew angle*, also known as the *shear strain*.

The sliding force of one material plane past another is referred to as *shear stress*. It is measured by the amount of force acting over one square centimeter or inch. Like tension and compression, the deformation of a body is proportional to the shear stress being imparted to it within a material's elastic range of behavior, and out of proportion in the material's plastic range of behavior. While shear strain is in some ways similar to strain induced by tension and compression, the ratio between shear stress and strain is less than that between tensile or compressive stress and strain – typically about 1/2.

If we take a body undergoing shear, for example the bracket in Figure 4.3.2, and take a free body diagram of it at the support, we find that in addition to the simple equation to solve for translational equilibrium there must also be reactions that keep the free body in rotational equilibrium. Therefore, any shear stress S will develop not only the reaction S_1 but also complementary forces S_R and S_L. These can then be summarized as shown. Here, the four shear forces are combined into two equal and opposite tensile and compressive forces. Note that *Shear always induces tension and compression in a structural member*. Materials weak in tension will fail under shear, typically along a 45° angle that represents the direction of the induced tensile force. Likewise, a thin material will fail by *buckling* when it undergoes shear – imagine a sheet of paper attempting to carry a weight at its end. The weight will find the most direct path to the ground, which in this case will tend to bend the paper out of the way.

Shear stress is measured by dividing the entire load in shear by the cross-sectional area of the member in the plane of the force.

253

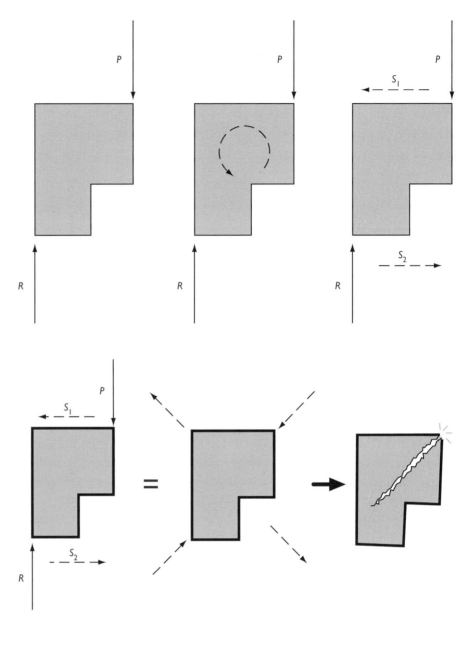

Figure 4.3.2. *Loading in shear typically induces a more complex set of internal reactions as the material develops resistance to both translational and rotational forces. Failure in shear is usually manifested by a diagonal cracking, which represents the resolution of the shear load and its reaction into diagonal compressive and tensile forces.*

Example: How large will the bolt shown in Figure 4.3.3 need to be to withstand the forces shown if it is fabricated in steel? Dense Southern Yellow Pine?

Solution: From Table 4.2.1, we know that the maximum allowable shear in steel is 844 kg/cm² (12,000 psi), whereas for Dense Southern Yellow Pine it is 9 kg/cm² (128 psi). The total shear acting on the bolt is:

$$900\,\text{kg} + 1350\,\text{kg} = 2250\,\text{kg} \qquad 2000\,\text{lb} + 3000\,\text{lb} = 5000\,\text{lb}$$

For steel, therefore, the required cross-sectional area will be:

$$\begin{array}{ll} 2250\,\text{kg}/(844\,\text{kg/cm}^2) & 5000\,\text{lb}/12{,}000\,\text{psi} \\ = 2.67\,\text{cm}^2 & = 0.4167\,\text{in.}^2 \end{array}$$

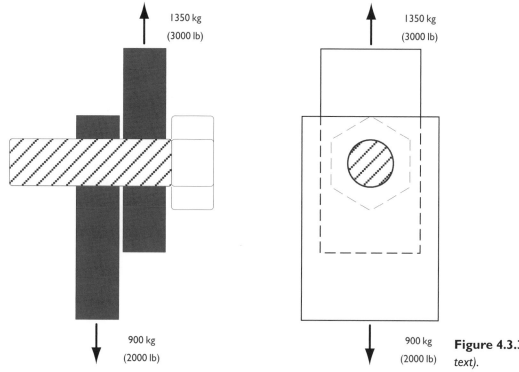

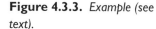

Figure 4.3.3. *Example (see text).*

or 0.4167 in.² Assuming a round bolt, the required radius will be:

$$\pi r^2 = 2.67 \, \text{cm}^2 \qquad \pi r^2 = 0.4167 \, \text{in.}^2$$
$$r^2 = 0.85 \, \text{cm}^2 \qquad r^2 = 0.132 \, \text{in.}^2$$
$$r = 0.92 \, \text{cm} \qquad r = 0.36 \, \text{in.}$$

Rounding up, the required radius for the bolt would be about a centimeter, or 3/8 in.

Using Southern Pine, we find that the required area would be:

$$2250 \, \text{kg}/(9 \, \text{kg/cm}^2) \qquad 5000 \, \text{lb}/128 \, \text{psi}$$
$$= 250 \, \text{cm}^2 \qquad = 39 \, \text{in.}^2$$

Assuming a square bolt, the required dimension will be:

$$\sqrt{250 \, \text{cm}^2} = 15.8 \, \text{cm} \qquad \sqrt{39 \, \text{in.}^2} = 6.25 \, \text{in.}$$

From this it can be seen why steel is preferred to pine for large structural connections.

Bending

Bending is intuitively understood – when we bend something we change its shape from flat to curved – but a good structural definition is more difficult to come by. A simple definition is this: an element in *bending* is transferring vertical loads over a horizontal distance or (vise versa) through internal stresses. Or, more generally, bending channels internal loads more or less perpendicular to the direction of force.

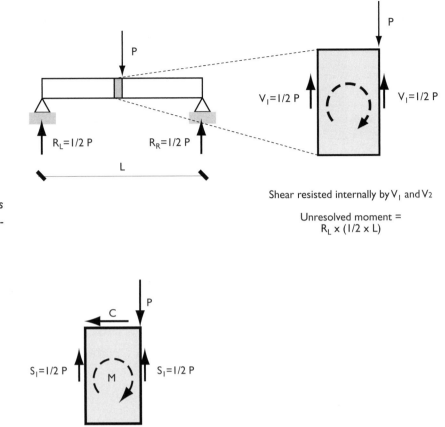

Figure 4.3.4. *In addition to shear, loading on a beam results in a moment that must be resisted by internal forces.*

Shear resisted internally by V_1 and V_2

Unresolved moment =
$R_L \times (1/2 \times L)$

Figure 4.3.5. *The loading in Figure 4.3.4 will result in an internal set of axial stresses – tension and compression – that work together to resist the 'twist' of the loading moment, twisting back by going into tension (pulling) on top, and into compression (pushing) on the bottom.*

What this means is that the shape of the material is resolving a large gap between the position of the load and the reaction(s). As shown in Figure 4.3.4, a free body of a beam taken at the point of loading reveals that reactions are insufficient to maintain rotational equilibrium. If *P* is located at the midspan, then R_1 will be equal to $1/2P$. To maintain translational equilibrium, P_1, the internal stress at the midpoint of the beam, will have to make up the difference, and will also be $1/2P$. However, there will be a lever arm acting on the midpoint equal to $R_1 \times 1/2$. Unless this is counteracted, the member will rotate. As there is no other force to resist this moment arm, the beam must develop an *internal moment* – a sort of 'reverse twist' that occurs within the material of the beam itself – to counteract this, equal but opposite to $R_1 \times 1/2$.

Since moments can be expressed as a coupled set of forces, the internal moment at *P* can also be shown as in Figure 4.3.5. This diagram shows the two internal shear reactions to keep the free body in translational equilibrium, and two opposing forces that keep the free body in rotational equilibrium – *tension* in the bottom of the beam, and *compression* in the top. The beam develops internal resisting moments when it is loaded, which take the form of a 'push' at the top and a 'pull' at the bottom. If we overload the

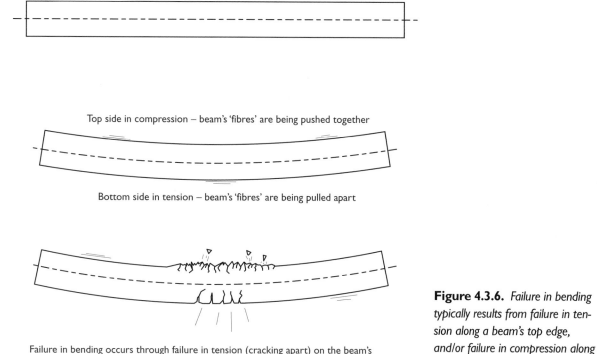

Figure 4.3.6. *Failure in bending typically results from failure in tension along a beam's top edge, and/or failure in compression along the beam's bottom edge.*

Top side in compression – beam's 'fibres' are being pushed together

Bottom side in tension – beam's 'fibres' are being pulled apart

Failure in bending occurs through failure in tension (cracking apart) on the beam's bottom edge, and through compression (crushing) on the top.

beam, we can see that the top begins to compress (or buckle) while the bottom tends to pull apart (Fig. 4.3.6). Bending is, therefore, really a state of simultaneous tension and compression spread across the section of a beam. Design for bending can use this principle to resolve the internal bending moment in terms of these two forces.

We can see from our diagram that the couple $(C_1 T_1)$ is related not only to the *span* of the member, but also to its *depth*, in that the internal moment induced by that couple must be equal to the moment induced by the reaction (Fig. 4.3.7):

$$R_1 \times (l/2) = M_1 = (C_1 \times d/2) + (T_1 \times d/2)$$

This idea of depth as integral to resisting bending moment is very important. The deeper a structural member, the more 'leverage' we have to resist the moment imparted by the reactions. The internal moment couple is actually distributed throughout the depth of the beam, with maximum tension occurring at the bottom 'fiber' and maximum tension occurring at the top as shown in Figure 4.3.7. The *area* of both triangles in this diagram must be equal to the *value* of the loading moment at any point in the beam. Note that the triangles' height and base are two different measures – the base measures maximum stress, while the height measures the depth of the beam. The area of each triangle can therefore be measured in kilogram-meters or foot-pounds, similar units to the maximum moment. The beam can resist greater moment either by accepting a greater maximum stress (increasing the triangles' areas by increasing their base) or by getting deeper (increasing the triangles' area by

257

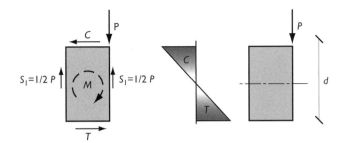

Figure 4.3.7. *The moment couple in Figure 4.3.5 is actually distributed throughout the cross-section of the beam – instead of two discrete vectors, the resulting tensile and compressive stresses are distributed across the beam's depth and can be thought of as two triangles of tension and compression vectors, as shown.*

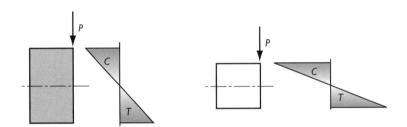

Figure 4.3.8. *Deeper beams result in greater efficiency, giving the resisting moment a taller triangle (depth) and thus a shorter base (stress) to achieve the same area. Shallower beams must develop a greater stress in the top and bottom edges of the beam to handle the same load.*

increasing their height) (Fig. 4.3.8). In the next chapter we'll see why increasing depth is even more effective than this diagram shows.

The dot-dash line in Figure 4.3.8 represents a region of the beam in which no tension or compression occur, known as the 'neutral axis.' Here, the beam's material is under no stress at all, while the beam's top and bottom edges are under the most stress.

Shear and bending diagrams

Given what we have just seen, it is relatively easy to find the maximum shear and bending values for a simple loaded beam. Such a beam can then be sized according to its maximum allowable shear stress and/or its maximum allowable tensile or compressive stress (covered in Section 4.4). Graphing the internal shear and bending along a beam is referred to as a 'shear/moment diagram,' and it is a useful tool for sizing and understanding how beams work. Shear/moment diagrams can be derived by mentally 'walking through' the beam under consideration and figuring what internal loads are needed to keep the beam in translational and rotational equilibrium at each key point.

For an example, take the beam in Figure 4.3.9, with simple supports and two loads of 13.5 kg (30 lb) and 22.5 kg (50 lb). If we solve for the reactions R_1 and

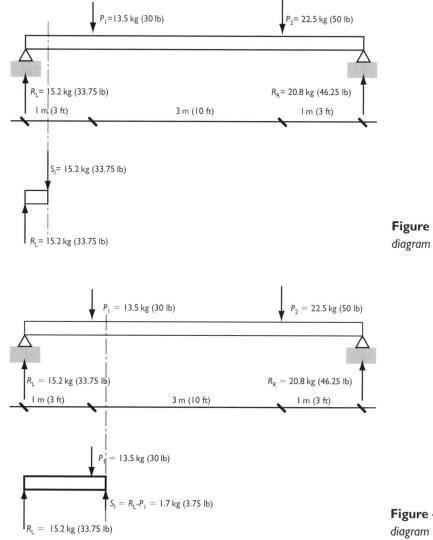

Figure 4.3.9. *Shear/moment diagram example (see text).*

Figure 4.3.10. *Shear/moment diagram example (see text).*

R_r we get the support reactions shown. If we then take a free body diagram of the left end of the beam, we find there must be an internal shear stress equal to R_L to maintain translational equilibrium – without such an internal force the left end of the beam would simply move in the direction of the reaction. This is true for any free body taken of the left end of the beam, so long as the section cut occurs 'before' the first load. At any point along this portion, an internal shear stress must develop to counteract the force of the reaction. Therefore, the shear stress in the left-most 1 m (3 ft) of the beam will be constant and equal to the size of the reaction, 15.2 kg (33.75 lb) as shown on the graph.

Then, if we take a free body to the right of the first load (Fig. 4.3.10), we find that the shear condition necessarily changes. Solving for translational equilibrium, we find that there must be an internal shear stress in the beam equal to the difference between the reaction and the first load, or 1.7 kg (3.75 lb). The internal shear changes at the load point. It follows that the shear stress will remain constant over the next 3 m (10 ft) segment of the beam at 1.7 kg (3.75 lb). However, a free body taken just to the right of the *second* load (Fig. 4.3.11) shows that the internal shear stress must again change to keep the free

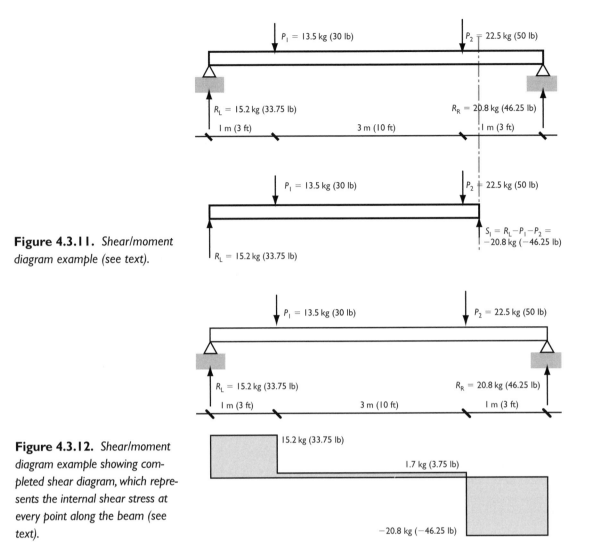

Figure 4.3.11. *Shear/moment diagram example (see text).*

Figure 4.3.12. *Shear/moment diagram example showing completed shear diagram, which represents the internal shear stress at every point along the beam (see text).*

body in equilibrium. In this case it will be the difference between the left-most reaction and the two forces, or −20.8 kg (−46.25 lb). Note that this is exactly the magnitude of the reaction at the right end of the beam, and a free body taken at the right-most support will show that the shear stress drops back to 0 at the (infinitesimal) point of the reaction. Interestingly, the completed shear diagram (Fig. 4.3.12) tells us that, even though the greatest single load on the beam is 22.5 kg (50 lb), the maximum internal *shear* in the beam is only 20.8 kg (46.25 lb).

The shear diagram can be intuitively understood by looking at the directions of the force arrows. Reading from the left, the reaction 'pushes' the internal shear up 15.2 kg (33.75 lb). The first force 'pushes' the internal shear down by 13.5 kg (30 lb). The second force 'pushes' it down a further 22.5 kg (50 lb), and the right reaction 'pushes' it up by 20.8 kg (46.25 lb). (While this isn't a rigorous description of the physics at work, it does help us to organize the cumulative effects of each load and gives us the correct diagram.)

If we follow the same procedure to find the internal *moment* at each point in the beam, we get a different – though related – diagram. This is complicated

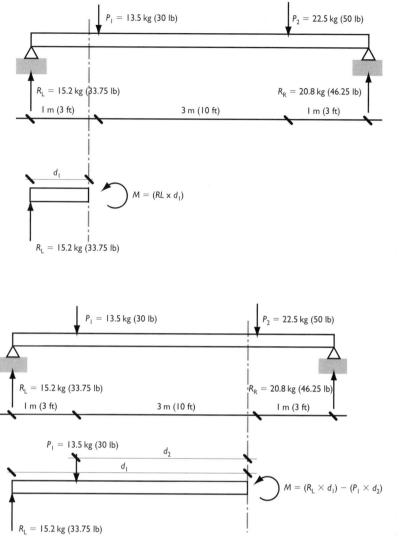

Figure 4.3.13. *Shear/moment diagram example (see text).*

Figure 4.3.14. *Shear/moment diagram example (see text).*

somewhat because we now have to consider the position of each 'cut' along the beam in addition to the sum of the forces; each force on the beam will produce an internal moment that changes as the cuts that we make for our free body diagrams get closer or further away. Beginning, again, at the left side of the diagram, we note that there can be no internal moment at the very edge of the beam, therefore the value at the left end is 0. However, the reaction immediately begins to induce a moment as our 'cut' moves to the right, equal by definition to 15.2 kg (33.75 lb) multiplied by whatever distance we've moved (Fig. 4.3.13). Therefore, at the point of the first load, 1 m (3 ft) in from the support, the internal moment must be 15.2 kg (33.75 lb) $\times$ 1 m (3 ft), or 15.2 kg-m (101.25 ft-lb). In a similar fashion, the first load will immediately induce a moment, in the *opposite* direction from that induced by the reaction (Fig. 4.3.14). (Note that the reaction 'twists' the piece of the beam we're looking at clockwise around the point we're cutting, while the load 'twists' it counter-clockwise. Since they're going in opposite directions, these two moments cancel one another out, rather than add to one another.) Therefore, a free body cut 1.2 m (4 ft) from the left reaction will show an internal moment that is the

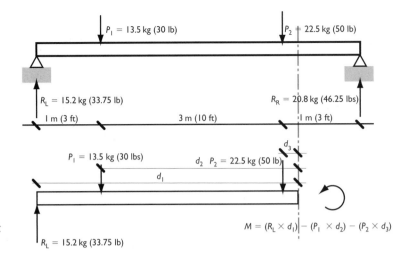

Figure 4.3.15. *Shear/moment diagram example (see text).*

difference between the moment induced by the reaction at that point, and that induced by the first load – in this case:

$$(15.2\,\text{kg} \times 1.2\,\text{m}) - (13.5\,\text{kg} \times 0.3\,\text{m}) \qquad (33.75\,\text{lb} \times 4\,\text{ft}) - (30\,\text{lb} \times 1\,\text{ft})$$
$$= 18.24\,\text{kg-m} - 4.05\,\text{kg-m} \qquad = 135\,\text{ft-lb} - 30\,\text{ft-lb}$$
$$= 14.2\,\text{kg-m} \qquad = 105\,\text{ft-lb}$$

The internal moment will thus increase *more slowly* over this portion of the beam, until at a point just before the second load it will be (Fig. 4.3.15):

$$(15.2\,\text{kg} \times 4\,\text{m}) - (13.5\,\text{kg} \times 3\,\text{m}) \qquad (33.75\,\text{lb} \times 13\,\text{ft}) - (30\,\text{lb} \times 10\,\text{ft})$$
$$= 60.8\,\text{kg-m} - 40.5\,\text{kg-m} \qquad = 438.75\,\text{ft-lb} - 300\,\text{ft-lb}$$
$$= 20.3\,\text{kg-m} \qquad = 138.75\,\text{ft-lb}$$

At this point, the *second* load will begin to induce a moment, in the same direction as the first load (Fig. 4.3.16), until by the extreme right end of the beam we will have:

$$(15.2\,\text{kg} \times 5\,\text{m}) - (13.5\,\text{kg} \times 4\,\text{m}) - (22.5\,\text{kg} \times 1\,\text{m})$$
$$(33.75\,\text{lb} \times 16\,\text{ft}) - (30\,\text{lb} \times 13\,\text{ft}) - (50\,\text{lb} \times 3\,\text{ft})$$
$$= 76\,\text{kg-m} - 54\,\text{kg-m} - 22.5\,\text{kg-m}$$
$$= 540\,\text{ft-lb} - 390\,\text{ft-lb} - 150\,\text{ft-lb} = 0\,\text{ft-lb} = 0\,\text{kg-m}$$

This is to be expected, since the connection, a pin, can't take any bending itself. (Note that there is a 0.5 kg rounding error in the metric example that we've eliminated.)

From this completed moment diagram (Fig. 4.3.16), we can see that the greatest *moment* in the beam occurs at the second load point, 20.3 kg-m (138.75 ft-lb).

There are numerous geometrical relationships between the shear and moment diagram that have to do with the relationships between load, span, and moment (Fig. 4.3.17). We can use these as shortcuts to quickly draw shear-moment diagrams. First, the *magnitude* of a given portion of a moment diagram at any point will be equivalent to the total *area* to the left or right of that cut in the

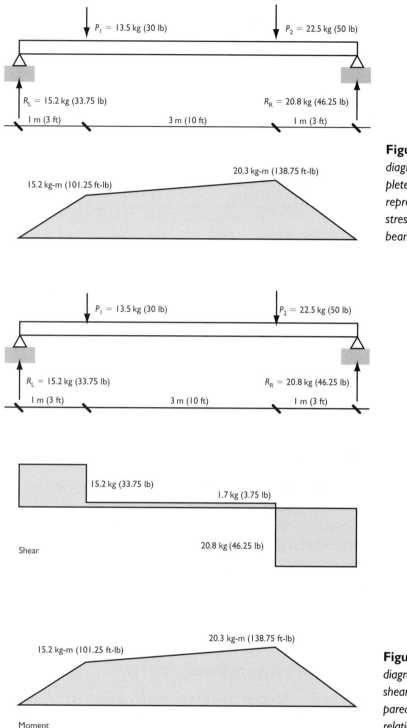

Figure 4.3.16. *Shear/moment diagram example showing completed moment diagram, which represents the internal bending stress at every point along the beam (see text).*

Figure 4.3.17. *Shear/moment diagram example showing final shear and moment diagrams, compared to show their geometrical relationships (see text).*

corresponding shear diagram. In this case, the moment at the first load point is 15.2 kg-m (101.25 ft-lb). This is equivalent to the area of the left-most portion of the shear diagram: 15.2 kg × 1 m (33.75 lb × 3 ft) = 15.2 kg-m (101.25 ft-lb).

Also, the *slope* of the moment diagram is always equivalent at a given point to the *magnitude* of the shear diagram at that point. For instance, the slope of the left-most portion of the moment diagram is 15.2 kg/m (33.75 lb/ft). Note that the central part of the moment diagram has a much shallower slope, in fact 1.7 kg/m (3.75 lb/ft). The right-most portion of the moment diagram has, in fact, a negative slope, as suggested by the shear diagram, −20.8 kg (−46.25 lb/ft).

This last point is useful, as the maximum moment must occur at a point of zero shear – representing a summit or valley in the moment diagram's slope. A moment diagram must inflect, or change direction, at a zero slope/zero shear point. This allows us to very quickly determine where the highest moment stress will be. If we look at all points of zero shear along a beam's diagram, and calculate the moments at only those points, we can guarantee that because of the geometry of the graph one of these will be the maximum moment value. When designing beams in bending, therefore, we are very interested in points of zero shear, since one of those will inevitably be the point of maximum moment. (Thinking this through, it becomes apparent that point loads are often locations of maximum moment, since they will often – though not always – 'push' the shear diagram across the zero line.)

Note, too, that for a distributed load, the complexity of line increases for each graph. Here, the *shear* value becomes a sloped line, and the *moment* value becomes a constant curve. Again, where the shear value is zero, the moment reaches its peak.

With practice, it becomes relatively simple to read shear and moment diagrams together, and to recognize patterns that emerge from combinations of point and distributed loads (Fig. 4.3.18). These patterns often show up in the forms of structural elements, for good reason. Recall that the most efficient way to resist bending is to provide a deep cross section, with enough distance to allow a significant internal moment to build up. Bending structures designed for efficiency thus do well to mimic the shape of their moment diagram, providing maximum resistance in the points of maximum bending stress. A well-known example of this strategy is shown in Figure 4.3.19. Here, the structural member is sized to provide the greatest depth at the point of maximum bending stress. Arguably, these shapes have an intuitively based esthetic to them that we recognize – either through experience or instinct – as reliable, strong, and perhaps therefore as 'beautiful'.

Frequently asked questions

It's great that there are shortcuts to drawing shear/moment diagrams, but I don't understand why these relationships work. Shear and bending are intricately related in a beam, since both develop from the same loads and reactions. The shortcuts to drawing shear and moment diagrams are graphic ways of revealing these. Think about the relationship of moment at any given point along a beam to that of shear – if we analyze it by the free body method, the shear at one end of a beam will be just the reaction, while the moment will be that same reaction times its distance to our analytical 'cut'. So the *value* of the moment at any point will be the reaction (or the shear stress) times its distance, which is also the formula for the 'area' of the shear diagram. Likewise, for every unit of measure we move the 'cut' along the beam, we gain a moment equal to the amount of shear times the unit of measure – also a definition of

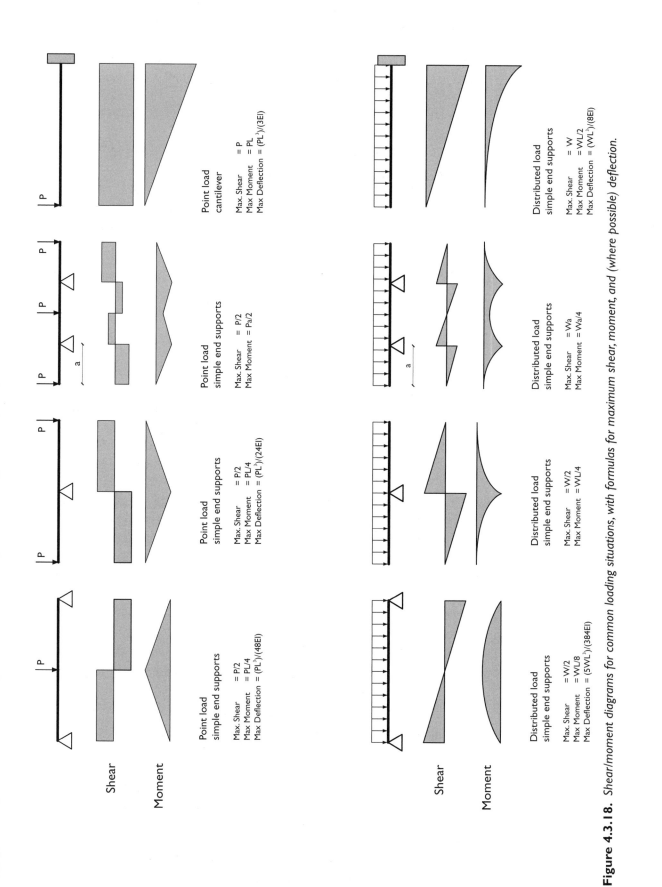

Shear

Moment

Point load
simple end supports

Max. Shear   = P/2
Max. Moment   = PL/4
Max Deflection = $(PL^3)/(48EI)$

Point load
simple end supports

Max. Shear   = P/2
Max. Moment   = PL/4
Max Deflection = $(PL^3)/(24EI)$

Point load
simple end supports

Max. Shear   = P/2
Max. Moment   = Pa/2

Point load
cantilever

Max. Shear   = P
Max. Moment   = PL
Max Deflection = $(PL^3)/(3EI)$

Distributed load
simple end supports

Max. Shear   = W/2
Max. Moment   = WL/8
Max Deflection = $(5WL^3)/(384EI)$

Distributed load
simple end supports

Max. Shear   = W/2
Max. Moment   = WL/4

Distributed load
simple end supports

Max. Shear   = Wa
Max. Moment   = Wa/4

Distributed load
simple end supports

Max. Shear   = W
Max. Moment   = WL/2
Max Deflection = $(WL^3)/(8EI)$

Figure 4.3.18. *Shear/moment diagrams for common loading situations, with formulas for maximum shear, moment, and (where possible) deflection.*

Figure 4.3.19. *Beam design often mimics the shape of moment diagrams to distribute material where it will do the most work. Here, a prototype school by Jean Prouve (1954) uses ideal cantilever shapes; deep at the root, tapering toward the tip, reflecting its shear and moment diagram (see Fig. 4.3.17). (From Benedikt Huber and Jean-Claude Steinegger, Jean Prouve).*

the shear diagram's slope. Note, too, that as we increase or move loads, both diagrams will change in ways that are necessarily related, since both rely on the magnitude and position of forces.

Glossary and formulas

Shear	An internal state of stress in which the particles of a material tend to slide past one another.
Bending	An internal state of stress in which loads are carried perpendicular to their direction. This is manifested by the development, within the structural member, of internal tension and compression.
Internal Moment	A force within a structural member that resists the 'twist' on it imparted by an external load.
Beam	A structural member that resists bending.
Force Couple	The development of axial forces perpendicular to an external load in a beam. Usually consists of an internal compressive force on the side toward the load, and an internal tensile force on the side away from the load.
Neutral Axis	A line through a beam that represents the 'axle' of a force couple. This line undergoes no tension or compression while the beam is in bending.

Further reading

Salvadori, M. (1963) Simple Shear (Section 5.3) and Simple Bending (Section 5.4), *Structure in Architecture: The Building of Buildings* (New York: Prentice-Hall), pp. 86–97.
Ambrose, J. and Parker, H. (2000) Bending (Section 2.2) and Properties of Sections (Sections 4.1–4.4), *Simplified Engineering for Architects and Builders* (New York: Wiley), pp. 43, 149–179.

4.4   Shape and strength: beams

Beams: Introduction	Definitions
	Anatomy of a typical beam
Forces within Beams	Reactions
	Resultant internal forces
Designing Beams	Use of shear-moment diagrams to determine
	internal forces
	Centroids and neutral axes
	Moment of inertia
	Section modulus

Shape and strength: cross section

In the last chapter, we examined the macro-behavior of beam elements – those in which the span is perpendicular to the applied load. We found ways of determining internal reactions, and we used those reactions to develop diagrams showing the internal states of shear and bending stress in simple beams.

While these diagrams are useful for finding the maximum internal stresses within members, they do not yet tell us how large beams need to be – and how they might be shaped in *cross section* – to resist these internal forces. In this chapter, we'll examine the micro-behavior of beam elements and look at ways of designing a beam's cross section to efficiently carry loads.

There are two principal ways that a beam can fail. Our job, predictably, is to ensure that neither of these come to pass. Beams may fail in *shear* if the internal shear stresses exceed the capacity of the material. However, beams may also fail in *bending*, and for most materials this tends to govern beam design.

As we saw when calculating moment and deflection diagrams, beams under loading change shape. As loads are applied, areas of the beam in tension elongate, those in compression shorten. The result is a characteristic curved shape that is intuitively recognizable. As we saw in previous chapters, materials are limited in the amount of tension and compression they can undergo, and a failure in bending tends to show characteristic cracking in the region in tension, and characteristic buckling in the region under compression.

One way to carry loads efficiently is to adjust the shape of the beam in the longitudinal axis, tuning the moment-resisting depth of an element where its bending moment is greatest, as we saw in Section 4.3. However, this does not often lead to shapes that can be fabricated or mass-produced easily, and this solution tends to dominate custom situations – large bridges, long-span roofs, etc. For the average structure, we are more interested in finding ways to

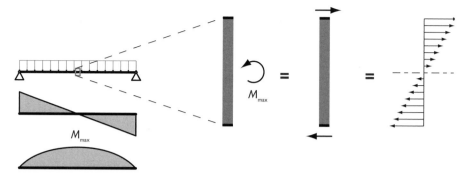

Figure 4.4.1. *Resistance to bending occurs in a beam through the development of tension in fibers above the neutral axis and compression in fibers below the neutral axis. The sum total of these fibers' capacity will determine the capacity of the beam itself.*

standardize structural shapes in the longitudinal direction, which has great advantages in fabrication (see, for instance, the description of steel rolling in Section 3.3).

To understand how the internal *moment* is resolved, recall that bending produces tension and compression in opposite faces of a structural member. In Figure 4.4.1, the internal moment has been translated into an equivalent *couple* of distributed, internal forces – the topmost triangle shows that this edge of the beam is in compression, the bottommost showing the other edge in tension. These two diagrams show the exact same static state – just in two different ways.

In a beam under loading, the internal moment is actually continuum of force that runs throughout the cross section of the beam – every 'fiber' of the beam material is either in compression or tension to varying degrees (note that we'll use the term 'fiber' to conveniently talk about very small portions of a beam shape, even though some of the materials we use in beams aren't fibrous). The maximum compression occurs in the topmost 'fiber' of the beam, the maximum tension in the bottommost. In between, each 'fiber' is in tension or compression *except* the very center fiber, where the graph shows that there is no stress at all. This fiber, the *neutral axis*, which for simple cross-sectional shapes (rectangles, circles, etc.) is located at the shape's centroid. Note that the area of each triangle is equivalent to the magnitude of a force running through the triangle's centroid that would, when coupled with the opposite force, produce the internal moment shown in Fig. 4.4.1.

The internal bending moment, as found in shear-moment diagrams, is therefore resisted best by the beam's capacity to resist simple tension and compression in its outer fibers or regions. If the same internal moment is applied to two beams – one narrow, one deep, we can see that the maximum stress in the outermost fiber will be considerably less in the deeper beam:

Example: *Find the maximum stress in each of the beam cross sections in Figure 4.4.2 if the internal moment in each is 1300 Nm (1000 ft-lb).*

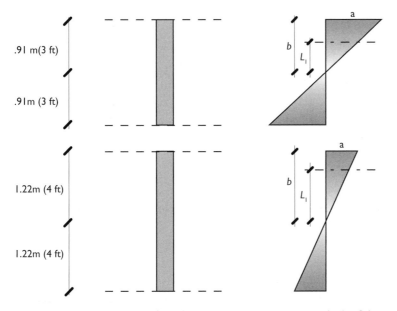

.91 m(3 ft)

.91m (3 ft)

1.22m (4 ft)

1.22m (4 ft)

Figure 4.4.2. *The mathematics of bending resistance requires us to think of the triangular area of stress and depth as a collection of forces that together have a moment arm about the neutral axis. The total resisting force times the average moment arm of each individual resisting fiber must equal the bending moment incurred by the loading and reactions for the beam to work.*

Recall that the internal moment can be expressed as the product of the area of two triangles multiplied by the perpendicular distance between their centroid and the neutral axis. In each case, therefore, we can find the length of the outer leg of each triangle (the maximum fiber stress) by backtracking from the internal moment:

$$1300\,\text{Nm} = (A_1 \times L_1) + (A_1 \times L_2)\quad 1000\,\text{ft-lb} = (A_1 \times L_1) + (A_1 \times L_2)$$

Since the beam is symmetrical about the neutral axis (we'll see cases later where this doesn't hold true), we also have:

$$650\,\text{Nm} = (A_1 \times L_1)\quad 500\,\text{ft-lb} = (A_1 \times L_1)$$

L_1 is the distance from the centroid of the triangle to the neutral axis, which by geometry is 1/3 the triangle's height, or 2 ft above the neutral axis. A_1 is simply the area of the triangle (1/2) ab. Since a represents the maximum stress, we will leave it as a variable. We thus have:

$$650\,\text{Nm} = (\tfrac{1}{2} ab) \times 0.61\,\text{m} \qquad\qquad 500\,\text{ft-lb} = (\tfrac{1}{2} ab) \times 2\,\text{ft}$$

$$650\,\text{Nm} = (1/2 \times 0.61\,\text{m} \times 0.91\,\text{m}) \times a \qquad 500\,\text{ft-lb} = (1/2 \times 2\,\text{ft} \times 3\,\text{ft}) \times a$$
$$650\,\text{Nm} = (0.29\,\text{m}^2) \times a \qquad\qquad 500\,\text{ft-lb} = (3\,\text{ft}^2) \times a$$
$$2500\,\text{N/m} = a \qquad\qquad 166.67\,\text{lb/ft} = a$$

The maximum fiber stress in the first example is, therefore, 2500 N/m (166.67 lb/ft). (Note that the units here are in loads per linear measure because of the two-dimensional nature of the problem. These aren't units we typically use, but here we're just making a point; ordinarily we'd measure stress in loads per unit of area, not length.)

Turning to the second, deeper example, and again backtracking from what we know about the internal moment, we find that the maximum fiber stress is:

$$650\,\text{Nm} = (\tfrac{1}{2}ab) \times (0.813\,\text{m}) \qquad\qquad 500\,\text{ft-lb} = (\tfrac{1}{2}ab) \times (2.67\,\text{ft})$$

$$650\,\text{Nm} = (1/2 \times 0.813\,\text{m} \times 1.220\,\text{m}) \times a \quad 500\,\text{ft-lb} = (1/2 \times 2.67\,\text{ft} \times 4\,\text{ft}) \times a$$
$$650\,\text{Nm} = 0.50\,\text{m}^2 \times a \qquad\qquad\qquad 500\,\text{ft-lb} = 5.33\,\text{ft} \times a$$
$$1300\,\text{N/m} = a \qquad\qquad\qquad\qquad 93.81\,\text{lb/ft} = a$$

We thus see that an increase in depth has an exponential effect on efficiency, as the depth of the beam figures twice in the calculation (note that we have not provided a figure for the beam's width, thus the extra term – m or ft in the final result).

As discussed above, it is not always possible to fabricate a beam to the most efficient structural depth or profile. Recall, however, that the tensile and compressive capacities of structural elements are determined by their cross-sectional area and their load capacity in lb/in.[2] We should, therefore, be able to increase a beam's efficiency not just by making it very *deep*, but also by giving it greater cross-sectional area *where* it needs to do the most work – at the outermost fibers of the structural section.

In other words, the same *quantity* of material can resist internal moments more efficiently if it is placed *further* from the neutral axis. One way to think about this is that the distance component of the moment from the external load can be resisted by a distance component of the material's distribution throughout its section, and if we can find a way to move more material to the top and bottom edges of a beam, it should be able to do more work with less mass.

An ideal beam shape, therefore, will deploy the majority of its material to the extreme top and bottom edges of its section. Work done by William Fairbairn in the early 19th century using rolled metal shapes led to the development, and eventually the standardization, of the instantly recognizable 'I-beam', with thick *flanges* and the narrowest *web* possible (Fig. 4.4.3). We'll now look at the mathematics behind Fairbairn's innovation, finding ways to measure how efficiently material is distributed throughout a beam section. This will involve some fairly abstract reasoning, but keep in mind that we're essentially looking to analyze what Fairbairn intuited – that shapes with more material at the edges can do more work per unit of cross-sectional area.

Three important measurements: centroid, moment of inertia, and section modulus

A key element of sizing structural beams is to determine the capacity of a given shape to resist internal moments. We do this with a number of formulas that quantify the properties of geometrical shapes, in particular the relative distance of the shape's areas in section from the neutral axis.

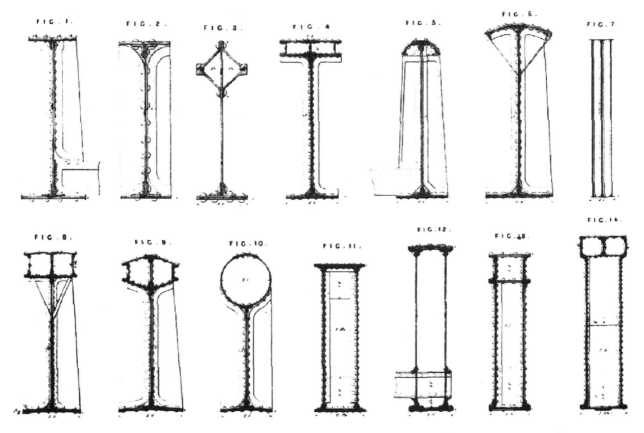

Figure 4.4.3. *The development of the I-shape occurred during the late 18th and early 19th century, and was finally perfected by British engineer William Fairbairn, who built up structurally efficient sections using cast and rolled iron plate.*

First among these is the *centroid*. This is a geometric property that essentially describes the center of gravity of a planar section. For symmetrical shapes, the centroid will lie at the intersection of the two axes of symmetry. For triangles, the centroid will lie at the intersection of lines drawn through the 1/3 points.

For shapes involving irregular geometry, the centroid must be calculated by breaking down the overall shape into smaller units whose centroid and area can be easily found. The areas of each of these sub-shapes are then multiplied by the distance from each sub-shape's centroid to an arbitrarily selected reference axis – usually the top or bottom of the shape for convenience. The sum of these area–distances are then divided by the total area of the shape, which give us the distance from the reference axis to the location of the centroid. One way to picture this is to think of the centroid as the *average* centroid of each sub-shape. The more area a sub-shape has, the greater its influence on the ultimate position of the overall centroid.

Example: *Find the centroid of the shape shown in Figure 4.4.4.*

Solution: The shape consists of two shapes that are symmetrical about the *y*-axis. Therefore the centroid will occur somewhere along the vertical axis

271

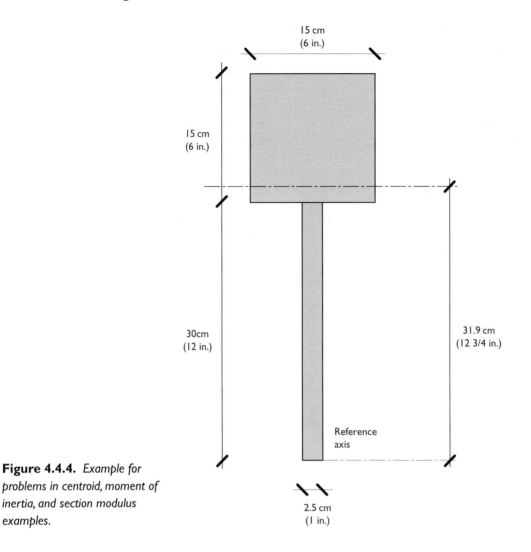

Figure 4.4.4. *Example for problems in centroid, moment of inertia, and section modulus examples.*

of symmetry. To find the distance between the centroid and the bottom edge of the shape, we take the areas of each shape – a 6 in. square at the top and a 12 in. × 1 in. rectangle at the base and multiply these by the distance between their respective centroids and the base of the shape:

Shape	Area	Distance from center to base	Area × distance
Square	15 cm ×15 cm = 225 cm² (6 in. × 6 in. = 36 in.²)	30 cm + ½ (15 cm)= 37.5 cm (12 in. + 1/2(6 in.) = 15 in.)	8437.5 cm³ (540 in.³)
Rectangle	30 cm × 2.5 cm = 75 cm² (12 in. × 1 in. = 12 in.²)	15 cm (6 in.)	1125 cm³ (72 in.³)
Total	300 cm² (48 in.²)		9562.5 cm³ (612 in.³)

We now divide the total (area × distance) by the total area to arrive at the 'leg' of the overall shape's centroid:

$$d = 9562.5 \text{ cm}^3/300 \text{ cm}^2 \qquad d = 612 \text{ in.}^3/48 \text{ in.}^2$$
$$= 31.9 \text{ cm} \qquad\qquad = 12 \text{ } 3/4 \text{ in.}$$

The centroid is an important sectional property as it determines the *neutral axis* of the section – the point at which there will be no bending-induced tension or compression, and the point at which internal tensile stresses will change to internal compressive forces in a beam under bending.

The *moment of inertia* is a (very) abstract property that combines the distance from the centroid and the areas of an infinite number of 'fibers' to arrive at a number, expressed in cm^4 or $in.^4$. The result is a measure of the average area $\times$ distance for every point in the beam's cross section. The moment of inertia of a shape may be calculated based on different axes depending on which direction the shape is being loaded from. This process again uses areas of sub-shapes and their 'lever arms' around the centroid. Shapes with large areas at great distances from the centroid will have high moments of inertia, while compact shapes will have very low moments of inertia.

To find a shape's moment of inertia, we multiply each fiber's infinitesimal cross-sectional area by the *square* of its distance from the centroid. The theoretical formula for a shape's moment of inertia is therefore:

$$I = \Sigma(az^2)$$

where a is an arbitrarily small area of the section and z is the distance from that area's centroid to the centroid of the overall section. Formulas for the moment of inertia of various shapes are derived using calculus, summing up the areas of individual points and multiplying them by the square of their distance from the centroid. We won't derive individual formulas for these, but the most useful formulae for finding I are given in Figure 4.4.5.

We can sum up or 'transfer' moments of inertia for various shapes using the formula

$$I = I_0 + Az^2$$

where I is the total moment of inertia of a shape about the desired centroid, I_0 is the moment of inertia of a sub-shape, A is the area of the sub-shape, and z is the distance from the centroid of the sub-shape to the centroid of the overall shape. This allows us to find the moment of inertia of complex shapes, provided we can break them down into simple components such as rectangles, triangles, etc.

Example: Find the total I_{X-X} for the shape shown in Figure 4.4.4.

Solution: First we find the I_{X-X} for each individual shape:

$$
\begin{aligned}
I_{X-X(top)} &= d^4/12 \\
&= (15\,cm)^4/12 \\
&= 50{,}625\,cm^4/12 \\
&= 4219\,cm^4
\end{aligned}
\qquad
\begin{aligned}
I_{X-X(top)} &= d^4/12 \\
&= (6\,in.)^4/12 \\
&= 1296\,in.^4/12 \\
&= 108\,in.^4
\end{aligned}
$$

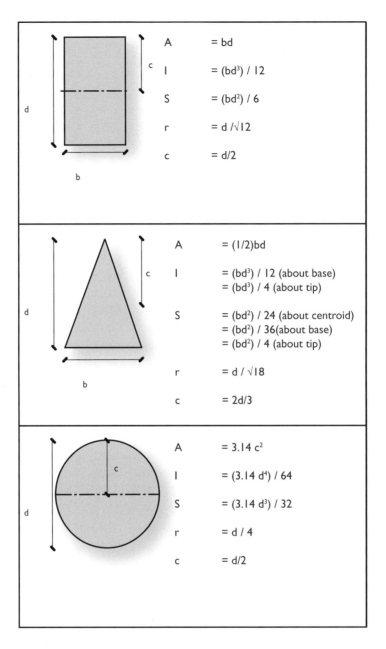

Figure 4.4.5. *Formulas for area (A), moment of inertia (I), section modulus (S), and centroid location (c) for typical structural shapes. Radius of Gyration (r) is covered in Section 4.5.*

$$I_{X-X(bottom)} = bd^3/12$$
$$= (2.5\,\text{cm})\,(30\,\text{cm})^3/12$$
$$= 67,500\,\text{cm}^4/12$$
$$= 5625\,\text{cm}^4$$

$$I_{X-X(bottom)} = bd^3/12$$
$$= (1\,\text{in.}) \times (12\,\text{in.})^3/12$$
$$= 1728\,\text{in.}^4/12$$
$$= 144\,\text{in.}^4$$

To combine these, we use the formula $I = I_0 + Az^2$. Remember that 'z' reflects the distance between a shape's own centroid and the centroid of the overall section. So for each shape, we figure the distance between its own centroid and the figure we arrived at in the previous centroid example:

$$I_{(top)} = I_0 + Az^2$$
$$= 4219\,\text{cm}^4 + 225\,\text{cm}^2\,(5.625\,\text{cm})^2$$
$$= 11,338\,\text{cm}^4$$

$$I_{(top)} = I_0 + Az^2$$
$$= 108\,\text{in.}^4 + 36\,\text{in.}^2\,(2.25\,\text{in.})^2$$
$$= 290.25\,\text{in.}^4$$

$$I_{(bottom)} = I_0 + Az^2$$
$$= 5625 \text{ cm}^4 + (30 \times 2.5)\text{cm}^2$$
$$(16.875 \text{ cm})^2$$
$$= 26,982 \text{ cm}^4$$

$$I_{(bottom)} = I_0 + Az^2$$
$$= 144 \text{ in.}^4 + 12 \text{ in.}^2 (6.75 \text{ in.})^2$$
$$= 690.75 \text{ in.}^4$$

$$I_{(total)} = 11,338 \text{ cm}^4 + 26,982 \text{ cm}^4$$
$$= 38,320 \text{ cm}^4$$

$$I_{(total)} = 290.25 \text{ in.}^4 + 690.75 \text{ in.}^4$$
$$= 981 \text{ in.}^4$$

Note that the lower shape, despite having much less area, adds a great deal more to the shape's moment of inertia by virtue of its centroid's distance from the overall shape's centroid.

A subtle refinement of the moment of inertia involves dividing I by the distance between the section's centroid and its farthest 'fiber'. This property is called the section modulus, and is represented by S, where

$$S = I/c$$

Section modulus is a truer representation of a shape's actual product of each fiber's area and distance from the neutral axis – it is measured in cm^3 or in.^3, rather than cm^4 or in.^4, and this directly reflects what we're really looking for – a measure of area times distance. To get to it, we need to use moment of inertia, but the real measure of a shape's structural capacity ends up being determined by S, section modulus.

The flexure formula

To understand the relevance of the section modulus, it is useful to return to our discussion regarding the development of internal moments within beams. This again involves a bit of abstract math – but the result will be a very simple way to calculate the moment-resisting capacity of a shape. Recall that the internal moment is equal in value to the combined areas of the two triangles shown in Figure 4.4.6. Note that the areas of the stress triangles (M) are defined by a maximum 'fiber stress', f, and by the distance 'c' between the furthest 'fiber' and the neutral axis:

$$M = 1/2 \ (f \times c)$$

Another way to think of this is to take each point of area in the section, find its fiber stress, and calculate its ability to develop a resisting moment based on its distance from the neutral axis. If we take an area 'a' that is at distance z from the neutral axis, we find that its fiber stress 'p' will be *proportional* to the maximum stress because of the triangle's slope, based on its position:

$$p = (f/c) \times z$$

The total internal stress over an area a, will thus be that stress multiplied by its own area:

$$p_a = (f/c) \times z \times a$$

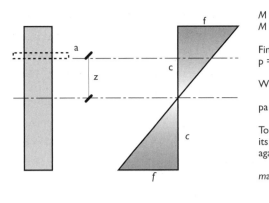

$$M \quad = 1/2\ (f \times c) \times 2$$
$$M \quad = fc$$

Find fiber stress (p) at a
$$p = (f/c) \times z$$

When this is spread over area 'a':

$$pa \quad = (f/c) \times z \times a$$

To find resisting moment of 'a', we add its distance to the neutral axis (z) once again:

$$ma \quad = (f/c) \times a \times z \times z$$
$$\quad = (f/c) \times a \times z^2$$

The total moment of the section will be:

$$M \quad = \Sigma\ (f/c)\ (az^2)$$
$$\quad = (f/c) \times \Sigma(az^2)$$
$$\quad = fI/c$$
$$\quad = fS$$

$$M \quad = fS$$

Figure 4.4.6. *Mathematical derivation of the flexure formula (see text).*

Again, this is a way of quantifying numerous small areas and the internal stress they will assume given their location in the cross section and the maximum fiber stress in the beam.

Each p_a will exert a *resisting moment* about the neutral axis equal to its total internal stress multiplied by its lever arm about the neutral axis. To find this, we multiply the total unit stress by its moment arm, which will be z, the distance between the centroid of *a* and the overall shape's neutral axis:

$$m_a = (f/c) \times z \times a \times z$$

Here we note that z figures twice, as previously noted. Depth counts twice because it helps determine the overall area *and* the length of the moment arm. The equation can now read:

$$m_a = (f/c) \times a \times z^2$$

To find the total resisting moment of a section, we therefore take the sum of each m_a:

$$M = \Sigma(f/c)\ (az^2)$$

Since f/c is constant, we can pull this out of the sum:

$$M = (f/c)\ \Sigma(az^2)$$

Note that the term on the left, $\Sigma(az^2)$, is the formula for moment of inertia ($I = \Sigma(az^2)$). We therefore can substitute *I* for these terms, after which we find:

$$M = fI/c$$

Here we find that I/c is equivalent to the section modulus, and we thus get:

$$M = fS$$

This surprisingly simple formula is called the *flexure formula*, and it tells us that the maximum capacity of a beam shape to carry moment is directly related to both its maximum allowable stress and to a measure of where its material is deployed through its section. Its derivation is, admittedly, a bit complex, but it's worth understanding where this remarkably simple formula comes from; to find it, we've basically thought about how a fiber's distance from a shape's neutral axis helps determine how much resisting work it can do. Fibers that are farther away from the neutral axis can do more, because they have a larger lever arm to help 'twist back' against a moment load.

The flexure formula means that we need to know only three things about a beam to properly size it – the *maximum moment* it undergoes, its *section modulus*, and the material's *maximum allowable fiber stress*. These last two quantities are routinely published by industry, and therefore the process of sizing a beam using handbooks is remarkably simple. Sample data on sectional shapes are shown in Table 4.4.1 and 4.4.2. For wood, we rely on a structural grading system that provides values for maximum 'extreme fiber in bending' stress, getting around the fact that values for wood in tension are not published. Note that concrete presents an unusual situation, in that steel reinforcing takes up the tension load. Therefore, we can't simply use the flexure formula to design concrete beams, and must instead find separate compressive and tensile capacities from the two materials. For the moment, we'll stick with steel and timber to cover the static principles involved.

Example: Size a beam in Select Structural Timber for the beam shown in Figure 4.4.7.

Solution: First, we'll analyze the beam to find its reactions, its shear diagram, and its moment diagram. From this, we will use the maximum moment, the

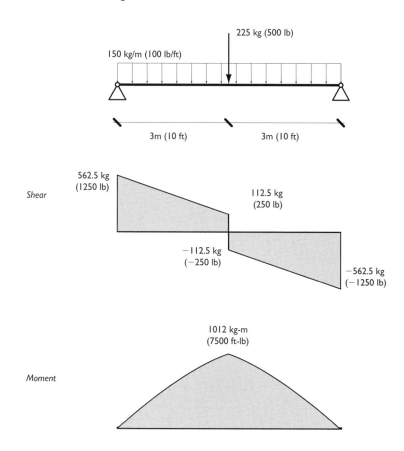

Figure 4.4.7. *Shear moment diagram for flexure formula example (see text).*

Table 4.4.1. Selected structural steel sections sorted by S, section modulus.

Designation		$Sx-x$		Weight		Depth		Flange width		Web thickness		Flange thickness	
Metric	US	cm³	in.³	kg/m	lb/ft	cm	in.	cm	in.	cm	in.	cm	in.
W250 × 25	W10 × 17	265.52	16.2	25	17	25.68	10.11	10.19	4.01	0.61	0.24	0.84	0.33
W250 × 28	W10 × 19	308.13	18.8	28	19	26.01	10.24	10.21	4.02	0.64	0.25	1.02	0.40
W250 × 39	W10 × 26	457.28	27.9	39	26	26.24	10.33	14.66	5.77	0.66	0.26	1.12	0.44
W310 × 39	W12 × 26	547.43	33.4	39	26	31.04	12.22	16.51	6.50	0.58	0.23	0.97	0.38
W250 × 49	W10 × 33	573.65	35.0	49	33	24.71	9.73	20.22	7.96	0.74	0.29	1.12	0.44
W310 × 45	W12 × 30	632.65	38.6	45	30	31.34	12.34	16.56	6.52	0.66	0.26	1.12	0.44
W360 × 45	W14 × 30	688.38	42.0	45	30	35.15	13.84	17.09	6.73	0.69	0.27	0.99	0.39
W250 × 58	W10 × 39	690.02	42.1	58	39	25.20	9.92	20.29	7.99	0.81	0.32	1.35	0.53
W360 × 51	W14 × 34	796.55	48.6	51	34	35.51	13.98	17.15	6.75	0.74	0.29	1.17	0.46
W310 × 60	W12 × 40	850.64	51.9	59	40	30.33	11.94	20.35	8.01	0.76	0.30	1.32	0.52
W250 × 73	W10 × 49	894.89	54.6	68	46	25.35	9.98	25.40	10.00	0.86	0.34	1.42	0.56
W410 × 53	W16 × 36	926.04	56.5	54	36	40.28	15.86	17.75	6.99	0.76	0.30	1.09	0.43
W310 × 67	W12 × 45	952.26	58.1	67	45	30.63	12.06	20.45	8.05	0.86	0.34	1.47	0.58
W360 × 64	W14 × 43	1027.65	62.7	64	43	34.70	13.66	20.32	8.00	0.79	0.31	1.35	0.53
W410 × 60	W16 × 40	1060.43	64.7	59	40	40.67	16.01	17.78	7.00	0.79	0.31	1.30	0.51
W460 × 60	W18 × 40	1121.08	68.4	59	40	45.47	17.90	15.29	6.02	0.81	0.32	1.35	0.53
W360 × 72	W14 × 48	1152.22	70.3	71	48	35.03	13.79	20.40	8.03	0.86	0.34	1.52	0.60
W310 × 79	W12 × 53	1157.13	70.6	79	53	30.63	12.06	25.40	10.00	0.89	0.35	1.47	0.58
W410 × 67	W16 × 45	1191.55	72.7	67	45	40.97	16.13	17.88	7.04	0.89	0.35	1.45	0.57
W460 × 68	W18 × 46	1291.53	78.8	68	46	45.87	18.06	15.39	6.06	0.91	0.36	1.55	0.61
W410 × 74	W16 × 50	1327.59	81.0	74	50	41.30	16.26	17.96	7.07	0.97	0.38	1.60	0.63
W250 × 115	W10 × 77	1407.9	85.9	114	77	26.92	10.60	25.91	10.20	1.35	0.53	2.21	0.87
W310 × 97	W12 × 65	1440.68	87.9	97	65	30.78	12.12	30.48	12.00	0.99	0.39	1.55	0.61
W460 × 74	W18 × 50	1457.07	88.9	74	50	45.69	17.99	19.05	7.50	0.91	0.36	1.45	0.57

(Continued)

maximum allowable stress f for our material, and the flexure formula to find our required section modulus. Then we will select a shape from the Table 4.4.2 that provides the required section modulus, S.

First, we find the reactions:

$$\Sigma M_R = 0 \quad \Sigma M_R = 0$$

$$((150\,\text{kg/m}) \times 6\,\text{m} \times 3\,\text{m}) + (225\,\text{kg} \times 3\,\text{m}) - (R_L \times 6\,\text{m}) = 0$$
$$((100\,\text{lb/ft}) \times 20\,\text{ft} \times 10\,\text{ft}) + (500\,\text{lb} \times 10\,\text{ft}) - (R_L \times 20\,\text{ft}) = 0$$
$$2700\,\text{kg-m} + 675\,\text{kg-m} - (R_L \times 6\,\text{m}) = 0 \quad 20{,}000\,\text{ft-lb} + 5000\,\text{ft-lb} - (R_L \times 20\,\text{ft}) = 0$$
$$3375\,\text{kg-m} = R_L \times 6\,\text{m} \quad 25{,}000\,\text{ft-lb} = R_L \times 20\,\text{ft}$$
$$R_L = 562.5\,\text{kg} \quad R_L = 1250\,\text{lb}$$

Table 4.4.1. (*Continued*)

Designation		$Sx-x$		Weight		Depth		Flange width		Web thickness		Flange thickness	
Metric	US	cm³	in.³	kg/m	lb/ft	cm	in.	cm	in.	cm	in.	cm	in.
W530 × 74	W21 × 50	1548.86	94.5	74	50	52.91	20.83	16.59	6.53	0.97	0.38	1.37	0.54
W310 × 107	W12 × 72	1596.39	97.4	107	72	31.12	12.25	30.58	12.04	1.09	0.43	1.70	0.67
W460 × 82	W18 × 55	1611.14	98.3	82	55	46.00	18.11	19.13	7.53	0.99	0.39	1.60	0.63
W250 × 131	W10 × 88	1614.42	98.5	131	88	27.53	10.84	26.09	10.27	1.55	0.61	2.51	0.99
W360 × 101	W14 × 68	1688.17	103.0	101	68	35.66	14.04	25.50	10.04	1.07	0.42	1.83	0.72
W460 × 89	W18 × 60	1770.12	108.0	89	60	46.33	18.24	19.20	7.56	1.07	0.42	1.78	0.70
W530 × 85	W21 × 57	1819.29	111.0	85	57	53.49	21.06	16.66	6.56	1.04	0.41	1.65	0.65
W360 × 110	W14 × 74	1835.68	112.0	110	74	35.99	14.17	25.58	10.07	1.14	0.45	2.01	0.79
W460 × 113	W18 × 76	2392.94	146.0	113	76	46.25	18.21	28.02	11.03	1.09	0.43	1.73	0.68
W530 × 109	W21 × 73	2474.89	151.0	109	73	53.95	21.24	21.08	8.30	1.17	0.46	1.88	0.74
W610 × 101	W24 × 68	2524.06	154.0	101	68	60.27	23.73	22.76	8.96	1.07	0.42	1.50	0.59
W310 × 179	W12 × 120	2671.57	163.0	178	120	33.32	13.12	31.29	12.32	1.80	0.71	2.79	1.10
W460 × 128	W18 × 86	2720.74	166.0	128	86	46.71	18.39	28.19	11.10	1.22	0.48	1.96	0.77
W530 × 123	W21 × 83	2802.69	171.0	123	83	54.43	21.43	21.23	8.36	1.32	0.52	2.13	0.84
W610 × 113	W24 × 76	2884.64	176.0	113	76	60.76	23.92	22.83	8.99	1.12	0.44	1.73	0.68
W310 × 202	W12 × 136	3048.54	186.0	202	136	34.06	13.41	31.50	12.40	2.01	0.79	3.18	1.25
W360 × 179	W14 × 120	3114.1	190.0	178	120	36.78	14.48	37.26	14.67	1.50	0.59	2.39	0.94
W610 × 125	W24 × 84	3212.44	196.0	125	84	61.21	24.10	22.91	9.02	1.19	0.47	1.96	0.77
W360 × 196	W14 × 132	3425.51	209.0	196	132	37.24	14.66	37.39	14.72	1.65	0.65	2.62	1.03
W690 × 125	W27 × 84	3491.07	213.0	125	84	67.84	26.71	25.30	9.96	1.17	0.46	1.63	0.64
W690 × 140	W27 × 94	3982.77	243.0	140	94	68.38	26.92	25.37	9.99	1.24	0.49	1.91	0.75
W760 × 147	W30 × 99	4408.91	269.0	147	99	75.31	29.65	26.67	10.50	1.32	0.52	1.70	0.67
W360 × 262	W14 × 176	4605.59	281.0	262	176	38.66	15.22	39.75	15.65	2.11	0.83	3.33	1.31
W760 × 173	W30 × 116	5392.31	329.0	172	116	76.23	30.01	26.67	10.50	1.45	0.57	2.16	0.85

Note: Consult AISC Handbook for full range of structural shapes.

From $\Sigma y = 0$ and from symmetry, we realize that both reactions must be equal, thus:

$$R_R = 562.5 \text{ kg (1250 lb)}$$

We now draw the shear diagram as shown. From left to right, we note that R_R will immediately impart a 1250 lb shear upward. This will gradually be countered by the distributed load. At the midpoint, the internal shear will equal:

$$562.5 \text{ kg} - (150 \text{ kg/m} \times 3 \text{ m}) \qquad 1250 \text{ lb} - (100 \text{ lb/ft} \times 10 \text{ ft})$$
$$= 112.5 \text{ kg} \qquad\qquad = 250 \text{ lb}$$

At this point, the single point load will impart a 'downward' shear, pushing the graphed line down below zero to −112.5 kg (−250 lb). From there, the distributed load will continue to impart its 150 kg/m (100 lb/ft) to the diagram, until the internal shear at the left reaction is equal to −562.5 kg (−1250 lb).

Table 4.4.2. Selected timber sections sorted by S, section modulus.

Designation		$Sx - x$		Weight per linear foot	
metric	US	cm³	in.³	kg	lb
25 × 75	1 × 3	12.80	0.78	0.70	0.47
25 × 100	1 × 4	25.10	1.53	0.95	0.64
50 × 75	2 × 3	25.61	1.56	1.40	0.94
75 × 75	3 × 3	42.68	2.60	2.26	1.52
50 × 100	2 × 4	50.19	3.06	1.90	1.28
25 × 150	1 × 6	61.97	3.78	1.49	1.00
75 × 100	3 × 4	83.66	5.10	3.17	2.13
25 × 200	1 × 8	107.69	6.57	1.96	1.32
100 × 100	4 × 4	117.12	7.15	4.43	2.98
50 × 150	2 × 6	123.95	7.56	2.97	2.00
25 × 250	1 × 10	175.30	10.70	2.51	1.69
75 × 150	3 × 6	206.58	12.60	4.97	3.34
50 × 200	2 × 8	215.37	13.14	3.93	2.64
25 × 300	1 × 12	259.29	15.82	3.05	2.05
100 × 150	4 × 6	289.22	17.65	6.96	4.68
50 × 250	2 × 10	350.59	21.39	5.01	3.37
75 × 200	3 × 8	358.96	21.90	6.56	4.41
150 × 150	6 × 6	454.48	27.73	10.93	7.35
100 × 200	4 × 8	502.54	30.66	9.17	6.17
50 × 300	2 × 12	518.59	31.64	6.10	4.10
75 × 250	3 × 10	584.32	35.65	8.36	5.62
50 × 350	2 × 14	719.37	43.89	7.18	4.83
100 × 250	4 × 10	818.05	49.91	11.57	7.78
150 × 200	6 × 8	845.11	51.56	14.91	10.03
75 × 300	3 × 12	864.32	52.73	10.17	6.84
200 × 200	8 × 8	1152.42	70.31	20.33	13.67
75 × 350	3 × 14	1198.95	73.15	11.97	8.05
100 × 300	4 × 12	1210.04	73.83	14.23	9.57
150 × 250	6 × 10	1355.93	82.73	18.88	12.70
75 × 400	3 × 16	1588.21	96.90	13.78	9.27
100 × 350	4 × 14	1678.52	102.41	16.77	11.28
200 × 250	8 × 10	1849.00	112.81	25.75	17.32
250 × 250	10 × 10	1874.95	114.40	32.62	21.94
150 × 300	6 × 12	1986.95	121.23	22.86	15.37
100 × 300	4 × 16	2223.49	135.66	19.30	12.98
200 × 300	8 × 12	2709.47	165.31	31.17	20.96
150 × 350	6 × 14	2738.15	167.06	26.84	18.05
250 × 300	10 × 12	3432.00	209.40	39.48	26.55
150 × 400	6 × 16	3609.56	220.23	30.81	20.72
200 × 350	8 × 14	3733.85	227.81	36.60	24.61
300 × 300	12 × 12	4154.52	253.48	47.79	32.14
150 × 450	6 × 18	4601.15	280.73	34.63	23.29
250 × 350	10 × 14	4729.54	288.56	46.35	31.17
200 × 400	8 × 16	4922.12	300.31	42.02	28.26
300 × 350	12 × 14	5725.23	349.31	56.10	37.73
250 × 400	10 × 16	6234.69	380.40	53.22	35.79
200 × 450	8 × 18	6274.30	382.81	47.44	31.90
300 × 400	12 × 16	7547.25	460.48	64.43	43.33
250 × 450	10 × 18	7947.44	484.90	60.09	40.41

Here, we note that the shear value is zero at the midpoint.

For the moment diagram, we recognize that the internal moment resisting the load will gradually increase from the left reaction to the midpoint, tapering off gradually as its slope reflects the diminishing value of the shear diagram. At the midpoint, its slope will change abruptly, and it will gradually diminish to the right end of the beam.

The maximum moment will occur at the point of zero-shear, the midpoint, and will be equal to the area under the shear diagram line to this point:

$$M_{max} = (112.5 \, kg \times 3 \, m) + 1/2 \, (450 \, kg \times 3 \, m)$$
$$M_{max} = (250 \, lb \times 10 \, ft) + 1/2 \, (1000 \, lb \times 10 \, ft)$$

Note that here we are summing up two areas – the area of the rectangle defined by the 112.5 kg (250 lb) value of the shear diagram at the midpoint and running left to the edge of the beam, and the triangle formed by the 562.5 kg (1250 lb) value at the left edge and running right to the midpoint. The height of this triangle must exclude the height of the rectangle, thus its value is:

$$562.5 \, kg - 112.5 \, kg = 450 \, kg \qquad 1250 \, lb - 250 \, lb = 1000 \, lb$$

Thus:

$$M_{max} = (112.5 \, kg \times 3 \, m) + 1/2 \, (450 \, kg \times 3 \, m) \quad M_{max} = (250 \, lb \times 10 \, ft) +$$
$$1/2 \, (1000 \, lb \times 10 \, ft)$$
$$M_{max} = 337.5 \, kg\text{-}m + 675 \, kg\text{-}m \quad M_{max} = 2500 \, ft\text{-}lb + 5000 \, ft\text{-}lb$$
$$M_{max} = 1012.5 \, kg\text{-}m \quad M_{max} = 7500 \, ft\text{-}lb$$

Having found the maximum moment, we need only the maximum allowable flexural stress for our beam's extreme fiber to find the required section modulus. From Table 4.2.1, we get that the allowable f for structural Pine or Douglas Fir is $84.37 \, kg/cm^2$ (1200psi).

We therefore have the flexure formula:
$$M = fS$$
$$(1012.5 \, kg\text{-}m \times 100 \, cm/m) = 84.37 \, kg/cm^2 \times S$$
$$101,250 \, kg\text{-}cm = 84.37 \, kg/cm^2 \times S$$
$$S = (101,250 \, kg\text{-}cm)/(84.37 \, kg/cm^2)$$
$$S = 1200 \, cm^3$$

And

$$M = fS$$
$$(7500 \, ft\text{-}lbs \times 12 \, in./ft/) = 1200 \, lb./in.^2 \times S$$
$$90,000 \, in\text{-}lbs = 1200 \, ib./in.^2 \times S$$
$$S = (90,000 \, in\text{-}lbs)/(1200 \, ib./in.^2)$$
$$S = 75 \, in^3$$

Note that for metric units we must multiply the moment value by 100 cm/m and for imperial units we must multiply the moment value M by 12 in./ft to coordinate terms on both sides of the equation. Note, too, that the kg (lb) figures on each side of the equation cancel each other out, and that by dividing inches by square inches gives us in.[3]

We must now turn to tables for structural timber to find a convenient beam size that will give us a section modulus of at least 900 cm^3 (56.25 in.^{3}). From the Table 4.4.2, we have several candidates:

Size		Section modulus		Weight	
Metric	US	cm^3	in.^{3}	kg/cm	lb/ft
200 × 200	8 × 8	1152.42	70.31	20.33	13.7
75 × 350	3 × 14	1198.95	73.15	11.97	8.05
100 × 300	4 × 12	1210.04	73.83	14.23	9.57
150 × 250	6 × 10	1355.93	82.73	18.88	12.7
75 × 400	3 × 16	1588.21	96.90	13.78	9.27

We could continue with greater and greater section moduli, though looking down the chart the majority of the larger sections will have much higher weights and/or depths. Our selection at this point will likely be based on our situation – we may want to limit the depth of the structural member to allow greater floor to ceiling height, or we may want to reduce weight (and cost). Any one of these sections will perform adequately from a structural perspective, however. If depth is an issue, the 200 × 200 beam saves us 50 mm over the next shallowest option. However, this is much heavier than some of its neighbors. If weight is our main concern, the 75 × 350 offers the lightest solution.

Deflection

Simply ensuring that a beam safely holds the load we've assumed for it doesn't necessarily mean it's the right structural member for the job. To get the basic principles behind beam design across, we've intentionally ignored a number of fine points of structural behavior that have to do with *serviceability*. Primary among these is the role of deflection, or how much a beam will move from its original position under loading. As we know from previous chapters, any material under loading will change shape. If the load is axial, the structural member will change length. For structural members in bending, the deflection will result in, predictably, bending. The member will curve due to the tension and compression in opposite edges. In most applications, there will be a limit to how far a member can deflect in this way before it becomes noticeable or causes problems. An important example of this is a flat roof – if the roof beams deflect enough, water will collect in the low points, adding unexpected weight.

In critical situations, the beam may be *cambered*, or curved in the direction opposite to the loading, before it's installed. In other situations, we may accept a certain amount of deflection in the structure and in many cases it may only be the visual effect of 'sagging' floors or beams that limits how far we allow structural members to deflect.

The math and physics behind deflection is complicated, but boils down to rules of thumb and some relatively simple deflection formulae. For most applications, we limit deflection to either 1/240 or 1/360 of the span. This is a common rule of thumb, and we find the deflection using the derived formulae shown along with shear and moment diagrams in Figure 4.4.7.

Note here that the connections of beams to their supports plays an important role in deflection. For a beam on simple, pin supports, only the beam itself can resist the deflection imparted by the load. But if we rigidly connect the beam to its supports, we can then 'recruit' the material of the support to resist bending, too. Rigid connections make for stiffer structures, and less deflection, a topic we'll take up in Section 4.8, Frames.

Just to prove the point, a number of related shapes are shown in Figure 4.4.9 (see page 285), with their moments of inertia and section moduli, and a mostly accurate measure of their efficiency shown for comparison. As Fairbairn predicted, the most efficient shapes are in fact those with most of their area at the extreme edges. Finally, keep in mind that material can be removed from the inefficient zone around the neutral axis in several ways, an example of which is shown in Figure 4.4.8.

Sizing beams: procedure

1. Determine loads on beam (see Section 4.1).
2. Find reactions using principles of rotational and translational equilibrium (see Section 4.1).
3. Draw Shear diagram based on loads and reactions (see Section 4.3).
4. Draw Moment diagram based on slopes and quantities in Shear diagram (see Section 4.3).
5. Determine maximum moment from Moment diagram (see Section 4.3).
6. Using maximum moment, use the flexure formula to determine required section modulus.
7. Find weight per linear foot of selected beam.
8. Repeat from step 1, now including additional weight of selected beam.
9. Check selected beam for ability to carry maximum shear based on cross-sectional area (see Section 4.3).
10. Check selected beam for deflection (usually $<1/240$ or $1/360$ span).

Frequently asked questions

If I-shaped beams are so efficient, why are other shapes ever used? In addition to carrying loads, we often ask beams to do other things – to connect to finishes, to hang connections, etc. While W-shapes are efficient, their wide flanges restrict connections to the web – where we'd like to make any connections that involve cutting into the beam's material. (Remember that the web is closest to the neutral axis and thus least stressed.) Channels and tees both offer easier access to the beam's web if we're trying to make a structural connection.

Why is it so important to limit deflection? Is it mostly a visual issue? Deflection occurs in two different ways depending on the load type. Something that is fixed or stored for a long period of time will cause a beam or floor to deflect constantly. This is rarely an issue beyond esthetics, although liquids may pond,

Figure 4.4.8. *Structural design often takes advantage of the neutral axis to eliminate material from the center 'web' of beams. Here, a motorway restaurant by Pier Luigi Nervi replaces much of its concrete beam's 'web' with window glass.*

objects may roll in disquieting ways, and any pipes connected to the structure may have their slopes changed (see Section 6.4, Plumbing). However, these beams will also deflect under live loading, which may include vibrations from footfall and machinery, or displacement due to wind. If large enough, these can be distracting to building occupants, the building can feel flimsy to them, and in extreme cases they may experience motion sickness. Likewise, if the building houses sensitive instruments these can be thrown off by remarkably small movements in the structure.

Glossary and formulas

Centroid	A measure of a shape's 'average' point in space or, more accurately, its center of gravity. This will correspond with the shape's neutral axis if it is employed as a beam, and is thus an important characteristic.
Moment of Inertia	Simply put, a weighted measure of a shape's area, accounting for both quantity of area and average distance of each point from the centroid. Formulae for typical shapes are readily available, and may be combined using the formula:

$$I_{\text{total}} = \Sigma(I_{\text{sub-shape}} + A_{\text{sub-shape}}z^2)$$

Where z is the distance from the sub-shapes' centroid to the overall shape's centroid.

Section Modulus	A refinement of moment of inertia that provides a more usable number for structural calculations by counting depth one fewer times. It is found by dividing a shape's moment of inertia by the distance from its centroid to its 'farthest fiber' (c):

$$S = I/c$$

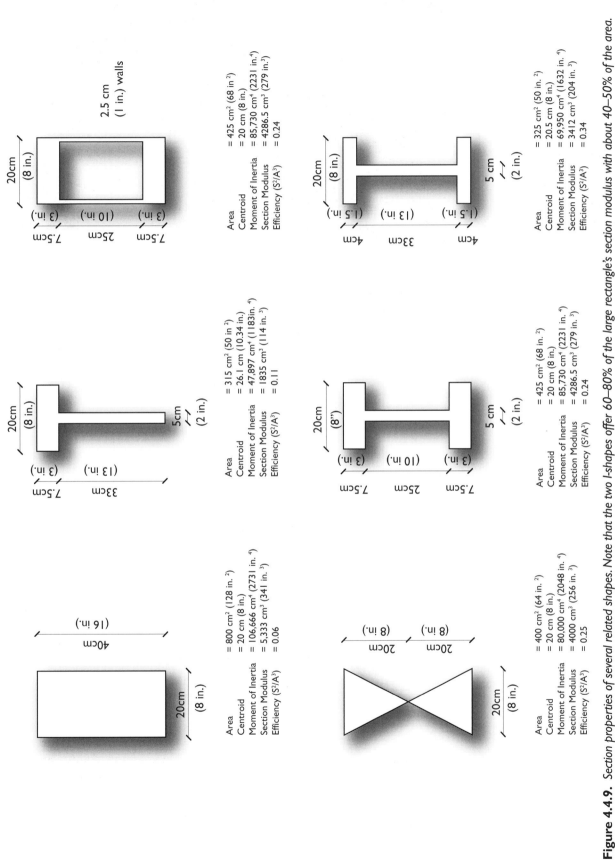

Figure 4.4.9. *Section properties of several related shapes. Note that the two I-shapes offer 60–80% of the large rectangle's section modulus with about 40–50% of the area.*

Flexure Formula	A simple formula that relates allowable stress, section modulus, and maximum allowable moment:

$$M = fS$$

The maximum allowable moment in any beam (M) is equal to the material's maximum allowable stress (f) multiplied by the section modulus of its cross-sectional shape (S).

Flanges	In beam design, top and bottom elements designed to put the most possible material in the most efficient places – far from the neutral axis.
Web	In beam design, an element designed to space flanges apart from one another, and thus from the neutral axis. This may be a solid plate, as in steel W-shapes, or a much lighter element, such as the bent metal bar in open web joists.

Further reading

Salvadori, M. (1963) Beams (Chapter 7), *Structure in Architecture: The Building of Buildings* (New York: Prentice-Hall), pp. 135–169.

Ambrose, J. and Parker, H. (2000) Investigation of Beams (Section 3.1–3.11), Frames (Section 60–135) and Wood Columns (Section 6.1–6.5), *Simplified Engineering for Architects and Builders* (New York: Wiley), pp. 212–228.

Allen, E. and Iano, J. (2002) Designing the Structure (Chapter 2), *The Architect's Studio Companion*, 3rd ed (New York: Wiley), pp. 47–137.

4.5   Column design

<table>
<tr><td>**Columns**</td><td>Definition
Unique properties as axially loaded members</td></tr>
<tr><td>**Buckling**</td><td>Why buckling occurs in columns
Ways to prevent columns from buckling</td></tr>
<tr><td>**Column Design**</td><td>Slenderness ratio
Radius of gyration
Effective column length and *K*</td></tr>
</table>

Introduction

In our discussion of axially loaded members from Section 4.2 (members in pure tension or compression along their long axis) we briefly discussed a caveat having to do with long compression members. For these situations, we can't simply assume the maximum allowable compressive strength without taking into account the likelihood of long, or slender members to bend and ultimately to buckle.

Buckling is a result of loads finding the shortest, most direct path to resolution. For a short column (a hockey puck, say), the most direct path will be to compress the 'column'. For a long column, the most direct path is more likely to fold the column out of the way – it will be easier for the force to bend the column than to compress it. As this occurs, the column may exceed its maximum bending strength and break. Typically, buckling causes failure by adding more compressive force through bending – recall that bending is really the development of a tension/compression couple across the section of a structural member.

Column failure is a particularly serious problem. If a beam collapses, it takes a relatively small area of floor with it – potentially fatal, but rarely catastrophic. If a column fails, it will take out a large *tributary area* – that is, the entire floor area whose loads 'flow' to that column. Column failures, therefore, are usually catastrophic, and factors of safety for these elements tend to be higher than for beams.

Column behavior

Mario Salvadori notes that, were it not for buckling, a column would be limited mostly by its deformation (Fig.4.5.1). A typical steel shape could conceivably support a large load at a height of over a mile before deflecting significantly. Take, for example, a standard steel beam with an area of 226 cm^2

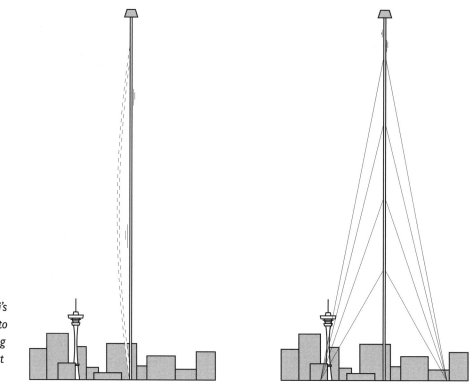

Figure 4.5.1. *Mario Salvadori's "Mile High Column" and a way to eliminate the problem of buckling by holding the column in place at various heights.*

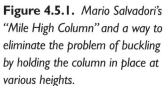

(35 in.^{2}) and a modulus of elasticity of 2,038,990 kg/cm^2 (29,000,000 psi). For a 1600 m (1 mile) high column carrying a load of 4500 kg (10,000 lb):

$e = PL/AE$ $e = PL/AE$

$e = ((4500\,\text{kg})\,(1600\,\text{m})\,(100\,\text{cm/m}))/$ $e = ((10,000\,\text{lb})\,(5280\,\text{ft})\,(12\,\text{in./ft}))/$
$((226\,\text{cm}^2)\,(2,038,990\,\text{kg/cm}^2))$ $((35\,\text{in.}^2)\,(29,000,000\,\text{psi}))$

$e = (4500 \times 1600 \times 100)\text{kg-cm}/$ $e = (10,000 \times 5280 \times 12)\text{lb-in.}/$
$(226 \times 2,038,990)\text{kg}$ $(35 \times 29,000,000)\text{lb}$

$e = 720,000,000\,\text{kg-cm}/$ $e = 633,600,000\,\text{lb-in.}/$
$460,811,740\,\text{kg}$ $1,015,000,000\,\text{lb}$

$e = 1.56\,\text{cm}$ $e = 0.62\,\text{in.}$

This is, of course, absurd. Our intuition tells us that a mile-high column will collapse. What is likely to happen? As shown in Figure 4.5.2, the column will flex in one direction or another over its length. As this happens, the center of gravity of the column will move out from under the center of the load. When this occurs, the load will no longer be imparting only an axial force on the column. It will also be imparting a *bending force* and the structure will go from being a simple column to being a complex *beam–column*, one that is carrying both axial and bending loads (Fig. 4.5.3).

Magnifying this problem, as the column flexes from its original position, the load will actually tend to push the column further out – and as the column moves

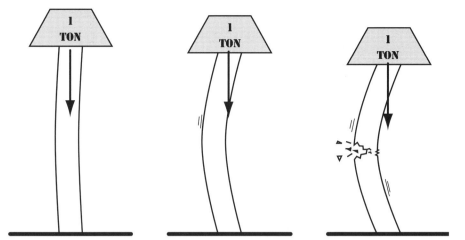

Figure 4.5.2. *Failure in buckling. As the column's material gets pushed aside by the weight, the column incurs a bending force which can eventually lead to failure that looks more like a beam – tension failure on one side, compression on the other.*

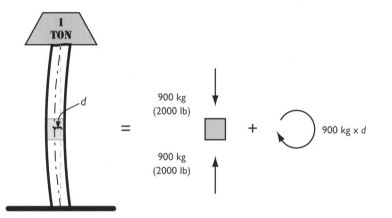

Figure 4.5.3. *The geometry of buckling. As the column 'moves' out of the load path, it begins to pick up a bending moment, defined by the load times the distance the column has moved.*

further, the moment induced by the load will increase. This creates a positive feedback loop that can cause column failure with a surprisingly small load.

Solving for a safe column load is mathematically complex and notoriously difficult. However, for our purposes, we can look at a handful of factors, and rely on handbooks, charts, and simple calculations to size columns with some confidence. Such calculations rely on empirical evidence more than theory – essentially documenting what's worked safely before. These calculations, like all structural calculations in this book, may be satisfactory for small-scale construction (and design studios), but past two stories most municipalities require professional engineering advice.

Column design: four factors

The tendency of columns to buckle is regulated by four factors – the column's *material*, its *shape*, its *slenderness ratio*, and its *end conditions*.

A column's *material* affects its tendency to flex in the first place, and its maximum bending load. Engineers begin to examine columns' likely behavior by figuring out how much the column can *deflect* under its initial loading – in other words, how much the column's center can move from its original position. If the material is fairly stiff, it will not move much to start with, and the progressive effects of loading and deflecting will be limited. Stiffness, remember, is measured by the modulus of elasticity, *E*, and thus a material with a higher *E* (e.g., steel) is from the start a more efficient choice for a column than a low one (e.g., aluminum) (see Section 4.2, Stresses).

Much like beam design, the cross-sectional *shape* of a column has a major influence on its ability to carry loads. While compressive strength is measured by simply dividing the allowable load by cross-sectional area, buckling resistance requires us to assess where the material is in that cross section. Area, of course, is critical, but so is location. With beams, we found the moment of inertia of various sections, which told us something about the distribution of material across a structural cross section. For columns, we use a related value, the *radius of gyration*. This value is equal to the square root of *I/A*, the moment of inertia divided by the area of the shape:

$$r = \sqrt{(I/A)}$$

The math behind this is tedious, but we can see that *r* is directly related to moment of inertia, and inversely proportional to a shape's area. It thus measures the quantity of matter, its location in a shape, and its efficiency in distribution. It can be thought of as the *average distance* of a shape's material from its neutral axis, while section modulus is the average *area times average distance* from the neutral axis. Interestingly, besides structural engineers, radius of gyration is extremely important to bowlers, who measure bowling balls in terms of their 'mass radius of gyration' along three axes. Somewhat like bowlers, we're interested in how columns will perform in multiple directions. While the column isn't spinning about multiple axes, like a bowling ball, there is no way to predict which direction it may begin to bend while under load. Thus, we must determine the worst case to design using *r*. For W-shapes, for example, we'll measure the radius of gyration with respect to the *weak, y–y* axis, since this will be less than the column's maximum performance for any other direction in which the column might buckle.

Note the difference between section modulus and radius of gyration. Section modulus divides one measure of *distance* out of moment of inertia (essentially one *z* out of Az^2) to arrive at a measure of *area times distance*. Radius of gyration divides the measure of *area* out of moment of inertia to arrive at a measure of *distance times distance*. It then takes the square root of this number to arrive at a pure *distance*, a measure strictly of how far, on average, a shape's material is from its neutral axis. While not strictly correct, it may be useful to think of radius of gyration as the *average width* of a section measured about a particular axis. Good column shapes, like good beam shapes, put the most material at the outer edges of the section. But, since we don't know which direction bending may start, it's not enough to just put the material on two edges. Instead, it has to be deployed *around* the outside of the column's shape. The most efficient column shapes are thus hollow tubes – square or round – that dispense entirely with a web and put *all* of their material at their outer edge. While W-shapes are often used instead of tubes for their lower fabrication costs, the best choices for column shapes are so-called 'compact' sections that tend to be square, with relatively deep flanges. Comparisons of related column shapes, with their section moduli, areas, and a reasonably accurate measure of their efficiency are given on page 455 (see Fig. 4.5.5).

Shape plays an additional role in column performance based on the location of the load. Most of our calculations will involve columns that are loaded along their center axis. The efficiency of a column is reduced if this load is applied eccentrically, that is, outside of the middle third of the column. An eccentric load will induce a bending moment in a column even before any deflection occurs.

Slenderness is the ratio of a column's length to its width. For simple rectangular sections, this is expressed as *l/d*, where *l* is the column length and *d* is the least dimension of the cross section. For complex sections, we replace *d* with *r*, the radius of gyration.

One of the simplest rules of thumb for column design is that the slenderness ratio of a steel compression column should never exceed 200, while that of a steel tension column should not exceed 240 for major members, and 300 for bracing members.

The role of slenderness in buckling was discovered in 1757 by a Swiss mathematician, Leonard Euler. The load at which a given column can be expected to fail in buckling is known as the *Euler Load* and for columns it is usually more important than the allowable compressive load. There are two paradoxes associated with Euler – first, that buckling is related solely to slenderness and a material's modulus of elasticity. The ultimate fiber strength of a material is *irrelevant* for column design. Thus, columns of a given length tend to be more nearly the same size than we might expect, no matter what the material. Stiffer materials may be more slender, but stronger materials may not be. The second paradox is that Euler developed his buckling formula long before any slender columns had been built – or even conceived. Columns in 1757 were universally made of stone, masonry, or timber. Buckling became an issue only with the arrival of iron and steel toward the end of the 1700s.

The final piece of the column puzzle relates to the end conditions. Structural members can be fixed to one another in three ways. They can be pinned, allowing rotation without translation, they can be fixed with a moment connection, allowing neither rotation nor translation, and they can be attached by a roller, allowing rotation and translation (see Section 4.8, Frames, for a full discussion of connections and their importance). These will affect the buckling tendencies of columns – fixed connections will inhibit the sort of bending that induces buckling by 'recruiting' the stiffness of the supporting material to resist bending, while 'looser' connections will allow columns to bend and thus buckle more

Column design

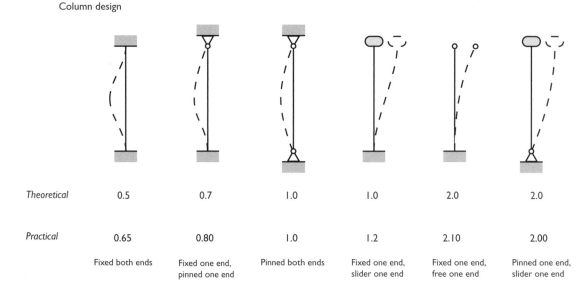

Theoretical	0.5	0.7	1.0	1.0	2.0	2.0
Practical	0.65	0.80	1.0	1.2	2.10	2.00
	Fixed both ends	Fixed one end, pinned one end	Pinned both ends	Fixed one end, slider one end	Fixed one end, free one end	Pinned one end, slider one end

Figure 4.5.5. *Modifying factors for column design based on end conditions (K) for use in the column formula (KL/r).*

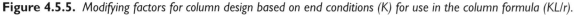

freely. Therefore, to design columns we first assign a multiplier to the column's actual length. This value, 'K', is assigned to each column depending on the end conditions (Fig. 4.5.5). This value modifies the length component of a column's slenderness ratio. A column that is simply pinned at each end has a K value of 1.0. A fixed connection at both ends results in a K value of 0.5, while an unfixed connection at one end results in a K value of 2.0. Thus, the end conditions can effectively reduce or extend a column's possible length by a factor of 2. What this means is that a column that is fixed at both ends will theoretically deflect only half the distance as a similar column with pinned connections at both ends.

In addition to the 'theoretical' K values, tables typically give 'recommended' values, indicating the complexity of actual behavior.

Column design
Because of the complexity of columns' theoretical behavior, and the catastrophic consequences of getting it wrong, governing bodies have simplified the process by publishing tables of empirically derived – and usually conservative – allowable stresses for columns of typical structural materials. Tables for steel are published by the American Institute of Steel Construction, while those for various types of timber are published by the National Lumber Manufacturers Association and the Southern Pine Association. Summary information for common shapes is shown in Tables 4.5.1 and 4.5.2. Note that these require us to know only the value for Kl.

Example: Design a column carrying 13,500 kg (30,000 lb) of floor load for a warehouse floor with story height of 6 m (20 ft) in Southern Pine (allowable load 105 kg/cm² or 1500 psi) and in A36 steel. The column is pinned at one end and fixed at the other.

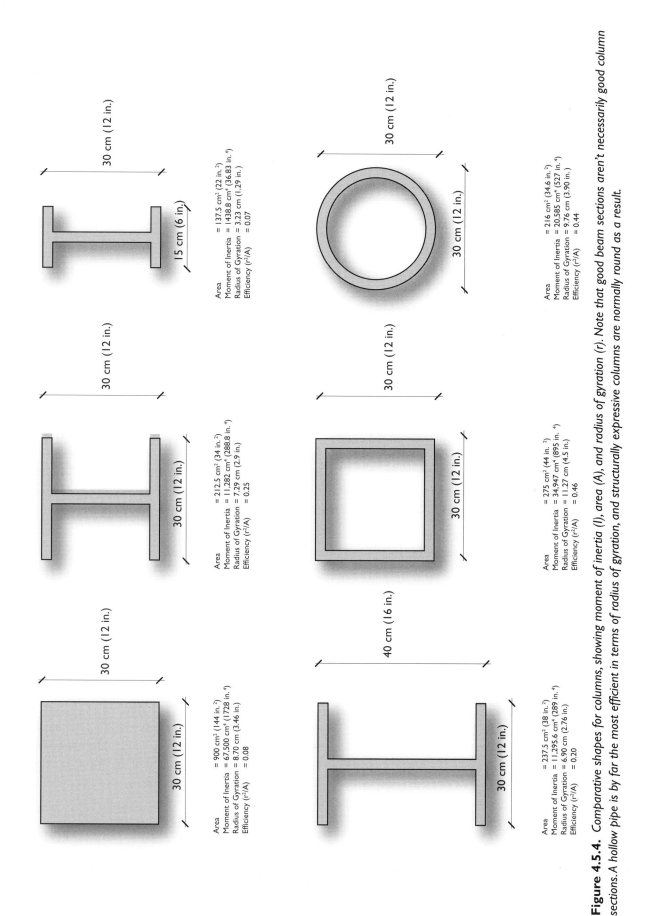

Figure 4.5.4. *Comparative shapes for columns, showing moment of inertia (I), area (A), and radius of gyration (r). Note that good beam sections aren't necessarily good column sections. A hollow pipe is by far the most efficient in terms of radius of gyration, and structurally expressive columns are normally round as a result.*

30 cm (12 in.)

30 cm (12 in.)

15 cm (6 in.)

Area = 137.5 cm² (22 in.²)
Moment of Inertia = 1438.8 cm⁴ (36.83 in.⁴)
Radius of Gyration = 3.23 cm (1.29 in.)
Efficiency (r²/A) = 0.07

30 cm (12 in.)

30 cm (12 in.)

30 cm (12 in.)

Area = 212.5 cm² (34 in.²)
Moment of Inertia = 11,282 cm⁴ (288.8 in.⁴)
Radius of Gyration = 7.29 cm (2.9 in.)
Efficiency (r²/A) = 0.25

30 cm (12 in.)

30 cm (12 in.)

Area = 900 cm² (144 in.²)
Moment of Inertia = 67,500 cm⁴ (1728 in.⁴)
Radius of Gyration = 8.70 cm (3.46 in.)
Efficiency (r²/A) = 0.08

30 cm (12 in.)

30 cm (12 in.)

Area = 216 cm² (34.6 in.²)
Moment of Inertia = 20,585 cm⁴ (527 in.⁴)
Radius of Gyration = 9.76 cm (3.90 in.)
Efficiency (r²/A) = 0.44

30 cm (12 in.)

Area = 275 cm² (44 in.²)
Moment of Inertia = 34,947 cm⁴ (895 in.⁴)
Radius of Gyration = 11.27 cm (4.5 in.)
Efficiency (r²/A) = 0.46

40 cm (16 in.)

30 cm (12 in.)

Area = 237.5 cm² (38 in.²)
Moment of Inertia = 11,295.6 cm⁴ (289 in.⁴)
Radius of Gyration = 6.90 cm (2.76 in.)
Efficiency (r²/A) = 0.20

Table 4.5.1. Allowable axial loading for selected A 36 steel column shapes.

| | | Effective unsupported length (Kl) with respect to least | | | | | | | | | | | | | | |
| | | 1.80 m (6 ft) | | 2.10 m (7 ft) | | 2.4 m (8 ft) | | 2.7 m (9 ft) | | 3.0 m (10 ft) | | 3.3 m (11 ft) | | 3.6 m (12 ft) | | 3.9 m (13 ft) | |
Nominal Metric size	Nominal Imperial size	kg (000)	lb (000)	kg (000)	lb (000)	kg (000)	lb (000)	kg (000)	lb (000)	kg (000)	lb (000)	kg (000)	lb (000)	kg (000)	lb (000)	kg (000)	lb (000)
W100 × 19	W4 × 13	28	62	26	57	23	51	20	45	18	39	14	32	12	27	10	23
W130 × 24	W5 × 16	37	83	36	79	33	74	31	69	29	64	26	58	23	52	21	46
W150 × 24	W6 × 16	38	85	36	81	35	78	33	74	32	70	29	65	27	60	25	55
W130 × 28	W5 × 19	44	97	41	92	39	87	36	81	34	75	31	69	28	62	25	55
W150 × 30	W6 × 20	49	109	47	105	45	101	43	96	41	91	38	85	36	80	33	74
W150 × 37	W6 × 25	62	137	59	132	57	126	54	120	51	114	48	107	45	100	42	93
W200 × 46	W8 × 31	80	178	78	174	76	169	74	164	72	159	69	154	67	148	64	142
W250 × 49	W10 × 33	85	189	83	184	81	179	78	173	75	167	72	161	70	155	67	149
W200 × 52	W8 × 35	90	201	89	197	86	191	84	186	81	180	78	174	76	168	73	162
W250 × 58	W10 × 39	101	224	98	218	95	212	93	206	90	199	87	193	83	185	80	178
W200 × 59	W8 × 40	104	230	101	225	99	219	96	213	93	206	90	200	87	193	83	185
W200 × 71	W8 × 48	125	277	122	270	119	264	116	257	112	249	108	241	105	233	101	224
W250 × 73	W10 × 49	130	289	128	284	126	279	123	273	121	268	118	262	115	256	112	249
W310 × 79	W12 × 53	140	312	138	307	135	301	133	295	130	288	127	282	124	275	120	267
W250 × 80	W10 × 54	144	319	141	313	139	308	136	302	133	296	130	289	127	282	124	275
W200 × 86	W8 × 58	151	335	147	327	144	319	140	311	136	302	132	293	127	283	123	273
W310 × 86	W12 × 58	154	342	151	336	149	330	145	323	142	316	139	309	136	302	132	294
W250 × 89	W10 × 60	160	355	157	349	154	343	151	336	148	329	145	322	141	314	138	307
W360 × 91	W14 × 61	162	359	158	352	155	345	152	338	149	331	145	323	142	315	138	306
W200 × 100	W8 × 67	174	387	171	379	167	370	162	360	158	350	153	339	148	328	142	316
W310 × 97	W12 × 65	175	389	173	384	171	379	168	373	165	367	162	361	160	355	157	348
W360 × 101	W14 × 68	180	400	177	393	173	385	170	377	166	369	162	360	158	351	154	342
W250 × 101	W10 × 68	181	402	178	395	175	388	171	381	168	373	164	365	161	357	157	348
W310 × 107	W12 × 72	194	431	191	425	189	420	186	413	183	407	180	400	177	393	174	386
W360 × 110	W14 × 74	196	436	193	429	189	421	185	412	181	403	177	394	173	384	168	373
W250 × 115	W10 × 77	204	454	201	447	198	439	194	431	190	422	186	413	182	404	177	394
W250 × 115	W10 × 77	205	456	202	448	198	440	194	432	191	424	186	414	182	405	178	395
W310 × 117	W12 × 79	213	473	210	467	207	461	204	454	201	447	198	439	194	432	191	424
W360 × 122	W14 × 82	217	482	213	474	209	465	205	456	201	446	196	435	191	425	186	413
W250 × 131	W10 × 88	234	521	231	513	227	504	223	495	218	485	214	475	209	464	204	453
W310 × 129	W12 × 87	235	522	232	515	229	508	225	501	222	493	218	485	215	477	211	468
W360 × 134	W14 × 90	246	547	243	541	241	536	239	530	236	524	233	517	230	511	227	504
W310 × 143	W12 × 96	259	575	256	568	252	560	248	552	245	544	241	535	237	526	232	516
W310 × 158	W12 × 106	286	636	283	628	279	620	275	611	271	602	266	592	262	582	257	572
W360 × 162	W14 × 109	297	661	294	654	291	647	288	640	285	633	282	626	278	618	274	609
W310 × 179	W12 × 120	324	721	320	712	316	702	311	692	307	682	302	671	297	660	292	648

radius of gyration – meters (feet) in kips and kg × 1000

4.2 m (14 ft)		4.5 m (15 ft)		4.8 m (16 ft)		5.1 m (17 ft)		5.4 m (18 ft)		5.7 m (19 ft)		6.0 m (20 ft)		6.3 m (21 ft)		6.6 m (22 ft)		7.0 m (23 ft)	
kg (000)	lb (000)	kg (000)	lb (000)	kg (000)	lb (000)	kg (000)	lb (000)	kg (000)	lb (000)	kg (000)	lb (000)	kg (000)	lb (000)	kg (000)	lb (000)	kg (000)	lb (000)	kg (000)	lb (000)
9	20	8	17	7	15														
18	39	15	34	14	30	12	27	11	24	9	21	9	19	8	18				
23	50	20	45	18	39	16	35	14	31	13	28	11	25	10	23	9	21	9	19
21	47	18	41	16	36	14	32	13	29	12	26	10	23	9	21				
30	67	27	61	24	54	22	48	19	42	17	38	15	34	14	31	13	28	12	26
38	85	35	77	31	69	27	61	25	55	22	49	20	44	18	40	16	36	15	33
61	136	59	130	55	123	53	117	50	110	46	102	43	95	39	87	36	79	32	72
64	142	61	135	57	127	54	120	50	112	46	103	43	95	39	86	35	78	32	72
70	155	67	148	63	141	60	133	56	125	53	117	49	109	45	100	41	91	37	83
77	170	73	162	69	153	65	145	61	135	57	126	52	116	48	106	43	96	40	88
80	177	77	170	72	161	69	153	65	144	60	134	56	125	52	115	47	105	43	96
97	215	93	206	89	197	84	187	79	176	74	165	69	154	64	143	59	131	54	120
109	242	106	235	103	228	99	221	96	213	92	205	89	197	85	188	81	180	77	171
117	260	113	252	110	244	106	235	102	227	98	218	94	209	90	199	85	189	81	179
121	268	117	260	114	253	110	244	106	236	102	227	98	218	94	209	90	200	86	190
118	262	113	251	108	239	103	228	97	215	91	202	85	189	79	175	72	161	66	147
129	286	125	277	121	269	117	260	113	250	108	241	104	231	99	221	95	210	90	199
135	299	131	290	126	281	122	272	118	263	114	254	110	244	105	234	100	223	95	212
134	297	130	288	126	279	121	269	117	259	112	248	107	237	102	226	97	215	91	203
137	304	131	292	126	279	119	265	113	251	106	236	99	221	93	206	86	190	78	174
153	341	150	334	147	326	144	319	140	311	136	303	133	295	129	286	125	277	121	268
149	332	145	322	140	311	135	301	130	289	125	278	120	266	114	253	108	241	102	227
153	339	149	330	144	320	140	310	135	299	130	289	125	278	120	267	115	255	109	242
170	378	167	370	163	362	159	354	155	345	151	336	147	327	143	318	139	308	135	299
163	363	158	352	153	341	148	329	143	317	137	304	131	292	125	278	119	265	113	250
173	384	168	373	163	362	158	351	153	339	147	327	142	315	136	302	130	289	124	275
173	385	168	374	163	363	158	352	153	340	148	328	142	316	136	303	131	290	124	276
187	415	183	407	179	398	175	389	171	380	167	370	162	360	158	350	153	339	148	328
181	402	175	389	170	377	163	363	158	351	152	337	145	323	139	308	132	293	125	277
199	442	194	430	188	417	182	405	176	392	170	378	164	364	157	349	151	335	144	319
207	459	203	450	198	440	194	430	189	420	184	409	179	398	174	386	169	376	164	364
224	497	220	489	217	482	213	474	210	466	206	458	202	449	198	440	194	432	190	422
228	506	223	496	219	486	214	475	209	464	203	452	198	440	193	428	187	416	181	403
252	561	248	550	242	538	237	526	231	514	226	502	220	489	214	475	208	462	202	448
270	601	266	592	262	583	258	574	254	564	249	554	245	544	240	533	235	523	230	512
286	636	281	624	275	611	269	597	263	584	256	569	250	555	243	540	236	525	222	493

(Continued)

Table 4.5.1. (*Continued*)

Effective unsupported length (*Kl*) with respect to least

Nominal Metric size	Nominal Imperial size	kg (000)	lbs (ft)	1.80 m (6 ft)		2.10 m (7 ft)		2.4 m (8 ft)		2.7 m (9 ft)		3.0 m (10 ft)		3.3 m (11 ft)		3.6 m (12 ft)	
				kg (000)	lb (000)	kg (000)	lb (000)	kg (000)	lb (000)	kg (000)	lb (000)	kg (000)	lb (000)	kg (000)	lb (000)	kg (000)	lb (000)
75 mm pipe	3 in. pipe	11.30	7.58	17	38	16	36	15	34	14	31	13	28	11	25	10	22
89 mm pipe	3.5 in. pipe	13.58	9.11	22	48	21	46	20	44	18	41	17	38	16	35	14	32
76 × 76 × 6.4	3 × 3 × 1/4	13.13	8.81	24	53	22	49	20	44	17	38	15	33	12	27	10	23
75 mm Ex. St. pipe	3 in. Ex. St. pipe	15.28	10.25	23	52	22	48	20	45	18	41	17	37	15	33	13	28
102 mm pipe	4 in. pipe	16.09	10.79	27	59	26	57	24	54	23	52	22	49	21	46	19	43
102 × 102 × 4.8	4 × 4 × 3/16	14.04	9.42	29	64	27	61	26	58	25	55	23	51	21	47	19	43
89 mm Ex. St. pipe	3.5 in. Ex. St. pipe	18.63	12.50	30	66	28	63	27	59	25	55	23	51	21	47	19	43
102 mm Ex. St. pipe	4 in. Ex. St. pipe	22.33	14.98	36	81	35	78	34	75	32	71	30	67	28	63	27	59
75 mm double Ex. St. pipe	3 in. double Ex. St. pipe	27.70	18.58	41	91	38	84	35	77	31	69	27	60	23	51	19	43
127 mm pipe	5 in. pipe	21.79	14.62	37	83	36	81	35	78	34	76	33	73	32	71	31	68
102 × 102 × 7.9	4 × 4 × 5/16	22.11	14.83	45	100	43	95	41	90	38	84	35	78	32	72	29	65
152 × 152 × 4.8	6 × 6 × 3/16	21.66	14.53	48	107	47	105	46	102	45	99	43	96	42	93	41	90
152 mm pipe	6 in. pipe	28.28	18.97	50	110	49	108	48	106	46	103	45	101	44	98	43	95
127 mm Ex. St. pipe	5 in. Ex. St. pipe	30.98	20.78	53	118	51	114	50	111	48	107	46	103	45	99	43	95
102 mm double Ex. St. pipe	4 in.double Ex. St. pipe	41.06	27.54	66	147	63	140	60	133	57	126	53	118	49	109	45	100
152 mm Ex. St. pipe	6 in. Ex. St. pipe	42.59	28.57	75	166	73	162	72	159	70	155	68	151	66	146	64	142
203 mm pipe	8 in. pipe	42.56	28.55	77	171	76	168	75	166	73	163	72	161	71	158	70	155
203 × 203 × 6.4	8 × 8 × 1/4	38.49	25.82	88	196	87	193	86	190	84	187	83	184	81	180	79	176
152 × 152 × 9.5	6 × 6 × 3/8	40.97	27.48	90	201	88	196	86	191	84	186	81	180	78	174	76	168
127 mm double Ex. St. pipe	5 in. double Ex. St. pipe	57.47	38.55	97	216	94	209	91	202	88	195	84	187	80	178	77	170
254 mm pipe	10 in pipe	60.35	40.48	111	246	109	243	108	241	107	238	106	235	104	232	103	229
203 mm Ex. St. pipe	8 in. Ex. St. pipe	64.68	43.39	117	259	115	255	113	251	111	247	109	243	108	239	105	234
203 × 203 × 9.5	8 × 8 × 3/8	56.05	37.60	129	286	126	281	125	277	122	272	120	267	118	262	115	256
152 mm double Ex. St. pipe	6 in. double Ex. St. pipe	79.25	53.16	138	306	135	299	131	292	128	284	124	275	120	266	116	257
310 mm pipe	12 in. pipe	73.88	49.56	136	303	135	301	135	299	133	296	132	293	131	291	130	288
254 × 254 × 7.9	10 × 10 × 5/16	60.15	40.35	140	311	139	308	137	305	135	301	134	297	132	293	130	289
254 mm Ex. St. pipe	10 in. Ex. St. pipe	81.60	54.74	149	332	148	328	146	325	144	321	143	318	141	314	139	309
310 mm Ex. St. pipe	12 in. Ex. St. pipe	97.53	65.42	180	400	179	397	177	394	176	390	174	387	172	383	171	379
203 mm double Ex. St. pipe	8 in. double Ex. St. pipe	107.96	72.42	194	431	191	424	188	417	185	410	181	403	178	395	174	387
305 × 305 × 9.5	12 × 12 × 3/8	86.61	58.10	204	453	202	449	200	445	198	441	197	437	195	433	193	428
254 × 254 × 12.7	10 × 10 × 1/2	93.11	62.46	216	481	214	476	212	471	209	465	207	459	203	452	201	446
356 × 356 × 9.5	14 × 14 × 3/8	101.83	68.31	241	536	240	533	238	529	236	525	234	521	233	517	231	513
305 × 305 × 12.7	12 × 12 × 1/2	113.40	76.07	267	593	265	588	262	583	260	577	257	571	255	566	252	559
356 × 356 × 12.7	14 × 14 × 1/2	133.69	89.68	317	704	315	699	312	694	310	689	308	684	305	678	302	672
406 × 406 × 12.7	16 × 16 × 1/2	154.00	103.30	367	815	365	810	362	805	360	800	358	795	356	790	353	785
406 × 406 × 15.9	16 × 16 × 5/8	189.88	127.37	451	1003	449	998	446	992	444	986	441	979	438	973	435	966

Ex. St.: extra strong.
Note: Consult AISC Steel Handbook for full range of structural shapes.
Structural tubing (square section) is typically graded to 46 ksi (shown here) instead of 36 ksi.

radius of gyration – meters (feet) in kips and kg × 1000

3.9 m (13 ft)		4.2 m (14 ft)		4.5 m (15 ft)		4.8 m (16 ft)		5.1 m (17 ft)		5.4 m (18 ft)		5.7 m (19 ft)		6.0 m (20 ft)		6.3 m (21 ft)		6.6 m (22 ft)		7.0 m (23 ft)	
kg (000)	lb (000)	kg (000)	lb (000)	kg (000)	lb (000)	kg (000)	lb (000)	kg (000)	lb (000)	kg (000)	lb (000)	kg (000)	lb (000)	kg (000)	lb (000)	kg (000)	lb (000)	kg (000)	lb (000)	kg (000)	lb (000)
9	19	7	16	6	14	5	12	5	11	5	10	4	9								
13	29	11	25	10	22	9	19	8	17	7	15	6	14	5	12	5	11	5	10		
9	19	8	17	7	15	6	13	5	11	5	10										
11	24	9	21	8	18	7	16	5	12	5	11										
18	40	16	36	15	33	13	29	12	26	10	23	9	21	9	19	8	17	7	15	6	14
18	39	16	35	14	30	12	27	11	24	9	21	9	19	8	17	7	16	6	14	6	13
17	38	15	33	13	29	11	25	10	23	9	20	8	18	7	16	6	14				
24	54	22	49	20	44	18	39	16	35	14	31	13	28	11	25	10	22	9	21	9	19
17	37	14	32	13	28	11	24	10	22												
29	65	29	64	26	58	25	55	23	51	21	47	19	43	18	39	16	36	14	32	13	30
26	58	23	51	20	44	18	39	15	34	14	31	13	28	11	25	10	23	9	21	9	19
39	87	37	83	36	80	34	76	32	72	31	68	29	64	27	60	25	56	23	51	19	43
41	92	40	89	39	86	37	82	36	79	34	75	32	71	30	67	28	63	27	59	25	55
41	91	39	86	36	81	34	76	32	71	29	65	27	59	24	54	22	48	20	44	18	41
41	91	36	81	32	70	28	62	25	55	22	49	20	44	18	40	16	37	15	33		
62	137	59	132	57	127	55	122	52	117	50	111	47	105	45	99	41	92	39	86	36	80
68	152	67	149	65	145	64	142	62	138	61	135	59	131	57	127	55	123	54	119	52	115
78	173	76	169	74	165	72	160	70	156	68	151	66	147	64	142	62	137	59	132	57	127
72	161	69	154	66	147	63	140	59	132	56	124	52	115	48	107	44	98	40	89	34	75
72	160	68	151	63	141	59	130	54	119	49	108	44	97	39	87	36	80	32	72	30	67
102	226	100	223	99	220	97	216	96	213	94	209	92	205	90	201	89	197	87	193	85	189
103	229	101	224	99	219	96	214	94	209	91	203	89	197	86	191	83	185	81	179	78	173
113	251	110	245	107	238	104	232	101	225	99	219	95	212	92	205	89	197	86	190	82	182
111	247	107	237	102	227	97	216	92	205	87	193	81	181	76	168	70	155	64	142	59	131
128	285	127	282	125	278	124	275	122	272	121	268	119	265	117	261	116	257	114	254	113	250
128	285	126	280	124	276	122	271	120	266	117	261	115	256	113	251	110	245	108	240	105	234
137	305	135	301	133	296	131	291	129	286	126	281	124	276	122	271	119	265	117	260	114	254
169	375	167	371	165	367	163	363	161	358	159	353	157	349	155	344	152	337	150	334	148	329
170	378	166	369	162	360	158	351	153	341	149	331	144	321	140	310	135	299	130	288	124	276
190	423	188	418	186	413	184	408	181	403	179	397	176	391	174	386	171	380	168	373	165	367
198	439	194	432	191	424	188	417	184	409	180	401	176	392	173	384	169	375	165	366	161	357
229	508	227	504	225	499	222	494	220	489	218	484	215	478	213	473	210	467	208	462	205	456
249	553	246	546	243	540	240	533	237	526	233	518	230	511	226	503	223	495	219	487	215	478
300	666	297	660	294	654	291	647	288	641	285	634	282	627	279	619	275	612	272	604	269	597
351	779	348	773	345	767	342	761	340	755	337	748	333	741	331	735	328	728	324	721	321	713
432	959	428	951	425	944	421	936	418	928	414	920	410	912	406	903	403	895	399	886	395	877

Note: Consult AISC Steel Handbook for full range of structural shapes.

Solution: From the chart shown in Figure 4.5.5, we find that a column pinned at one end and fixed at the other has a recommended design value for *K* of 0.80. The column's *effective length* is, therefore:

$$L_e = KL \qquad\qquad L_e = KL$$
$$L_e = (0.80)\,(6\,m) \qquad L_e = (0.80)\,(20\,ft)$$
$$L_e = 4.8\,m \qquad\qquad L_e = 16\,ft$$

For Southern Pine, we read from the table of allowable axial loads in Table 4.5.2. Note that there are no 4.8 m (16 ft) listings for anything less than an 150 × 200 (6 × 8) member. Reading down under the 4.8 m column, we find that the first column that can safely carry a load greater than 13,500 kg (30,000 lb) is a 200 × 200 (8 × 8), which can carry up to 14,500 kg.

From the table of allowable axial loads for steel, we read down the table under 4.8 m (16 ft) and find – almost immediately – that a W130 × 24 (W5 × 16) will just do the job. Looking further down the chart, there are no smaller or lighter members, and thus this will be our best choice.

For multi-story buildings, we must design based on the accumulated, or *tributary* load carried by each segment of the column. This is, of course, additive as we go down the building, as each column-story picks up additional load at each floor level. Columns at ground level are often, therefore, larger than those at the top level of high buildings. We often find, however that it is more economical to design for the worst case, and to continue that column shape up the entire frame. This allows elevational consistency, standardization, and economies of scale at the price of weight.

Example: Find acceptable A36 steel column sizes at the roof, top floor, and ground floor of a 10-story building. The tributary area for each floor is 58 m² (625 ft². Floor loading is 488 kg/m² (100 lb/ft²), roof loading is 122 kg/m² (25 lb/ft²), and each story is 5 m (15 ft high) with fixed connections at top and bottom.

Solution: Each column will have an effective length that is reduced by having fixed connections at both ends. From the table of *K*s, we get that the effective length of each column will be:

$$(0.65) \times 5\,m = 3.25\,m \qquad (0.65) \times 15\,ft = 9.75\,ft$$

Each column will therefore have an effective length of 3.25 m (3.3 m or 10 ft rounded up).

Beginning at the roof, we find that the topmost column will carry a load of:

$$(58\,m^2) \times 122\,kg/m^2 \qquad (625\,ft^2) \times 25\,lb/ft^2$$
$$= 7076\,kg \qquad\qquad = 15,625\,lb$$

Table 4.5.2. Allowable axial loading for selected Southern Pine/Douglas Fir column sizes.

Nominal size Metric	Nominal size Imperial	1.80 m (6 ft) kg (000)	1.80 m (6 ft) lb (000)	2.4 m (8 ft) kg (000)	2.4 m (8 ft) lb (000)	3.0 m (10 ft) kg (000)	3.0 m (10 ft) lb (000)	3.6 m (12 ft) kg (000)	3.6 m (12 ft) lb (000)	4.2 m (14 ft) kg (000)	4.2 m (14 ft) lb (000)	4.8 m (16 ft) kg (000)	4.8 m (16 ft) lb (000)	5.4 m (18 ft) kg (000)	5.4 m (18 ft) lb (000)	6.0 m (20 ft) kg (000)	6.0 m (20 ft) lb (000)
						Effective unsupported length (Kl) with respect to least radius of gyration – meters (feet) in kips and kg × 1000											
100 × 100	4 × 4	5.0	11.1	3.3	7.3	2.2	4.9	1.6	3.5	1.2	2.6						
100 × 150	4 × 6	7.8	17.4	5.1	11.4	3.5	7.8	2.5	5.5	1.9	4.1						
100 × 200	4 × 8	10.3	22.9	6.8	15.1	4.6	10.2	3.3	7.3	2.9	6.5						
150 × 150	6 × 6	12.4	27.6	11.2	24.8	9.4	20.9	7.6	16.9	6.0	13.4						
150 × 200	6 × 8	16.9	37.6	15.3	33.9	12.8	28.5	10.4	23.1	8.2	18.3	6.6	14.6	5.4	11.9	4.4	9.8
150 × 250	6 × 10	21.4	47.6	19.4	43.0	16.2	36.1	13.1	29.2	10.4	23.1	8.3	18.5	6.8	15.0	6.0	13.4
200 × 200	8 × 8	24.3	54.0	23.2	51.5	21.6	48.1	19.6	43.5	17.1	38.0	14.5	32.3	12.3	27.4	10.4	23.1
200 × 250	8 × 10	30.8	68.4	29.4	65.3	27.5	61.0	24.8	55.1	21.6	48.1	18.5	41.0	15.6	34.7	13.2	29.3
200 × 300	8 × 12	37.3	82.8	35.6	79.0	33.2	73.8	30.0	66.7	26.2	58.2	22.3	49.6	18.9	42.0	15.9	35.4
250 × 300	10 × 10	39.8	88.4	38.7	85.9	37.4	83.0	35.6	79.0	33.1	73.6	30.2	67.0	27.0	60.0	23.8	52.9
250 × 300	10 × 12	48.2	107.0	46.8	104.0	45.0	100.0	43.0	95.6	40.1	89.1	36.5	81.2	32.7	72.6	28.8	64.0
250 × 350	10 × 14	56.7	126.0	54.9	122.0	53.1	118.0	50.4	112.0	47.3	105.0	42.9	95.3	38.4	85.3	33.8	75.1
300 × 300	12 × 12	58.5	130.0	57.6	128.0	56.3	125.0	54.9	122.0	52.7	117.0	50.0	111.0	46.8	104.0	43.0	95.6
350 × 350	14 × 14	81.0	180.0	80.1	178.0	79.2	176.0	77.4	172.0	75.6	168.0	73.4	163.0	70.2	156.0	66.6	148.0
400 × 400	16 × 16	107.1	238.0	106.2	236.0	105.3	234.0	103.5	230.0	101.7	226.0	99.9	222.0	97.2	216.0	93.6	208.0

Figure 4.5.6. *Columns showing the additive effects of multiple floors. As the tributary load increases, the columns step out toward the building's base, reflecting the need for greater cross-sectional area. (Note that stepping out in one direction does nothing to increase the column's slenderness ratio, which isn't always a problem with short story heights).*
Promontory Apartments, Chicago. Mies van der Rohe, Architect; Frank Kornacker, Engineer.

Scanning across Table 4.5.1, we find that we are at the very low end of the spectrum. The smallest shape listed, a W4 × 13 wide flange, 3 m (10 ft) in length, will carry a safe load of 17,550 kg (39,000 lb), more than twice our load.

Just below the top floor, the first 'serious' column will carry both the roof load we've just found, and the load of the top floor:

$$P = P_{\text{roof}} + P_{10}$$
$$P = 7076\,\text{kg} + (488\,\text{kg/m}^2) \times 58\,\text{m}^2$$
$$P = 7076\,\text{kg} + 28{,}304\,\text{kg}$$
$$P = 35{,}380\,\text{kg}$$

$$P = P_{\text{roof}} + P_{10}$$
$$P = 15{,}625\,\text{lb} + (100\,\text{lb/ft}^2) \times 625\,\text{ft}^2$$
$$P = 15{,}625\,\text{lb} + 62{,}500\,\text{lb}$$
$$P = 78{,}125\,\text{lb}$$

Figure 4.5.7. *Column theory as architectural expression. Note the gradual thickening of columns toward the base, and the use of intermediate tension columns to support the second floor, opening up the ground floor. Riverside Plaza, Chicago. Bruce Graham/SOM, Architect; Fazlur Khan/SOM, Engineer.*

Again looking at Table 4.5.1, we now find that we must jump to a W150 × 30 (W6 × 20).

It is now a simple matter to calculate the total tributary area on the ground floor column:

$$P_{\text{ground}} = P_{\text{roof}} + 9 \times (P_{\text{typical}}) \qquad P_{\text{ground}} = P_{\text{roof}} + 9 \times (P_{\text{typical}})$$
$$P_{\text{ground}} = 7076\,\text{kg} + 9\,(35{,}380\,\text{kg}) \qquad P_{\text{ground}} = 15{,}625\,\text{lb} + 9\,(62{,}500\,\text{lb})$$
$$P_{\text{ground}} = 7076\,\text{kg} + 303{,}750\,\text{kg} \qquad P_{\text{ground}} = 15{,}625\,\text{lb} + 562{,}500\,\text{lb}$$
$$P_{\text{ground}} = 310{,}826\,\text{kg} \qquad\qquad P_{\text{ground}} = 578{,}125\,\text{lb}$$

Here, a W310 × 158 (W12 × 106) would work, carrying a safe load of 271,000 kg (602,000 lb) for the effective length.

Figure 4.5.8. *A structurally expressive skylon, wider at the middle to counteract buckling forces at La Villette, Paris. Bernard Tschumi, Architect; Peter Rice, Engineer.*

In practice, significant reductions are often allowed in the assumed live load of a multi-story structure, and codes assume that there will be a significant diversity factor – that all floors will not be fully loaded all at the same time. In buildings over seven stories, for instance, columns are assumed to carry only half of the normally calculated live load.

Nevertheless, we see that the accumulation of loading over a tall building creates a difference in the required sizes of columns at the top and base. This, of course, is inconvenient if we want to open up the ground level for, say, a lobby. Skyscrapers will sometimes use transfer girders, or collecting piers, to open up the ground floor, but these may become so deep because of the shear stresses involved that they themselves take up an entire story. Likewise, very tall buildings will often use rooftop heating, ventilation, and air conditioning (HVAC) plants to feed air downward through column shafts. As the structural columns taper toward the top, ductwork, tapers toward the base, making more efficient use of a consistent section in plan. Occasionally, building columns will express the fact that they taper toward the ground – in particular some work by Bruce Graham and Fazlur Khan of SOM in Chicago during the 1960s and 1970s experimented with subtle uses of columns as structurally expressive elements in high rises (Figs. 4.5.6 and 4.5.7).

While these column charts will suffice for preliminary design, there are often situations where we must calculate the total radius of gyration for additive shapes – angles bolted to one another, for instance. In these cases, we rely on tables that give allowable unit stresses for various Kl/r ratios, typically reductions from the allowable compressive strength as the ratio gets larger.

One final design note. Since long columns are essentially designed for both compression and bending loads, their behavior is somewhat like simply loaded beams. Therefore, it is often beneficial to design columns of varying section, thicker in the middle of the 'span', with narrower sections at the edges. Renzo Piano and Santiago Calatrava in particular use this aspect of column behavior to often spectacular effect, and the 'skylon', or tapering column, is an often-used device in high-tech design (Fig. 4.5.8).

Glossary and formulas

Column	Technically, any axially loaded member. Usually a vertical member carrying gravity loads and designed to resist both compression and buckling.
End Conditions	How a column is connected to the beams or supports at its ends. Because these play a role in how much or little the column can move, they are important considerations in how well the column will resist buckling.
Radius of Gyration	Basically, a measurement of a column shape's efficiency. Radius of gyration measures the average distance of a shape's area from its centroid, giving a usable measure of the column's 'average width.' Radius of gyration is defined by:

$$r = \sqrt{(I/A)}$$

where *I* is the shape's moment of inertia and *A* is the shape's area. Note that we must usually find *r* for the *weakest* axis.

Skylon	A column that is widest at the middle, tapering toward both ends. This is a 'true' column shape that acknowledges the role of bending in determining column performance, and is often used to dramatic visual effect.
Slenderness Ratio	A measure of a column's length divided by either its narrowest width or by its radius of gyration in the weakest axis. Generally we use the formula:

$$kl/r$$

where *k* is a multiplier based on the end conditions of the column, *l* is the column length in inches (or cm), and *r* is the shape's radius of gyration in inches or cm. This number then guides us through charts of allowable loads for a given material to select a shape.

Tributary Area	The total area of floor plate that 'flows' into a column. In multi-story buildings, this will include the weight and loads of every floor plate above the column in question. Figured on each floor by assuming each column will carry an area defined by the centerlines of each surrounding bay.

Further reading

Salvadori, M. and Heller, R. (1963) Basic States of Stress (Chapter 5), *Structure in Architecture: The Building of Buildings* (New York: Prentice-Hall), pp. 83–87.

Ambrose, J. and Parker, H. (2000) Investigation of Beams and Frames – Compression Members (Section 3.1–3.11), *Simplified Engineering for Architects and Builders* (New York: Wiley), pp. 122–135.

Allen, E. and Iano, J. (2002) Designing the Structure (Chapter 2), *The Architect's Studio Companion*, 3rd ed (New York: Wiley), pp. 47–137.

Mainstone, R.J. (2001) Supports, Walls, and Foundations (Chapter 10), *Developments in Structural Form*, 2nd ed (Oxford: Architectural Press), pp. 175–185.

Sandaker, B.N. and Eggen, A.P. (1992) The Column (Chapter 5), *The Structural Basis of Architecture* (New York: Whitney), pp. 109–130.

4.6 Slabs and plates

Slabs and Plates	Difference between one- and two-way action
	What this means for slab design?
Floor Systems	Wood
	Steel
	Concrete
Plates	Folded plates and simple shell theory
	When is a plate a beam?

Introduction

Thus far we have discussed only one-dimensional structural elements – columns, beams, and cables. While these are the major elements of a skeleton structure, we have still not dealt with a key element – the floor. The 'tools' we have thus far – beams, columns trusses, etc., handle the major work of structures, collecting and transferring loads to the ground. Slabs are more complex than beams or columns, as they work in two dimensions instead of one, but the loads they carry individually are relatively small compared with larger structural members. While not as glamorous as beams or columns, slabs can play a key role in architectural expression – floors often constitute the bulk of a building structure's weight, and thus their performance often needs to be particularly efficient.

Floors and other horizontal planes are described structurally as *slabs* or *plates*. Their mathematical behavior is complex, but the basics are quite simple, and slabs have been in use for long enough that an extensive body of empirical evidence makes it possible to specify, rather than engineer, slabs for most situations.

To begin to understand slab behavior, consider a typical floor. With simple beam calculations, we could figure out a structural system composed entirely of one-dimensional beams (Fig. 4.6.1). Assuming they had some thickness, we could cover an entire floor with steel W-shapes.

This, of course, strikes us as a very heavy solution, since we are used to seeing floor structures that have a much thinner floor thickness than the beams that carry them. How can this be? The answer lies in the slab's two-dimensional nature. Roughly speaking, where a beam transfers load along its length alone, a slab is capable of transferring loads in two dimension, and its monolithic nature means that each individual 'slice' is assisted in carrying its load by the 'slices' of slab next to it.

To understand why, we need to remind ourselves about *deflection*, the tendency of structural members to change shape under loading. A structural member under loading changes shape – a beam will curve slightly, which is

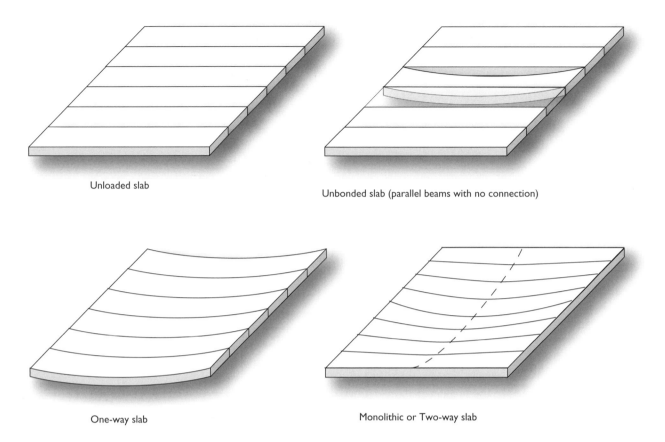

Figure 4.6.1. *Basic slab theory. Slabs work more efficiently than beams because of their monolithic nature. When one element undergoes bending, it forces the elements around it into bending as well, and their resistance to deflection helps carry the load. Two-way slabs add to this efficiency further, by carrying the load and resisting deflection in two axes.*

another way of saying that the top edge compresses while the bottom edge elongates. The amount that a beam deflects under load is, we recall, directly proportional to the load and length of the beam, and inversely proportional to the material's modulus of elasticity and the shape's moment of inertia.

Now, looking at Figure 4.6.1, note that, under loading, one 'slice' of the slab will deflect a certain distance at its midpoint. Note, too, that if the slab is monolithic, its neighbors must, by necessity, deflect nearly the same amount – slightly less, but a considerable amount. The amount that the adjacent slice deflects will depend on the material's stiffness – a very rigid material will tend to 'recruit' more assistance from the slice next to it than one that is spongy. This means that this adjacent slice, working backward from the deflection, must be carrying nearly the same load as the original slice. We can work our way to the edge of the slab, and note that each individual slice carries some percentage of the original load, diminishing until we get to the (supported) edge of the slab. Thus, the single load that we've applied at the center is carried not just by the 'beam' of the middle slice, but by *each slice in turn* throughout the slab.

Each 'slice' helps carry the load in two ways. If we think through the mechanism that transfers the load from one slice to another, we realize that each slice will deflect as noted above, but it will also twist. This twist means that each subsequent slice deflects a bit less, and thus carries a bit less of the load.

One-way vs. two-way slabs

We can look at this another way. Imagine that we divide the slab not just in one direction, but in both directions, so that the load occurs at the intersection of two slices – one longitudinal, and one transverse. Again, we note that the deflection in each slice must be equal. Working backward through the deflection equations, we realize that both slices are carrying a significant portion of the load, and thus the load is essentially 'split' in two directions. Here, too, note that adjacent slices in both directions will contribute significantly to carrying the load, thus increasing the slab's efficiency further.

From deflection equations, we can see that the stiffness of a beam is inversely proportional to the cube of its length. It follows that a beam twice as long will deflect eight times as much. This applies to slabs as well. Slabs that are much longer than they are wide will tend to do most of the carrying work in one direction. A slab with a ratio of 2:1 will resolve 8/9 of its load along its short dimension, and only 1/9 of its load along the long direction. This is another way of saying that loads will always 'seek' the shortest distance to a support. For slabs with an aspect ratio of about 5:1, two-way behavior essentially disappears, and the slab acts as a *one-way slab*, still more efficient than a series of unconnected beams, but less efficient than a more squarish bay.

It follows that a square bay should always have the most efficient two-way performance, and thus the thinnest slab. There are a number of reasons, however, why we might choose column grids that are more rectangular – the shape of program spaces, the shape of the site, or the need to distribute services.

In small applications, we can fine-tune our materials to take advantage of this two-way performance. Plywood is the best example of this. Wood on its own has a distinct structural grain – in one direction. If we were to build a floor plate out of a single, thin skin of wood on its own, it would essentially work as a one-way slab. Any two-way behavior would run up against the weakness of wood in bending across its grain. Plywood intentionally alternates the grain pattern in the thin sheets of wood that make up its cross section, offering an inherent capability for two way plate action.

This two-way behavior works well on its own in relatively light materials – wood or steel decking, for example. However, in denser materials such as concrete, even the most efficient flat slab may still prove to be quite heavy. For example, using empirical data, we find that a 6 m (20 ft) square bay – not terribly large – requires a flat slab of nearly 23 cm (9 in.). When made of solid concrete, this becomes quite heavy, requiring much larger columns and foundations than a more lightweight solution. Additionally, it is quite possible that a slab this heavy will be in danger of punching through around the column due to the enormous shear stresses at work. We may need to add even more

Figure 4.6.2. *One of the limiting factors in slab design is the high shear stress that can develop between a flat plate and a supporting column. A typical solution is to spread the column out at the intersection and/or to add a flat drop panel. Both of these have the effect of spreading the shear across a wider area – the cylinder that is formed by the circumference of the column capital and the depth of the slab. From Leonard Michaels. Request sent to Reinhold.*

weight in the form of a *column cap* that basically provides more sectional area to resist the punching shear between slab and column (Fig. 4.6.2). (Note that, for a typical gridded structural system, a single column will carry the load of an entire bay: $4 \times 1/4 = 1$).

We are, therefore, tempted to find ways to increase the performance of the slab over that of a simple flat plate. To do this, we usually borrow from our knowledge of beam behavior. Remember that we improved the performance of a simple rectangular beam by adding cross-sectional area at the extreme edges, away from the neutral axes. This increased the moment of inertia (and therefore the section modulus) while reducing the required quantity of material. We can, in fact, do the same thing with slabs, by essentially taking out material from near the slab's neutral axis. By getting rid of this 'lazy' mass, we concentrate the material where it does the most good – at the edges.

An ideal slab section is shown in Figure 4.6.3. Here, we have eliminated mass from around the neutral axis, leaving the slab solid at its top and bottom edges. The moment of inertia of the slab is thus actually increased while its mass is reduced. We can therefore expect much better performance with far less weight.

The problems with this ideal shape are twofold. First, it is difficult to form out of sitecast concrete, as we would need to 'float' formwork boxes to get the voids, and then find a way to remove them. (Precast concrete often gets around this by flat casting slabs, and then drilling holes out of the center). Second, it

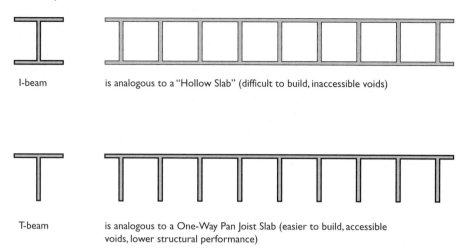

Slabs and plates

I-beam — is analogous to a "Hollow Slab" (difficult to build, inaccessible voids)

T-beam — is analogous to a One-Way Pan Joist Slab (easier to build, accessible voids, lower structural performance)

Figure 4.6.3. *Slab theory is analogous to beam theory, in that the cross-sectional shape can be fine tuned to provide greater section modulus for less material. While an ideal slab would repeat an I-beam shape across its width, the constructional difficulties involved in making voids within the slab mean that most structurally efficient slabs are composed of more easily built 'T' shapes.*

provides voids in the slab that are inaccessible. This is in part a maintenance issue, but it is also a waste of good sectional space. While slabs like this have been built using Styrofoam inserts (a technique pioneered by engineer August Komendant for the floor of Louis Kahn's Kimbell Art Museum), it requires careful coordination of reinforcing steel and is rarely used.

To get around the constructional and fabricational difficulties of the hollow slab, and to provide usable void space, concrete slabs are often poured in 'T' shapes such as those shown at the bottom of Figure 4.6.3, providing downstand 'joists' that raise the shape's moment of inertia while providing good-sized, accessible voids. These typically come in two forms – one-way pan joists and two-way waffle slabs. Pan joists often allow carefully coordinated ductwork, piping, and lighting to occupy the same depth as the structure. Waffle slabs offer less integrative possibilities, but are often used to hold lighting. Both systems offer some measure of architectural interest, as they provide a structural grain to the space below. There are obvious tradeoffs between one-way and two-way systems; where the former allow useful void space they are less efficient structurally.

Slab construction

Because slabs cover large areas, cost becomes a determining factor in the materials we can use. While steel is occasionally used for relatively small applications, we almost invariably use concrete or a combination of steel decking with poured concrete floor slabs in large applications. For residential scales, wood comes conveniently in slab form, as plywood. Usually this is placed as a sub-floor, with a finish layer above it. Plywood will typically carry an APA Rating telling a contractor how far it can span. While plywood spans a reasonable distance, it is usually combined with joists (often 2 × 6 or deeper) to create a one-way system. This one-way system typically rests on bearing walls at either end. Because this configuration is so widely used, wood manufacturers regularly produce tables showing safe spans for various wood systems.

For larger floors, or for projects requiring fire resistance, reinforced concrete tends to be used more for floor slabs, as it is relatively cheap and performs other functions (vibration and sound control) in addition to its structural performance. If the building frame is concrete, we typically just form slabs to be monolithic with the main structure. This has the advantage of providing moment connections between slabs and beams. If, however, the building is steel framed, we usually pour a relatively thin layer of concrete over a corrugated steel deck. The deck can be bolted or welded to the frame, and it provides a natural 'tray' in which to pour the concrete. The finished slab is thus actually a composite member, and studs can be welded to the deck to ensure that the steel deck and the concrete slab work together as a one-way system.

While plywood is the simplest way to make a concrete form, there are numerous commercial products that use metal to create temporary forms for one-way and two-way slabs. These 'pans' are placed on a temporary floor, 'tanked' at the edges, and used to create voids in a deep concrete slab. Because of their finish, they can create architecturally acceptable surfaces, and can be re-used. These systems are thus quite economical. Typical lightweight floor and roof construction types are shown in Figure 4.6.4, while options for heavier, concrete types are shown in Figure 4.6.5.

Two-way 'waffle slabs' are a particularly efficient type of slab, as they provide monolithic behavior in both directions (Fig. 4.6.6). An intriguing refinement in two-way slab construction was carried out by Pier Luigi Nervi in a number of factory projects in the 1950s (Figs. 4.6.7 and 4.6.8). Nervi used 'ferro-cemento' pans, made by bending a wire mesh over a mold, and then spraying lightweight cement over the resulting shape. Because these could be – sort of – mass-produced, and because they could be made in virtually any shape, the resulting buildings have interesting ceiling patterns. In one case (the Gatti Wool Mill) the resulting 'joists' conform to the lines of isostatic stress found in a typical two-way slab.

Plates and slabs present a number of calculation problems, and while they do not represent the potential for catastrophic failure found in columns, they are again usually sized empirically, based on charts and handbooks that essentially document what sizes have safely been used in what conditions previously. The structural charts following Chapter 4 include two charts that show relationships between span and depth for typical flooring conditions. Post-tensioning can allow significant long spans in slabs, but the work of a long span is generally more economical when done by beams and girders. For these reasons, slabs are usually designed for relatively short spans, and they are only mathematically calculated if unusual loading or support conditions are anticipated. In normal situations, standard loading and typical spans and supports will allow sizing by chart or rule of thumb.

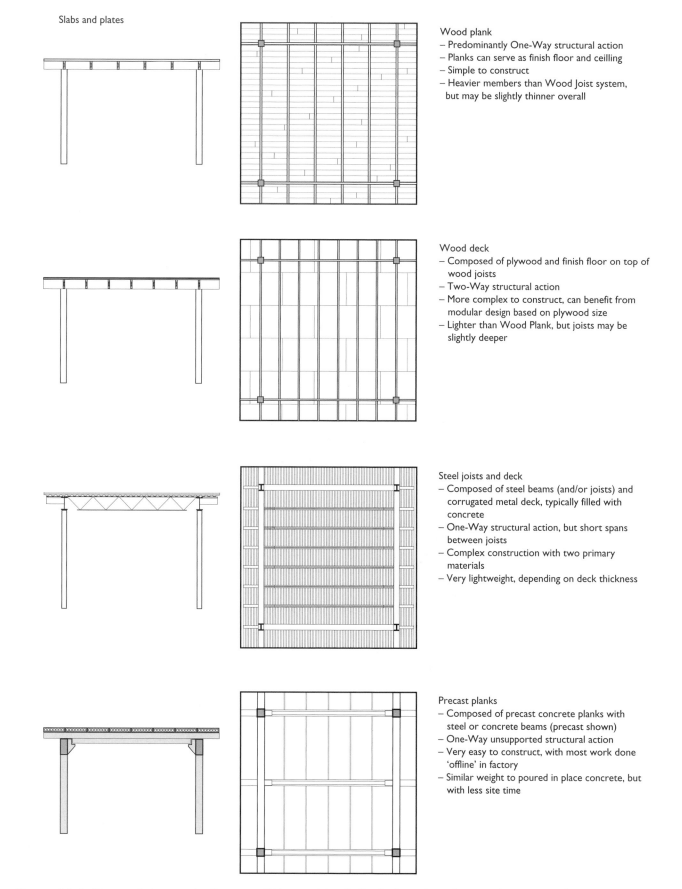

Slabs and plates

Wood plank
- Predominantly One-Way structural action
- Planks can serve as finish floor and ceilling
- Simple to construct
- Heavier members than Wood Joist system, but may be slightly thinner overall

Wood deck
- Composed of plywood and finish floor on top of wood joists
- Two-Way structural action
- More complex to construct, can benefit from modular design based on plywood size
- Lighter than Wood Plank, but joists may be slightly deeper

Steel joists and deck
- Composed of steel beams (and/or joists) and corrugated metal deck, typically filled with concrete
- One-Way structural action, but short spans between joists
- Complex construction with two primary materials
- Very lightweight, depending on deck thickness

Precast planks
- Composed of precast concrete planks with steel or concrete beams (precast shown)
- One-Way unsupported structural action
- Very easy to construct, with most work done 'offline' in factory
- Similar weight to poured in place concrete, but with less site time

Figure 4.6.4. *Floors and plates made of non-monolithic materials will often be layered to gain as much two-way performance as possible. Four common types are shown here.*

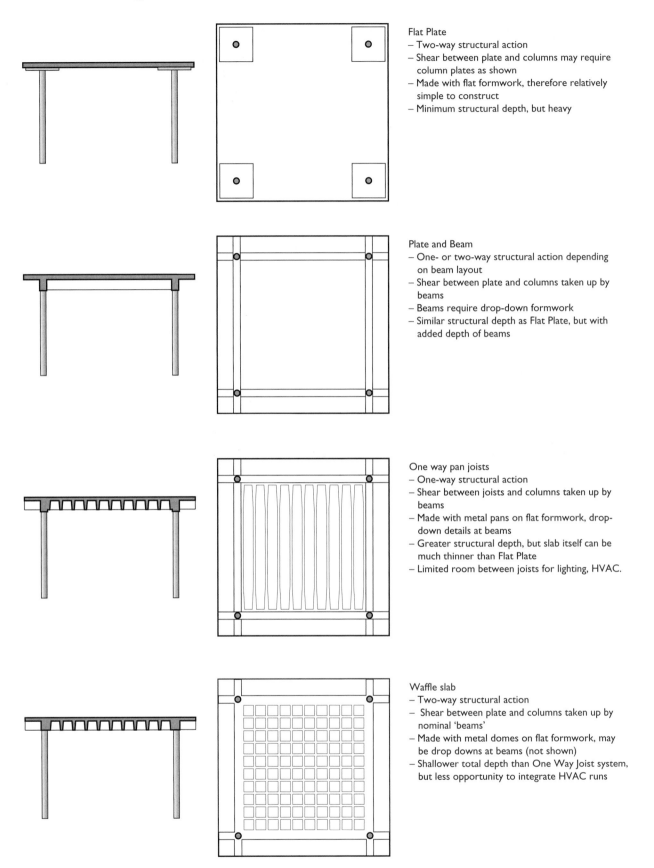

Flat Plate
- Two-way structural action
- Shear between plate and columns may require column plates as shown
- Made with flat formwork, therefore relatively simple to construct
- Minimum structural depth, but heavy

Plate and Beam
- One- or two-way structural action depending on beam layout
- Shear between plate and columns taken up by beams
- Beams require drop-down formwork
- Similar structural depth as Flat Plate, but with added depth of beams

One way pan joists
- One-way structural action
- Shear between joists and columns taken up by beams
- Made with metal pans on flat formwork, drop-down details at beams
- Greater structural depth, but slab itself can be much thinner than Flat Plate
- Limited room between joists for lighting, HVAC.

Waffle slab
- Two-way structural action
- Shear between plate and columns taken up by nominal 'beams'
- Made with metal domes on flat formwork, may be drop downs at beams (not shown)
- Shallower total depth than One Way Joist system, but less opportunity to integrate HVAC runs

Figure 4.6.5. *Because of its monolithic nature, concrete is a naturally efficient choice for floor and roof construction. The challenges of forming and pouring, however, limit its use to the four basic types shown here.*

Figure 4.6.6. *A typical two-way ('waffle') slab.*

High-performance slabs and shapes

In addition to using formwork to shape slab sections, we can actually 'fold' flat plates to achieve extremely good one- and two-way performance. The reason for this can be demonstrated by simply holding a piece of paper as shown in Figure 4.6.9. Here, because we are adding a vertical dimension the paper, it will naturally act as a cantilever beam. If we put a load on the end, the top fibers will go into tension, and the bottom fibers will go into compression. Our holding the paper provides a moment connection at the paper beam's root, and with very little material we can carry a fairly heavy load.

Using the same principle, we can use 'folded plates' to carry great loads with minimal material. Corrugated roof decks are the smallest-scale example of this, but large-scale concrete plates have been used for aircraft hangars, sports arenas, and grandstand roofs (see Section 4.9, Long Spans). In each case the vertical depth of a folded planar element separates top and bottom fibers, and the 'plate' actually acts like a very efficient beam.

Frequently asked questions

Why are the dimensions of waffle slabs limited to sizes like 2 ft and 4 ft square? Because waffle slabs are poured using metal pans for formwork, we're limited to a fairly standard set of pan sizes to actually form the slab. We could custom

313

Figure 4.6.7. *An experimental concrete floor system designed by Pier Luigi Nervi for the Gatti Wool Factory in Rome (1953). By using custom-shaped pans (of light cement and wire), Nervi was able to re-configure a standard waffle slab so that its ribs followed the lines of static 'flow' from slab to column.*

Figure 4.6.8. *Another expressive floor slab by Nervi. This one, for a tobacco factory in Bologna (1952) thickens the ribs of a waffle slab where they meet supporting beams – and where they experience the greatest shear stress.*

make a whole set of pans to whatever dimensions we wanted, but this would incur a fairly substantial cost. We can tune the distance between the pans (or 'domes') if wider ribs are acceptable. One-way metal pans can telescope, so their length is variable.

Did Le Corbusier invent the 'Dom-Ino' slab? Not really. Corbusier's 1914 drawing of a concrete slab construction system shows very thin floor plates and no column capitals (Fig. 4.6.10). Given the technology of the day it's unlikely that the system as drawn would have worked. As described above, the spans might have been achievable given adequate steel reinforcement, but the weight of the slabs themselves might well have caused the supporting columns to punch through. By 1922, the Swiss engineer and designer Robert Maillart patented a system of gridded steel reinforcement that allowed very small column caps, approximating the

315

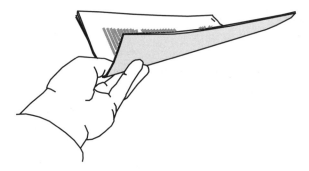

Figure 4.6.9. *A simple folded plate. Adding depth to the shape of a sheet of paper by folding or bending it allows the paper to develop bending resistance, with tension at the top and compression at the base.*

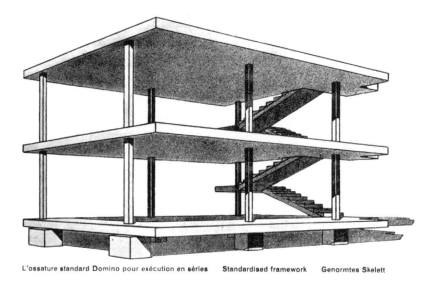

L'ossature standard Domino pour exécution en séries   Standardised framework   Genormtes Skelett

Figure 4.6.10. *A prototypical slab construction system, the 'Dom-Ino' by Le Corbusier (1914).*

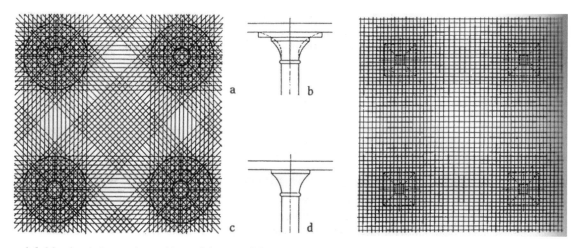

Figure 4.6.11. *A solution to the problem of shear in slab connections by Robert Maillart (1923) using reinforcing patterns to limit the size of column capitals.*

skinny edges of Corbusier's proposal (Fig. 4.6.11). It's interesting to note that Maillart had built experiments in this form of construction by 1913, suggesting that the Dom-Ino was as much a reflection of cutting edge concrete engineering as it was invention.

What is precast planking? Precast floor planks are an economical way to lay a floor. They are essentially wide, flat rectangles of concrete that can be trucked to a job site and laid by crane. Their proportions give them some two-way plate action, so they're reasonably efficient, but their performance can be enhanced by pouring a *topping slab*, which consists of a layer of concrete that bonds to steel cables or studs in the top of the precast planks. They can also be made more efficient by coring out round cylinders from around their neutral axes − so-called *hollow-core slabs*, and by threading steel cables through these hollows and tightening them against the plank ends. This is called *post-tensioning* and is a common method of building parking decks, in particular.

Glossary and formulas

Column Cap	A conical or rectilinear element between a column and a floor plate that is designed to spread the shear force between the two over a wider cross-sectional area.
Folded Plate	A thin, planar structural system that relies on 'folds' or bends in its cross section to develop bending resistance.
One-Way Slab (or Plate)	A thin, planar structural system that gains most of its structural performance from simple bending resistance along the axis of the span.
Pan Joists	In concrete construction, a system of downstand concrete joists made by pouring concrete between long, linear metal pans placed upside down.
Plate	A thin slab. Slab denotes a heavy, thick material, while plate is more descriptive of metal or wood.
Slab	A structural member that gains some of its performance by two-way resistance to bending.
Two-Way Slab (or Plate)	A thin, planar structural system that gains its structural performance from a combination of bending along *and across* the axis of the span.
Waffle Slab	A two-way concrete slab system made by pouring concrete between square 'domes' to form a network of intersecting concrete joists.

Further reading

Bill, M. (1949) *Robert Maillart* (Zurich: Verlag).
Nervi, P.L. (1958) *Structures* (New York: F.W. Dodge), pp. 98–103.
Salvadori, M. (1975) Grids, Plates, and Folded Plates (Chapter 10), *Structure in Architecture: The Art of Building*, 2nd ed (Englewood Cliffs: Prentice-Hall), pp. 239–292.

4.7   Foundations

Soils	Rock
	Gravel
	Clay
	Fill
Foundation Types	Spread footings
	Mats and displacement
	Piles
Design Process	Rules of thumb and calculations

Introduction

We have now investigated the major elements of building *superstructures*, that is, the portions of a building's structure that are above ground. While these elements are of most interest to us as architects, since they affect the functioning and appearance of the building, it is arguably the *substructure*, or the collection of structural elements *below* ground level, that is most crucial to a building's longevity.

Substructures include foundation walls around basements, as well as structural elements designed to transmit the building load to the earth around and under it. Because of this, the nature and condition of the soil in and around the building site is critically important, and we often rely on the expertise of geotechnical and civil engineers to do the actual design of our foundations. However, a basic knowledge of how these elements operate is critical to understanding the termination of our building structures, and to appreciate the cost and resources that must be devoted to a building's substructure.

Soils

A fond myth about building science is that our structures are 'firmly' rooted to solid earth, and that once fixed, they are stable. While this is true for a very limited number of structures – those that are anchored or screwed into bedrock – the vast majority of buildings essentially float in a variety of soil types, and in fact all buildings move over time. This is known as *settlement*, and in most cases it can be controlled, minimized, or made imperceptible. The Leaning Tower of Pisa is perhaps the most famous example of settlement gone awry. This tower's failure is not in the structure itself, but rather in the understanding of the ground's capability to carry the intense load of the tower equally across its site (Fig. 4.7.1).

Soils resist loading by a combination of compression and shear. Soil particles develop friction as they move past one another under loading, and the surface

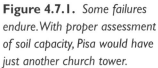

Figure 4.7.1. *Some failures endure. With proper assessment of soil capacity, Pisa would have just another church tower.*

shapes and roughness of these particles determines their ability to resist loads.

Soils are usually divided into five types. Rock (or *bedrock*) is monolithic, solid and depending on its composition either fiercely resistant to crushing or vulnerable to point loads. *Sands and gravels* are coarse, granular and *non-plastic* – that is, they do not 'give' easily. Rather, they fail by crushing of the material itself, and therefore they tend to be good load-resistive soils. *Clays* are fine,

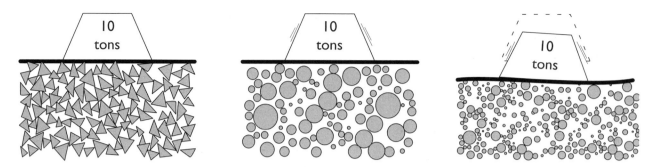

Figure 4.7.2. *Simple soil physics. Bearing capacity depends on the size of an average soil grain, its compressive capacity, and the friction it can develop with its surrounding grains. Soil that is coarse, rough, and densely packed (e.g., gravel) performs better than soil that is fine, smooth, and loosely packed (e.g., clay). Soil that is subject to liquefaction (sand, for example) may lose most of its bearing capacity and behave more like a fluid than a solid, likely resulting in extensive damage or failure.*

granular and (usually) plastic, meaning that they fail gradually, and that they cease deformation if a load is removed. They are vulnerable to settlement. *Silts* behave unpredictably, like sand or clay depending on their grain size. Finally, *organics* are composed of decaying vegetation, with little or no resistance to crushing.

Soils originate in either *residual* or *sedimentary* processes. Residual processes involve the gradual weathering of rock, and tend to leave reliable, undisturbed soils. Sedimentary processes bring soil to a site from other sources through rivers, glaciers, etc., and while they often leave good tillable earth, they are often unreliable structural soils.

Rock, sand, or gravel tend to be the best soils for basic foundations (Fig. 4.7.2). Their non-plastic nature means that their resistance to crushing is reliable, and they will provide a generally stable base. Silts and clays, because of their plasticity, settle immediately upon application of loading, and their final overall strength and resistance to settling is, at best, guesswork. Likewise, silts and clays are vulnerable to *liquefaction*. If they get wet, their grains get covered with a lubricating film of water, and their strength is greatly reduced. As they become saturated, silts and clays act more like a liquid than a solid, meaning that buildings built on top of them will 'float'.

The transition from solid to liquid is gradual as a soil's moisture content increases. Intermediate, *viscous* stages are dangerous as well as the final, liquid state. Thus, clays and silts are generally considered poor soils on which to build.

Boring, testing, and improvement

The first action on a jobsite is thus often a series of test borings, done under the supervision of a civil engineer. A core sample is usually taken from various locations on the construction site – often in a grid pattern, but also in likely areas of structural necessity (see Section 1.3, Site ecology). Inconsistencies between borings often require intermediate tests to establish where subsurface pockets of good – or bad – soil occur.

In addition to identification, geotechnical engineers will provide tests to show the density, moisture content, and granularity of the recovered soils. Each of these affect reliability and bearing capacity. The location, type, and strength of any bedrock reached will also be noted. A final report is issued to the client, who then issues the report to the design team, in particular the structural engineer.

For smaller construction, test pits or trenches may substitute for borings. In each of these cases, holes are manually dug across the site to establish soil conditions near the surface. These have the advantage of locating actual strata of soil, rather than just point locations.

Very rarely do we build large projects on soils as we find them. More often, some simple measures taken at the beginning of construction can greatly improve the performance of a building's substructure.

Cutting and Filling involves sculpting the site to allow placement of level structures. For large projects, loose organic soil is always removed from any location that will receive bearing pads or slabs. In general, we try to equalize the amount of cutting and filling of usable soil on a site to avoid expensive inhaul or outhaul. Thus, with a large enough site, we may add landscape elements using soil excavated from foundations. For large jobs (particularly midrise buildings with large footprints) we may cart off poor soil and replace it with a fairly large quantity of sand or gravel. Note, however, that this poor soil needs to go somewhere, and the fiscal and environmental penalties of this usually suggest working in some way with what we have to hand.

Densification and Compaction are techniques for improving the performance of soils as we find them on a site. At the very least, we typically roll soil on which we will pour slabs, to compact it and make it perform more monolithically. However, more involved techniques include the use of vibrating rollers, which can compact sand to a depth of 2 m (6 ft). For deeper compaction, vibrating piles and probes can compact sands to a depth of 12 m (40 ft). Occasionally these devices are coupled with saturation, so that the soil liquefies, permitting rapid consolidation, after which it is drained to form a tighter, denser underpinning. Perhaps the most radical form of compaction involves dropping multi-ton weights from heights of up to 30 m. While extremely efficient, this technique is limited to areas without neighbors, whose structures might be damaged by the seismic force imparted to the soil. For clay soils, a similar technique known as *surcharging* works by piling weight on to the site equivalent to the estimated load of the final building. The clay is thus permanently deformed to (approximately) the level imparted by the structure. While effective, this process is time consuming and requires 'borrowing' loose fill for weight – often expensive. Surcharging is usually limited to relatively lightweight structures that cover a large footprint.

Grouting involves the injection of liquid cement into known underground cavities or fissures. It can also be used to solidify porous rock for either drainage or structural reasons, or to stabilize loose sand and gravel.

Drainage is the most common soil improvement. Removing water from existing soil – and keeping it out – allows the soil particles to achieve dry bonding, adding friction to their resisting capabilities. Providing permanent drainage and/or water exclusion at the site perimeter can prevent soil from liquifying, or from developing water films that reduce its strength.

Finally, soils can be reinforced using plastic rods or ribs that are threaded into the ground. Similarly, *geomembranes* can be placed under new soil to direct or control water infiltration.

Foundation types

In addition to a wide variety of potential soil types, we tend to put a number of different types of structural load into the ground. The pattern of support for a house, for example, is dramatically different from that of a large office building. In general, we have two types of foundations – *distributed* and *point load* – that support walls, slabs, and columns respectively.

The simplest type of foundation is a *spread footing* (Fig. 4.7.3). This is usually a concrete pad that seeks to spread the load from a wall or column out over an area of soil sufficient to support it. This can be visualized as the design of a column capital in reverse; once again we are concerned with the tendency of the column or wall to punch through the footing, although here we are concerned with taking the concentrated vertical load of the column and spreading it out into what essentially is a reverse slab. The footing must be very rigid, so that it distributes the load of the column evenly. For columns, the footing is usually square, while for walls it is typically a rectangle that is more or less centered on the wall itself. Like slabs, care must be taken to ensure that columns do not shear through the footing, and the use of intermediate 'feet' and reinforcing steel recalls column caps in floor construction (Fig. 4.7.4). At the edges of a site, the footings must be designed to stay within the site boundaries, meaning that additional structural members may be required to form what is, essentially, a cantilevered footing. Often, footings will be connected by *grade beams* to ensure that they all settle evenly. Spread footings work best on sands and gravels, where resistance can be accurately predicted and where plastic deformation does not occur.

Mat foundations provide a spread footing for the entire structure at once, connecting all columns and walls with a single, monolithic concrete slab. This has the advantage of equalizing pressure on the soil throughout the site, and it is thus good for sites with varying or locally unpredictable conditions. Mat foundations are also quite good for silt or clay soils, as they are supported not only by the soils' resistance to compression, but also by *displacement* – essentially the building can be made to 'float' in viscous or liquid soil. (This is usually called

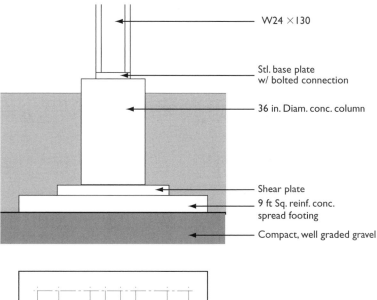

W24 ×130

Stl. base plate
w/ bolted connection

36 in. Diam. conc. column

Shear plate

9 ft Sq. reinf. conc.
spread footing

Compact, well graded gravel

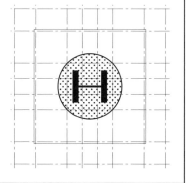

Figure 4.7.3. *A typical spread footing works like a column capital in reverse, spreading a point load out over an area large enough to absorb the weight without settling excessively or failing.*

a *raft foundation* or, in extreme cases, a *tank*.) Generally, careful calculation is needed to determine the final settlement of the finished building, and care needs to be taken when planning for utility interfaces in the foundation walls. Small-scale foundation types are shown in Figure 4.7.5.

Pile Foundations support loads either by carrying them deep into the ground to bedrock, or by friction with surrounding soil. In either case, they usually consist of woodpiles or steel or concrete shafts that are inserted through the soil by excavation, drilling, or pounding. *Pile Caps* are spread footings under columns or walls that sit atop a group of piles, rather than just on ground. These are necessary as placement of piles is inexact at best; the cap allows some tolerance for the piles final positions in relation to the column (Fig. 4.7.6). *Bearing piles* are essentially long columns that carry loads past poor soil to rock. Occasionally these need to be supplemented by bells or cones to spread the load out across the surface of the rock. This is accomplished by remote excavating machinery that is sent down a drill shaft. More common are *friction piles*, which are simply driven into the ground until the friction between the soil and the pile itself becomes great enough to support building loads. Pile foundations present some problems, in that their end conditions can only be assumed – the pile might be sitting on bedrock, or it might have simply reached a particularly dense strata of hardpan. For tall buildings, caissons are usually drilled, and an inspector (either mechanical or human) is lowered into the void to sample the base

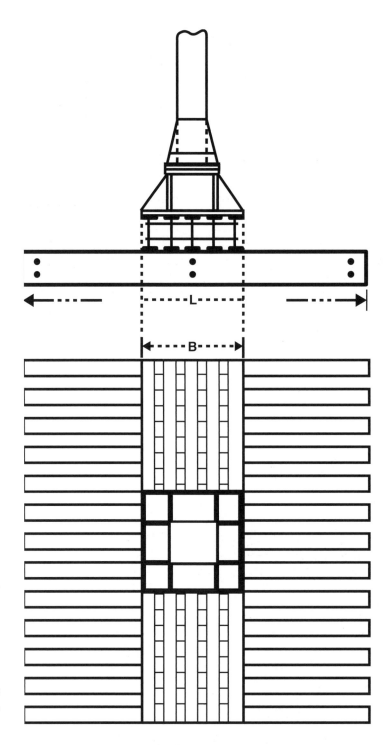

Figure 4.7.4. *The spread footing is almost entirely an invention of 19th-century Chicago, where tall, heavy buildings were built on very poor soil. Readily available steel rail sections were used for their good bending capacity, given the lack of reliable concrete technology at the time.*

condition. The caisson is later filled with concrete. Pile foundations and other larger-scale types are shown in Figure 4.7.7.

Retaining Walls are built to separate a basement from soil and moisture outside. They are usually load bearing, and are supported by spread footings, mats, or pile caps. Because they resist soil pressure, or the tendency of loose soil to spread under its own weight, retaining walls must be designed as vertical cantilevers. Often, the area around them must be cleared of unacceptable soil, and *backfilled* with sand or gravel that allows moisture to percolate and drain away from the building face.

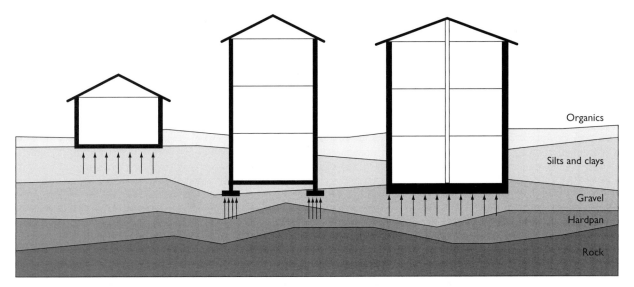

Figure 4.7.5. *Simple foundation techniques that rely on simple bearing. From left, a simple slab on grade, spread footings (wall or column) and a mat foundation.*

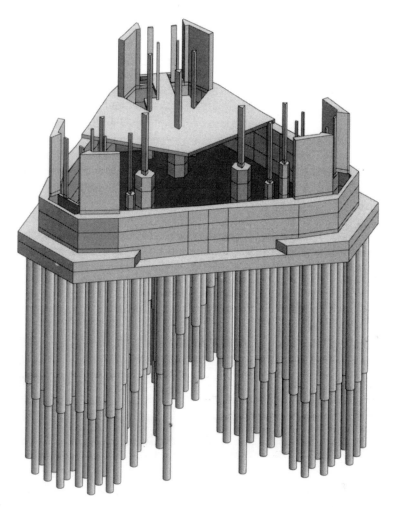

Figure 4.7.6. *Axonometric of a typical pile system, showing the thick concrete pile cap that transfers loading from columns to the numerous soil pilings.*

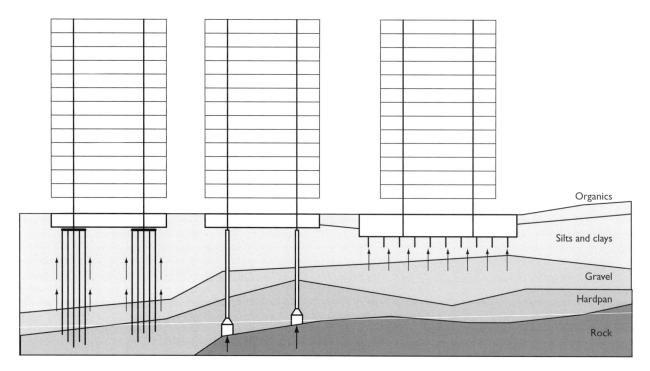

Figure 4.7.7. *For larger buildings or for poor soil, more complex foundation techniques may be required. Piles may support the building's weight by developing friction with the surrounding soil, or caissons may be dug down to a reliable rock strata and filled with concrete. In extreme situations, a displacement foundation may literally 'float' the building in very poor or liquefied soil.*

Sheet Piles are piles driven to provide an underground wall. These are often formed of bent steel plate, and while usually temporary, they can be used to retain undesirable soil away from a foundation wall. Any retaining wall or sheet pile must be adequately *shored*, or prevented from collapse by tipping. This can be accomplished by diagonal bracing, by *dead men* drilled into the earth from the wall, or by *soldier beams and anchors* that work by tension.

Basic foundation design

Foundations, particularly spread footings, can be quickly estimated if the total load of the building and the conditions of the soil below are known. Table 4.7.1 shows allowable bearing pressures for a variety of soil types (note the range of performance between soft soils and sound rock – this explains why caissons and drilled piers are often economical). If the total weight on a column, wall, or floor is known, this figure can be divided by the allowable ton/ft^2 given in this chart to estimate the required area of a spread footing. Further calculations to ensure the shear capacity of the slab/column connection is required.

There are circumstances where the weight of a building cannot be supported by the surrounding soil. In this case, a different system must be designed, taking the load of the building down to a point at which the soil material will suffice. For shallow strata, it is sometimes economical to excavate a deep basement, as hardpan material is often only a few yards beneath the surface. However for deep strata, this situation calls for piers or piles.

Table 4.7.1. Allowable bearing loads on various soil types.

Soil type	Allowable bearing (kg/m2)	Allowable bearing (ton/ft2)
Sound rock	585,900	60
Medium rock	390,600	40
Intermediate rock	195,300	20
Well-cemented hardpan	117,180	12
Compact, well-graded gravel	97,650	10
Poorly-cemented hardpan	78,120	8
Compact gravel	78,120	8
Loose gravel	58,590	6
Weathered or porous rock	19,530–78,120	2–8
Coarse sand	29,295–58,690	3–6
Hard clay	48,825	5
Gravel/sand mix	39,060	4
Fine sand	19,530–39,060	2–4
Fill	19,530–39,060	2–4
Dense silt	29,295	3
Medium clay	19,530	2
Medium silt	14,647	1.5

Example: Develop foundation strategies for each strata for the building shown in Figure 4.7.8. Assume the loading for each floor is 488 kg/m2 (100 lb/ft2).

Solution: We first find the total weight that must bear on each column's foundation. Since each bay is square, each central column will hold up one bay's worth of load, and each edge column will hold half of one bay's load. Given the bay size, this will be:

$$P = \text{(no. of stories)} \times \text{(bay area)} \times \text{(loading/m}^2\text{)}$$
$$= 20 \times 100\,\text{m}^2 \times 488\,\text{kg/m}^2$$
$$= 976,000\,\text{kg}$$

$$P = \text{(no. of stories)} \times \text{(bay area)} \times \text{(loading/ft}^2\text{)}$$
$$= 20 \times 900\,\text{ft}^2 \times 100\,\text{lb/ft}^2$$
$$= 1,800,000\,\text{lb}$$
$$= 900\,\text{ton}$$

Now we examine what area it would take to safely spread this load over each of the four strata. To do this, we can take a systematic approach, using a chart to list soil strata, safe bearing load, and the resulting area ($A = P/f_{all}$):

Strata	Total load, P kg (ton)	Allowable load load, f_{all} kg/m² (lb/ft²)	$A = P/f_{all}$ m² (ft²)
Silt	976,000 (900)	14,647 (1.5)	66.6 (717)
Clay	976,000 (900)	48,825 (5)	20.0 (215)
Gravel	976,000 (900)	78,120 (8)	12.5 (134)
Sound rock	976,000 (900)	585,900 (60)	1.70 (18.0)

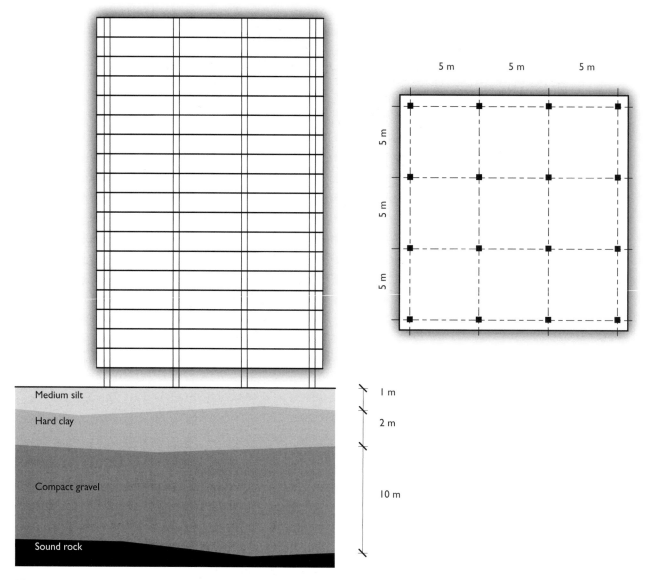

Figure 4.7.8. *Foundation example (see text).*

Note that we can – barely – support the building on a set of large pads $8\,m^2$ on the layer of dense silt. Given the shallow nature of this layer, though, it might well be more economical to excavate to the layer of clay, where we'd need spread foundations of only $4.5\,m^2$, or to gravel, where the foundations would only need to be $3.5\,m^2$. Excavating down to sound rock would allow caissons with a radius of only $0.73\,m$. Our decision would be affected by local concrete prices vs. the cost of labor to excavate these strata.

Foundation failures

Most foundation failures occur because of *settlement* or its inverse, *heaving*. Settlement occurs primarily when the bearing strength of the soil is altered, usually by water. Soft, wet soil offers much less resistance because of the lubricating effect of water, and foundations will often sink a significant

Figure 4.7.9. *What happens when foundations go bad. In this case, neighboring construction allowed the soil that had supported this bank building to slide. With nothing to bear upon, the footings collapsed, bringing down most of the building with it.*

amount after saturation from flooding, etc. The classic case is of subsidence occurring after a pipe leak, for example. If flooding occurs locally, for instance by saturation of the soil from a poorly placed gutter, the footing may bridge over a locally weak area. However, if the footing fails, the portion of the building above may sink while the remainder of the building remains in place, causing cracking of brickwork, interior finishes, and structural members.

A notorious failure is the saturation – and dissolution – of limestone by newly introduced water. The discovery of limestone in a boring test may in itself disqualify a potential site.

New construction must be done carefully in tight confines to ensure that neighboring foundations are not undermined (Fig. 4.7.9). Likewise, the imposition of a new load in a tight urban site may compress soils beneath other buildings, also causing subsidence.

Heaving occurs when a foundation is installed above the local frost line. As soil below freezes, it can displace the surface by an inch or more. The constant freeze-thaw motion will often cause buildings to settle differentially over time. Most commonly, porch foundations on old houses were often simple surface beams. When attached to a house on a basement foundation, the constant differential movement and settlement can lead to the porch's foundation settling further than the main one, causing the porch to slope away from the house.

Glossary and formulas

Substructure	The part of a building's structure below the ground floor.
Settlement	The tendency of a structure to work its way down through the ground, often the result of a change in composition of the soil (e.g., from flooding) or inadequately designed foundations.
Sand	Coarse, granular soil composed of small grains.
Gravel	Coarse, granular soil composed of large grains.
Clay	Fine, granular soil that is subject to plastic behavior.
Silts	Fine soil that becomes suspended in water that flows rather than holding its shape (and is therefore structurally dangerous).
Organics	Decaying vegetation or peat with little capability of resisting loads.
Boring	A test drilling that procures a long cylindrical sample of earth.
Cutting and Filling	The process of, respectively, removing and adding earth to a site.
Densification	Compacting a site's soil to achieve better structural performance.
Grouting	Adding cement or concrete to soil to increase its structural capacity, or to repair fissures or voids.
Geomembrane	A filter-like fabric used to control or direct water flow on a site.
Spread Footing	A foundation type that works like an inverted slab, taking the point load of a column or pier and distributing it over an area of foundation 'pad' (usually concrete) so that the soil is not stressed past its capacity.
Mat Foundation	A foundation type that uses the entire footprint of a building to spread its load over the soil below. Typically used for large volume, low-rise buildings where the foundation can be combined with the ground floor slab.
Raft Foundation	A foundation type that works by displacement, essentially 'floating' the building in the soil.
Pile Foundation	A foundation type that uses long, usually cylindrical rods (piles) to either reach a firmer soil below, or develop bearing through friction with the surrounding soil.
Pile Cap	A slab or mat that rests on a number of piles, spreading the load of a column or pier over them.

Caissons	Drilled or excavated voids in the ground that are later filled with concrete, creating a large, pile-like foundation.
Retaining Walls	Foundation type that creates a vertical drop in the ground. Retaining walls must be designed as cantilevers to resist the overturning moment of the 'held-back' soil.
Sheet Piles	Planar elements that are driven into the ground to form an underground wall. Typically made of large-scale corrugated steel.
Heaving	Uplift in the ground caused by freezing or other soil expansion.

Further reading

Gupton, C.P. (1994) Soil Mechanics and Foundations (Sections 6.1–6.63), in Frederick S. Merritt and Jonathan T. Ricketts, *Building Design and Construction Handbook*, 5th ed (New York: McGraw-Hill).

Mainstone, R.J. (2001) Supports, Walls, and Foundations (Chapter 10), *Developments in Structural Form* (Oxford: Architectural Press), pp. 175–192.

Salvadori, M. (1979) The Part of the Building You Don't See (Chapter 7), *The Art of Construction* (Chicago: Chicago Review Press), pp. 51–56.

4.8 Frames

Synergy in Frame Structures	What defines a frame Fixed vs. hinged frames and why these matter
Joints in Frames	Hinges in wood, steel, and concrete Fixed (moment) connections in wood, steel, and concrete
Frame Behavior	Interaction of columns and beams Effects of hinges and fixed joints
Lateral Stability	How frames resist horizontal forces (wind, seismic) What we can do to assist this

Introduction: frames and synergy of structural elements

We've now covered all the major structural elements in a typical multi-story building – slabs, beams and girders, columns and foundations. However, when these are assembled into a structural system, there are some remaining fine points that we need to know to accurately assess how the overall structure – the *frame* will behave. A *frame* is a system of horizontal and vertical structural members tied together in order to collectively resist both vertical and horizontal forces. Frames can be further divided into a number of sub-types, generally *fixed* and *hinged*. As high-performance steel and concrete frames have been developed and perfected in the last century, the frame has also become a primary element in the architectural expression of high-rise buildings (Fig. 4.8.1).

Throughout most of history, column and beam structures were assembled by simply stacking the best available structural material – either wood or stone – in the form of piers and *lintels*, or simple beams spanning over openings.

Crucially, most of these structures did not provide for a fixed connection between column and lintel. While stone construction often included a key and channel connection between the two, and wood construction would tie or pin these members together, these connections were both quite flexible, and they allowed a great deal of movement – both rotational and translational – between beam and column (Fig. 4.8.2).

For simple loading, this does not present much of a problem. However, in extreme circumstances – large storms with high winds, for instance, or earthquakes – the lateral movement in such a system could easily cause the lintel to slide or rock off of its connection to the column. This method of collapse

Figure 4.8.1. *The structural frame has been one of the defining architectural expressions of high-rise construction. Mies van der Rohe's Lake Shore Drive Apartments (1949) pioneered the frame as a compositional element.*

is particularly dangerous, as it tends to crush anything inside the building footprint *and* a shadow area where the upper floor(s) rotate down.

As an example, a 6.9 magnitude earthquake on the Loma Prieta Fault near San Francisco in 1989 caused 63 fatalities. The same scale earthquake in Tajikistan in 1998 killed more than 5000. San Francisco's stringent seismic design codes mandate frames that resist the type of horizontal loading that occurs during the shaking of an earthquake. Buildings near the Tajikistan earthquake were built of brick and of precast concrete with inadequate connections to columns, and they tended to collapse in classic fashion onto adjacent sites and streets.

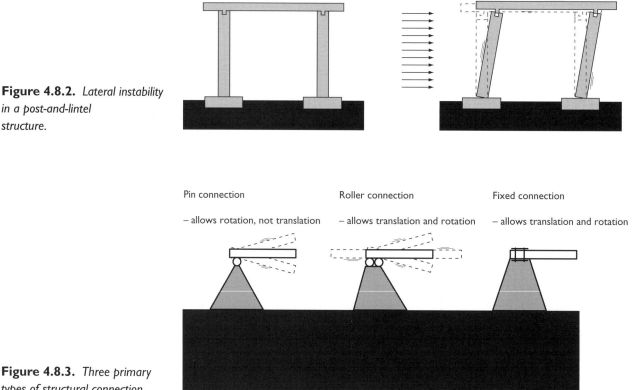

Figure 4.8.2. *Lateral instability in a post-and-lintel structure.*

Figure 4.8.3. *Three primary types of structural connection.*

Connections

Fixed frames have beams and columns connected rigidly, allowing neither translational nor rotational movement between members. Members in a hinged frame are connected with pins, allowing rotational movement between beams and columns.

It is worth reminding ourselves of the three ways that structural members can be connected. In Section 4.1, we noted that there are three basic types of joints – *pins* that allow members to rotate but not translate, *moment connections* that allow neither translation nor rotation relative to one another, and *rollers* that allow only translation (Fig. 4.8.3).

Frames behave in dramatically different ways depending on which of these connections are used and where. Not surprisingly, frames with fixed connections are generally stiffer than frames with hinges. However, they also impart more complex forces into their foundations, and they are more complicated to solve.

A frame with hinged connections between columns, beams, and foundations is shown in Figure 4.8.4. As shown, this frame will be very loose under loading, and the beam will deflect significantly. More importantly, a stiff breeze will impart a lateral force to the frame, which will have no resistance. The beam will rotate with respect to the columns (it will *rack*), which will rotate with respect to the ground connections, and the frame will collapse.

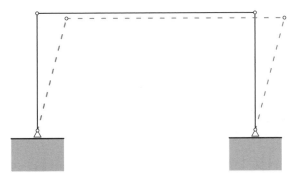

Unbraced (hinged) frame

Figure 4.8.4. *A simple hinged frame will, like the unbraced post-and-lintel system, easily collapse on itself if subjected to lateral loading.*

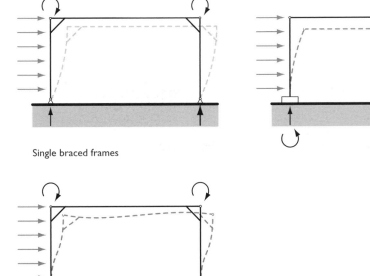

Single braced frames

Doubly braced frame (indeterminate)

Figures 4.8.5. *Basic frame theory considers the relative effects of stiffening connections between members, and between members and the substructure. The more rigid the connections, the more the individual members' resistance to deflection is 'recruited' into stiffening the frame.*

Figure 4.8.5 shows more promising arrangements. First, the beam can be attached by fixed connections to the columns, which can in turn be pinned to the ground. As the beam is loaded, the fixed connections maintain the 90° angle between beam and columns. However, since the beam does deflect, this means that the columns must deflect as well. If the columns were not fixed against translation at the ground, they would tend to spread out, being twisted by the loading of the beam. However, since they are pinned, there must be a horizontal force at the ground that resists this *thrust*, or horizontal push. This thrust can be resisted by buttresses or a tie rod that essentially makes the frame work against itself, resolving the horizontal forces internally, or it can simply be taken up by the connections to the ground.

A doubly braced frame offers greater stiffness. Here, the columns are connected to the beam and ground by fixed connections. Not only do the columns stay in one place, they also maintain their 90° relationship with the beam and the ground. Thus, they do not start bending until some distance up the column. In fact, this *inflection point* occurs halfway up the column for the situation shown, which is why k for a column fixed at both ends is (theoretically) 0.5. Also note, however, that in addition to the thrust, the ground connection must resist a bending moment, keeping the column straight when the load is trying to force it to twist. This, again, requires extra foundation structure.

If fixed connections offer so much structural efficiency, why would we ever use pinned connections in a frame? For one thing, we often do not want to impart bending loads into foundations, as constant movement back and forth may weaken the soil under a footing, or compact it to a point where the footing is no longer fully bearing. This is particularly serious in bridge design, where constant live load changes can create significant movement.

Another reason that pins have been used historically is that, prior to sophisticated computer analysis, there has been no way to fully calculate the reactions in a beam fixed at more than one point. In this case, finding the reactions using simple methods is impossible, as there is no point at which we know the moment will be 0. These are called *indeterminate structures*, and while they are now easy to calculate using computer simulation, for centuries they presented an enormous problem, often leading to the use of pins simply to create a determinant structure.

Multiple frames

The synergy of two or more frames acting in concert with one another has some advantages. First, if we are able to add some reasonably stiff connections between columns and beams, the frames will begin to resist lateral loading through synergy. A load on one side of the multiple frames in Figure 4.8.6 will be resisted by each of the columns connected to the top beam, as shown. Note that the frame is rotating a little around each column, and thus the stiffness of the connections, the beam material, and the column material are all being recruited to help resist the deflection. Resisting deflection allows resistance to load, and the lateral load will end up being carried by the multiple columns to ensure that the frame remains in equilibrium. If the lateral force is large enough, the windward columns may resist the lateral load by going into tension. When this happens, the frame will rotate if the foundation isn't capable of sustaining the uplift load.

Note that the frame with pinned connections resists movement (*sidesway*) only by the stiffness of the ground joint, while the frame with fixed connections throughout resists by the stiffness of both. Also note that, for significant winds, there may be a fairly serious moment to resist that attempts to tip the entire frame over. In this case, the windward ground connection may go into tension, while the leeward connection may experience much greater compression. Adding multiple bays to the frame helps resist uplift and racking by spreading the lateral force out over several connections, and by providing reactions with larger moment arms – a wind blowing against the multi-bay

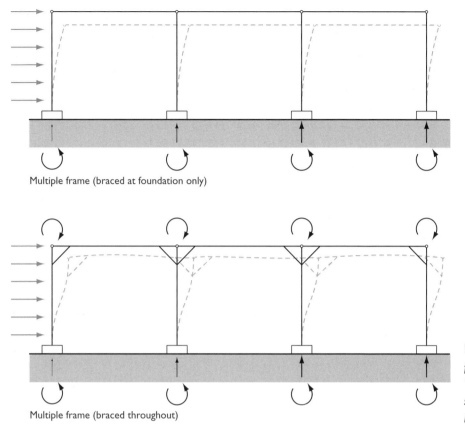

Multiple frame (braced at foundation only)

Multiple frame (braced throughout)

Figure 4.8.6. *Multiple frames provide the added benefit of the 'table-leg' principle, with compression in the 'back' columns assisting in resisting a lateral load.*

frames at the bottom of Figure 4.8.6 will have to overcome very large-resisting moments that can develop between the back columns and their relatively long distance from the front columns. This is known as the *table-leg* principle, and it allows relatively weak connections to work synergetically to resist wind forces along the length of a structure.

One final note. If we look inside the members of a fixed frame, we find a subtle variation on the standard shear and moment diagrams we've calculated previously. Note, for instance, that the column in Figure 4.8.6, while predominantly in axial compression, is also in bending. If we were to draw a diagram showing the compression loads in its cross section, we would essentially add a relatively small bending diagram (top) to a simple compression value (bottom). Likewise, the columns will resist bending in part through a compressive reaction at the beam. Thus, in addition to the primary bending action we expect from beams, we would add a small block of compression to the beam. Note that this moves the neutral axis slightly, and might require a bit of extra reinforcement along the top (compressed) edge.

Determinacy vs. indeterminacy and frame synergy

Thus far we have intentionally dealt with structural members whose support conditions make them fairly easy to calculate reactions and, thus, internal moments. This has involved assuming simple connections for beams, with pins at their ends to give us conditions of zero moment. As noted above, we frequently attach beams to columns with *fixed* connections that can transmit considerable moment from beam to column. With the inclusion of stiff joints, we are now in a mathematical realm that goes beyond the fairly straightforward algebra that has allowed us to quickly find reactions as noted above.

There are ways to calculate the resulting moment and shear diagrams in the frame, however. These involve more complex engineering than the scope of this book, but we can at least look at the effects of fixed connections on a relatively simple frame. Such an illustration will also give us some insight into how frames can 'recruit' the stiffness of individual members to perform better than a simply supported beam.

The first frame in Figure 4.8.7, for example, shows a stiff connection between a beam and columns of approximately the same stiffness. Simplifying somewhat, the resulting moment diagram will approximate the shape shown, reversing the traditional moment diagram of a distributed load with simple supports. Here, the maximum moment will occur at the *ends* of the beam rather than in the middle. Again, the math behind this is complex, but we can describe this phenomenon as 'moment attraction', in that bending moment will tend to 'collect' around the stiffest connections or elements in a frame. In this case, the fixed corners of the frame are more capable of carrying moment than the center of the beam, and will experience the highest internal bending. Note that the columns, too, participate in carrying the bending load by carrying some of the resisting moment. Here, we've hinged the 'feet' of the frame, and the moment diagram (now read vertically) decreases to zero at these points. Note, too, that the moment must be the same value in the beam and the column at the connection (for this situation, the moment here will be the maximum for the frame – $wl^2/8$).

Now, understanding the phenomena of 'moment attraction', we can logically show what happens to our frame if we change the relative stiffness of one or more frame elements. If we apply the same load as shown previously to a frame with significantly weaker columns, the columns will begin to bend, changing the shape of the moment diagram as they move away from the frame's ideal shape. The result will be a moment curve as shown. Note that the curve remains the same – the distance between the valley of the moment diagram across the beam and its value at the columns remains $wl^2/8$, but the curve has slipped down so that the moment transferred across the fixed connection now imparts to the column a much smaller bending load. Note, too, that for an infinitely weak column, the moment diagram will have to start at 0, and we'll get a moment diagram on the beam that will equal that of a beam with simple, pin supports and a maximum internal moment of $wl^2/8$.

If, on the other hand, we weaken the *beam* and stiffen the columns, we get quite the opposite effect. Now, the columns are capable of taking quite a bit of bending load, and the need to equalize moment values across the fixed connection means that, as the columns get relatively stiffer in relation to the beam, we tend to *reduce* the maximum moment at the beam's center. In fact, if we add a hinge to the center of the beam, we get the final condition shown in Figure 4.8.7, in

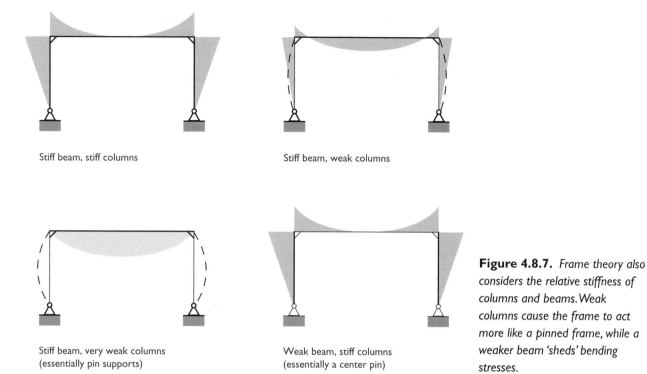

Stiff beam, stiff columns

Stiff beam, weak columns

Stiff beam, very weak columns
(essentially pin supports)

Weak beam, stiff columns
(essentially a center pin)

Figure 4.8.7. *Frame theory also considers the relative stiffness of columns and beams. Weak columns cause the frame to act more like a pinned frame, while a weaker beam 'sheds' bending stresses.*

which the moment curve reverses, and the maximum internal bending stress of $wl^2/8$ now occurs at the two fixed connections. This suggests the structural shape as shown, a common arrangement for relatively long-span frames.

In all cases, note that the bending forces at work will tend to spread the columns apart at their bases. This *thrust* has to be resisted by either robust ground connections, or by tying the column bases to one another with a ground beam to enable the two thrusts to cancel one another out.

Lateral resistance: large scale

So far we've assumed that we can, in fact, develop a fixed connection between beam and column. In practice, there are essentially four methods to do this (Fig. 4.8.8).

In the first, we can build a *diaphragm wall* connecting one or more members with the ground. This wall needs to be a stiff plane, one that resists *racking*, or conversion to a skewed parallelogram. If a lateral force is applied, the diaphragm wall will go into shear, carrying the lateral load into the ground via a shear-resistant foundation. Typical residential construction, for example, uses sheets of plywood on external walls to brace simple stud walls. Nailed connections, no matter how good, must be assumed to provide only pins, while plywood's planar nature means that it is excellent against racking. In larger-scale applications, this principle is applied in *shear walls*, often made of concrete. The effectiveness of these elements is entirely dependent on their length, along which shear resistance can develop.

The second type of laterally resistant member is a diagonal brace, essentially making a joint into a moment connection by triangulating the beam and column.

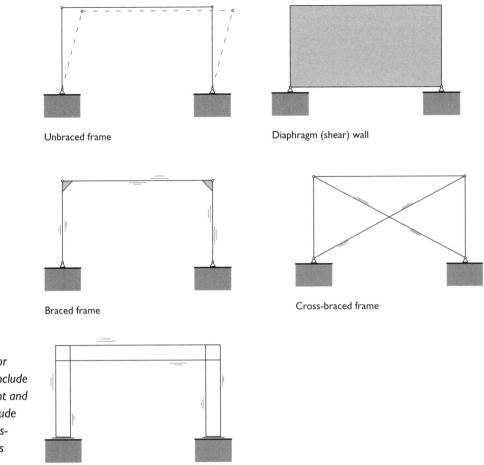

Unbraced frame

Diaphragm (shear) wall

Braced frame

Cross-braced frame

Figure 4.8.8. *Strategies for providing lateral resistance include stiff or braced joints (moment and braced frames), but also include lighter solutions such as cross-bracing, and heavier solutions such as diaphragm walls.*

Moment frame

The result, a *braced frame* offers the advantage of clear sectional area, though potentially limited head height in the corners. This is most common in timber construction.

The third type shown is triangulation via *cross-bracing*, or physically connecting the pin between a beam and column with the pin at ground level. If cross-braced in both directions, these members can be simple tension elements, often just cables. A load from one direction will cause one cable to go into tension, while the other goes slack, and the tight cable will triangulate the frame, preventing movement. This is often the lightest solution, but presents conflicts with circulation through the frame.

Finally, we can provide adequate stiffness for most situations by simply oversizing the structural members involved and ensuring that they are able to connect with one another over a reasonably large-sectional area. *Moment Connections* are bulky, and often require oversized beams and columns, but they offer the advantage of open bays. In steel, these are often achieved by welding on additional plates that essentially extend one member's flanges across the perpendicular member's section, creating a *moment box* that offers considerably rigidity.

In general, multiple frames perform best when lateral resistance is evenly distributed throughout the footprint (Fig. 4.8.9). Uneven lateral resistance can

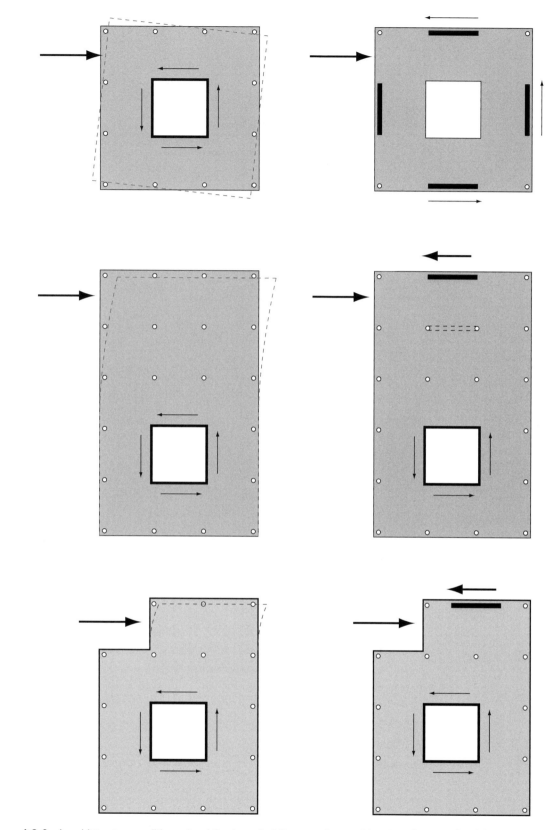

Figure 4.8.9. *In addition to overall lateral stability, large buildings require consideration of torsional stability, or the resistance of a frame to twisting. Here, general principles include providing stiffness on the perimeter of a building structure to gain leverage around the core, and providing additional stiffness to weak or asymmetrical areas if they are unavoidable.*

Figure 4.8.10. *Chicago architecture of the post-war area contains numerous examples of the frame used as architectural device. The Sears Tower (Bruce Graham and Fazlur Khan of SOM, 1961) uses moment frames bundled into nine tubes, essentially super-scale columns with the majority of their stiffness on their perimeter.*

cause the entire building to twist. Because this twisting is essentially a moment force about the center of the footprint, it follows that the most effective lateral bracing locations are at the extreme edges of the building. However, this is often where we want the greatest transparency, and so compromise is often inevitable.

Large-scale frames often revert to familiar structural types. The Sears Tower, for example, relies on hundreds of moment connections at its perimeter and through its floorplate to provide lateral stability. However, these connections are concentrated on the lines of a large nine-square grid, essentially turning the frame into a gigantic column with internal bracing (Fig. 4.8.10).

Likewise, the John Hancock Tower, also in Chicago, relies on an external system of cross-bracing that, again, acts like a very large column with most of its material deployed along the outside edge in a structurally efficient pattern (Fig. 4.8.11).

Figure 4.8.11. *The John Hancock Tower (Bruce Graham and Fazlur Khan of SOM) uses cross bracing for both its lateral stability and its gravity system, lightening its total weight considerably.*

A final, more modestly scaled Chicago example is the Inland Steel Building, shown in Figure 4.8.12. The structure of Inland Steel is a single bay deep, and nine bays long. The structure resists lateral forces in the E–W direction through its large external core, which has a very stiff, cross-braced frame behind its stainless steel skin. Because this core is placed asymmetrically, the columns of Inland Steel are rectangles that are long in the E–W direction, offering a reasonable amount of shear resistance at the unbalanced end. Shear resistance in the N–S direction comes from the interaction of multiple frames connected to one another by fixed joints (Fig. 4.8.13).

Glossary and formulas

Determinate Structure   A structure whose supporting conditions can be easily figured algebraically. For simple beams, this requires supports to be pinned, so that $\Sigma M = 0$ can be established.

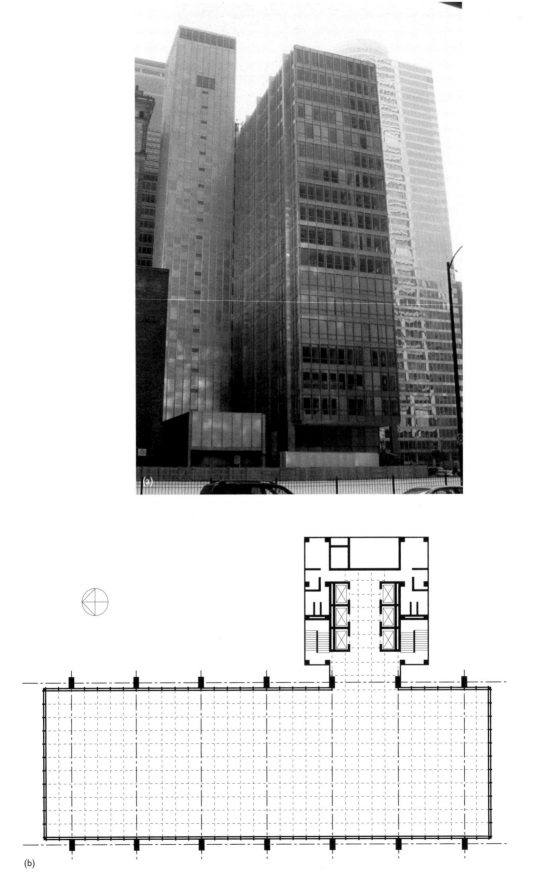

Figure 4.8.12. *Still one of the most elegant buildings in Chicago, Inland Steel used stiff connections and a heavily braced core tower to deal with the lateral stability and weak-arm torsion problems inherent in its shape.*

Figure 4.8.13. *Model of a typical moment connection at Inland Steel's perimeter. Additional steel plates have been added to the column to carry the geometry of the beam through, creating a 'moment box.' This provides the stiffness to keep the building frame from twisting unevenly due to the asymmetrical bracing in the core. (Model by Doug Conroy and Asa Westphal.)*

Indeterminate Structure	A structure whose supporting conditions cannot be calculated algebraically, typically because fixed connections offer the capacity to take moment stresses.
Cross-Bracing	A method of providing lateral resistance to frames by triangulating a rectangular bay. Often this is done using steel cables, rods, or compact sections. When the frame undergoes lateral loading, the diagonal cross-bracing will go into tension or compression and will transmit the lateral load directly to the frame's supports.
Braced Frame	A method of providing lateral resistance to frames by triangulating the corners of a rectangular bay. This ensures that the corners themselves will remain rigid, and that any lateral force will be absorbed by a combination of the vertical members going in to bending and the horizontal member undergoing axial load.
Diaphragm Walls	Planar, vertical panels designed to provide lateral stiffness to a structure. Essentially, shear walls work like cantilevers tipped up on their ends, absorbing lateral loads by going in to bending and transmitting the loads to a foundation. Typically made of reinforced concrete in large-scale construction, or plywood in smaller-scale buildings.

Racking	The tendency of a frame to change shape by skewing when undergoing lateral loading.
Thrust	Horizontal forces at the base of a frame (or any other structure) incurred due to the frame's stiffness. As loads deform a stiff frame, its 'feet' will tend to spread out because of the joints' rotations.
Moment Attraction	The phenomenon under which stiff members tend to develop the highest bending stresses in a frame. As weaker members shrug off bending forces by deforming, stiffer members are left carrying the bending load as they hold their geometry.
Inflection Point	The point in a bending structure at which the resulting curvature changes from one direction to the other.
Moment Connections	Another term for fixed connections, more accurately describing the fact that they can carry bending moment from one member to another due to their stiffness.
Frame	A system of horizontal and vertical structural members that collectively resist gravity and lateral forces more effectively than they would on their own.
Lateral Stability	The second order of magnitude of structural design, after gravity resistance. Simply put, the ability of a structure to resist sideways forces.

Further reading

Ali, M. (2001) *Art of the Skyscraper: The Genius of Fazlur Khan* (New York: Rizzoli).

Jordy, W.H. (1986) Masonry Block and Metal Skeleton: Chicago and the 'Commercial Style', in *American Buildings and Their Architects: Volume 4, Progressive and Academic Ideas at the Turn of the Twentieth Century* (New York: Oxford University Press).

Salvadori, M. (1975) Frames and Arches (Chapter 8), *Structure in Architecture: The Building of Buildings* (Englewood Cliffs: Prentice-Hall), pp. 178–202.

Sandaker, B.N. and Eggen, A.P. (1992) The Frame: Cooperation Between the Column and the Beam (Chapter 6), *The Structural Basis of Architecture* (New York: Whitney Library of Design), pp. 131–148.

4.9 Long-span structures

Long Span	Qualitative differences between long spans and simple frames History and case studies
Long Span in Bending	Folded plates Hybrid beams
Long Span in Compression	Arches Vaults Shells
Long Span in Tension	Cable-stayed roofs Suspension structures Membranes

Long spans: principles and history

Long-Span Systems are structural systems whose dimensions exceed the limits of standard beams and slabs and thus require changes to their geometry, configuration, or shape to more effectively or safely carry loading. In general, we run into long spans in large-volume buildings, such as sports arenas, aircraft hangars, etc., however the principles of long-span design occasionally crop up in high rises or smaller-scale applications.

In general, long-span systems tend toward a handful of basic types, relying on principles of bending, compression, or tension to carry roof or floor loads over large distances. As spans get greater, the architectural implications of such systems become more onerous, as pure structural forms are often necessary at the outer limits of a given type's technology.

Long-span structures existed in the ancient world, but advances in long-span design only occurred after the industrial revolution, with new materials and structural design methods. Until the use of analytical techniques in the 19th century, the great spans of the world were few – the Pantheon and St. Peter's in Rome, the Duomo in Florence, the Hagia Sophia in Istanbul, and St. Paul's Cathedral in London were the major surviving domes, exceeded only in 1866 by the shed of St. Pancras Station in London. Since then, advances in steel and concrete, along with rapidly developing analysis and design techniques, have enabled explosive growth in the scale of long-span structures – currently domes with spans of over 130 m (400 ft) are relatively common, while suspension bridges with 10 times that span have been built worldwide.

Long-span development underwent a tremendous growth in sophistication during two phases – the railway-led period of the mid-19th century and the aircraft-led period of WWII and the decades after. In the first, iron and steel construction played a role in responding to the need for new bridges and sheds

4   Structural design

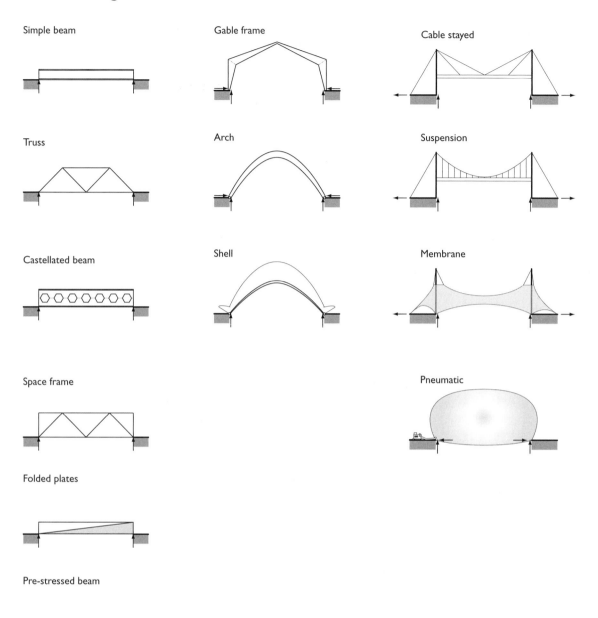

Simple beam

Truss

Castellated beam

Space frame

Folded plates

Pre-stressed beam

Gable frame

Arch

Shell

Cable stayed

Suspension

Membrane

Pneumatic

Figure 4.9.1. *Types of long span structures organized by main structural behavior: bending, compression, and tension.*

to accommodate locomotives, while in the second the extraordinary wingspans of the post-war jets forced engineers to develop spans for hangars that ultimately found their way into terminal buildings and (later) sports arenas. The most commonly used types of long spans are shown in Figure 4.9.1.

Long spans in bending

While complex in their structural behavior, long-span systems that operate as, essentially, efficient beams comprise an immediately recognizable form. Spans for wood beams are generally limited to around 9 m, or 30 ft; simple concrete systems offer bay sizes up to about 20 m (70 ft), while basic steel joists and beams can span up to about 45 m (150 ft). All of these systems up to these spans can rely on simple, unadorned beam theory, with efficiently designed cross sections to provide resistance to tensile and compressive forces at the bottom and top of the beam. However, past a certain point the weight of the structure itself will superimpose a dead load that begins to render the beam inefficient, and at a certain point the beam will not be able to carry even its own weight. At this point, bending structures must be designed to eliminate as much of their own dead load as possible while maintaining a high-section modulus.

The simplest way to do this is to remove portions of the statically inefficient web, leaving the outer edges (flanges) intact. This can be accomplished by cutting holes out of a steel beam, or casting voids in a concrete beam. In both cases, the resulting openings must be located on or near the beam's neutral axis. Steel beams lend themselves to a particular technique known as *castellation*, in which a zigzag hexagonal cut is made in the web of a beam, which is then welded back together so that the resulting 'tabs' attach to one another. This creates open hexagonal voids in the beam, and increasing the overall depth (and thus the section modulus) using the same weight of material. (With plasma cutting, the shape doesn't need to have the geometric efficiency of hexagons – circles or other shapes are just as easy and have the same effect.) Another method of increasing section modulus while decreasing weight is by *trussing* the span, using axially loaded members to resist the internal shear that develops between areas in tension and those in compression. Here, the 'web' is eliminated in favor of rods and/or cables arranged to form triangular panels. The bending load is thus transmitted in part by tension and compression in the truss' 'flanges' (called 'chords'), and in part by axial forces in the web members. This adds considerably to the efficiency of the beam – wood trusses can span up to 70 m (220 ft), while steel trusses are capable of spans up to 90 m (300 ft) (Fig. 4.9.2).

Analogous to the truss is the *space frame*, developed by Konrad Wachsmann in the 1950s (Fig. 4.9.3). Space frames are essentially trusses that span in two dimensions, with intersecting sections. A space frame has the same relationship to a truss as a slab has to a beam; because the trusses of a space frame intersect each other (typically at 90°), they brace one another, preventing twisting, and they transmit some of their stiffness to other elements under load. The resistance to 'twisting' that is added by the cross members prevents deflection, which increases the efficiency of the span. Because of this, the primary limitations of space frames are the compressive abilities of their internal members. Since the frame can itself provide internal bracing, space frames can be extremely efficient, and can span up to 110 m (300 ft).

Concrete can be poured – with some difficulty – into truss shapes, however its ability to take any pourable form allows an even greater efficiency in the form of *folded plates*. These forms use bending principles to combine the web of a concrete beam with the slab of (usually) a concrete roof, often in the form of a curved or sloped plane. The bottom area of the 'folded plate' thus becomes analogous to the tension region of a beam, while the top goes into compression. Fundamentally, this principle is the same as holding a sheet of paper with a curve or fold in it – without the fold the paper cannot carry its own weight,

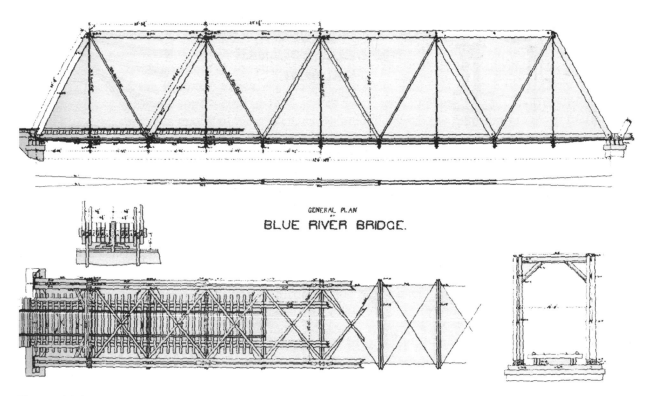

GENERAL PLAN
of
BLUE RIVER BRIDGE.

Figure 4.9.2. *A truss works by replacing a beam's web with a network of axially loaded members, arranged in triangular panels. Note that the compressive members in the 'web' are larger at the truss' ends, as they carry greater loads.*

Figure 4.9.3. *Space frames can be thought of as two-directional trusses, combining the efficiency of lightweight webs with the two-dimensional structural action of slabs. Here, Mies van der Rohe's project for a Chicago Convention Hall.*

however once it is given a cross section it develops a section modulus and can carry considerable load. While folded plates are generally limited to about 55 m (180 ft) of span, note that they can serve as enclosure, thus saving the cost of a separate roof applied to a traditional beam or joist system ft (Fig. 4.9.4).

A slightly more complex method of increasing a concrete beam's efficiency is through the introduction of additional steel members in areas undergoing

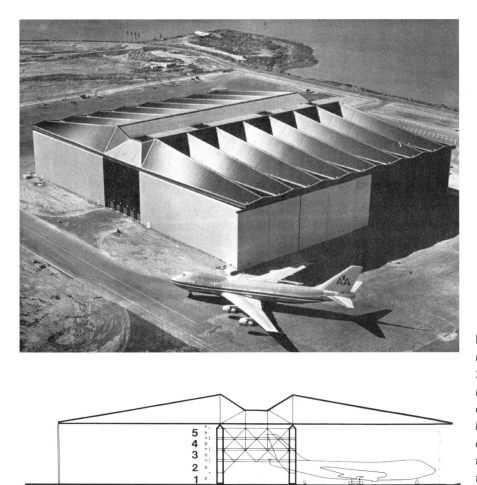

Figure 4.9.4. *A folded plate roof atop an aircraft hangar in San Francisco, CA. While the exterior walls disguise the building's overall structural performance, the hangar's section reveals that the corrugated roof assumes cantilever shape, providing depth at the root while eliminating the dead weight of a solid beam.*

tension. In *post-tensioned* beams, rubber or metal ducts are cast into the member in strategic locations. After curing, steel cables are threaded through these ducts and tightened using jacks or drills. Once tight, these cables take additional tensile load (this can also be thought of as putting the beam into artificially induced compression, taking the job of absorbing tension). In precast situations, these cables may be tightened against a formwork first, and released against the concrete after it has cured. This is known as *pre-tensioning*. The generic name for this technique is *pre-stressing*, denoting the fact that the concrete is assisted by the steel before it undergoes its service load.

Long spans in compression

While bending structures work well for multiple floor plates, we are often faced with programs that require greater span over a single level. For these purposes, it is often more efficient to change not the cross section of a structural member, but its longitudinal section. This can reduce internal bending forces and can load the structure *axially*, that is, putting it into almost pure tension or compression. As we saw in our discussion of axial loads, these funicular (or near-funicular) shapes behave relatively simply, and typically require less material than structures in bending.

The simplest compression long-span structures are *arches*, and the history of this type illuminates some of its finer structural points. First, imagine a typical frame with a single horizontal beam. If the beam were bent as in Figure 4.9.5, it would behave somewhat differently than before. In addition to the bending load, it would, because of its angle, carry some of the load in compression, in other words, directly along its longitudinal axis. It would also begin to push out at its base, against the columns supporting it – again, because of its angle and the resulting horizontal vector at its connection. This type of structure is called a *gable frame*, and it can be a relatively efficient (and because of its simple geometry, cheap) way to span a space – up to 100 ft for wood, or about 200 ft for steel. Note, however, that the frame will tend to push out at its base. This must be resisted either by robust supports that offer horizontal resistance, by a 'tie' between the two supports that cancels out one thrust with the other, or by a moment connection at the top that prevents the two legs from spreading.

If we increase the angle of the gable enough, we end up with a very tall frame – really almost a column – that carries its load almost vertically, and with less and less outward thrust at its base as it gets taller. Alternatively, if we add folds to the beam, we can make it so that it connects to its supporting columns almost vertically, again transmitting less thrust and more axial load (Fig. 4.9.6). If we take this idea to its logical limit, and introduce an infinite number of small bends to the beam, we find that a distributed load can be carried more or less axially along the entire length, subtly shifting at each infinitesimal 'joint' until it arrives at the end, where it will be tangential to the vertical support. This is an arch at its most pure; it will carry a gravity load over a span in compression (more or less, depending on its geometry), and it will impart a horizontal thrust at its base that is inversely proportional to its height.

Over history, the arch developed from very basic construction techniques. Ancient construction originally used stone lintels to span doorways and windows in walls. As these grew larger, they exceeded the capacity of stone in bending, and builders learned to replace them with *voussoirs*, or stones cut on a slant and keyed to one another. This eliminated bending, forcing loads to be carried strictly by the shear capacity of the stone, but it required stones to be cut deeply into walls to provide enough load to counter the tendency of the voussoirs to rotate and collapse. Eventually, lintels became sloped themselves and builders realized that curving the lintel could effectively 'turn' the force inside into a nearly vertical one, eliminating bending almost entirely. Romans perfected the semi-circular arch, a shape that was easy to construct with centering to support the arch as it went up, but relying on a single keystone at the center to tie the two halves of the arch together, preventing them from falling inward on one another.

While the semi-circle is easy to construct, it is not the ideal shape for an arch carrying a simple, distributed load. The ideal shape – a catenary curve – reflects the constant addition of load to the resultant force vector, turning it toward vertical more rapidly than a circular shape (Figs. 4.9.7 and 4.9.8). A circular arch thus tends to have much more bending at its center, which can result in failure

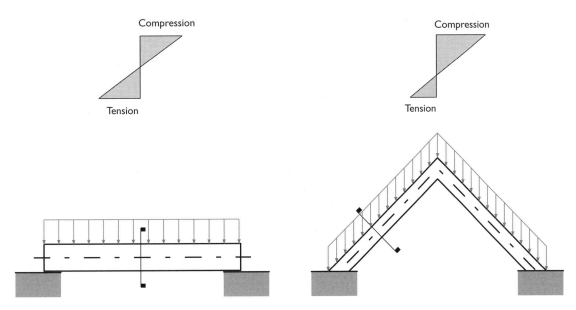

Figure 4.9.5. *Development of arch structural action. A distributed load carried on a beam produces pure bending action. If the beam is peaked, the stress diagram is shifted into compression.*

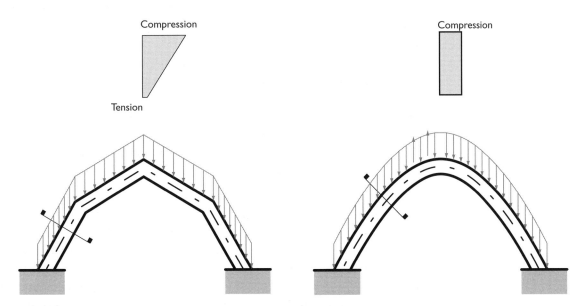

Figure 4.9.6. *Development of arch structural action. In a gabled frame, the entire section may end up in compression, however the lingering bending action in the straight portions will again cause a progressive development – the bottom will be in less compression than the top. In a pure funicular arch, the entire section will experience equal compressive stress.*

in tension at the base of the arch. The 'slipped keystone' that is occasionally seen in Roman architecture is a result of this failure (and may well have been the inspiration for the Mannerist 'slipped keystone' in the Renaissance).

An arch of any shape can be turned into a three-dimensional structure by either extruding its curve along a line (a *generatrix*) or by rotating it about a point. In the first case the result is a *vault*, while in the second the result is a dome. In both instances, the structure will need something at the base to resist the outward thrust inherent in the system. Vaults may be tied with a tension member across the span (essentially turning the vault into a beam with no web), or buttressed

Figure 4.9.7. *A funicular arch shape in steel: the Garabit Viaduct by Gustave Eiffel (1884). Note the pin connections at the base, and the 'spread' of the structure at the base to resist considerable wind pressure.*

Figure 4.9.8. *A funicular arch shape in concrete: the Airship Hangar at Orly, designed by Euegene Freyssenet, 1923. Note that the support strategy here is the opposite of the Garabit Viaduct – the arch gets thicker toward the base, creating moment connections. Any bending in the arch (from lateral loading, for instance) was taken up by this connection, rather than by the arch itself.*

by angled walls on the exterior. Domes have the advantage that their outward thrust can be counteracted by circumferential tension members – one of the keys to Brunelleschi's dome over the Florence Cathedral is that it is literally wrapped with miles of iron chain to prevent it from splaying out.

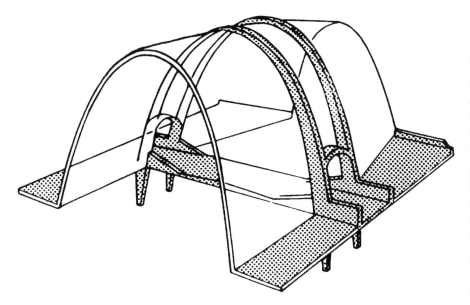

Figure 4.9.9. *An early concrete shell by Swiss engineer Robert Maillart (1939). The thin concrete surface is able to carry its own weight because of its curvature, and the surrounding frame (rarely shown in photographs) that holds the shell's shape and prevents it from flattening. Like most one-way shells, this one works by developing beam action along its length – the top of the shell is largely in compression, the bottom in tension.*

Compressive structures in three dimensions that rely only on surface stresses – shear, compression, and tension – to resolve their loading are referred to as *shells*. These are typically much thinner than vaults or domes, and they must be shaped to ensure that they do not create any internal bending forces (Figs. 4.9.9 and 4.9.10). Folded plates, while their macro-scale performance is similar to a beam, are actually shells when viewed at a small scale – all of their forces can be

Figure 4.9.10. *Zarzeula Racecourse by the Spanish engineer Eduardo Torroja clearly shows its shell geometry – the longer span is cantilevered from supports at the rear of the stand, where the sectional 'fold' gets deeper to allow a significant resisting moment to develop.*

resolved as shear, tension, or compression on their surface. Curved shells can be easily mistaken for domes or vaults, notably at the Kimbell Art Museum by Louis Kahn, where the roof structures 'look' like roman vaults, but behave like thin folded plates. However, there are advantages in *double-curved* shells, in which both the cross section and the generatrix are curves. In these cases, the resulting form will resist deformation in two axes, making it particularly strong. To visualize this, imagine crushing both a toilet paper roll and a tennis ball, each cut in half. While both may have similarly deep cross sections, the tennis ball is inherently stronger. When it is loaded, it develops tension around its base that the toilet paper roll can't. The roll fails, typically, along one line, while the tennis ball must fail at multiple points.

Long spans in tension

While compressive long-span structures are subject to the same buckling concerns as compressive axial elements (columns), tensile structures have no such drawbacks, and thus can be extremely efficient. Because buckling is not a concern, tensile long-span members can be designed simply for axial loading, and materials good in tension such as steel can thus exploit their natural strengths.

The difficulty with tension structures is that we are, invariably, interested in holding things *up* above the earth's surface, and to resist the pull of gravity, tension structures by necessity must pull *upward*, meaning that they typically need to be supported by long compressive structures – columns, arches, or masts – that rise further above the elements we need to support. Since we are usually interested in minimizing the number of these often intrusive elements, they will

Figure 4.9.11. *A dramatic cable-stayed structure. Note that while the cables themselves are quite light, the roof must be sized to take a significant compressive load. As the cable 'pulls' to keep the roof up, the roof itself must be sized to avoid buckling.*

typically carry large loads, absorbing numerous resultants from tension members. Thus, while the tensile structure itself may be efficient, there often come with a very bulky set of compressive elements to hold them up, and our job is often to try to balance light and heavy in these situations.

The simplest tension structure is a cable-stayed deck. Here, a compressive mast supports one or more tension members, usually a cable but occasionally a bar or rod, that is in turn attached directly to a roof or deck we are trying to support. There will usually be a balance between wanting a shallow angle to limit the height of the mast, and wanting a steeper angle to enable the cable to perform efficiently. An additional concern is that the tension member will tend to pull the roof back toward its anchor point, inducing compressive loads in the otherwise lightweight roof deck (Fig. 4.9.11). However even these drawbacks are relatively minor. Tension systems are limited in dimension only by the deflection of the cables, allowing spans of well over 150 m (500 ft). Likewise, the inherent triangular geometry of cabling can add lateral stability to a system, allowing designers to use very simple pin joints for connections rather than moment joints.

While rare in architectural applications, the equivalent of an arch in tension is a particularly efficient way to span very large distances. A 'cable arch' or suspension system involves one or more cables draped over compressive towers and usually anchored to the ground beyond. Between the towers, a deck can be suspended by tension members attached to the main cables (Fig. 4.9.12). Because the main cables will naturally assume a funicular shape for a distributed load they will always carry the loads in pure tension, and will self-adjust based on differential loading. Thus, suspension systems are inherently flexible, and must be designed to take significant movement. In turning the span into an axial load, suspension systems necessarily incur a significant horizontal thrust, tending to pull the towers toward one another in a typical span. This is usually resisted by

Figure 4.9.12. *A rare example of a architectural suspension structure, the Burgo Paper Mill by Nervi. In this case, the roof might have been more efficiently carried by a more traditional system, but the result is a clear statement of the complex forces at work in a suspension structure – note the towers 'lean' that helps counteract the tendency of the cables to pull them toward one another.*

anchoring the cable to the earth on the opposite side of the towers, and by providing some dead weight to the cable system outside of the supports. To achieve a reasonable efficiency in the main cables, this 'backspan' must be significant – ideally one half of the main span, but at least one-third, as a rule of thumb.

Like compression structures, tension structures can be extruded or spun to create three-dimensional elements. The most interesting of these are membrane structures, conceptually similar to concrete shells, which rely entirely on surface tension in all directions. These of course must be held up by elements such as masts or ground anchors at higher elevations, and to do any work structurally they must be *pretensioned*, that is, the membrane must be stretched and held tight. In practice this can be quite simple – an umbrella, for instance, is pretensioned against both uplift (wind) and loading (rain) by extending the metal frame beneath, which is attached to the fabric's extreme edges. To gain maximum efficiency, the membrane must be doubly curved, or stretched both in and out of plane; it must assume a three-dimensional shape to direct any vertical loading (Fig. 4.9.13). Like their two-dimensional brethren, membrane structures are primarily limited in span by their deflection, although they are particularly vulnerable to wind and must be designed for both gravity and wind-driven uplift.

A particular form of membrane structures are *pneumatics*, which rely on differential air pressure to pretension an enclosed membrane. The space being spanned can itself be pressurized, requiring careful control of air balancing, or the membrane can be formed in tubes or 'pillows,' enclosing within the system pressurized air that pretensions the surface and makes the system rigid (Fig. 4.9.14). In addition to the energy required to maintain pressure in these

Figure 4.9.13. *A membrane structure by Frei Otto (West German Pavilion, Montreal EXPO 1967).*

Figure 4.9.14. *A pneumatic structure (Fuji Pavilion, Osaka EXPO 1970) that used pressurized tubes to avoid the need for complicated revolving doors and pressure maintenance devices.*

systems, their design must be careful to ensure that they are properly restrained, usually by cables or mooring lines. While these are vulnerable to collapse under asymmetrical loading (extreme wind), snow or impact (puncture), pneumatic structures are lightweight enough that they will fail slowly, allowing occupants plenty of time to evacuate.

Long-spans architecturally considered

Long spans are often considered their own unique architectural problem – while much of what architects do involves stacking floors on top of one another, with a program such as an arena or an aircraft hangar we have a naturally thrilling space to work with. But while extreme engineering holds its own interest, architects have found ways to make large volume or wide-spanning spaces relate to human scale as well. Architecturally successful long spans tend to not only reveal the spatial drama inherent in such a structural leap, but to also break the scale of such a space down, through the use of structural modules, revealed patterns of statics or construction, and particularly through expressive detailing that allows an intuitive understanding of the principles involved in the structure's span and assembly.

Perhaps the greatest master of the long span was the Italian *constructeur* Pier Luigi Nervi, the designer of the Borgo Paper Mill cited above. Nervi was trained as both an engineer and an architect, but he made much of his living by actually constructing, as well. Over his career, Nervi developed a language of concrete (and, to a lesser extent, steel) that was capable of both great span and human detail. Nervi often wrote of the importance of geometrical order in his work, and of the need to communicate both the structural performance and the work of its builders to a structure's occupants. Speaking in 1965, he suggested the following:

> '... the relationship between technology and aesthetics that we found in the great buildings of the past has remained intact. It seems to me that this relationship can be defined in the following manner: the objective data of the problem, technology and statics, suggest the solutions and the forms; the aesthetic sensitivity of the designer, who understand their intrinsic beauty and validity, welcomes the suggestion and models it, emphasizes it, proportions it, in a personal manner which constitutes the artistic element in architecture.'

Frequently asked questions

In looking through the structural charts in the appendix, it looks like geodesic domes are really inefficient. Aren't they supposed to be super-light? The charts show the relationship of total depth to span. By that measure, geodesic domes are very inefficient – there are shallower ways to span almost any given distance. That's because most geodesic domes have a spherical geometry, which as we've seen isn't an ideal structural shape. However, geodesic domes are quite efficient in terms of *weight*; they use multiple nodes and connections to very effectively distribute both gravity and lateral loads across the dome's surface, eliminating a great deal of a classic dome's dead weight. While not totally accurate, a geodesic dome can be thought of as a space frame (already an efficient structure) wrapped around a sphere (not the most efficient structural shape, but doubly curved and therefore inherently strong).

What's the largest-span building in the world? That depends on the way 'largest' is measured. The longest single-span roof is currently the Georgia Dome in Atlanta, GA, which uses a tensegrity system (a variant on a space frame that uses truss principles to gain height in addition to span) to span just over 250 m (840 ft) with a membrane roof. The longest-span compression roof remains the Louisiana Superdome in New Orleans, which uses arched trusses to span 207 m (680 ft). But these pale in comparison to almost any suspension bridge; currently the longest suspension span in the world is the Akashi Kaikyo Bridge in Japan, which is 1991 m between towers (about 5400 ft). Still other ways to think about the 'largest span' include roof area, in which case the 85,000 m^2 fabric and glass roof of the Munich Olympic Stadium, built in 1972, remains the largest. Boeing's aircraft factory in Everett, Washington, holds the record for total volume, at over 13 million cm^3 (450 million ft^3), though its largest individual structural bays are a relatively small 450 ft.

Glossary and formulas

Arch	A structural member that is curved to ensure that the majority of its material will be in compression when loaded.
Cable-Stayed	A structural system that uses linear cables to directly support a roof or beam.
Castellated Beam	A beam, usually steel, that has been cut lengthwise near the neutral axis and reassembled so that it gains depth without gaining weight.
Dome	A doubly curved shell in which both curves open in the same direction.
Double Curved	A surface that is curved in more than one plane. Such surfaces provide great resistance to deformation through their material strength. A dome is the simplest of these.
Folded Plate	A surface whose sectional geometry has been modified to give it structural depth, allowing it to span as a beam.
Gable Frame	A linear structural member that is angled or bent to transfer some of its load from bending into compression.
Membrane	A structural member that relies on surface stresses in tension and shear only to achieve its span. Compare with a *shell*, which uses tension, compression, and shear.
Pneumatic	A structural system that relies on air pressure to keep a thin membrane in constant tension, enabling it to span considerable distances.
Pre-Stressing	The use of tensioned steel in concrete beams to absorb much of the beam's tensile stress.
Shell	A three-dimensional compression structure whose geometry ensures that all loads are resolved through surface stresses, thus requiring little in the way of buttressing.
Space Frame	A network of trusses arranged at an angle to one another and interconnected to span in two dimensions.
Suspension	A structural system that uses a main cable and smaller 'hangars' to support a roof or beam. The main cable in suspension structures will take on a characteristic funicular shape, approximating a catenary shape as more hangars are added.
Thrust	An inevitable consequence of two-dimensional arched structures. The geometry of these systems creates a resultant force – outward in compression structures, inward in tension structures – that must be countered for the structure to stand.

Truss	A bending member that replaces the solid web of a beam with a network of axially loaded members, usually arranged in triangular panels.
Vault	A three-dimensional arch, with the arch's shape extruded perpendicular to its section. Like an arch, a vault implies a thrust that must be countered at its base.

Further reading

Goldsmith, M. (1987) *Myron Goldsmith: Buildings and Concepts* (New York: Rizzoli), pp. 8–22.

Wilkinson, C. (1996) *Supersheds: The Architecture of Long-Span, Large-Volume Buildings* (Oxford/ Boston: Butterworth Architecture).

Petroski, H. (1982) *To Engineer is Human: The Role of Failure in Successful Design* (New York: Random House).

Siegel, C. (1962) *Structure and Form in Modern Architecture* (New York: Reinhold).

Robbin, T. (1996) *Engineering a New Architecture* (New Haven: Yale).

Salvadori, M. (1990) *The Art of Construction: Projects and Principles for Beginning Engineers and Architects*, 3rd ed (Chicago: Chicago Review Press).

Nervi, P.L. *Aesthetics and Technology in Building: The Charles Eliot Norton Lectures, 1961–1962* (Cambridge: Harvard University Press, 1965).

4.10 Appendix: Structural sizing charts for preliminary design

Introduction

Chapter 4 gives a fairly thorough introduction to the physics of building structures, and in a few cases (beam, column, and foundation design) it provides a rough process for preliminary sizing of structural elements.

However, during the design process, architects and engineers often need to get a general idea about how large a structural member might be, or what material options are for a particular situations. For about 50 years, there has been a tradition of handbook charts that provide vastly simplified, easy-to-use information on rough structural sizing based on experience and some analysis. While it's important to know the theory behind these elements, it's also important to be able to quickly assess what the consequences of certain spans or loading might be. In that spirit, the following charts compile information from several sources (including Henry J. Cowan's *Architectural Structures*, which used diagrams by Philip Corkill, Edward Allen, and Joseph Iano's *Architect's Studio Companion*, and Odd Albert's charts in 1940s era *Architectural Graphic Standards*.)

To allow for easier comparison, we've combined charts for various systems into more comprehensive diagrams based on typology – beams, columns,

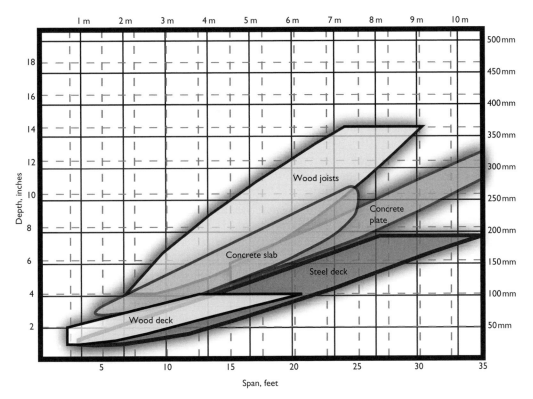

Figure 4.10.1. *Short span floor systems (less than 35 ft).*

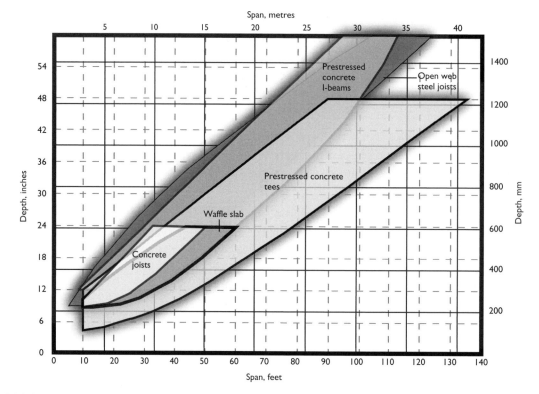

Figure 4.10.2. *Long span floor systems.*

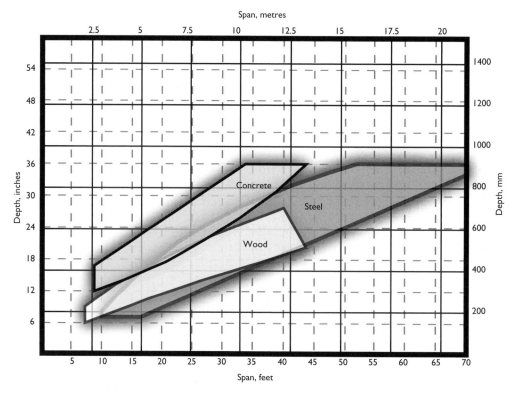

Figure 4.10.3. *Normal span beams (less than 70 ft).*

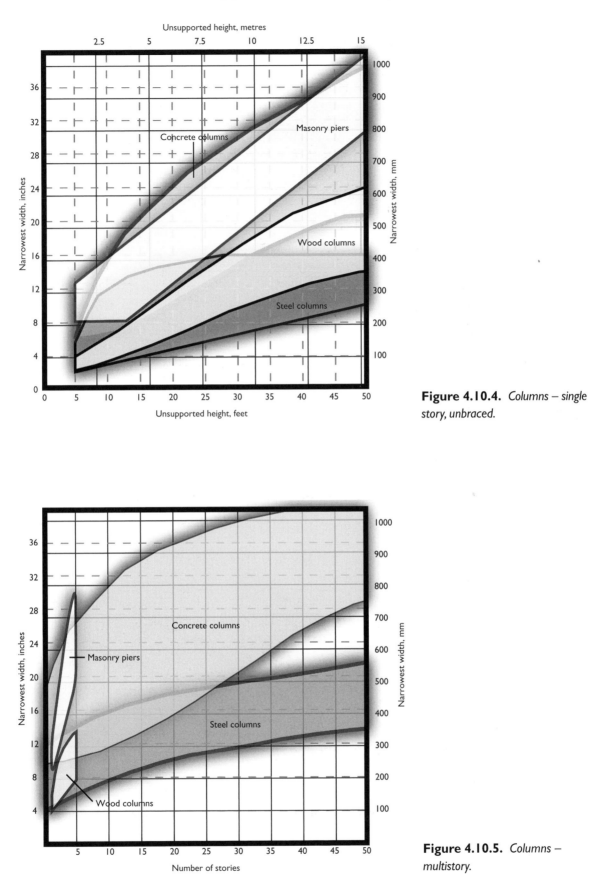

Figure 4.10.4. *Columns – single story, unbraced.*

Figure 4.10.5. *Columns – multistory.*

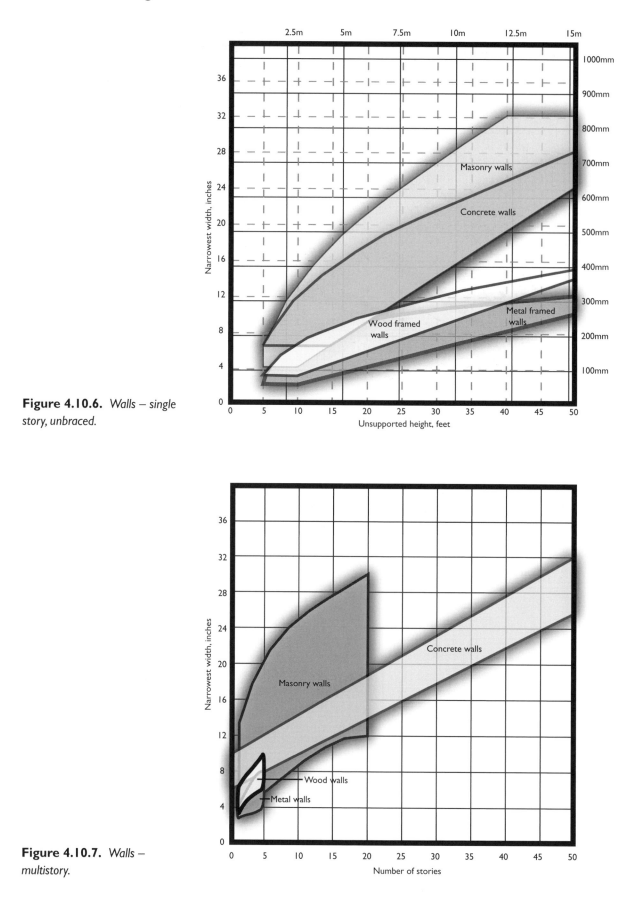

Figure 4.10.6. *Walls — single story, unbraced.*

Figure 4.10.7. *Walls — multistory.*

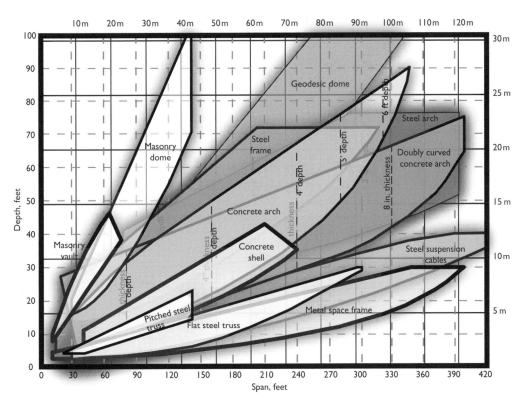

Figure 4.10.8. *Long span roofs.*

walls, short-span floors, long-span floors, and long-span roofs. Elements can be roughly sized by reading the span across the horizontal axes, and finding required depth vertically. In all cases, the charts assume normal loads, standard connections and shapes, and standard specification materials.

These charts are intended for use as only preliminary design aids, and are – obviously – no substitute for proper consultation with engineering professionals.

CHAPTER **5**

Building Components

5.1   Building envelope

Purpose of the Building Envelope	The elements and human comfort Regional differences Water, wind, heat, cold ice and condensation Active and passive enclosures
Building Enclosure Components	Roofs Walls Foundations
Assembly/Sequence	The general contractor Site, foundation, structure, roof, skin

Introduction to building envelope

The building envelope is what we most commonly think of as creating architecture. This is the exterior enclosure, providing the form, materiality and image of the building. Obviously there are innumerable other factors involved in the creation of architecture, but the envelope or shell of any structure typically deals with more issues than any other part of a building. The primary issues being: structure (at times), warmth, dryness, ventilation, wind protection, daylight, view, interior and exterior space making, entry, contextual relationship, scale, texture, color, etc.

One primary goal of understanding envelope is a comprehensive approach to design. Too frequently planning takes up the majority of design time, with the section and skin qualities of projects being ill considered and rushed. Much more time is spent during the development and documentation phases of a project figuring out the enclosure – and building envelopes poorly designed in schematics rarely get much better if they were not well conceived from the beginning. Also keep in mind that no one perceives a building in plan; they mostly see the vertical surfaces.

Another goal of envelope design is durability, and the most destructive and seemingly unstoppable enemy of enclosure is water. Most of your time designing the technical aspects of enclosure will be spent understanding how moisture can move through the system. All buildings are made of relatively small components – the largest of which are about 4 ft × 8 ft (1.2 m × 2.4 m) with the remainder being considerably smaller. Each joint between materials is a potential leak, and moisture has many ways to move through any gap in the system, six ways are most typical: gravity, capillary action, pressure differential, water vapor, thermal expansion and percolation.

Finally, enclosure systems control thermal movement. Heat and cold move through the enclosure in many ways and different methods are required to deal with each type of thermal movement. A thorough understanding of the technical issues confronting building envelope design is necessary in order to achieve any aesthetic goals. In addition, the technical issues are inseparable from the aesthetic issues – each seems to feed the needs of the other, which is the goal of any sophisticated, elegantly conceived building design.

Purpose of the building envelope

The core purpose of the building envelope is to increase comfort for inhabitants above the conditions found in the exterior environment. This can mean many things, but is mainly involved with moisture and temperature control. Sun, wind, air temperature and precipitation are the primary weather elements to be controlled, along with security from intruders – animal, human or insect. This seemingly simple task becomes more difficult due to the changing conditions of the exterior environment throughout the seasons; the same enclosure that works well trapping the heat in winter can become unbearably hot in the summer. Enclosures that transform themselves are much more difficult to build, and tend to allow moisture in, and as we've discussed can vastly decrease durability. Thus the cycle of increasingly complex enclosures to solve multiple problems continues on.

The severity and specific type of these problems has much to with regional differences in climate, the same solutions do not work everywhere. Therefore it is not only necessary to know how to deal with varying seasonal conditions in one place, but to know the particular conditions of the place you are building.

While we may think of the most critical element of human comfort to be thermal control, the most difficult to deal with is water. As was stated earlier, moisture has 6 ways to move through any gap in the system (Fig. 5.1.1).

Gravity simply moves water through horizontal openings and can be easily dealt with – the most effective way is to keep the surface sloped to keep water moving, rather than sitting and eventually eating its way through a surface.

Capillary Action occurs when the space separating two open surfaces is small, so moisture is drawn into the gap. The best way to deal with this is avoid small gaps and create discontinuities or air gaps in any gaps that do exist. This is also related to surface tension, which allows water to cling to surfaces, creating flow on the underside of soffits and overhangs. This places water in positions where protection might not be covered – a drip edge condition at the outer edge of overhangs solves this problem.

Pressure Differential is the most common leakage problem. If the pressure on the outside of the building is higher than on the inside, water will eventually flow in. This condition is combated by using a rain screen – an air space between the outer skin and inner enclosure that is kept pressure equalized by not tightly

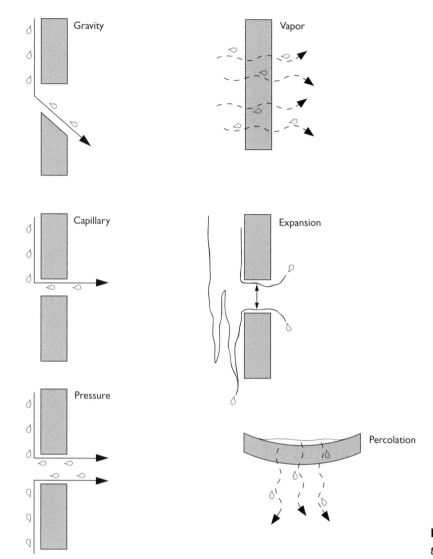

Figure 5.1.1. *Water movement through a surface.*

sealing the space between the outer wall and outdoors (Figs. 5.1.2 and 5.1.3) – therefore the water will not be drawn through the outer wall and the inner wall does not need to deal with moisture protection. Wind pressure may also contribute to this with water approaching a surface at high speed, the momentum carrying the water through any small opening. Covers or baffles can prevent this type of penetration.

Water Vapor can move airborne moisture into spaces through any opening small enough for air to pass. Porous surfaces can also draw moisture in if they are below the relative humidity of the surrounding air. This type of moisture penetration tends to trap humidity inside of surfaces where it can condense into water or freeze and expand.

Thermal Expansion occurs when water infiltrates a gap, then freezes and expands – forcing the gap wider and letting additional moisture inside. This is a particular problem of areas that experience frequent freeze–thaw cycles. Over time a very small opening can become quite large, or cracks can form that threaten the structural integrity of a building component.

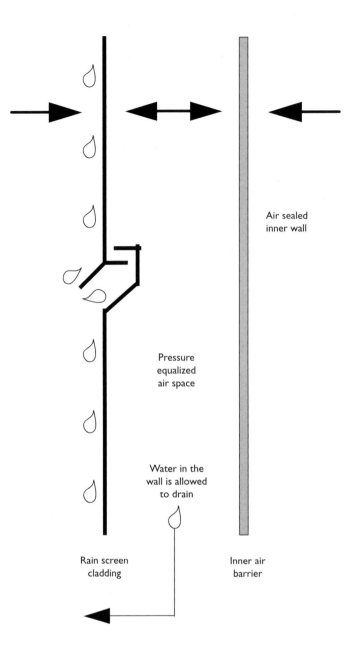

Air sealed
inner wall

Pressure
equalized
air space

Water in the
wall is allowed
to drain

Rain screen
cladding

Inner air
barrier

Figure 5.1.2. *Rain screen elements.*

Percolation is an issue of standing water that eventually finds its way through any porosity in the exterior cladding. Water almost always eventually wins in this situation, as it tends to eat away at most materials through expanding and shrinking or freeze–thaw cycles. The goal is to always keep the water moving off of building surfaces.

Thermal protection in the enclosure comes from insulating against air temperature and mitigating solar radiation. Insulation is a simple process; the key is to keep the insulation continuous and consistent. It makes little sense to insulate one part of the enclosure much more heavily than another, because the heat or cold will find its way through the weak point in the system. This gets more difficult when there are many different components to the exterior skin, creating the need to know how the varying pieces relate to one another's thermal performance. Most manufacturers publish their performance ratings and sources such as *Graphic Standards* and *Architects Data* list common thermal performances

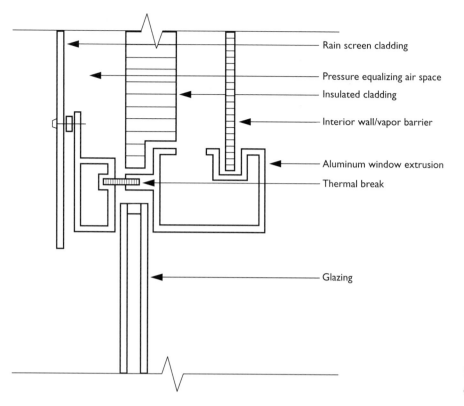

Rain screen cladding

Pressure equalizing air space

Insulated cladding

Interior wall/vapor barrier

Aluminum window extrusion

Thermal break

Glazing

Figure 5.1.3. *Rain screen detail.*

of building assemblies. Many municipalities now require a performance assessment of any new building's enclosure system to ensure minimum standards of energy efficiency. Another purpose of insulation is protection against condensation, or keeping the dew point out of the interior of wall surfaces, where moisture will collect. Proper use and understanding of vapor retarders will also assist in this regard – remember, the vapor retarder always goes on the warm side of the wall, and this is typically the inside of the building insulation. The inside of the building is where the humidity is coming from that will cause condensation; this is only not true in tropical climates where the exterior heat and humidity are extreme and there are few situations where the interior needs to be heated. In colder climates keeping condensation out of the building requires a 'thermal break' at all conditions where metal passes from inside to outside, including all aluminum window assemblies (see Fig. 5.1.3).

Mitigating solar radiation requires an understanding of where the sun is at different times of the day and year. Depending on the climate, location and season solar radiation can be very desirable or very undesirable. Because conditions change throughout the year, but the sun's movement is completely predictable, it is possible to use shading and solar collection strategies to get the wanted sun and exclude the unwanted solar conditions. These strategies can be passive or active, and affect the building enclosure, siting, and landscaping.

Building enclosure systems

The components of a building's enclosure system are generally broken down into roofs, walls, and foundations. These each deal with the movement of water and thermal transmission in different ways.

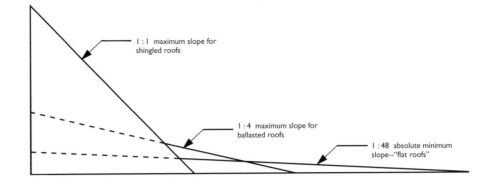

Figure 5.1.4. *Common maximum and minimum roof slope angles.*

Roofs

Since they are most exposed to falling rain, and since their vulnerability to gravity-caused flow is greatest, roofs are the most important area of concern regarding water infiltration. Historically, damp climates have developed surprisingly successful indigenous responses to heavy rainfall. Typically these include roofs with slopes proportional to the amount of rainfall received – steeper roofs in damper climates – and sophisticated devices for preventing water seepage, including bundled or layered grasses that wick water down the roof, and clay tiles designed to capture and direct water locally.

For residential applications, the gold standard of waterproofing is still the sloped roof, which relies on gravity to induce a flow down and away from habitable spaces. A typical sloped roof at this scale will include a deck of plywood, a layer of waterproofing, and overlapped shingles, which are positioned such that each shingle will cover the nail holes of the shingle beneath it. Shingles may be wood, asphalt, metal, or clay, but in each case they will be impervious and fairly dense, to provide protection to the deck below and to resist being blown off by a heavy wind (which, of course, is often accompanied by heavy rains). Such roofs must be pitched to at least 1 in 3, or about 18 degrees. Steeper roofs will induce faster flowing water, and therefore shingles that are made of compositional material (asphalt in particular) will deteriorate more quickly on steep roofs. Generally, shingled roofs are no steeper than 45° (Fig. 5.1.4). The layer of waterproofing beneath is unlikely to get wet from water soaking through the shingles, but prevents wind-driven water that may get under the shingled layer from permeating into the roof structure. Current membranes include materials that self-heal around nail holes, preventing a common leak source, and are generally overlapped, like shingles, to ensure full coverage and watertight joints.

Flashing

Where sloped roofs intersect, their shapes will create valleys through which large quantities of water may be channeled. These areas are particularly vulnerable as the deck below will be mitered, the waterproofing layer must either be cut or creased, and shingles will overlap in tight quarters where good workmanship may not be achievable. Therefore, roofs are typically *flashed* wherever their surface folds – at either a ridge or valley. Flashing normally consists of light-gauge

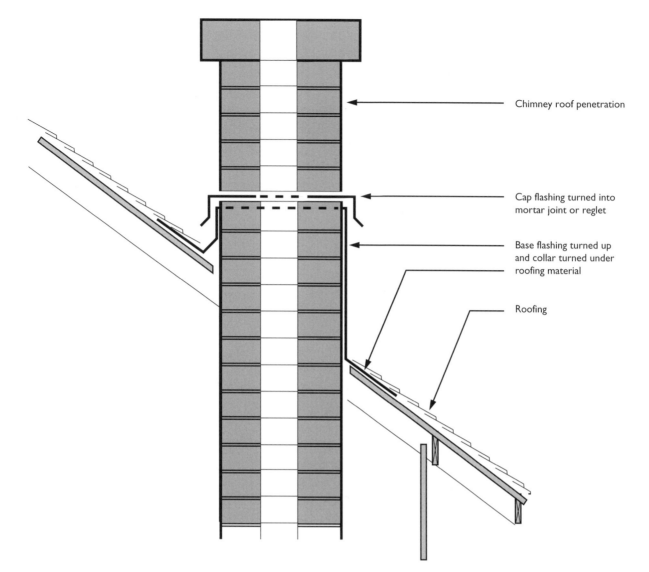

Chimney roof penetration

Cap flashing turned into
mortar joint or reglet

Base flashing turned up
and collar turned under
roofing material

Roofing

Figure 5.1.5. *Roof penetration flashing.*

metal sheeting that can easily be crimped or folded, although for residential applications this may just be an additional sheet of waterproofing membrane. At valleys flashing is tucked under both planes of shingles, which may then be mitered
or overlapped on top of it. Flashing is also used where elements such as chimneys or stack vents penetrate the roof (Fig. 5.1.5). Here, the lightweight metal is
attached to the protruding object well above the roof level, and run underneath
the shingle layer. While water will inevitably flow down the flashing and under the
shingles, it will then be on top of the waterproof membrane and will work
its way down the roof. For masonry penetrations, flashing may be set into a
mortar joint – which must then itself be flashed to keep water from working its
way into the brick. Where differential movement is anticipated, surfaces may
have cap and valley flashing, where two sheets overlap one another. Flashing
is generally part of a two-part strategy for water exclusion that relies on a
generally watertight outer layer and a backup system that will capture whatever small amount of water may penetrate that layer. Generally, flashing is
composed of galvanized or stainless steel, although copper is occasionally used
in high-end installations. Aluminum, because of its tendency to oxidize in water,

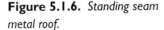

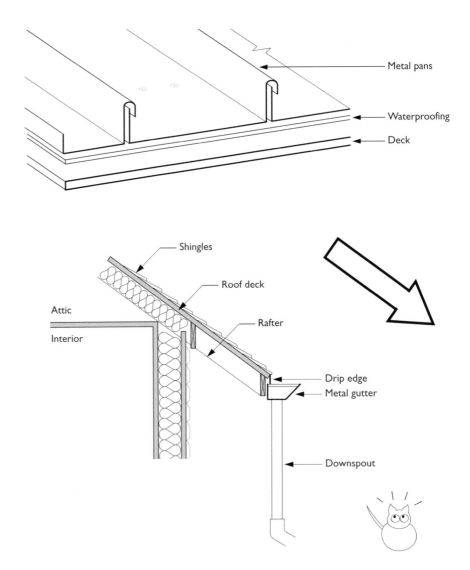

Figure 5.1.6. *Standing seam metal roof.*

Figure 5.1.7. *Eaves and gutters.*

is less often used. A variant on the standard sloped roof is a *standing seam metal roof*, which can be thought of as a roof system made of flashing (Fig. 5.1.6). Pans of light-gauge metal are laid over a roof and are seamed to one another by folding the edges of each pan up and into one another.

Eaves and gutters
Typical sloped roofs will extend past a building's exterior wall, providing a certain separation between the large flow of water off the edge and the vulnerable top of the wall itself (Fig. 5.1.7). This *eave* brings with it some problems that must typically be addressed. First, despite the guarantee of the overhang, the junction between eave and wall must still be made watertight, typically by taking the wall's waterproofing layer (see below) up past the junction several inches. Additional problems, however, occur in cold climates. In particular, snow on the upper portion of the roof, above heated, occupied spaces, will often melt, running down the roof's surface and hitting the roof above the eave, which is of course unheated. At this point it may freeze and water flowing down the roof may be dammed (Fig. 5.1.8). Eventually, this may force water up under the shingles,

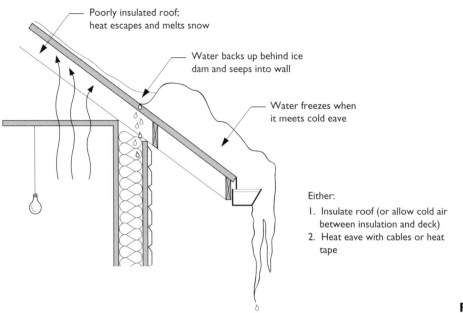

Poorly insulated roof;
heat escapes and melts snow

Water backs up behind ice
dam and seeps into wall

Water freezes when
it meets cold eave

Either:
1. Insulate roof (or allow cold air
   between insulation and deck)
2. Heat eave with cables or heat
   tape

Figure 5.1.8. *Ice dams.*

where it may sit until it works its way into the roof through nail holes causing leaking into the exterior wall. Such a condition, known as an *ice dam* can be quite destructive, as freezing water can lift shingles, separate wall cladding, and push off fascia panels. To prevent this from occurring, the roof may be designed as a *cold roof*, with the insulation held back to the ceiling or at least 25 mm (1 in.) away from the bottom of the roof deck. Outside air is then brought in through ventilation holes at the edge of the roof, or through the attic, preventing snow from melting in the first place. Alternatively, there are products for heating eaves and creating channels for water to flow through, and proper maintenance including raking vulnerable areas of snow may help prevent damming.

At the roof edge, it is important to quickly move water away from vulnerable edges, to prevent water being driven under the waterproof layer by wind or capillary action. At its simplest, the edge of a pitched roof may have a simple *drip* edge, an angled piece of metal that moves water about 25 mm (1 in.) away from the roof edge, preventing it from running down the side of the fascia. However, this can still be a sizable quantity of water, and good practice will usually call for gutters to move this away from the equally vulnerable foundation wall below.

While sloped roofs have an inherent advantage, in that they use gravity to move water toward the building edge, the majority of commercial and industrial structures use flat roofs. While there are inherent problems with these, there are also well-tested methods of collecting, directing and eliminating rainwater for low-slope roofs. First, there is really no such thing as a 'flat' roof. All roofs use slopes to move water toward building edges or drains. In general, flat roofs actually have local slopes of 3–6.5 mm (1/8–1/4 in.) per foot. This can be achieved by using pre-formed rigid insulation, allowing the structure to be flat and standardized. Drains and outlets can be placed to minimize the total depth of the roof slope, giving the appearance of flatness. Codes will often limit the area of roof that can be directed to a single drain, ensuring that if one becomes clogged – a virtual guarantee over the lifetime of a building – the collected water will eventually spill over into adjacent drain tributaries and the total load will not be too great for the structure below.

Like sloped roofs, the buildup of the roof structure itself is designed to keep water from percolating into the structure while it is moving toward a drain. However, in flat roof installations water may be moving much more slowly, and it is more likely that water will end up standing on the roof at some point in its lifetime. A waterproof layer is therefore applied that is both more permanent and more reliably leak proof than on sloped elements. This layer may be a felt and asphalt hybrid, in which layers of fabric are alternated with 'mops' of hot tar, providing a monolithic but flexible layer that can, during hot weather, automatically self-heal. In the past 20 years, higher-end installations (in particular where the volatile installation presents a comfort problem) have tended to use membrane roofing, in which a rubberized or plastic layer is rolled out onto the roof. Seams between sheets are then welded together, again providing a waterproof layer. The reliance on welding and the ease with which these membrane surfaces can be damaged, however, require careful installation and maintenance. In many cases, a layer of ballast – usually round gravel – will be placed atop the membrane for both protection and uplift resistance in a strong wind. EPDM can also be mechanically fixed to the structure below, which eliminates the need for ballast but requires care in placing bolts through the membrane.

Drains are installed at the low points of local roof slope. Their detailing is critical to roof performance, as they invariably involve a penetration through the waterproof layer (Fig. 5.1.9). Typically, the waterproofing is laid over a base plate, and sealed to it with mastic or adhesive. The drain cap is then bolted on top of the waterproofing, through the mastic to the base plate below. The tight clamp of the drain cap and the sloped shape of the base plate ensure that the majority of water will flow, via gravity, into the drain itself, while the base plate will tend to 'catch' any water that happens to get under the membrane and direct it, too, to the drain. Drains must usually have a slotted collector to prevent leaves and debris from getting into the drainpipe itself, enabling a worker to visually inspect and manually clear each drain from the rooftop. Most codes will require at least two drains from any rooftop surface, to allow drainage in the event that one becomes clogged. Once below the roof, stormwater is carried through a dedicated sewer that must not become contaminated with sanitary waste, and can be discharged to an untreated municipal sewer that runs off the property, or to holding ponds on site. Note that drainpipes must typically be insulated to prevent condensation in the winter, as their contents will often be runoff from snow and ice that has accumulated on the roof.

A simple solution for discharging rooftop stormwater is a *scupper*, or a channel off the edge of a rooftop into a gutter or simply away from the building surface. These are often unsightly, however, and run the risk of discharging small amounts of water vertically down the face of a building, marring its appearance. Likewise, for large flat roofs, the necessary slope to the edge of a building places the greatest volume of water at the building's most vulnerable point – where

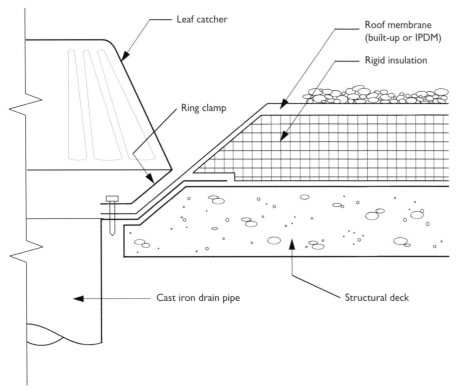

Leaf catcher

Roof membrane
(built-up or IPDM)

Rigid insulation

Ring clamp

Cast iron drain pipe

Structural deck

Figure 5.1.9. *Roof drain detail.*

the roof and exterior wall intersect. It is therefore common on flat roofs to employ roof drains toward the center of the roof, with slopes arranged to keep the smallest volume of water at the building edges, and in fact to contain it slightly to prevent it from being blown down the sides of buildings. At its simplest, this may be a light metal gravel stop that lies on top of a sealed membrane edge, and is only high enough to contain the necessary ballast for the roof. In larger installations, however, it is common to 'tank' the rooftop by running the waterproofing up a *parapet*, or continuation of the exterior wall up past the roof surface (Fig. 5.1.10). This prevents rooftop water from getting into the exterior wall construction by raising the vulnerable top edge of the wall, and it provides a reliable side to the rooftop 'tank' if the waterproofing layer runs up it some ways. Additional advantages to a parapet are aesthetic – a consistent line across the roofscape – and safety related, as workers on top of the roof are protected by the height of the parapet wall. The upper edge of the parapet must itself be waterproofed, usually by a layer of metal flashing that covers the wall's cross section completely, and by a coping, which may be stone, masonry, or metal. The coping provides a firm connection between the flashing and the wall, while the flashing's base may be integrated with the rooftop flashing, forming a continuous liner for the rooftop volume (Fig. 5.1.11).

Walls

Because water is naturally shed off of vertical walls by gravity, they present somewhat less of a waterproofing problem than roofs. However, steps must still

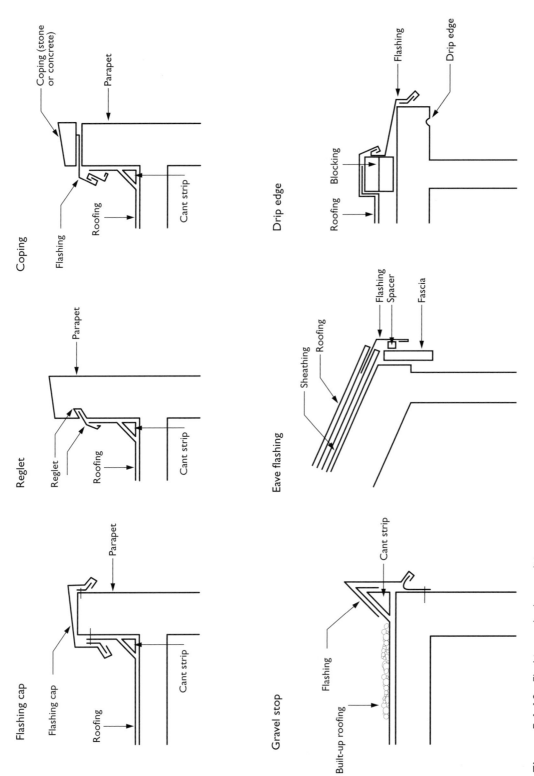

Figure 5.1.10. *Flashing and edge conditions.*

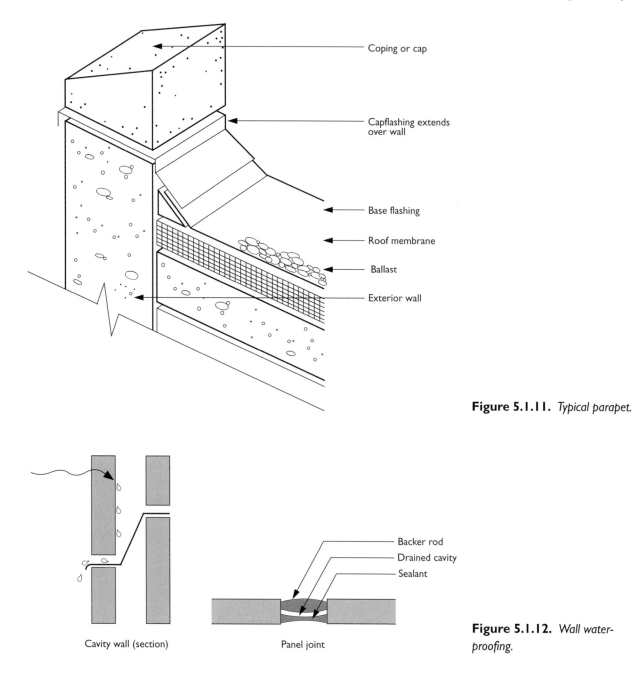

Coping or cap

Capflashing extends over wall

Base flashing

Roof membrane

Ballast

Exterior wall

Figure 5.1.11. *Typical parapet.*

Backer rod
Drained cavity
Sealant

Cavity wall (section)

Panel joint

Figure 5.1.12. *Wall waterproofing.*

be taken to ensure that water does not penetrate wall assemblies by either wind pressure or capillary action. Porous materials such as concrete or stone must either be waterproofed, usually by a liquid sealer that will eventually deteriorate, or else it must be backed up by a dedicated waterproof membrane. Typically, a 'belt and braces' approach involves sealing the exterior as well as possible, and then providing a backup layer that both excludes and directs water down through the wall and out away from the building (Fig. 5.1.12). Brick cavity walls, for example, provide a sloped flashing and *weep holes* at their base, permitting the moisture that inevitably penetrates through the porous outer bricklayer to fall by gravity and be led out of the wall (Fig. 5.1.13). Where exterior elements join, they are typically sealed with an elastomeric compound or sealant that rigidly adheres to both surfaces and excludes water. This is typically backed up by a *backer rod* that is wedged into the joint, again providing a backup exclusion

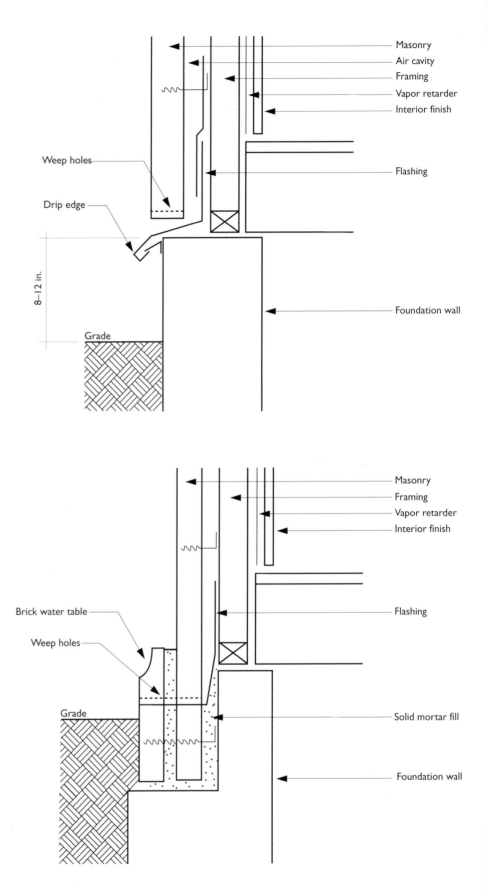

Masonry
Air cavity
Framing
Vapor retarder
Interior finish

Weep holes

Flashing

Drip edge

8–12 in.

Grade

Foundation wall

Masonry
Framing
Vapor retarder
Interior finish

Brick water table

Flashing

Weep holes

Grade

Solid mortar fill

Foundation wall

Figure 5.1.13. *Masonry veneer flashing.*

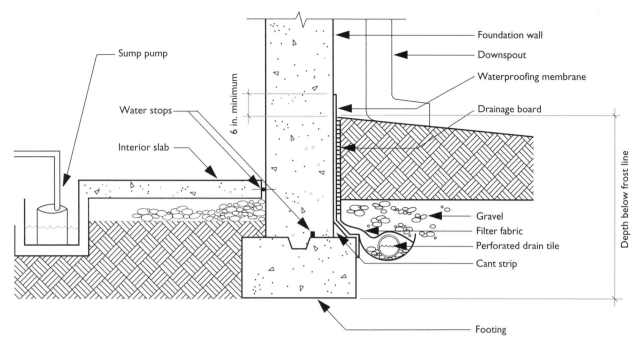

Figure 5.1.14. *Foundation waterproofing.*

system for water that might get past the manually applied – and therefore likely flawed – sealant joint. The backer rod also provides resistance to the sealant, so it will compress and fill the joint properly.

Other areas of concern in exterior walls include projections, which may gather water and direct it into the exterior wall assembly in one of two ways, and base conditions. On the top of a horizontal projection, an inadvertent slope toward the building will direct water in by gravity. This can be corrected by designing in an outward slope, or by flashing the top of the projection into the exterior wall with a positive vertical. More insidious is water that flows across the bottom of a horizontal projection by capillary action. This can very easily continue flowing past the top of an exterior wall assembly if the underside joint is flawed. Providing a drip edge on the lower face of any projection prevents water from traversing this surface. Finally, the point of contact between an exterior wall and the ground surface is a notorious area for water infiltration, as porous materials such as concrete can easily wick ground water up into the wall, leaving unsightly stains or, worse, standing water inside the wall assembly. Good practice includes a dedicated break at the ground level.

Foundations

Foundations carry two major concerns – they are underground and therefore in constant contact with soil that may be damp on a daily basis, and they are covered, which means that repairs are quite costly. Generally, foundations are waterproofed in three ways – by treating the exterior of the basement walls and floors with an exclusionary membrane or coating, by modifying the surrounding soil to encourage drainage away from the building line, and by capturing water at the footing (Fig. 5.1.14). The waterproof layer may be a simple 'mop' of asphalt or a rubberized membrane – in either case it must extend down to and over the top of all footings, as well as rising up the exterior wall above the ground line to exclude water flowing across the surface. It is generally protected by a layer of rigid insulation or other protection board to prevent its being damaged by site work after installation. Waterproofing of slabs is usually accomplished by laying a gravel bed atop the excavated surface, which allows water to fall away from the bottom of the slab by gravity, and then laying a vapor barrier above the gravel to prevent cold, moist air from seeping through the slab. An additional layer of cardboard impregnated with bentonite may also be used – bentonite expands when wet, forming a seal that is impervious to water. Penetrations through the foundation or slab must be protected in ways that allow for flawed installation, usually by a combination of grout, sealant, and bentonite.

Just as the slab may be kept dry by a layer of gravel, the foundation itself can be protected by backfilling with gravel rather than soil, forcing any water that percolates through the ground to fall by gravity away from the foundation wall. To capture water falling through this gravel fill, a drainage tile is placed around the perimeter of the foundation, usually at the level of the footing's top surface. Drainage tile is basically a perforated pipe, which captures water and discharges it away from the building underground or into a storm sewer. It typically requires a filter fabric over its top, perforated side to keep sand, dirt, and vermin that might cause a clog from entering, and it, like all drain and waste piping, must be sloped to fall between 3 and 6.5 mm (1/8–1/4 in.) per foot of run.

In areas where the ground freezes a foundation system must be constructed that sits on earth that will not freeze, or is below the 'frost line'. This depth varies throughout the world, it is 1065 mm (42 in.) in the Upper Midwest of the US and 450 mm (18 in.) in Southeast England, and must be a depth that the frost line has never and will never reach. The reason a building foundation must set below this line is due to the expansion of water when it turns to ice, if this expansion were to occur under the foundation it would 'heave' and cause the foundation to crack. This condition is seen in older buildings built incorrectly, and in conditions where the grade around an existing structure has been changed to expose a section of foundation wall previously covered with earth. The freezing condition is very powerful and can 'heave' and blow apart the heaviest of structures.

Finally, the best protection for foundations is to prevent water from reaching them in the first place. In residential situations, gutters that are sized properly, that discharge away from the building line, and that are kept clean will prevent most water from ever reaching the foundation wall, particularly with an eaved roof. Likewise, proper site grading to ensure that water flows away from, rather than toward the building perimeter will prevent surface water from ever reaching the foundation wall. A final piece of insurance is a *sump pump*, located in a low spot in the basement that turns on when it detects a pumpable volume of water.

Assembly/Sequence

When preparing documentation for a building the architect, and their consultants, are responsible for describing all of the components of a building and their assembly. However, the means, methods and sequence of construction are at the discretion of the contractor – this is not only because they are the most qualified to establish these, but also because it is their liability if things go wrong. The architect typically does not build the structures they design, and this becomes most apparent when dealing with a general contractor. The general contractor determines the cost of the project and how to put it together; they hire all of the subcontractors, order all of the materials, obtain all of the permits, and take the risks involved with construction. This is not a liability most architects would want, we're responsible for our own errors and omissions insurance in case what we've drawn is built as drawn, but doesn't perform acceptably. The general contractor is usually not contractually tied to the architect in any way; architects are simply the owner's representatives doing site 'observation' (the term 'inspection' is often avoided for fear of additional liability). The owner hires the architect and contractor separately and has the architect act as their expert in the field protecting their interests.

This stated, the architect must know the construction sequence in order to prepare drawings that can be built correctly. Buildings are obviously built from the ground up, but there are some notable exceptions when dealing with building enclosure. Site clearing, underground drainage and utilities are first, followed by foundation systems. Next is the basic wall structure, then the roof structure. Roof enclosure typically follows structural frame construction, due to the desire to get the interior dry as soon as possible for construction staging and material storage. The wall enclosure goes up next, again to get the inside dry enough to start the more delicate parts of interior construction. Lastly the glass and doors go into seal-up the interior and provide security for more valuable materials and tools. Careful sequencing sometimes needs to take place so that large-scale assemblies are inside before final enclosure takes place, an example would be on a job site where the stair fabrications will not fit through the door. A debate would likely ensue about whether to tear down part of the wall or cut the stairs in half and re-weld them later. The architect would typically not direct which option to take, but could remind the contractor that the specifications on the stair welds would be difficult to meet in a site fabricated welding condition.

Regardless of what the construction documents state, if you have drawn something impossible to make there will be little sympathy from the contractor or the owner. The architect may end up re-designing it quickly and for free, along with losing credibility with the client and the contractor. Additionally, the re-design may be less attractive than the original and cost more. This can make a simple mistake or oversight extremely costly. Think about how the process of assembly will work in the field as if you had to put it together yourself.

Frequently asked questions

What side of the wall does the vapor retarder go on?

The vapor retarder is intended to keep moisture from migrating into the walls and ceiling of a building structure. This moisture moves through permeable surfaces in the form of airborne humidity. In temperate, cold and hot/dry climates this humidity is greatest on the inside of the structure – so the retarder goes on the inside of the insulation. In very warm and humid climates the humidity can be greater on the outside of the building for the majority of the time, causing the vapor retarder to go on the outside of the structure. Occasionally it is recommended to eliminate the vapor retarder entirely in these situations.

What is Hydrostatic pressure?

Hydrostatic pressure occurs when the moisture in the surrounding soil presses against a building's foundation walls. Most soils retain some moisture, except coarse sands and gravel, causing foundations to be under some hydrostatic pressure constantly. This can cause foundation walls to leak or even buckle and fail over time. It is critical to give the water an alternate route, which is usually done by creating an air gap between the soil and wall that drops the moisture to a drain tile.

Conclusion

More lawsuits involve water penetration than any other single building failure. Usually the problem can be traced back to an attempt to save construction costs (by, in some cases, eliminating flashing or sealant) or an attempt to retrofit waterproofing strategies to a design that failed to recognize potential infiltration at the start. Keeping in mind the six paths that water can get into a building at all times is good practice no matter what system is being considered.

Glossary and formulas

Backer rod	A flexible foam extrusion that is pushed into gaps to prevent sealant from passing through the opening. It also allows compression of the sealant to form a more reliable joint.
Bentonite	A clay material that expands when wet, forming a seal that is impervious to water.
Capillary action	Water movement occurring when the space separating two open surfaces is small, so moisture is drawn into the gap
EPDM	Ethylene Propylene Diene Monomer is a sheet rubber roofing material for use on flat roof installations.
Flashing	Used for waterproofing roof conditions, it normally consists of light-gauge metal sheeting that can easily be crimped or folded
Freeze–thaw cycle	Temperature shifts that allow moisture to freeze and expand, then melt and flow into gaps. It is a particular difficulty of building in temperate climates where the temperature frequently drifts above and below freezing.

Frost line	The depth the ground in a location is subject to freezing. A building foundation must set below this line is due to the expansion of water when it turns to ice, if this expansion were to occur under the foundation it would 'heave' and cause the foundation to crack.
Hydrostatic pressure	Pressure of moisture/water in the soil pushing against the foundation walls.
Ice dam	Melted snow that re-freezes at the edge of a roof assembly, causing a dam that pushes subsequent ice freezing under the shingles. This ice will destroy the roofing components and potentially re-melt into the building assembly.
Parapet	A continuation of the exterior wall up past the roof surface.
Rain screen	An exterior enclosure system with an air space between the outer skin and inner enclosure that is kept pressure equalized.
Scupper	A channel off the edge of a rooftop into a gutter or simply away from the building surface.
Thermal break	A discontinuity inserted into a material assembly to prevent conductive materials from transferring temperature from outside to inside, creating a condensation problem. The inserted material, usually a plastic or polycarbonate, must not conduct temperature well.
Vapor retarder	A waterproof membrane that prevents humidity from passing into an exterior wall cavity.

Further reading

Bassler, B. ed. (2000) Thermal and Moisture Protection (Chapter 7), *Architectural Graphic Standards Student Edition*, 9th ed (New York: Wiley), pp. 210, 214, 216–248.

Ernst and Peter Neufert (2000) *Architect's Data*, 3rd ed (London, UK: Blackwell Science), pp. 51–61, 72–81, 111–116.

5.2 Curtain walls

History	The curtain wall from 1851
Principles	Structure
	Lateral support
	Modularity
	Connections
	Environmental enclosure
Solid Systems	Pre-cast concrete
	GRC/GFRP
	Metal
Glass Systems	Glass material
	Capture techniques
	Subframe and wind support
Hybrid Systems	Structural glazing
	Double skins

History

Until the 1890s, the idea of 'cladding' a building structure would not have made much sense to builders or architects. The outer layer of any building was generally its environmental enclosure and its structure, as the vast majority of buildings relied on bearing exterior walls for support. This, of course, was due to the preponderance of masonry and timber as building materials, both of which work well in compression, but not so well in tension or (in the case of masonry) bending.

However, the advent of steel construction in the late 19th century offered the potential for a lightweight, skeletal construction independent from the outer wall; that wall could thus also be lightweight, skinny, and composed of material that wasn't necessarily structural. Architects of early skyscrapers quickly recognized the potential for large plates of glass on the building's exterior, usually cantilevered off of an internal steel structure with only enough solid material on the skin to hold the glass in place, and to give some sense of security to building occupants (Fig. 5.2.1).

Throughout the early 20th century, building skins underwent a complex balancing act between the desire (partly aesthetic) for transparency and the simultaneous expense (both financial and environmental) of glass. Advances in interior climate control and glass production were balanced by the growing affordability of electric lighting between 1900 and about 1939, however after WWII the availability of insulated glass and the invention of the float

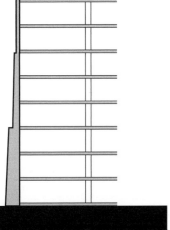

Bearing wall
  Exterior wall supports floors
  Thickest at base
  Punched windows
  Heavy

Curtain wall
  Floors support Exterior wall
  Thin throughout--allows open ground floor
  Skin can be transparent, translucent or opaque
  Very light

Figure 5.2.1. *The fundamental difference between curtain walls and bearing walls. Curtain walls are a relatively recent phenomenon (developed and perfected in the 1890s), but they account for most large-scale construction today.*

glass process combined to make transparent, vitreous skins affordable in their construction and life cycle.

The 'glass box' was one of modernism's greatest promises – and starkest failures. While the crisp aesthetics of such buildings as Mies van der Rohe's Lake Shore Drive Apartments (Figs. 5.2.2 and 5.2.3) seemed to fulfill early experiments in transparent buildings, the rapid industrialization of glass cladding meant that this was a default choice for cheap, speculative office towers the world over through the 1970s. Shoddy or poorly designed glass curtain walls doomed the all glass skin for reasons both aesthetic and environmental, the latter in response to the 1973 energy crisis. Since then, there have been notable advances in building cladding – including a return of the solid (though not bearing) skin aligned with the postmodernist aesthetic of the late 1970s and early 1980s, and a re-engagement of the glass skin by architects and engineers keen to refine its aesthetics and fix its environmental shortcomings.

Principles

A 'curtain wall' is, essentially, any environmental separation that is hung from a building structure. While we tend to associate curtain walls with glass, it is also common to use solid paneling in much the same way. In all cases, there is a hierarchy of issues that must be understood to design a successful cladding system – the cladding's gravity-resisting structure, its resistance to wind or lateral loads, its modularity and size, connections between its components and its structure, and how it filters the outside environment.

Structurally, curtain walls depend on the building frame for their support. While lightweight, curtain walls still have a significant mass, and connections to the

Figure 5.2.2. *A clear demonstration of the curtain wall's configuration and assembly; a panel is lifted into place on Mies van der Rohe's 1949 Lake Shore Drive Apartments, to be filled later by glass panes.*

frame must be robust while allowing for installation and movement. Often, curtain walls will have a *subframe* of aluminum or lightweight steel that will mediate between the building structure and the panels of the wall itself. This subframe is usually tied to the structure at key points, often using steel angle connections attached to a metal frame, or embedded in a concrete structure. This connection must be designed to accept a fair amount of thermal movement, particularly for aluminum systems, since the exterior skin may be exposed to very different temperatures than the interior. Usually, a system of slotted connections allows for this, while also permitting tolerance and adjustment during installation.

A second important structural consideration is the curtain wall's resistance to lateral – usually wind – loading. Because of its lightweight and large vertical area, building cladding is vulnerable to wind pressure. Cladding systems must resist

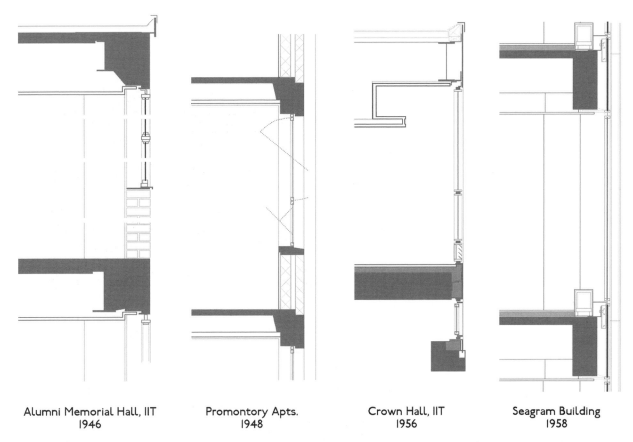

| Alumni Memorial Hall, IIT
1946 | Promontory Apts.
1948 | Crown Hall, IIT
1956 | Seagram Building
1958 |

Figure 5.2.3. *Mies' buildings after WWII show the gradual development and standardization of the industrialized curtain wall, as the building skin gradually emerged from the confines of the structural frame.*

the 'push' of a wind in toward the building, but more importantly they must resist negative wind pressure that might suck the cladding system off the building structure. Connections to the building frame must therefore be designed for tension, compression, and bending, while the system itself must have some depth to convert wind loading into a bending load – the subframe or panels must act like a vertical beam in these instances. For particularly tall or broad installations, cladding systems may have substantial trusses behind them, not so much to hold them up as to ensure their integrity in high winds.

In conjunction with the cladding system's structural performance, a key factor in the design of curtain walls is their modularity. Generally, the task of the cladding system is to cover broad areas of the building's exterior surface in as efficient a method as possible, so we typically seek materials that are economical in relatively flat, planar areas. This favors materials that are produced in sheets (aluminum or steel, or glass). Sizes of panels are limited by both manufacture (glass, for instance, which must fit into annealing ovens) and transport (panels are usually delivered by truck). Subframes, however, are generally composed of linear elements – like the building structure, but on a smaller scale. These elements are thus typically made of rolled or extruded materials such as steel or aluminum. Aluminum, in particular, lends itself to curtain walls particularly well, as the tight tolerances of the extrusion process allows very precise channels and fittings that can be used to grip plates of glass or metal. When the subframe is expressed on

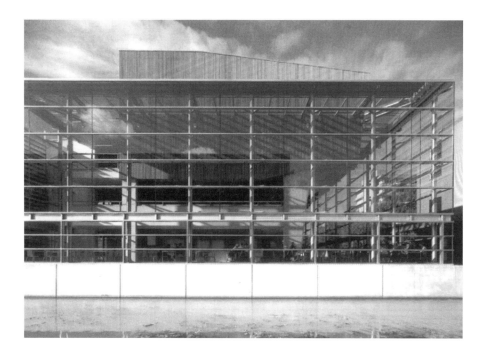

Figure 5.2.4. *A typical (though thoughtfully composed) glass curtain wall.*

the outside face of the curtain wall, its elements are called *mullions* (vertical) and *transoms* (horizontal). A typical aluminum mullion system is shown in Figure 5.2.4. Curtain walls built with individual mullion planar elements are called 'stick-built' while those with panel and mullions assembled in the factory are called 'panelized'.

A good deal of effort often goes into the connections between the flat plate elements of a curtain wall and its linear supports. Here, we are concerned both with the structural connections and the ability of the joint to keep out intemperate air and all forms of water. For metal panels, we may rely on the precision of an aluminum mullion to accept a folded or crimped edge of an aluminum sheet. However we almost always include some form of transitional material – usually neoprene – to allow for some movement, installation tolerance, and air and water exclusion. For glass panels, this neoprene serves the additional role of protecting the glass from bearing directly on the aluminum, which could cause cracking and breakage. With the addition of a *pressure plate*, the neoprene serves to hold the glass in place by friction, a more robust environmental attachment and a structurally more forgiving one. In some cases – so-called 'slick skins', glass may simply be adhered to the mullion's surface with silicone adhesive.

The curtain wall's primary function, of course, is environmental separation. We usually want to provide a system that keeps rain out, that keeps an environmental barrier between interior, conditioned air and exterior air, and that admits only useful quantities of light. As noted below, this equation is changing as energy performance becomes a more important element of building design, and curtain walls have therefore increased in complexity. Advanced curtain walls may include provisions for allowing exterior air to filter in when its temperature and humidity are within acceptable ranges, may include insulating glass in addition to insulated solid panels, and may include solar shading, either within the system itself or as an outrigger structure.

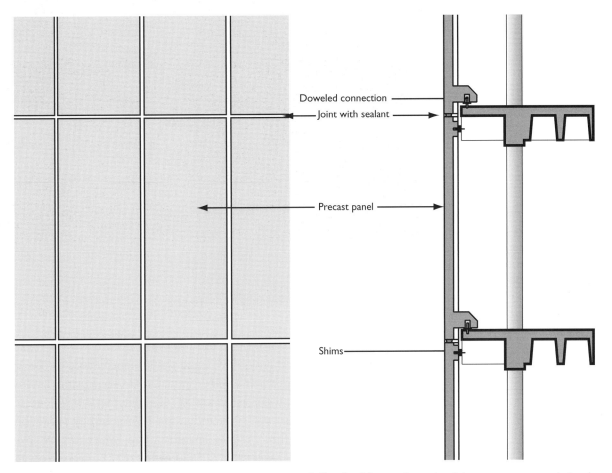

Figure 5.2.5. *Anatomy of a typical pre-cast concrete curtain wall. Panels of factory formed or job-cast concrete are hoisted into position on anchors pre-set into the building structure. Panels can then be shimmed into precise position and their joints sealed.*

Solid curtain walls

At its simplest, a curtain wall may simply consist of solid, pre-cast concrete panels, attached at their top and base to a steel or concrete frame behind. This is inexpensive, and a certain measure of quality control is obtainable if the concrete is pre-cast in environmentally controlled conditions. It is also speedy, as the panels can be formed independently of the construction process, trucked to the site as needed, and hoisted by crane quickly. However, it is usually not possible to obtain particularly fine detailing with concrete in general, as its aggregate size prohibits small elements from forming properly. Likewise, there is an economic tendency when using pre-cast to eschew variety in favor of (often extreme) modularity. Pre-cast can, however, be used as a substrate for other materials, notably stone, and designers can take advantage of its controlled production to ensure remarkable consistency and arrangement in cladding panels. Pre-cast panels are typically bolted to plates embedded in concrete structures, or welded onto steel structures (Fig. 5.2.5). Their attachments generally leave room for maneuvering once in place, with slotted connections for bolts and space for shims or packing (Fig. 5.2.6).

Figure 5.2.6. *Pre-cast panels assembled on a concrete frame, showing joint detail and tolerance gap between panels and floor slab.*

Other solid materials that are often used as cladding include glass-reinforced plastic and concrete (GRP and GFRC), and sheet metal, which can be super-formed with ribs or brake shaped with crimped edges to provide dimensional stability and rigidity. Small deformations in reflective metal may lead to 'oil-canning,' or large waves in the surface that are highlighted by reflection patterns. Metal panels are thus typically limited in size, which will be inversely proportional to its gauge, or thickness. Solid panels may be through bolted to steel or aluminum subframes, or they may be 'captured' mechanically with aluminum channels and neoprene seals. Insulation will typically be required behind these panels, or may be incorporated into its depth by hollows or double skins.

Glass curtain walls

Since the Reliance Building of 1895, the aesthetic and performance potential for lightweight, glass building skins has been an almost primal goal of modernist architecture. Throughout the 1920s, German modernism – expressionism in particular, expressed an almost religious devotion to the ideal of a crystalline building – this despite the fact that glass and framing technology was almost medieval at the time. Until the 1910s, most glass was formed by the cylinder or crown method, both involving extensive hand production and labor. Commercial building glass used an energy-intensive casting and polishing process, which limited its use to only the highest end installations. Beginning in 1914, progress in 'drawing' glass from vats, and later in more efficient polishing processes, meant that glass' relative price dropped throughout the century, often as result of military innovations during wartime. By 1960, with the development of float processes (in which glass is cast atop a layer of molten tin, assuring a perfectly smooth finish) its price had dropped so precipitously that it became, by default, the cheapest way to clad large tower blocks.

However, the material development of glass was only part of the curtain wall story. Ways to physically attach the glass to the building structure also presented

a variety of problems. Glass is both heavy and fragile, and it must thus be supported by a robust yet flexible system, able to hold large, weighty panes in place,
yet with enough give to prevent the glass from bending and therefore breaking.
In 1851, the Crystal Palace relied on wood frames and manually placed putty to
adhere the glass to its structure. This was fine for a temporary exhibition structure that could (and did) leak ferociously. The Reliance Building, 40 years later,
used cast terra cotta, again with a clay-like putty, to hold its 36 sq. ft panes in
place, with better results. A major development in lightening the substructure
for glass panes came about in 1919, when the Hallidie Building in San Francisco
by Willis Polk used steel straps and rods to hold up its extensive (and, unfortunately, south facing) seven story glass façade. Steel continued as the framing
material of choice for glass skins well past WWII, despite its relative weight,
crude detailing and nasty tendency to corrode unless carefully maintained. Likewise, putty remained the only available sealant until the fall in rubber prices after
wartime. In fact, as late as 1951 the most technically advanced curtain walls (at
for instance, Eero Saarinen's GM Technical Center) used steel and putty to hold
single layers of glass in place and, where aesthetically necessary, covered this
with bent aluminum plates.

Three developments after WWII revolutionized glass skins, creating the modern
curtain wall as we know it. First, aluminum's price dropped dramatically, and
extruding mills began producing standard (and thus cheap) sectional shapes for
architectural production. Second, aircraft technology gave high-quality sealants
to architecture, including neoprene, which has proven less vulnerable to weathering than rubber or putty. Third, after decades of failure, glass manufacturers
began to produce reliable insulating glass, using two sheets of plate glass separated by metal spacers and filled with inert gases.

In its contemporary form, the standard glazed curtain wall consists of four
main components: the glass itself, a system of metal (usually aluminum) mullions and transoms that keep the glass in place, sealants or gaskets that provide an environmental connection between glass and mullion, and a set of
connections that transfer the weight of the entire cladding system to the building structure (Fig. 5.2.7).

The glass itself will generally be tempered, that is, heated to near melting and
then cooled quickly. This essentially post-tensions the outer layer of glass, adding
strength and causing it to shatter into small, harmless grains if broken. Glass may
be tinted to reduce interior glare, or fritted. Frit is a baked-on ceramic coating
that can be applied in a variety of densities, including a full, opaque coat or
lighter, dotted or striped patterns to reduce the amount of light transmitted
through a pane. Two sheets of glass may be also be laminated together with a
plastic interlayer. This adds a factor of safety in the event of breakage, and provides an acoustic separation. Plate glass is generally available in sizes up to a maximum of around $10\,m^2$ ($100\,ft^2$) although widths are limited to around $3.65\,m$
($12\,ft$) in any one direction. This is due both to the size of available annealing
ovens, and to the need to transport plates on commercially available trucks.

Transoms and mullions are typically made of aluminum, which can easily be
extruded to very precise tolerances. A standard curtain wall element will

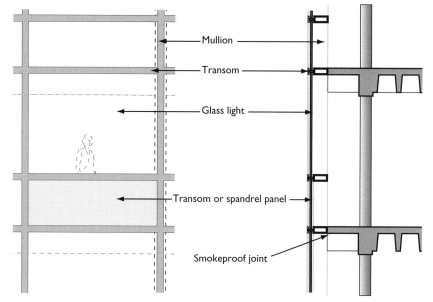

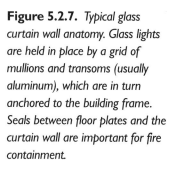

Figure 5.2.7. *Typical glass curtain wall anatomy. Glass lights are held in place by a grid of mullions and transoms (usually aluminum), which are in turn anchored to the building frame. Seals between floor plates and the curtain wall are important for fire containment.*

include a 'box' and a set of grips. The box may vary in size from 2 to 6 in. wide, and from 3 to 12 in. in depth (Fig. 5.2.8). Generally, extrusions must be circumscribed by a circle no larger than 14 in. in diameter, the width of the largest commercially available extruding dies. The box may contain integral channels, usually on the inside, that allow precise connections between 'sticks'. The grips are typically formed on one side by the short end of the box, which is grooved to accept a sealer or gasket, and by a plate that is generally bolted onto a ridge that sticks out from the short side of the box. Plates are then covered by a continuous cover strip, which provides a smooth finish on the exterior. Aesthetics may dictate that either vertical or horizontal elements be suppressed, and these can be composed of simply a box, with or without ridge, siliconed to the back of the glass. To avoid thermal bridges, mullion sections may include neoprene gaskets that separate elements that come in contact with outside air from those that contact the interior.

Gaskets between the aluminum mullion system and the glass panels are usually neoprene, although silicone is also used occasionally. Generally, these elements provide a friction fit between the two materials that supports the glass while allowing it to move a bit, preventing any violent gripping action that could break it (Figs. 5.2.9 and 5.2.10). The entire system must be supported both vertically and laterally by either the building structure, or (for large or tall spaces) a separate substructure designed to transmit these forces. Again, wind is generally the greatest concern, as large flat surfaces will act as sails, either driving the cladding wall into the building structure or sucking it away. At its simplest, these connections can be simple steel angles that bolt to the mullions and to concrete floor slabs, however large systems may employ steel trusses, cable systems, or large freestanding columns to ensure stability.

Recent developments

Among current standards in curtain wall practice are *rain screens*, or cladding systems that rely on a 'loose fit' exterior layer to provide a pressurized zone that resists rain intrusion, and engineered shading systems that exclude direct

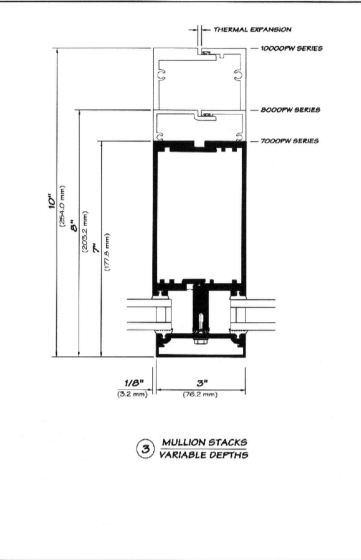

Figure 5.2.8. *Detail of a typical stock aluminum mullion system.*

Scale: 6"=1'0"   C3-6   Wausau 2000

sunlight during particularly warm periods of the year or working day. Rain screens are covered in Section 5.1.

Structural Glazing eliminates mullions, using the inherent strength of glass in tension to support itself. While cladding a building in nothing but a glass sheath has been a dream of modernists since Mies van der Rohe's so-called 'glass skyscraper' projects of 1922, it took a combination of float glass, annealing, and innovations in sealants and connections to bring this ideal to reality. In 1972, Foster Associates' headquarters for Willis Faber and Dumas in Ipswich, England, was the first large-scale installation of an entirely mullion-free glass wall.

The principle behind structural glazing is simple (Fig. 5.2.11). Plates of glass are suspended from the roof slab of a structure, and are connected to one another

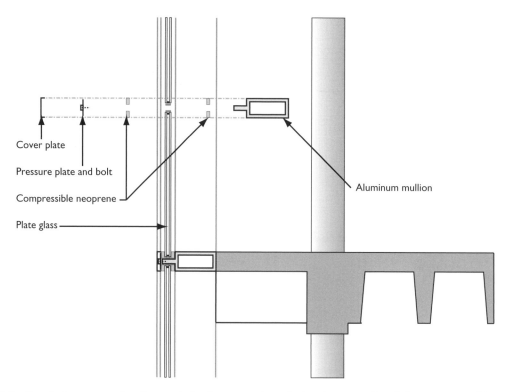

Figure 5.2.9. *Detailed anatomy of a glass and aluminum curtain wall, showing assembly of glass, compressible neoprene, and aluminum mullion.*

Figure 5.2.10. *A metal and glass curtain wall from the 1950s that remains a particularly elegant example; the Crown Zellerbach Building in San Francisco.*

at corners, by either patch plates (square pieces of metal with through bolts) or 'spiders' (steel elements with four connections) (Fig. 5.2.12). The glass literally hangs from the top of the building, relying on trusses or glass fins to keep it stable against lateral loading from wind. Because each sheet is connected to three others at its top, a single pane breaking will simply force the redistribution of gravity loads, and will not cause the entire column to collapse. Sheets of glass are siliconed to one another at their edges to provide an environmental enclosure,

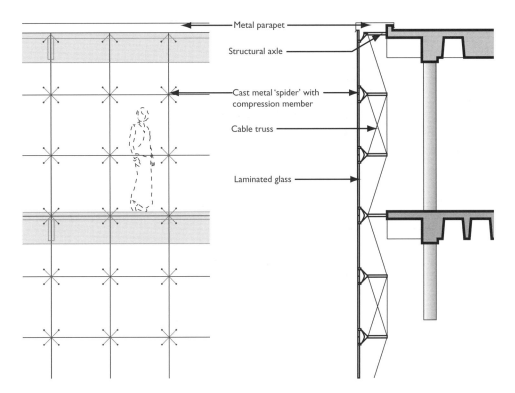

Figure 5.2.11. *Anatomy of a typical structural glass system. Each column of the glass skin is hung from a single axle fitting, while a wind bracing system (here a cable truss, but in some applications glass fins) prevents lateral loading from tearing the glass from the building frame.*

and bolt connections use ball-in-socket joints to permit glass panels to rotate slightly, preventing breakage by 'giving.' A similar strategy must be adopted at the top, where sheets of glass are typically supported by a single axle, allowing the entire column to rotate very slightly, rather than gripping the glass and causing breakage. A base detail typically allows the wall to 'ride' up and down from thermal expansion.

Double Skins. While glass cladding systems have become both affordable and constructionally efficient, their environmental performance, even when insulated glass is used, In climates where either extreme cold or extreme heat is prevalent for part of the year (i.e., about 75% of the USA), thin curtain walls incur, by their very nature, a substantial energy penalty. This, of course, is in addition to the embodied energy inherent in a system made of (energy intensive) aluminum and (energy intensive) glass.

Beginning in the late 1970s, in response to the growing impact of the energy crisis, environmental engineers began to investigate the potential for *thick curtain walls*, that is, with depth that would permit the introduction of cleverly deployed shading, air movement and/or encapsulation. The thinking was that these strategies could be deployed to improve the efficiency of glass skins, permitting the aesthetic and lighting benefits that curtain walls offered while eliminating much of the life cycle performance penalty that they entailed. Integral *shading*, of course, adopted a standard climate response strategy, essentially bolting on metal fins, shelves, or louvers in response to solar geometry – vertical on east,

Figure 5.2.12. *A structurally glazed skin showing connection details.*

west and north, sides to keep low sun and its attendant glare out, horizontal to keep low winter sun in and high summer sun out. In 1978, the Occidental Chemical Building in Niagara Falls took this strategy one step further.

Occidental's strategy was based on the failure of standard, venetian-blind responses to summer heat. The problem with internal blinds is that they block direct sunlight, but also absorb direct solar radiation, which is then discharged inside the building. Occidental's designers relocated a screen of fixed aluminum louvers, placing them between two glass skins – one a 'storefront' system at the edge of the office floor plate, the other a glass curtain wall hung about 2 ft beyond the slab, creating a vertical shaft between the two skins. Summer sun would hit the louvers and warm the air in the shaft, which would then rise and be ejected through a vent at roof level. Thus, the building got the full benefit of natural daylight with no appreciable heat gain, as the hot air around the louvers was exhausted directly to the outside. In the winter, the system could simply be closed up, and the hot air generated by the sun would serve as a super efficient insulator.

While effective, this system was expensive to build, and it provided only a limited environmental benefit. Double skins remained experimental until the 1990s,

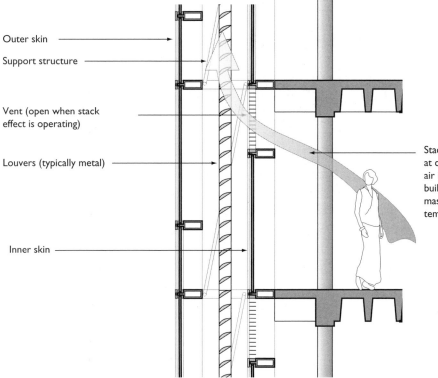

Outer skin

Support structure

Vent (open when stack
effect is operating)

Louvers (typically metal)

Inner skin

Stack effect exhausts hot air
at ceiling level. Replacement
air is drawn from center of
building, which is thermally
massive and therefore
tempered

Figure 5.2.13. *Anatomy of a typical double (ventilated) skin. Double skins use solar energy to develop a stack effect. As heated air rises through the cavity, it can be used to draw air from occupied spaces. During cold weather, the skin can be shut tight to provide an insulating barrier, while in temperate weather both layers can be open, allowing fresh air into the building.*

when energy prices in Germany forced engineers to look at the efficiency of their designs holistically. Led by engineers such as ARUP and Kaiser Bautechnik, the double skin made a comeback in a slightly modified form. Instead of sealing the interior skin, these second generation systems included vents in the inner, office skin. With the advent of heavy computer use, heating offices became a non-issue – this happened naturally from CRT displays, high-speed processors, etc. Cooling, however, became a year-round issue, and the vents in the inner skin allowed the rising air in the external shaft to pull exhaust air from the office, usually at the ceiling where hot air would tend to collect. Shafts within concrete cores provided a source of naturally tempered supply air, which could be used to make up the volume extracted by the double skin wall (Fig. 5.2.13).

This system has now become standard practice in Germany, and is catching on elsewhere (Fig. 5.2.14). Perhaps the most advanced double skin system is Renzo Piano's Debis Tower in Berlin (see Fig. 2.1.10), where east and west facades rely on a complex layering of operable glass panels, terra cotta shading bars, and interior vented window units. Digital controls permit the skin to tune itself to the exterior climate – on a moderate day, both layers can open to permit outside air into offices. On hot days, the outer skin closes, and the interior skin opens, sucking hot air out of offices and out the top of the building. On cold days, the skin can close up entirely, creating an insulating layer.

Figure 5.2.14. *Double skins offer visual depth and a refined texture, in addition to their environmental benefits. (World Trade Tower, Hannover Thomas Herzog, 1998)*

Double skins do present detailing problems, particularly around issues of maintenance and fire prevention. Contemporary designs typically include enough width for worker access, and may provide steel grates for cleaning personnel to stand on at each floor. Fire is a more pressing issue – most codes will not permit more than three consecutive floors to open on to a shaft without intensive fire protection. While the 'solar engine' will work at this reduced scale, it loses a great deal of efficiency. European codes have changed to permit larger external shafts provided they are sprinklered and have fire shutters at every three to four floors.

Frequently asked questions

Every so often a tall building is in the news for losing panes of glass. What causes this?
One of the most notorious building failures of all time was the loss of glass from the John Hancock Tower in Boston, designed by I.M. Pei. Large panes of glass

popped out of the building skin and crashed to the street below – ultimately, the skin had to be replaced while the building stood covered in plywood. While some speculated that the building was racking excessively due to unforeseen wind behavior, the problem turned out to involve weakening in the glass panels themselves. Similarly, the shedding of large marble panels in the Standard Oil (now Amoco) building in Chicago turned out to be due to the unforeseen effects of that city's climatic extremes; as the panels expanded and contracted during winter and summer, the physical bonds within the marble deteriorated. Eventually, when it was noted that many panels were cracked and that some were bowing by as much as 1 in. from true, the skin was replaced. In both of these cases, unanticipated stresses within the material proved to be disastrous, and the lessons from both involve knowing how a particular cladding system or material will work in a given situation. Cladding failures from basic principles are relatively rare – we know now how to waterproof building skins, how to make them stand up, and how to have them resist wind. Where failures occur, they are often the result of failing to properly anticipate the synergetic effects of climate, movement, and loading.

Isn't Aluminum a good conductor of heat and an energy-intensive material? Why would you use it in an environmental enclosure – won't it drain heat in winter and transmit it in summer? Yes, it will do both. Aluminum is an almost unavoidable material in precision curtain walls, however, due to its ease of formation (through extrusion) and its robust structural performance (nearly that of steel). Its considerable drawbacks include its grossly inefficient production and its ability to transmit heat (note that good cookware is made of aluminum for precisely this latter property). Curtain walls will almost always include a thermal break within an aluminum section to provide better insulating performance. This usually occurs between the pressure plate and the 'root' of the backup section. In terms of embodied energy, it is best to keep in mind the up-front ecological cost of aluminum, and to make sure that it is being used in the most efficient ways possible. A pound of aluminum can do the work of roughly 15 pounds of wood, if used properly. Shapes that eliminate 'lazy' material and that maximize performance per pound are thus crucial to the design of aluminum components.

Glossary and formulas

Curtain wall	Any lightweight building enclosure that is fully supported by the building's structure.
Double skin	A catch-all term for a number of curtain wall types that rely on an intermediate air space between inside and outside for environmental performance – in some cases just insulation, in other cases solar-powered air movement.
Gasket	A soft material, usually rubber or neoprene, that is compressed into a gap between a cladding panel and its support, providing an environmental seal and, often, a friction-based structural connection.

Mullion	A linear element that provides support and environmental closure to a curtain wall's panels. Strictly speaking, the vertical members of a curtain wall's subframe are called mullions, while horizontal members are called *transoms*.
Pressure plate	In glass curtain walls, a metal plate attached opposite the main body of the mullion that compresses a neoprene or rubber gasket against the glass panels, providing a robust connection.
Structural glazing	A cladding technique that relies on the inherent tensile strength of glass, supporting a glass 'curtain' from the top with only lateral bracing below.
Subframe	A structural system designed to transfer the gravity and lateral loads experienced by the cladding system to the building's structure.

Further reading

Schittich, C. ed. (2001) In *Detail: Building Skins, Concepts, Layers, Materials* (Basel: Birkhauser).

Rice, P. and Dutton, H. (1995) *Structural Glass*, 2nd ed (London: Spon).

Harris, J. and Wiggington, M. (2002) *Intelligent Skins* (Oxford: Architectural Press).

Danz, E. (1967) *Sun Protection: An International Architectural Survey* (New York: Praeger).

Hunt, W.D. (1958) *The Contemporary Curtain Wall: Its Design, Fabrication, and Erection* (New York: F.W. Dodge).

5.3   Interior finish materials

Interior Finish Materials	Walls
	Ceilings
	Floors
	Openings
Material Assemblies	Plaster
	Gypsum board
	Wood panels
	Tile
	Terrazzo
	Wood flooring
	Resilient flooring
	Carpet
	Acoustical ceilings
Decision-Making	Ethics
	Design
	Quality

Introduction to interior finishes

Architectural space is defined by the elements of enclosure and structure. Beyond the definition of the shape, size, openings and light is the consideration of inhabitation by *people*. Decisions about the interior finishes control the perceived quality and emphasis of the space. Regardless of the shape of a space, the finishes will almost always have more impact than the form. This will be amplified by the way in which those finish materials are detailed and assembled (Fig. 5.3.1). Design does not stop once the configuration of the building is determined – far from it, the vast majority of the decisions will be made beyond this point. We often hear that 'design' is only 10% of the architect's job, and that's true if your perception of design is only the schematic layout. However, almost every decision you make, and every contractor/client/building official call or meeting is part of the design process. Operating in this mode of thinking is difficult, but it is the only way to produce truly excellent work.

Interior finish materials

While any material you construct inside a building may in some way be considered a finish material, the focus of this discussion will be on the primary interior surfaces – walls, floors and ceilings. The finishes may be thought of as the interior cladding of the building, which is fundamentally different than the exterior. While the exterior is largely driven by environmental performance balanced with cost and aesthetic concerns, the interior is driven by aesthetics mixed with a variety of durability, cost and performance concerns.

Figure 5.3.1. *British Arts Center, 1970, Yale University, New Haven, CT, Louis Kahn.*

Walls generally consist of Plaster, Gypsum Board, Wood Panels, Glass, Tile, and various Metal or Plastic coatings on a substrate. Other materials, such as Concrete or Masonry, can be used but are typically considered as exterior materials brought inside. Glass is usually installed as an interior partition assembly as opposed to exterior style cladding brought indoors.

Ceilings can use many of the same finishes as walls, the most common being Gypsum Board and Wood. Acoustical ceilings are the other frequently used finish material and offer a wide range of options.

Floors are hard or soft surfaces, with gradients in between. Tile, Stone, Terrazzo, Wood, Resilient Flooring and Carpet are the most common choices. Concrete is again used, but is still primarily an exposed structural material and not specifically an interior finish.

Doors and windows, while not traditionally considered part of the interior finishes, have many varieties and trim options that need to be considered in terms of their impact on the interior environment.

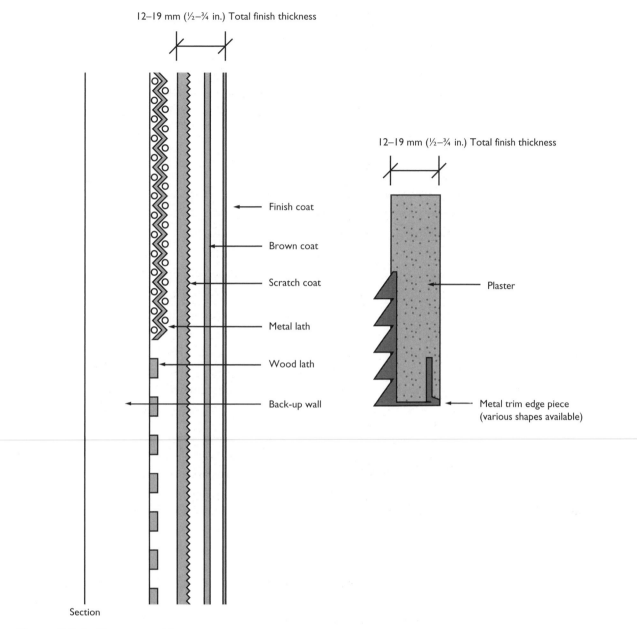

12–19 mm (½–¾ in.) Total finish thickness

Finish coat

Brown coat

Scratch coat

Metal lath

Wood lath

Back-up wall

Section

12–19 mm (½–¾ in.) Total finish thickness

Plaster

Metal trim edge piece
(various shapes available)

Figure 5.3.2. *Plaster assembly.*

Material assemblies

Plaster is a cementitious material that is spread over metal lath, gypsum board lath, or wood lath strips. There are 2 types of plaster – gypsum plaster, which is lighter weight but only suitable for interior uses, and cement plaster or stucco, which is made with Portland cement and can be used on exterior surfaces (Fig. 5.3.2). Plaster can be applied over wood, metal or block back-up walls, but the weight of the material needs to be considered. Ceiling applications can be on direct applied furring or suspended on wires and tracks, similar to acoustic ceilings.

Plaster is applied typically in 3 coats – scratch coat, brown coat and finish coat. The scratch coat is first providing coverage and bonding to the lath. It is made rough on the surface or 'scratched' to provide a bonding texture for subsequent layers. The brown coat levels the plaster out to the majority of its final thickness. Sometimes the brown coat is done before the scratch coat has set and is referred to as 2-coat plaster. The finish coat is a thin surface that is troweled smooth and covers the metal trim that protects the edges. Typical thickness is between 12.5 and 19 mm (1/2 and 3/4 in.).

The metal trim pieces protect edges and corners, and provide a screed to finish the plaster to the correct thickness. Control joints also need to be installed into plaster, because it acts like concrete in terms of movement and cracking. Aspect ratios closest to 1:1 are best, with longer runs possible, but risk of cracking increases the thinner the material gets.

Gypsum Board has a compressed gypsum powder core that is faced with a paper cover material that adds performance and allows for finishing. Boards come in modular sizes and are commonly applied over frame construction or on furring strips. Gypsum can be applied directly to block or concrete surfaces, but trapped moisture will damage the boards, it is difficult to get a perfectly level surface, and more difficult to fasten the board to concrete. Differential movement is also better accommodated with an intermediate furring piece that can allow for some flex. Ceiling applications also work on direct applied furring or suspended on wires and tracks, similar to acoustic ceilings.

Gypsum boards come in various types that can provide for additional water (green board) or fire resistance (type x) if needed. Panels are typically screwed in place with tapered edges butting one another. Joint tape is applied to resist movement and cracking, then joint compound is applied over the surface in multiple layers to provide a monolithic smooth surface (Fig. 5.3.3). Metal trim pieces are used at the corners and edges to protect against damage and provide reveal joints where desired or needed for movement. For wet situations where tile will be installed, a cement board (such as Durock) is used that will not degrade under heavy moisture and has a rough finish to help mechanically bond with the tile mortar.

Wood Panels are applied over frame construction or furring and are typically plywood or MDF (medium density fiberboard) cores with wood veneer faces. Wood paneling is similar to gypsum board in installation, but the fasteners and joints cannot be hidden under joint compound. The edge conditions become critical with wood and the potential for differential movement needs to be carefully considered (Fig. 5.3.4). Edges can be covered with a wood finished tape or hardwood strips, the strips are always preferable but will only be done if specifically requested. Reveal joints or splines are commonly used between panels to allow for movement and variations in grain patterns. Veneer patterns can be specified along with the desired layout. Remember that different species of wood have varying grain characteristics and the 'figure' or pattern of the grain depends on the manner in which it was cut from the tree. There are also a great number of options for how veneers can be laid out that affect the look

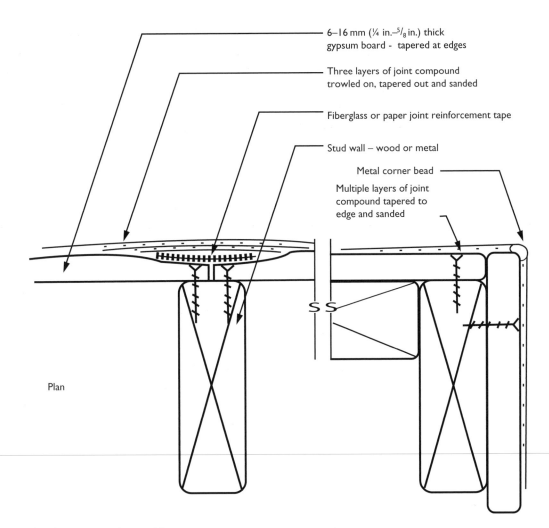

6–16 mm (¼ in.–⁵/₈ in.) thick
gypsum board - tapered at edges

Three layers of joint compound
trowled on, tapered out and sanded

Fiberglass or paper joint reinforcement tape

Stud wall – wood or metal

Metal corner bead

Multiple layers of joint
compound tapered to
edge and sanded

Plan

Figure 5.3.3. *Gypsum board assembly.*

of the final product (Fig. 5.3.5). Plastic and metal veneers on MDF can also be used and follow the same assembly logic as wood veneers.

Tile refers to small modular surfacing units typically made from fired ceramic materials or glass. They come in a wide variety of shapes and sizes, are very durable, waterproof, cleanable, and can be used on walls, floors and ceilings (Fig. 5.3.6). Tile comes in a few standard types based on use and look. Ceramic mosaic tiles are usually small units made from clay materials and can be glazed or unglazed. They are typically 3–8 mm (1/8–1/4 in.) thick and can be used on walls/ceilings or floors. Glazed wall tile is often larger in size and is normally closer to the 3 mm (1/8 in.) thickness. Glazed tiles have glossy or matte surfaces, various textures, and almost any color due to the glazes applied and bonded to the tile through firing. Unglazed tiles derive their color and finish from the base material and coloring agents mixed into the tile before firing. Tiles can also be pressed with patterns to create a textured surface. Quarry and paver tile are unglazed, normally colored in more natural earth tones and can be used in interior or exterior applications. Quarry and paver tiles are thicker than standard ceramic tiles, ranging from 12.5 to 25 mm (1/2 to 1 in.) thick. Glass tiles have become much more popular recently, and come in various sizes and finishes. They are either cast in molds or cut from a cold sheet and polished. Glass tiles

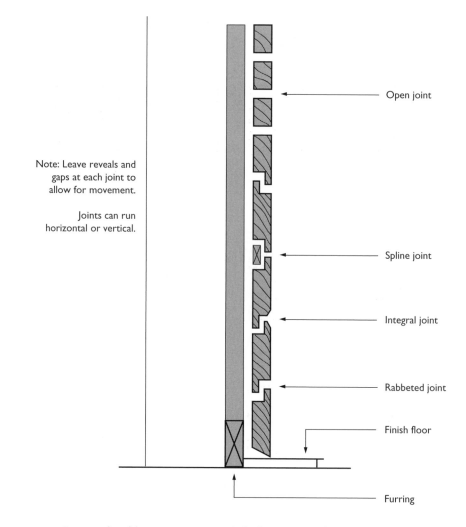

Note: Leave reveals and
gaps at each joint to
allow for movement.

Joints can run
horizontal or vertical.

Open joint

Spline joint

Integral joint

Rabbeted joint

Finish floor

Furring

Figure 5.3.4. *Wood wall finish assembly.*

are just as durable as ceramic, with little concern for surface breaking because the vulnerability of glass is in flex and surface tiles are protected from this by being set in mortar. Glass is also non-porous, meaning moisture and mildew will not collect in the surface of tiles. They are installed in a similar fashion to ceramic tile, with particular care being needed during grouting.

Tile is applied over a waterproof base material with mortar or adhesives. Thin-set mortars 3–8 mm (1/8–1/4 in.) thick are most common in flat conditions, with thicker mortars used to create sloped surfaces. Once set in place, grout is troweled between the joints making the tile joints waterproof and smooth.

Terrazzo is a hard cementitious floor material made of stone chips in a cement matrix that is ground to a polished finish. The size and color of the stone chips affect the look of the floor, along with the color of the matrix – making almost any look possible. The mixture is poured onto the sub-base of sand or concrete then ground and polished smooth once set (Fig. 5.3.7). Limited vertical surfaces can also be created, but the grinding process is more difficult. Terrazzo is extremely durable, yet has the cracking characteristics of concrete and needs to have control joints considered carefully. Joints are handled with divider strips typically of zinc alloy, brass or plastic. These allow for changes in color to be poured and can have neoprene gaskets installed for movement. Older terrazzo is thick set with a 50 mm (2 in.) plus underbed of concrete material and a

Face grain patterns

Veneer grain matching patterns

Figure 5.3.5. *Wood grain and matching patterns.*

12.5 mm (1/2 in.) topcoat of the terrazzo surface. Newer terrazzo is commonly thin-set as 1/4 in. of finish material directly over a concrete base. Pre-cast terrazzo shapes are available as wall bases and window sills, along with stair treads, shower bases and tiles.

Wood Flooring is a strip or block flooring of durable wood species. They are manufactured carefully to avoid cracking and warping, and are engineered to form a uniform surface. There are many species of wood used for flooring – the most common traditional types being oak, maple, beech, pecan, birch, southern pine and douglas fir. Many newer floors use species such as cherry, recycled exotic woods, bamboo and palm wood. Cork is also a wood floor finish, but comes in fairly thin tiles that are considered resilient flooring.

Strip Flooring is the most common type in a tongue and groove (T&G) configuration (Fig. 5.3.8). The T&G arrangement allows for the floor to fit tighter together and to be nailed down in a concealed manner. Thicknesses range from 8 up to 43.5 mm (5/16 in. up to 53/32 in.). The thicker the floor the more durable, which seems obvious, but it also has to do with how many times the floor can be refinished. The critical dimension in refinishing is the thickness from the top to the tongue; once this is too thin the floor will crack to the tongue and groove point and be ruined. Thin floors can be refinished once, where thicker

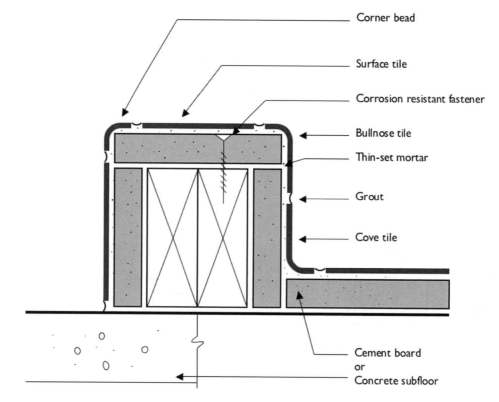

Corner bead

Surface tile

Corrosion resistant fastener

Bullnose tile

Thin-set mortar

Grout

Cove tile

Cement board
or
Concrete subfloor

Figure 5.3.6. *Ceramic tile installation.*

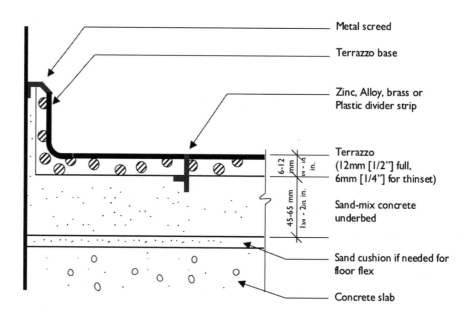

Metal screed

Terrazzo base

Zinc, Alloy, brass or
Plastic divider strip

Terrazzo
(12mm [1/2"] full,
6mm [1/4"] for thinset)

Sand-mix concrete
underbed

Sand cushion if needed for
floor flex

Concrete slab

Figure 5.3.7. *Terrazzo installation.*

floors have many more opportunities to be revived. Wood floors need to have room to expand at the edges, so the floors stop short of the wall and have base trim cover the gap. This can be a problem in situations where you want to change the base condition in an existing installation because often when you pull the old base a large gap is exposed. Top finishes are done with a polyurethane sealer in a matte or glossy finish.

Installation can take place directly over a concrete slab on plywood underlayment or on sleepers to provide some moisture ventilation. The underlayment must be firm when on open joists to prevent shifting and creaking. Sleepers

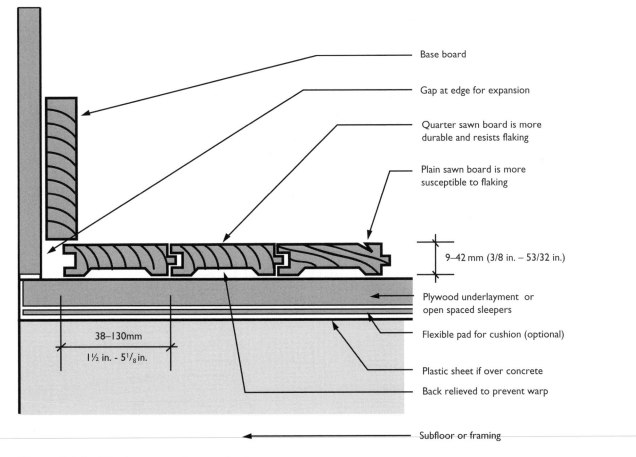

Base board

Gap at edge for expansion

Quarter sawn board is more durable and resists flaking

Plain sawn board is more susceptible to flaking

9–42 mm (3/8 in. – 53/32 in.)

Plywood underlayment or open spaced sleepers

38–130mm

1½ in. - 5⅛ in.

Flexible pad for cushion (optional)

Plastic sheet if over concrete

Back relieved to prevent warp

Subfloor or framing

Figure 5.3.8. *Wood tongue and groove flooring.*

can be cushioned with neoprene pads for comfort, but the sleepers should be rigid enough to not flex in small areas, again causing creaking problems.

Resilient Flooring is a thin material that comes in tiles or sheets applied directly to slabs or an underlayment board. Thicknesses are typically about 3 mm (1/8 in.). The resilience allows the material to not dent and provides some comfort and warmth. It is often an inexpensive solution to utility areas, high traffic corridors and classrooms, but there are higher and lower-quality resilient floors depending on the application. The most common types are vinyl sheets, vinyl tiles, cork tiles, rubber tiles, and linoleum sheets and tiles. They are normally glued down and can be easily cut to fit. Other types of modular vinyl tiles can be mixed with harder materials, such as quartz, to produce durable flooring that is not as flexible, but can be easily cut and adhered to the subfloor.

Carpet can be made from a wide variety of fibers bonded or woven to continuous backings (Fig. 5.3.9). Wool, acrylic, nylon, polyester, olefin, and cotton are used to achieve certain effects – aesthetic, performance and cost. Carpet is generally divided into 2 categories, residential and commercial. Carpet comes in rolls and tiles, and can have a variety of backing pads for comfort. Beyond the fiber material, carpet is judged by the face finish and weight. Weight is simply the thickness and density, the higher the weight the better

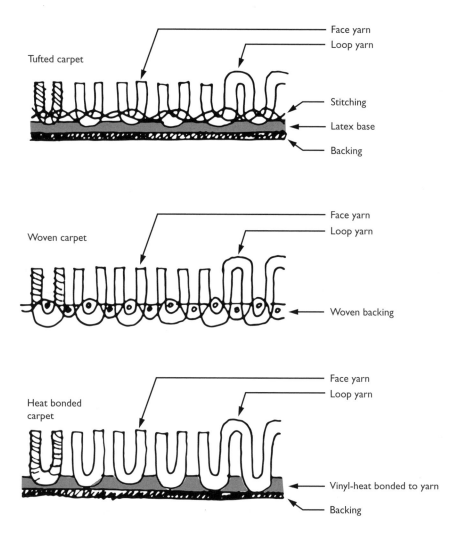

Tufted carpet

Face yarn
Loop yarn

Stitching
Latex base
Backing

Woven carpet

Face yarn
Loop yarn

Woven backing

Heat bonded carpet

Face yarn
Loop yarn

Vinyl-heat bonded to yarn
Backing

Figure 5.3.9. *Carpet fabrication.*

the quality and durability. Face finish is the loop or cut of the yarn. Loop carpets keep a continuous strand of yarn running through the weave and are very durable, cut carpet exposes the edge of the yarn and tend to be softer and a bit less durable. Berber is a commonly used term to describe loose loop carpet for residential applications – loose for comfort, loop for inexpensive. Commercial manufacturers have become increasingly sophisticated and now produce multi-leveled loop and cut patterns with 'tip sheared' finishes (cutting just a portion of the loop) as well. Carpet is colored and patterned in two primary ways – solution dyed or piece dyed, with combinations of the two happening on some patterned carpets. Solution dyed means the fibers are colored before the yarn is extruded, piece dyed is after the final carpet is woven. Solution dye is far more durable, colorfast, and resistant to fading. Piece dyeing is currently the most popular method, with carpet sent through the dyeing process before the final backing is applied. Piece dying is sometimes done over a solution dyed carpet to achieve an over-pattern rather than weaving it in. Carpet is unavoidable due to its inexpensive overall cost, comfort and acoustical value. Flooring is a decision that affects 1/3 of the entire interior surface area of your projects, use carpet and other flooring materials as an integral part of the design project, not an afterthought or something to be handed off as unimportant.

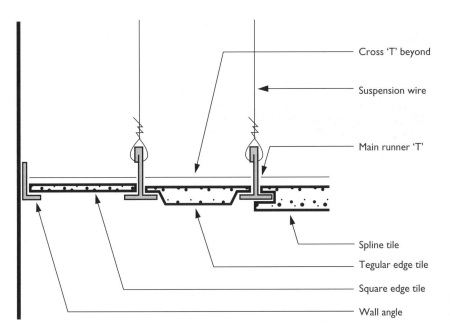

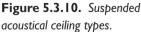

Figure 5.3.10. *Suspended acoustical ceiling types.*

Acoustical Ceilings consist of fibrous material molded into modular tiles that are suspended in a metal grid (Fig. 5.3.10). These systems are commonly used to provide flexibility and access to mechanical systems and lighting. The ceiling plane can be easily suspended after installation of ducts, plumbing, electrical, communications, fire suppression, etc. – providing ample space to hide it all without the contractors needing to keep it clean and organized. Remember this when you decide to save money on a project by eliminating the acoustical ceiling and just trying to keep the 'stuff' up there organized – by the time you're done it can cost more. Ceiling tiles are typically 600 by 600 mm or 600 by 1200 mm (2 ft $\times$ 2 ft or 2 ft $\times$ 4 ft) and the grids can be fully exposed, partly recessed (known as tegular edge tiles), or concealed (spline systems). The grids can also be regular or narrow profile. These are progressively more expensive. Tiles also differ in quality and finish, and have varying qualities of sound absorption and fire resistance. Remember that if you paint a ceiling tile, the porous surface becomes sealed, reducing the acoustical performance. The grid is hung from the ceiling deck or structural members above with thin metals wires that are twisted around the support channels and runners. Ceilings are leveled with a rotating laser that inscribes a path of light at the edges of a space. Other ceiling materials may be hung using the grid system such as metal, wood, or gypsum board assemblies.

Frequently asked questions

Why do so many buildings use bland patterned carpet as the floor finish?

There are a number of reasons why carpet is so popular, the primary one being cost. Carpet is one of the cheapest floor finishes available. It also assists in acoustical damping and is more effective than most ceiling options at absorbing sound. Carpet is comfortable to walk on because of this resilient quality and tends to show dirt less than many hard finish floors. Maintenance is relatively easy, with vacuuming being easier and less slippery than mopping, and if carpet tile is used a small area can be replaced easily if stained or damaged. The bland quality often comes from the desire to hide stains. It would obviously be a bad idea to use white or black carpet due to staining, so the medium tone colors and patterns extend this logic to mask the color and pattern of likely staining. If you install an essentially pre-stained floor finish it may look less dramatic on day one, but it will look about the same on day 500.

How do you decide when to use a suspended acoustical ceiling?

This is a common problem, because designers frequently want to leave everything exposed and have hard surface floors ceilings and walls. While this may meet aesthetic goals it rarely meets acoustical or budgetary concerns. Often there is a question of choices, will the floor be absorptive (carpet) or the ceiling (acoustic tile), because something needs to absorb the sound and no one likes carpet on the walls anymore. This choice is sometimes solved by the need to conceal building systems, such as lights, ducts, conduit, etc., above a suspended ceiling. Hard surface ceilings like gypsum board look good until you install hinged access panels everywhere to get at mechanical systems. Acoustical ceilings allow for free access anywhere service is needed and solve the acoustical problem. Remember that ceiling grids typically come in modules of 600 by 600 mm or 600 by 1200 mm (2 ft × 2 ft or 2 ft × 4 ft), and that these grids benefit from lining up with other parts of the space design rather than randomly blanketing a ceiling.

Conclusion: decision-making

Every designer must be able to make decisions from an endless variety of choices of finish materials. How would one go about making these decisions when it is impossible to know all of the choices? The answer has to do with limiting the set of options and continually searching for better ways to achieve your goals. Limiting options means you will have preferences that you go to first because you have tested the results in projects. You will also learn these from the first offices you work in – a critical point. While you will continually broaden your lexicon of materials, it takes a vast amount of time learning how to specify, detail and assemble. Determining what is good in a set of material choices is built on an ethic of sorts – designers must have opinions about what is better and worse in a subjective arena. Clients will constantly ask your opinion about aesthetic decisions and you must be able to deliver a confident assessment of your choices. You will also need to build-up your knowledge base about what choices are both available and acceptable. The kinds of things you look at when visiting buildings will change over time to include specific materials and details. It's a process that never ends – you will pick apart your own and others projects to constantly improve what you're doing. This is normal and is part of being a designer – be discreet while evaluating the work of others and be relentless in improving your own.

Glossary and formulas

Acoustical ceilings	Consist of fibrous material molded into modular tiles that are suspended in a metal grid.

Carpet	Absorptive flooring material that can be made from a wide variety of fibers bonded or woven to continuous backings.
Gypsum board	Construction finish board that has a compressed gypsum powder core faced with a paper cover material that adds performance and allows for finishing.
Plaster	A cementitious material that is spread over metal lath, gypsum board lath, or wood lath strips.
Resilient flooring	A thin floor finish material that comes in tiles or sheets applied directly to slabs or an underlayment board.
Terrazzo	A hard cementitious floor material made of stone chips in a cement matrix that is ground to a polished finish.
Tile	Refers to small modular surfacing units typically made from fired ceramic materials or glass, although resilient flooring materials, carpet, and acoustical ceiling panels are also made in tile configurations.
Wood flooring	A strip or block finish flooring of durable wood species.
Wood panels	Wall or ceiling panels that are applied over frame construction or furring and are typically plywood or MDF cores with wood veneer faces.

Further reading

Ching, F.D.K. and Adams, C. (2001) Finishes (Chapter 10), *Building Construction Illustrated*, 3rd edn (New York, NY: John Wiley & Sons).

Ramsey, Sleeper (2000) Finishes (Chapter 9), *Architectural Graphic Standards*, 10th ed (New York, NY: John Wiley & Sons).

5.4 Site design and construction

Heidi Hohmann, ASLA

Introduction	Site design
Exterior Surfaces	'Hard' versus 'Soft' surfaces
	slopes
Types of Hard Surfaces	
Plants and Planting	Lawns and lawn alternatives
	space-defining planting
Decision-Making	

Introduction

If site analysis is part of the design process, then site design should obviously be part of the design product. At the very least, a building's siting directs pedestrian access, controls storm water, and conveys a visitor's first impression of the building and interior spaces to come. On the other end of the spectrum, a landscape around a building can be designed as part of a holistic spatial experience. In other words, spatial design does not necessarily end at a building wall, but rather extends into the landscape around it, integrating interior and exterior design.

Exterior landscape design can be as simple as a sidewalk and a few street trees and as complex as a stormwater catchment system that diverts water from building rooftops and parking lots into a constructed wetland designed for aquifer recharge and as wildlife habitat. Like building design, landscape design has its own set of opportunities and constraints, which primarily differ from architectural concerns in that they address issues of living species and ecological systems. As a result in its most expanded sense, landscape design becomes an activity in its own right, performed by the allied profession of landscape architecture, and supported by specialists in other fields, such as horticulture, soil science, and conservation ecology. In general, however, landscape architecture includes the design of exterior space such as plazas, terraces, sitting areas, parking lots, lawns, and parks surrounding buildings, as well as more extensive and programmed landscapes such as playing fields, gardens, forests, wetlands, and storm drainage systems.

This section provides some very basic guidelines and information about exterior landscape treatments, both 'hardscape' and 'plantscape,' for the most common architectural applications. For larger, more complex issues of site design and management, especially those that address the requirements of plants and ecosystems, it may be necessary to consult other resources or other professionals. Though consultation with a landscape architect may seem like an 'extra' expense, remember that a beautiful and ecologically sound landscape design can be a way to provide your client with value-added design.

Table 5.4.1 Recommended slopes and cross slopes for typical surface applications.

	Recommended slope (%)	Maximum slope (%)	Minimum slope (%)
Paved areas			
Sidewalk, longitudinal slope	1–5	10	0.5
Sidewalk, cross slope	2	4	1
Terraces, patios, etc.	1	2	0.5
Driveway, longitudinal slope	1–10	0.5	10
Parking lot, longitudinal slope	2–3	5	0.5
Parking lot, cross slope	2–3	10	0.5
Road, longitudinal slope	2–10	20	1
Road crown	2	3	1
Lawn/unpaved areas			
Lawns	5–10	30 (approx 3:1)	1
Mowed slopes	20	30 (approx 3:1)	–
Planted beds	3–5	10	1
Athletic fields, generally	1	2	0.5

Exterior planting and paving materials

Landscape materials for building surrounds can be divided into two major types. 'Hard' surfacing and paving is most often used for pedestrian and vehicular access and where durability for traffic is required, such as roads, sidewalks, paths, patios and terraces. 'Soft' surfacing, such as lawn and beds planted with groundcover or shrubs are most often used in larger areas where pedestrian traffic is dispersed or recreational. In general, planted areas are also more pervious than most pavements, allowing water to better permeate their surfaces and percolate into the soil and groundwater below.

For both pavement and planted areas, the slope or gradient of surfaces is very important for access and drainage. In general, exterior grades generally range from 1% to 20%. Surfaces with a gradient of less than 1% are difficult to construct to drain properly and surfaces of more than 25% are difficult for pedestrians and vehicles to navigate and for lawn mowers to maintain. To provide ADA accessibility, paved surfaces should generally be 5% or less, though grades of 8.33% are permitted with appropriate handrails and landings (see Section 2.2). Table 5.4.1 shows recommended slopes and cross slopes for typical surface applications.

Hardscape/pavement

In general, all pavements are layered constructions, consisting of a prepared subgrade, an aggregate base, and a wear or surface layer. *Subgrade* is the soil beneath the pavement, usually prepared through cutting, compaction or leveling to meet the designed slopes and elevations for proper surface drainage. *Aggregate base* is placed on the subgrade to transfer the pavement load to the subgrade, provide a level setting surface, and to create a well-drained base that reduces the heaving effects of the freeze–thaw cycles. Depth of aggregate therefore depends on frost depth and load requirements. In colder climates aggregate base depth may be 6–8 in., with an extra layer of coarser sub-base

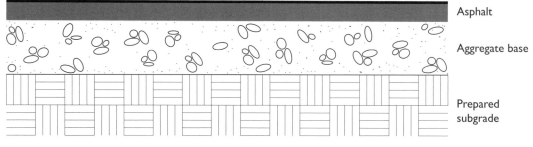

Figure 5.4.1. *Flexible monolithic paving.*

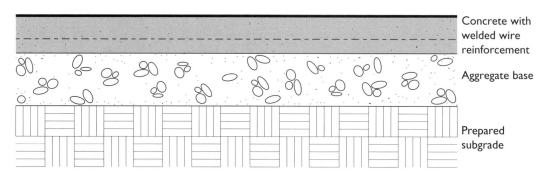

Figure 5.4.2. *Rigid monolithic paving.*

gravel below it if heavy loads are anticipated. In warm climates, a light duty pedestrian pavement might simply consist of a *wear layer* of flagstone pavers set in a few inches of sand that serves as both structural support and as setting bed. Pavements are further classified as rigid or flexible and may be either considered to be of monolithic construction (composed of a single, seamless construction) or unit construction (made of individual paving units).

Flexible pavements are so-called because they are able to move, expand and contract in response to freeze–thaw cycles. They generally consist of thinner monolithic or unit surfaces applied over thicker aggregate bases. *Monolithic flexible pavements* (Fig. 5.4.1) include bound aggregate and polymer pavements such as asphalt or rubberized athletic surfaces which are applied in smooth, extruded sheets 1½–4 in. thick over a prepared base. Depth of surface pavement depends on load. Asphalt pavement for roads, for example, is thicker, often applied in two layers, a tack coat and a wear layer, over the aggregate base.

Flexible unit pavements include brick, concrete and stone pavers of various thicknesses (1½ – 4 in., depending on the material structure of the paver itself) butt-jointed and set in a sand setting bed atop a prepared aggregate base (Fig. 5.4.2). The wide variety of colors, sizes, textures, and patterns in which unit pavers can be placed make unit paving a popular way to show a designer's creativity, provided one guards against excess. Heavier loads require thicker unit pavers, so that road applications utilizing brick, concrete or granite pavers might use units anywhere from 3 to 8 in. thick.

The butt joint construction and sand-swept joints of flexible unit pavement makes flexible unit pavements pervious to water. *Porous paving* is an increasingly

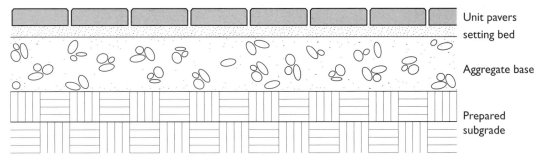

Unit pavers
setting bed

Aggregate base

Prepared
subgrade

Figure 5.4.3. *Flexible unit paving.*

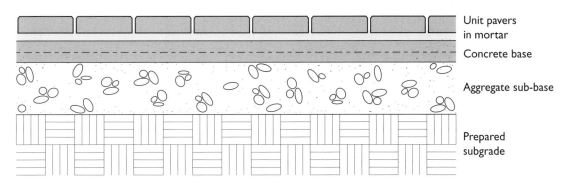

Unit pavers
in mortar

Concrete base

Aggregate sub-base

Prepared
subgrade

Figure 5.4.4. *Rigid unit paving.*

important subclass of flexible paving designed to be even more permeable to storm water, and includes simple aggregate pavement such as stone dust or graded aggregate/fine mixtures that can be compacted into firm surfaces. Plant and polymer binders are now being added to these mixtures to make them more durable in public spaces. Other porous pavings include extremely coarse aggregate asphalt surfaces and specially shaped, gridded pavers, designed to be interspersed with gravel or turf. However, the efficacy of these different pavers varies widely based on different climatic zones, so it's wise to find and follow local methods in constructing porous pavings.

Rigid monolithic pavement usually means reinforced concrete pavement, cast in place atop aggregate base (Fig. 5.4.3). Rigid concrete pavement, in contrast to flexible pavements, generally require a somewhat thinner aggregate base layer, at least in warmer climates, because it distributes loads more evenly; aggregate base here serves to provide a uniform and level subgrade. To allow its rigid nature to accommodate freeze–thaw cycle movement, concrete pavement is constructed with expansion joints (polymer-sealed and felt or Styrofoam-filled gaps between pours) approximately every 25 ft. Control joints (scored cuts in the pavement surface) are also used every 5–10 ft, depending on aesthetics and local construction practices, to prevent random cracking of the concrete pavement surfaces. *Rigid unit pavement* is simply individual stone, brick, or cast concrete paving units glued or mortared to a reinforced concrete base (Fig. 5.4.4). Rigid unit pavement sometimes provides a more manicured or 'finished' appearance than dry-laid flexible unit paving, and allows the use of larger, and thinner, almost veneer-like paving units, and is often used in urban plaza settings.

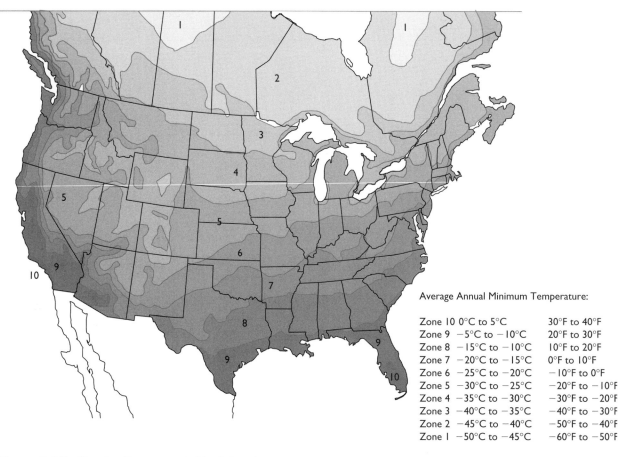

Average Annual Minimum Temperature:

Zone 10 0°C to 5°C	30°F to 40°F
Zone 9 −5°C to −10°C	20°F to 30°F
Zone 8 −15°C to −10°C	10°F to 20°F
Zone 7 −20°C to −15°C	0°F to 10°F
Zone 6 −25°C to −20°C	−10°F to 0°F
Zone 5 −30°C to −25°C	−20°F to −10°F
Zone 4 −35°C to −30°C	−30°F to −20°F
Zone 3 −40°C to −35°C	−40°F to −30°F
Zone 2 −45°C to −40°C	−50°F to −40°F
Zone 1 −50°C to −45°C	−60°F to −50°F

Figure 5.4.5. *Plant hardiness zones in North America.*

Landscape/plants and planting

In contrast to pavement, planted surfaces or 'natural' landscape can provide major benefits in exterior spaces, including, but not limited to, seasonal changes of color, form and texture; microclimate modification; and, as noted earlier, an increased ability to manage stormwater run-off on site. Planting strategies range from simple plantings of turf or groundcover to more extensive designs such as groves, perennial borders, or rain gardens. Unlike paving, plants are living things, and as such have key requirements for their survival. These include an adequate healthy soil (non-compacted, pH-neutral, rich in organic material); sun (a *minimum* of 4 h/day for shade tolerant species) and adequate water. In other words, plants cannot be planted right next to buildings, under building overhangs, in narrow courtyards that only receive light at high noon, and other inhospitable places.

In addition, it is important to choose plants that are suited for your site's climate, usually described as the site's USDA Hardiness Zone (Fig. 5.4.5). Using plants that are native to your site is also often a good idea, because these plants are adapted to local seasonal extremes and soil types, support local wildlife, and express the regional character of the building site. Native plants are best obtained from local nurseries and seed suppliers, to ensure the plants are truly indigenous to the area. Invasive, non-native species should be avoided at all costs.

Since Le Corbusier, expanses of green turf have often been used as a foil for hard-edged contemporary building styles, or as a stand-in for 'nature' in urban

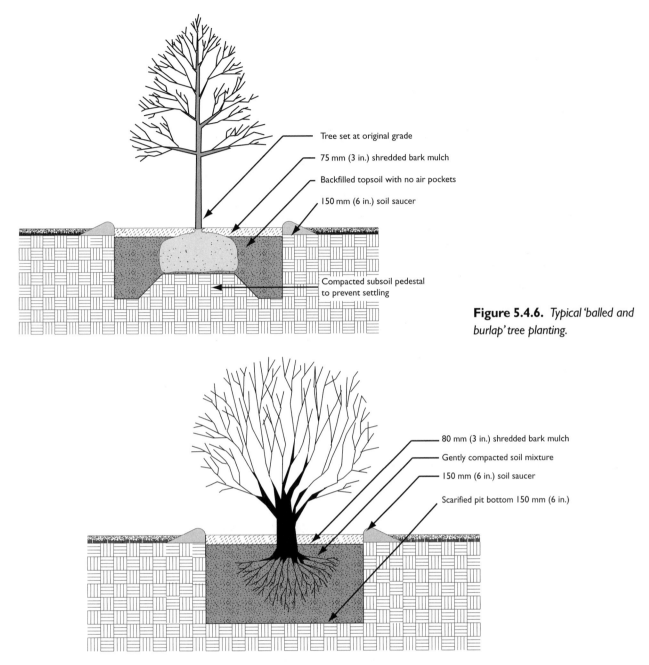

Tree set at original grade

75 mm (3 in.) shredded bark mulch

Backfilled topsoil with no air pockets

150 mm (6 in.) soil saucer

Compacted subsoil pedestal to prevent settling

Figure 5.4.6. *Typical 'balled and burlap' tree planting.*

80 mm (3 in.) shredded bark mulch

Gently compacted soil mixture

150 mm (6 in.) soil saucer

Scarified pit bottom 150 mm (6 in.)

Figure 5.4.7. *Typical bare root shrub planting.*

settings. As a result, today *lawn* is often a 'default' landscape condition. Lawns are most commonly created by sodding or, more economically and conveniently in larger areas or on steep slopes, by seeding. Lawn is a poor choice, however, for high-traffic areas; and in low maintenance situations, since it requires high inputs of mowing, irrigation, and herbicide and fertilizer to maintain a sufficiently lush appearance.

However, lawn alternatives do exist, especially for no traffic areas or for foundation plantings. The most common alternatives are a variety of *groundcovers*, which include low-growing plants and vines, such as English ivy (*Hedera helix*), periwinkle (*Vinca minor*); native prairie grasses; and prostrate shrubs such as

Table 5.4.2 Typical landscape materials.

Landscape surface	Advantages	Disadvantages
Concrete	Easily installed, common material Relatively inexpensive Multiple finishes, textures, colors Long lasting Hard, non-resilient surface Adaptable to curvilinear forms	Requires joints Can be ugly Difficult to color consistently Cracks easily
Asphalt	Easily installed, common material Relatively inexpensive Durable, low maintenance Adaptable to curvilinear forms Can be made porous Good for bike/walking paths	Edges will disintegrate if unsupported Can be ugly Can soften in warm weather Soluble by petroleum-based liquids
Brick pavers	Non-glare, non-skid surface Wide color range Good scale Easily repaired if dry laid	Higher installation cost Susceptible to settlement if dry laid Susceptible to spalling
Concrete pavers	Multiple types, sizes, forms available Wide color range Easily repaired if dry laid	Higher installation cost Susceptible to settlement if dry laid
Granite pavers	Hard and dense Very durable and permanent, supports heavy traffic Variety of color, finishes available	Hardness makes it difficult to work with Relatively expensive
Compacted aggregate	Relatively inexpensive/economical Local sources of aggregate help circulation routes blend into larger environment	Requires replenishment every few years Requires edging to hold material
Turfgrass/lawn	Easily installed, common material Relatively inexpensive, especially if seeded Well drained; pervious	Does not hold up under high traffic Not drought or heat tolerant Expensive to maintain and irrigate
Organic mulch	Relatively inexpensive Quiet, cushioned walking or playing surface Compatible with natural surroundings	Does not hold up under high traffic Not permanent; degrades, requiring annual or bi-annual replenishment
Turf blocks/gridded pavers	Similar to turf, but can withstand light vehicular traffic	Requires higher maintenance Less viable in northern climates

juniper (*Juniperus* spp.) or fragrant sumac (*Rhus aromatica*). Groundcovers can be good choices on steeper slopes or where less maintenance over time is required or desired. The spacing of groundcover plants must be carefully worked out to both minimize the time to full area coverage and to avoid bare spots, and a mulch of shredded bark, wood chips, or compost over a weed barrier should be installed under plants to prevent weed growth until plants are well established and reach mature, ground-covering size. Mulch also provides other benefits for plants such as conserving soil moisture and moderating temperature.

Table 5.4.3 Typical landscape plant materials.

Landscape surface	Advantages	Disadvantages
Container trees	Establish quickly Healthier over time	Take years to mature Roots can circle if contained too long
Balled and burlapped trees	Roots won't 'circle' Hardier	Roots may be damaged by digging out Can be slow to recover from transplanting
Bare-root shrubs	Less expensive Establish faster than container plants; better long-term health	Sensitive to seasonal planting Flowers and leafs not apparent at planting
Container shrubs	Verifiable leaf and plant color Wider variety available Can be planted year-round	May be root-bound More expensive
Contained groundcover	Good for large areas Sturdier at planting	Bare patches must be avoided by careful design Slow to fill in
Flats	Economical, quick to plant	Small root balls may dry quickly
Seeds	Cheapest Can be grown locally, thus adapted to local conditions Random patterns easily achievable	Pattern can be hard to control Long growing period
Hydroseeding	Large areas easy to plant Can be used on difficult slopes	Choice of seed may be limited Unattractive initially due to des
Sod	Instant groundcover Even coverage	Must be installed quickly after delivery Can't be used on steep slopes or large areas

Plants needn't just serve as surface treatments; *trees* and *shrubs* can be used architecturally to create spatial enclosure or separation; to provide shade for building facades or exterior spaces; to control circulation; and to provide visual screening. In other words, plants can be used spatially just as architectural materials can be – and often their purchase and installation costs are less than that for other built materials. Trees and shrubs are available from nurseries as dormant bareroot stock; in containers as young, growing plants; and when more mature and larger, as balled and burlapped plants. These three conditions require slightly different planting techniques as seen in Figures 5.4.6 and 5.4.7. Proper installation is important to plant survival and thriftiness. Key factors to consider are plant spacing, to allow for full growth, especially for specimen trees and digging adequately sized holes or trenches in appropriate, amended soils.

Decision-making

The designer's choice of exterior landscape materials is far more varied than the ubiquity of concrete, asphalt, and lawn would imply. While these three exterior materials are easily installed and relatively inexpensive, other materials – especially local stone and native plants – may, in fact, be less expensive and more visually interesting. And, of course, when dealing with plants, but also when dealing with pavement materials, climatic regions also influence a material's advantages and disadvantages. Some of these are summarized in Table 5.4.2 and 5.4.3.

Glossary and formulas

Aggregate base	Gravel or coarse rock placed between subgrade and pavement.
Flexible pavements	Pavements that can move, expand, and contract without damage or cracking.
Flexible unit pavements	Bricks, stones, or concrete units set atop a sand setting bed and aggregate base.
Groundcovers	Lawn alternatives that offer leafy or flowering plants covering a broad area.
Lawn	Grass surface created by sodding or seeding.
Monolithic flexible pavements	Extruded pavement designed to accept minor movements.
Porous paving	Paving that allows water (stormwater in particular) to percolate through to the soil below.
Rigid monolithic pavement	Solid hard surface, usually reinforced concrete, atop an aggregate base.
Rigid unit pavement	Individual bricks, stones, or concrete units glued or mortared to a reinforced concrete base.
Subgrade	Soil beneath pavement.
Wear layer	A light duty pavement of pavers simply set in sand.

Further reading

Harris, C.W. and Dines, N.T. eds. (1988) *Time-Saver Standards for Landscape Architecture: Design and Construction Data* (New York: McGraw-Hill).

Simonds, J.O. (1983) *Landscape Architecture: A Manual of Site Planning and Design* (New York: McGraw-Hill).

Walker, T.D. (1992) *Site Design and Construction Detailing* (New York: Van Nostrand Reinhold).

5.5 Detailing

<table>
<tr><td colspan="2">Introduction</td></tr>
<tr><td>Six Principles</td><td>Fit
Organization
Consistency
Robustness
Durability
Finish</td></tr>
<tr><td>Balancing</td><td>Economics and quality</td></tr>
<tr><td>Conclusion</td><td>Five classic details and why they're worth studying</td></tr>
</table>

Introduction

When designing buildings architects are faced with a vast myriad of component choices. While most of the buildings architects deal with are custom, they are largely assembled of mass produced, pre-manufactured pieces. This is necessary in order to maintain both a consistency of performance and to keep costs under control, however it can lead to a frustrating lack of choices when alternatives to the standards are desired. Further, it can create a bland similarity between buildings that use the same kit of parts for every situation. One of the first tasks for any designer is to learn the wide range of standards that are offered for building assembly; this takes years to begin and really never ends as new products are constantly introduced. Once the range of commercially produced options are known then it can be determined when something custom is desired. The process of custom design requires an understanding of the means of production and the materials available. This is time consuming, but is the only way to produce results that extend beyond the range of mass produced choices for building materials.

To some extent, nearly every architect-led design ends up being customized to some degree, and it is in this realm – in how we *render our designs in real materials* – that really good architects separate themselves from the pack. The jobsite and the world of users are our buildings' toughest hurdles. As designers, the more we understand how buildings are manufactured, put together, and then used and perceived, the more convincing our designs will often be. Most architects have the experience of traveling to see a recent building that's been in the magazines only to be sorely disappointed. Good photography can hide a multitude of sins, but buildings that stand up to experience are, we think, the real test. Our attention to how things are fabricated, put together, and perceived really comes home in two areas – *detailing*, or the art of figuring out how best to assemble building components for a visual and serviceable result, and *custom fabrication*, or knowing what tools and materials we have to hand to solve spatial, visual, and functional issues that aren't covered by typically available building components. We'll cover fabrication in the next chapter, but *detailing* itself is one of the great traditions and crafts of the profession, and deserves its own discussion first.

Detailing

Perhaps no one is more famous for their building details than Mies van der Rohe. But it's instructive to note that his famous quote – 'God is in the details' – was actually borrowed from an old American Puritan saying – 'The Devil is in the details'. Both of these views are, in our view, absolutely true, in that the best and worst architectural experiences often occur at the level of tactility, where we recognize how parts come together, how they're finished, how our hands, feet, or eyes are invited to rest on them. If the architect has gotten it right, if he or she has understood fully the peculiarities of the material, how it will be put in place on the jobsite, how it will weather, settle, move, shrink, expand, etc., over time, the detail stands a chance of being a rich, expressive experience. If, however, the detail is less than well thought through, a misalignment or imperfect placement during construction – or an unanticipated movement or deterioration over time – may stick out and inflect people's perception of the building's durability. Humans are instinctively judgmental about structures and shelter, and the less we play to this sensibility the less aesthetically satisfying our buildings will be.

Principles

When we sit down with a blank sheet of trace and begin thinking about how components of a building will come together, there are six basic considerations we should have to ensure that the detail will perform well, be reasonably efficient to construct, and maintain its appearance. In no particular order, these include *fit*, *organization*, *consistency*, *robustness*, *durability*, and *finish*.

To begin with, it is important to recognize the role of tolerance and *fit* on the job site (Fig. 5.5.1). Precision is easy to achieve in an office, less so in the controlled chaos of construction. The straight lines we draw have to be put in place by machinery and human hands, often under intense schedule pressure and in hazardous conditions. Some of the materials we work with – concrete in particular – are sloppy and even crude, while others – aluminum or glass – come from fabrication shops or factories with much more control. Any material will have generally recognized *tolerances* that tell us how accurately we can expect it to be placed on the job site. These tolerances come in two forms – locational and dimensional. Location tolerances are often based on the type of structure or subframe being used, and recognize that some degree of inaccuracy in construction is inevitable. Dimensional tolerances tell us how accurately made we can expect a material to be – how close a component will come to the drawings, essentially. Materials may sag, for example, while in transit, or may shrink while curing. The more we're aware of these, the more we can design around them. Concrete, for example, has notoriously low tolerances due to its liquid nature and the difficulty of placing heavy formwork accurately.

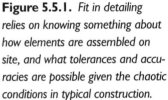

Figure 5.5.1. *Fit in detailing relies on knowing something about how elements are assembled on site, and what tolerances and accuracies are possible given the chaotic conditions in typical construction.*

Trying to rely on a precise location or surface in a concrete element, therefore, isn't wise. Instead, we typically design connections to concrete with plenty of adjustability, so that even if the concrete isn't quite where we expect it, there will be ways for contractors to correct the error later on, by *shimming* elements to their proper elevation or by adjusting bolts in slotted connections. In aluminum, or steel, however, we can design to a fairly tight tolerance and expect the final product to be much closer in location and dimension to what we've assumed. If we're after a precise aesthetic in a concrete building, we may not express the concrete itself, for example. It will be easier to attach steel or aluminum edges, for instance, at any exposed slab edge to give the floor a reliably true 'line' in the elevation. At the same time, there is inherent drama in the play of a slightly funky concrete structure against the precision of metal, and we may want to expose the imperfect concrete and set it against the more accurate systems. In this case, we want to make sure that we leave enough space between the two materials to prevent a wild inaccuracy in the concrete from affecting the trueness of the metal.

This brings up the second key consideration; any exercise in detailing is essentially about *organization* (Fig. 5.5.2). Tolerance and fit are an important element in this, but overall every detail we do is the result of absorbing and organizing information about finishes, supports, fixings, and assembly processes. A logical detail will almost always be a visually appealing one, since it will give the impression that the building has been carefully put together. This can also be thought of as bolstering the craft of the construction site with the craft of the drafting

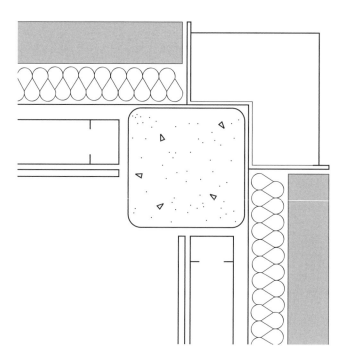

Figure 5.5.2. *A properly organized detail allows plenty of room for materials, fixings, and tools during assembly.*

table. How can we think through the assembly process to give everything enough room, not only in the finished detail, but also as it is being put together? One way to do this is to think through each component, often working from the building structure out, considering each element and understanding how much space it will need to be cleanly placed and attached. We typically run into trouble when we try to do too much in too small a space – when we forget about the width of door frames, for example, or about the extension of a stair's handrail, or the clearance needed for a worker's wrench to tighten a bolt. When we have multiple materials, or multiple systems, a classic drafting aphorism is to give each piece its own space, to separate pieces that do different things, and to remember that what we're drawing has to get built by machines or human hands. Drawing is actually a good tool for thinking this way – if we find it difficult to clearly draw through a detail, it's probably complex enough to be trouble in the field. Accept that good details take a bit of space, figure out where that space can be had, and let the detail be what it needs to be. Think logically, get all the information on each piece, and draw through them sequentially, considering what the actual processes for fixing each component will be.

Consistency is something often taken for granted – when we draw a curtain wall, for instance, we often just assume that each panel will have the same color, or the same finish. Many building products, however, will vary in ways that can be visually jarring (Fig. 5.5.3). Sometimes this is obvious; wood or marble, for example, have natural grains in them that are both unpredictable and part of the material's aesthetic appeal. Other materials have consistency issues that we might easily forget. Concrete is notoriously fickle, as its color and texture can change dramatically with small variations in temperature and humidity. Over a 21-day curing period, we absolutely can't know how a rainy day, a cold night, or a dry spell will affect the color of the pour. Even material that we use *because* of its consistency can be problematic – anodized aluminum can vary in color enough from the start of one dip to the end to be noticeable. There are two

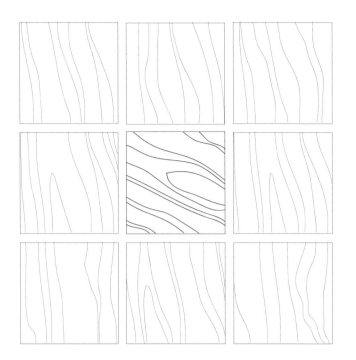

Figure 5.5.3. *Consistency is an important aspect of materials selection and placement. Woods, stones, and other natural materials present fairly obvious issues of color and grain matching, but materials such as concrete and even aluminum must be selected carefully for finish, color, and texture to ensure that no piece 'sticks out' from its cohorts.*

approaches to dealing with this. One is to fight the nature of all materials to have some variation in their appearance or color, and to write tight specifications – often at a fiscal and environmental cost of rejecting material solely on a visual basis. A more productive method is to recognize that, like tolerance, variation in material is a given. Building in time during construction, for example, to shuffle stone tiling so that differently colored batches are intermixed (called 'quilting') will spread the variation out, rather than turning it into a visible line in the floor. Likewise, understanding the veining patterns of stone or wood paneling leads us to think carefully about how we lay out an elevation – we can book match or randomly intermix rather than risking the unintentional patterning effects of a purely sequential layout.

Nothing gives away the illusion of a carefully crafted, solid building more than a detail that appears 'flimsy' (Fig. 5.5.4). Robust detailing involves thinking structurally at a small scale, ensuring that elements are securely fastened to the building or to a subframe and that they themselves are sturdy enough to resist the inevitable bumps that will occur during construction and during the life of the building. Secure fastening involves finding a 'path' for each piece of the detail that can take gravity and lateral loads – rarely on the scales we've discussed in Chapter 4, but just as important. Fastening only one end of a panel, for example, creates a small-scale cantilever, with the relatively large bending moment at the root just as if it were a large beam. We can expect the panel, over its lifetime, to twist out of plumb over time if its subjected to large enough loads. Often, the inclusion of an intermediate structure of light-gauge steel or wood will trade off some space in section for the security of

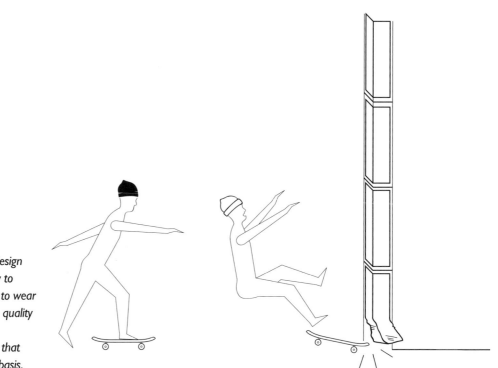

Figure 5.5.4. *Structural design on a small scale is necessary to ensure that details stand up to wear and tear – 'robustness' is the quality of a well-engineered set of connection and components that can resist impact on a daily basis.*

widely available, reliable fixing points. Likewise, components themselves need to be designed to take loads, often from unanticipated sources. We may need to reinforce them around connection points to avoid shear failure, for example, and we may need to think through how the material will behave under high-wind loading, or when a cart runs into it. Typical examples of this thinking include crimping or bending the edges of metal panels 90° to give their edges some rigidity, installing heavier duty plasterboard in areas likely to be impacted by traffic, including kick boards at wall bases to resist accidental shoe scuffs, and reinforcing corners with additional substructure or (better) metal guards.

This last suggestion touches on the durability of a detail or material – how will it hold up through weathering and/or constant use (Fig. 5.5.5)? While there's no such thing as a 'maintenance free' material or system, there are materials that can take everyday punishment without losing their integrity more easily than others. Stone, for example, if detailed to the right thickness and anchored correctly, can shed rain, constant human touch, intense sunlight, and freeze–thaw cycles. But it's an expensive material, particularly if detailed correctly. Cement stucco might be a much cheaper alternative, but this material may not perform as well over time – if it's penetrated by water, for example, it may lose its adhesion, and it won't resist impacts as well. Over the building's lifetime, the initial cost of stone may easily repay itself by maintaining its appearance. Some materials do need more frequent maintenance – concrete, for example, should be water sealed regularly, while exterior wood will need painting every 8–12 years. Weathering is also a consideration when detailing around materials. Concrete, for instance, can easily be stained if it's exposed to regular flows of water. Draining a roof by using scuppers through a pre-cast wall, therefore, needs to be done carefully, to ensure that the

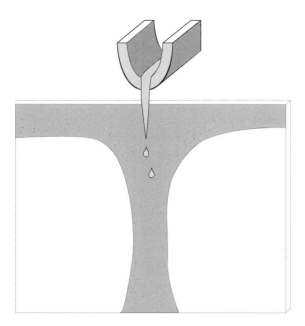

Figure 5.5.5. *Durability has to do with the material itself – can it withstand scratching, puncturing, and bending? Often we'll specify different materials for different levels of wear – higher grade drywall, wood panels, or sheet metal where walls may get hit by carts or chairs, for example. Weathering is a particularly difficult issue, and the design of gutters, overflows, and scuppers can, if done poorly, set up materials for staining.*

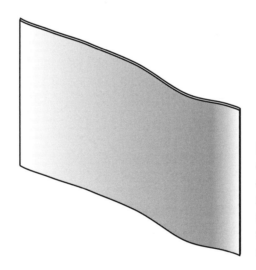

Figure 5.5.6. *Finishes can amplify or suppress issues in detailing. Reflective surfaces are notorious for highlighting poor fit or warped planes, while dark colors tend to hide less-than-ideal workmanship.*

water shoots well clear of the wall and isn't blown back by prevailing winds. Brick walls in contact with soil can wick water up into pores within the material, eventually leading to an integral water stain. Weathering can add to a building's appearance if handled correctly; oxidized copper, for instance, is invariably seen as a patina while oxidized steel is seen as 'rusty'. Knowing how well a material will hold up to the site's climate and its uses is important to making good decisions.

Finally, there are aspects to a material's finish that are important to its perception (Fig. 5.5.6). Some materials by their appearance connote strength (concrete, no matter how thin), others appear honed or polished (stainless steel, for instance). The human eye interprets these in unforgiving ways – it tends to like a match between what it sees and how the mind behind it interprets how the building is held up. Shiny, polished materials can appear either refined or chintzy, depending on where and how they're used. Too much of one or the other can be visually boring or overstimulating. Likewise, both ends of the spectrum have their own unique issues. Coarser materials, because they tend to absorb or diffuse light, tend to flatten visually and can often benefit from relief or patterning. More honed materials, because they tend to reflect light, must be very carefully placed, as errors in positioning or orientation will be multiplied. Reflective glass walls, for example, can seem very flimsy if the reflections in them warp excessively, or don't match up from one pane to another. Worse, polished metal panels that 'oil can' or warp even slightly will appear highly distorted due to the variation in reflected light that results. Here in particular, a backup structure that allows for precise placement and offers robust support can reduce the problem. In general, bright or light finishes tend to amplify the quality of design and assembly – if either of these are questionable for reasons of cost or skill, a less reflective or darker palette is often advisable.

Balancing

All of the above principles seem obvious – all of our details ought to be the robust, well fit, visually appropriate and durable details that are the hallmark of some of the most enduring buildings we study. Why, then, is shoddy detailing so prevalent?

The answer is, of course, that cost and time often mitigate against the perfect detail, and that the tradeoff for a building that's on time and on budget is often a compromise or the pressure-driven abandonment of one or more of these principles. Often this will be a straightforward zero-sum game – stone panels, for instance, are more robust, durable and (arguably) visually engaging than cement stucco. But they cost a great deal more per unit of area, and they take more time to quarry, erect, and affix. Likewise, there is almost a one-to-one ratio between the time available to set concrete and its formwork and the quality of the finished product. No project has an infinite time frame or (unfortunately) an infinite budget, and one of the profession's really valuable skills is the wisdom to know what can be re-designed, cut, refined or changed to achieve savings in cost or schedule while minimizing the impact to the building's durability or its aesthetics. Ethically, we also need to balance the long-term health of the building with short-term desires for something visually striking or, from our client's point of view, constructionally expedient.

As with many other aspects of design, some of this wisdom comes from a fluency in materials and methods – knowing how parts will be put together, how they will interact, and what their physical properties will allow. What we don't know we can often glean from contractors or subcontractors, who will often have an incentive to find solutions that will save them and their clients time and money without impacting the project's quality. Often, meetings in the midst of a budget crisis will produce some of the job's most innovative solutions, despite their inherent stress. It's also true that this pressure can, in fact, produce better solutions than those we might come up with otherwise;

Figures 5.5.7 and 5.5.8 *Mies van der Rohe's Farnsworth House in Plano, IL, is a minimalist pair of planes with living spaces perched tenuously between. To emphasize the crisp, tight spatial concept, connections between steel columns and beams were welded and ground, so that no bolts or connections are visible. Steel window frames were set just inside the structural frame, offering a very subtle – almost unnoticeable – hierarchy.*

details that are refined under this pressure may well be cleaner, simpler, and less fussy than those drawn through only once.

The balance we usually seek in detailing is between economics (including cost and fabrication/construction time), performance (including functionality and durability), and aesthetics (how it looks on day one, and through the service life

Figure 5.5.9. *In contrast to Mies' Farnsworth House, Louis Kahn's Kimbell Art Museum in ort Worth, TX, adopted an intensive program of expression, with pour lines in concrete detailed to show just how its pours were sequences. Aluminum and travertine finishes were attached with reveals and shadow lines to show that they were clearly assembled after the concrete frame.*

Figure 5.5.10. *Renzo Piano's Menil Museum in Houston, TX, fit simple wood siding into a steel frame, allowing it to relate to the clapboard houses in its neighborhood. The boards are aligned with the front of the column's flanges, so that the beam's indentation creates a reveal, or break, in the wall. Elements of the roof form overhead show the building's internal rhythm.*

Figure 5.5.11. *Detail can be structurally expressive. Here, Peter Berhrens AEG Turbinfabrik in Berlin (1909) used steel 'knuckles' to allow the frame above to move without disrupting the foundations. Behrens obviously recognized the chance to put this structural principle on display, attaching the knuckle to a bench-like base and slipping the factory windows behind the steel frame.*

of the building). Often, clients will need to be reminded that this last element is important, though the pressure of cost occasionally makes it an attractive target.

Conclusion

Good detailing is the result of experience, logical, disciplined thought, and a firm grasp of the physics involved in joining materials together. Most architects only develop a really good detail sense after a few projects, and in this sense detailing is very much like a language – vocabulary is good and relatively easy to learn, but fluency can only happen with repetition and practice. A fully educated architect is one who has taken the time to look at buildings with a mental microscope in addition to a wide-angled lens, and who has developed a sense of how the particulars of a building's assembly can have a dialogue with the generalities of form, rhythm, and style. Keeping in mind the six principles listed above – *fit, organization, consistency, robustness, durability,* and *finish* – is a good start toward developing a sense of how things go together best. Historically, details have

Figure 5.5.12. *Corbusier's Swiss Pavilion at the Cite Universitaire in Paris blends glass, concrete, stone, and metal into a rich pattern that has both regularity and variety. The cladding is set just outboard of the solid wall, again telling us something about how the building was assembled and how it works. The end wall is plain, but it isn't inarticulate – the pattern of stonework describes the building section by revealing the floor locations. Finally, while the building could have been held up by a simple pier, the curvilinear shape at the base actually tells us – subtly – about the building's lateral stability, with two 'flanges' at the outer edges in the short (therefore weaker) direction of the building above.*

played a large role in expressing the aesthetic, functional, structural, and constructional 'stories' of architecture (Figs. 5.5.7–5.5.12).

Further reading

Ford, E.R. (1990 & 1996) *The Details of Modern Architecture* (Cambridge: MIT Press).

5.6 Custom fabrication

Component Design	Construction – standard vs. custom
	Innovation
	Responsibility
Production	Extrusions
	Metal castings
	Sheet metal forming
	Composites
	Glass
Prototypes and Testing	Research design and development
	Performance and aesthetic criteria
	Types of testing
	Virtual and real prototyping

Component design

Standardization in the construction industry has by and large been a good thing. It's possible to build buildings more efficiently, to have them operate more predictably, and to repair and maintain them more systematically as the industry has streamlined and coordinated its offerings. Much of our work today involves specification rather than design – selecting products and components with reliable sizes, interfaces, and performance and handing over at least some part of our building's appearance and operation to a well-cataloged, standard product.

There are times, however, when what's available on the shelf won't do, when there's a unique problem to solve, or when we just aren't satisfied with the standard offerings. In those instances, when we go off the chart and out of the catalog, architectural design can be its most rewarding – and its most difficult. When we find ourselves having to come up with custom details, or to design custom components, we no longer have the safety of a manufacturers testing or warranty behind us. Instead we have to rely on what we know about materials, about fabrication methods, and about the end use of the element. We're more exposed to liability here, but we're also able – if we know what we're doing – to really innovate and to solve problems in ways that are both creative and collaborative. There are also opportunities in custom component design to learn first hand how things are really made, always a valuable experience.

Often, the process of custom design will start with an existing product or system that, for whatever reason, doesn't meet the needs at hand. We may be able to work with a supplier or fabricator to make subtle alterations – at a cost – to existing products that will bring them in line with what our needs are. Some manufacturers are more open to this process than others; there are liabilities involved with any variation of a product that hasn't been thoroughly tested, and changing dimensions or components may not work with the way a factory line is set up. Still, there are manufacturers who appreciate the push that such projects provide, and many will be willing to at least meet to discuss what can be done if there's a large enough sale to be made (sometimes the results will improve the product's appeal – if one project needs a particular modification there may be similar opportunities for the manufacturer elsewhere). In these cases, setting up a worksession with a company's product engineers, designers, or factory foremen can be a valuable way forward in finding out what would be involved with a 'semi-custom' component. Often this is surprisingly easy; aluminum extrusion, for example, can be done to order with a custom extrusion using a unique die. Since the process chews up dies rapidly, the cost of a custom section can be easily amortized over the size of the project – in a large enough job, the extruder might go through a steel die anyway. In this case, the only excess costs involved are the design and tooling of the custom die.

In other instances, there won't be a product anything like the component we need, and we may need to look at custom designing a building element from scratch. This is more risky territory, as we won't necessarily have to hand the experience of a manufacturer that comes with 'tweaking' an existing product. We may try to find a company that produces components made from a similar material – a steel fabricator, for instance, if we think the component might be best made from that – or that produces something with a similar function – a laboratory furniture manufacture, perhaps, if we're designing a security station. In any case, it's advisable to agree on a fairly detailed program with the client, and to find expertise in fabrication, installation, and performance.

Production

We've discussed typical building materials in Chapter 3, but it is worth summarizing a handful of production processes that we often rely on when designing custom components (Figs. 5.6.1–5.6.4). These are drawn from Michael Stacey's 2001 book *Component Design*, which is highly recommended as a more thorough introduction to the possibilities inherent in designing building elements from first principles.

All building materials are either *cast*, *rolled*, *extruded*, *sawn*, or *carved*. At its most basic, component design includes working with a carpenter to design a simple set of cuts and joints in wood to build a cabinet, for example, or a door. At this level, all the aspects of component design are present, but in a relatively low-risk environment – we have a 'program' for the component (to hold plates, for example, or to open and close), we have a material with definitive properties and fabricational tendencies (wood is relatively weak but easy to carve, and it is readily available in both linear and planar forms), and we have expertise to hand in the carpenter, who can help guide us to a solution that balances what we want to achieve with what's possible to do in wood. We may, for instance, ask for advice in terms of cabinet door thickness, or

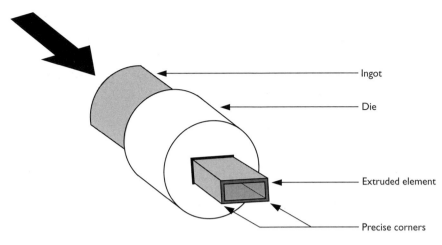

Ingot

Die

Extruded element

Precise corners

Figure 5.6.1. *Extrusion processes produce constant sections, with sharp corners and very smooth surfaces.*

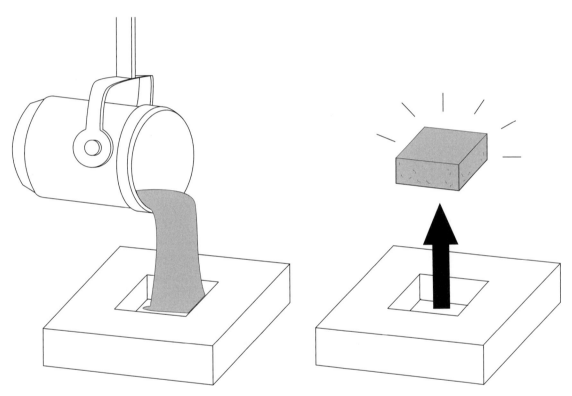

Figure 5.6.2. *Casting produces three-dimensional shapes, with options for smooth or rough surfaces depending on the molding process. It relies on mass production of similar objects for its economic viability.*

proper hinges, or how best to finish a door opening. A really good carpenter may offer more opportunities than a journeyman.

In much the same way, materials such as steel, aluminum, and fiberglass all have distinct properties and fabricational tendencies based on how they're made and where they come from.

Organic materials are either mined, quarried, or harvested. Hard materials such as stone and wood can be sawn to achieve planar or linear elements. Wood, additionally, can be laid up with resins to form strong plywood. Both stone and

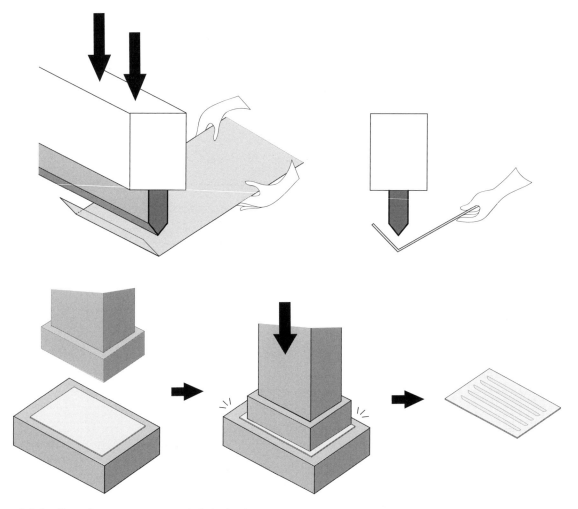

Figure 5.6.3. *Sheet forming processes include brake-shaping, which involves crimping edges of sheet or plate metal in a brake press. This is typically a hand process, but it may be supplemented by CNC cutting of the metal elements. Stamping or pressing uses pressure to impress a pattern into a sheet. This can be used to give the resulting component additional rigidity and/or texture.*

wood are subject to variations in color and pattern, which can be visually rich or distracting depending on how they're anticipated. Both can be hand carved or sawn to achieve very fine tolerances and details. Wood, because it's softer, can be more easily worked by hand and it is thus an excellent material for ornamentation and small-scale structure – house framing, for example, is a uniquely suited use of wood's linear production processes and its ease of cutting and jointing. Both wood and stone are limited in size by the scale of cutting operations, and must therefore be assembled in panels for planar applications.

Some organic materials – in particular concrete and clay – can be *cast* or *molded* after their extraction. Both processes involve making a negative *form* into which the material can be pressed or poured and allowed to cure or dry. This can be a time consuming process, but if forms can be mass produced it can be a very economical one. Cost savings occur through production efficiency, and therefore these materials benefit from repetition. Terra cotta ornamentation in the early 1900s, for example, produced building skins that were highly repetitive, using a few patterns many times. Many architects

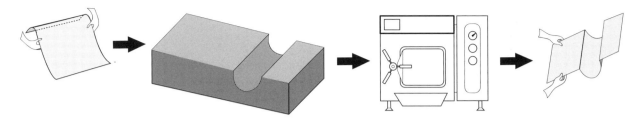

Figure 5.6.4. *Composite materials are laid up as sheets of fabric over a mold or jig. Baking in an autoclave allows resins – either impregnated in the fabric or added – to hold fabric fibres in a stiff matrix. This is a labor-intensive process, but it can produce components of remarkable strength and accuracy.*

(notably Daniel Burnham in Chicago) were able to exploit these properties to create highly unified, rhythmic building facades that were relatively economical because of their repetitive nature. Concrete offers particular opportunities and problems, as noted in Section 3.5.

Metals offer the most flexibility in terms of forming and shaping. Depending on their resistance to deformation, aluminum and steel alloys can be *rolled* into standard shapes, *extruded* through dies into standard or custom sections, *bent* or *brake shaped* into forms based on sheets or plates, or *cast* using heat and molds into custom forms. Rolling is limited, because of the tooling involved, to standard shapes, but extrusion offers almost unlimited possibilities because of the relatively low cost of producing dies. While the initial cost for tooling is substantial (between US$10,000 and US$20,000 for a custom die), in a large job this is essentially amortized over the total linear feet produced, which may make it quite affordable. Dies are usually limited to 36 cm (14 in.) in diameter, and the section must allow for smooth, regular 'flow' of the metal through the die. But the result can be a very precise section custom designed to meet the particular needs of the project. Bending (and stretch forming) take metal sheet or plate and induce permanent (i.e. plastic) deformation around a shaped billet. This is an efficient process for curved plates or sheets. Steel tubes or structural sections may be bent using machinery that induces deformation around a mold, or by heating small sections of the steel and drawing the element along a gently radiused track. Brake shaping uses a hydraulic or mechanical press with a long blade to force a bend into a metal sheet or plate. This is convenient for shallow box sections or lightweight framing. Sheets may be *stamped* using a positive mold, or they may be formed into molds by air pressure or vacuum, all of which can permanently deform patterns into the flat material. Finally, by melting metal and pouring it into robust, heat-proof molds, it can be cast into a permanent three-dimensional form. This can be time and labor intensive, but if the mold can survive multiple castings, or if molds can be mass produced, casting can be reasonably affordable.

Another cast material is glass. While glass can be custom cast, the expense of re-tooling usually leaves us with standard sheets and blocks with which to design. Glass can be custom fabricated primarily by cutting or by layering additional material such as ceramic frit. But plate glass can also be bent to very precise tolerances in bending ovens, where the glass is slowly heated to near its melting point and allowed to gradually drape over a heat-proof mold. This is limited by the size of heating ovens to about 4 m (12 ft) in any direction.

Other materials offer more generous fabrication possibilities. In particular, composites such as fibreglass or carbon fibre are generally laid up by arranging sheets of the fibrous material over one another in a resin matrix. This can be done over a mold of considerably complexity, allowing very detailed and geometrically complicated shapes. Following layup, the element is cured, typically with heat, and the result is a piece that is rigid, lightweight, and dimensionally stable. Composites are particularly useful for their structural properties, as the sheets of fibre can be laid up directionally. Areas of particular stress can receive additional layers of fibre fabric, or the direction of the fabric can be tuned to the directions of anticipated structural loading, making the final pieces uniquely tuned to their load-bearing task. Composites remain expensive, as they are labor intensive and difficult to mass produce without complex tooling. Material costs for carbon fiber have priced that material out of most architectural applications, but continued efficiencies in production promise lower costs in the future.

Recent developments in CAD/CAM production have significantly changed the parameters involved in mass producing building components. While mass production has historically encouraged elements with dimensional consistency, due to the fixed nature of tooling, dies, and forms, the introduction of computer-driven cutters and routers has allowed much greater freedom in mass production. Plasma or arc cutters, for instance, can be programmed to not only cut a variety of shapes from a metal plate; they can also be programmed to figure out how to do this with minimal waste. Planar steel elements cut to a variety of shapes and dimensions, therefore, may be nearly as economical to produce as elements cut to a consistent pattern. Likewise, the ability of three-dimensional printers to quickly form individual prototypes of cornstarch or plastic has allowed mass production of differently shaped molds for metal castings, altering the economics of this process, which has historically been limited to producing identical copies from the same mold to achieve any measure of economy.

Prototyping, testing, and mock-ups

Depending on the complexity of the component that's being custom fabricated, we may need to go through a number of steps to design and test it that go well beyond the drawing board. Clients may be concerned about the functionality, appearance, or durability of the new piece, and as designers we'll want some assurance that the design we're contemplating will actually work in the situation we're designing for. Professional liability in this realm is also a concern – with standardized products and installations the manufacturer and contractor will bear most of the responsibility for the component, at least for a given warranty period. But in cases where we've designed something untried and untested, we bear a considerable responsibility for how it performs – and the component may well undergo more scrutiny than it would if it were a standard piece. Therefore, we'll often undergo a more rigorous program of research and testing for custom components.

This process usually begins with research and development. We may start with similar products, or with components that have parallel functions or manufacturing processes. Installers, fabricators and manufacturers may all serve as useful resources in laying out the new component's performance requirements, materials, and configuration. Brainstorming with engineers or designers who manufacture a similar product is often the most productive way of moving forward, and many companies will gladly take on such a project if it gives them an opportunity to expand their product line. This process will typically lead to a set of criteria for performance, cost, delivery, and aesthetics. As the design progresses, we'll often exchange information with a production team consisting of drawings, models, or CAD visualizations from the designers, and shop drawings from the manufacturer. Shop drawings show very clearly the intended dimensions, materials, and configuration of what the manufacturer understands they are to produce, and our role gradually shifts to reviewing these drawings and commenting on them.

For large or particularly critical components, designers will usually agree on a testing program to ensure that the final product appears, fits, and works as expected. The simplest tests involve *prototypes*, or single pieces that show clearly what the manufacturer intends to produce. Seeing a component in three dimensions often brings up important issues of appearance, fit, and texture that can't be deduced from drawings, no matter how detailed. Prototypes may be made of the intended materials, or they may be carved from foam or wood, depending on the expense and workability of the material involved (aluminum or steel castings, for instance, may need to be carved from wood first to make molds). A more involved test involves a *mock-up*, which is a full-scale installation of the component into its intended surroundings. This may occur on a portion of the building that has been completed, or it may require a separate construction. Issues here include appearance, fit, and texture, but also compatibility with surrounding components and systems. How a prefabricated panel attaches to a building frame, and how much it can be adjusted, for instance, is a typical mockup issue. Mockups may also test on-site procedures, such as forming and curing times for concrete. Most concrete installations will require a mockup panel that includes typical formwork details, textures, and colors. These panels are usually required on-site, ensuring that the subcontractor works within the conditions that will exist during the actual placement of the project's concrete.

More involved tests may be required to ensure that a component performs under unusual or stressful conditions. In particular, custom designs for fire-rated walls, doors, or windows may need to be tested to ensure that they will remain intact if exposed to the extreme heat of a building fire. In this case, a testing agency will be contracted to assemble a test rig, place the component or assembly in the rig, and expose it to a standard temperature for a given period of time – usually 1, 2, or 4h. If the element passes, the agency gives it a rating, and it can then be used to meet containment or integrity requirements of a building code. While expensive, these tests are valuable for manufacturers, as they provide new details that can be reliably specified in future projects; testing agencies keep and publish libraries of fire tests in particular that can be specified or copied. Other outside testing may include service-ability tests, in which a mechanical component may be actuated thousands of times to simulate a lifetime's use, water exclusion tests, in which cladding systems are subjected to torrents of wind-driven rain (often using aircraft engines to simulate hurricane forces), or structural tests, in which elements are loaded to an agreed upon multiple of their anticipated loading to check for deflection and integrity.

Developments in virtual simulation have made CAD modeling an important tool in assessing the appropriateness and performance of custom fabricated components and building elements. Structural design in particular can be very closely approximated for complex forms, and much of the required testing for static performance can be done digitally, saving the expense of multiple proto-types. Illumination, airflow, acoustics and heat transfer are among the other performance characteristics that can be reliably modeled in virtual environ-ments. However, for many of these codes and clients will still insist, with some justification, that a physical test be carried out as well to ensure performance in the complex environment of the job site and the finished building. Virtual models are, in the end, only as accurate as the information that goes into them, and are thus subject to the potential human error that comes from fail-ing to fully account for important – but perhaps not obvious – aspects of their surroundings. Where digital simulation has proven most useful in this phase is in construction integration, as three-dimensional files from architects, engin-eers, consultants and landscape architects can be 'overlaid' with one another and checked for conflicts – cabling running through structure, for example, or pipes that are larger than the wall specified for them are among the errors that can be 'caught' by current CAD programs. Rapid prototyping is another area where digital technology has made this phase quicker and more efficient, as laser cutters and three-dimensional printers can very rapidly produce complex shapes and forms that allow us to assess components' spatial attributes.

Conclusions

For a certain breed of architect, custom fabrication is the best part of the job. Working directly with people who know materials and processes intimately is both challenging and productive, and it can be an unbeatable opportunity to better educate yourself about the ways and means with which we build. In an era where specification has taken over much of our design time, there is a unique reward in being able to point to a finished building element and tell the whole story – from 'program' through design, fabrication, and installation. Likewise, digital tools that enable mass customization and extensive virtual testing have given us unprecedented opportunities to design elements that are uniquely suited to solving particular problems, and to get the design of these elements absolutely, incontrovertibly *correct*. Much of the work of leading con-temporary architects – including Norman Foster, Renzo Piano and Nicholas Grimshaw, and more formally radical designers such as Frank Gehry, SHoP, and Zaha Hadid – owe their unique designs to their willingness to go 'off track' and design key elements from scratch, rather than simply selecting them.

There are limits, however, to the effectiveness of custom design. It is invariably time consuming, because of the additional days or weeks needed for design and tooling. Likewise, in most cases custom components will incur additional costs in both design and fabrication. The risks involved in an element that doesn't work because of an unforeseen condition can also discourage such innovation. Like detailing, then, custom fabrication of building components is very often a matter of knowing when the added attention, care, and risk of invention is warranted, and when more expedient, 'off-the-shelf' solutions can be accepted or assimilated into a design.

Glossary and formulas

Brake forming (or shaping)	A process that forms permanent angles in sheet or plate by stressing the material past its elastic limit.
Casting	Material fabrication that involves pouring liquid into a mold and allowing it to either cool, dry, or cure into a solid. Typically used for concrete (curing), steel, glass, or iron (cooling).
Extrusion	Material fabrication that takes advantage of a material's ductility by pushing it through a die. Allows precise corners and details. Typically used for Aluminum, neoprene, and rubber, among others.
Mockup	A full scale assembly of a series of components or systems designed to test fit, appearance, and tolerance. Often done on the job site to ensure adequate modeling of conditions.
Plate	Thick gauge metal in planar form.
Prototype	A full scale model of a component, system, or junction designed to test the physical and material implications of its design.
Rolling	Material fabrication that takes place through the use of friction rollers. The material may be heated prior to rolling to increase its 'flow'. Typically used for steel.
Sheet	Narrow gauge metal in planar form.
Stretch-forming	A process that forms a permanent bend in metal by stressing the material past its elastic limit.

Further reading

Stacey, M. (2001) *Component Design* (Oxford, UK: Architectural Press).

CHAPTER **6**

Building Services

6.1 Environmental control: passive ventilation

Wind Movement	Exterior conditions
	Principles of air flow
	Pressure, eddies and direction
	General opening placement
	Air jets
Natural Air Flow in Buildings	Ventilation – health/comfort/ structure
	Stack effect principles
Passive Ventilation Systems	Bio-climatic chart review
	Cross ventilation
	Specific window opening locations & sizes
	Wind catchers
	Night cooled mass
	Mechanically assisted systems

Introduction to passive ventilation

Most decisions affecting the energy use of a building happen during schematic design. The basic form and siting of a building determines most of its efficiency potential and trying to make changes to overall shape or location late in project development is difficult or impossible. Therefore a basic understanding of how to work with the environment can affect the earliest stages of design, whiles other architectural issues are also being considered synthetically.

Passive ventilation is one of the areas of building design most affected by siting and building configuration. It is also one of the areas that can be most beneficial to reducing energy consumption.

The mechanics of wind flow are relatively easy to understand as are the way openings in buildings affect air movement and interior comfort. The rules of how to make buildings comfortable passively have been around since building began; there was simply no other choice until relatively recently. So why don't we always use these basic systems? The answer is odd – it's largely due to efficiency. When using mechanical cooling systems the goal is often to keep the building envelope as tightly sealed as possible to prevent inefficient losses of conditioned air. Once the sealed mechanical systems became the norm the passive systems became less important.

We now better understand the need to reduce our dependence on active building systems and the energy they require. We've also created problems due to sealing buildings too tightly, recycling bad air and trapping harmful air-borne illnesses. Passive ventilation systems are increasingly being used in lieu of or as hybrids with mechanical systems to create more efficient and healthful environments.

Wind movement

Exterior Conditions such as vegetation, adjacent buildings, and landforms can greatly affect wind direction and speed. Most prevailing wind direction and speed information comes from airport locations, which may not accurately represent your local site conditions. Look at the land to analyze this like you would the other basic site conditions.

The difficulty in determining how to place openings is deciding where the wind will be coming from and how fast it will be traveling when you want to use it. This is affected by everything from how you landscape the site to what buildings may be constructed around your project in the future – so you must be able to reasonably assess how your site will be developed and what surrounding development may take place. Openings may need to be oversized on day one so that tree growth or neighboring buildings won't reduce the required air movement in your building during its life cycle. Also keep in mind that insect screens can reduce airflow through a window by up to half.

Wind approaching a building slows and compresses as it hits the front face. This wind then diverts and flows around the sides of the building. As it flows around the sides it begins to separate from the surface and create negative pressure along these sides. Once it passes the building it creates eddies flowing in a circular pattern back toward the rear of the structure. The rear of the building is also in negative pressure, but not as much as the sides. (Fig. 6.1.1(a)) The goal in placing openings is to take advantage of the natural tendency of wind to create these zones of positive and negative pressure.

Opening placed front and back (or *windward* and *leeward*) sides of a building will allow air to cross ventilate and form small eddies back toward the main wind direction. Placing openings in the sidewalls instead of the back will utilize the greater negative pressure at the exterior sides to draw air through the building more efficiently. This also mixes the air through the interior better (Fig. 6.1.1(b), (c)).

Winds that strike a building at an oblique angle flow better through buildings with openings on three sides rather than two (Fig. 6.1.1(d), (e)). But if the wind approaches from the side without windows all openings are in negative pressure, eliminating good ventilation (Fig. 6.1.1(f)).

When only one side of a building can be opened the windows should be as far apart as possible and the building should try to sit at an oblique angle to the wind. Short projections beside the windows can enhance the positive and negative pressures to improve airflow (Fig. 6.1.1(g)). The airflow in this situation needs to be kept from eddying back out of the first opening, therefore reducing air intake (Fig. 6.1.1(h)).

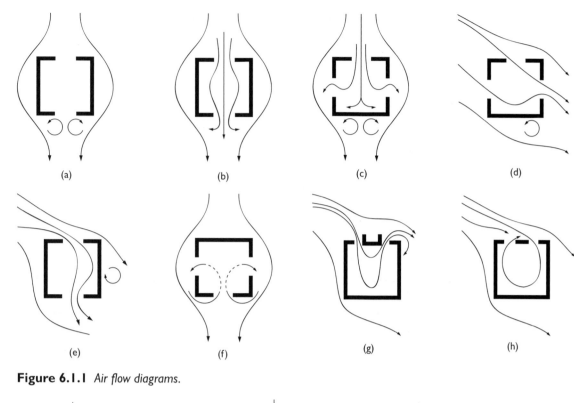

Figure 6.1.1 *Air flow diagrams.*

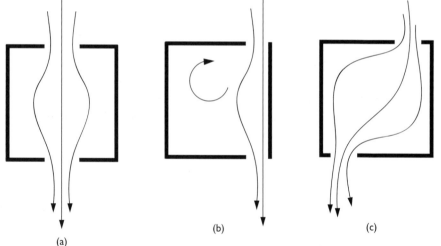

Figure 6.1.2. *Air jet diagrams.*

As a basic rule of thumb the intake and exit sizes of windows should be equal to maximize airflow. To get lower airflow, but better air circulation reduce the outlet size somewhat – but greater than a 60–40% ratio greatly reduces overall airflow.

Air passing through a room creates an *air jet*, an accelerated flow of wind traveling a set path – openings in the center run the jet free or open from attaching to a surface (Fig. 6.1.2(a)). Openings along walls or ceilings causes the air jet to cling to the surface removing heat from that surface more rapidly than an open jet, which can be a valuable way to cool a radiant surface (Fig. 6.1.2(b)). Overall airflow mixing is maximized by offsetting intake and outlet locations; this promotes both surface cooling and room air changes (Fig. 6.1.2(c)).

Air flow in buildings

The three basic functions of passive ventilation are to promote health, increase comfort with air circulation, and remove heat from structural elements. *Health* requires enough fresh outdoor air be changed with the stale indoor air to resist air-borne germs/bacteria/mold, etc. from building up. *Comfort* is achieved through evaporative and convective heat losses from adequate air movement. *Structural cooling* moves heat away from surfaces where it has built before it radiates that heat into the structure – this really qualifies as comfort also, but it's easier to explain it separately.

At times wind flow cannot be achieved through window openings or there is a desire to enhance flow through other passive means. The *stack effect* creates airflow by using the thermal principles of airflow. The density of air lessens as it warms causing it to rise. Cooler air is drawn into the slight vacuum caused by the air displacement and tends to be drawn up after the warm air. Creating a chimney that separates lower cooler air from higher warmer air enhances stack effect – the top of the stack is allowed to heat, drawing warmer air up into it. Cool air flows into the lower space and up the chimney starting a natural convective loop of air movement. The bigger the stack the more air movement, atriums can be used as the chimney to create this effect. Also, placing the openings at the top of the vent in the suction zone of the prevailing winds will increase airflow. Houses in Middle Eastern countries use this system traditionally and it has been used in various ways in modern buildings as well (Fig. 6.1.3).

The minimum rate of *air changes* per hour in a room is determined by code and tends to be about 7. This means that every hour *all* of the air in that room has been renewed 7 times. This rate is based in very basic health requirements and not comfort – codes are largely unconcerned with comfort, they're trying to prevent dangers like Legionnaires disease (named after the first recognized

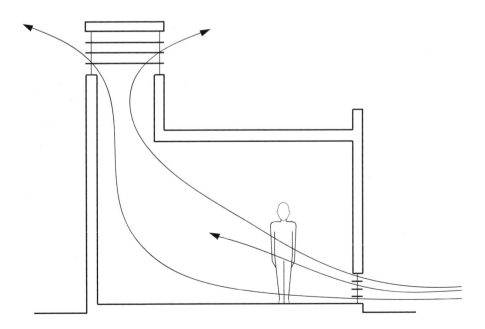

Figure 6.1.3. *Stack effect.*

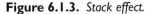

outbreak of the sometimes fatal respiratory disease at an American Legion Convention in Philadelphia in 1976). For comfort the number of changes should be about 30. There are sources, such as *Graphic Standards and Architect's Data*, that have charts to assist in window sizing for varying air changes per hour.

Passive ventilation systems

The Bio-Climatic Chart is based on how to achieve comfort through the factors affecting the human body, or how to reach the 'comfort zone' (see Section 1.1: Human Factors). The 'COMFORT ZONE' is a defined combination of factors – air movement, air temperature, relative humidity, and radiation where a human body with average clothing at rest will be comfortable. Passive ventilation can be figured into the wind speed area at the top of the bio-climatic chart and its effectiveness will depend on the climate zone of your building.

Cross Ventilation is the most effective way to move air through a building for comfort. The effectiveness is largely dependent on the difference in temperature between the inside and outside. Structures tend to build up heat due to people, lights, equipment, solar radiation, and other factors – but if the air outside is warmer than the air inside it is not going to cool the space no matter how hard it blows through. Using basic charts of the buildings heat load (the combination of factors heating the building) along with wind speed and temperature differential between inside and outside can determine the size of openings required (see *Sun, Wind & Light* by Brown + DeKay). During the complex process of designing buildings you either need to learn how to do this or hire knowledgeable consultants that can assist you. At a minimum you need to know that this is all possible and viable as a solution.

The design of window openings for passive ventilation should be based on a number of factors (Fig. 6.1.4):

1. First the wind needs to be able to get to the opening. This may mean the opening needs to occur high in the wall, low in the wall or from one side only.
2. The air then needs to flow to where it's needed – the velocity may be right based on the bio-climatic chart, but if it's on the ceiling or floor no people are being touched by the air. Think about where the people will be in a room and adjust openings to run air past the core and head of their body.
3. A variety of openings may be needed to both cool people and cool the wall/ceiling surfaces. The surfaces most needing cooling jets are typically the ceiling and west walls – the areas heated by the sun the most during the warmest part of the year. The amount of cooling needed depends on the insulation value of those surfaces, but it makes little sense to cool the floor if it's the coolest surface in the room already.
4. Air supply in a mechanical system usually follows the rule of supply high/return low, when cooling is the primary concern and the opposite when heating is the main factor. This is because cool air falls and warm air rises – therefore you might think to place inlet windows high in order to let the

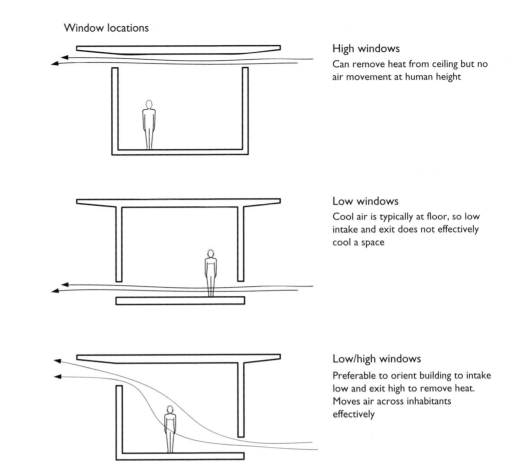

Window locations

High windows
Can remove heat from ceiling but no air movement at human height

Low windows
Cool air is typically at floor, so low intake and exit does not effectively cool a space

Low/high windows
Preferable to orient building to intake low and exit high to remove heat. Moves air across inhabitants effectively

Figure 6.1.4. *Window locations for wind flow.*

cool air fall and place outlet windows low. However with airflow through a building the opposite is usually true – you want to evacuate the warm air and it's already on the ceiling, so you need to supply low and evacuate the warm air up high. This allows greater air mixing than if you supplied high and evacuated high – which would cause an air jet at the ceiling.

Wind catchers allow buildings in dense areas or where low winds are unavailable to draw wind down from higher areas (Fig. 6.1.5). This has benefits and liabilities, the first liability being the need to evacuate warm air high. This is usually solved by creating a chimney to evacuate warm air and baffles to direct the air down into the space rather than straight to the chimney. The benefit of wind catchers is that wind typically is at a higher velocity farther from the drag of the ground, so it can be directed at higher velocities down into the space.

In more sophisticated versions of passive cooling, systems like night cooled mass may be used. This operates on the principle of thermal mass temperature shift – like a thermal wall that stores heat during the day and radiates it back at night. In a night cooled mass, the building structure absorbs heat during the day as a closed system and at night vents are opened using airflow evacuate the stored heat. The mass is then cool for the next morning until it begins to store heat again. During cooler months the heat can be retained and used to warm the building. This system requires substantial enough diurnal temperature shifts for enough of the year to make it feasible (Fig. 6.1.6).

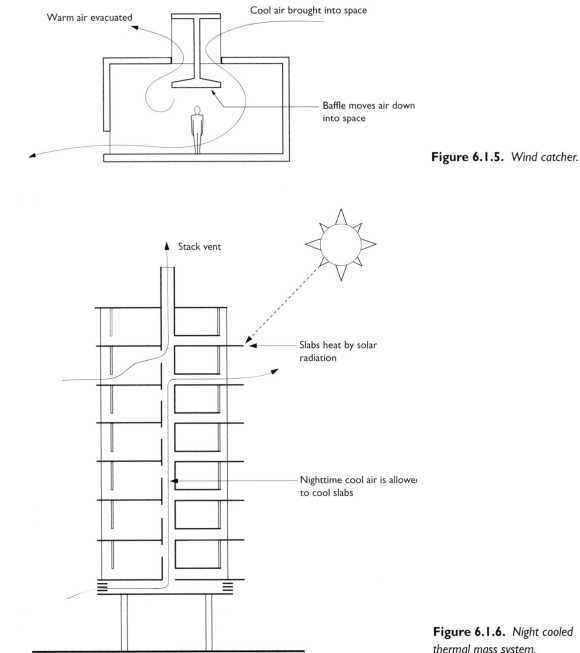

Warm air evacuated

Cool air brought into space

Baffle moves air down
into space

Figure 6.1.5. *Wind catcher.*

Stack vent

Slabs heat by solar
radiation

Nighttime cool air is allowed
to cool slabs

Figure 6.1.6. *Night cooled
thermal mass system.*

Passive cooling systems are often hybridized with some components of a mechanical system to improve performance. The most common of these are fans that assist in air movement when wind is not adequate. A common and very useful type is the basic ceiling fan – pushing warm air down in the winter and pulling cool air up in the summer (Fig. 6.1.7). Most people don't use the fans this way, but they effectively work in the summer for evaporative airflow in down mode or to circulate in up mode. The better version of drawing the cool air up and evacuating warm air is the attic vent fan. The problem with ceiling fans in the up mode is that the warm air has no place to go; the attic fan pushes the warm air up and out of the structure while pulling cooler air in. These are very effective systems that can mechanically enhance passive ventilation systems with low energy output. Other hybrid systems like

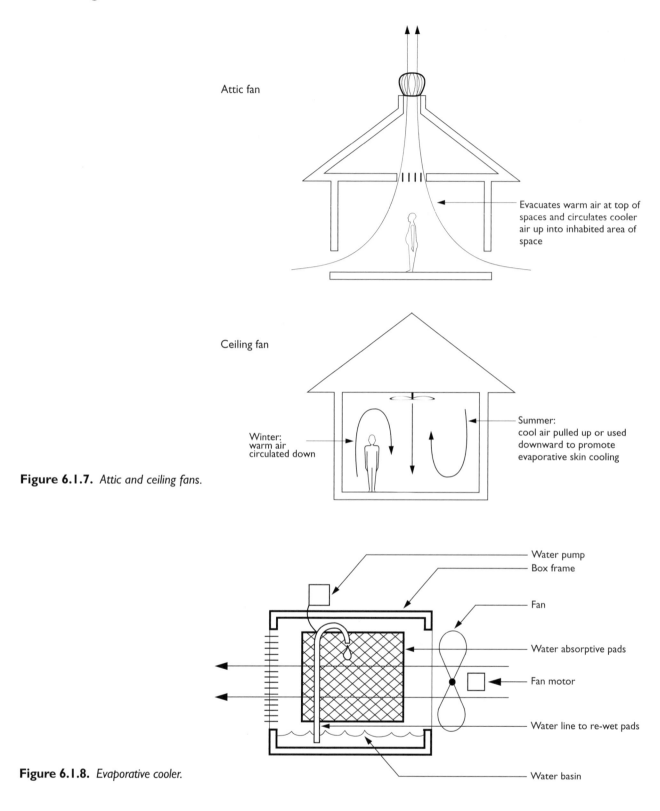

Figure 6.1.7. *Attic and ceiling fans.*

Figure 6.1.8. *Evaporative cooler.*

evaporative coolers (swamp coolers) can work well in hot and dry climate zones by adding moisture and airflow to dry air (Fig. 6.1.8). The system works by pumping water into absorptive pads that are being wetted with a pump, and blowing air across the pads with a fan. The system can lower the temperature in a space by 6.5°C (20°F) as the water evaporates from the pads, and they use one-fourth the energy of refrigerated systems.

Frequently asked questions

'How do you determine how much wind a site will get and where it will come from?'
The NOAA (National Oceanographic and Atmospheric Administration) in the USA and the Met Office in the UK provide national weather forecasting and meteorological history for most regions. This information includes prevailing wind speed and direction by month; however, it is typically taken from airports or other open areas. Local sites often have conditions that modify wind direction, such as hills, trees, buildings, etc. that must be taken into account. These conditions can speed or slow wind, along with changing the prevailing direction. Since it is normally impossible to survey a site for a yearlong period to test these conditions there is a certain amount of guesswork involved in determining wind speed and direction. Often it is helpful to ask someone locally about conditions or to hire a consultant who is knowledgeable about local conditions.

'Where should windows be placed to maximize cooling effects?'
This is a complex problem that involves both local conditions and the form of the building; however, there are some fundamental rules. First you must know where the wind is coming from during the warm months of the year. Then you need to consider where inhabitants are in the spaces, so that wind can be moved across them and not just into the building. Lastly it is typically best to take cool air in low and exhaust it high, so warm air that is rising in a space will be moved out of the space. Consider the shape of the interior space and study the airflow diagrams to maximize air speed, mix, and location.

Conclusion

Passive ventilation acts as a logical time tested system of dealing with human comfort that had fallen out of favor for 50 of the last 10,000 or so years of making buildings. We happen to be arriving at the end of that 50-year period, with rising concerns over energy costs and the need to reduce the impact of building energy consumption, but there is still resistance to hybridizing passive and active systems. The reason is due to the unpredictability of weather factors such as wind speed and air temperature. A mechanical system is reliable to cool a room, and trying a different approach that may cause an owner discomfort is difficult to propose. Architects are the primary decision makers that push forward the types of mechanical systems our designs will incorporate. No one else will lead us back to sensibly considering building systems if we don't begin the process ourselves. This requires education of us first to the capabilities of passive environmental control systems and then to our clients of the reliability and long-term benefits of lower impact approaches to building.

Glossary and formulas

Air changes	Indicate the number of times all of the air in a space has been renewed. It is typically measured by the number of changes per hour.
Air jet	An accelerated flow of wind traveling a set path through a space.

Cross Ventilation	Air moving into and through a space, rather than at the corners or edges. This is frequently enhanced by having narrower spaces with windows on opposite sides.
Leeward side	The back or opposite side of a building from the direction of prevailing wind at that time.
Stack effect	Creates airflow by using the thermal principles of airflow. The density of air lessens as it warms causing it to rise. Cooler air is drawn into the slight vacuum caused by the air displacement and tends to be drawn up after the warm air.
Wind catchers	Allow buildings in dense areas or where low winds are unavailable to draw wind down from higher areas. This is usually accomplished through a tower that directs wind down into the space.
Wind eddy	The tendency of a fluid medium such as wind to slow and swirl off of the main flow at the edges.
Windward side	The front or exposed side of a building from the direction of prevailing wind at that time.

Further reading

Brown, G.Z. and Mark DeKay. (2001) *Sun, Wind & Light: Architectural Design Strategies*, 2nd ed(New York, NY: John Wiley and Sons, Inc).

6.2 Environmental control: active ventilation

HVAC Systems	All air systems
	All water systems
	Direct expansion systems (refrigerant systems)
Mechanical Air Flow in Buildings	Air distribution systems
	High vs. low supply and return
	Throw, spread and fall
	Ductwork and diffusers
Refrigeration & Heat Transfer	The refrigeration cycle
	Cooling
	Heat pump
	Chiller and cooling tower

Introduction to active ventilation

Active ventilation refers to HVAC (Heating, Ventilation, and Air Conditioning) systems that use energy to function. Most buildings use a combination of active and passive systems in practice. While passive systems can have a major impact on the interior environment, active systems are usually needed to effectively maintain comfort in all situations. This, however, is the appropriate order to think about the problem of comfort – passive first with support from active, not the other way around.

The purpose of HVAC systems is to adjust air temperature, radiant temperatures, relative humidity, and air motion to put human inhabitants into the 'comfort zone'. This can be done in numerous ways and must take into account several factors during system selection:

- initial cost, performance, and long-term expense of the system,
- fuel and power sources required to run the system,
- size and location of the equipment,
- heating or cooling medium used,
- distribution and return systems – particularly the size,
- outlet size, type, and locations,
- humidity, fresh air, and filtering,
- noise and vibration control.

Keep in mind that by the time you're selecting mechanical systems you may already be past the point of making the major siting and formal decisions that will determine how efficient or inefficient your building will be.

HVAC systems

There are three basic types of HVAC systems: All Air, All Water, and Direct Expansion or Refrigerant systems. All systems follow the same issues listed above in system selection, but handle them in different ways.

All Air Systems have the heating or refrigerating units control the quality of the air, from heat to cold and humidity to filtering. This air is then delivered through ducts to the final room destination. Common types are single and double duct systems.

Single duct systems force either warm or cold air at a constant temperature through low velocity ducts to the spaces. Variable airflow systems use dampers at the outlets to control airflow based on the needs of the space. Reheat systems can also heat air right at the point of delivery to avoid loss of heat in the ducts.

Double duct systems deliver both warm and cold air simultaneously to mixing units that create the appropriate temperature to deliver to the space. This mixing takes place with thermostatically controlled dampers run from a thermostat. This is usually a high velocity system to reduce duct sizes. Mixing units or VAV (variable air volume) boxes may serve different individual spaces or zones of a building (Fig. 6.2.1).

All Water Systems deliver hot or chilled water to spaces, which runs in smaller piping than air ducts. This water runs into fan coil units that blow air over the hot or cold coils of fluid to heat or cool the space. Radiators are also used without the fans to heat spaces. Ventilation or air changes must be supplied separately from the system to get fresh air into the spaces.

Two pipe systems circulate either hot or cold water in then out of the space.

Four pipe systems circulate both hot and cold water simultaneously in separate circuits to provide necessary heating and cooling to different parts of a building.

Direct Expansion Systems (Refrigerant Systems) are self-contained units used on rooftop or through wall applications. These systems can eliminate ductwork and can serve individual needs of spaces without providing unnecessary capacity – in other words you only run what you need. Small sections of ductwork can also be used to distribute air from a centrally located unit. Cooling

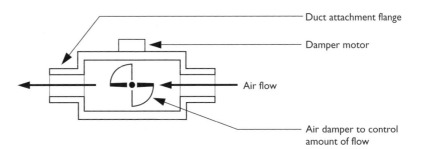

Figure 6.2.1. *VAV box.*

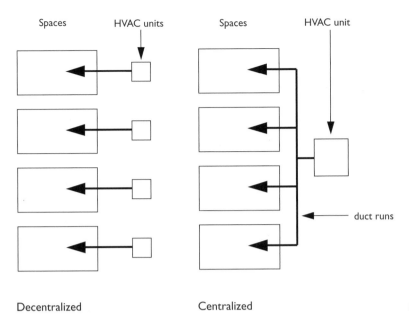

Spaces   HVAC units   Spaces   HVAC unit

duct runs

Decentralized   Centralized

Figure 6.2.2. *Air distribution systems.*

is provided by air cooled condensers or chiller units which require an indoor to outdoor loop. Heating is accomplished by gas or oil furnaces, electric heaters, or heat pumps.

A *heat pump* is an electrically powered heating and cooling unit. It uses an evaporative cooling cycle to absorb and transfer indoor heat to the outdoors for cooling. For heating energy is drawn from the outdoor air by reversing the cooling cycle and switching the heat exchange functions of the condenser and evaporator (this will be covered in more detail below). Heat pumps work well in mild climates where heat and cooling loads are equal. Additional difficulties arise when used in below freezing temperatures.

Air flow in buildings

Air Distribution Systems can be centralized or de-centralized which affects the method of distribution. De-centralized units often require little distribution runs or ductwork because they can blow air directly into the space. Centralized systems require a more extensive distribution system, which means there is less equipment but more duct runs (Fig. 6.2.2).

Air duct systems require more space than water systems and must be thought of early in the design process in order to work with structural systems, lights, wall layouts and other services. These various systems can take large amounts of space above a ceiling and need to be considered with the structural system (Fig. 6.2.3).

Ductwork distribution typically runs vertically in a chase to feed a floor and horizontally in the floor or ceiling to feed spaces within each floor. This system can be reversed with main feeds horizontally and individual feeds

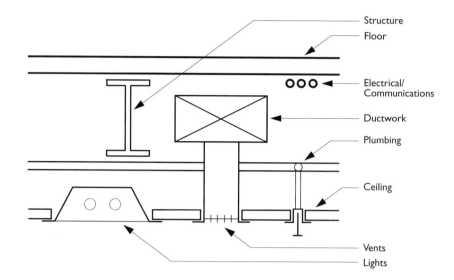

Figure 6.2.3. *Ceiling space requirements.*

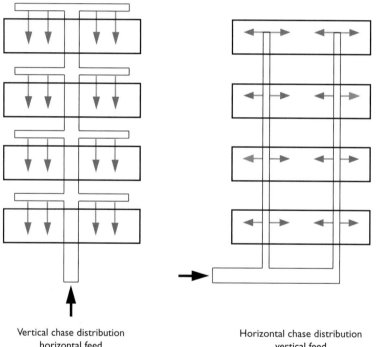

Figure 6.2.4. *Ductwork chase distribution types.*

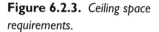

Vertical chase distribution
horizontal feed

Horizontal chase distribution
vertical feed

vertically, but it is much less common as multiple vertical chases are required in the right locations to distribute air (Fig. 6.2.4).

Horizontal distribution patterns are typically defined as radial, perimeter or lateral.

Radial patterns use minimal duct runs, but rely on unobstructed space.

Perimeter loop systems work well to resist exterior heat/cold loads and are typically fed from the floor.

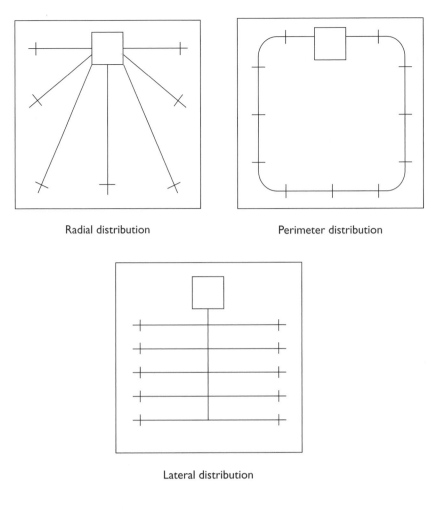

Radial distribution   Perimeter distribution

Lateral distribution

Figure 6.2.5. *Horizontal ductwork patterns.*

Lateral systems use the most duct run, but accommodate flexible distribution patterns, structural obstructions and segmented spaces on a floor (Fig. 6.2.5).

High vs. Low Supply and Return affects the efficiency of the system at different times of the year (Fig. 6.2.6). The basic rule of thumb in cold climates is to supply low and return high, this puts warm into the space at the bottom and as it naturally rises it returns into the system. The problem is in warm weather you are trying to supply cold air low and it wants to stay low rather than mix into the space – making the system inefficient during this cycle of the system. The opposite is true in warm climates when supply is typically high to allow cool air to fall into the space. In cool weather the high supply keep the warm air at the ceiling. The typical way to deal with these problems are to increase the velocity of the air during the off cycle to blow past the natural tendency of the air temperature rise and fall, an inefficient means of solving this issue. This is certainly an area where you should be trying to use the most effective passive systems and use the mechanical systems to deal with conditions that the passive systems don't handle as well. Also, creating hybrid systems such as radiant heat at the base of cold window or wall surfaces with air systems elsewhere can improve performance and efficiency.

Throw, Spread and Fall are the actions of the air once it enters the space. Outlets should be located to distribute air comfortably, without drafts, and

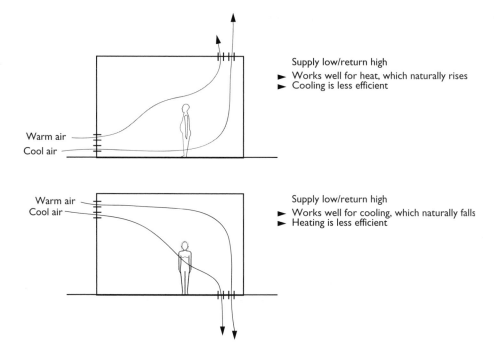

Supply low/return high
▶ Works well for heat, which naturally rises
▶ Cooling is less efficient

Warm air
Cool air

Warm air
Cool air

Supply low/return high
▶ Works well for cooling, which naturally falls
▶ Heating is less efficient

Figure 6.2.6. *High vs. low supply and return.*

without stratification. Throw distance and spread must be considered along with avoiding obstructions to airflow. The standard throw of air into a room should be 3/4 of the total depth. At the 3/4 point the air should be at head height or approximately 1.8 m (6 ft) above the floor. Air is typically blown toward the exterior wall where the cooled or heated air can reduce the radiant temperature of the surface. Registers should be placed to supply air evenly into a space; therefore they sit away from sidewalls and far enough apart to mix with minimal overlap (Fig. 6.2.7).

Registers and Diffusers are arranged to create the desired effects of airflow. Diffusers typically supply air at the ceiling and have curved fins to run air away from the source. Registers are air supply grilles with usually operable damper fins to control air direction. Registers are typically wall or floor mounted (Fig. 6.2.8). Return grilles are most often open grates or straight fins that simply pull air back into the system. The returns are placed away from the supply to not short circuit the airflow through the space.

A common problem with ceiling and high-wall diffusers are dirt marks or smudging that occurs when small particles of dust are repeatedly blown across a surface. This can be prevented by not placing wall diffusers too close to ceilings and using materials that will not stain or trap dust particles.

Refrigeration & heat transfer

The Refrigeration Cycle is a process that moves heat from one place to another. Kitchen refrigerators move heat from the storage area to the surrounding room. Air conditioners move heat from the rooms to the outdoors. A large quantity of heat is required to change the state of liquid to steam; this is

High vs. low supply/return

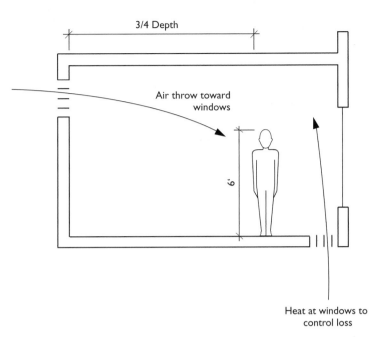

Figure 6.2.7. *Air throw.*

Horizontal ductwork patterns

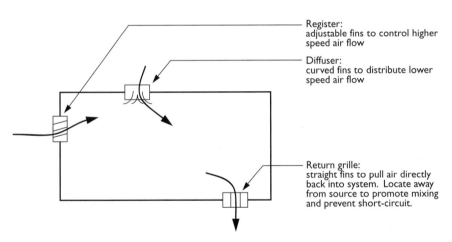

Figure 6.2.8. *Registers, diffuser, and return grilles.*

referred to as latent heat. Latent heat is the key to moving large quantities of heat with small amounts of refrigerant. To move heat from an area of low temperature to an area of high temperature (for instance, 24°C [75°F] inside to 35°C [95°F] outside) refrigeration equipment needs to change the boiling temperature of the refrigerant. This is accomplished by changing the pressure of the refrigerant (which is why refrigerators go bad because the compressor fails).

During the *Cooling* cycle an evaporator coil absorbs heat from its surroundings, heated refrigerant within the coil evaporates internally. The refrigerant vapor is drawn into a compressor where pressure and, therefore, boiling (or condensing) temperature are increased. The refrigerant vapor is then

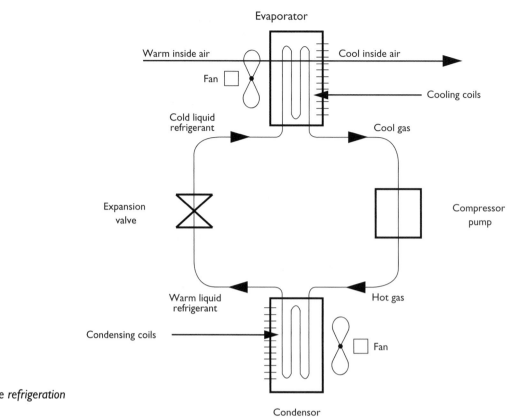

Figure 6.2.9. *The refrigeration cycle.*

discharged into a condenser coil, where it gives up the latent heat absorbed in the evaporator and returns to a liquid state. Finally, liquid refrigerant circulates through an expansion valve, where pressure and evaporation temperature are reduced; the cycle is then repeated (Fig. 6.2.9).

A *Heat Pump* reverses the cooling cycle to extract heat from a low temperature source, such as outside air, to heat a building. The basic equipment is unchanged with the exception of a four-way reversing valve and controls that permit the condenser and evaporator to exchange functions.

Chiller and Cooling Towers – In large buildings it is impractical to move heat with air only because ducts would become too large. Therefore a chiller is added to the evaporator, and chilled water is circulated to air handling units throughout the building. Cooling towers increase efficiency by keeping the temperature of the outdoor exchange lower, by using at huge scale the evaporation of water to lower the exterior temperature that the refrigerant coil goes through (say 29°C [85°F] water rather than 35°C [95°F] air) (Fig. 6.2.10).

Frequently asked questions

'How do you determine the air distribution pattern in a building?'
Air distribution tends to follow two sets of decisions; whether to supply high or low and what pattern to run the ductwork. Ideally you supply high and return

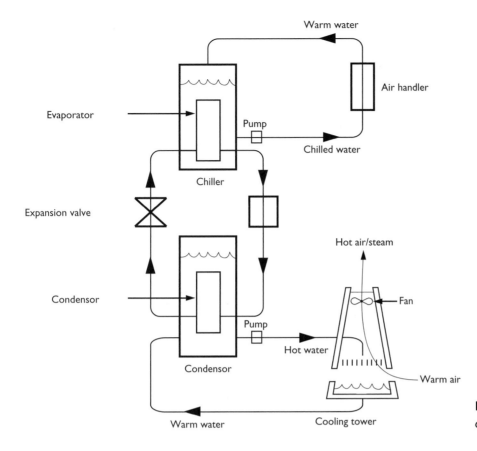

Figure 6.2.10. *Chiller and cooling tower arrangement.*

low when the primary load on a building is cooling and the reverse when the primary load is heating. This is designed to work with the natural tendency of warm air to rise and cool air to fall. Often there is no option, because the building configuration will only allow supply ducts to be run at the ceiling. Determining how you want air distribution to work can effect early design decisions if you want to run distribution under the floor. Duct patterns matter most when they are exposed. Sometimes the pattern you desire to see will not be the best layout for duct length economy or to maximize efficiency of the system. When ducts are concealed you typically run them in the shortest pattern to minimize thermal loss, reduce material cost, keep fan velocities lower, and get supply to the exterior edges of a space where the heat gain/loss is the greatest.

'How do you tell whether a vent is for supply or return in an existing space?'
First check to see if air is blowing out or sucking into a vent if it is within reach. Often they are not within reach or the system is not running, but you can also usually tell just by looking at them. Supply vents tend to have baffles or fins that control the direction of airflow, while return vents are normally grilles that simply collect air at lower velocities. Any curved or adjustable louver will be for supply whether it is on the floor, wall or ceiling. Long linear vents are also normally supply, and any vent at the floor or ceiling next to a window opening is typically supply. Large square or rectangular grilles with egg crate fin patterns are for return, as they are designed to pull air in from all directions and generally limit debris being sucked into the system.

Conclusion

Mechanical ventilation systems are unavoidable in most building conditions, but much can be done to lessen their impact and expense. Don't automatically assume that buildings will be completely active, use the strategies of siting and form to improve performance long before you're selecting what system to use. Employ mechanical consultants that are skilled in the use of passive and active systems early in the design process to maximize the effects of passive and active strategies. Consider the specific conditions of the activities and locations of people in a building to provide comfort where it's most needed rather than indiscriminately spreading the same HVAC conditions everywhere, or worse where it's not needed at all. Finally, understand the strategies to maximize the performance of building systems. Most buildings could be run with half the energy they currently consume if they had been designed with efficiency and energy conservation in mind. This may cost more initially to construct, but the long-term costs and impact on the environment can be vastly improved.

Glossary and formulas

All Air Systems	Have the heating or refrigerating units control the quality of the air, from heat to cold and humidity to filtering.
All Water Systems	Deliver hot or chilled water to spaces, which runs in smaller piping than air ducts. Water is then run to radiators or fan coil units to distribute heating and cooling.
Diffuser	A louvered vent that distributes air into a space from the mechanical system. They typically supply air at the ceiling and have curved fins to run air away from the source.
Direct Expansion Systems (Refrigerant Systems)	Are self-contained units used on rooftop or through wall applications.
Heat pump	An electrically powered heating and cooling unit. It uses an evaporative cooling cycle to absorb and transfer indoor heat to the outdoors for cooling.
HVAC	Heating, Ventilation, and Air Conditioning. An active system of climate control.
Plenum	In construction this is a space that is used for air transfer in lieu of a duct. It typically occurs above the suspended ceiling or in a space below the floor.
Registers	Are air supply vents with operable damper fins to control air direction.
Throw	The distance air is 'thrown' into a room from a diffuser.

Further Reading

Bassler, B. (ed.) (2000) Mechanical (Chapter 15), *Architectural Graphic Standards*, 10th ed (New York, NY: Wiley).

Ernst and Peter Neufert. (2000) *Architect's Data*, 3rd ed. (London, UK: Blackwell Science). pp. 95–109.

6.3 Environmental control: illumination

Perception of Light	Anatomy
	Color
	Contrast
History	Thomas Edison and the incandescent bulb
	Fluorescent bulb development
	High performance lamps
Fixtures/Lamps	Lamp sources
	Properties
	Fixture types
	Light control

Introduction to illumination

Illumination, either natural or artificial, creates the conditions by which we can use our sight. Most of our information about the world comes from sight and it is the primary means by which we perceive and judge space. Traditionally buildings were designed with little artificial light (such as lamps or fires) and needed to utilize sunlight as the primary source of illumination. Since the invention of artificial lighting we have extended the ability of a building to function without sunlight, but have often neglected providing adequate provisions for daylighting. This significantly impacts issues of health and well being, along with energy consumption.

We covered the topic of daylighting during Solar Geometry, and now concern ourselves with artificial lighting. As noted in the daylighting section, approximately 50% of most building's energy consumption comes from artificial lighting – so this area offers some of the most significant impact on energy efficiency. Also critical is the way lighting affects the way a structure is perceived. This is a concern that is normally not fully considered during design, particularly in school, and is too often a last minute concern. Consider this – the area that primarily affects the way anyone perceives a space and impacts most of the energy consumption is frequently poorly executed. Why would that be the case? The answer is that it can be ignored in favor of the myriad other concerns that are not as tangible as bricks and mortar. This is certainly one of the complex issues that define sophisticated practitioners (Fig. 6.3.1).

Perception of light

Light passes through the lens of the eye and focuses onto the retina at the back of the sphere. The retina is made up of light sensitive receptors, rods, and cones, which transmit information for the brain to interpret. The rods

Figure 6.3.1. *Castelvecchio Museum, 1954–1967, Verona, Italy, Carlo Scarpa.*

gather around the edges of the retina and function to capture low light levels and movement, they do not gather information on color. The cones are closer to the center of the retina and function at higher light levels to perceive color and detail (Fig. 6.3.2). The level of light and contrast of surroundings controls the way the eye perceives an image. Too much contrast and the eye cannot focus on either the dark or light objects, too little contrast and objects cannot be discerned from one another. The iris of the eye adjusts to varying light levels rather quickly, but when presented with extremes will try to balance between the two – making both light and dark objects difficult to see.

When moving from very light to very dark spaces the eye also needs to change from one type of sight system to another. Cones work on the photopic or higher light level system, while rods work on the scotopic or lower light level range. Quick shifts between the two create problems because it can take as much as 40 min for the rods to fully adjust to low light levels.

Human eyes evolved in sunlight and therefore perceive that quality of light as 'normal'. Artificial lights vary in color temperature from sunlight and therefore affect the way color is seen. The color of the light that is reflected by an

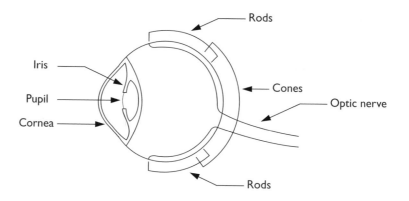

Figure 6.3.2. *Eye diagram.*

object establishes what color we see. When the light source varies in color (or wavelengths of color) from sunlight we see the same object differently because of the color of the light that is reflected. Visible light is actually in a small range of the electromagnetic spectrum and the wavelength of light rays determines the color perception of objects (Fig. 6.3.3). Sunlight waves in the visible range run from violet to red as discovered by Newton in 1678 and commonly portrayed by a rainbow as ROYGBIV (red, orange, yellow, green, blue, indigo, violet) – all colors in equal proportion from the sun is seen as 'white' light. Firelight is seen as more red because it is deficient in shorter wavelengths, and is likely the reason we like incandescent bulbs better than fluorescent, because it is similar to fire or lamplight in color rendition.

History

Thomas Edison is typically credited with the invention of the electric light in 1879, however it was commonly known that heating a filament would produce light. The problem was the filament would oxidize and burn out quickly, making the application not commercially viable. Edison perfected the use of tungsten as the filament, which burns at 2480°C (4500°F) without melting. The bulb is filled with a low-pressure gas, such as argon, that prevents the metal combining with oxygen and oxidizing (Fig. 6.3.4). These bulbs have remained virtually unchanged and last approximately 1000 h, but are very inefficient with 6% of the energy going to light and 94% to heat. By 1900 electric lights were common in American and British households.

Fluorescent light experiments had occurred in the mid 1800s, but the first commercially viable lamps were not developed until 1934 by Arthur Compton. Fluorescent lamps work by passing an electric current through a gas; in this case electrons hit atoms of mercury vapor in the tube causing them to emit ultra-violet light (Fig. 6.3.5). These invisible rays hit a phosphor coating on the inside of the tube, causing the atoms in the phosphor to emit white light. The conversion of light from ultraviolet to visible white is known as fluorescence. Fluorescent light is more efficient than incandescent and does not produce as much heat, but the mercury vapor is considered a toxic material. Currently there is a common fee per bulb to dispose of fluorescent bulbs because of the mercury content. Fluorescent bulbs also tend to be more blue/green and create odd color

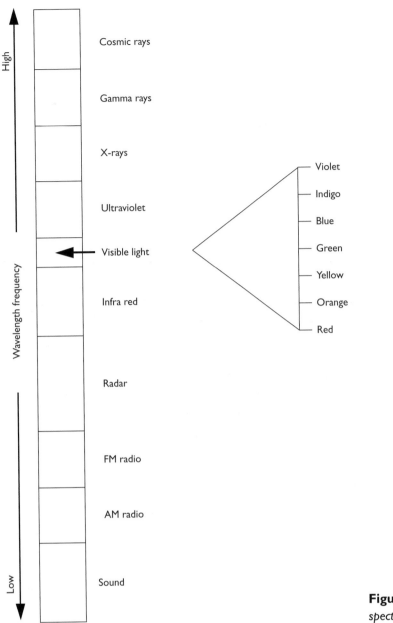

Figure 6.3.3. *Electromagnetic spectrum.*

renditions, making people and food appear less appealing. Improvements have been made in the color rendition, but they are not perfect yet and have a higher initial cost. Finally, the alternating current running through the gas can give a perceptible flicker to the lights, which can be made more troubling by an alternating vibration in older monitor screens – at times causing a type of motion sickness. This can be mitigated by using multiple light sources, including incandescent lights, and using indirect lights to cover individuals in a space.

Other types of filament lights have been developed to increase the efficiency, size, and light output of lamps. Most innovations consist of the type and pressure of gas used in the lamp. Early examples of these were the tungsten halogen lamps developed for car headlights, which burn brighter due to different gases and pressure being used in the lamp. Metal halide, mercury

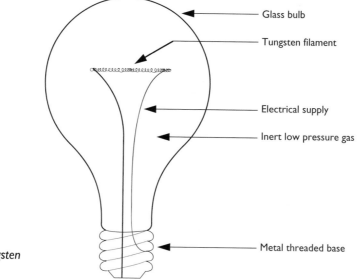

Figure 6.3.4. *Typical tungsten lamp anatomy.*

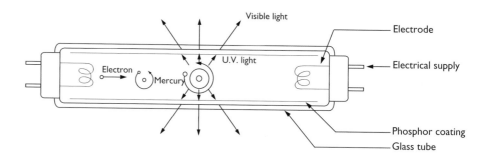

Figure 6.3.5. *Typical fluorescent lamp anatomy.*

vapor, and high-pressure sodium lamps are widely used commercially and can extend the life of filament bulbs considerably, but have various color rendition qualities.

LED (light emitting diode) lamps have recently become more common in the lighting industry (Fig. 6.3.6). Practical LEDs of visible spectrum light were first developed by Nick Holonyak Jr. at the University of Illinois in 1962. They have taken over the task of most signage indicator illumination and are becoming more common in general lighting applications. A light emitting diode is a semi-conductor diode that converts electric energy into electromagnetic radiation at visible wavelengths of light. They currently last twice as long as the best fluorescent bulbs (about 10 years of normal use) and twenty times longer than the best incandescent lamps. The efficiency is better than incandescent, but still behind fluorescent bulbs so they are currently more expensive to run. This is a problem being worked on, and while the industry feels the compact fluorescent bulb is as efficient as it will probably get, the LED will likely become much brighter and more efficient in time – surpassing fluorescent in short order. They can be made in many colors, and the small scale and plastic lenses make then much more durable than other light sources using glass bulb or tubes.

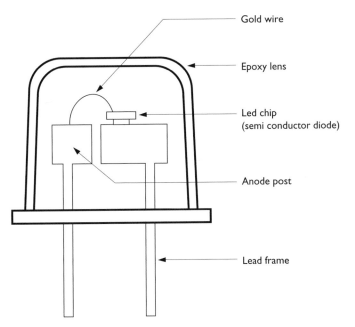

Gold wire

Epoxy lens

Led chip
(semi conductor diode)

Anode post

Lead frame

Figure 6.3.6. *L.E.D. (light emitting diode) diagram.*

Fixtures/lamps

When choosing lighting there are a number of factors to be considered. Some primary issues are: the task being performed, the quality or mood of the space desired, where the focus is in a space, the efficiency of the solution, and what creates security.

The types of lighting can be categorized into six basic configurations (Fig. 6.3.7):

1. Downlight – Virtually all downlights
2. Partial Downlight – Mostly downlight with some up or bounced light
3. Diffuse – Equal light distribution in all directions
4. Up/Downlight – Roughly equal distribution both up and down
5. Partial Uplight – Mostly up light with some downlight
6. Uplight – Virtually all uplights

Each of these has its benefits and liabilities; most lighting solutions use a combination of these along with natural light. A certain desired amount of uniformity is typically sought which tends to overlap lighting sources. This is in part because the intensity of light falls away in direct proportion to the distance from the light source. Light directly under a source is brightest and dims quickly; overlapping keeps the light level more even and prevents too much contrast from developing (Fig. 6.3.8). The idea is to get the right amount of light where you want it and not waste energy over-lighting areas that don't require it. In the 1970s many offices had light levels at consistently high levels of 100 footcandles or more. Studies had shown that this improved the ability to accomplish tasks, but in practice the intensity fostered fatigue and became an immense energy consumer. Understanding the correct amount of light needed for the task and focusing that light where needed is more efficient and produces more comfortable environments. Remember that some variation is also helpful for productivity and stress relief.

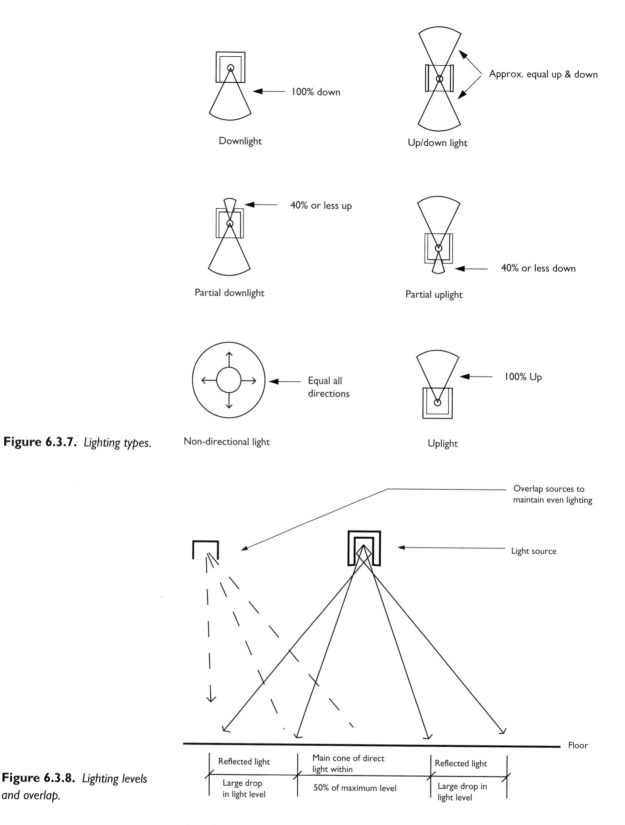

Figure 6.3.7. *Lighting types.*

Figure 6.3.8. *Lighting levels and overlap.*

Another common issue to deal with when selecting lights is glare. Glare is primarily a problem of excessive contrast that creates difficulty or discomfort focusing on an object or task. There are two main types of glare, direct and reflected (or veiling). Direct glare comes from a light source in the field of vision. This can be either from view directly to a lamp or bright window. Shielding or diffusing the light source typically prevents direct glare. The methods that limit

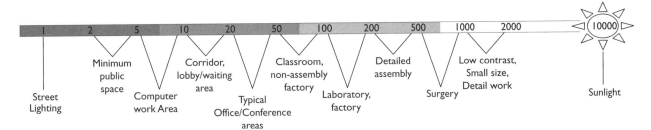

Figure 6.3.9. *Typical footcandles for different activities.*

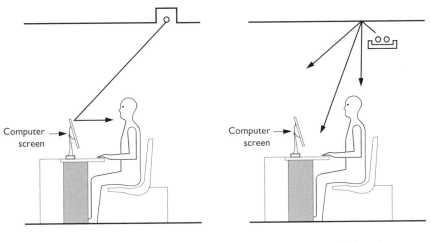

Veiling glare from
direct light source

Veiling glare avoided through
use of indirect lighting

Figure 6.3.10. *Veiling glare.*

glare also cut down on the amount of light given off and negatively impact efficiency, so a balance between putting enough light where desired while not directly viewing the source must be achieved (Fig. 6.3.9).

Reflected or *veiling glare* is primarily a problem with computer screens, due to the fact that they can have a glossy surface. Even matte finish flat or laptop screens have some difficulty with veiling glare, but to a lesser degree than older glass curved screens. Reflected glare can be difficult to predict because computer locations are not always known in advance and can change, added is the problem that the reflection comes from a source behind the viewer (Fig. 6.3.10). Locating light sources so that the cutoff angle is greater than 45 degrees downward prevents most veiling glare from direct fixtures while uplighting has also been used effectively to eliminate most artificially produced glare problems. The other difficulty comes from bright windows, which are desirable sources of natural light but can produce high levels of glare. Light shelves and louvers limit much of the direct sunlight into a space, but will not prevent a bright reflective light source from showing up on a computer screen. Proper orientation of the occupants relative to windows is necessary in order to utilize natural lighting. Some screening at the work surface can occur to mitigate problems at the user instead of the source, but as always, properly educating clients and managing expectations is critical when using large amounts of natural light in a work environment.

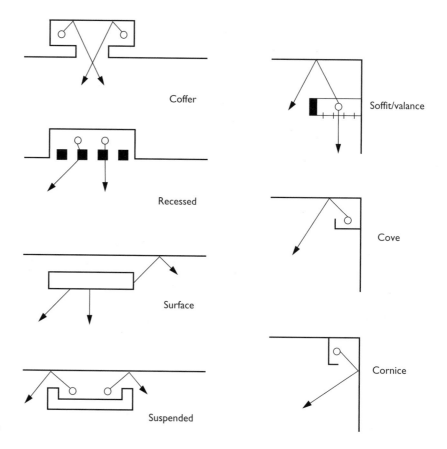

Figure 6.3.11. *Light locations.*

Light location can occur recessed in the ceiling, flush, surface mounted, or suspended, along with combinations of systems. Edge or wall conditions can be handled with soffit, cove, cornice or valance lighting (Fig. 6.3.11). Each of these locations affects the way the light is perceived and the quality of the space in a room. Consider multiple options beyond simply mounting standard grids of lights in the ceiling.

Switching lamps on and off can be done in a variety of ways. The simple one-way wall switch is the most common – being a simple connection between a toggle style switch and the fixtures connected to it. Three-way switches allow for a light source to be controlled from two locations, frequently found in residential applications at the top and base of stairs for example. In commercial applications lights are often controlled from a central bank of switches or electrical box, preventing undesirable personal freedoms of the occupants. Switches can also be keyed for the operation of facilities personnel only. Digital switches and dimmers, along with computer controlled timing systems and photocell zoning are becoming standard in large scale building applications.

Frequently asked questions

'How do I determine how much light is needed in the various parts of a building?' There are numerous references, such as *Architect's Data* and *Graphic Standards*, which have charts of typical footcandles for various activities. These give a starting point for where to focus the light for a specified activity, however, there are other factors that need to be weighed. One is the amount of

natural light which is available during the times the building will be used, often times the specified level may be attainable with minimal additional illumination. It's also important to understand the specific task being undertaken in the space, categories such as 'office' do not make clear what is being done and can encourage general lighting levels which are too high everywhere. A rule of thumb is to keep general lighting lower to conserve energy and to light specific task areas more heavily. Also provide enough separate circuits and adjustability to allow lights to be lowered or turned off when an area is not in use.

Conclusion

Lighting considerations often have as much impact on the quality of space as form or assembly, yet are too frequently overlooked. Lighting also offers the greatest impact on building energy efficiency and is a primary concern of passive design strategies. Much of the information on lighting principles can be found in text and photos, but nothing substitutes for experiential learning in this area. Pay specific attention to the quality of light in spaces you like and dislike, begin building an experiential set of criteria for what makes light quality good or bad. These lessons will be used often and sometimes intuitively when designing projects. Use multiple types of lights for different purposes, provide adjustability and get the light to where it's needed for activities, rather than generally illuminating spaces that don't need light everywhere.

Glossary and formulas

Brightness	Is the density of light being reflected, transmitted or emitted from a surface. It is measured in Footlamberts – which is footcandles × reflectance factor. This is a more comprehensive way of judging the intensity of the light, but is less frequently used due to the difficulty of measuring the reflectance factor. Footcandles can be measured more directly and objectively, if less accurately for perception.
Candela	A measure of a light source's intensity, often referred to as candlepower it is originally based on the light of a wax candle.
Color Temperature	Lamps are measured by color temperature, which is a rating of the frequency of light wavelengths. Different wavelengths reflect colors differently off of surfaces, so the color temperature of light affects the way your eye perceives colors in a space.
Footcandle	A unit of measure of the intensity of light falling on a surface, equal to one lumen per square foot. Originally based on the intensity of a candle one foot from a surface. The metric version is called a Lux, which equals lumens per square meter. This is the most common measurement we use to determine how bright a space is. This can be an inexact science due to

	issues such as contrast, reflectivity of surfaces, whether you can see the light source, etc.
Glare	Primarily a problem of excessive contrast that creates difficulty or discomfort focusing on an object or task. Veiling glare refers to the reflected glare that can occur on a computer screen from light sources behind the user.
Lamp	Is the term used to indicate the bulb that actually emits the illumination. Therefore if you specify a 'light' only, a fixture will arrive without the bulb.
LED	A light emitting diode is a semiconductor diode that converts electric energy into electromagnetic radiation at visible wavelengths of light.
Light	Is the term generally used for the fixture that houses the lamp (or bulb) that produces the actual illumination.
Lumen	A measure of luminous flux – or the rate of flow of light per unit of time. Light efficiency is measured in lumens per watt, a ratio of light output relative to energy input.

For example, a 60-watt incandescent lamp produces 900 lumens; that is, 900 lumens/60 watts = 15 lumens/watt. A 40-watt fluorescent lamp produces 3000 lumens; that is, 3000 lumens/40 watts = 75 lumens/watt, much more efficient than the incandescent.

Further Reading

Ramsey and Sleeper. (2000) *Architectural Graphic Standards*, 10th ed. (New York, NY: John Wiley & Sons). pp. 47–62.

Ernst and Peter Neufert. (2000) *Architect's Data*, 3rd ed (London, UK: Blackwell Science). pp. 24–26, 141–150.

6.4 Plumbing

- **History**
- **Supply**   Principles
                         Fixtures
- **Waste**   Drainage
- **Design Standards**   Fixture heights
                         Clearance

Introduction and history

Perhaps the least elevated of all architectural discussions is how to get clean, healthy water into buildings for various functions, and how to dispose of waste-water, sewage and other health-critical contaminants. Despite its rather gross implications, plumbing is a key factor in the design of any building of reasonable size, and the proper provision of fresh, clean water and safe disposal channels is among the most significant health and safety issues faced by designers.

Anyone who has had their water service interrupted recognizes instantly the importance of fresh water for drinking and cleaning, and perhaps more importantly the vital need to quickly and efficiently dispose of human waste. Yet until the 1860s, deaths from diseases caused by poor sanitation from typhus and cholera were epidemic.

Sanitation is one of the few areas in which ancient builders actually exceeded the abilities of subsequent centuries, and the reform movements that arose in the late 19th century for the most part only demanded a return to standards of cleanliness and sanitation enjoyed by the Romans. While sewage disposal adopted the time-honored technique of throwing a chamberpot's contents into the street, that street was invariably sloped toward a central channel, regularly flushed by flowing water and engineered to flow into underground sewer lines. Fresh water from aqueducts was available throughout most large Roman cities, and the separation of drinking water from mountain springs and the effluent cast into rivers worked reasonably well.

However the aqueducts built by the Romans were still in use throughout the middle ages, while the sewers crumbled. The middle ages – and subsequent centuries – were horrifically unclean by modern standards, with human and animal waste piled in streets and only slowly oozing toward streams and rivers. Roman principles of discharge and flow were largely forgotten, and formal disposal practices ranged from communal cesspits to residential gardens. In cities, the only formal requirements for sanitation were that citizens were usually required to warn passers-by before dumping chamberpots from upper stories.

Continual epidemics of water-borne diseases from cross-contamination of drinking water with human waste was exacerbated by the intense urban migrations of the industrial revolution. Reform movements in the middle of the 19th century found deplorable conditions in working class housing, with

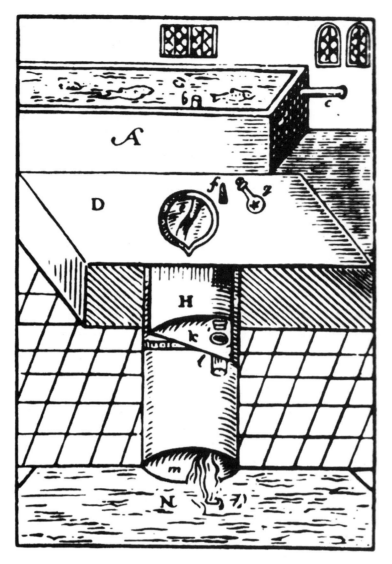

Figure 6.4.1. *An early (ca. 1600) attempt at sanitary removal of human waste. All plumbing essentially moves this problem along – usually to a municipal treatment plant, but in this case just to a local stream. Note the inhabitants of the supply reservoir.*

underground cesspits commonly leaching into nearby wells and similarly grave problems in cities such as London and New York. While common scientific opinion at the time focused on 'miasmas', or foul air as the cause of disease, there was a growing understanding that clean drinking water and proper waste disposal were essential to controlling disease.

The single most important innovation in urban sanitation was the water closet, which presented an efficient way to remove liquid and solid waste by relying on the flow of fast running, high volume water through properly sized pipes. While rudimentary fixtures had been put into use as early as 1596 (Fig. 6.4.1), the first patent on a water closet was issued in London to Alexander Cumming in 1775, using an iron bowl with a leather valve at its base covering a waste pipe and an overhead reservoir of water that emptied into the top of the bowl. By operating a lever, the user could simultaneously open the valve and start the flow of water, washing waste into the pipe below. Numerous improvements on this basic principle were paralleled by advances in piped supply water, purification using sand beds to filter out algae and organisms and rudimentary sewage disposal and treatment. Pipes which had been made of clay and wood were gradually replaced by cast iron, which offered less porous surfaces and more robust connections.

Principles

Today, the provision and disposal of water relies on the same basic principles as the Roman sewers, albeit with advances in supply, disposal and treatment that add efficiency and reliability. All systems rely on tapping water from a natural source, and storing it in a way that adds pressure to the distribution system. Most buildings tap into a public source through a meter, which controls pressure within pipes inside. Supply fixtures rely on this built-up pressure, allowing water out through dedicated fixtures. Once out of the supply system, water is considered waste, and is taken out of the building through dedicated sanitary sewage systems, to be either disposed of or treated chemically and biologically.

While these basic principles are fairly simple, major health and safety issues require careful design and installation. Most importantly, fixtures are designed to avoid both cross-contamination of fresh water with waste, and to prevent noxious gases from public sewers from backing up into occupied areas. Likewise, plumbing systems must be designed to avoid leaks and backups, and to encourage rapid flow into sewers – waste pipes don't benefit from the pressurization inherent in supply systems and must be designed to induce adequate speed and volume to prevent solids from settling. Finally, the intense forces involved with hydraulic and hydrostatic pressure must be taken into account when designing systems and fixtures.

Supply – Potability, treatment, and distribution. Potable water is typically available from a municipal source, although in rural areas it may be necessary to drill a well if a public source is not convenient. Well water must often be treated to remove bacteria and mineral deposits and it is vulnerable to plumes of ground-borne pollution. Of particular concern is the presence of calcium carbonate ($CaCO_3$), which causes 'hardness'. Hard water prevents other substances (soap, detergent, and shampoo in particular) from dissolving, making washing difficult. It can also precipitate in boilers, water tanks and tableware. Softening by chemical treatment, usually done in municipal water facilities, may thus require significant mechanical space in a building fed by well water.

In addition to harmful biological or chemical substances, municipal treatment removes objectionable material that can cause turbidity (very fine powders suspended in water), color, odors, or bad tastes. From this point forward, it is imperative that all pipes, fixtures, and tanks be sterile, to prevent bacteria breeding in the supply. Backflow and siphonage are two major concerns. Backflow involves contamination of the water supply from a foreign source (a gasoline tank that leeches into a buried pipe, for instance.) Back siphonage occurs when a fixture backs up into the supply faucet, contaminating the sterile supply water with potentially foul water from a basin or tub. This can be prevented by a mandated air gap between an overflow drain and a faucet.

Municipal water is typically pumped to a tower, whose height pressurizes the supply system. Systems must have enough pressure to overcome friction within

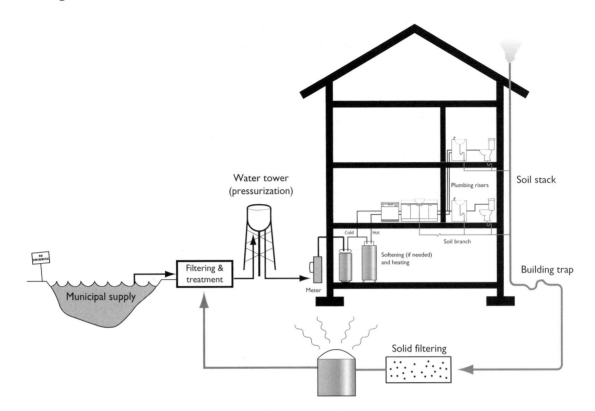

Figure 6.4.2. *Water supply and waste in a typical small-scale installation.*

pipes and at bends, (which can significantly reduce flow) but must not be so highly pressured that caps or fixtures break. (Fire hydrants, for instance, are always put on a separate public line from domestic and commercial supply that is typically much higher pressure).

Residential supply typically enters a building at a single meter, where its flow is recorded (Fig. 6.4.2). Codes mandate a main shutoff valve near the supply's entrance so that the entire system can be shut down and purged in an emergency. Larger-scale buildings must typically have two separate systems, one for regular supply and the other for fire suppression, to ensure full sprinkler protection even if the regular supply is shut off, and may use a rooftop tank or pumps to ensure that both systems are pressurized. Supply water will typically be split into two systems: cold water that is supplied at the temperature at which it enters the house, and hot water that is heated in a heater. Buildings that use steam heat will have a third system that runs through a boiler. Heaters may be standard storage types, which use a gas or electric heating element to warm water in 30–400l (10–100) gallon insulated tanks, or on-demand, which use heating elements to heat water as it enters the system. On-demand heaters are generally more efficient, as there is no heat loss during storage, and are not limited in the quantity of hot water they provide.

Pipes

Depending on a building's age, intended use, and resources, supply pipe may be made of PVC, iron, steel, brass or copper. Pieces of metal pipe can be brazed (lightly welded), ensuring a more permanent connection, but this is much more expensive than plastic (PVC) pipe, which can be assembled using contact cement. Iron and steel pipe will corrode over time, particularly if the supply water is slightly acidic.

All pipe is manufactured in straight runs, with connecting elements and bends accomplished by pre-manufactured components. Flow through, into and out of piped systems is controlled by valves, also known as faucets or cocks. Long runs of pipe, particularly those carrying heated or chilled water, must have expansion joints at about every 15 m (50 ft), while systems that experience rapid changes in water flow or direction will typically be supplied with air chambers that cushion water flow and prevent water 'hammer'.

Once inside a building, it is desirable to maintain temperature within a pipe. Hot water pipes that travel a great distance are usually wrapped in fiberglass insulation, and any pipe in an exterior wall or chase must be insulated to prevent freezing. Water expands, and frozen pipes will often burst, flooding whatever is upstream of the frozen portion. Occasionally electric heating of pipes will ensure constant flow, but more typically pipe runs will be located well inside a building floor plate. All municipal pipes will be put below the frost line, meaning that supply water will rarely be much warmer or colder than 10°C (55°F) throughout the year.

Fixtures

Sinks and faucets. Most municipal codes will require minimum numbers of various types of fixtures, particularly water closets, urinals sinks, and drinking fountains (Table 6.4.1). In the past 10 years, codes have been altered to include additional fixtures for women's bathrooms, recognizing the lopsided advantage of urinals in bathroom efficiency. For most occupancies, the requirement will work out to one toilet for every 20–30 male occupants, and one toilet for every 15-female occupants. This varies, however, with intensity of use. Assembly buildings typically have far more onerous fixture requirements per population, due to their heavily punctuated use at intermissions, end of performances, etc. Most codes require that any establishments that sell food have restrooms for dedicated customer use.

Water closets are more complex, as they require significant pressure to remove solid waste (Fig. 6.4.3). Generally, they come in two types – tanks, which rely on a reservoir to supply pressured water to the bowl, and valves, which rely on the pressure of the building's plumbing system (Fig. 6.4.4). In both cases, the bowl's contents are flushed out by simultaneously supplying fresh water to the bowl and supercharging the waste line with high-pressure water, creating a siphon that literally pulls the contents of the bowl into the drain pipe. The siphon can be created either by injecting the drain with pressured supply, or by vortex action, in which supply water is directed into the bowl to induce rotation as the bowl drains, creating a low-pressure jet in the middle of the waste stream. Tank fixtures will include both a floating shutoff valve that stops incoming water when the tank reaches a certain level, and a flapper valve that uses the pressure of the tank water to seal the drain to the bowl.

Table 6.4.1. Typical assumptions for fixtures in common building occupancies.

Occupancy	Water Closets		Urinals		Sinks	
	Provide	Then	Provide	Then	Provide	Then
Assembly-male	3 for first 400 patrons	1 for every 500 patrons	3 for first 400 patrons	1 for every 300 patrons	3 for first 750 patrons	1 for each 500 patrons
Assembly-female	8 for first 400 patrons	2 for every 300 patrons				
Dwelling Units	1–2 per dwelling	1 for every			1 per W.C.	
Factories	3 for first 50 persons	30 persons			1 for every 12 persons	
Institutional-male	1 for every 25 persons		1 for every 50 persons		1 for every 40 persons	
Institutional-female	1 for every 20 persons				1 for every 40 persons	
Office Buildings	3 for first 55 employees	1 for every 40 employees	1 for every 50 males		1 for every 40 employees	
Restaurants	3 for first 300 patrons	1 for every 200 patrons	1 for every 150 males		3 for first 400 patrons	1 for every 400 patrons
Schools—Nursery	2 for first 50 students	1 for every 50 students			2 for first 50 students	1 for every 50 students
Schools-male	1 for every 30 students		1 for every 75 students		1 for every 35 students	
Schools-female	1 for every 25 students				1 for every 35 students	
Secondary and University-male	1 for every 40 students		1 for every 35 students		1 for every 40 students	
Secondary and University-female	1 for every 30 students				1 for every 40 students	

Source: IAMPO.

Plumbing engineers will also typically be responsible for other piped services such as natural gas, laboratory gases, compressed air and vacuum, and sprinkler systems.

Waste

Venting, collection, and connection to sewers. Waste lines are more complicated than supply lines because they rely only on gravity, not pressure, to work. Thus, there are additional considerations in their layout, as a leak in a waste line is a significantly greater hazard. In designing for waste, it is advisable to keep the pipe system simple, with no bends or shifts, as clogs in a gravity system can lead to enormous head pressures and explosive failure.

Waste water systems have two features that prevent noxious sewer gases from entering a building. All drains are typically required by codes to have traps, 50–100 mm (2–4 in.) U-shaped bends in drain pipes that reliably hold

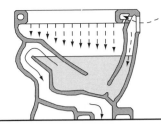

Washdown bowl relies on displacement to remove solids from bowl. Inexpensive but easily clogged

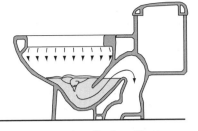

Siphon vortex uses shaped bowl to achieve low-pressure whirlpool to evacuate bowl. Moderate price, reasonably free from clogging

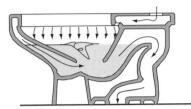

Siphon Jet uses directed flow of water to create siphonic action. Expensive but less prone to clogs

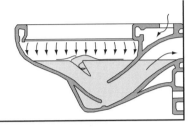

Blowout Flush uses pressure of building pipes to evacuate bowl. A flush valve is required meaning added expense, but spatially more efficient due to lack of tank

Figure 6.4.3. *Types of toilet fixtures.*

    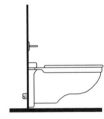

Floor-mounted
Integral tank

Least expensive
Easy installation
Compact section
No support needed in wall

Floor-mounted
Separate tank

Less expensive
Large capacity
Easy maintenance
Bulky configuration
No support needed in wall

Floor-mounted
Flush valve

Excellent performance
More expensive
Compact
Visible flush valve hardware
No support needed in wall

Wall-mounted
Integral tank

Less expensive
Bulky
Support needed in wall
Easy to clean floor

Wall-mounted
Flush valve

Most expensive
Compact
Support needed in wall
Easy to clean floor
Concealed hardware

Figure 6.4.4. *Tank and Valve locations on typical toilet fixtures.*

enough water to form an airtight seal. For this to contain gases, air pressure on both sides of the seal must be roughly equal, and therefore waste pipes must have vents to the outside that will prevent pressure from building up behind traps (Fig. 6.4.5). In small buildings this can be accomplished simply by extending the main vertical drain (the *soil stack*) through the roof (the *stack vent*), however larger buildings with multiple fixture washrooms are usually required to provide a separate pipe, called a *vent stack* that runs parallel to the soil stack. The two pipes can usually connect to one another above the highest fixture on a floor and below the lowest (Fig. 6.4.6).

Horizontal runs of drain pipes must be placed at a slope that is neither so shallow that water won't run, nor so quickly that the water filters away from slower moving particulates. Most codes require horizontal runs of between 1% and 4%. Cleanouts are usually required near any elbow and at each stack's connection

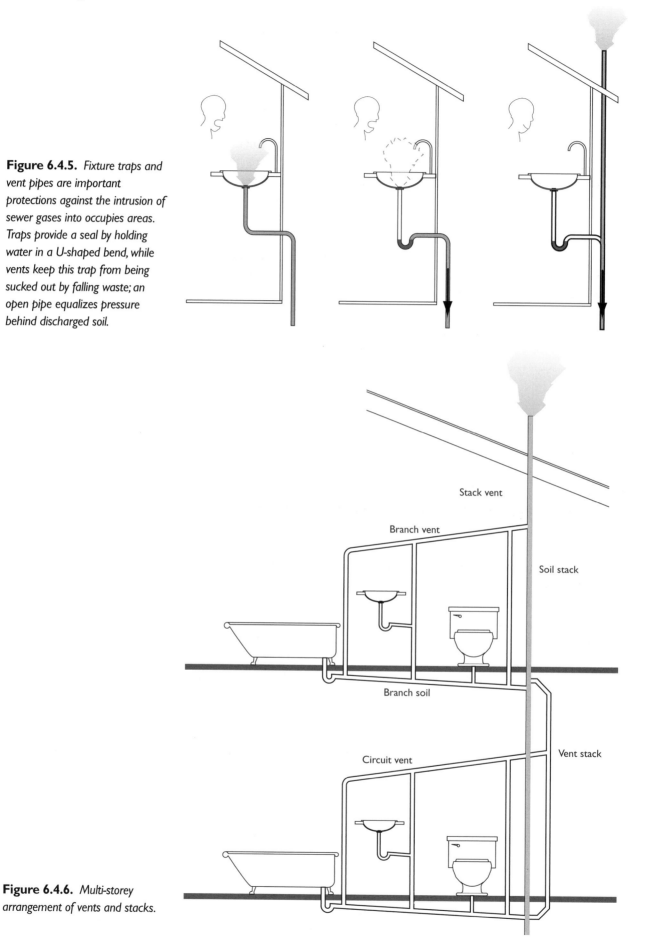

Figure 6.4.5. *Fixture traps and vent pipes are important protections against the intrusion of sewer gases into occupies areas. Traps provide a seal by holding water in a U-shaped bend, while vents keep this trap from being sucked out by falling waste; an open pipe equalizes pressure behind discharged soil.*

Figure 6.4.6. *Multi-storey arrangement of vents and stacks.*

to the main sewer. These allow a plumber to easily run a metal snake into drain pipes to remove blockages.

A main building sewer will typically collect all vertical stacks, and will flow at 1–2% slope from the building to a public sewer. Again, straight runs are preferable, and codes will often require manholes or cleanouts for bends. A *building trap* is usually required immediately prior to the sewer's leaving the footprint of the building. Codes may also require a grease trap between the final stack and the main sewer, to intercept potentially fouling cooking grease and similar substances from entering the public system. Sewer pipes are usually cast iron, concrete or tile, and they must be impervious to roots. Buildings in rural areas will often need to essentially treat wastewater on site using either a septic tank that allows solids to settle out of the effluent, which then leeches out into a tile field or sand filter. Bacteria in the tank itself will gradually digest the remaining solid matter, which must eventually be removed manually.

A separate waste system for rainwater drainage (*storm sewer*) is required to be separate from the system described above (*sanitary sewer*). This is discussed under Building Hydrology (Section 5.2).

Fixture design and layout

While architect's rarely design or lay out plumbing themselves, the results are second only to structural design in their direct impact on the spaces of a building. Bathrooms are one of the few places where people will be guaranteed to physically interact with our designs, and therefore knowing a few parameters going in is likely to reinforce the resulting quality of a design.

From a space planning point of view, it is important to remember that plumbing is typically buried in walls, and these walls (plumbing or chase walls) must be designed to accommodate some rather large pipe. It is common to assume an 200 mm (8 in.) clear space in all plumbing walls for medium to large scale buildings, and to lay out toilet rooms so that this larger wall can serve more than one space. The cost of piping also suggests that toilet rooms, showers, kitchens, etc., should be clustered together, eliminating long supply runs, and long waste runs. Supply and waste pipes are run through ceilings only as a last resort, as they can be noisy and potentially leaky.

Esthetics will often determine the selection of fixtures, however keep in mind that the American Disability Act (ADA) requires significant alterations to standard mounting heights and accessible areas:

Fixture type	Mounting height	Nearest distance to wall
Toilet	450 mm (18 in.)	450 mm (18 in.) from centerline (for grab bars this is both max and min)
Urinals	430 mm (17 in.) with elongated rim	450 mm (18 in.) from centerline

Fixture type	Mounting height	Nearest distance to wall
Lavatory	810 mm (32 in.) (optimum) 860 mm (34 in.) max 735 mm (29 in.) for ADA compliant fixture	450 mm (18 in.) 430 mm (17 in.) minimum – hot pipes must be insulated below fixture
Drinking fountain	900 mm (36 in.) max to spout	760 mm × 1220 mm (30 in. × 48 in.) clear approach
Shower	1010 mm (40 in.) max for controls, no more than 505 mm (20 in.) reach from bench	900 mm (36 in.) minimum square floor plan

Codes will also typically provide minimum requirements for the number of fixtures based on occupancy type. These are usually expressed in terms of fixtures per occupant, which is in turn determined by fire code occupancies. For most building types, these should be calculated per floor, as they usually offer a small – and useful – redundancy. Buildings with expected peak flows such as theaters or arenas often demand significantly higher fixture counts than may be expected, and in all cases provision should be made for gender inequality – women's restrooms should have higher fixture counts due to the efficiency of urinals vs. ordinary toilets (Figs. 6.4.7–6.4.9).

Frequently asked questions

Do restrooms need to stack in a multi-story building?
Not necessarily, but there are maintenance and economic reasons why we typically stack restrooms above one another whenever possible. First, plumbing is expensive in labor and materials costs. Adding enough number of pipes to take water and waste service to remote parts of a building will be costly. A more serious reason, however, has to do with head pressure in waste stacks. Shifting waste stacks requires a horizontal run of pipe, which must be slopes between 1:50 and 1:100. In long runs this will eat ceiling space quickly. But consider what can happen if something gets stuck in the elbow between vertical and horizontal pipes. If the stack is tall enough, water and waste may back up. If the backup is tall enough, the head pressure that results may be enough to burst the pipe at the vulnerable elbow. Anything immediately below the break will be deluged with the contents of the waste stack – not a pleasant thing for owner or architect. As a result, where possible we stack restrooms and other plumbing fixtures, or at the very least make sure that waste stacks transition over unoccupied – and easily cleanable – spaces.

What's a waterless urinal?
Waterless urinals use an oil trap and rely on the relatively light weight of human waste to migrate through the trap and into the waste stack. They require occasional maintenance to ensure that the trap has a usable oil level, but save very large amounts of water.

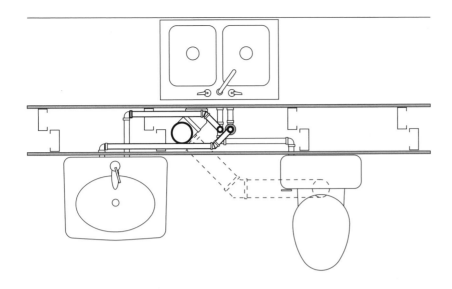

Figure 6.4.7. *Typical plumbing chase, showing need for coordination and space for both pipes and access.*

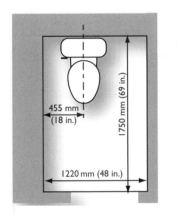

Accessible toilet stall – minimum

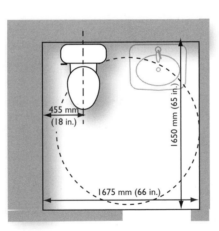

Accessible toilet stallt–preferred

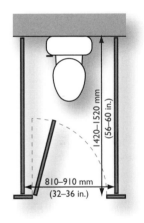

Non-accessible toilet stall

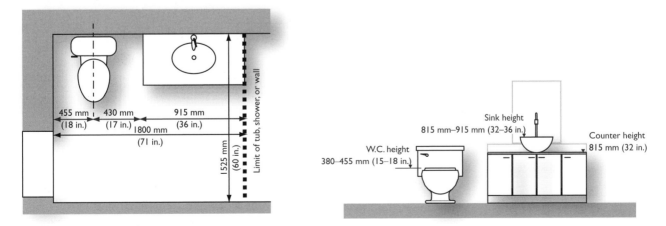

Figure 6.4.8. *Standard arrangements of toilets and lavatories to ensure access.*

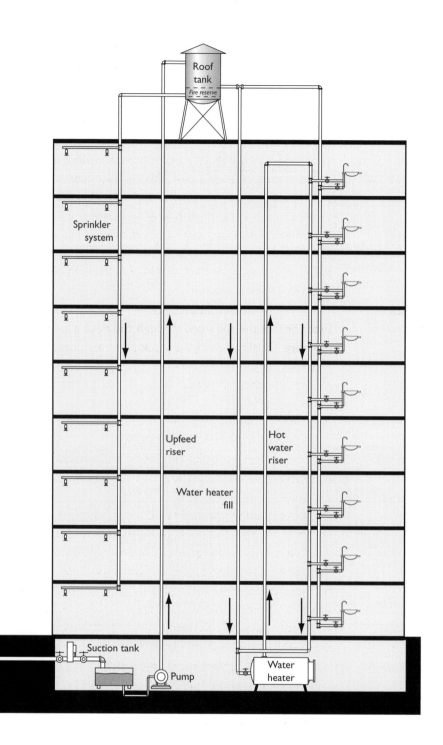

Figure 6.4.9. *Tall buildings require dedicated roof tanks to provide adequate pressure on all floors. Often, this will include provision for a dedicated fire reserve, to charge the sprinkler system, at the lowest portion of the tank.*

Glossary and formulas

Backflow	Contamination of water supply from a foreign source.
Building Trap	A U-shaped bend immediately downstream from a waste pipe's exit point from a building system. First line of defense against sewer gases migrating into occupied spaces.
Fixture	Any fixed equipment that offers users an interface with fresh water or a sewer. Includes *water closets*, *lavatories*, *urinals*, *mop sinks*, *showers*, *and bathtubs* and others such

	as laboratory faucets. Numbers of each type in public and commercial facilities are mandated by code.
Flush Valve	Type of water closet that uses house supply pressure to evacuate its bowl. Mostly commercial and institutional uses.
Hard Water	Water with high levels of calcium carbonate or similar minerals that prevent dissolution of soaps, etc.
Lavatory	Internationally accepted term for hand washing sink.
Sanitary Sewer	The opposite of what it says. Waste pipes that carry solid and liquid waste to municipal treatment facilities or on-site remediation (leach fields, septic tanks, etc.)
Siphonage	Contamination of a water supply through a faucet or fixture submerged in foul water. Broadly speaking, the tendency of water to 'pull' itself uphill for short distances if its net effect is downhill.
Soil Stack	The main vertical drain in a multi-story building.
Stack Vent	Extension of the *soil stack* through the roof, allowing pressure equalization in the stack and thus preventing water in *traps* from being siphoned out. Not to be confused with a *vent stack*, although this is a notorious exam question.
Storm Sewer	A drainage system for rainwater. Must typically be separated entirely from *sanitary sewer*.
Tank Fixture	Type of water closet that relies on a reservoir of water to evacuate its bowl. Mostly residential uses due to low pressure.
Trap	A U-shaped bend immediately downstream from a fixture in the waste pipe. Water is left in this pipe after use, which prevents sewer gas from escaping through fixture.
Urinal	Plumbing fixture that allows sanitary evacuation of liquid human waste. While experiments in the 1970s proposed these for women, human anatomy makes these, for better or worse, male-only fixtures in most situations.
Vent Stack	A separate, parallel pip to the *soil stack* in large installations that provides pressure equalization to fixtures throughout a system, preventing traps from being siphoned out. Connected to the soil stack above the highest fixture on a floor.
Water Closet	Internationally accepted term for toilet. Any device that allows sanitary evacuation of solid human waste.

Further reading

Stein, B. Reynolds, J.S. Grondzik, W.T. and Alison G. Kwok, *Mechanical and Electrical Equipment for Buildings*. (New York: Wiley, 2005).

6.5 Environmental control: acoustics

Sound	Physics
	Decibels
	Frequency
	Loudness
	'Air-borne' vs. 'Structure-borne' sound
	Reflectance
	Reverberation
Transmission/Assembly	Tuning space
	Sight lines
	Paths of travel
	Echo – flutter
	Absorption
	Isolation
	Focus
	Diffusion
	Shadow
	Mass
	Insulation
	Stagger

Introduction to acoustics

Sound affects the quality of all spaces we inhabit. Many sounds are desirable, such as listening to music or having a conversation – however once that becomes someone else's music or conversation it can move from being just sound to being noise. Everyone has had the experience of going to a restaurant and having great food, but experiencing too much noise. This is a problem that can be and should be avoidable by any skilled designer. The quality of the sound is also important to the experience of place – a medieval church benefits from long echoes when an organ fugue is being played, but is a terrible place to hold multiple conversations. Architects control the quality of sound by the decisions we make about design, yet are often unaware of what the result will be. Understanding the way sound travels and can be controlled gives the designer not only the ability to avoid mistakes, but also another tool to use in improving the quality of space.

Sound

Sound travels in waves from a vibrating source through an elastic medium. Air is the most common medium for transfer of sound, known as 'air-borne sound', but any material that can vibrate will transmit sound. Therefore virtually any

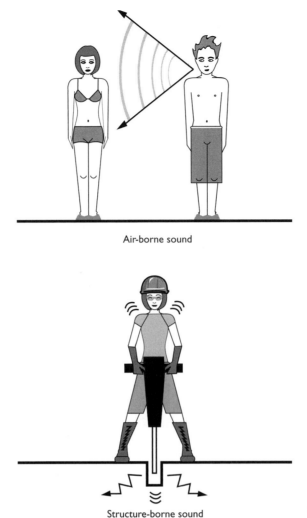

Air-borne sound

Structure-borne sound

Figure 6.5.1. *Types of sound.*

part of a building can transmit audible sound if it is set in motion within the frequency of human hearing. This type of sound transfer is known as 'structure-borne sound'. Both need to be considered in every project (Fig. 6.5.1).

Sound emanates equally outward from its source until reflected or absorbed by an object. We hear sounds directly from the source first, then reflections of the sound bouncing off surfaces (Fig. 6.5.2). Sound that travels further requires longer arriving, and the time gap between the first and subsequent sounds is what determines how 'live' or 'dead' a space is. Live spaces have longer reverberations and dead spaces absorb most reflections – each is appropriate for different activities.

Decibel (dB) is a measurement of sound intensity from the lower limit of perception (0) to above the threshold of pain (140). It is based on a logarithmic scale with differences in perception based on a subjective scale. The decibel levels of two noise sources happening at one time cannot be added directly, but there is a scale used to indicate the result of adding two sounds together. If the difference between two sounds is between 0 and 1 dB you add 3 to the higher decibel level. If the difference is between 2 and 3 you add 2 dB to the higher level, and

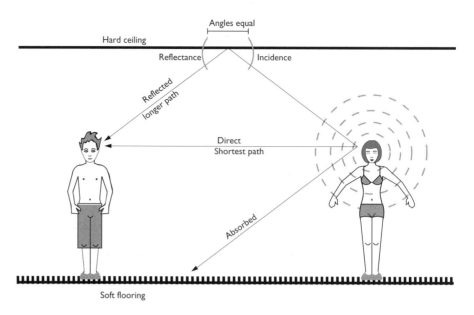

Figure 6.5.2. *Basic sound path diagram.*

Decibel level changes and perception in sound

Decibel Amount (dB)	Average perception of difference
3	Hard to notice difference
5	Clearly noticeable difference
10	2 times as loud
15	3 times as loud
20	4 times as loud

For example 50 dB to 53 dB results in no noticeable difference
50 dB to 60 dB results in a sound perceived as twice as loud
50dB to 70dB results in a sound perceived as four times as loud.

Figure 6.5.3. *Perception of changes in decibel level.*

if it is between 4 and 9 you add 1 dB. Anything above 10 dB difference adds nothing to the higher level. So 50 + 30 dB = 50 dB of perceived sound, and 50 + 50 dB = 53 dB of perceived sound (Fig. 6.5.3).

The *frequency* of human hearing is measured on a hertz scale measuring pitch between about 16 and 16,000 Hz (Fig. 6.5.4). We hear and understand speech most clearly in the middle of that range, while sounds at the upper and lower ranges of the scale are less clear and eventually pass into inaudible. Human speech is a narrower band than what we hear, but covers a broad range of the audible frequency range.

Loudness is a relative scale of the perceived volume of sound. Sounds at the same decibel level but different frequencies do not always sound equally loud. We tend to perceive sounds at the middle range of frequencies as louder,

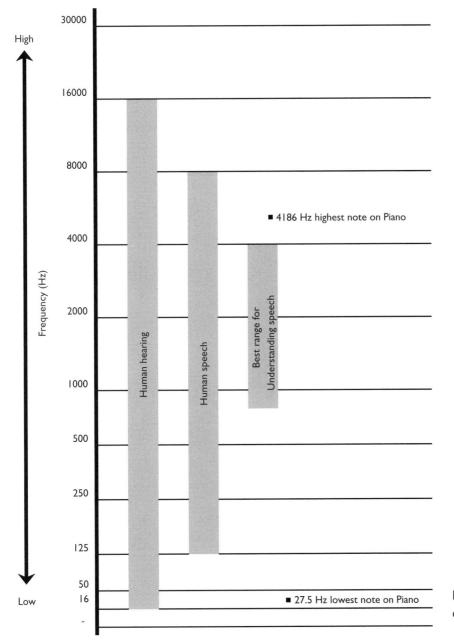

Figure 6.5.4. *Sound frequency of human hearing and speech.*

while sounds of the same decibel level at the upper and lower ends of the frequency scale are perceived as much more quiet. So hitting a key in the middle of a piano will sound louder than a key hit at the upper or lower end with the same force (Fig. 6.5.5).

Reverberation comes from multiple reflections of a sound – creating a lasting perceptible effect. This can be desirable at times, but tends to cause a lack of clarity in understanding speech. Broadcast studios tend to desire no reverberations at all, which makes speech much more crisp and articulate. Orchestral halls and churches benefit from the longest reverberations where music articulation desires a blending of sounds. Typical spaces with some speech needs fall into the lower end of the reverberation times (Fig. 6.5.6).

Decibel Level (dB)	Typical source	Perception
140	Shotgun blast	Very painful
130	Jet engine @ 30 m (100 ft)	Threshold of pain
120	Thunder	Sound can be felt
110	Jackhammer	
100	Rock concert	Very loud
90	Circular saw	
80	Shouting match	
70	Vacuum cleaner	Loud
60	Typical open office	Normal
50	Face to face conversion	Outlet
40	Outlet office	
30	Library	Very quiet
20	Whisper	
10	Butterfly	Barely perceptible
0		Not audible

(Left margin annotations: "Hearing Damage" arrow at 110–120 level; "Hearing Risk" arrow at 80–90 level)

Figure 6.5.5. *Decibel levels and perception.*

Transmission/assembly

We acoustically design space to improve the sound we want and limit the sound we don't. Improving the sound we want comes from understanding what needs to be reflected and what needs to be absorbed – and how much of each. This is tuning the space and can be thought of in terms of designing a musical instrument. It should be noted that different instruments are better for differing purposes and that is true of building acoustics as well – a space designed for an orchestra will be somewhat 'live' or have longer reverberations, and not be well suited for recording speech when you desire crisp annunciation without reverberation. It is possible to convert spaces by modifying the reflective/absorptive surfaces, but requires significant effort if the space is large. It is also important to consider dynamic systems as well as static ones – meaning people wear absorptive clothes that change the reflectance of interior surfaces. A full concert hall sounds different than an empty one, and a full one in the summer has a different sound than the same hall in the winter due to the thickness and porosity of the clothing.

Limiting sound between spaces, or acoustic separation, is also a primary concern of building design and can be most easily accomplished during schematics rather than later. Simply considering the relationship between noisy spaces and the best ways to limit undesired sound transmission based on adjacency is better than trying to insulate a bad layout. This is very important in mixed-use spaces where you may have a concert practice room next to a

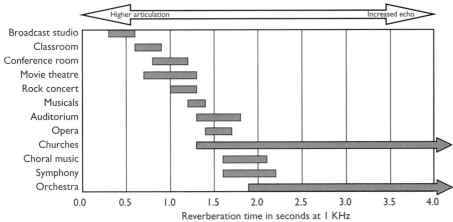

Figure 6.5.6. *Typical ideal reverberation times.*

classroom or office, but even the location of the mechanical room can have a major impact on sound transmission. For example, if you are laying out 2 music practice spaces with a bathroom and storage area, the preferred arrangement would put the bath and storage between the practice rooms. This allows the layout to limit sound transmission rather than having to heavily insulate walls between two directly adjacent practice rooms.

Material use for acoustical control falls into two types: lightweight sound absorbing materials for echo and reverberation control, and heavy impermeable materials for sound transmission control. Each serves a different purpose and both may be required to achieve the desired results. Lightweight materials generally trap air in an acoustical blanket, which captures sound waves within the open cells and prevents it from traveling back into the space. Heavy materials are designed to limit sound transmission through and into an adjacent space.

The most direct path of sound travel is directly from the source to the listener and is related to the sight line of a viewer. Auditorium design is the easiest way to describe tuning desirable sound transmission, as the principles are easily viewed and relate to every other condition of transmitting sound. In an auditorium people up front are receiving mostly direct sound, however in the back reflected sounds become more critical (Fig. 6.5.7). In every case there is a direct sound and reflected sounds, and the differential between the two needs to be controlled so the experience from front to back is similar. As sound travels at a constant speed in a space it is possible to calculate the distance from direct sound to reflectance, and adjust the shape of a space to respond to the desired reverberation (Figs. 6.5.8 and 6.5.9). Shadow occurs when balconies are too deep and stop reverberations from the ceiling reaching the seats below.

Problems with tuning come from issues such as poor reverberation times, along with echo and flutter. Echo occurs in spaces beginning with parallel walls at 18 m (60 ft) apart, where the direct sound and reverberations are heard as separate sounds. Flutter occurs in smaller spaces where sound reverberates back and forth off parallel hard surfaces causing a quick succession of short echoes. The shape of a surface can also cause undesirable focusing or diffusion of a sound.

The other area of concern is isolating sound between spaces. Because sound can travel in two ways, through air or structure, and each must be considered

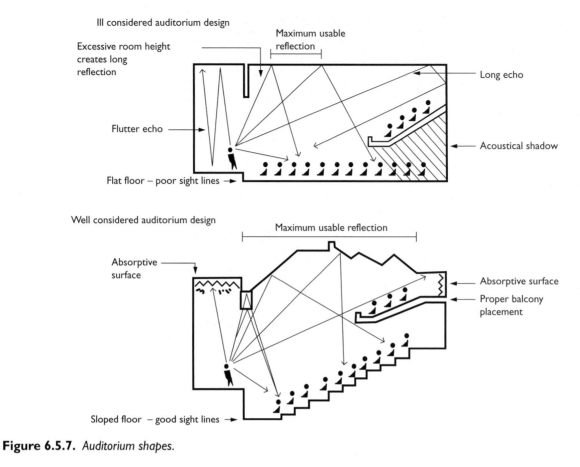

III considered auditorium design

Excessive room height
creates long
reflection

Maximum usable
reflection

Long echo

Flutter echo

Acoustical shadow

Flat floor – poor sight lines →

Well considered auditorium design

Maximum usable reflection

Absorptive
surface

Absorptive surface

Proper balcony
placement

Sloped floor – good sight lines →

Figure 6.5.7. *Auditorium shapes.*

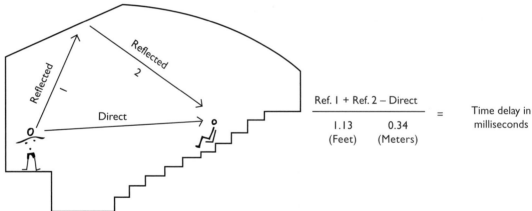

Reflected
1

Reflected
2

Direct

$$\frac{\text{Ref. 1} + \text{Ref. 2} - \text{Direct}}{1.13 \qquad 0.34} = \text{Time delay in milliseconds}$$
$$\text{(Feet)} \quad \text{(Meters)}$$

Figure 6.5.8. *Reverberation time.*

in different ways (Fig. 6.5.10). Air-borne sound can travel through any opening between spaces, even if it's not a direct path. If an air duct serves two spaces, sound will travel into a vent then reflect off the metal and transmit into the adjacent space – or farther. Any gap is vulnerable and can allow sound to move easily through it. The mass of a material also factors into transmission – the more mass the better it is able to limit overall transmission. Thin materials can often absorb sound, but can begin to vibrate themselves – turning air-borne sound into structure-borne sound. A combination of absorptive materials and mass typically is required to limit transmission. STC or sound transmission coefficient is the measure of sound reduction through a membrane. The higher the number, the better the sound reduction (Fig. 6.5.11).

Figure 6.5.9. *CY Stephens auditorium. Iowa State University, Ames, IA, USA (1969).*

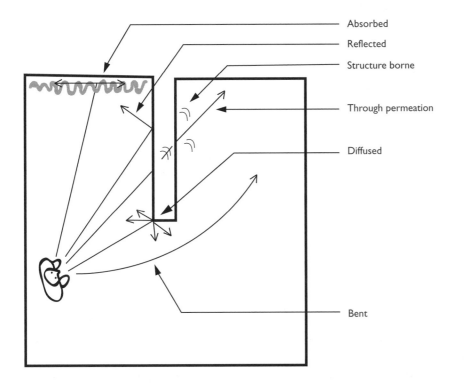

Figure 6.5.10. *Sound behavior in a Space.*

Staggering construction to prevent sound transmission is critical – this is mostly common sense, but requires some diligence to make the construction documents completely clear. If you don't draw or specify complete separation of components it will likely be constructed incorrectly, and a single breach in the system can transmit a large amount of sound. This includes items such as structural elements, outlets, cabinets, and ductwork (Fig. 6.5.12).

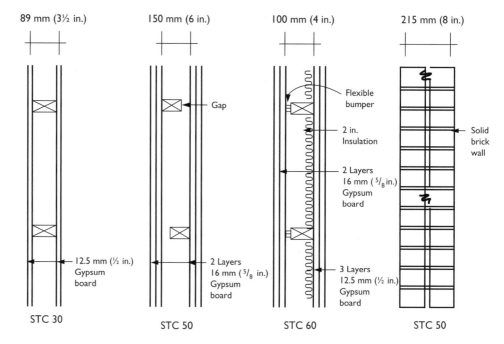

Figure 6.5.11. *Typical STCs.*

89 mm (3½ in.)   150 mm (6 in.)   100 mm (4 in.)   215 mm (8 in.)

Gap

Flexible bumper

2 in. Insulation

2 Layers 16 mm (⁵⁄₈ in.) Gypsum board

Solid brick wall

12.5 mm (½ in.) Gypsum board

2 Layers 16 mm (⁵⁄₈ in.) Gypsum board

3 Layers 12.5 mm (½ in.) Gypsum board

STC 30   STC 50   STC 60   STC 50

White noise refers to masking sounds introduced into a space to limit the perception of background noise. This is achieved by creating a background sound that interferes with the one you are trying to limit – the hope is that your introduced noise is less distracting than the original sound. It works quite effectively in most cases, as your ears tend to filter relatively high levels of sound as long as they are consistent. An acoustical consultant does this best, as you need to be precise about the type and level of the white noise.

Frequently asked questions

'What makes some spaces sound lively while others sound dead?'
Sound quality in a space is affected primarily by reflected sound waves. Direct sounds reach you regardless of the shape or reflectance of a space, but if there is no reflected sound the space will seem dead. The lively quality of a space is provided by the second or reflected sound. Very absorptive surfaces that prevent reflected sounds cause dead sounding spaces, which is often desirable where clarity of speech is important. Multiple reflections of sound make a space seem lively; however, this can also make a space seem noisy if there is too much reflected sound from many sources. Large historic churches are often the liveliest of spaces because there are many hard reflected surfaces that are far away from the listener, causing many long delayed reflected sounds.

'Can structure-borne sound become air-borne sound?'
Yes, and air-borne sounds can also become structure borne. Structure-borne sounds simply vibrate an elastic medium such as the ground or a building structure rather than the air, but these vibrating structures tend to cause the air to vibrate which makes the sound become airborne. This can often happen after the structure-borne sound has traveled far through a building, causing air-borne sounds at the top level from a motor running in the basement. Loud air-borne

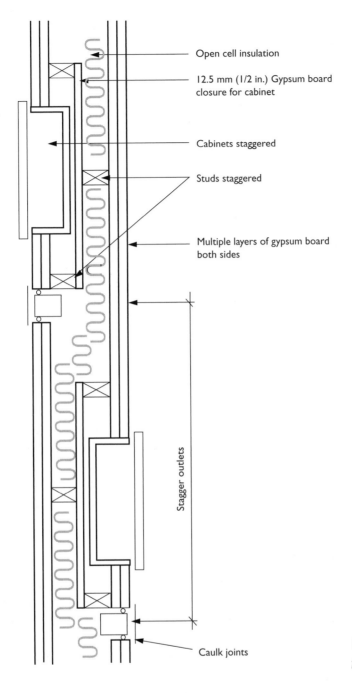

Open cell insulation

12.5 mm (1/2 in.) Gypsum board closure for cabinet

Cabinets staggered

Studs staggered

Multiple layers of gypsum board both sides

Stagger outlets

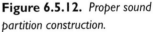

Caulk joints

Figure 6.5.12. *Proper sound partition construction.*

sounds can also cause waves strong enough to vibrate structure, which is commonly seen when airplanes rattle windows in a building when they pass overhead.

Conclusion

Sound quality is an important part and, as we frequently note, often overlooked part of building design. We've all had bad experiences with poor acoustics, and it is an area under the architect's control – no one else in the process is paying attention to this aspect of design unless a specific acoustical consultant has been hired. Different intended uses of a space can be enhanced or ruined depending on how the acoustics are considered, and while existing spaces can be modified to perform better acoustically it is always more difficult and less effective than planning ahead. Consider the user groups of a project, the shapes and arrangement of rooms, the materials being used on various surfaces and the potential for structure borne or outside environmental sounds. Acoustics are a powerful experiential tool that can enrich the quality of every project when properly considered.

Glossary and formulas

Air-borne sound	Sound traveling in waves from a vibrating source through the elastic medium of air.
Decibel (dB)	A measurement of sound intensity from the lower limit of perception (0) to above the threshold of pain (140).
Echo	Occurs in spaces where the direct sound and reverberations are heard as distinguishable separate sounds.
Flutter	Occurs in small spaces where sound reverberates back and forth off parallel hard surfaces causing a quick succession of short echoes.
Frequency	Human hearing is measured on a hertz scale measuring frequency of pitch between about 16 and 16,000 Hz.
Loudness	A relative scale of the perceived volume of sound.
Reverberation	Comes from multiple reflections of a sound, creating a lasting perceptible effect.
Sight line	Is both the direct view from the sound source to the intended audience, but also the direct path of sound travel. In other words, if you can see the source you can hear it directly, if you cannot see the source you are hearing reflected or indirect sounds only.
STC	Sound transmission coefficient is the measure of sound reduction through a membrane. The higher the number, the better the sound reduction.
Structure-borne sound	Sound traveling in waves from a vibrating source through an elastic medium of a building's structure or the ground.

Further Reading

Charles M. Salter Associates. (1998) *Acoustics: Architecture, Engineering, the Environment* (San Francisco, CA: William Stout). pp. 27–43.

Ramsey and Sleeper.(2000) *Architectural Graphic Standards*, 10th ed (New York, NY: John Wiley & Sons). pp. 63–72.

Ernst and Peter Neufert. (2000) *Architect's Data*, 3rd ed (London, UK: Blackwell Science). pp. 117–124.

6.6 Electrical and data services

History	Influence of need for architectural lighting
	Supply and demand pricing
	Development of standardized, municipal utility services
Principles	Current, voltage and resistance (Ohm's law)
	Municipal supply
	Switches and distribution
Devices and Systems	Wiring
	Outlets
	Switches
	Safety

Electrical services – history

Of all building services, electrical is both the most recent and most hazardous. Prior to the 1880s, the only source of lighting and energy within buildings was fire, whether in the form of a hearth, a gas lamp, or a wood stove. Municipal services provided street lighting as early as 1881. While early electrical service was often shoddy and nearly always operated by inexperienced (and thus often quite dangerous) companies in the 1890s, by the turn of the century Edison had established a monopoly in most cities, providing reasonable safe, often subsidized electric current to commercial and residential customers.

Like water, electricity is typically brought to a building site from a municipal source, although on-site generation does occur, whether through integrated generators or solar panels. Generation is predominantly done at a power plant by heating water in a boiler, and using the pressure from the resulting steam to turn turbines. These in turn provide motive power to a generator, which generates current by rapidly rotating wire coils through a magnetic field. Even with a century of advancement, electrical generation is at its best only 40% efficient. Most of the energy that goes into a power plant, whether nuclear, coal, gas or oil, ends up being wasted as heat.

Three terms describe the quantity and flow of electricity, and it is useful to think of these in terms of flowing water (Fig. 6.6.1). The *voltage* in a system (V) is analogous to the pressure in a piped system, the *current* (I) is analogous to flow, and the *resistance* (R) is analogous to friction. For electricity, these are measured in volts, amperes, and ohms, respectively, and are related by Ohm's law, which states that the current flowing in a circuit will be proportional to the voltage (pressure), and inversely proportional to the resistance (friction):

$$I = V/R$$

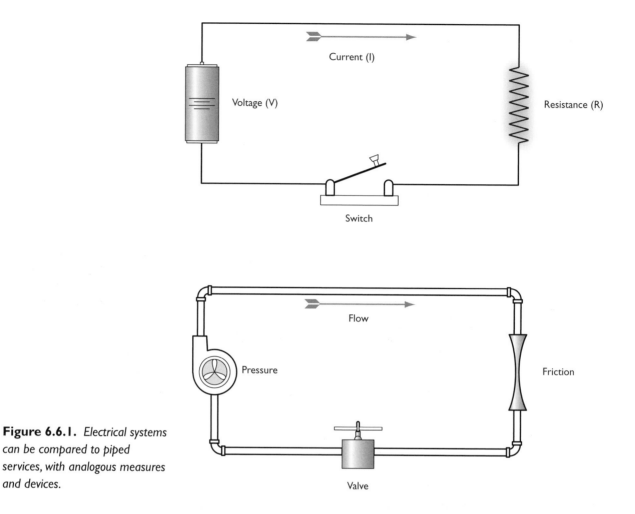

Figure 6.6.1. *Electrical systems can be compared to piped services, with analogous measures and devices.*

Electric fixtures are rated by their capacity for voltage – the amount of 'push' they can take – but they will also typically be rated for their resistance, that is, the amount of 'friction' they offer to current passing through. Wiring is generally rated in terms of current – how much 'flow' it can safely take. Appliances and fixtures use a differential in voltage between two sides of an electrical circuit to induce electrical flow, powering motors, illuminating filaments, etc. Current is additive, that is, every voltage drop on a circuit will 'pull' more amperage. Thus, the current running through a given circuit will be:

$$I_{total} = (V_1R_1 + V_2R_2 + \ldots + V_nR_n)$$

More appliances, fixtures, or other elements that provide resistance and a voltage differential will pull more amperage through the system (Fig. 6.6.2). One of our greatest concerns is making sure that we don't add so many of these to a circuit that the amperage 'pulled' through wiring is greater than that wiring's safe capacity.

The distribution of electricity relied on the development of AC, or 'alternating current'. While direct current (DC) is relatively simple, its voltage cannot be changed. Alternating current, on the other hand, allows easy 'stepping' up and down of voltage, so that a single generating plant can send out very high voltage current to substations, which can then send out moderate voltage to individual customers, where it can then be stepped down to relatively low voltage

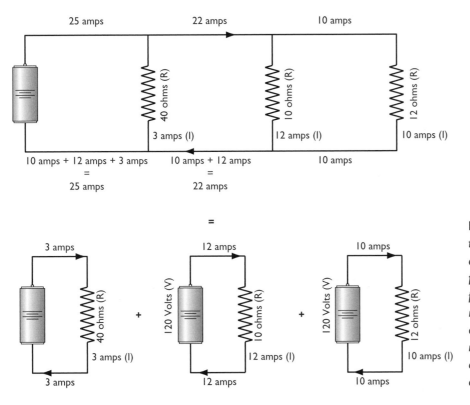

Figure 6.6.2. *Basic current theory. The flow of electricity across voltage drops (appliances, fixtures, etc.) pulls current in inverse proportion to the amount of resistance each drop offers. This effect is additive, meaning that multiple appliances on one circuit can quickly add up to a very large current.*

current. This development led to an implosion of electrical prices in the early 20th century, permitting its widespread throughout urban areas.

Appliances and systems within a building use the difference in voltage between a combination of supply wires to create a 'voltage drop,' or a difference in potential energy. Electricity will flow across this voltage drop. Some appliances will use high resistance elements to create heat or light, while others will use the flow of electrons to induce motion in magnetic motors, the opposite of the generation process. Solid state equipment will transform the incoming electricity much further, using micro-currents to manipulate relays, transistors, or microprocessors.

While practices and components have been developed to be generally safe, electricity poses some obvious and preventable hazards. First and foremost is the risk of electrocution, in which the body comes in contact with a voltage drop that can cause paralysis and death. This can occur both through direct contact with electric wires, but it can also occur when a building element or appliance is accidentally charged. A more common hazard is fire. Resistance causes heat, and if electricity is pushed or pulled through a wire or appliance at a greater rate than anticipated, heat from resistance can build quickly, igniting nearby material. Likewise, a faulty connection can cause electricity to jump across an unintentional voltage drop, causing sparks that can start fires. Electrical codes are therefore geared toward isolating elements of electrical supply, limiting the flow of current, and guaranteeing standards of connection.

Supply

Municipal power in the United States has been standardized, with three major supply elements to every building – two 'hot,' and one 'neutral.' The neutral line is grounded – no electric potential exists between it and the ground. The two 'hot' cables carry alternating current in interlocking phases, so that at any given moment the potential between either one and the ground is 120 V, but the potential between the two of them is 240 V. This allows two different voltages within the building. Small appliances, lights, and other light-duty fixtures use 120 V, while larger appliances such as ovens, water heaters, washers and dryers use 240 V. Transformers will typically be required to step down the voltage from municipal supply lines, and these may be provided either by the utility or within the building site itself.

The three wires enter a building either underground, or through an exterior conduit (a metal pipe that protects the wires and serves as an automatic ground). At their entrance to the building, most codes require both a *meter* and a *shutoff*. The shutoff is generally located downstream from the meter, so that any faults, or 'leakage' of electricity through a bad connection is registered. The meter itself reads the flow of current, recorded as current (sometimes peak) load, and total power delivered. This is measured in kilowatt-hours.

Electric power is metered at the entrance to a building, much like water. Because electricity must be used instantaneously, electric companies typically charge based not only on the total quantity of electricity provided (usually measured in kilowatt-hours, or kWh), but also on the *peak demand* of a given customer. Power is easy to supply at low levels, but times of maximum usage, particularly hot days when many customers may be using air conditioners, determine the required capacity of power plants. Therefore, utilities typically charge a higher rate for peak time usage, reflecting the overhead cost of maintaining a plant sized for this greater demand, along with the basic charge for the number of kilowatt hours. Large customers may therefore benefit from *demand control*, which monitors usage during peak times and adjusts electricity usage accordingly – water heaters, for example, may be set to a lower temperature during the day, and battery chargers may be programmed to operate only at night. At its most sophisticated, demand control may compare fuel costs with utility costs, and shift supply from a municipal source to an on-site generator.

Once inside a building, electricity flows through three elements – *Control, Wiring, and Fixtures*. Control systems take power from either a utility or on-site source, transform its voltage, and direct it to various runs of cables and circuits.

To avoid transmission loss, electricity arrives at a building at a very high voltage – often 2400–13,200 V. (Recall that Ohm's law says that the amperage, or flow of current, is directly proportional to its voltage – so this represents a very big 'push' through very thick, dedicated high-voltage lines). Needless to say, this would quickly burn out typical household fixtures, which are usually rated for changes in potential of 120 or 240 V. A *transformer* is therefore needed between the utility supply and the customer, usually one that drops to 240 V for residential buildings, or 480 V for larger commercial consumers. Upon entering a building, electricity is sent through a switchboard, which provides dedicated circuits at high and low voltage that can then be distributed appropriately throughout the building. For residential service, there will

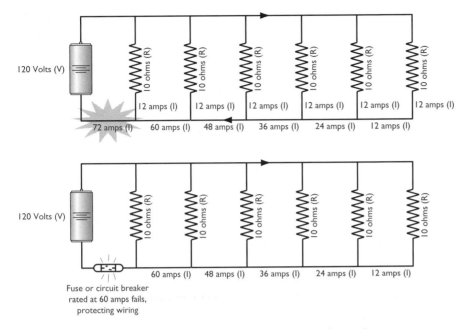

Figure 6.6.3. *Overloading a circuit with multiple appliances can draw a dangerous current. Wiring in particular is rated for varying levels of amperage, which if exceeded can cause excessive heat and fire. Fuses and circuit breakers are designed to sense when a preset level of current is exceeded, at which point they break the circuit and prevent a dangerous condition.*

usually be a panelboard composed of circuit breakers and switches that divides loads into 120 and 240-V circuits. 120-V power is provided by running a single 'hot' wire and a neutral, while 240-V power is provided by running two 'hot' wires each charged with 120 V – one positive, one negative, for a total voltage drop of 240 V. Commercial service will use a similar technique to provide service up to 480 V.

Circuit breakers are designed to allow the passage of current up to a given rating, usually 100, 150, 200, 400, and 600 amp. Current flowing through a wire produces heat, and therefore circuits can overheat and catch fire if the amperage passing through them is too high. Wire is therefore rated according to the maximum amperage it can safely handle, and must be connected to a similarly rated *circuit breaker*. This device, much like the fuses it has replaced, senses when amperage goes above a given load, and mechanically 'trips' to break the circuit. Adding too many appliances to a circuit will therefore trip a circuit breaker, shutting down the circuit and preventing a possible fire from overloaded and thus overheated wires (Fig. 6.6.3). This arrangement also prevents a *short circuit*, where two wires with a voltage differential accidentally come into contact (Fig. 6.6.4). From Ohm's law, it can be seen that this condition is quite dangerous – with little resistance offered by regular wires, the voltage will induce a very high amperage, leading quickly to overheating and fire. Because this amperage will exceed the rating of a circuit breaker, however, the circuit will be turned off quickly if properly connected.

These conditions were handled in older houses by fuse boxes, using disposable, screw-in fuses that would fail at given amperages. However the reliance

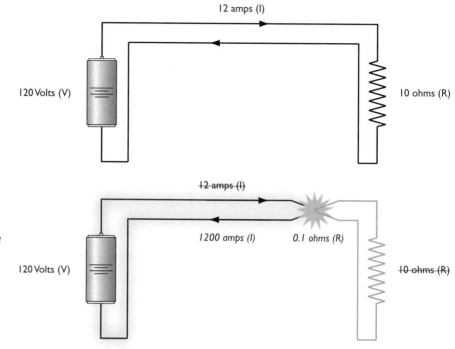

Figure 6.6.4. *Fuses and circuit breakers also prevent short circuits, which occur when positive and negative (or neutral) wires accidentally come in contact with one another. If this occurs, the resistance is nearly zero, and the resulting large current can quickly cause a fire.*

of these devices on untrained owners to replace fuses with the correct rating and type created an inherently dangerous situation. In particular, the common practice of replacing a blown fuse with a copper coin led, predictably, to disastrous consequences. Insurance companies have understandably led the move toward more foolproof circuit breakers to protect residential and smaller commercial and institutional systems or branches. Circuit breakers are typically contained in a *panelboard*, which allows easy access in a central location (Fig. 6.6.5).

Larger scale installations will use dedicated switchgear instead of circuit panelboards, based on similar principles but often with much higher amperage to feed larger cables. These systems lead to smaller, more familiar panelboards in distributed electrical closets throughout a building. Switchgear will usually include dedicated circuits for high-voltage equipment such as elevators. In all cases, electrical codes will require a fairly large clear floor space in front of any panelboard or switch to permit an electrician space to work and to ensure that they will not be trapped against a door or wall during accidental contact with a 'hot' wire in the panel.

Wiring

Because even the largest typical electric wire in an architectural application is usually around 4 in. in diameter, consideration of wiring paths and configuration is often left strictly up to electrical engineers or electricians themselves. Cable is inherently flexible, and it can be snaked in very tight spaces. Therefore, electrical supply tends to be easier to integrate than larger systems such as air handling and plumbing. A basic understanding of wiring principles, however, can often lead to more efficient and cheaper installations. All wiring

Figure 6.6.5. *At typical panelboard, which serves as both a distribution panel and a central point for disconnecting individual circuits.*

is rated according to the maximum current it can safely carry, determined by its resulting temperature. High current cable must be thermally insulated to prevent possible ignition of surrounding materials, while low current cable may require little if any thermal protection.

Two basic factors influence all wiring design – insulation and grounding. 'Hot' wires leading to typical interior appliances at 120 V can kill a person in wet conditions, and therefore all charged cables must have a non-conducting insulating jacket. This may be as simple as a rubber or plastic sleeve for low voltage wire, but may also include glass tubing, fiberglass casings or dedicated rubber insulators that separate charged cabling from a box-like enclosure. This ensures that any contact with the cable will not allow current to jump across the potential difference between circuit and ground through the person.

Grounding is a bit more complicated, but equally important. Most domestic electrical systems include a dedicated neutral wire for 120 V supply, which is connected directly to a lead running into the surrounding earth, guaranteeing that the building will not develop a potential voltage drop with its surroundings. The supply charge, however, will always seek and find the easiest and most direct path to the neutral ground, whether it is the intended wire or not. If, for

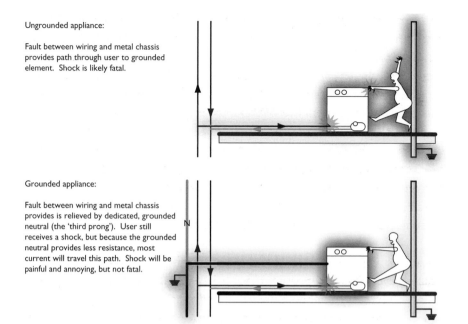

Ungrounded appliance:

Fault between wiring and metal chassis
provides path through user to grounded
element. Shock is likely fatal.

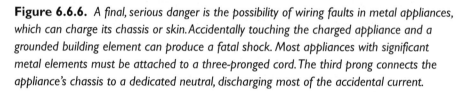

Grounded appliance:

Fault between wiring and metal chassis
provides is relieved by dedicated, grounded
neutral (the 'third prong'). User still
receives a shock, but because the grounded
neutral provides less resistance, most
current will travel this path. Shock will be
painful and annoying, but not fatal.

Figure 6.6.6. *A final, serious danger is the possibility of wiring faults in metal appliances, which can charge its chassis or skin. Accidentally touching the charged appliance and a grounded building element can produce a fatal shock. Most appliances with significant metal elements must be attached to a three-pronged cord. The third prong connects the appliance's chassis to a dedicated neutral, discharging most of the accidental current.*

example, a wire within an appliance comes in contact with an external, conducting surface (e.g., a steel dishwasher), that external surface becomes a potential hazard (Fig. 6.6.6). A person touching that surface and another grounded piece of metal – a sink faucet, for instance – will instantly become part of a 120 V circuit. Appliances are therefore typically required to connect potentially conducting surfaces to a dedicated ground wire, and such appliances must have a three-pronged plug. This third prong connects to a second dedicated ground circuit within the building, often tied to a copper water pipe, that will discharge any such unintentional circuit.

Wiring comes in a variety of sizes and configurations. (Note that the distinction between cable and wire is one of size – smaller than 6-gauge is called wire, larger is called cable.) In all cases, the resistance of wire or bus is inversely proportional to its cross sectional area – just as a wide pipe allows more water to flow through, a wide cable allows more amperage. Ratings are given based on the maximum amperage that can safely be carried at a given temperature, a combination of the cable's material, insulation, and location.

Large installations will often use a *busduct* to run from their main switchgear. This consists of flat copper or aluminum bars, stacked atop one another and insulated by rubber or plastic separators. While technically unlimited, ordinary busduct is often rated up to 4000 amp, and can be configured to allow circuits to directly plug into its metal bars.

Most commercial installations are required by code to run wiring through rigid *conduit*, usually metal, that provides protection to the flexible conductors inside. Conduit is rated in three categories based on its strength – rigid steel, intermediate metal conduit, and electric metal tubing. While the former is more robust, the latter lends itself to easier bending. In addition to preventing damage to wiring, conduit provides a naturally fireproof environment, and it can be easily grounded, providing a quick, safe path for current from a damaged wire inside. Because of its smooth interior surface, conduit allows wire to be literally pulled through a building, meaning that cabling can be easily retrofitted. While available in up to 4 in. diameter, most installations will use 1–2 in. conduit to run from panelboards. Aluminum conduit is lighter, but more subject to corrosion and reaction with concrete.

Cable and wiring may also be run in *raceways*, metal trays that support flexible cables and wires and protect them from snagging. In addition to power, raceways often carry telecommunication and data cabling, though these are usually required to run in physically separate compartments from power cables, to prevent short circuiting that could energize telecommunications equipment. Raceways may be located within ceiling spaces, within rooms and corridors themselves, or under a floor. This last application is particularly useful for data and power intensive programs, such as trading floors, as access to the cabling can be easily accomplished without shutting down large areas to maneuver ladders for access to the ceiling. Raised floor systems have become common in the past 20 years, usually relying on a standardized grid of floor tiles attached to vertical posts.

Another way to protect wiring and cable is by a dedicated metal sleeve, called *armor*, that is factory wrapped around the conductors. *Armored cable* provides integral protection to individual wires by wrapping them in spiral-metal shields. Both conduit and cable armor provide a convenient grounding strategy, in that they can both be easily attached to a grounded circuit. Being metal, they will carry any load induced by a fault safely to ground. However, both armor and conduit must be carefully cut and fitted to avoid damaging cable within, either from installation or from rubbing.

At its simplest, wiring will consist simply of a metal conductor wrapped by an insulator – typically strands of copper surrounded by rubber or plastic. Older installations may contain raw wiring, insulated by glass 'knobs' connected to the building structure. Wiring that is to be pulled through conduit will have a nylon sleeve surrounding the rubber insulation, to avoid friction or snagging within the conduit.

Outlets and switches

Again like plumbing, electrical services are only as useful as their interface with occupied spaces. Numerous standards exist for the installation of end-use attachments. In general, wire or cable will be attached at the point of use to a junction box that is firmly connected to the building structure. This is usually accomplished by metal arms or bridges that attach to adjacent studs and allow some horizontal adjustment, but boxes are also frequently cast into concrete slabs and fitted into brick walls. Electrical boxes are made of steel or aluminum, and include punched openings on all sides to allow cable entry from a convenient angle. Typically the cable will be attached with some slack to the box, so that it does not get pulled or snagged if the box moves over time. Once inside the box, the cable will unwrap and connect directly to an outlet, a switch, or the wires inside of an electrical device.

Boxes, and thus switches and outlets, come in several standard sizes, referred to by the number of columns of available connections – a *one-gang* outlet contains a vertically arranged pair (or gang) of connections, a *two-gang* outlet contains two pairs, etc. Plugs (or *receptacles*) come in a variety of shapes and configurations, keyed to the power requirements of a given electrical appliance. Large motors, for example, may have plugs that can only be fit into outlets providing adequate voltage with proper phasing.

Two types of electrical receptacle and plug include important safety features for daily use. A *three-pronged* plug is used wherever a significant amount of conducting metal is used in the electrical device itself. As described above, the third prong is a dedicated ground circuit, connected directly to the metal structure or component of an electric device, that ensures that any 'stray' current will have an easy connection to ground. While a user may still receive a shock, the majority of the current will flow through the third prong, eliminating any fatal amperage.

Similarly, a *ground-fault indicator*, or *ground-fault-circuit interrupt* (GFI or GFCI) includes a device that compares current flowing into an outlet vs. current returning through an outlet. In the event that there is a significant difference, the device will automatically trip, stopping power flow through the circuit. This is also designed to protect users who contact an electrified device and a ground, in particular where water is present (Fig. 6.6.7). Because water conducts so well, a 120 V shock through a bathtub, for instance, draws enough amperage to be fatal. A user who drops an electrified device in a bathtub will be protected, however, by a GFI, which will recognize the current 'dump' outside the circuit and shut off within half a second.

Codes will typically require that a GFI outlet be provided within 450 mm (18 in.) of any sink, guaranteeing safe electric power and discouraging users from stretching cords to other outlets without GFCI outlets. Similarly, codes mandate a certain number and placement of outlets in any room, both to ensure access and to discourage the use of extension cords, which can be tripping hazards and which, over time, may wear and cause short circuits or fires, for example when placed under carpets.

Outlets and switches must be placed for convenient usage. A common household danger is the use of multiple extension cords and surge protectors to make up for a lack of easily accessible outlets, and proper provision in places that are likely to be available (i.e., not blocked by furniture) is by far the easiest way to prevent this. Likewise, switches must be properly located in intuitive places to allow easy use and access. While electricians or electrical engineers will typically lay out circuits and wiring paths, architects should consider locations of

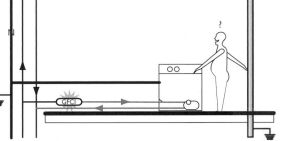

Ground fault circuit interrupt

Fault between wiring and metal chassis is detected by GFCI as current flow between wires doesn't balance. The interrupt trips, breaking the circuit and protecting the user. Appliance won't work, but user will receive only a very brief, non-lethal shock.

Figure 6.6.7. *The danger of charged appliances and grounded occupants can also be eliminated with GFCIs, which sense any 'leakage' of current and shut down the entire circuit if this occurs. GFCIs are often required near sinks and bathtubs, where accidents involving appliances, water, and grounded pipes are possible.*

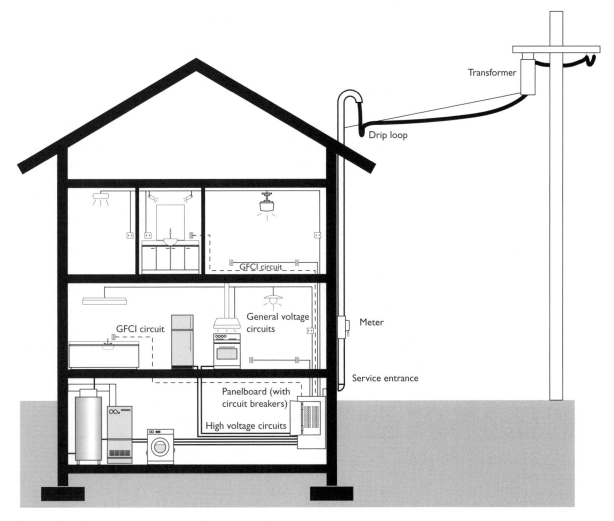

Figure 6.6.8. *Anatomy of a typical electrical installation.*

all elements for their functional and esthetic implications (Fig. 6.6.8). A typical electrical plan, as shown in Figure 6.6.9, will include general placement within rooms, and will show schematic representations of circuits, including paths from switches to lights and outlets. Both outlets and switches must be accessible to both standing occupants and wheelchair users. Common mounting heights and locations are shown in Figure 6.6.10.

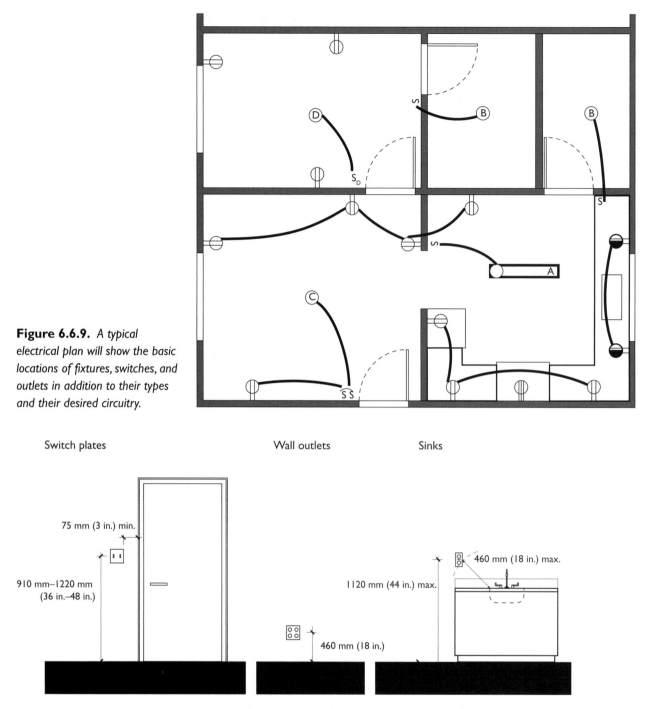

Figure 6.6.9. *A typical electrical plan will show the basic locations of fixtures, switches, and outlets in addition to their types and their desired circuitry.*

Switch plates   Wall outlets   Sinks

75 mm (3 in.) min.

910 mm–1220 mm
(36 in.–48 in.)

1120 mm (44 in.) max.

460 mm (18 in.) max.

460 mm (18 in.)

Figure 6.6.10. *Typical mounting heights and locations for common electrical interfaces.*

Frequently asked questions

I have a three-pronged plug but can only find a two-pronged outlet. Is it safe to just file off the third prong of the plug?

Not if there is a fault in the appliance you are plugging in. The third prong connects to the ground circuit in the building and will safely discharge any current that accidentally runs through the metal chassis or skin of the appliance or fixture. The third prong is there to ensure that the appliance is *only* plugged in to a grounded outlet.

How safe is old wiring? Does it need to be replaced if the building is being renovated?
Not necessarily. Old wiring may have several problems, which need to be investigated. Most importantly, insulation on cables or wires can deteriorate, particularly older rubber and plastic coatings. If this frays or cracks, the 'hot' wire may come in contact with other wires, or with metal elements of the building structure. Likewise, constant tugging due to small building movements can pull wires out of place and lead to exposed ends. Wires themselves, being made of copper (or sometimes aluminum) are not prone to deterioration, but may corrode if exposed to water. Any of these can lead to a dangerous situation.

Given the proliferation of electronic office equipment in the last 15 years, isn't it dangerous to add so many computers, monitors, printers, etc., to electrical systems designed for previous generations?
The multiple surge protectors and extension cords that seem to define the office desktop today certainly don't look safe. But once these loads get back to the building system, they tend not to produce overloads. This is because electronic equipment (other than cathode-ray tube (CRT) monitors) tends to use very low voltages. Even a handful of CPUs on a circuit, for example, won't require nearly the voltage drop of an old electric typewriter. While the number of devices has grown, the power they use has dropped significantly.

Glossary and formulas

Alternating Current	Electrical supply that reverses polarity rapidly. This offers advantages in transmission and safety.
Armored Cable	Insulated cable with an additional, spiral-metal coating.
Busduct	High capacity power 'cabling' consisting of flat, insulated metal plates.
Cable	Drawn metal larger than 6-gauge.
Circuit Breaker	A mechanism designed to break a circuit if a certain level of current is exceeded. Circuit breakers are available in a range of current ratings.
Conduit	Metal tube through which insulated cable can be pulled, providing a protected path.
Current	A measure of the flow rate of electricity in a circuit, measured in amperes (or 'amps').
Demand Control	Building management systems that adjust electrical usage based on peak rate structures.
Direct Current	Electrical supply that occurs at a constant positive/negative polarity (compare with Alternating Current).
Fuse	A small metal filament, usually encased in glass, designed to melt if a precise level of current is run through it. While still available, fuses have largely been replaced in new construction by circuit breakers.
Ground-Fault-Circuit-Interrupt (GFCI)	A special outlet that contains a mechanical device capable of recognizing a sudden 'dump' of

current and quickly breaking the circuit. This prevents a user from being electrocuted by accidentally completing a circuit, and is typically required in wet areas such as kitchens or bathrooms.

Grounding	Wiring designed to discharge any electrical potential from a building, appliance, or fixture into the earth, bypassing any users or objects that would be harmed by such a current.
Insulation	In electrical instances, non-conducting material designed to isolate wire, cable, or busduct from users and potentially conducting building elements.
Junction Box	A metal box designed to provide a safe connection between a cable and its outlet. Contains attachments for a face plate, connections to the building substructure (often wall studs, e.g.), and openings for cable access.
One- (or Two-, Three-, or Four-) Gang	A measure of the number of outlets in a face plate. One-gang contains two, vertically stacked outlets, Two-gang contains four, etc. These may be power outlets, or data, telecommunication, or indicator components.
Peak Demand	Pricing policy often put in place by utilities that charges extra for use during particularly intensive periods.
Raceways	Flat trays in which insulated cable can be laid, providing easy access.
Resistance	A measure of a circuit's 'friction' or impedance of current flow. Measured in ohms.
Three-Pronged Plug	A plug that contains a dedicated ground wire, designed to connect with a building's grounded circuit. This is capable of diverting any stray current in a faulty appliance to the ground, minimizing hazards for users.
Transformer	An electrical device that 'steps down' supply voltage. Used to draw usable voltages from municipal supplies.
Voltage	A measure of the 'pressure' within an electrical circuit, measured in Volts. Also a rating of the safe voltage for an appliance or fixture.
Wire	Drawn metal smaller than 6-gauge.

Further reading

Bannon, James M. Electrical Systems, in *Mechanical and Electrical Equipment for Buildings* 10th edn. New York: Wiley, 2005.

Bibliography

A necessarily incomplete list of books and sources based on our own libraries and other publications we've consulted for this book. Particularly valuable references are marked with a "*" and are recommended as important elements of a good technical library.

Ali, M. (2001) *Art of the Skyscraper: The Genius of Fazlur Khan* (New York, NY: Rizzoli).

*Allen, E. and Iano, J. (2002) *The Architect's Studio Companion*, 3rd ed. (New York, NY: Wiley).

*Allen, E. and Iano, J. (2004) *Fundamentals of Building Construction: Materials and Methods* (Hoboken, NJ: John Wiley & Sons).

*Ambrose, J. and Parker, H. (2000) *Simplified Engineering for Architects and Builders* (New York, NY: Wiley, 2000).

Bachman, L.R. (2003) *Integrated Buildings: The Systems Basis of Architecture* (New York, NY: John Wiley & Sons).

Bill, M. (1949) *Robert Maillart* (Zurich, Switzerland: Verlag).

Breyer, D. (1980) *Design of Wood Structures* (New York, NY: McGraw-Hill).

*Brown, G.Z. and DeKay, M. (2001) *Sun, Wind & Light: Architectural Design Strategies*, 2nd ed (New York, NY: John Wiley & Sons).

Cerver, F.A. (1997) *The Architecture of Glass: Shaping Light* (New York, NY: Watson Guptil).

Charles M. Salter Associates (1998) *Acoustics: Architecture, Engineering, the Environment* (San Francisco, CA: William Stout).

*Ching, F.D.K. (2001) *Building Construction Illustrated* (New York, NY: John Wiley & Sons).

D'Agostino, F.R. (1982) *Mechanical and Electrical Systems in Building* (Reston, VA: Reston Pub. Co.).

Danz, E. (1967) *Sun Protection: An International Architectural Survey* (New York, NY: Praeger).

Davison, B. and Owens, G. (2003) *Steel Designer's Manual* (Oxford, UK: Blackwell Science Ltd.).

DeChiara, J. (1990) *Timesaver Standards for Building Types* (New York, NY: McGraw-Hill).

*DeChiara, J. (2001) *Timesaver Standards for Interior Design and Space Planning* (New York, NY: McGraw-Hill).

Diffrient, N. (1974–1981) *Humanscale 1,2,3–4,5,6–7,8,9* (Cambridge, MA: MIT Press).

Eggen, A.P. and Sandaker, B.N. (1995) *Steel, Structure, and Architecture* (New York, NY: Watson Guptil Publications).

*Ernst and Neufert, P. (2000) *Architect's Data*, 3rd ed (London, UK: Blackwell Science).

*Evan Terry Associates, P.C. (2002) *Pocket Guide to the ADA* Revised edition (New York, NY: Wiley).

FAO (1989) *Design Manual on Basic Wood Harvesting Technology* (Rome, Italy: FAO).

Ford, E.R. (1990, 1996) *The Details of Modern Architecture* (Cambridge, MA: MIT Press).

Frohlich, B. ed. (2002) *Concrete Architecture: Design and Construction* (Berlin, Germany: Birkhauser).

Goldsmith, M. (1987) *Myron Goldsmith: Buildings and Concepts* (New York, NY: Rizzoli).

Harris, J. and Wiggington, M. (2002) *Intelligent Skins* (Oxford, UK: Architectural Press).

Hawkes, D., McDonald, J. and Steemers, K. (2002) *The Selective Environment* (New York, NY: Spon Press).

Hayward, A., Weare, F. and Oakhill, A. (2002) *Steel Detailers' Manual* (Oxford, UK: Blackwell Science Ltd.).

Hendry, A.W. and Khalaf, F.M. (2001) *Masonry Wall Construction* (New York, NY/ London, UK: SPON Press).

*Henry Dreyfuss Associates (2002) *The Measure of Man and Woman: Human Factors in Design* (New York, NY: Wiley).

Hunt, W.D. (1958) *The Contemporary Curtain Wall: Its Design, Fabrication, and Erection* (New York, NY: F.W. Dodge).

LeCuyer, A. (2003) *Steel and Beyond – New Strategies for Metals in Architecture* (Berlin, Germany: Birkhauser).

Lefteri, C. (2003) *Wood: Materials for Inspirational Design* (Mies, Switzerland: RotoVision SA).

Levin, E. (1972) *The International Guide to Wood Selection* (New York, NY: Drake Publishers).

Mainstone, R.J. (2001) *Developments in Structural Form*, 2nd ed (Oxford, UK: Architectural Press).

Bibliography

Manual of Steel Construction: Allowable Stress Design (Chicago, IL: American Institute of Steel Construction, 1994).

Margolius, I. (2002) *Architects + Engineers = Structures* (Chichester, UK: Wiley-Academy).

*Merritt, F.S. and Ricketts, J.T. (1994) *Building Design and Construction Handbook*, 5th ed (New York, NY: McGraw-Hill).

Nervi, P.L. (1956) *Structures* (New York, NY: F.W. Dodge).

Nervi, P.L. (1965) *Aesthetics and Technology in Building: The Charles Eliot Norton Lectures, 1961–1962* (Cambridge, MA: Harvard University Press).

*Olgyay, V. (1963) *Design with Climate: Bioclimatic Approach to Architectural Regionalism* (Princeton, NJ: Princeton University Press).

Osterberg, A.E. and Kain, D.J. (2002) *Access for Everyone: A Guide to Accessibility with References to ADAAG* (Ames, IA: Iowa State University Facilities Planning & Management).

Panero, J. and Zelnik, M. (1979) *Human Dimensions & Interior Space.* (New York, NY: Whitney Library of Design).

Peña, W., Parshall, S. and Kelly, K. (1987) *Problem Seeking: An Architectural Programming Primer* (Washington, WA: AIA Press).

Petroski, H. (1982) *To Engineer is Human: The Role of Failure in Successful Design* (New York, NY: Random House).

Pfiefer, Ramcke, Achtziger and Zilch (2001) *Masonry Construction Manual* (Basel, Switzerland/Boston, UK/Berlin, Germany: Birkhauser).

*Ramsey, C.G. and Sleeper, H.R. (1994, 2001) *Architectural Graphic Standards*, 9th or 10th ed (New York, NY: John Wiley & Sons).

Rice, P. and Dutton, H. (1995) *Structural Glass*, 2nd ed (London, UK; Spon).

Robbins, T. (1996) *Engineering a New Architecture* (New Haven, CT: Yale).

*Salvadori, M. (1963) *Structure in Architecture: The Building of Buildings* (Englewood Cliffs, NJ: Prentice-Hall).

Salvadori, M. (1979) *The Art of Construction* (Chicago, IL: Chicago Review Press).

Sandaker, B.N. and Eggen, A.P. (1992) *The Structural Basis of Architecture* (New York, NY: Whitney).

Schittich, C. ed. (2001) *In Detail: Building Skins, Concepts, Layers, Materials* (Basel, Switzerland: Birkhauser).

Siebein, G.W. (1986) *Man Technology and Environment, A Primer in the Environmental Technologies*, 2nd ed (Gainesville, FL: University of Florida).

Siegel, C. (1962) *Structure and Form in Modern Architecture* (New York, NY: Reinhold).

*Stacey, M. (2001) *Component Design* (Oxford, UK: Architectural Press).

Strakosch, G.R. ed. (1998) *The Vertical Transportation Handbook* (New York, NY: Wiley).

Templer, J. (1992) *The Staircase: Studies of Hazards, Falls, and Safer Design* (Cambridge, MA: MIT Press).

U.S. Green Building Council (2005) *LEED – NC, Technical Review Workshop for New Construction*.

White, E.T. (c1983) *Site Analysis: Diagramming Information for Architectural Design* (Tucson, AZ: Architectural Media).

Wiggington, M. (1996) *Glass in Architecture* (London, UK: Phaidon).

Wilkinson, C. (1996) *Supersheds: The Architecture of Long-Span, Large-Volume Buildings* (Oxford/Boston, UK: Butterworth Architecture).

Index

Index

Index